THE KHMER KINGS

AND THE HISTORY OF CAMBODIA
BOOK I
1ST CENTURY TO 1595:
FUNAN, CHENLA, ANGKOR, AND LONGVEK PERIODS

THE KHMER KINGS
AND THE HISTORY OF CAMBODIA
BOOK I
1ST CENTURY TO 1595:
FUNAN, CHENLA, ANGKOR, AND LONGVEK PERIODS

ព្រះមហាក្សត្រខ្មែរ
អម្បូលក្សត្រខ្មែរ
ព្រះមហាក្សត្រខ្មែរទាំងអស់

Kenneth T. So
(So Khong Thay)
សោ ខុង ថៃ

蘇康泰

DatASIA Press
www.DatASIA.us

About the Cover and the artistic creation of the special scripts
My drawing of Suryavarman II shown on the front cover was based on the bas-relief of Paramavishnuloka at the Angkor Wat, South Gallery, West Wing. The front and back covers were designed by Jacqueline So. The font for the title shown herein as **THE KHMER KINGS AND THE HISTORY OF CAMBODIA** was inspired Khmer characters, albeit flipped around and/or manipulated to look like particular Roman letters.

Kenneth T. So
The Khmer Kings and The History of Cambodia
Book I
1st Century to 1595: Funan, Chenla, Angkor, and Longvek Periods

DatASIA Press — www.DatASIA.us
First Edition
ISBN 978-1-934431-36-8
Library of Congress Pre-Assigned Control Number: 2017949243

To my family: Theany, Elizabeth, Jacqueline, and Angelica

Your steadfast support and encouragement
gave me the strength to work tirelessly,
and it is for this reason that
I enjoyed writing this
book so much.

The achievement of a man is not measured by what he has accomplished during his lifetime, but by what he has left as his legacy after he has departed the world.

Catvāry Ārya Satyāni (Sanskrit)

Cattāri Ariyo Saccāni (Pali)

Chatuk Arei Sachak/ចតុអរិយសច្ច: (Khmer)

The Four Noble Truths (English)

Dukkha (ទុក្ខ: Suffering): All lives are subject to Dukkha

Cause of Dukkha (សមុទយ: Samudaya): Desire (តណ្ហា) is the root causes of Dukkha

Cessation of Dukkha (និរោធ: Nirhodha): Eliminate desire

Steps to eliminate desire (មគ្គ: Magga):

Apply the Noble Eightfold Path [Ārya Astanga Marga (Sanskrit)/Ariyo Aṭṭhaṅgiko Maggo (Pāli)]

- *Right Understanding*
- *Right Thought*
- *Right Speech*
- *Right Conduct/Action*
- *Right Livelihood*
- *Right Effort*
- *Right Attentiveness/Mindfulness*
- *Right Concentration/Meditation*

CONTENTS

THE KHMER KINGS AND THE HISTORY OF CAMBODIA

LIST OF TABLES

THE KHMER KINGS AND THE HISTORY OF CAMBODIA

LIST OF ILLUSTRATIONS

THE KHMER KINGS AND THE HISTORY OF CAMBODIA

LIST OF ABBREVIATIONS AND ACRONYMS

AEF: Ang Eng Fragment. The document was composed under King Ang Eng. It was submitted to King Chulaloke of Siam, also known as Rama I (1782-1809) for approval first before it could be officially released. It is called Fragment because sections of the original work were destroyed.

APSARA: Autorité pour la Protection du Site et l'Aménagement de la Région d'Angkor, but known in English as Authority for the Protection and Management of Angkor and the Region of Siem Reap.

BE: ពុទ្ធសករាជ — Buddha Era, known as Buddh Sakarach (BE began in 543 AD).

CS: ចុល្លសករាជ — Cula Sakarach. CS began in 638 AD.

EFEO: École Française d'Extrême-Orient.

GLT: Google Language Tools.

LIDAR: Light Detection And Ranging. It is a laser light that is used as a surveying method to measure the distance to a target to be studied.

LP/LPC: Luang Praseut/Luang Praseut Chronicle.

MSL: Ming Shi-lu. It is a Chinese imperial annals with over 400,000 pages that recorded events under the Ming dynasty. The Chinese called them "Ming Real/True Records." The annals covered 13 out of 15 reigns.

NC: Nong Chronicle. It was composed in 1818 by Oknha Vongsa Sarapech Nong, an official at the court of Ang Chan II, to cover the period between 1414 and 1819. The chronicle was presented to King Mongkut in 1855, which was later translated in Thai and published in 1868. The version was reprinted in Bangkok in 1914 under the name Prachum Phongsavadan, Vol 1. The chronicle was used as the basis for the French translation, which was known as the Nong Chronicle. After obtaining permission from King Norodom in 1863, Doudart de Lagrée had the chronicle of Oknha Vongsa Sarapech Nong phonetically spelled in roman alphabets by Col de Monteiro, which he completed in 1866.

SE: Saka Era, also known as Moha Sakarach (មហាសករាជ) or Sakarach Thom, which means Grand Era. Saka was probably introduced into Cambodia by the earlier Indians and Brahman settlers who came to Funan. The word Saka was carved along the numerical value 605 on the K.127 Inscription, which thus showed the earliest use of the number zero. As a background, the Saka Era originated under the reign of King Shaka after his victory over Ujjayin which was the capital of the Avanti Kingdom. The current location of Ujjayin would have been in Madhya Pradesh in India. The Saka Era began in 78 AD.

GEOGRAPHICAL NAMES

THE KHMER KINGS AND THE HISTORY OF CAMBODIA

Amarendrapura: Located in the Angkor Thom region around the Western Baray.

Amoghapura: Probably located in present-day Phimai, Thailand.

Amrak Kirinbaur (អម្រាក់គិរិន្ទបុរ): Located in present-day Kampong Chhnang.

Angkor Borei (អង្គរបុរី): Possibly an ancient capital of Funan located in present-day Takeo according to Michael Vickery.

Aninditapura: Same as Baladityapura. Located close to Kampong Thom, near the village of Sambor Prey Kuk.

Asantuk (អសន្ទុក) Provinces: Comprised of 24 counties such as Staung (ស្ទោង), Chikreng (ជីក្រែង), Prohm Tep (ព្រហ្មទេព), Prasat Dorp (ប្រាសាទដប់), Prey Kdei (ព្រៃក្តី), Sra-ngé (ស្រង៉ែ), Chheu Teal (ឈើទាល), Ngaun (ងន), Kampong Leng (កំពង់លែង), Koh Ker (កោះកេរ្ត៍ or គាស់កែ), Preah Kan (ព្រះកាន), Puthi Rong (ពោធិរោង), Sen (សែន), Nakor (នគរ), Mlu Prey (ម្លូព្រៃ), Choam Ksant (ជាំខ្សាន្ត), Veari Saen (វារីសែន), Prey Sambuor (ព្រៃសំបួរ), Kampoul Pich (កំពូលពេជ្រ), Preah Trasap (ព្រះត្រសប់), Tbeng (ត្បែង), Preah Khleang (ព្រះឃ្លាំង), and Kauk Seh (គោកសេះ).

Ayutthaya: The precursor of modern Thailand. The kingdom was founded in 1351 by U-Thong from Lavo (or Lupbori, an outpost of the Khmer capital and a study center for Khmer civilization such as Buddhism and Hinduism). George Coedès believed U-Thong belonged to a family of Môn or Khmer origins. Professor Wilaiwan Khanittanan of the Department of Linguistic at the Thammasat University said that U-Thong married a Khmer princess from Suphanburi, the sister of Prince Pha-Ngua who would later become King Borommaracha I.

Ba Phnom (បាភ្នំ, in ancient time): Comprised of 7 counties such as Koh (កោះ), Mechong (មេចុង), Mekorng (មេកង), Svay Teap (ស្វាយទាប), Ramduol (រំដួល), Kandal (កណ្តាល), and one undetermined county. Believed to be the capital of Funan, located south of the confluence of the Mekong and Tonlé Sap Rivers in Prey Veng.

Baladityapura: Same as Aninditapura. Located close to Kampong Thom, near the village of Sambor Prey Kuk.

Bampenh Reach or Kamping Reach: Ancient name of a village near Angkor Thom that was mentioned in the legend of Ta Trasâk Paêm.

Banteay Prey Nokor (បន្ទាយព្រៃនគរ): Located in present-day Kampong Cham.

Baray Teuk Thla (បារាយទឹកថ្លា): West Baray located at Angkor and considered to be the largest reservoir with a dimension of 2.2 x 8.0 km.

Baschimborei (បស្ចឹមបុរី): Present-day Prachinburi, Thailand.

Bati: Located in present-day Takeo.

Bhimapura: Present-day Phimai in Thailand.

Boeung Tea (បឹងទា): Meaning Duck Lake. Also called Boeung Totea/Toteung (បឹងទទា/បឹងទទឹង), which means Partridge/Unconventional Lakes.

Boribaur (បរិបូណ៌): Literally, it means Plentiful. Located in present-day Kampong Chhnang.

Braḥ Nagar Hluoṅ or Preah Nokor Luong: Angkor Thom.

Cakrankapura: Probably in present-day Phimai in Thailand.

Caturmukh or Chaktomouk (ចតុមុខ): Confluence of the Mekong, Tonlé Sap, and Bassac Rivers in Phnom Penh.

Chakling: Champa province corresponding to present-day Phan Rang, Vietnam. The name was published in the Chinese Imperial Annals Chu-fan-chih by Chao Ju-kua in 1225.

Ch'a-nan (查南): Recorded by Zhou Daguan to indicate Kampong Chhnang.

Chen Ching: Champa (per Ma Duanlin, the famous author of the 1317 Chinese encyclopedia); see also Tchen-ch'eng.

Chen-li-fu: Chanthaburi, Thailand. The name was published in the Chinese Imperial Annals Chu-fan-chih by Chao Ju-kua in 1225.

Chenla (真臘): Land of the Khmers; Post Funan, predating Kambuja and Cambodia.

Chen-pu (真蒲): Recorded by Zhou Daguan to indicate Baria (present-day Ba Ria-Vaung Tau in Vietnam).

Chhlong (ឆ្លូង): Located in Kratié province near Laos.

Chia-lo-hsi: See Kia-lo-hi.

Chiangdong-Chiangthong: Ancient name of Luang Prabang, Laos.

Chiao Chi or Chiao Chou: Tonkin.

Chok Gargyar: Also called Lingapura, located near Koh Ker about 100 miles north east of Angkor. Koh Keh is officially spelled កោះកេរ្តិ៍ in Khmer, which means heritage island. Because there is no island in the area, could Koh Ker possibly be intended to mean "to dig and repair" (កាស់កែ) instead?

Dvaravati: Môn Kingdom.

Dviradapura: Located near present-day Longvek.

Eyntapath Moha Nokor (ឥន្ទ្រយក្សមហានគរ): Angkor Thom. The name came from the Sanskrit Indraprastha Maha Nagara, which means City of Indra of the Great Kingdom.

Fo-hsuen (佛村): Recorded by Zhou Daguan to indicate present-day Pursat. Literally, it means village of the Buddha. Zhou Daguan must have mistranslated the name Pursat (ពោធិ៍សាត់), which signified drifting banyan tree, for bodhisattva (ពោធិសត្វ) which signified Buddha.

Funan (扶南): Land of the Khmers; predating Chenla, Kambuja, and Cambodia.

Hariharalaya: Located in Roluos, approximately 15 km southeast of Siem Reap.

Haripunjaya: Present-day Lamphun, Thailand.

Indrapatha Nagara: Angkor.

Indraprashta: Legendary city founded by Pandavas, the son of Pandu in the Indian epic Mahabharata.

Isanapura: Original capital of Jayavarman I, located in present-day Sambor in Kratié.

Kambuja: Land of the Khmers; Post Funan and Chenla, predating Cambodia.

Kampong Hav (កំពង់ហៅ): Literally, it means Calling Shore. It is located near Longvek.

Kan-p'ang hsui (干傍取): It was recorded by Zhou Daguan to indicate Kampong Chei, which means Port of Victory. It was located 20 km from Angkor Thom.

Karen country: Northern part of Laos.

Kia-lo-hi: Grahi, a vassal state of Srivijaya. The name was published in the Chinese Imperial Annals Chu-fan-chih by Chao Ju-kua in 1225.

Ko-lo: Name of Kok Thlok (ancient Cambodia) in Chinese, which the Vietnamese called Co-luc.

Kok Thlok (កុកធ្លុក): Ancient Cambodia.

Krâng: Located in Kampong Chhnang.

Kreang Leav (ក្រាំងលាវ): The ancient name of the village was Prey Puon (ព្រៃពួន). It is located in the district of Rolea Pha-ea (រលាផ្អើ) in Kampong Chhnang.

K'un-lun (崑崙): It was recorded by Zhou Daguan to indicate Koh Tralach (present-day Con Son, Vietnam).

Lan Na: Ancient kingdom founded by Mangrai with Chiang Mai as its capital. Mangrai moved his capital to Chiang Mai on 27 March 1292, but the construction of his residency did not start until 19 April 1296 due to the war with the Mongols.

Lankadvipa: Sri Lanka.

Lan Xang: Original name of present-day Laos which means million elephants, founded in 1353.

Lavarattha: Believed to be Haripunjaya in present-day Lamphun, Thailand.

Lavo, Louvo, or Lo-ho: Present-day Lopburi in Thailand.

Ligor: Corresponding to present-day Nakhon Sri Thammarat, Thailand.

Lingapura: Also called Chok Gargyar, located near Koh Ker about 100 miles north east of Angkor.

Lobok Srot (Inscription): Located in ancient province of Sambor in Kratié.

Luzhenla (陸真臘): Upper Chenla or Land Chenla.

Madhyadesa: Located in northern India near the Himalaya.

Ma-lo-wen: Malyang per Khmer inscription or Mou-liang per Zhou Daguan, a place located south of Battambang. The name was published in the Chinese Imperial Annals Chu-fan-chih by Chao Ju-kua in 1225.

Malyang: Corresponding to present-day Battambang (see Ma-lo-wen).

Mlu Prey (ម្លូព្រៃ): Near Preah Vihear.

Mofu: Original country of Hun Tien, believed to be in the Malay Peninsula, according to Paul Pelliot.

Mou-liang: See Ma-lo-wen.

Mount Mahendra: Phnom Kulen, the location where Jayavarman II chose to declare his independence and emancipation of Kambuja from Java in 802.

Muang Rat: Located in the eastern territory of Sukhothai, probably in present-day Uttaradit in Thailand.

Muang Sawa: Ancient name of Luang Prabang, Laos.

Nagara Jayasri: City name given by Jayavarman VII, which means luminous/fortunate city of victory, where the temple Preah Khan is located.

Nafuna: Believed to be in the region of Kampot.

Nakhong Luang: Angkor.

Narapatidesa: A region believed to be in Burma.

Ngeh-an: North central coast of present-day Vietnam. The name was published in the Chinese Imperial Annals Chu-fan-chih by Chao Ju-kua in 1225.

Nokor Kok Thlok (នគរកុកធ្លុក): Literally, it means the land of the Thlok trees which was the name of ancient Cambodia.

Nokor Reach Seima (នគររាជសីមា): Ancient province of Cambodia. Present-day Nakhon Ratchasima or Korat, Thailand.

Nom Van monastery: Located near Korat, Thailand.

O Keo (អូរកែវ): Literally, it means Important Creek or Cherished Creek. It must be noted that the spelling of this ancient port of Funan is shown in literature as Oc Eo, which in my opinion was misspelled. The place is currently located in Ba The (Thoai Son) district, Barach (Long Xuyen) city, and An Giang province in Vietnam.

Oc Eo: Misspelled name of O Keo, an ancient port in Funan located near the Mekong delta.

Padāgūcām: Prāp cām or Prāp Jhām (ប្រាបចាម). According to Michael Vickery this place was the present-day Chaktomouk, Cambodia.

Pagan: Ancient name for Burma/Myarnma.

Panduranga: See Rajapura.

P'an-P'an: Located in present-day Chumphon in Thailand.

Pataliputra: Corresponding to present-day Patna, India.

Pegu: Môn capital in lower part of present-day Burma/Myanmar.

Phnom Banan: Located in khum "sub-district" Kantuk (កន្ទុ) of srok "district" Sangker and in the province of Battambang.

Phnom Ksach Sâ (ភ្នំឃ្យាច់ស): Literally, it means White Sand Mountain. It was the capital of Funan according to Dr. Hema Goonatilake. It is presently located in Prey Veng.

Phnom Preah Reach Troap (ភ្នំព្រះរាជទ្រព្យ): Literally, it means Mount of the King's Wealth. The third pagoda was built on this location by King Ang Chan I. It is located in Samrong Tong (សំរោងទង) in Kampong Speu.

Phum Tean (ភូមិទាន): Literally, it means Village of Goodwill/Offering or Village of Candles. It is located in present-day Kandal, Cambodia.

Po Nagar: Ancient Champa province corresponding to present-day Nha Trang in Vietnam. The name was published in the Chinese Imperial Annals Chu-fan-chih by Chao Ju-kua in 1225.

Polonnaruwa: Ancient capital city of Sri Lanka.

Polou (婆鑪): Upper Chenla or Land Chenla.

Prāp Jhām (ប្រាបឈាម) or **Prāp cām** (ប្រាបចាម): Prior name of Tonlé Chaktomouk Bopear (ទន្លេចតុមុខបុព្វា). According to Michael Vickery, which he spelled Prāp Jhām (ប្រាបឈាម, which means "covering with blood of the defeated enemy") or Prāp cām which means "to put down the Cham" because the area was known as the Cham River.

Prayaga: Corresponding to present-day Allahabad, located in Uttar Pradesh, India.

Preah Khan of Kampong Svay: Located about 100 km east of Angkor in the Preah Vihear province.

Preah Theat Preah Srei (Inscription): Located in ancient province of Thbong Khmum in Kratié.

Prèk Touch (ប្រែកតូច): Located in Samrong Tong in Kampong Speu.

Prey Ngo-nguy (ព្រៃងងុយ): Literally, it means Sleepy Forest. It is located in Kampong Chhnang.

Prey Puon (ព្រៃពួន): Literally, it means Hidden Forest. The village was located in the ancient province of Samrong Tong, which is now called Kreang Leav (គ្រាំងលាវ). It is located in the district of Rolea Pha-ea (រលាផ្អៀ), in Kampong Chhnang.

P'u-kan: Pagan, ancient name for Burma/Myarnma. The name was published in the Chinese Imperial Annals Chu-fan-chih by Chao Ju-kua in 1225.

Pursat (ពោធិសាត់, **in ancient time**): Comprised of 6 counties such as Chau Ponhea Suorkealauk (ចៅពញាស្ងួ តារលោក), Krakor (ក្រគរ), Krorng (ក្រុង), Thporng (ថ្ពង), Khlong (ខ្លុង), Tang (តាំង), and Samrè (សំរែ).

Puth Oream/Ureal (ពោធិឪរាម/ឧរាល): Village located in Kandal Stung district in Kandal province.

Rajapura: Ancient city in Champa corresponding to present-day Phan Rang in Vietnam. The name was published in the Chinese Imperial Annals Chu-fan-chih by Chao Ju-kua in 1225.

Reachea Dak: Ancient name of a village near the temple of Preah Khan that was mentioned in the legend of Ta Trasâk Paêm.

Reachtheani (រាជធានី): Royal Capital.

Ro Ang Seila Bat (រអាងសីលាបាទ): Present-day Sa Keo in Thailand.

Rolea Pha-ea (រលាផ្អៀ): District located in Kampong Chhnang.

Sambhupura: Capital of Jayavarman I (was originally named Isanapura), located in present-day Sambor in Kratié.

San-fo-t'si: See Srivijaya.

San-lo or Sien-lo: Siam people. The name was published in the Chinese Imperial Annals Chu-fan-chih by Chao Ju-kua in 1225.

Sawankhalok: District of the present-day province of Sukhothai, Thailand.

Shuizhenla (水真臘): Lower Chenla or Water Chenla.

Singpuri: Lopburi in Thailand.

Snam Khsach Koukhan: Undetermined location in Laos.

Srah Preah Thommoker (ព្រះធម្មករិ្ដ): Literally, it means Heritage Pond because King Ang Chan I wanted to remind people that his father, Thommo Reachea, had the work started when he was alive. It is located in Puth Oream village in Samrong Tong in Kampong Speu.

Srei Sâ Chhor (ស្រីសឈរ): Literally, it means White Lady Standing. The place was named in honor of Neak Mneang Peou, the favorite and number one concubine of Srei Sokonthor Bat (1504-1512). The name was changed from Basan. It is located in present-day Kampong Cham.

Srei Santhor (ស្រីសន្ធរ): Literally, it means Pleasant Lady. It was changed from Srei Sa Chhor, which previously was called Basan. It is located in present-day Kampong Cham.

Sri Satchanalai: Present-day Sawankhalok in Thailand.

Sri Sodararajadhani or **Siri Sandhara**: Srei Santhor.

Sri Sodharapura: Corrupted name of Sri Yasodharapura, which is Angkor Thom.

Srivijaya: Ancient city in Sumatra, Indonesia.

Stung Raung Touk (ស្ទឹងរោងទូក): Literally, it means Boat Storage River. It was the name of the Tonle Sap River in front of the Citadel of Longvek that was proclaimed by King Ang Chan I because a hangar was built on the river to store the royal boats.

Stung Saen (ស្ទឹងសែន): Meaning river of offering "to the spirits." Located in the province of Kampong Svay.

Sukhothai: Ancient kingdom located in mid-western part of present-day Thailand. The foundation of Sukhothai started with a Muang Rat lord. The location of Muang Rat is probably in present-day Uttaradit in Thailand.

Tambralinga: See Ligor.

Tamrapura: Located near Tomu (Ba Phnom), the capital of Funan.

Tchen-ch'eng (占城): Recorded by Zhou Daguan to indicate Champa; see also Cheng Ching.

Teng-liu-mei: See Ligor (name published in the Chinese Imperial Annals Chu-fan-chih by Chao Ju-kua in 1225).

Tep Maha Nokor: Bangkok.

Than-hoa: Located south of present-day Hanoi, Vietnam.

Tomu: Capital of Funan, conquerred by Chenla, that George Coedès identified as Ba Phnom.

Thbong Khmum (ត្បូងឃ្មុំ, in ancient time): Comprised of 5 counties and four sub-counties such as Tuol Angkunh (ទួលអង្គុញ), Dambè (ដំបែ), Phnom Preah (ភ្នំព្រះ), Tvear Lo (ទ្វារលោ), Tvear Pheakdei (ទ្វារភក្ដី), Cheung Kuor (ជើងគួរ), Chrey Prahar (ព្រៃប្រហារ), Tvear Raung (ទ្វាររោង), and Tvear Riel (ទ្វាររៀល).

Trapeang Phlong: Located in the Parrot's Beak region at the border of Cambodia and Vietnam.

Treang (ត្រាំង, in ancient time): Comprised of 6 counties such as Peam (ពាម), Prey Cheung (ព្រៃជើង), Choan Chum (ជាន់ជុំ), Banteay Meas (បន្ទាយមាស), Srè Ronaung (ស្រែរនោង), and Tabour (តាបូរ).

Tun-Sun: Same as Dvaravati, which was the name of Môn Kingdom.

Tuol Kreang (ទួលក្រាំង): Located in Kampong Chhnang.

Vat Kok Khpous (វត្តកុកខ្ពស់): Literally, it means Pagoda of a Tall Heron. Also called Kok Svay Chek and it is located near Siem Reap.

Vat Phu (វត្តភ្នំ): Ancient capital of Chenla located in present-day Laos between eastern border of Thailand and northern border of Cambodia.

Vat Preah Nippean (វត្តព្រះនិព្វាន): Literally, it means Nirvana Temple. It was built by Srei Sokonthor Bat after his favorite concubine, Mneang Peou, recovered from her illness. Located in Srei Santhor.

Vat Preah Puth Leay Leakhana (វត្តព្រះពុទ្ធលាយលក្ខណ): The name of the pagoda means the Buddha had signs of characteristic qualities such as those shown in his palm, in the bottom of his feet, etc. Located in Kampong Chhnang.

Vat Preah Eynt Tep Nimitt (វត្តព្រះឥន្ទទេពនិមិត្ត): Literally, it means Apparition of Brahma. The second pagoda built by King Ang Chan I. Located in Longvek.

Vat Prey Bang (វត្តព្រៃបាំង): Literally, it means Temple Hidden by Forest. It was changed from Vat Preah Nippean. Located in Srei Santhor, next to present-day National Road No.8.

Vat Traleng Keng (វត្តត្រឡែងកែង): Literally, it means Four-Faced Pagoda. It was built in 1530 in Longvek. The first pagoda built by King Ang Chan I to house the statue of the Buddha made from the branch of a gagī (គគី, koki) tree and a block of stone that the king found sitting on that tree. The statue was carved with the Buddha having four faces and four backs fused into one body sitting on the stone.

Vijaya: Capital of Champa, located in present-day Binh Dinh, Vietnam.

Vrah Prang (ព្រះប្រាង្គ): Name found at Vat Phu, which means Holy Tower or Holy Pyramid. This name was attributed as the original name for Angkor Wat.

Vrah Thkval or Preah Thkal (ព្រះថ្កល់): Literally, it means Elevated God. It was the original name given to Vat Phu by the founder Jayavarman VI. It was also called Preah Phnom.

Vyadhapura: Capital of Funan, located at the foot of Ba Phnom in Prey Veng according to George Coedès; but at either Ba Phnom or Angkor Borei in Takeo according to Michael Vickery.

Wa country: northern part of Laos.

Wat Preah Po Mean Bon: Literally, it means Pagoda of the Holy Banyan Tree with Merits. The pagoda was built in 1534 by Ang Chan I (Borom Reachea III) to commemorate the Khmer victory over the Ayutthayan army. The name of the pagoda may have been distorted to its current name, Wat Preah Puth Mean Bon (Pagoda of the Buddha with Merits), which is located in Phnom Penh.

Wat Toap Poat Chambak (វត្តទ័ពពាក់ចំបក់): Literally, it means Temple Encircled by the Army. Ang Chan I had the pagoda built in 1535 in Bati (present-day Kandal Stung district) near the Chambak tree to commemorate the discovery of the Royal Sacred Sword. It is located in Phum Tean village (ភូមិទាន), in Kandal.

Wendan (文單): Land Chenla.

Wiang Chaiprakan: Ancient city located in present-day Fang in the northern part of Chiang Mai in Thailand.

Wiangchan: Old name of Vientiane.

Yasodharapura: Present-day Phnom Bakheng.

OFFICIAL TITLES

Akkamohasena (អគ្គមហាសេនា): Prime Minister.

Arahant (អរហន្ត): Buddha's disciples.

Asura: Inhabitants of the underworld, demons.

Bakou: Brahman.

Bhagavan: Chaplain.

Bhavavarman (ភវវរ្ម័ន): Protector of Shiva (whose armor was Shiva).

Brahmapurohita (ព្រហ្មបុរោហិត): Brahman Chief.

Chakravatin (ចក្រវាទិន): Universal Ruler.

Deva: God.

Devaraja (ទេវរាជ): God-King

Dhuli Jeng Vrah Kamrateng Añ (ធូលីជើងព្រះកំម្រតេងអញ): The dust of the feet of the Lord.

God (phi fā) of Chao Muang Sri Sodharapura: Jayavarman VIII. According to George Coedès, Sri Sodharapura was the corrupted name of Sri Yasodharapura, the ancient name of Angkor Thom. Sriyasodharapura was changed to Sriy-Sodharapura, then to Sri Sodharapura. The epithet was mentioned in the Vat Mahadhatu inscription of Sukhothai that is currently preserved at the National Library of Thailand in Bangkok. This Khmer king bestowed the title of *Kamratēng Añ Phā Muang Sri Indrapatīndrāditya* to the Tai Chieftain Pho Khun Pha Muang Chao of Muang Rat.

Hanuman: Monkey god.

Hara: Shiva.

Harihara: Image of Shiva and Vishnu merged into one body.

Harirak Reamea Issarathipadei (ហរិរក្សរាមាធិបតី): Title of Ang Duong, which means "one who is sovereign, powerful, charming, protector of Indra.

Isanavarman (ឦសានវរ្ម័ន): Protector of Lord Shiva (whose armor was the Lord Shiva).

Kalahom: Ancient Siam title for Minister of Defense.

Kamratēng Añ Phā Muang Sri Indrapatīndrāditya: Title equivalent to a king or vice-king that Jayavaeman VIII bestowed to the Tai Chieftain Pho Khun Pha Muang Chao of Muang Rat accompanied by the sword Jaiyasri and his daughter named Nang Sikharamahadevi in marriage to the Tai chieftain.

Khun Luong Preah Sdach Samuha Senathipadei (ឃុនល្វងព្រះស្តេចសមុហាសេនាធិបតី): Honorific title equivalent to a Lord that Srei Sokhonthor Bat bestowed to his brother-in-law Kân.

Kshatrya: Royalty.

Mahatthai (មហាតថៃ): Ministry of Interior.

Mahendravarman (មហេន្ទ្រវរ្ម័ន): Protector of the Great Indra (whose armor was the Great Indra).

Me Smeung (មេស្មឹង): A person who acted as the medium between human beings and supernatural beings (genies).

Neak Ta (អ្នកតា): Equivalent to a genie.

Okña/Oknha (ឧកញ៉ា): Noble title given by the king to high officials in ancient time. This title is watered down in modern time, post-UNTAC, and is no longer considered as prestigious and noble as it was in ancient time.

Okña/Oknha Chakrei (ឧកញ៉ាចក្រី): Minister of the Army (responsible for transportation of soldiers and war equipments by land route).

Okña/Oknha Kralahom (ឧកញ៉ាក្រឡាហោម): Minister of the Marine (responsible for transportation of soldiers and war equipments by boats).

Okña/Oknha Veang (ឧកញ៉ាវាំង): Minister of the Royal Palace and Finance (responsible for finance and safeguarding of the royal treasury).

Phra Khlang: Ancient Siam title for Minister of Treasury.

Preah (ព្រះ): Prefix used for honorific title mostly reserved for members of the royal family, clergy (monks), and god. It is a high form of respect.

Prohm Borohet (Brahmapurohita — ព្រហ្មបុរោហិត): Brahman Chief.

Purohita (បុរោហិត): Chief Priest (Brahman Chief).

Ravana: Antagonist of Rama.

Samdech (សម្តេច): Prefix given by the king to high officials with distinguished careers as well as to highest ranking monks and also to certain members of the royal family. Rank of 10 *poan*.

Samdech Preah Sangkhareach (សម្តេចព្រះសង្ឃរាជ): Supreme monk patriarch.

Samuha Nayok: Prime Minister (ancient title in Siam).

Snâm Êk (ស្នំឯក): Concubine of the first order (favorite concubine).

Srutavarman (ស្រុតវរ្ម័ន): Protector of Vedas (whose armor was the Vedas).

Tep Thoroni: Title attributed to the queen of Sukhothai (according to Micheal Vickery).

Uparaja (ឧបរាជ): The term was composed of the Sanskrit words *upa*, which means "secondary," and *raja*, which means "king." Literally, the term means "secondary king or vice-king." This term comes to designate a Crown Prince as heir apparent to the king.

Upayuvaraja (ឧបយុវរាជ): The term was composed of the Sanskrit words *upayuva*, which means "twice," and *raja*, which means "king." Literally, the term means "being king twice." Originally, the term referred to a king who had abdicated and then returned to reign again. However, politics came into play when the king wanted to remove one of the princes, usually a brother, from the line of succession by giving him the title *Upayuvaraja* to indicate that he would no longer be considered as heir to the throne. The title is considered to be higher than Uparaja but viewed as having less power.

Vrah kamrateng añ: Title equivalent to a lord or a king.

Yama: Lord of the Death.

GLOSSARY

THE KHMER KINGS AND THE HISTORY OF CAMBODIA

Apsara: Khmer female spirit dancer with exceptional beauty. A beautiful divine female being and/or spirit who likes to entertain and/or seduce gods, god-like beings, or kings. Apsara sculptures adorn temple walls throughout Angkor. As a comparison, Apsara is akin to the nymph in Greek mythologies.

Cetiya (បេតិយ): Stupa.

Ch'u-ku (芋姑): It is believed Zhou Daguan described Hinayanist monks.

Jayabuddhamahanatha: Name given by Jayavarman VII to 23 statues scattered over the Khmer Empire which means in glory to Buddha, the great savior.

Kambojavasala: The name of residential Khmer quarter in Sri Lanka mentioned on the inscription left by King Nissankamalla.

Khom (ខម): Khom is a Môn word to designate Khmer.

Makara: It is a kind of shark or swordfish that is also known by the name Chlām Makara (ឆ្លមមករ), or just Chlām, or Trī Thkar (ត្រីថ្កr). The fish was portrayed in Khmer arts in the middle of the seventh century of the style of Sambor Prey Kuk. The Makara symbol was used in ancient Khmer banners.

Pan-ch'i (斑詰): It is believed that Zhou Daguan described Brahmanism.

Pa-zhong-wei (八忠惟): Because of his unfamiliarity with the customs and religion in Kambuja, Zhou Daguan called these practitioners Taoists. However, Paul Pelliot and Finot believed they belonged to the Shaivite faith called Pashupata that was referred in the epic of Mahabharata. The Pashupata movement was especially influential between the 7th and 14th centuries.

Preah Khan Reach: Sacred Sword used for the coronation ceremony of Khmer kings. Its whereabouts is now unknown. The Sword disappeared somewhere between the period of the Khmer Republic (1970-1975) and Prince Norodom Sihanouk's return to the Royal Palace in Phnom Penh on 10 September 1975.

Tripitaka: Three baskets of the Buddhist scriptures that include Vinaya Pitika (Discipline), Sutra (Discourse), and Abhidharma (Special Doctrine).

PREFACE

The journey of my book was 40 years in the making. I wanted to write a book about the history of Cambodia, but 40 years ago I was not mature enough to understand the intricacies of politics. As the years ticked away I was more and more anxious to start my project, but the opportunity was not right because I was too busy holding a full-time job, going to graduate school, and raising my family at the same time. I finally decided in June 2008 to start my project, which was dear to my heart for half of my life. It took me nine years to write this book. I wanted this book to be as thorough as possible and I did not want to leave any gaps in the Khmer history. As a result, it took about 20,000 hours and 500,000 words to complete my work. Due to its enormous size, I decided to split the work into two books as follows:

1. The Khmer Kings and the History of Cambodia — Book I: 1st Century to 1595 (Funan, Chenla, Angkor, and Longvek Periods)

2. The Khmer Kings and the History of Cambodia — Book II: 1595 to Contemporary Period

When I decided to write the history of Cambodia, I did not want it to be simply a history book filled up with dates and events without considering how they were related. I wanted it to be a cultural history book as well. For that reason, I utilized the expressive narrative method to write this book. Through my narration, I attempt to relate historical and cultural events, presenting them to the readers in a manner of a story that formed the fabric and foundation of the Cambodian society. My book is not a pure history book in the conventional sense. It is a history book injected with my personal analyses and some relevant personal stories. It is necessary for me to take this approach because of the complexity of the issues and the many anecdotes, mostly historical but some of them personal, that needed to be told. There are many articles about Cambodia that are published in journals but they are read by academicians and a few people only. For this book, it is important for me to analyze the information published in academic journals and/or books to further clarify and provide my personal understanding on these subjects.

I am a synthesizer and systems integrator of information. I research historical information written by historians and journalists and then put them together into a coherent narrative story. I believe in imageries because pictures are the best way of enhancing communication and retaining information. I am fully aware that it is very easy to get confused by all of the names of the kings; to get mixed up by the different times of events that occurred during the course of history; and to get lost by all of the names of unfamiliar cities, provinces, and countries of ancient time. As a consequence, I developed genealogy trees with specific reigning dates and provided illustrations as a visual guide to help the readers trace the lineages of the Khmer monarchs and locate the places described in the book. It is my firm belief that imagery enhances the pleasure of reading this book and facilitates its understanding. For this book, I decided to take the unconventional approach concerning footnotes. I decided to do away with footnotes, but instead I inserted the annotations in-between brackets in the body of the texts. Because most people erroneously think that footnotes are not important, they tend to skip and not read them. During my research, I found a lot of valuable information through the references in the footnotes.

I am a self-taught historian. I am trained in the professional fields of engineering as a rocket scientist and systems management. I am blessed to be able to combine my Cambodian upbringing of eastern philosophy with my curiosity and western education to look at history through a different perspective. My background enables me to ask questions that are complementary to those formulated by professional historians. It also allowed me the freedom to deviate and raise questions without feeling the constraint and pressure that are normally imposed on professional historians. My job is that of a synthesizer and my purpose is to organize and break down the history of Cambodia into a clear timeline that is easy to understand and follow. I gathered the data provided by historians and narrowed down the most probable causes of events that took place. This method enabled me to identify the names of monarchs during the period in history that had not been satisfactorily resolved. I do not want my book to be overwhelmed with technical data and impressive phraseology to render it unreadable, thus becoming uninteresting to the majority of the people; at the same time, I do not want my book to be too scholarly and academic but I do not want it to be too simple either that will offer no value added. I try to balance the book between the technical aspects of it and the story telling so that it would render the book less painful to read. However, because of the names and places in ancient Cambodia that are mostly unfamiliar to foreigners and non-academic readers, it is necessary that the book needs to be read more than once in order to grasp the whole history. Also, whenever possible I will provide the Chinese and/or Khmer names to accompany the names written in the Roman alphabets. I hope that I find the right balance to provide the readers a sense of fulfillment after they have finished reading the book.

One of the most important parts of writing a book is to decide on its topic and its title. I already knew that I wanted to write a book about the history of Cambodia, but I struggled with what title to give to my book. After multiple iterations, I finally settled on *The Khmer Kings and the History of Cambodia* because the history of Cambodia is essentially the history of the Khmer kings. Because half of the book deals with the ancient period, I wanted to capture some of the enigmas and unresolved mysteries that still surround the history of Cambodia, with an accompanying title in Khmer language. A modern Khmer translation would be too simple and not intriguing enough. I decided to use the ancient Khmer language to accompany the English title for "The Khmer Kings" shown on page iii. The ancient Khmer title says *Ampall Kurung Khmer (អម្បាល់ក្រុងខ្មែរ)*, which means *All the Khmer Kings*.

My keen interest in Cambodia's history did not start until the Khmer Rouge took over the country in 1975. I was an engineering student in the United States at the time Cambodia fell to the communist Khmer Rouge. My mother left Cambodia a month before its fall and my father left on the last plane to Bangkok. Like many Cambodians overseas, I followed the events on the news that showed the mass exodus of people leaving Phnom Penh by force. I worried about the fate of my two older brothers and their families, and a younger sister still living in Phnom Penh. I thought about my grandmother, cousins, aunts, and uncles who were not prepared for the Khmer Rouge's collective revenge on mostly innocent people. They all thought that the Khmer Rouge conquerors who were Khmers like them would be compassionate, kind, gentle, and polite as our culture and tradition had taught us. They soon realized that the Khmer Rouge were a new breed of people full of hatred and savagery in their blood. Like most Cambodians who lost members of their families in this tragedy, I also lost mine when the Khmer Rouge killed my older brother after they found out he was a medical doctor. It was a senseless execution. From that moment on, I started to collect news and books written on Cambodia. I wanted to know more about our history, beyond what I was taught as a youngster in high school. I wanted to understand what caused the Khmer Rouge to behave so savagely.

My plan to write this book has fomented in my mind for a long time but I felt that I needed to know more about the history of Cambodia and its neighbor in order to write a thorough, meaningful, and different story that had already been tackled by others. In the meantime, I was busy writing articles for *Khmer Conscience*, a bilingual publication that was published during the United Nations Transitional Authority of Cambodia (UNTAC) in 1992. The purpose of the publication was to educate Khmer people on democracy. My involvement with Khmer Conscience and other essays that I wrote pushed my interest further for the need to understand Khmer history. This contemporary period of the Khmer history is discussed in Book II.

My purpose for writing *The Khmer Kings and the History of Cambodia* is partly due to my own frustration of finding a book that tells a compelling, interesting, and comprehensive history of Cambodia while simultaneously shows a complete lineage of the Khmer kings from the Funan period to the present time. There are such books that have already been written by many eminent scholars but they are either partially outdated, incomplete in certain areas of information, not organized to my liking, too scholarly and academic, or not easily readable. My purpose is to thoroughly trace the lineages of all of the Khmer kings with detailed genealogy trees; to reassess some old beliefs or theories made by previous scholars — such as *Hun Tien* being *Kaundinya* and Funan as a backward country before the arrival of the Brahmans; to clear up some information that were previously confusing or unresolved — such as identifying the name of the Khmer king that was beheaded by the maharaja of Zabag (King of Java); to reveal the mystery behind the origin of Jayaviravarman who overthrew Udayadityavarman I and waged war against Suryavarman I for eight years; to bring out information that is obscure to the limelight; to identify who was the Leper King that ruled Cambodia during the Angkor period; to explain the merit of accessions through the rule of ambilateral descent system; to provide my own explanation for the meaning of the name Chenla; to analyze the story of Neak Ta Khleang Moeung from a psychological point of view; to connect some of the missing links between royal lineages; to clear up unresolved issues that remain; to provide complementary and alternative point of views and inject some of my personal findings and understanding of events of the history of Southeast Asia; to provide my own analysis of why Pol Pot behaved in such a ruthless manner; and most of all, to make the reading of history fun again.

Most history books about Cambodia were written for the Funan, Chenla, and Angkor periods up to the reign of Jayavarman Paramesvara; or for the post Angkor period starting from Chau Ponhea Yat. The contemporary period can be found in many books but in most cases, it is excluded in the overall Cambodian history. History experts on Cambodia avoid writing in details about the period between the end of Jayavarman Paramesvara's reign and Chau Ponhea Yat's accession to the throne. The reasons for this omission are many, but the main one is due to the lack of information for this troubling period. Events covering this period were ambiguous and very uncertain. This period has not been well explored and leaves a big gap in the Khmer history to this day. I feel that it is important to expand the knowledge and discuss in depth about the events in this turbulent time because it affects the understanding of the post Angkor period. Oliver William Wolters, continuing on the work of George Coedès, had done a magnificent job analyzing this period in his article *The Khmer King at Basan (1371-3) and the Restoration of the Cambodian Chronology during the Fourteenth and Fifteenth Centuries*. His work was mostly based on the records published in the Chinese Imperial Annals Ming Shi-lu (*MSL*). However, his analysis was still incomplete and unresolved concerning the identities of the Khmer monarchs. Most of all, he had not discussed the identity and origin of Ponhea Yat. Claude Jacques also discussed the period after Jayavarman VII in his article, *Les Derniers Siècle d'Angkor*, but his emphasis was mostly about Indravarman II. Like his mentor George Coedès and other historians such as Adhémard Leclère, Lawrence Palmer Briggs, and Mak Phoeun, Claude Jacques would not commit to the origin and exact relationship between Ponhea Yat and his predecessors. Michael Vickery is the only historian who had written extensively about the events leading to Chau Ponhea Yat's accession to the throne. Vickery's discovery of a lost chronicle of Ayutthaya that he found in the National Library of Thailand in Bangkok in 1971 enabled him to unmask some of the mysteries surrounding the events that took place during that tumultuous period. He wrote a comprehensive article analyzing this period in a paper called *The 2/k.125 Fragment, a Lost Chronicle of Ayutthaya*. Equipped with Vickery's paper, I decided to probe further on the relationships between Ayutthaya and Angkor, as well as between Borommaracha II and Chau Ponhea Yat. When the *2/k.125 Fragment* is combined with the Chinese Imperial Annals *MSL* during this ambiguous period, a clearer picture of Cambodia history emerges. The *2/k.125 Fragment* was the missing piece that needed to complete the puzzle.

In order to understand the relationship between the Khmers and the Thais, it is necessary to understand the origin of the Thai people. I have dedicated a generous portion of this book on the history of Thailand. U-Thong was considered by Thais to be the founder of Thailand. George Coedès said that he belonged to a family of Môn or Khmer origin. According to Wilaiwan Khanittanan of the Department of Linguistic, Faculty of Liberal Arts Thammasat University, U-Thong married a Khmer princess from Suphanburi which was a Khmer province during the Angkor period. He must have married her to consolidate his power when he founded Ayutthaya and reigned as King Ramathibodi. The Khmer princess also had a brother named Pha-ngua, who went on to become King Borommaracha of Ayutthaya according to David K. Wyatt. The connection between the Khmer royal bloodlines of Cambodia and Ayutthaya is undeniable and has not been fully investigated and written about in history books. The Thai kings with Khmer royal bloodlines coming from these two branches (the U-Thong/Ramathibodi and Pha-ngua/Borommaracha branches) were propagated all the way down to King Si Saowaphak (1610), and possibly as far as to King Narai (1656-1688). The connection between the Ayutthayan and Khmer royal bloodlines is discussed in Chapter 6 under *Chronology of Khmer King by Adhémard Leclère*; in Chapter 8 under *The U-Thong and Suphanburi Dynasties and their Connections to Khmer Royal Bloodlines*; and in Book II during the post Longvek period under *Royal Khmer Bloodlines of Ayutthayan Kings*.

The *2/k.125 Fragment* has shown that Chau Ponhea Yat descended from the line of the Khmer princess and U-Thong/Ramathibodi, believed to be of Môn or Môn-Khmer origin according to George Coedès. King Ramaracha was the grandson of Ramathibodi/Khmer princess and father of Chau Ponhea Yat. Ramaracha was overthrown by his second cousin Nakhon In (from the branch of Pha-ngua/Borommaracha) who reigned as Intharacha when he acceded to the throne. According to the Luang Praseut Chronicle (*LPC*), Intharacha sent Ramaracha into exile to Padāgūcām. As to the *2/k.125 Fragment*, it said that Braḥ Rām Cau (Ramaracha) was sent into exile to Chaktomouk (present-day Phnom Penh). Vickery has done a magnificent job demonstrating that Padāgūcām, mentioned in the *LPC*, was Chaktomouk by breaking down the word Padāgūcām to *prāp jhām*. *Prāp* means "to put down" or "to conquer." According to Vickery, *Prāp Jhām* means "to put down the Cham" as the area was also known as the Cham River. As a background, the Cambodian chronicles said that after Chau Ponhea Yat arrived in Chaktomouk in 1433 he decreed that the four confluent rivers called *Prāp Jhām* (ព្រាបចាម ឬ ព្រាបឈាម), be renamed to *Tonlé Chaktomouk Bopear* (ទន្លេចតុមុខបួព័). Therefore, there was a historical connection between Padāgūcām, Prāp Jhām, and Chaktomouk.

It was customary in ancient time that a king removed from power by one of his relatives would be sent into exile to live in a friendly or vassal country, which was the case for the Khmer kings Srei Reachea and Srei Soriyotei. With the intervention of King Borommatrailokanat (1448-1488) of Ayutthaya, Uparaja Thommo Reachea had his half-brother Srei Reachea (the legitimate king) and his nephew Srei Soriyotei (the rebellious and self-proclaimed king) sent into exile to Ayutthaya. In the same manner, when the *2/k.125 Fragment* mentioned that Braḥ Rām Cau (Ramaracha) was sent into exile by the king of Ayutthaya to Chaktomouk, Cambodia must have been in friendly terms with Ayutthaya. During the reigning periods between Ramathibodi (1351-1369) and Ramaracha (1395-1409), Cambodia seemed to be still in good relations with Ayutthaya because there were no indications showing any conflicts between the two countries. If Ramaracha were exiled to Padāgūcām (Chaktomouk) in 1409, as stated in the *LP* Chronicle, then the event would have occurred under the reign of Lompong Reachea (1409-1416). It must be remembered that the Cambodian chronicles are really ambiguous during this period. The *LP* Chronicle said that Nakhon In (who later became King Intharacha) toppled his nephew, King Ramaracha, and exiled him to Cambodia.

As history has shown, a good relationship between two countries could suddenly turn into enmity when a new ruler took over. The relationship between Ayutthaya and Cambodia must have gone sour after Borom Reamea became king in 1425. When Thommasoka succeeded Borom Reamea in 1429 Intharacha decided to launch an aggressive attack at Angkor. The Cambodian chronicles said that Ponhea Yat was in the service of King Thommasoka and that the Khmer king gave him a troop to command to fight the Ayutthayan army. The Cambodian chronicles did not state the exact relationship between Thommasoka and Ponhea Yat, except to say that Ponhea Yat was of royal blood. If we take the *2/k.125 Fragment* to be true, then Ponhea Yat (son of Ramaracha from the branch of Khmer princess of Suphanburi and U-Thong/Ramathibodi of Môn or Môn-Khmer) was the antagonist of Intharacha (son of Pha-ngua, a Khmer prince from Suphanburi who succeeded his brother-in-law Ramathibodi as King Borommaracha I). Could it be possible that Intharacha launched an attack at Angkor because he felt threatened by Ramaracha and Ponhea Yat? The war between Ayutthaya and Angkor before the accession of Chau Ponhea Yat could in a sense be considered a civil war between the Khmer royal branch of Suphanburi and the Khmer royal branch of Angkor. Thommasoka was the last Khmer king descending from the royal bloodline of Angkor. When Chau Ponhea Yat took up the mantle after Thommasoka was killed, the war between Angkor and Ayutthaya truly became a civil war between the Suphanburi-Lopburi branch of Khmer Princess/U-Thong (Ramathibodi) and the Suphanburi branch of Pha-ngua (Borommaracha I).

Before he acceded to the throne and became King Rama VI, Crown Prince Maha Vajiravudh conducted a survey of the cities of Kamphaeng Phet, Sawankhalok, Sukhothai, and Phitsanulok. His findings were published by Piriya Krairiksh in a paper called *A Historiography of Sukhothai Art: a Framework in Need of Revision*. The Crown Prince mentioned that the Khmer language was practiced in the early Sukhothai period, at least until the reign of King Lithai (1340-1357 or 1346/7-1368/74). By extension, it can be deduced that the Khmer language was also practiced in Suphanburi and possibly in Ayutthaya at least under the reign of King Ramathibodi. During that period, the Khmer language was considered elitist and appreciated in the royal and noble circles. It was very likely that the Ayutthayan kings, princes, and noble families during that period practiced the Khmer language, in combination with the early Thai language, in a similar way that the British used the French language in the old England court.

It is not a coincidence that the prefix *Chau Ponhea*, a term coming from Ayutthaya, was introduced into Cambodia during the reign of Chau Ponhea Yat. Prior to this period, there were no Khmer monarchs utilizing this prefix. The letter King Ang Chan I sent to King Chairacha of Ayutthaya in 1536, which mentioned that King Ramathibodi II was his uncle, tends to support the *2/k.125 Fragment*, which stated that Chau Ponhea Yat was the son of Ramaracha, which in turn reinforces the credibility of the document. The Cambodian concept of family relationships is different than the concept used by the Western standard. Because Chau Ponhea Yat was the son of King Ramaracha (from the branch of the Khmer princess from Suphanburi who married U-Thong/Ramathibodi), then King Ramathibodi II (from the branch of Pha-ngua/Borommaracha I, the Khmer prince from Suphanburi and brother of the Khmer princess) would be considered his nephew in the Cambodian concept of ranked order. Ang Chan I, who was the grandson of Chau Ponhea Yat, would therefore be considered the nephew of Ramathibodi II. In contrast, the Western concept would consider Ang Chan I and Ramathibodi II as fourth cousin once removed. The ranked order in family relationships is considered very important in the Cambodian concept and also in the Asian concept in general.

Even though Book I covers only up to the end of the Longvek period (1594/1595), I decided to include the entire history of Thailand in this book for the purpose of better understanding the history of Cambodia. Throughout this book, Ayutthaya and Ayutthayan are used from 1351 to 1767. The foundation of the

Kingdom of Ayutthaya started in 1351 by U-Thong, believed to be of Môn or Môn-Khmer origin according to George Coedès, who reigned as King Ramathibodi. The Ayutthaya period is considered to have ended under the Ban Phlu Luang Dynasty, with Borommaracha V (1758-1767) as the last king. The word "Siam" is used from 1767, starting from the Thonburi period under the reign of Taksin, to 1939 when Prime Minister Phibunsongkhram declared that Siam would be renamed Thailand as a political move to encompass Tai people outside of Siam. Except for a brief period under the turbulent time between 1945 and 1949, "Thailand" was reverted to "Siam" but I will use the words "Thailand" and "Thai" from 1939. Cambodians and Khmers are used interchangeably throughout this book. The words Tonkin and Annam referred to Vietnam in general. Geographically, Tonkin covered the northern area with its capital located in Hanoi while Annam covered the southern area with its capital located in Hue.

During my research for this book, I encountered many obstacles and difficulties in reporting the timelines for the reigns of the Khmer kings. The difficulties were due to some sources giving conflicting dates for their reigns. The conflicting dates were due to many reasons, but a few of those were as follows:

1. **Uncertainty of Khmer Kings or of their Reigns during the Angkor Period**

    The name of Sdach Kamluong (Leper King) has not been satisfactorily resolved and the identities of two kings, Udayadityavarman I and Jayaviravarman, that battled Suryavarman I for the throne of Angkor are still being debated.

2. **Confusing Records Used in the 14th and 15th Centuries**

    The genealogy that is most uncertain and confusing occurred during the 14th and 15th centuries. Records during these periods were destroyed due to many wars. To reestablish the records, King Ponhea Yat (1432-1463) convened his ministers and tried to reconstruct past historical events by memories, but they could only go back 27 years into the past. Therefore, the events prior to 1405 were very uncertain. I had to reconstruct the events of those periods based on the Chinese records and Laotian chronicles. Most of the events have been reported by previous scholars, but because of the confusing and unclear situations, they only reported the accounts without much elaboration.

    Pertaining to Book II that covered the reign of King Ang Eng, it must be noted that the king made an attempt to reconstruct the royal chronology during the above confusing periods. The dates in the *Ang Eng Document* (also called *Ang Eng Fragment* because sections of the original work were destroyed) that were submitted in 1796 to Rama I of Thailand were reported in animal years without specifying their numerical years in the Saka, Buddhist, or Christian era. This led to different interpretations by historians on the reigns of the Khmer kings during the confusing period of the 14th and 15th centuries. The *Nong Royal Chronicle of Cambodia,* which was produced after the *Ang Eng Fragment,* again reported the years only in animal signs. Additionally, it differed in certain areas from the *Ang Eng Fragment,* which further led to more confusion.

Conventions Used to Transliterate Khmer or Related Khmer Names

Names in Khmer or related to Khmer will be transliterated using the method devised by Savaros (Pou) Lewitz in her publication, *Note sur la Translittération du Cambodgien*. In order to make the reading of the texts easier and less foreign to readers, they will be transliterated only once whenever possible. In certain cases, I may have to repeat the transliterated names in order to avoid confusions. Standard Romanized texts will replace repeated names that have already been transliterated. The transliterated method prescribed by Lewitz is reproduced herein in Table 1 to facilitate the reader in deciphering the names mentioned in this book. Names derived from the Chinese transliteration, especially those predating the apparition of the Khmer epigraphies in the early 7th century, will not be transliterated further.

It must be noted that whenever possible, Vietnamese names will be written in the Vietnamese language for the first time but they will be written in the English language thereafter for easier reading.

Table 1. Convention Prescribed by Savaros (Pou) Lewitz for the Transliteration of Khmer Names

ក k	ខ kh	គ g	ឃ gh	ង ṅ
ច c	ឆ ch	ជ j	ឈ jh	ញ ñ
ដ ṭ	ឋ ប ṭh	ឌ ḍ	ឍ ḍh	ណ ṇ
ត t	ថ th	ទ d	ធ dh	ន n
ប p	ផ ph	ព b	ភ bh	ម m
យ y	រ r	ល l	វ v	ស s (ś or ṣ)	ហ h	ឡ ḷ	អ a
ហ្វ hv	ហ្ន hn	ហ្ម hm	ហ្ល hl	ស្ស sh			
ឫ ṛ	ឬ ṝ	ឭ ḷ	ឮ ḹ				

Inherent Wovel a	ា ā	ិ i	ី ī	ឹ ĭ	ឺ ī̆	�ុ u	ូ ū	ួ uo	ើ oe
ឿ īoe	ៀ īe	េ e	ែ ae	ៃ ai	ោ o	ៅ au	ំ ṃ	ះ ḥ	
ö	ô	ō	ៈ ơ	ó	ŏrŏ	(o)	ő	ő	។ o2	ៗ o1	។ល។ //l

Examples:

1. Nārāy(n) Rājā = នារាយណ៍រាជា   2. Srī Suriyovaṅs = ស្រីសុរិយោវង្ស   3. ñăr = ញ៉ារ   4. Sraḥ = ស្រះ
4. Sra· = ស្រ: 5. Catumukh = ចតុមុខ   6. Jayajeṭṭhā = ជ័យជេដ្ឋា   8. Aṅg Nan' = អង្គនន់
9. Narottam = នរោត្តម   10. Sīsuvatthi = ស៊ីសុវត្ថិ   11. Paṅgāp' = បង្កប់

Conventions Used to Classify the Reigns of the Khmer Kings

One of the considerations I have made in this book is to differentiate kings, regents, and usurpers. Another consideration is the classification on the reigned orders of the kings. The following are the conventions I use:

1. I put a number in front of each king to indicate the order of his reign.
2. For example, **40 Jayavarman VII** indicated that Jayavarman VII was the 40th king that I identified in the Khmer history.
3. All rulers in the Funan period are classified as kings.
4. Non-consecrated legitimate rulers of royal blood, even for short reigns, are classified as kings.
5. Regents are not considered kings and will be put in brackets.
6. Usurpers are not considered kings and will be put in brackets, except for the following:
   a. Usurpers of royal blood and consecrated are classified as kings.
   b. A usurper who married the daughter or wife of the previous king that he killed or deposed to legitimize his reign is considered a king. For example, even though Indravarman III was a usurper and not of royal blood, he is considered a king, because he married the daughter of

the king that he deposed. Sdach Kân is not considered a king because he is an outright usurper who never married any of the king's daughters.

7. Legendary kings such as Ta Trasâk Paêm and Ta Suos will only be used for reference points and will not be classified as historical kings.

For each king, whenever possible I will list his secondary name; the capitals where he resided or reigned; his relationship to his predecessors; the dates of his birth and death; his posthumous name; the temples or monuments he had built; and his religion. I will omit any of the above data if no definite information is available.

Personal Preference on how to Cite References

I am well aware that most authors prefer to partition their references within each chapter. I do not believe there is a right or wrong way on how to cite references, but as a personal preference I prefer to deviate from the norm by listing the references into one grouping. Additionally, I use my own personal method to cite a reference by placing it in superscript within brackets. If I cited a specific case or event that I described in my book, then I will also provide the page number(s) separated by a comma after the reference number. If there are more than one references, I will cite them all within the same brackets and separated by a semi colon. My purpose for doing so is to be transparent about my sources of information. Below are the examples on how I cited my references:

- **Citing Reference 1**: In the genealogy chart, Coedès indicated that Bhavavarman I was the son of Prithivindravarman and his cousin Chitrasena was the son of Viravarman.[1]
- **Citing Reference 6 on Page 16**: The map illustrating the Funan Empire is shown in Figure 11.[6,p16]
- **Citing Reference 111 on Pages 150 to 152**: The timeline reported in the *Essai de Tableau Chronologique de la Période Post-Angkorienne* by Mak Phoeun[110,pp150-152] does not seem to take into account the events mentioned in the Ming Shi-lu (MSL).
- **Citing Reference 5 with Footnote 3 on Pages 101 to 102**: However, Vickery also wrote that the name *Kaundinya* was mentioned in many inscriptions, such as K.5, K.263, K.268, K. 483, K. 528, K. 669, and K. 806 as noted below:[5,footnote3,pp101-102]
- **Citing Reference 7 on Pages 288-289 with Notation 1**: Based on the Khmer Inscription K.27 that was discovered by Étienne Aymonier.[7,pp288-289,note1]
- **Citing References 1 and 3**2: Coedès indicated in the genealogy chart that Viravarman and Prithivindravarman were the sons of Rudravarman.[1; 32]
- **Citing Reference1 on Page 115, Reference 6 on Page 122, and Reference 75 on Page 11**: Vrahmaloka (K.393)[1,p115; 6,p122; 75,p11]

Influences of the Kings' Wives and Princes' Wives

The Cambodian chronicles and all information about the history of Cambodia never mentioned the roles or influences the wives had on their kings or princes, except for the case of Jayarajadevi and Indradevi. We know that Jayarajadevi had a great impact on Jayavarman VII. The Cambodian chronicles never directly mentioned about the influence of Srei Sokonthor Bat's concubine, Neak Mneang Peou, over the king but it was implied that she had a great influence over him. It was because of Neak Mneang Peou that Srei Sokonthor Bat elevated her brother Kân and her father Neay Kim to high ranking officials and noble titles of Oknha Meun Sneha Chom Chith and Preah Pichey Neak (with the title of Uk Luong Montrei Sneha), respectively. Besides that, we are mostly left in the dark on what kind of influences the wives of the Uparaja, or the Upayuvaraja, or the kings had on their husbands. I venture to guess that many of the wars between royal siblings or royal families could have been caused by jealousies from the wives who wanted their sons to be kings. Probably many of the fratricidal wars, that were one of the major causes for the downfall of Cambodia, could have been prevented if the rule of succession were firmly and clearly established. A clearly defined rule of succession would prevent the manipulation of the system which was subjective.

Final Note

When writing about history, everything must be put in perspective, and into its proper context. In ancient times, Westerners and even the Chinese described Southeast Asians as barbarians primarily based on the way they dressed. Most of the natives were half-naked on the upper bodies. One must understand that it was the climate that dictated how they dressed. Unlike the Europeans and the Chinese, whose native climates were much cooler and thus required them to cover their entire bodies in clothing. The Southeast Asians (also the Egyptians) who live in warm climate cannot dress in the same manner as the Europeans. When the Europeans and the Chinese came in contacts with the Southeast Asians in earlier centuries, their first impression was to label these natives as barbarians without considering the fact that they had built sophisticated monuments. It was only after the invention of air conditioning systems and the interactions with Westerners that culture and traditions started to change in Southeast Asia. Even in the 21st century, some men still prefer to bare their upper bodies while staying at home and the reason has mainly to do with the weather being too hot. Some men in the countryside still work shirtless to cool off their bodies.

The main history of Cambodia has already been written, but I feel that some events have not been covered. If I can make an analogy I would compare the Khmer history to the Mekong River. The river's source originates from the plateau of Tibet. As the river flows through many countries, its main body is fed by small streams and grows to its full size to form the Mekong River. Like the Mekong River, the Khmer history is well known by historians, but the many events — like the small streams feeding to the main body of the river — that fed to the history of Cambodia have not been well-discussed. This book is written to cover many of the events that occurred in the Khmer history.

ACKNOWLEDGMENTS

THE KHMER KINGS AND THE HISTORY OF CAMBODIA

I am very humble and honored for the support and encouragement that His departed Majesty King Father Norodom Sihanouk (Preah Borom Ratanak Kaudh), Her Majesty Queen Mother Norodom Monineath Sihanouk, and King Norodom Sihamoni had given me concerning my effort to write *The Khmer Kings and the History of Cambodia*. The letters of appreciation from their Majesties are reproduced in Appendix 1.

I am eternally indebted to my wife Theany and my three daughters Elizabeth, Jacqueline, and Angelica for supporting and encouraging me to write this book and also for some editing work. My wife was so patient with me while I wrote this book for the last nine years. I had papers, books, and all sorts of documents scattered all over the place and never once did she complain about the mess I made around the house. She also accompanied me to the all of the meetings and book club conferences in both, the USA and France, while I was working on this project. I am very thankful for the feedback I received from my family for the improvement of my book.

I am forever grateful to my parents So Bun Hor and Tan Laâm who had provided me with their support and the necessary means to achieve my education. Their primary concern was for me to get an education and they would not hesitate to make many sacrifices for me to achieve that goal. I would like to also thank my American families, the Jaggers and the Lusks, who took me into their homes and provided me with love, kindness, and comfort when I was working in Tennessee in the summers and winters while the Khmer Rouge was persecuting the Khmer people in Cambodia.

I am very thankful for the feedback and editing I received from my very dear friend James Gerrand. I greatly treasure our friendship that goes back for almost thirty years. He was kind enough to agree to read and edit a major portion of my draft. He made valuable suggestions and recommendations which enabled me to improve the content of my book.

I am very appreciative for the help I received from Professors Khing Hoc Dy and Vong Sotheara. I am very thankful for their guidance for the proper translation of ancient Khmer words and spelling of Khmer names.

I thank Ryan Arneson for reviewing and editing a large portion of my book and my brother Kelvin So (So Khong Leng) with whom I had conversations concerning the progress of my book. I am eternally thankful to my friend Shuh Yi Chern who had spent a lot of time with me going over the pronunciations and meanings of the Chinese words that I reproduced in this book. Without his help I would have never been able to achieve the results shown in this book. He was so patient and very generous spending his time with me. I am eternally grateful to Professor Sar Peou who was my Khmer teacher. His dedication to teaching had imparted my thirst for knowledge in Khmer. He is my guru. I would like to thank Kent Davis for his advice and for agreeing to publish this book.

George Coedès' magnitude of work about Southeast Asia but particularly about Cambodia revealed the secret of Angkor, thus opening up the understanding of Khmer history to the rest of the world. Coedès is one of the great minds and epigraphists on Southeast Asia. I would like to thank him and all scholars and historians who have written on Cambodia.

I would like to acknowledge my thanks and deep appreciation to Antiquariaat Sanderus for allowing me to reproduce the image of the 1747 Dutch map of the Citadel of Longvek; to Alex Whitaker for letting me use the image of the constellation; and to Google for agreeing to let me reproduce the image of the Angkor Wat complex as viewed from the sky.

I entered monkhood for a short time at the Wat Khmer San Jose and studied under the late Venerable Preah Kru Chum Choeum in the fall of 1996. I am very grateful to his venerable for accepting me as his student and allowing me to stay in his temple and sleep by the side of his bed during my time as a bikkhu. Finally, I am eternally indebted to the late Venerable Preah Kru Sumedhavansa Oung Mean Candavanno at Vatt Buddhikarama in Washington, D.C. (Cambodian Buddhist temple located in Silver Spring, Maryland) because he was the person who had the most impact on me about my belief in Buddhism. He was so articulate and clear in his explanations about Buddhism and the teaching of the Lord Buddha. The more I conversed with Preah Kru Ong Mean, the more I wanted to know about Buddhism. He was the source of my inspiration.

This book is dedicated to the Khmer people who are the guardians of the Khmer culture and tradition.

Brief Description of
Present-Day Cambodia

The official name of Cambodia is the Kingdom of Cambodia with Norodom Sihamoni as its constitutional monarch. The country, with its superficies of 181,035 square kilometers, is located in Southeast Asia between latitudes 10°/15°N and longitudes 102°/108°E within the tropics. It is bordered on the east-southeast by Vietnam, on the west-northwest by Thailand, and on the northeast by Laos (Figure 1). The Cambodian people are called Khmers. As of this writing, the population in Cambodia is estimated to be over 15 million with over 90 percent of them practicing Theravada Buddhism. Phnom Penh is the capital and it is located at the confluent of the Mekong, Bassac, and Tonle Sap Rivers called Tonlé Chaktomouk (river of four faces).

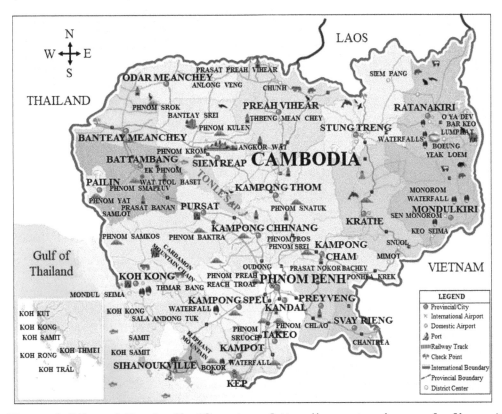

Figure 1. Map of Cambodia (Courtesy: https://www.tourismcambodia.org)

The temperature in Cambodia ranges between 20° and 40°C (68° and 104°F) with November being the coldest month and April the hottest month. Cambodia's climate is divided into the dry and wet seasons. The dry season starts in November and ends in April. The wet season starts in May-June and ends in October.

Due to water management and modern techniques, Cambodia is able to practice rice cultivation four times per year such as short wet season from mid-April to end of August; medium wet season from mid-August to end of February; long wet season from beginning of June to end of February; and dry season from beginning of December to end of March. The chart indicating the temperature climate and rice cultivation period is shown in Figure 2.

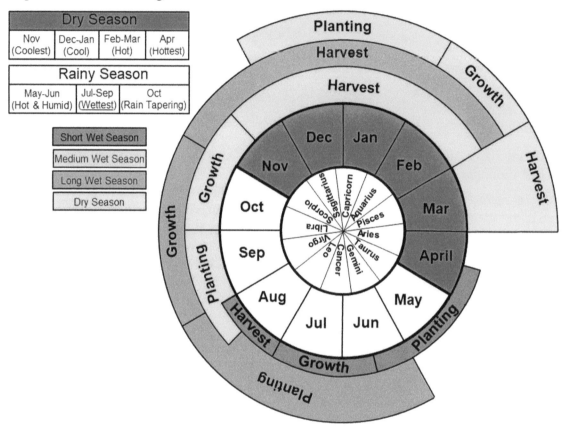

Figure 2. Climate and Rice Cultivation during Wet and Dry Seasons in Cambodia
(Based on Cambodia Ministry of Agriculture, Forestry, and Fisheries, 2012)

Cambodia has the largest fresh water lake in Southeast Asia, which is called Boeung Tonlé Sap (Freshwater 'River' Lake as opposed to salty lake), also known as the Great Lake. There is one feature about the Great Lake that is unique in the world. In the dry season the water flowed out of the lake and emptied into the ocean, but in the monsoon season the rivers (Tonlé Sap, Mékong, and Bassac) sizes swelled and reversed courses; with the Tonlé Sap River carried the water back into the Great Lake. It is for this reason that the lake superficies increase about fourfold in the monsoon season to 10,800 square kilometers from its dry season of about 2,700 square kilometers. In the past the lake had the greatest concentration of fish in the world living in the water per cubic meter. Henri Mouhot was so astonished by the abundance of fish that he wrote in his journal that *the fish were crushed under the boats*. Due to overfishing and lack of management control, the fish are much scarcer nowadays. In the same way, Cambodia was covered by about seventy percent of forest prior to 1993 but nowadays the uncontrolled deforestation perpetrated by the lumber industry has reduced the forest to 30-40 percent. Many faunas that served as refuge for wild animals are disappearing rapidly.

Cambodia is famed for Angkor Wat and many of its temples scattered over an area of approximately 1,000 square kilometers in the Angkor region. The other iconic landmarks are the temples of Bayon, Ta Prohm, Preah Khan, Banteay Srei, and Preah Vihear just to name a few. Many international organizations such as the United Nations Educational, Scientific and Cultural Organization (UNESCO) and École Française d'Extrême-Orient (EFEO) as well as countries like India, Japan, Australia, New Zealand, Hungary, Germany, the United Kingdom, and China are cooperating with the Autorité pour la Protection du Site et l'Aménagement de la Région d'Angkor (APSARA; but known in English as Authority for the Protection and Management of Angkor and the Region of Siem Reap) to work to restore the temples.

SUMMARY

THE KHMER KINGS AND THE HISTORY OF CAMBODIA

The history of Cambodia that has been written demands an update with a fresh analysis and new point of views. Recent evidence shows that Funan was already an advanced maritime society before the arrival of the Indian Brahmans. Stories of Funan ships more than fifty meters in length with the capacity to carry 1,000 tons of cargo were mentioned in the Chinese records. The Chinese had been using Funan ships for long distance because the Chinese ships were not large enough. In 1968, Dr. Georges Olivier mentioned that before the Indian migration, the Khmers — especially the ethnic *Kouys* and *Samrès* — had an advanced culture and were already proficient and knowledgeable in the art of extracting iron and gold from iron ores. The tradition of utilizing the expertise of the Kouys was still carried on by King Ang Chan I when he employed them to build war equipment.

Funan must have been a great seafaring country due to some evidences that existed between the ancient Khmer kingdom and Maya in South America. Lawrence Palmer Briggs stated the following about the contact between Funan and Maya:

> *However, an even wider range of Khmer influence is dimly emerging from the pages of unwritten history. The exhibition shown by the American Museum of Natural History on the occasion of the International Congress of Americanists in 1949, opened a completely new chapter by demonstrating the existence of cultural links, surprisingly close in some instances, between the Maya and Mexican area and ancient Cambodia. These contacts seem to have been established at the time of the kingdom of Fu-nan and to have ended only with the political collapse of the Khmer empire shortly after A.D. 1200. They imply the former existence of a powerful Khmer maritime activity, of which we had, so far, only a few vague indications in old Chinese reports.*

The connection between Funan and the Mayan culture had brought Michael D. Coe to give his opinion on this subject. Even though Coe admits in his book *Angkor and the Khmer Civilization* the similarity of Angkor temples architecture with that of Mexico (temples in the southeastern region) and that of Guatemala (temples in the northern region), he still dismisses any connections between the Maya and Angkor culture.

Concerning his contribution to the Southeast Asia study, and particularly to the history of Cambodia, there is nobody equal to George Coedès, especially in the field of epigraphy. He has enriched the world with his insights and expert knowledge in the ancient Khmer civilization. His work is of the utmost respect by scholars and is of great influence to researchers of Southeast Asian study all over the world. However, lately some of his theses or assumptions have been challenged by scholars like Michael Vickery — one of the experts on the history of ancient Cambodia. Also, the modern theory of the Nusantao Maritime Trading and Communication Network (NMTCN) exposed by the American anthropologist Wilhelm Soheim II has put into questions some of the assumptions made by Coedès and other scholars that came before and after him. Two of Vickery's essays that caught my attention were *Funan Reviewed: Deconstructing the Ancients* and *Coedès' Histories of Cambodia*. Both essays are highly recommended for anybody who is truly interested in expanding his or her knowledge on Cambodia's history. Before Vickery and Wilhelm, nobody was brave enough to challenge and deconstruct Cocdès's words. The theory that Funan was somewhat of a backward country until the arrival of the Indian Brahmans was accepted as truthful and left unchallenged for decades. This belief is now questionable based on more careful examinations of the Chinese accounts on Funan and also on Wilhelm's theory of the NMTCN (*Nusantao Maritime Trading and Communication Network*). He summarized his theory as follows:

> *... I now define Nusantao as natives of Southeast Asia, and their descendants, with a maritime-oriented culture from their beginnings, these beginnings probably in southeastern Island Southeast Asia around 5000 BC or possibly earlier. Most of the Nusantao probably spoke a related or pre-Austronesian language, but there were likely some who spoke a non-Austronesian language as well... I did not consider non-maritime Austronesian-speakers as Nusantao.*

Furthermore, Wilhelm stated that because of their philosophical training, the European reflected negatively on the culture of Southeast Asia. He made a powerful and convincing statement as follows:

> *This general conclusion that the Southeast Asian cultural region was backward was based not on an objective and independent analysis of the data, but on the prevailing philosophy of the late Victorian Age and the unconscious predisposition of the European and European-oriented archaeologists who were doing the research in and on Southeast Asian prehistory. The culture of western Europe was considered as the peak of civilization to that time, with the known cultural history which led to that peak — including the early historic Middle East to Greece to Rome — being the ideal path for culture to follow. The greater the difference and distance of a culture from that path, as expressed in the prehistoric artifacts and known history, the farther behind the ideal that culture was. What was known of Southeast Asian prehistoric artifacts and living ethnic groups indicated that they were very different from those of Europe, and thus were primitive.*

It is perplexing how the name *Hun Tien* (混填), described in the Chinese Imperial Records as the first king of Funan (扶南), came to be transcribed as *Kaundinya*. George Coedès transcribed the Chinese words to *Chiao Chen Ju (or Kiao Tchen You)* and then to *Kaundinya* in Sanskrit. Hun Tien had only two syllables while Chiao Chen Ju or Kaundinya (Kaun-din-ya) had three syllables. The answer to this bothersome question could be found in Michael Vickery's articles: *Funan Reviewed: Deconstructing the Ancients* and *Coedès' Histories of Cambodia* as well as in another article called *Kingdom of Funan*. I relied on a Chinese native (see Acknowledgments) and on the Google Language Tools (GLT) to help me decipher the Chinese pronunciation, which was reconstructed according to Edwin George Pulleyblank (*Lexicon of Reconstructed Pronouncition in Early Middle Chinese, and Early Mandarin. UCB Press, Vancouver, pp. 135 and 306, 1991*). As I listened to the pronunciation in the GLT, no detection for the three syllables that Coedès assigned to the words *Hun Tien* could be heard. This was also confirmed by the native Chinese that I consulted and interviewed for this book. Coedès left the transcriptions of other descendants of *Hun Tien* such as *Hun P'an Huang* (混盤況), *Hun P'an* (混盤盤), *Fan Shih Man* (范師蔓), *Fan Chin Sheng* (范金生), *Fan Chan* (范旃), *Fan Chang* (范長), and *Fan Xun* (范尋) faithfully to their original names. The question then ensued as to why Coedès chose to only transcribe the name of the first Funan king to a Sanskrit name, thus connoting he was of Indian origin? Vickery argued that *Hun* may be a Môn-Khmer or prehistoric Austronesian title or clan name used by the earlier Funan kings. He further speculated that George Coedès and Paul Pelliot, the French sinologist who translated the Chinese records on Funan, may have been influenced by their works and had preconceived ideas that Funan was founded by Brahmans. After examining and listening to the evidence of how the Chinese words 混塡 are pronounced, I tend to concur with Vickery's point of view on this issue. Vickery went further in his writing by claiming that there was no Indian by the name of Kaundinya who came to Funan. He said:

> *It is certain that no real 'Kaundinya' ever went from India, or from anywhere else, to Funan at any time, and this so-called second Kaundinya simply shows us that by the 4th-5th century, after two centuries of contact with India, the Funan rulers were taking on Indian garb, and had adopted the Indian Kaundinya legend as their own, updating their origin legend to incorporate elements of Indian origin legends.*

However, Vickery also wrote that the name *Kaundinya* was mentioned in many inscriptions, such as K.5, K.263, K.268, K. 483, K. 528, K. 669, and K. 806 as noted below:

> *The title 'Preah Bat/brah pada was unknown in Funan; in fact it was not even in use in the epigraphy of the 7ᵗʰ-8ᵗʰ century Chenla period, and although common in Angkor was not accorded to Kaundinya in any of the Angkor inscriptions in which that name is found."*

An observation must be made. Prior to Coedès' transcription of the words "Hun Tien" to "Kundinya", Paul Pelliot had already attempted to suggest that *Hun* was meant to be *Kaun,* and that *Tien* was the same as *Dien.* Therefore, *Hun Tien* was *Kaun-Dien* or *Kaun-Dyn.* It must be noted that in some Cambodian historical records, *Kaundinya* is also called *Preah Bat Kaundyn.* The acceptance and belief of *Kaundinya* as the first Funan king is so entrenched in the Khmer society and imprinted in the culture that it is impossible to undo it. For the purpose of this book, *Hun Tien* and *Kaundinya* are used interchangeably. However, it must be noted that *Hun Tien* is the original and primary name of the first king of Funan.

Most of what is known during the *Funan* (扶南) and *Chenla* (真臘) periods came from the Chinese Imperial Records. Combining these records with the Khmer sources, Cham sources, and archaeological excavations throughout Southeast Asia, a very broad understanding on the history of Funan and Chenla emerges.

China exchanged embassies and special envoys with Funan from the 3rd to the 7th centuries AD, and also with Chenla, from the 7th to the 8th centuries AD. These events were recorded in the *History of the Three Kingdoms* (Sanguo Zhi Li-shi, 三國志歷史) by Chen Shou (陳壽) in 289; in the *Annals of the Southern Qi* (Nan Qi Shu, 南齊書) by Xiao Zixian (蕭子顯, 485-537); in the *Annals of the Liang* (Liang Shu, 梁書) by Yao Cha (姚察) and Yao Siliáan (姚思廉) in 636; and in the *Annals of the Jin* (Jin Shu, 晉書) by Fang Xuanling (房玄齡) in 648. The French sinologist, Paul Pelliot, collected the information from these Chinese archives and published his work called *Fou-Nan* in the Bulletin de l'École Française d'Extrême-Orient in 1903.

Chinese texts, dating as far back as the first century AD, mentioned the existence of two main states located in the lower valley of the Mekong. The two states were Funan and Chenla. Coedès suggested that the word *Funan* was a Chinese pronunciation of the Môn-Khmer word *Phnom* which means mountain in Khmer, but his theory has not been universally accepted by scholars.

The people of Funan and Chenla, who are classified as belonging to the Austro-Asiatic race, must have spoken the language belonging to the Môn-Khmer family because that was the most prevalent spoken language in that region. In the early period, Southeast Asia was predominantly composed of Funanese, Khmer (Chenla), Môn, Puy, Malay, Cham, and Annamese/Tonkinese. The Funanese, especially the Khmer and the Môn were closely related. The Annamese/Tonkinese, before its sinization for a millennium by China from 100 BC to 900 AD, were an amalgamation of people with the languages related to the Môn-Khmer family.

It must be understood that Brahmans in ancient time were men of knowledge who understood mathematics, cosmology, sciences, art, literature, and philosophy. They could be equated to the great philosophers, mathematicians, and inventors of ancient Greece like Archimedes, or of the Renaissance period, like Leonardo da Vinci.

There is some confusion as to who was the founder of the Khmer civilization. Some books mentioned Kaundinya, the son of King Adityavaṁsa "Itapah," whom the Chinese called *Hun Tien* and the Cambodian called *Preah Thong*, as the first Khmer king. The legend says that Kaundinya was banished from Indraprashta, which was located about twenty miles south of the city of Delhi in India. He married Princess Soma, whom the Chinese called *Liu Yeh*, the daughter of the local king named *Nagaraja* (Dragon/Serpent King). Some other books mentioned Kambu Svayambhuva, a Hindu hermit, as the founder of the Khmer civilization. He took Mera, an *Apsara* (celestial nymph) of great beauty and elegance, as his wife.

The seemingly contradiction in these two legends was caused by the lack of explanation of the origins of Kaundinya and Kambu. The Lunar Dynasty — which drew its inspiration from the Hindu epic *Mahabharata* with Krishna as the Avatar (incarnation) of Vishnu, the Supreme God in the Hindu religion — was created when Kaundinya married Princess Soma, the Naga princess and native of Funan. The Solar Dynasty — which drew its inspiration from another Hindu epic, the *Ramayana*, where Rama was another embodiment or incarnation of Vishnu — was created when Kambu married Mera, an Apsara and native of Chenla. It must be noted that the cultural events in the story of *Ramayana* preceded that of the *Mahabharata*.

Because Chenla was a vassal state of Funan during the earlier period, then, chronologically speaking, Kaundinya would be considered the first Khmer king. However, the name *Kaundinya* never existed, per se. The name was a rendition that George Coedès derived from the name *Hun Tien* mentioned in the *Chinese Imperial Dynasty Records*.

A legend resembling the Kaundinya and Soma's union was told by the Pallava kings of Kanchi who ruled south India for over 500 years from the 4th century to the end of the 9th century AD. Is the Khmer legend borrowed from that of the Pallava legend that was brought in by the earlier Brahman settlers? The name Pallava was derived from the Sanskrit word *Pallavam* that means "branch," and refers to a new branch of dynasty founded by Aa-thondaimaan Ilanthiraiyan, the son of Karikala Chola, in the early 2nd century AD. Therefore, the Pallava dynasty was an offshoot of the Chola dynasty. Khmer scripts were derived from the Pallava scripts.

Funan became an empire under the reign of Fan Shih Man (205-225), a great general who served under Hun Pan, the last descendant of Hun Tien. The known Funan period lasted for about five hundred years, from the later part of the 1st century of the Common era to 540 until Chenla, a vassal state, rebelled and replaced Funan as the new master of the region. Compilations of all historical records indicate a total of thirteen known Funan rulers. The Funan Empire faded into the background and finally disappeared from historical records.

The Chenla period lasted for about two and a half centuries, from 540 to 802. Chenla was mentioned for the first time in the *Annals of the Sui* (Sui Shu - 隋書) in 636. It must be noted that the name *Chenla* is equivalent to Kambuja, Kamvuja, Kambujadesa, and Cambodia. Chenla, still a vassal state of Funan, became more confident as its power started to rise under the reign of Srutavarman (435-495). He was credited for starting the process of liberating Chenla from the domination of Funan. The rise of Chenla's power coincided with the undefined line of successions and broken line of new Funan rulers. The ascendancy of each new Funan ruler to the throne never seemed to go smoothly. Chenla, with its more stable government, took advantage of the situation and started its conquest over Funan. The role was now reversed and Chenla subjugated Funan to a vassal state. Bhavavarman I (550-600) is considered the first Chenla king who ruled over Funan. The domination and annexation of Funan by Chenla was completed under the reign of Isanavarman (611-640) in 627, but some former vassal states of Funan were still outside of Chenla's influence. Chenla was divided after Jayavarman I because he did not leave a male heir to succeed him. Chinese records indicate that after 707, Chenla was divided into Upper Chenla or Land Chenla (Luzhenla, 陸真臘; also called Wendan, 文單; or Polou, 婆鏤) and Lower Chenla or Water Chenla (Shuizhenla, 水真臘). The breakup of Chenla brought chaos and civil wars into the region. Srivijaya (Java) invaded Water Chenla and subjugated the country to a vassal state before Jayavarman II declared Kambuja's independence from Java.

A new emerging period sprung up and Angkor, also known as the Kambuja Period, replaced Chenla as the dominant state in the region. The name *Kambuja* (or *Kambujadesa*) was probably given in honor to the Indian hermit Kambu, the founder of the Solar Dynasty. Because Jayavarman II wanted to start a new era under his reign and intended to sever his relationship with Java [according to L.S. Thind in his article on Ancient Kaboj Rashtra, the name Java was derived from the Sanskrit words Yava Dwipa, which means island of grain or of millet; furthermore, the Indian word for millet is Java], the king may have decided to give his country a new name. Kambuja may have been chosen for the reason given above, but it may also be chosen in homage to the country called Kamboja, mentioned by the Indian Emperor Asoka as well as in the Indian epic *Mahabharata*. Historians classified the Angkor period from the beginning of Jayavarman II's reign in 802 to the Ayutthaya invasion of Angkor in 1431. The name *Angkor* came from the Sanskrit word *Nagara* or Khmer word *Nokor,* meaning "city." Angkor was not the original name of the city. It came only later after the Angkor period. Because Angkor was the ancient capital city of Khmer kings, in my opinion I believe that people may have later combined the words Ang (as Preah Ang to indicate a king) and Nokor (city) to form *Angnokor* and over time it may have been shortened to Angkor. The period prior to Ayutthaya invasion of Angkor is considered to be the Golden Age of the Khmer civilization.

Historians considered Jayavarman II (802-850) to be the founder of the Khmer Empire under the Angkor period. Jayavarman II elevated himself from a simple monarch to a *Chakravatin*, a Universal Ruler. He became a *Devaraja*, "God-King," through a sacred ritual conducted by Sivakaivalya that he learned from a Brahman named Hiranyadama from Mlu Prey (Present-day Preah Vihear, Cambodia). Hiranyadama would teach the sacred Devaraja ritual to Sivakaivalya only with the promise that Jayavarman II would make Sivakaivalya a *Brahmapurohita* (*Prohm Borohet*; "Brahman Chief") and that the position would be hereditary. The reason Hiranyadama demanded it to be hereditary was because he did not want the sacred rituals with its powerful magic to fall into the wrong hands. Outside the kingship, the purohita position was probably the most important and influential one in the government. Therefore, the history of Cambodia during the Angkor period was also shaped by the hereditary sacerdotal families of Sivakaivalya, at least until Suryavarman I reformed the system because he felt that the families were becoming too powerful.

The First Angkor Dynasty (802-1080) started under Jayavarman II (802-850) which marked the period of unification. Indravarman I (877-889) was credited for starting grandiose projects that left a legacy for future kings of Angkor to follow. He was a king with a vision. His reign started out smoothly but the period of instability ensued after the death of Yasovarman I. Jayavaman IV, as regent, rebelled against Harshavarman I. War between three kings erupted after the death of Jayavarman V with Jayaviravarman (Narapativiravarman) overthrew his brother Udayadityavarman I (Jayayudhavarman) immediately after he acceded to the throne. Suryavarman I declared himself king and finally defeated Jayaviravarman in 1011. Afterward, the calming period was established. The First Angkor Dynasty ended under the reign of Harshavarman III (1066-1080). Angkor flourished and a new dynasty unrelated to previous Angkor dynasties emerged. This is known as the Second Angkor Dynasty or the Mahidharapura Dynasty (1080-1160) whose first king was Jayavarman VI (1080-1107). The progenitor of the dynasty was a vassal king of Angkor named Hiranyavarman who ruled over Mahidharapura (near present-day Phimai in Thailand). This period reached its grandeur during the reign of Suryavarman II (1113-1150). It is known as the Great Empire Period with the temple of Angkor Wat built in dedication to Vishnu. The period ended under Dharanindravarman II (1150-1160). The Third Angkor Dynasty (1160-1431) started with the merging of the Mahidharapura Dynasty that included the old Lunar and Solar Dynasties under the reign of Yasovarman II (1160-1165). This period reached its crescendo and cumulated to the greatest Khmer territory expansion under the great leadership of Jayavarman VII (1181-1219). Afterward, it went into a declining period and ended with the Ayutthayan sacking of Angkor in 1431 and its abandonment thereafter.

The timeline between Jayavarman Paramesvara or Jayavarman IX (during which time the last epigraphy was recorded) and Ponhea Yat is very ambiguous. The story of a sweet cucumber gardener who became King Ta Trasâk Paêm was injected during this period. The story of Ta Trasâk Paêm seems to be based on a legend borrowed from Burma combined with a historical Khmer king, Indravarman III, who usurped the throne from his predecessor. In my opinion, the reigning periods for Ta Trasâk Paêm and Nippean Bat reported in the Cambodian chronicles are inaccurate. Most of the sources reported — and possibly copied from one another — that Ta Trasâk Paêm reigned from 1336 to 1340 and that Nippean Bat succeeded his father from 1340 to 1346. This timeline seems to be improbable because Nippean Bat would have been at the most three years old when he succeeded his father because Ta Trasâk Paêm married Princess Chant Vara Vattey, the daughter of King Paramathakemaraja (Preah Sihanu Reach according to legend or Jayavarman Paramesvara according to the chronology of the Cambodian chronicles), right after he was nominated king. The most probable reigning timeline between the above uncertain periods is discussed in Chapter 6 under *Reconstruction of Lost Records*.

Historically, the royal successions in Cambodia were passed down through the female lines. However, from time to time, there were troubled periods when the patrilineal sides challenged the matrilineal sides for successions. After Jayavarman II, an attempt was made to adopt the line of successions through the paternal side. As a result, claims and counterclaims for the legitimacies of the accession to the thrones were always in dispute. That was one of the reasons for the downfall of the Khmer Empire. The Angkor period adopted the ambilateral descent system for the line of succession. The Encyclopaedia of Britannica defines the ambilateral descent system as "patrilineal and matrilineal principles both operate at the societal level, but at the level of the individual various rules or choices define a person as belonging to either the mother's or the father's group. In some ambilateral descent systems, marriage broadens one's choice of lineage to include those of one's mother- or father-in-law." The history of Cambodia could be better understood if one could suspend for a moment the modern concept of succession where the son of a monarch succeeded his father after he had passed away. By visualizing how the ambilateral descent system was adopted in the Angkor period, some of the ambiguities in the line of successions become clearer and make more sense. Michael Vickery, in his paper *Some Remarks on Early State Formation in Cambodia*, provides further explanation on how the ambilateral descent system worked during the Angkor period. He said that the "kingship pass through individuals of the same generation before descending to the next generation."

It would be misguided to think that the people during the Funan, Chenla, and Angkor periods enthusiastically embraced Brahmanism as their religion. The cult of Devaraja with the monarch as the universal ruler was created under the auspices of Brahmanism. The religion was used as a tool for the kings, Brahmans, and families of the upper class to control people of the lower class. Concerning the religion, the inscriptions during the above periods mentioned mostly about the cult of Devaraja and the worship of linga that were the core belief of Brahmanism. These practices were mainly reserved for the kings, Brahmans, and the noble families but not for people of low stature. Sanskrit, the language of high learning used in Brahmanism to perform sacred rituals and official functions was controlled by the Brahmans and people of the upper class. The language was considered sacred and beyond the reach of commoners. There were no Brahmans assigned to teach Sanskrit or Brahmanism to the people at the local level. People during the above periods were more familiar with the animistic practices of worshiping spirits and dead ancestors than Vishnu or Shiva. Buddhism had briefly found its voice during the above periods but did not endure because of the control exercised by the Brahman priests to preserve

Brahmanism and of their resistance to sharing power. Brahman priests started to lose their grips under the reign of Suryavarman I when he appointed people of Vishnuist and Buddhist backgrounds to positions of equal importance to balance out the influence of Brahmans who controlled Cambodia since the time of Jayavarman II. Probably sensing the ever increasing influence of Brahmans, Suryavarman I decided to divest some of the entrenched powers of the house of Sivakaivalya that had produced the hereditary position of purohita (Chief Brahman) since the reign of Jayavarman II. People of lower stature had always had an affinity for Buddhism. It was Dharanindravarman II who started Buddhism but it was Jayavarman VII who firmly implemented it as the state religion. After Jayavarman VII, Buddhism was temporarily displaced by Brahmanism until it found its renaissance under future kings who sponsored and embraced Buddhism again. With the state sponsored, Buddhism was diffused to the masses without hindrance and it became the religion embraced by the majority of Khmer people. Under Buddhism, temples were built and served as worship and learning centers under the guidance and teaching of monks. Pali and Khmer languages were taught to commoners. Reading and writing were no longer reserved for the privilege of the upper-class families.

The "Post Angkor Period" from 1432 to 1847 took Cambodia further into a declining period with Thailand and Vietnam gaining more territory at the expense of Cambodia. During this period, there were civil wars where Khmer kings or princes called on either Thailand or Vietnam for help in settling their disputes for the thrones. This Book I covers only up to the period of Longvek which ended in 1594/1595. The Post Longvek to the Contemporary period is addressed in Book II.

The fall of Angkor did not provide the coup de grâce to Cambodia. The kingdom was still relatively strong after the Angkor period up until the fall of Longvek in 1594. Cambodia had embraced Buddhism for centuries, and during its course it had developed a tradition and culture that shaped the Khmer society. When Naresuan attacked Cambodia he was not just content to bring down Longvek. He wanted to make sure that Cambodia would not be in a position to pose a threat to Ayutthaya in the future. For that reason, Naresuan took all the Khmer treasures (such as sacred manuscripts, chronicles, books of code of laws, custom and tradition, skilled people, and a great number of Khmer families to Ayutthaya). The purpose of uprooting Khmer families from Cambodia was threefold: the first one was to prevent future Khmer kings from raising an army against Ayutthaya; the second one was to reduce able bodies from working on the land; and the third one was to hurt Cambodia economically because with less people working on the land would mean less revenue for the state, thus preventing the king from building an effective army. Without the code of laws, Cambodia was not able to rule the country properly and as a result the country slowly fell into a state of decadence.

CHAPTER 1

THE KHMER KINGS AND THE HISTORY OF CAMBODIA

GENESIS

Indian-style kingdoms were formed by assembling many local groups — each possessing its guardian genie or god of the soil — under the authority of a single or indianized-native chief. Often this organization was accompanied by the establishment, on a natural or artificial mountain, of the cult of an Indian divinity intimately associated with the royal person and symbolizing the unity of the kingdom. This custom, associated with the original foundation of a kingdom or royal dynasty, is witnessed in all the Indian kingdoms of the Indochinese Peninsula. It reconciled the native cult of spirits on the heights with the Indian concept of royalty, and gave the population, assembled under one sovereign, a sort of national god, intimately associated with the monarchy. We have here a typical example of how India, in spreading her civilization to the Indochinese Peninsula, knew how to make foreign beliefs and cults her own and assimilate them — an example that illustrates the relative parts played by Indian and native elements in the formation of the ancient Indochinese civilizations and the manner in which these two elements interacted.

The Indianized States of Southeast Asia
George Coedès[1,pp26-27]

HISTORICAL RECORDS, KHMER LEGENDS, SYMBOLISM, AND SETTLEMENT

Chinese Imperial Dynasty Records

The earliest mention of *Funan* (扶南), a country considered to be the root of the Khmer civilization, was first recorded in the *Chinese Imperial Dynasty Records*. The Chinese Emperor Sun Chuan (孫權) sent two envoys named Kang Tai (康泰) and Chu Ying (朱應) to gather information about Funan before the middle of the 3rd century AD. They arrived at the court of Funan between 245 and 250 AD, during the reign of Fan Xun (范尋). After returning to China, these two envoys published a book and a report of their mission. Chu Ying wrote a report on Funan, but unfortunately his original work was lost. However, Funan must have been of great interest and importance to the Chinese for their scholars and historians to quote Chu Ying's work throughout the Chinese dynastic history. Yao Cha (姚察) and Yao Silian (姚思廉) recorded the event reported by Chu Ying in the *Annals of the Liang* (Liang Shu — 梁書) in 636 AD.[2; 3] It said that a man named Hun Tien (混填) from the southern country called Jiao (徼) had a dream about a genie. Hun Tien believed in the worship of spirit. In the dream the genie gave him a divine bow and told him to take a large merchant ship and sail away. The next morning he went to the temple and found the divine bow at the foot of a tree. Then he embarked on a large merchant ship and sailed to sea. The genie blew the wind and directed the ship to reach Funan. Upon seeing the ship arriving at her shore, Queen Liu Yeh (柳葉 — translated by Paul Pelliot to mean "Willow Leaf") ordered to have the ship seized. Hun Tien grabbed the divine bow and fired the arrow, which pierced Liu Yeh's ship from side to side. Frightened, Liu Yeh surrendered herself and Hun Tien took her as his wife.[2; 4] Hun Tien started the custom of covering the naked bodies of Funan's women with a piece of cloth.

In Paul Pelliot's original translation he said that Hun Tien came from a country of *Mofu* instead of *Jiao*. In another Chinese historical record, Hun Tien was quoted as coming from a country called *Heng-tie*. In his essay *Funan Reviewed: Deconstructing the Ancients*,[5] Michael Vickery mentioned that Pelliot considered the Chinese characters for *Mo* and *Heng* as well as *Fu* and *Tie* to be quite similar that one can easily substitute one word for another. After copying and recopying from one source to another over the centuries, it is understandable that the two similar Chinese characters could be mixed up, considering that the Chinese scribes may not be familiar with the geography of the region. Based on his language expertise and understanding of how the Chinese transcribed foreign names, Pelliot decided to combine the two words and chose to call it *Mo-tie* as Hun Tien's country of origin. According to Vickery, this word by itself is not easily identifiable, but the Chinese source provided a clue that *Heng-tie* was located southeast of another country called *Yeou-po,* and that this latter was in turn situated approximately 5,000 *li* southeast of India. The distance of 5,000 *li* is equivalent to about 2,000 km. In this case, the east coast of the present-day Malay Peninsula would most likely be the country where Hun Tien came from. Because he came from the Malay Peninsula and worshipped a spirit and not Hindu deities, it is very unlikely that Hun Tien was a Brahman as Coedès had suggested. This event seems to suggest that the foundation of Funan predated the establishment of the Brahmanic faith, culture, and tradition in the region. It must be noted that during this period, the people living in the Malay Peninsula and Funan were probably of similar background or of the same Austro Asian race. The second century Chinese sources described the Malay kingdom as tributary to Funan. Was Hun Tien, who came from the Malay Peninsula, a vassal prince of Funan? One could deduce that the story took place around the first century AD or even earlier based on the Chinese sources mentioning other historical figures in the second century AD, which in turn may have been based on earlier sources. As to the meaning of the name *Liu Yeh*, Vickery mentioned that even Pelliot was troubled by his translation of "Willow Leaf" because the tree does not exist in Cambodia. Some scholars have suggested another translation for *Liu Yeh*. They observed that due to the similarity between the Chinese characters for willow (柳) and coconut (椰), the transcriber could easily interchange the two words and could thus render *Yiu Yeh* (椰葉 — Coconut Leaf) to *Liu Yeh* (柳葉 — Willow Leaf). Willow and coconut are not only similar in Chinese characters but they are also similar in Chinese pronunciation.

The Brahmans must have come to Funan sometime between the first/second and early third centuries because the influence of India over Funan was firmly implanted around the period of Fan Xun's reign (244-287 AD). Chu Ying mentioned that books written in a language similar to Indian scriptures were found in the Funan library.[6, p19] This implies that Funan was an advanced society because a library is a repository of knowledge. The scriptures must have been of Kushan origin that predated the earliest Khmer inscriptions (K.600) found at Angkor Borei (dated 611 AD) which were based on the Pallava scripts. Georges Maspero believed that Kushan scripts were probably introduced into Funan around the time of Fan Shih Man (205-225 AD).

Khmer Legends

Many variations of the legend of *Srok Khmer* (Khmer Country) — also called *Nokor Kok Thlok* (Land of the Thlok trees) — were told and passed down from generation to generation. Many of the legends seemed to be created between the 11th and 12th centuries.

The legends placed the founders of the Khmer civilization such as Kaundinya, Preah Thong, Soma, and Neang Neak (Lady Naga/Serpent) to the time of Angkor. Other legends attributed Preah Ket Mealea (identified by scholars as Suryavarman II) as the founder of Nokor Kok Thlok and founder of Angkor Wat. Without the historical knowledge, people viewed Angkor Wat as the genesis of the Khmer civilization. It must be noted that people in the post-Angkorian time were not aware that Angkor Wat was built by Suryavarman II in the 12th century. Events, times, and places seem to be mixed up, which gives suspicion that many of the various versions of the legend were probably spinoffs of the same source and created at a much later date.

The events told in the legends did not correspond to the times and places where those personalities existed. As reported by Adhémar Leclère in his book *Histoire du Cambodge*,[7] there is the legend of the Chvea Pream [it must be noted that Chvea indicates people of Malay origin and Cham are people from Champa] who came from *Pareanosey* (Vanarasi/Benares) and founded Nokor Kok Thlok in 473 BC. However, the word Chvea used by the Khmer in this case must have been intended for Brahman and not for Malay people [Pream means Brahman], as is currently understood.

The legend mentioned the founder's name and his six descendants. It said that *Youyou Vormonti*, which Leclère transcribed as Jayavarman (Youyou pronounced Yaya, which could mean Jaya and Vormonti may be a variation of Varman), reigned for 50 years. His son, *Kaveala Reach Kaumar*, succeeded him. He reigned for 20 years. The third king, *Sauriya Vormonti* (Suryavarman), reigned for another 20 years. The fourth king, *Thornintrea Vormonti* (Dharanindravarman), also reigned for 20 years. The fifth king, *Atity Vormonti* (Adityavarman), also reigned for 20 years. Finally, the sixth king with the name of *Assachey* reigned for only 11 years before Preah Thong overthrew him.

The legend of the Chvea Pream and his six descendants must have been based on some historical facts but on the wrong period. It must be observed that *Youyou Vormonti*, probably referring to Jayavarman VI (1080-1107); *Sauriya Vormonti*, probably referring to Suryavarman II (1107-1113); *Thornintrea Vormonti*, probably referring to Dharanindravarman II (1150-1160); and *Atity Vormonti*, probably referring to Udayadityavarman II (1050-1066) were the historical names of Khmer kings in the Angkor period. Considering how closely the legend matched the historical facts, it is likely that the legend could have been invented any time after the 13th centuries or possibly during the reign of Ang Chan I because he was the last king who completed the unfinished bas-reliefs on the North Wing of the East Gallery and the East Wing of North Gallery.

Up to this date, there are no records of any Indian settlements in the Funan and Mekong delta region 473 years before the Common era. The second, third, fourth, and fifth kings who reigned exactly for 20 years each seems very unusual. The word Chvea to indicate a Brahman is completely inaccurate. An argument can be made that it was convenient to choose the city of Benares in the Indian state of Uttar Pradesh, as the birthplace of the *Chvea Pream Youyou Vormonti* (Jayavarman) because of its reputation as the holiest Hindu city [and also as the oldest continuously inhabited city in the world]. The famous city surely must have been known to the people living in Southeast Asia, especially after the contacts with Indian Brahmans. It must be noted that the original names of the kings before their translations to Sanskrit are Khmer sounding names rather than Chvea or Cham.

The origin of Preah Thong as reported by Adhémard Leclère provided another variation of the legend. The legend said that the king of Indraprashta had five male children. Indraprashta was the legendary city founded by Pandavas, the son of Pandu in the Indian epic *Mahabharata*. The battle scene between the Pandavas and Kauravas are depicted on the bas-relief at Angkor Wat (South side of West Gallery). It was no coincidence that the Lunar Dynasty, which was founded during the Funan period, drew its inspiration from the Hindu epic *Mahabharata*. Some of the places mentioned in the *Mahabharata* were based on actual locations or regions of India. Indraprashta was considered to be the first Delhi city and its location was about 20 miles south of the current city of Delhi in India.

According to the legend, the king of Indraprashta decided to give some territories away to his four older children, so they could govern them as their fiefdoms, but kept his kingdom for his favorite youngest son. When his youngest son reached adulthood, the king abdicated in favor of his favorite son. He would have supreme power over all four of his older brothers. Three of his brothers accepted their fates with only the remaining one, Preah Thong, who refused to attend the crowning ceremony of his younger brother [coincidentally, Norodom Ranariddh was absent during the crowning ceremony of his younger half-brother Norodom Sihamoni]. The father thought of sending his four obedient children to fight Preah Thong but changed his mind because he realized that the rebelled prince was very popular and also had the support of the people. Instead he decided to banish Preah Thong and all his supporters out of the country. Branded as the person who broke away from his religion, Preah Thong and his supporters moved east and reached a place named *Kok Thlok* (Dry land of the Thlok trees). The legend said that the land was already occupied by the Cham. Preah Thong and his people could not coexist with the Cham. Battles erupted and with the help of the natives, Preah Thong and his people chased the Cham from Kok Thlok. The Cham fled all the way to Champassak in present-day Laos. His defeat of the Cham left him as the only victor and Preah Thong became king of Kok Thlok. He took Neang Neak (Lady Naga/Serpent), also called Soma (the daughter of the Naga King), as his bride. The legend said that the Naga King drank part of the ocean to create a dry land as a wedding gift for his daughter and Preah Thong. The legend of the Naga King's draining of the ocean was probably based on the phenomenon of the Tonlé Sap discharging its water from the lake, accumulated to its full size and capacity (six times the size of the dry season) during the monsoon wet season (May-October), to the Mekong River during the dry season from November to April. The drainage of the lake would provide enough dry land for people to use for six months before another dry-wet seasonal cycle started again. This story of the Naga King's drainage of the ocean is unique to Cambodia because the phenomenon of water reversing its course to discharge into a lake, instead of into the ocean, and then reverting to the river six months later to discharge into the ocean does not exist anywhere in the world. This phenomenon was associated with the folklore of Preah Thong as the first Khmer king. From that moment on, the union between native Khmers and Indian people were formed.

It must be noted that there is some historical basis to the legend. The natives may have combined the historical fact of the Môn-Khmer migration from the Tibetan region and their settlements in Southeast Asia with the story in the *Mahabharata*. The Môns and the Khmers left the upper reaches of the Mekong around the Tibetan region before the beginning of the Common era. The Môn came down along the Salween River first to settle in the Menam Valley. The Khmers followed the Môns and settled in the middle of the Mekong Valley. The battle between the Pandavas and Kauravas, known as the battle of Kurukshetra, has its origin in the *Mahabharata*. Similar to Preah Thong, Prince Pandu rebelled against his older brother, King Dhritarashtra, by forming his own dynastic branch called the Pandava. Both brothers were the sons of King Kuru and descended from the Kaurava dynasty. As noted earlier, the legend of Preah Thong seems to have been created around the 11th century, which coincidentally corresponded to the period of trade expansions between the Chola Empire of south India and Southeast Asia. Coedès' mention of Tamil legends that spoke of a Chola king marrying the daughter of the Naga king was quite reminiscent of the Kaundinya-Soma/Preah Thong-Neang Neak story. A Funan coin of Angkor Borei showing a serpent coiling around a tree on the obverse side and a dancing mythical bird Garuda on the reverse side in shown in Figure 3 (personal collection). Was the serpent a symbolic representation of Soma, the Naga/Serpent princess? Both the garuda and the serpent are found throughout Khmer culture, adorning temples from the Angkor time to the present. Additional coins during the Angkor Borei period are presented in Appendix 2.

Figure 3. Funan Coin of Angkor Borei
(Personal Collection)

The Symbol of the Seven-Headed Naga

In the Cambodian tradition and culture, Naga/Serpent has always been respected as it was used in drawings, carvings, and statues to protect the Buddha during his meditation. The seven-headed serpent is a symbol representing strength, power, guardian of protection, and all things related to the seven scales of harmony in nature.

If Naga sculptures were made in the Funan era, none of them survived. The Naga sculptures that survive to the present time dated back to the Angkor period. The Naga was usually represented as a three, seven, or nine headed serpent. Seven-headed serpent was the most commonly found in literature, on carving walls, and on statues. Why was Naga chosen as the symbol for the native king of Kok Thlok, and afterward as the seven-headed serpent that adorned most of Khmer monuments? The seven-headed serpent was also used as a symbol to protect Buddha during his state of meditation.

George Coedès believed that the Naga legend had its origin in the court of the Pallavas.[6,p27; 8] The copperplate found in the time of the Pallava dynasty mentioned the story of Asvatthaman marrying a Naga. They produced a son and he became the founder of the Pallava dynasty. Coedès also cited several works in Indian mythology where a king married a Naga. Among the Southeast Asian and Indian culture, Naga is a very powerful symbol. Coedès believed that Naga represented the rainbow as a symbol of Indra's arch reaching across the realm of the gods, linking it to the world of the humans. The rainbow is called Inthanou (ឥន្ធនូ = Indra + Thnou) in Cambodian, which means "the bow of Indra." The Chinese equivalent to the Naga is the dragon. Rainbow has played a role in mythology due to its beauty and mystery. Therefore, using the seven-headed serpent to represent rainbow fits well within the concept and belief of Hindu mythology. In Hindu mythology, Indradhanush (rainbow) represents the bow of Indra as the God of lightning, thunder, and rain. The seven-headed serpent could represent the seven colors in a rainbow (red, orange, yellow, green, blue, indigo, and violet).

Ancient Khmers, especially during the Angkor period, were well versed in cosmology and astrology as it was attested by Zhou Daguan during his one-year living in Cambodia near the end of the 13th century. He said that Khmer men understood astronomy and knew how to calculate the time for the eclipses of the moon and sun. Astrology and naga played a big part in Khmer culture. The seven-headed serpent could also symbolize the seven days in a week with each day represented by a different angel. Sunday represents Tungsa Tevy riding a garuda[9] (mythological bird as shown in Figure 3); she carries *Kâng Chak* (Sudarshana Chakra — a spinning serrated disc used by Vishnu to symbolize wisdom/thought) in her right hand and a conch shell (Shankha — used by Vishnu to symbolize creation) in her left hand. Monday represents Koreak Tevy riding a tiger;[9] she carries a sword in her right hand and a cane in her left hand (to symbolize authority). Tuesday represents Reaksa Tevy riding a horse;[9] she carries a trident in her right hand and a bow in her left hand (to symbolize authority). Wednesday represents Modar Tevy riding a donkey;[9] she carries a needle in her right hand and a cane in her left hand (to symbolize maturity and wisdom). Thursday represents Keriny Tevy riding an elephant;[9] she carries a harpoon in her right hand and a weapon in her left hand (to symbolize authority). Friday represents Kemira Tevy riding a water buffalo;[9] she carries a sword in her right hand and a musical instrument in her left hand (to symbolize authority and harmony). Saturday represents Mohurea Tevy riding a peacock;[9] she carries *Kâng Chak* in her right hand and a trident in her left hand (to symbolize wisdom and authority).

The Chinese Imperial Records mentioned that its court received a Funan envoy in 243 AD with presents such as musicians and products of the country. Funan must have been very proud of its music for the king to send his musicians to entertain the China Imperial court. Funan's music had such an impact on China that in 244 AD, under the reign of the Chinese Emperor Sun Chuan, a place to house Funan music was set up. The office was outside the capital of Nanjing (ancient capital of China). Gungwu Wang, the prominent Singaporean professor wrote that "Fu-nan music and musicians were cherished."[10, 11] Based on this account, Funan must have understood musical notes. Music had been a part of the Khmer culture since the dawn of history. Funan music may have even been adopted and incorporated into Chinese music. Because of Funan's understanding of music, the seven-headed serpent could also be a representation of the seven notes in a musical scale.

Indian Settlement in the Funan/Mekong Delta

Many scholars recognize the unique territorial position that Funan occupied in ancient time, especially the port of O Keo (misspelled by scholars as Oc Eo) located near the Mekong delta. A note must be made concerning the spelling of this ancient port in Funan. This port is spelled by scholars and in all historical books as "Oc Eo." It is my contention that the port should be spelled "O Keo," which means "important creek" or "cherished creek" in Khmer. Oc Eo does not have any meaning in the Khmer language.

Commerce between China and India made Funan even more important after China was split into three kingdoms (三國時) between 184 and 280 AD. The three kingdoms were Cao Wei (曹魏), Shu Han (蜀漢), and Dong Wu (東吳). The war prevented the Wu from using the land route controlled by the Wei to do commerce with the west. As a consequence, the Wu started to use the maritime route to do commerce with India, as far away as the Middle East. Funan was the natural resting point for the Chinese merchants to take a break before proceeding on their second leg of voyage to India through the Strait of Malacca. Due to the long and difficult voyage, merchants coming from the Middle East and India would stop in Funan and rest before continuing to China. As a result, Funan became prosperous. Albrecht Dihle, the German scholar, has theorized that O Keo may be the port city of Kattigara mentioned by Ptolemy in the 2nd century. Excavation at O Keo has found Funan coins (Personal collection shown in Figure 4) as well as golden coins portraying the Roman Emperor Antonius Pius in 152 AD. Ned Seidler sketched the various treasure (which included the coins shown in Figure 4) found on the ancient port city of Funan, O Keo, in the March 1971 issue of the National Geographic.[12] The finding suggests that trades between Rome and Asia had passed through Funan. O Keo was a bustling port city. Additional coins dating during the Funan period are shown in Appendix 2.

Jacob E. Conner, the former American Council at Saigon in 1912 speculated that the mineral riches of Funan may have enticed Brahmans to venture farther from India in search of new wealth.[13] The ruby mine located in the province of Pailin in Cambodia which is still being mined today, could have been a source of attraction for Brahmans to venture out of India to come to Funan. Cambodia used to also be known by the name Sovannaphum (Gold Region/Country). The current province of Korat (Thailand), which at one time was a Khmer territory had its gold mined in the district of Chettorach.[14,p137] Was gold that was found in Funan enough to lure Brahmans from India to seek new lives and settle in Funan? In his book *The Indianized States of Southeast Asia*, Coedès stated that "around the beginning of the Christian Era, Southeast Asia was the 'land of gold' toward which the Indian navigators sailed."[1,pxv]

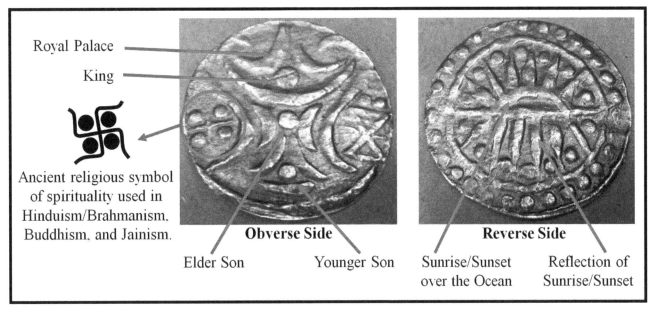

Figure 4. Funan Coin Found at O Keo (Oc Eo)
Obverse side shows the king in his royal palace stretching his arms with his children
below him as if to indicate they were the future rulers and/or heirs of the kingdom.
The sign (parts of the lines were effaced) to the right side of the king and his children
is an ancient Indian religious symbol used throughout India, East Asia, and Southeast Asia.
Reverse side shows the sunrise/sunset and its reflection over the ocean horizon.
(Personal Collection)

CHAPTER 2

THE KHMER KINGS AND THE HISTORY OF CAMBODIA

WHERE DID THE KHMERS COME FROM?

The history of Ancient Cambodia is now comparatively well authenticated. The continuity of history from the earliest times to the present is better established in Cambodia than in Egypt, and there is no more reason to doubt that the modern Cambodian is the true descendant of the ancient Khmer than that the modern inhabitants of Greece and Italy are descended, at least in part, from the ancient Greeks and Romans. As far as chronology is concerned, the author knows of no country whose history can be so completely and so accurately written from the inscriptions. From the beginning of the ninth to nearly the middle of the fourteenth century — the period in which all the great monuments were built — the inscriptions furnish an unbroken line of kings, with the approximate, when not the exact, dates of their reigns and generally their relationship to their predecessors. Chinese writers supplement these inscriptions with sometimes more detailed information, more or less regularly from the first part of the third to early in the fourteenth century.

The Ancient Khmer Empire
Lawrence Palmer Briggs[6,p4]

THE LANGUAGE AND THE PEOPLE

The Môn-Khmer Language

Who are the Khmers? Where did they come from? Earlier evidence suggests the Môns and Khmers originated from the northern region somewhere near the Himalaya.[15,p2] The Khmer people came from the upper reaches of the Mekong — around the Tibetan region — and Salween Rivers at the dawn of history. The Môns who were cousins of the Khmers migrated earlier from the same region to the east and settled around the Tenasserim Coast bordering along the Andaman Sea. The Khmers followed the Môns but continued farther eastward and settled around the middle reaches of the Mekong Valley.[16,p15] According to Coedès, the Chams came from the northwestern region by sea and settled on the east coast of Southeast Asia around 500 BC to 0 AD. After their settlements, the Khmers founded the Chenla state. The renown French scholar, Alfred Foucher, placed the land of ancient Kambojas (Kamboja desha) — probably the ancestors of the Khmers — in the vicinity of the Himalaya in Tibet.[17,p271] The map of the early Southeast Asia that depicts the general area of the Funan state as well as the route of the Môn-Khmer migration and their region of settlements is shown in Figure 5 (the generated map was based on References 17 and 19).

The Chinese texts dating as far back as the first century AD mention the existence of two main states located in the lower Menam valley of the Mekong. Apparently, these states were Funan/Chenla and Champa. It can therefore be assumed that these states may have existed even before the first century AD, which suggests that the Môns and Khmers (as well as the Chams) had come down to this region before the Common era.In order to trace the origin of the Khmer, one must follow where its language came from. The Môn-Khmer language is classified under the category of Austro-Asiatic language, a combination of the Latin word Austro (south) and Greek word Asia, thus South-Asia. Under the Austro-Asiatic language family, scholars have identified 147 languages that fall under the Môn-Khmer languages and 21 languages under the Munda languages. Two-thirds of those languages are considered to be endangered because of the small percentage of people practicing them. Gérard Diffloh, Ilia Peiros, and a few other scholars classified the Môn-Khmer languages under the following sub-categories (Figure 6):[18]

1. Northern Môn-Khmer (38 languages): Khasic, Khmuic, and Palaungo-Pakanic
    1.1   Khasic (3 languages): They are spoken in Eastern India and Bangladesh
    1.2   Khmuic (13 languages): They are spoken in Laos and Thailand
    1.3   Palaungo-Pakanic (22 languages): They are spoken in Myanmar, Southern China, Northern Thailand, and Northern Laos.
2. Nuclear Môn-Khmer (109 languages)
    2.1   Eastern Môn-Khmer (67 languages)
        2.1.1   One or two Khmer languages are spoken in Cambodia, Thailand, and Vietnam
        2.1.2   6 Pearic languages are spoken in Cambodia
        2.1.3   19 Katuic languages are spoken in Cambodia, Thailand, Laos, and Vietnam
        2.1.4   40 Khmero-Bahnaric languages are spoken in Cambodia, Laos, and Vietnam
    2.2   Vieto-Muong (10 languages): There are 10 Vietic languages spoken in Vietnam and Laos
    2.3   Southern Môn-Khmer (6 languages): There are 6 Nicobarese languages spoken on the Nicobar Islands of India territory
    2.4   Aslian (19 languages): There are 19 Aslian languages spoken in Malaysia and Thailand
    2.5   Monic (2 languages)
        2.5.1   One Môn language is spoken in Myanmar
        2.5.2   One Nyahkur language is spoken in Thailand
    2.6   Palyu (One language): One Palya language is spoken in Southern China
    2.7   Unclassified (4 languages): There are 4 unclassified languages considered to be of Môn-Khmer family that are spoken in China

The Khasic language of the Northern Môn-Khmer classification is one of the principal languages spoken in present-day Meghalaya in India, bordering Bengladesh. It is one of the rarest surviving Môn-Khmer languages that are still surviving and being practiced in India. Khasi was originally a spoken language only; it did not have its own script. It was one of the oldest Môn-Khmer languages and Meghalaya may possibly be the birthplace of the Khmers living in present-day Cambodia, Thailand, and Vietnam.

The interaction between the people of Funan with the Khmers (who could possibly come from the region of present-day Meghalaya in India), as far back as the first century BC or even earlier, resulted in the adoption of the Môn-Khmer language for usage as the functioning language — based on indirect evidence from Tun-Sun (Dvaravati) and on some epigraphies dating back to the Chenla period. The Môn-Khmer languages introduced by the Khmers dominated the region covering an area spanning from Funan-Chenla to Annam to the north and to Puy to the west. It was only after the arrival of the Indian Brahmans that Sanskrit was introduced into the Funan and Chenla high societies. The introduction of the Hindu religion, culture, and literature merged and coexisted with the indigenous lifestyles and habits of the Funan and Chenla inhabitants. The above events, most likely took place during the first to the second centuries AD. Chenla started out as a vassal state of Funan and remained under its subjugation until 550 AD before their roles were reversed.

Before the Chinese military rebel Chao T'o (Zhao Tuo) proclaimed himself King of Nan-yueh (Nam Viet) in 207 BC, the people of Red River delta bearing the name of Lo (Lac) were the original inhabitants of the region. They spoke Môn-Khmer languages. Regarding the Vietnamese language, Coedès made the following statement:[19,pp28-29]

> *With regard to Vietnamese, which has a tonal system very similar to that of the T'ai languages, but a vocabulary of largely Mon-Khmer origin, discussion has centered on whether it should be regarded as a T'ai or a Mon-Khmer language. The point to be decided was whether it was more likely that a Mon-Khmer language without tones had adopted the T'ai tonal system, or whether a T'ai language had borrowed a large part of its vocabulary from the Mon-Khmer group. In either case, the theory arrived at was that of a 'mixed' language. But it has now been observed that tones may arise in Chinese and in T'ai as a result of phonetic changes, and the same may have been true of the Mon-Khmer spoken languages, which were originally toneless; so that the presence of tones in Vietnamese no longer prevents it from being regarded as belonging to the Mon-Khmer family, with which it has the major part of its basic vocabulary in common. Indeed it may now be assumed to be a Mon-Khmer language in which a tonal system similar to that of the T'ai languages has arisen. ...For while the ancestry of the Mons, the Khmers, the Chams, and the mountain people related to them stretches far back into Neolithic past, that of the Vietnamese does not go back any earlier than the bronze age, and the Tibeto-Burmans and the T'ais do not appear in Indochina until much later, after the beginning of the Christian era.*

Ethnic Tribes

According to the study conducted by Georges Olivier of the École Française d'Extrême Orient (EFEO) in 1968,[20; 21] the Khmers are made up of multiple ethnic tribes. Khmer, Lao, and Cham belong to the Asian group classified as "Brown Skin" with rounded eyes, dark skin, and speaking atonal language of common origin called Môn-Khmer. In contrast, Chinese, Vietnamese, and Thai belong to the Asian group classified as "Yellow Skin" of the Mongoloid type with slit eyes, lighter skin, and speaking tonal language. It must be noted that Olivier probably intended to refer to the Tai people, who make up one of the major ethnic groups of the entire Thai population, when he used the word Thai. He probably intended to distinguish the native Lao from the Loa of Tai origin.

Adrien Pannetier stated that Khmer was the product of interactions and mixed marriages between the local people (as numerated below) and Indians who migrated to this Southeast region. As one goes up the rivers and away from the cities, there were less inter-marriages between these ethnic groups. Olivier said that Khmer represents a local ethnicity of the Southeast region, which is distinctly different from the Chinese ethnicity that came progressively from China. Additionally, the Chinese communities tend to concentrate only in cities where they conduct their businesses. Over the centuries, the Khmers were strongly influenced by the religion and culture of Indian origins.

Before the Indian migration, the local people (especially the Kouys and Samrès) were already expert at extracting iron and gold from iron ores. They already knew how to work on metal. They had their own culture that was quite advanced already. The Khmers acquired new knowledge, culture, language, and scripts with the constant arrivals of Indians who came to do commerce in this Southeastern part of Asia after the first century AD, probably around the middle of the third century. Many things that the Indians brought were found to be compatible and complementary by the Khmers, which led to the peaceful acceptance and coexistence between the two ethnic groups. While the Chinese were mostly concerned with commerce, the Indians were primarily concerned with spreading the Hindu and Buddhist religions, as well as "colonizing" these countries.

Henri Mouhot, the great French explorer who stumbled upon Angkor Wat in 1860 after the temple had been hidden in the jungle for over 500 years, appreciated the hard working quality and character of the Samrè people. The only people in the region that he could equate to the qualities of the Samrè were those of the Vietnamese. A study done by Frédéric Bourdier in 1995 listed the Khmer ethnic population from the province of Ratanakiri, as shown in Table 2:[20]

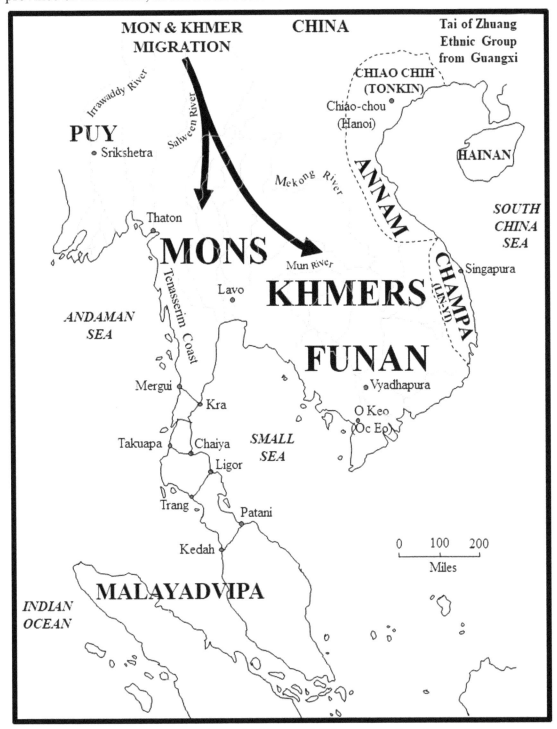

**Figure 5. The Migration of Môns and Khmers to Southeast Asia
in the Early Period (Map based on References 17 and 19)**

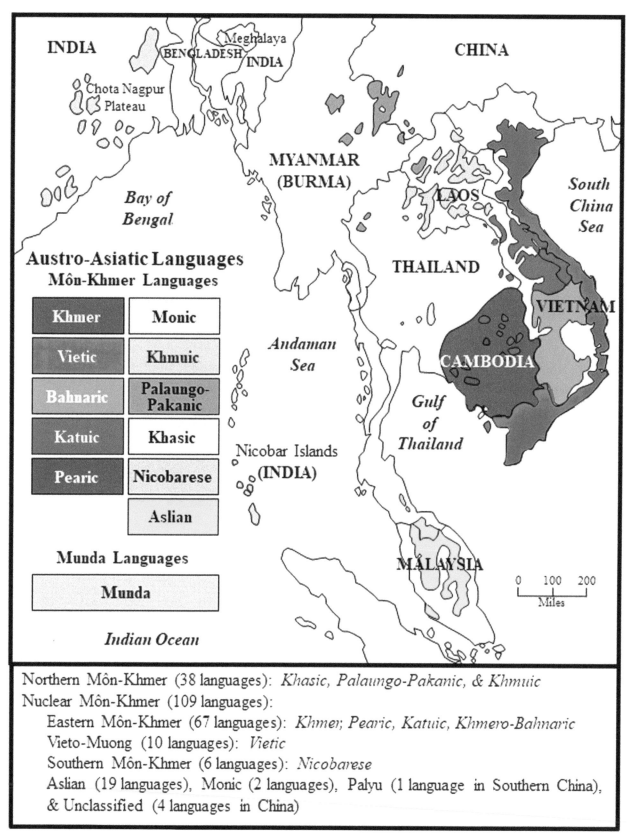

Northern Môn-Khmer (38 languages): *Khasic, Palaungo-Pakanic, & Khmuic*
Nuclear Môn-Khmer (109 languages):
    Eastern Môn-Khmer (67 languages): *Khmer, Pearic, Katuic, Khmero-Bahnaric*
    Vieto-Muong (10 languages): *Vietic*
    Southern Môn-Khmer (6 languages): *Nicobarese*
    Aslian (19 languages), Monic (2 languages), Palyu (1 language in Southern China),
    & Unclassified (4 languages in China)

**Figure 6. Map of the Môn-Khmer Language Spoken in South Asia
(Map extracted from Ref. 18 and based on the studies of
Gérard Diffloh, Elia Peiros, and various scholars)**

Ethnicity	Population	Linguistic Grouping
Tampuan	16,368	Môn-Khmer
Jaraï	14,040	Malayo-Polynesian
Krūng	13,430	Môn-Khmer
Khmer	9,396	Khmer
Lao	6,467	Lao
Brao	5,328	Môn-Khmer
Krachach	2,164	
Kravet	1,210	
Vietnamese	753	Vietnamese
Chinese	190	Chinese
Lum	41	Môn-Khmer
Mnong	32	

Table 2. Khmer Ethnic Population from the Province of Ratanakiri (Adapted from Frédéric Bordier's 1995 Study, Ref. 20)

The study conducted by Dr. Georges Olivier defining the Khmers from different ethnic tribes were:[20]

Northern Region

Kouy — They live in Preah Vihear, Stung Treng, and in the northern regions of Kompong Thom. They are also found in eastern Thailand and southern Laos, which were once part of the Khmer Empire. In Thailand, they are called *Souy*. The word *Kouy* means "man," which connotes "free man." They have a culture that was more advanced than the other tribes. They knew how to work on metal and were experts on how to extract iron and gold from iron and gold ores. Historically they were the metal workers and builders of weapons. They speak Môn-Khmer language family.

North-Western Region

Samrè — They have dark skin and most of them are found in the northern region of Siem Reap, near the Phnom Kulen. Another group of Samrè lives among the Kouys. The Samrè people were so well assimilated within the Khmer society that they lost their own dialect. In contrast to the traditional legend saying that *Ta Trasâk Paêm* was a gardener of sweet cucumbers, it was reported in some circles that he was a leader of the Samrè tribe who led his people to overthrow King Preah Sihanu-Reach (which would correspond to King Paramesvara according to the Cambodian Chronicles). He then married the king's daughter to legitimize his accession to the throne. After his usurpation, he moved his palace to Banteay Samrè. Historically, the Samrès were used as slaves or soldiers. They were used to transport stones from Phnom Kulen to build temples in the Angkor region. They were the guardians and trainers of elephants. Like the Kouys, they were good metal workers and strong warriors.

Western Region

Péar (aka Porrs) — They are made up of two groups: 1) The western group, located between Pailin and Kranhung; and 2) the eastern group, located in the northern Cardamone mountain region — on the western side of the village of Rovieng. The Péars are considered to be distinct from the Kouys. The name Péar means "man of color." Anthropologic analysis has determined that the Péars were the descendants of the Samrès. Khmer kings gave them some hunting land in the western part of Cambodia. They lived and mixed with the ***Chongs*** (aka Chhâng). Nowadays, the Chongs can be found only in Thailand [according to Leclère,[7,p126] the Chongs were found in the provinces of Kampong Som, Chanborei (present-day Chanthaburi in Thailand), and Rayang (present-day Rayong in Thailand)]. Khmer kings recruited the Samrès and Péars to fight wars. They were strong warriors. In the 16th and 17th centuries, 10,000 strong men were formed from the recruit of Samrè and Péar tribes.

Southern Region

Soach — They live in the Kompong Som and western part of Kampot. Their dialect is similar to the Samrès and the Péars. They were related to the Chongs who lived on the southern side of the Cardamone mountain region (called Chong Khnâng Phnom), south of the Péars. They have have dark skins with small stature and curly hairs who live mostly in Malaysia Peninsula and speak an Austro-Asiatic language. Most of them fled and went to live in the province of Trat in Thailand.

North-Eastern and Eastern Regions

1. **Kravet** (aka Khrêk) — They live in actual areas of Cambodia and Laos.
2. **Brao** (aka Préous) — They mix with the **Krûngs** and live in areas that include actual Cambodia, Laos, and Vietnam. Most of this tribe is found in Stung Trèng and Ratanakiri.
3. **Tampuan** — They live in actual area around the city of Bokéo. Most of them live in northeast of Ratanakiri. They speak Môn-Khmer language family. They are classified as Khmer Loeu. Zirconium was discovered in 1925 in this area. There were 5,000 mining wells counted in 1937.
4. **Mnong** (aka Phnong) — They live in Mondulkiri, but the majority of the population is concentrated in Vietnam, in Central Highlands and Binh Phuoc. They speak the Bahnaric languages, which belong to the Môn-Khmer language family.[22]
5. **Stieng** — They live south of the Mnong tribe. They are classified as Khmer Loeu.
6. **Jaraï** — They live farther east of all the above tribes, between actual Cambodia and Vietnam. They were persecuted by the Chams.

Khmers are an amalgam of many ethnic tribes. The arrival of Indian Brahmans reinforced and contributed to Khmer unity and dominance of Southeast Asia. The culture of the Khmer people and the widespread of the Môn-Khmer languages throughout Southeast Asia were a good fit with the Indian Brahman culture. The knowledge in cosmology and literature possessed by the Brahmans would provide the catalyst to unite different ethnic tribes under one common entity, leading to the birth of the Khmer civilization. Sanskrit was used for the first time as the centralized and functional language to unite and govern the Khmer nation. It was Sanskrit, the sacred language of high learning that brought about the prominence and respect of the Khmer civilization. Pali was introduced into the Khmer language when Buddhism was brought to Cambodia. According to George Coedès, Pali appeared in Cambodia for the first time in 1309 under the reign of Indrajayavarman after Indravarman III abdicated in favor of his brother-in-law.[19,p195; 23] However, Buddhism which was associated with Pali appeared in Cambodia as early as the 5th century during the reign of Kaundinya Jayavarman (478-514).

The existence of Funan was revealed to the world by the French sinologist Paul Pelliot through his published work in 1903, *Le Fou-nan*.[24] The earliest use of the word Funan that appeared in Chinese historical archives came most likely from the accounts of the Chinese envoys Kang Tai and Chu Ying for their mission to Funan that took place under the reign of the Fan Xun (240-310). Chu Ying mentioned that books found in the Funan libraries were written in language resembling that of India.[6,p19] Georges Maspero believed that these early writings were probably based on the Kushan scripts and introduced into Funan around the time of Fan Shih Man (205-225). The Kushan scripts were different from the earliest Khmer inscriptions found at Angkor Borei. These Khmer inscriptions, dated 611 AD, were the earliest system of writing based on the Pallava scripts that appeared in Southeast Asia. All Indian scripts descended from the Brahmi or Magadha family; all Southeast Asian scripts descended from the Pallava scripts. The French scholar and physician Jean Filliozat who was fluent in Sanskrit, Pali, Tibetan, and Tamil did a study on the evolution of the Southeast Asian scripts.[25,pp446-448] He used the Pallava script *ta* as the prototype to show how it branched out to different Southeast Asian scripts. An adaptation of the Filliozat's Pallava *Akshara ta* tree is presented in Figure 7.[25,p448; 26] Since they first appeared around the 6th century, the evolution of Khmer scripts had made nine more transformations until they reached the present-day form. The names and classification of the evolution of Khmer scripts are shown in Table 3.[26] Thai scripts that branched out from Khmer scripts appeared during the reign of King Ram Khamhaeng (1239-1298), but the authenticity of the Ram Khamhaeng stele had been questioned by leading scholars like Michael Vickery, Michael Wright, and Piriya Krairiksh. The controversy of the Ram Khamhaeng Inscriptions is discussed with more details in Chapter 9.

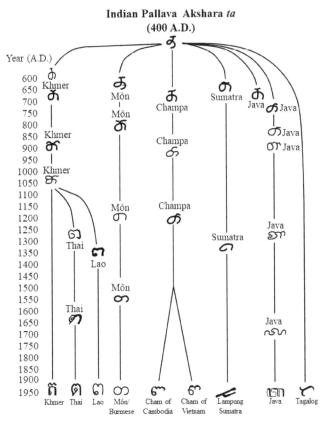

Figure 7. Example of Script *ta* Evolution in Southeast Asia
Originated from the Indian Pallava Abugidary
(Adapted from Ref. 26 of Jean Filliozat's Pallava Prototype 1953)

Table 3. Khmer Scripts Evolution from the 6th Century to the Present Day
(Adaped from Reference 26)

Type	Name/ Classification	Era (A.D.)	Khmer Scripts
I	Han Chey	6th Century	
II	Veal Kan Teng	End 6th Century/ Early 7th Century	
III	Ang Chomney Kor	667	
IV	Inn Kor Sey	970	
V	Preah Keo	1002	
VI	Nor Korr	1066	
VII	Banteay Chmar	12th Century	
VIII	Angkor Wat	13th Century	
IX	Post Angkor	1702	
X	Present	Present-Day	

CHAPTER 3

THE KHMER KINGS AND THE HISTORY OF CAMBODIA

KHMER TRADITIONAL CALENDAR

In this country, as in our own, there are men who understand astronomy and can calculate the eclipses of the sun and of the moon. However, a system different from ours determines the length of each month. In certain years, they must needs resort to an intercalary month, but this can only be the ninth month — and this I am unable to understand. Every night is divided into five watches. A cycle consists of seven days, analogous to the Chinese k'ai-pi chien ch'u. ... The twelve animals of the cycle correspond with those in China, but are named differently. Thus the horse is called pu-sai (Khmer, bhu sèh); the cock is man (Khmer, man); the pig is shih-lu (Khmer, cruk); the ox is ko (Khmer, kô); et cetera.

The Customs of Cambodia
Chou Ta-Kuan[27,pX]

THE METHODOLOGY AND THE DIFFERENT CALENDAR SYSTEMS

The Khmer Calendar System

Ancient Cambodians understood the moon and solar movements which enabled them to create calendars. The understanding of the Khmer calendar *Chankitek* is necessary to properly convert the dates used in ancient Khmer inscriptions to the Gregorian calendar dates. *Chankitek* calendar means "moon calendar," but this term is misleading because the Khmer calendar uses a combination of the lunar and solar dates. To be properly correct, it should be called lunisolar calendar or *Chansoryakitek* calendar. The lunar dates are determined by the movement of the moon, which synchronizes with the number of days the earth goes around the sun in a year. This Khmer accounting system is used to synchronize with the Gregorian calendar system to prevent the years from shifting.

Khmer history was originally recorded in *Moha Sakaraj* or simply *Saka* (known in Khmer as *Sakarach Thom,* which means Grand Era). *Saka* was probably introduced into Cambodia by the earlier Indians and Brahman settlers who came to Funan. The word *Saka* was carved along the numerical value *605* on the K.127 Inscription, which thus showed the earliest use of the number zero [this subject is discussed in Book II under the reign of Sisowath Monivong because the discovery was made by George Coedès in 1931]. As a background, the Saka Era originated under the reign of King Shaka after his victory over Ujjayin which was the capital of the Avanti Kingdom. The current location of Ujjayin would have been in Madhya Pradesh in India. The Saka Era began in 78 AD.

Eventually a new epoch, called the *Chul Sakarach* (or *Cula Sakaraj*, noted as *CS* — also known as the Little Era), was introduced in Cambodia and used along with the *SE*. It was believed it was Srei Soriyovong (1416-1425) who introduced *CS* into the calendar system. *CS* was still in use until the reign of Srei Soriyopor (1601-1618). The beginning for *CS* corresponded to the Gregorian date of 22 March 638 AD. As a background, because of the diversity of how the Cula calendar was applied the Indian government decided in 1957 to establish a unifying calendar by fixing the starting new year either on March 22 (for a normal year) or on March 21 (for a leap year). The updated methodology used for the Indian calendar is independent of the methodology used for the Cambodian calendar.

When Buddhism finally replaced Brahmanism, the calendar system changed one more time and the *Buddhist Era (BE)* replaced the *Saka Era*, but sometime *CS* and *SE* were still used along with *BE*. The Buddhist Era was based on the time the Buddha entered Nirvana. There are two schools of thought concerning when the Buddha was born. According to the Long Chronology or Ceylonese Chronology, 543 BC is considered to be the year when the Buddha achieved the ultimate stage in the realization of Nirvana. Only the countries that practice Theravada Buddhism — which include Sri Lanka, Burma, Cambodia, Laos, and Thailand — adopt this chronology. They believe that the Buddha entered Nirvana around 12-17 April. Therefore, this time frame is considered as the starting new year for the Buddhist calendar. Because the Buddha had lived to the age of 80 years before he entered Nirvana, therefore he was born in 623 BC [543 + 80]. In contrast to the above belief, Western and Indian historians tied the date of Nirvana with the date of the consecration of the Emperor Asoka of India. His consecration was in 268 BC. Historians call this the "Corrected Long Chronology" or "Corrected Ceylonese Chronology." According to this new school of thought, the Nirvana date is determined to occur 218 years before Emperor Asoka's consecration. Therefore, the Buddha's birth date is reported in most literatures as 566 BC (218 + 268 + 80 = 566).

Converting Non-Gregorian Era to Gregorian/Common Era

The current reference point for the Khmer calendar is the Khmer New Year, which for the modern era starts either on the 13th or 14th of April. The Buddhist year starts in April of the Gregorian year, which corresponds to the sign of Aries. Table 4 below shows a very rough approximation on how to convert the years from the different Non-Gregorian eras such as Saka, Cula, and Buddhist to the Common Era (CE) or Anno Domini (AD). Table 4 is divided into the periods prior and post adoption of the Buddhist calendar, which occurred probably around 1863 under the French protectorate. Theoretically, the Buddhist years would not be applicable for conversion from the Cula and Saka years but the methodology used for post Buddhist calendar could be similarly applied in this case.

Table 4. Conversion from Common Era to Other Eras Used in Cambodia

Non-Gregorian Era	Gregorian/Common Era (CE) or Anno Domini (AD)				
	Before Adoption of Buddhist Calendar (~1863)		After Adoption of Buddhist Calendar (~1863)		
	January 1 - March 21	March 22 - December 31	January 1 - March 21	March 22 - April 12/13	April 13/14 - December 31
Buddh Sakaraj or Buddhist Era (BE)	N/A	N/A	AD = BE - 543		AD = BE - 544
Chul Sakaraj (CS)	AD = CS + 639	AD = CS + 638	AD = CS + 639	AD = CS + 638	
Moha Sakaraj or Saka Era (SE)	AD = (SE + 78)/(SE + 79)				

For AD year it must be noted that the Saka and Cula eras occurred after the Common era while the Buddhist era preceded it. The new year for CS is specifically stated as March 22 while that for SE is not given. As a result, the AD conversion pertaining to the SE can only be given as a range between two bounding years.

To determine the AD year for the Saka calendar, 78 and 79 must be added separately to the SE year to bound the date. The AD year must range between "SE + 78" and "SE + 79".

To determine the AD year for the Cula calendar, 639 must be added to the CS year for event occurring before March 22; and 638 must be added for event occurring after March 22.

For the Buddhist calendar, the AD year is obtained by subtracting 543 from the BE year for event occurring before April 13 or 14; and 544 must be subtracted from the BE year for event occurring after April 13 or 14.

Why was the new year celebration changed from November (as mentioned by Zhou Daguan during his yearly stay at Angkor in 1296) to the present-day month of April? There were two schools of thought concerning this subject. Some scholars speculated that due to the precession, the dates had been moved from the month of November to April. This theory cannot be true because it takes approximately 25,920 years for the precession to complete a full-year cycle or 2,160 years to advance one month. Only 720 years have elapsed from the time Zhou Daguan visited Angkor in 1296 to the present day. Therefore according to my calculation, the precession has only advanced by 0.333 month or approximately 10 days. The second speculation said it was the French Colonial government that moved the new year to April because they wanted people to rest and celebrate after the harvesting season and before the start of the rainy season. This theory may or may not be true. From my understanding and research on this subject, I believe that the switch for the new year from November to April was due to the use of the Buddhist calendar system. The new year celebration reported by Zhou Daguan was based on the first lunar month of Meakasé which fell mostly in the month of November in the Gregorian calendar. When the calendar system was switched from the Cula and Saka eras to the Buddhist era, the first month of Meakasé which corresponded to November and used as the beginning of the year was discarded and replaced with the month of April.

For example, the date reported in the Cambodian chronicle for the accession of Ang Chan I that was reported in the Buddhist, Saka, and Cula eras could be determined using the calculation shown in Reference 28. The Cambodian chronicle mentioned that Ang Chan I acceded to the throne in 2073 of the Buddhist era, 1451 of the Saka era, 891 of the Cula era, in the year of the Ox, on Thursday of the 11th day of the waxing moon, in the month of Phalguna.[29,p149] Khin Sok stated that the above date would correspond to 1529 AD, but based on Table 4 and on my own calculation, the corresponding Gregorian date had to be 10 March 1530 to fit the above dates (except for the Buddhist date). There was no date in 1529 AD that would fall on Thursday in the month of March (or February or April) of the 11th day of the waxing moon.[28]

Metonic 19-Year Cycle and Khmer 10-Year Cycle Systems

An example of a Metonic 19-year cycle and 10-year cycle systems is shown in Table 5. Khmer calendar used both the lunar and solar system calendars. Based on References 30 and 31, a method has been devised to calculate and convert the days, months, and years from the Gregorian calendar to those used in the Khmer calendar. Khmer used the Metonic cycle system to synchronize the lunar and solar dates. The Greek mathematician and astronomer Meton of Athens introduced the system of calculation in 432 BC, now known as the Metonic cycle (also called Enneadecaeteris), after he discovered that it took 19 solar years or 228 solar months to coincide with 235 lunar months. The year that has 365 days is considered a normal year and the one with 366 days is a leap year. Five leap years occur within the span of a 19-solar-year. As a consequence, five extra days are added to the total number of days in a 19-solar-year. A normal lunar year has 29 days for each of the following Khmer six months: *Meakasé* មិគសិរ *(1st)*, *Meak* មាឃ *(3rd)*, *Chaet* ចេត្រ *(5th)*, *Chais* ជេស្ឋ *(7th)*, *Srap* ស្រាពណ៍ *(9th)*, and *Asoch* អស្សុជ *(11th)*; and 30 days for each of the remaining six months: *Bos* បុស្ស *(2nd)*, *Phalkun* ផល្គុន *(4th)*, *Pisak* ពិសាខ *(6th)*, *Asadh* អាសាឍ *(8th)*, *Phutrobot* ភទ្របទ *(10th)*, and *Kadeuk* កត្តិក *(12th)*. The seven months discrepancy between the solar and lunar months resulted in an additional seven days that must be added to the total days of the 235 lunar months. The arithmetic required for the synchronization of the solar and lunar system of accounting is shown below:

Number of days in 19 solar years = [(19 x 365) + 5] or [(14 x 365) + (5 x 366)] = 6940 days
Number of days in 235 lunar months = (117 x 29) + (118 x 30) + 7 = 6940 days

Table 5. Metonic 19-Year Cycle and Khmer 10-Year Cycle Systems

GREGORIAN CALENDAR		19-YEAR CYCLE		ERAS USED IN KHMER CHRONOLOGY			KHMER 10-YEAR CYCLE		ANIMAL	
Common Era (AD)		Enneadecaeretics		Small or Cula Sakaraj (CS)	Grand or Saka Era (SE)	Buddhist Era (BE)	SAK Year	Name	Year	Sign
1997	1 Jan-21Mar	1(2)	Leap Day	1358		2540	8	Ardaksak (អដ្ឋសិក)	1	Rat Chout (ជូត)
	22 Mar-13Apr				1918-1919					
	14 Apr-31 Dec			1359		2541	9	Noppaksak (នព្វសិក)	2	Ox Chhleuv (ឆ្លូវ)
1998	1 Jan-21Mar	2	None							
	22 Mar-13Apr				1919-1920					
	14 Apr-31 Dec			1360		2542	10	Somrithiksak (សំរិទ្ធិសិក)	3	Tiger Khal (ខាល)
1999	1 Jan-21Mar	3(3)	Leap Month							
	22 Mar-13Apr				1920-1921					
	14 Apr-31 Dec			1361		2543	1	Aeksak (ឯកសិក)	4	Hare Thos (ថោះ)
2000(1)	1 Jan-21Mar	4(2)	Leap Day							
	22 Mar-13Apr				1921-1922					
	14 Apr-31 Dec			1362		2544	2	Tosak (ទោសិក)	5	Dragon Raung (រោង)
2001	1 Jan-21Mar	5	None							
	22 Mar-13Apr				1922-1923					
	14 Apr-31 Dec			1363		2545	3	Treysak (ត្រីសិក)	6	Snake Masanh (ម្សាញ់)
2002	1 Jan-21Mar	6(3)	Leap Month							
	22 Mar-13Apr				1923-1924					
	14 Apr-31 Dec			1364		2546	4	Chaktvasak (ចត្វាសិក)	7	Horse Momy (មមី)
2003	1 Jan-21Mar	7	None							
	22 Mar-13Apr				1924-1925					
	14 Apr-31 Dec			1365		2547	5	Panhjaksak (បញ្ចសិក)	8	Goat Momé (មមែ)
2004(1)	1 Jan-21Mar	8(3)	Leap Month							
	22 Mar-13Apr				1925-1926					
	14 Apr-31 Dec			1366		2548	6	Chhorsak (ឆសិក)	9	Monkey Vauk (វក)
2005	1 Jan-21Mar	9	None							
	22 Mar-13Apr				1926-1927					
	14 Apr-31 Dec			1367		2549	7	Sabpaksak (សប្ដសិក)	10	Rooster Rokar (រកា)
2006	1 Jan-21Mar	10(2)	Leap Day							
	22 Mar-13Apr				1927-1928					
	14 Apr-31 Dec			1368		2550	8	Ardaksak (អដ្ឋសិក)	11	Dog Chor (ច)
2007	1 Jan-21Mar	11(3)	Leap Month							
	22 Mar-13Apr				1928-1929					
	14 Apr-31 Dec			1369		2551	9	Noppaksak (នព្វសិក)	12	Pig Kaor (កុរ)
2008(1)	1 Jan-21Mar	12	None							
	22 Mar-13Apr				1929-1930					
	14 Apr-31 Dec			1370		2552	10	Somrithiksak (សំរិទ្ធិសិក)	1	Rat Chout (ជូត)
2009	1 Jan-21Mar	13	None							
	22 Mar-13Apr				1930-1931					
	14 Apr-31 Dec			1371		2553	1	Aeksak (ឯកសិក)	2	Ox Chhleuv (ឆ្លូវ)
2010	1 Jan-21Mar	14(3)	Leap Month							
	22 Mar-13Apr				1931-1932					
	14 Apr-31 Dec			1372		2554	2	Tosak (ទោសិក)	3	Tiger Khal (ខាល)
2011	1 Jan-21Mar	15	None							
	22 Mar-13Apr				1932-1933					
	14 Apr-31 Dec			1373		2555	3	Treysak (ត្រីសិក)	4	Hare Thos (ថោះ)
2012	1 Jan-21Mar	16	None							
	22 Mar-13Apr				1933-1934					
	14 Apr-31 Dec			1374		2556	4	Chaktvasak (ចត្វាសិក)	5	Dragon Raung (រោង)
2013	1 Jan-21Mar	17(3)	Leap Month							
	22 Mar-13Apr				1934-1935					
	14 Apr-31 Dec			1375		2557	5	Panhjaksak (បញ្ចសិក)	6	Snake Masanh (ម្សាញ់)
2014	1 Jan-21Mar	18	None							
	22 Mar-13Apr				1935-1936					
	14 Apr-31 Dec			1376		2558	6	Chhorsak (ឆសិក)	7	Horse Momy (មមី)
2015	1 Jan-21Mar	19(3)	Leap Month							
	22 Mar-13Apr				1936-1937					
	14 Apr-31 Dec			1377		2559	7	Sabpaksak (សប្ដសិក)	8	Goat Momé (មមែ)

Notes: 1. Leap year occurred on 2000, 2004, 2008, and 2012 (add one extra day for the month of February).
    2. Leap days occurred on year 1, 4, and 10 of the Metonic 19-year cycle (add one extra day for the month of Chais, see Table 6).
    3. Leap months occurred on year 3, 6, 8, 11, 14, 17, and 19 of the Metonic 19-year cycle. On these years, the month of Asadh is replaced by the months of Pakthameasadh and Tutayeasadh.

Based on historical data, 1997 is the first year of the Metonic 19-year cycle. Therefore, 2015 is the last years of the cycle. The chart shows the relationship between the Gregorian calendar and the Khmer system of accounting used in the lunisolar calendar. The Sak year used in the Khmer calendar is based on a 10-year cycle. The names of the years, starting from the first year are *Aeksak (ឯកស័ក)*, *Tosak (ទោស័ក)*, *Treisak (ត្រីស័ក)*, *Chaktvasak (ចត្វាស័ក)*, *Panhjaksak (បញ្ចស័ក)*, *Chhorsak (ឆស័ក)*, *Sabpaksak (សប្ដស័ក)*, *Ardaksak (អដ្ឋស័ក)*, *Noppaksak (នព្វស័ក)*, and *Somrithiksak (សំរឹទ្ធិស័ក)*. The animal years are based on a 12-year cycle. The names of the animals, starting from the first year are *Chout (ជូត — Rat)*, *Chhleuv (ឆ្លូវ — Ox)*, *Khal (ខាល — Tiger)*, *Thos (ថោះ — Hare)*, *Raung (រោង — Dragon)*, *Massagne (ម្សាញ់ — Snake)*, *Momi (មមី — Horse)*, *Momé (មមែ — Goat)*, *Vauk (វក — Monkey)*, *Rokar (រកា — Rooster)*, *Chor (ច — Dog)*, *Koar (កុរ — Pig)*. The Buddhist years are transitioning in the Gregorian years either on April 13 or 14. After the 19-year cycle is completed, a new cycle will start at the point where the last cycle left off and continues in the same manner for another 19-year cycle. The determination of a leap year in the Gregorian calendar is the following: 1) It is a leap year if the year is evenly divisible by four; 2) That year is not a leap year if it is evenly divisible by 100; 3) Unless that year is also evenly divisible by 400, then it is a leap year. The years 1600, 2000, 2004, 2008, and 2012 are leap years while the years 1700, 1800, 1900 are not. Three leap-days and seven leap-months occur within the Metonic 19-year cycle. The three leap-days occurred on the 1st, 4th, and 10th years. The seven leap-months occurred on the 3rd, 6th, 8th, 11th, 14th, 17th, and 19th years.

Khmer Lunar Days/Months

Except for the month of February that has 28 days for a non-leap year and 29 days for a leap year, the solar months have either 30 or 31 days. The Khmer lunar months have either 29 or 30 days. Within each month, the days are broken into two phases — the waxing moon and waning moon phases.

The waxing moon is called *Keurt (កើត)*, meaning to be born or to rise. The first day of the waxing moon is called 1 *Keurt*. The last day of the waxing moon, which is the full moon is called 15 *Keurt*. After the full moon, the counting is discontinued and starts anew with 1 *Rauch (រោច)* to indicate the first day of the waning moon. The end of the waning moon will be either 14 *Rauch* or 15 *Rauch*, depending on the month.

Table 6 shows the Khmer and Sanskrit names for the lunar months and their corresponding number of days. When the year has a leap day, an extra day is added to the seventh Khmer month *Chais (ជេស្ឋ)*. Therefore, the 7th month will have 30 days instead of the customary 29 days. When the year has a leap month, the 8th Khmer month *Asadh (អាសាឍ)* will be replaced by two months, namely *Pakthameasadh (បឋមាសាឍ)* and *Tutayeasadh (ទុតិយាសាឍ)*. Both months will have 30 days each.

Table 6. Lunar Months and Lunar Days

LUNAR MONTH			NUMBER OF DAYS IN A LUNAR MONTH		
Number	Khmer Name	Sanskrit Name	Normal Year	Year with Leap Day	Year with Leap Month
1	Meakasé មិគសិរ	Margashirsha	(29 Days) 1-15 K & 1-14 R	(29 Days) 1-15 K & 1-14 R	(29 Days) 1-15 K & 1-14 R
2	Bos បុស្ស	Pausha	(30 Days) 1-15 K & 1-15 R	(30 Days) 1-15 K & 1-15 R	(30 Days) 1-15 K & 1-15 R
3	Meak មាឃ	Magha	(29 Days) 1-15 K & 1-14 R	(29 Days) 1-15 K & 1-14 R	(29 Days) 1-15 K & 1-14 R
4	Phalkun ផល្គុន	Phalguna	(30 Days) 1-15 K & 1-15 R	(30 Days) 1-15 K & 1-15 R	(30 Days) 1-15 K & 1-15 R
5	Chaet ចេត្រ	Chaitra	(29 Days) 1-15 K & 1-14 R	(29 Days) 1-15 K & 1-14 R	(29 Days) 1-15 K & 1-14 R
6	Pisak ពិសាខ	Saisakha	(30 Days) 1-15 K & 1-15 R	(30 Days) 1-15 K & 1-15 R	(30 Days) 1-15 K & 1-15 R
7	Chais ជេស្ឋ	Jyaishtha	(29 Days) 1-15 K & 1-14 R	(30 Days) 1-15 K & 1-15 R	(29 Days) 1-15 K & 1-14 R
8	Asadh អាសាឍ	Ashadha	(30 Days) 1-15 K & 1-15 R	(30 Days) 1-15 K & 1-15 R	N/A
8.1	Pakthameasadh បឋមអាសាឍ	Badhamasadh (Ashadha I)	N/A	N/A	(30 Days) 1-15 K & 1-15 R
8.2	Tutayeasadh ទុតិយាសាឍ	Thitiyasadh (Ashadha II)	N/A	N/A	(30 Days) 1-15 K & 1-15 R
9	Srap ស្រាពណ៌	Sravanag	(29 Days) 1-15 K & 1-14 R	(29 Days) 1-15 K & 1-14 R	(29 Days) 1-15 K & 1-14 R
10	Phutrobot ភទ្របទ	Bhadrapada	(30 Days) 1-15 K & 1-15 R	(30 Days) 1-15 K & 1-15 R	(30 Days) 1-15 K & 1-15 R
11	Asoch អស្សុជ	Ashvina	(29 Days) 1-15 K & 1-14 R	(29 Days) 1-15 K & 1-14 R	(29 Days) 1-15 K & 1-14 R
12	Kadeuk កត្តិក	Kartika	(30 Days) 1-15 K & 1-15 R	(30 Days) 1-15 K & 1-15 R	(30 Days) 1-15 K & 1-15 R

K = Keurt កើត (Day on the Waxing Moon)
R = Rauch រោច (Day on the Waning Moon)

Gregorian Months and Correspondence with Khmer Lunar Months

Cambodia has created Khmer names corresponding to the months used in the Gregorian calendar. Because the Lunar calendar is also used in conjunction with the Gregorian calendar, I developed a table to correlate the months pertained to the Lunar calendar with those used in Gregorian calendar. As mentioned above and shown in Table 6, when the year falls on a leap month an extra month is added to the Lunar calendar to keep up the synchronization with the Gregorian calendar. The correspondence between the Gregorian months and Lunar months are shown in Table 7. It must also be noted that Cambodia was divided into two seasons, with the monsoon wet season occurring from May to October and the dry season occurring from November to April. The Cambodian festivals and Buddhist religious celebrations are usually practiced based on their Lunar calendar.

Table 7. Gregorian Months and Correspondence with the Khmer Lunar Months

Gregorian Month		Khmer Lunar Month		Season	Cambodian Festivals or Religious Celebrations
English	Khmer	Normal Year	Year with Leap Month		
January	កម្ភៈ (Meakara)	បុស្ស-មាឃ (Bos-Meak)	បុស្ស-មាឃ (Bos-Meak)	Dry	
February	កម្ភៈ (Kompheak)	មាឃ-ផល្គុន (Meak-Phalkun)	មាឃ-ផល្គុន (Meak-Phalkun)	Dry	មាឃបូជា (Meak Bochea: celebrating on the full moon of the 3rd lunar month, which usually falls in February or early March to commemorate the day when 1,250 Bhikkhus were ordained by the Buddha)
March	មិនា (Mina)	ផល្គុន-ចេត្រ (Phalkun-Chaet)	ផល្គុន-ចេត្រ (Phalkun-Chaet)		
April	មេសា (Mésa)	ចេត្រ-ពិសាខ (Chaet-Pisak)	ចេត្រ-ពិសាខ (Chaet-Pisak)		ចូលឆ្នាំខ្មែរ (Chaul Chhnam Khmer: Cambodian New Year; usually celebrated on 13 or 14 April)
May	ឧសភា (Ussaphea)	ពិសាខ-ជេស្ឋ (Pisak-Chais)	ពិសាខ-ជេស្ឋ (Pisak-Chais)	Mansoon (Wet)	• ព្រះរាជពិធីច្រត់ព្រះនង្គ័ល (Royal Ploughing Ceremony: 4th day of the waning moon) • វិសាខបូជា (Visak Bochea: 15th day of the waxing moon; celebrating Buddha's enlightenment)
June	មិថុនា (Mithona)	ជេស្ឋ-អាសាឍ (Chais-Asadh)	ជេស្ឋ-បឋមាសាឍ (Chais-Pakthameasach)		
July	កក្កដា (Kakda)	អាសាឍ-ស្រាពណ៍ (Asadh-Srap)	បឋមាសាឍ-ទុតិយាសាឍ (Pakthameasach-Tutayeasach)		• ចូលព្រះវស្សា/ចេញព្រះវស្សា (Chaul Preah Vossa: Rain Retreat or Buddhist Lent starts 1 Rauch of Asadh or Tutayeasadh to Chenh Preah Vossa on 15 Keurt of Asoch)
August	សីហា (Seiha)	ស្រាពណ៍-ភទ្របទ (Srap-Phutrobot)	ទុតិយាសាឍ-ស្រាពណ៍ (Tutayeasach-Srap)		• ភ្ជុំបិណ្ឌ (Pchum Bèn; memorial day celebrating the ancestors. It started on the 16th day of Phutrobot (on 1 Rauch) and lasted for 15 days (15 Rauch). This 15th day is called Pchum Bèn.
September	កញ្ញា (Kaña)	ភទ្របទ-អស្សុជ (Phutrobot-Asoch)	ស្រាពណ៍-ភទ្របទ (Srap-Phutrobot)		• កឋិន (Kathin: started on 1 Rauch of Asoch; usually celebrated for 29 days by offering safron robes to monks who exited Rain Retreat; it lasted from October to November)
October	តុលា (Tula)	អស្សុជ-កត្ដិក (Asoch-Kadeuk)	ភទ្របទ-អស្សុជ (Putrobot-Asoch)		
November	វិច្ឆិកា (Vichka)	កត្ដិក-មិគសិរ (Kadeuk-Meakasé)	អស្សុជ-កត្ដិក (Asoch-Kadeuk)	Dry	បុណ្យអុំទូក (Bonn Om Touk: boat racing water festival, which ccurred on the full moon of Kadeuk (November) to celebrate the reversing of the flow of Tonle Sap and Mekong River)
December	ធ្នូ (Thnou)	មិគសិរ-បុស្ស (Meakasé-Bos)	កត្ដិក-មិគសិរ (Kadeuké-Meakasé)		

Determining the Year of the Khmer 10-Year Cycle for a Given Cula or Moha Sakaraj

Prior to using the Gregorian and Buddhist years, Cambodia recorded the events in term of the Cula Sakarach (CS) or Moha Sakarach (Saka Era = SE) accompanied by the order of the year in the Khmer 10-year cycle system. For example, the Cambodian chronicle recorded that after 13 years of reign Ang Chan I was consecrated in 1451 SE, 891 CS, the first decade (of the 10-year cycle system) that the author of the chronicle converted to 2073 of the Buddhist era (BE) or 1529 AD.[29,p149] The CS and SE used a modulus of 10 (as in a 10-year cycle system). When 1451 SE or 891 CS is divided by 10, its remainder is 1. The number one is the first decade quoted in the chronicle. When the calendar was switched from the Cula and Saka to the Buddhist calendar, it was not necessary to use the 10-year cycle but it was kept in the system probably for historical reason and as a habit of performing the calculation. To be correct, the 10-year cycle should be in sync with the Cula and Saka years but it seems that someone decided to sync it with the Buddhist years instead. How did the author of the chronicle come up with 2073 BE or 1529 AD for the date that corresponded to 1451 SE or 891 CS? The formula in Table 4 was used for the verification of the above conversion date from SE and CS to BE or AD. Table 8 shows a truncated version for the conversation and/or correlation between the AD, SE, CS, and BE years in relationship to the 12-year animal signs and the Khmer 10-year cycle system. Additional information about Chankitek calendar, Buddhist, Cula, and Saka eras can be obtained from References 30 and 31.

Table 8. Truncated Version Showing the Correlation between Gregorian, Saka, Cula, and Buddhist Years in Relationship to the 12-Year Animal Signs and Khmer 10-Year Cycle System

GREGORIAN AD YEAR		CULA YEAR	SAKA YEAR	BUDDHIST YEAR	ANIMAL YEAR	KHMER 10-YEAR CYCLE
1527	Jan 1-Mar 21	888	1448-1449	2070	DOG	ARDAKSAK
	Mar 22-Apr 12/13					
	Apr 12/13-Dec 31	889		2071	PIG	NOPPAKSAK
1528	Jan 1-Mar 21		1449-1450			
	Mar 22-Apr 12/13					
	Apr 12/13-Dec 31	890		2072	RAT	SOMRITHIKSAK
1529	Jan 1-Mar 21		1450-1451			
	Mar 22-Apr 12/13					
	Apr 12/13-Dec 31	891		2073	OX	AEKSAK
1530	Jan 1-Mar 21		1451-1452			
	Mar 22-Apr 12/13					
	Apr 12/13-Dec 31	892		2074	TIGER	TOSAK
1531	Jan 1-Mar 21		1452-1453			
	Mar 22-Apr 12/13					
	Apr 12/13-Dec 31	893		2075	HARE	TREYSAK
1532	Jan 1-Mar 21		1453-1454			
	Mar 22-Apr 12/13					
	Apr 12/13-Dec 31	894		2076	DRAGON	CHAKTVASAK
1533	Jan 1-Mar 21		1454-1455			
	Mar 22-Apr 12/13					
	Apr 12/13-Dec 31	895		2077	SNAKE	PANHJAKSAK
1534	Jan 1-Mar 21		1455-1456			
	Mar 22-Apr 12/13					
	Apr 12/13-Dec 31	896		2078	HORSE	CHHORSAK
1535	Jan 1-Mar 21		1456-1457			
	Mar 22-Apr 12/13					
	Apr 12/13-Dec 31	897		2079	GOAT	SABPAKSAK
1536	Jan 1-Mar 21		1457-1458			
	Mar 22-Apr 12/13					
	Apr 12/13-Dec 31	898		2080	MONKEY	ARDAKSAK
1537	Jan 1-Mar 21		1458-1459			
	Mar 22-Apr 12/13					
	Apr 12/13-Dec 31	899		2081	ROOSTER	NOPPAKSAK
1538	Jan 1-Mar 21		1459-1460			
	Mar 22-Apr 12/13					
	Apr 12/13-Dec 31	900		2082	DOG	SOMRITHIKSAK
1539	Jan 1-Mar 21		1460-1461			
	Mar 22-Apr 12/13	901				
	Apr 12/13-Dec 31			2083	PIG	AEKSAK
1540 to 2007		901-902 to 1368-1369	1461-1462 to 1928-1929	2083 to 2551	PIG to PIG	AEKSAK to NOPPAKSAK
2008	Jan 1-Mar 21	1369	1929-1930	2551	PIG	NOPPAKSAK
	Mar 22-Apr 12/13					
	Apr 12/13-Dec 31	1370		2552	RAT	SOMRITHIKSAK
2009	Jan 1-Mar 21		1930-1931			
	Mar 22-Apr 12/13					
	Apr 12/13-Dec 31	1371		2553	OX	AEKSAK
2010	Jan 1-Mar 21		1931-1932			
	Mar 22-Apr 12/13					
	Apr 12/13-Dec 31	1372		2554	TIGER	TOSAK
2011	Jan 1-Mar 21		1932-1933			
	Mar 22-Apr 12/13					
	Apr 12/13-Dec 31	1373		2555	HARE	TREYSAK
2012	Jan 1-Mar 21		1933-1934			
	Mar 22-Apr 12/13					
	Apr 12/13-Dec 31	1374		2556	DRAGON	CHAKTVASAK
2013	Jan 1-Mar 21		1934-1935			
	Mar 22-Apr 12/13					
	Apr 12/13-Dec 31	1375		2557	SNAKE	PANHJAKSAK
2014	Jan 1-Mar 21		1935-1936			
	Mar 22-Apr 12/13					
	Apr 12/13-Dec 31	1376		2558	HORSE	CHHORSAK
2015	Jan 1-Mar 21		1936-1937			
	Mar 22-Apr 12/13					
	Apr 12/13-Dec 31	1377		2559	GOAT	SABPAKSAK
2016	Jan 1-Mar 21		1937-1938			
	Mar 22-Apr 12/13					
	Apr 12/13-Dec 31	1378		2560	MONKEY	ARDAKSAK
2017	Jan 1-Mar 21		1938-1939			
	Mar 22-Apr 12/13					
	Apr 12/13-Dec 31	1379		2561	ROOSTER	NOPPAKSAK
2018	Jan 1-Mar 21		1939-1940			
	Mar 22-Apr 12/13					
	Apr 12/13-Dec 31	1380		2562	DOG	SOMRITHIKSAK
2019	Jan 1-Mar 21		1940-1941			

Determining the Animal Sign for a Given Buddhist Era (BE), Cula Sakaraj (CS), or Saka Era (SE)

In order to determine the animal sign for a given year in the BE or CS, it is first necessary to know the animal sign for a specific known year. Take the Buddhist year 2561 BE where the new year started on 14 April in the early morning, which corresponded to the year of the Rooster. Take 2561 modulo 12 to obtain the remainder, which in this case would be 5 [(2561/12) = (213 x 12) +5 = 2556 + 5]. To determine the animal sign for a given year in the Buddhist era, add 5 to the BE year and then take a modulus of 12. The remainder is the animal year. Using the above described method, 2017 AD would correspond to the 10th animal year which is the Rooster [(2561 + 5)/12 = (213 x 12) + 10 = 2556 + 10]. Take another example, such as 2541 BE (1997-1998 AD), to determine the animal sign for that year. Add 5 to 2541 would give 2546; its modulo 12 would yielded 2 as the remainder, which in this case would correspond to the year of the Ox.

A similar method can be applied to the CS or SE to obtain the animal sign for any given year, but it must be used cautiously due to the uncertainty of the new year starting dates for these eras. It is assumed that the new year for CS started on 22 March 638 AD but the exact date for the new year for SE is uncertain. To determine the animal sign for the CS year, it is first necessary to convert 638 AD to the BE year. Using Table 4, the BE year for 22 March 638 AD corresponded to 1182 BE (BE = AD + 544 = 638 + 544 = 1182). Add 5 to 1182 to obtain 1187. Take 1187 modulo 12 to obtain the remainder, which in this case is 11 [(1187/12) = (98 x 12) + 11]. The animal signs for the beginning of the Cula epoch were bounded between the 11th and 12th animal years (Dog and Pig). As an example, 1377 CS which corresponded to 2015-2016 would fall on the animal year of the Goat. The following is the math to determine the animal year for 1377 CS: 1) Add 11 to 1377 to obtain 1388; 2) Take 1388 modulo 12 to obtain 8 as the remainder [(1388/12) = (115 x 12) + 8]; the 8th animal year is the Goat. The same principal can be applied to the Saka year but the mechanic to obtain the result is less certain because it could be off by one animal year.

Three examples of the synchronizations between the Khmer lunisolar calendars and the Gregorian calendars for the years 1997 AD (2540-2541 BE), 2015 AD (2558-2559 BE), and 2016 AD (2559-2560 BE) are shown in Figures 8, 9, and 10 respectively. Overlapping years occur between the Khmer and Gregorian calendars because Khmer New Year started either on April 13 or April 14. The determination of the date for the new year has nothing to do with the lunar calendar, but rather with the number of days in the solar calendar. The number of days in a year is 365 for a normal year and 366 for a leap year. The determination for the date of the new year is based on the date of the previous new year. As an example, the New Year's date for 2015 AD is calculated as follows:

1. The New Year's date for 2014 AD fell on April 14.
2. Number of days from 15 April 2014 to 31 December 2014 = 261 days
3. Number of days in 2015 AD before the Khmer New Year = 365 – 261 = 104 days
4. Number of days from 1 January 2015 to 31 March 2015 = 90 days
5. Remaining number of days in April = 104 – 90 = 14 days
6. Therefore, the Khmer New Year for 2015 AD is April 14.

It must be noted that approximately 6 hrs and 12 min was added to the starting time for each new year to compensate for the one-day shift of the leap year that occurred every four years.

The year 1997 AD was chosen because it represented the first year of the Metonic 19-year cycle. For 1997 AD, the Khmer New Year falls on April 13, which corresponded to *Thgnay 8 Keurt* (8th day of the waxing moon), *Khèr Chaet* (the month of Chaitra), *Chhnam Chhleuv* 2541 BE (year of the ox, 2541 of the Buddhist era), and *Noppaksak* year (9th Sak year of the Khmer 10-year cycle). Because 2541 BE fell on the year with a leap day, therefore one additional day must be added to the 29 days for the month of Chais (7th lunar month).

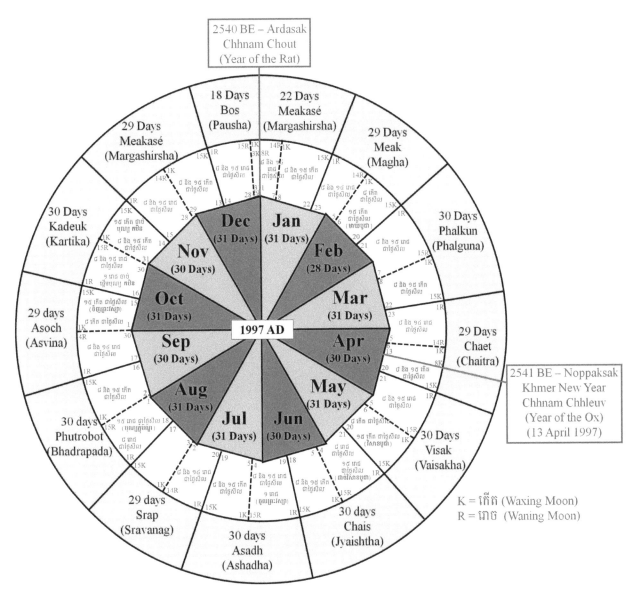

Figure 8. Correspondence Between 2540-2541 BE and 1997 AD in Khmer Lunisolar Calendar

The year 2015 AD was chosen because it represented the last year of the Metonic 19-year cycle. For 2015 AD, the Khmer New Year falls on April 14, which corresponded to *Thgnay 11 Rauch* (11th day of the waning moon), *Khèr Chaet* (the month of Chaitra), *Chhnam Momé* 2559 BE (year of the goat, 2559 of the Buddhist era), and *Sabpaksak* year (7th Sak year of the Khmer 10-year cycle). Because 2559 BE fell on the year with a leap month, therefore the month of Asadh (8th lunar month) must be replaced by the months of Pakthameasadh and Tutayeasadh with both months having 30 days each.

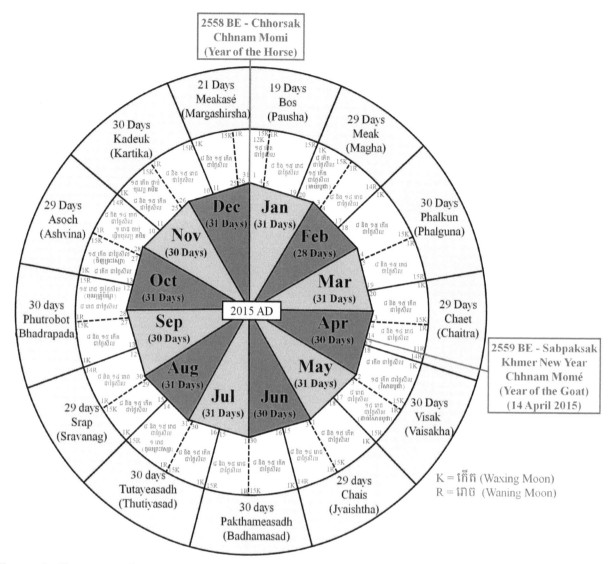

Figure 9. Correspondence Between 2558-2559 BE and 2015 AD in Khmer Lunisolar Calendar

The year 2016 AD was chosen because it started over as the beginning for the next Metonic 19-year cycle. For 2016 AD, the Khmer New Year falls on April 13, which corresponded to *Thgnay 7 Keurt* (7th day of the waxing moon), *Khèr Chaet* (the month of Chaitra), *Chhnam Vauk* 2560 BE (year of the monkey, 2560 of the Buddhist era), and *Ardaksak* year (8th Sak year of the Khmer 10-year cycle). It must be noted that 2016 AD was a leap year where the month of February had 29 days. 2560 BE fell on the year with a leap day. Therefore, one additional day must be added to the 29 days for the month of Chais (7th lunar month).

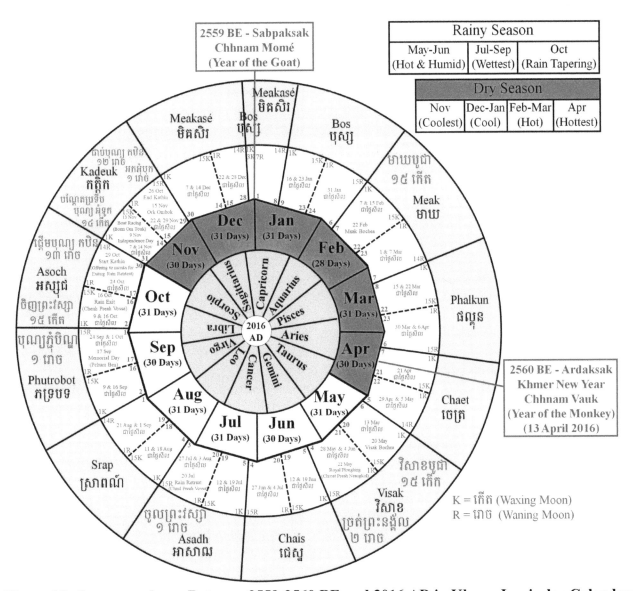

Figure 10. Correspondence Between 2559-2560 BE and 2016 AD in Khmer Lunisolar Calendar

Khmers during the Angkorian time did not celebrate the New Year on April 13 or 14. Zhou Daguan mentioned in his report that Cambodia celebrated the New Year on the tenth of the Chinese moon that he called *Chia-te* (*Kartika* in Sanskrit and *Kadeuk* in Khmer), which corresponded to the month of November. He wrote a report on the customs of Cambodia after he spent almost an entire year in Angkor. The dates Zhou Daguan left and then returned to China were mentioned in his report as follows:[27]

In the sixth moon of the year i-wei of the yuan-ch'eng epoch (July 14 to August 11, 1295) the holy Son of Heaven sent an ambassador to recall these people to their sense of duty and designated me as his travelling companion. On the second moon of following year ping-chen (March 5 to April 3, 1296) we left Ming-chou (Ning-po) and on the twentieth (March 24, 1296) put out to sea from the estuary of Wen-chou. On the fifteenth day of the third moon (April 18, 1296) we arrived at Champa. From now on, halfway through our journey, we were harassed by contrary winds, which delayed our arrival until autumn, at the seven moon (August 1 to 29, 1296). After receiving homage and accomplishing the purpose of our embassy, we returned to our ship on the sixth moon of the year ting-yu of the period ta-te (June 21 to July 20, 1297). On the twelfth day of the eighth moon (August 30, 1297) we finally dropped anchor at Sau-ming (Ning-p'o). Certain it is that in so short a time the customs and peculiarities of this country could not have been revealed to us in all their details; however, we were at least in a position to outline its principal characteristics.

During his stay in Angkor, Zhou Daguan recorded the dates of different festivals that Khmer people celebrated throughout the year. He mentioned of Khmer men who understood astronomy. He also gave a brief description of the way Khmer calendar was calculated. Below is the translation of his chronicle:[27,p29]

In Cambodia the New Year begins with the tenth Chinese moon, and is called chia-te (Sanskrit: Kārttika). In front of the royal palace a great platform is erected, sufficient to hold more than a thousand persons, and decorated from end to end with lanterns and flowers. Opposite this, some hundred and twenty feet distant, rises a lofty scaffold, put together of pieces of wood, shaped like the scaffolds used in building stupas, and towering to a height of one hundred and twenty feet. Every night from three to six of these structures arise. Rockets and firecrackers are placed on top of these – all this at great expense to the provinces and the noble families. As night comes on, the King is besought to take part in the spectacle. The rockets are fired, and the crackers touched off. The rockets can be seen at a distance of thirteen kilometers: the fire-crackers, large as swivel-guns, shake the whole city with their explosions. Mandarins and nobles are put to considerable expense to provide torches and areca nuts. Foreign ambassadors are also invited by the King to enjoy the spectacle, which comes to an end after a fortnight.

Every month a festival is held. The fourth month they have ball games. With the ninth month comes the ya lieh (rap riep) or census, when the entire population of the kingdom is summoned to the capital and passed in review before the royal palace. With the fifth month comes the ceremony of "bringing water to the Buddhas". Then Buddhas are carried from all over the kingdom, water is procured, and the ruler lends a hand in laving them. The festival of floats marks the sixth month, with the King enthroned on a belvedere to enjoy the spectacle. "The burning of the rice" marks the seventh month. This is the season for harvesting the new rice, which is brought to the South Gate and burned as a sacrifice to the Buddha. Countless women arrive in carts or on elephants to watch this ceremony, but the ruler is not to be seen. The eighth is the month of ai-lan (räm), or dancing. Every day actors and musicians are summoned to the royal palace to perform the ai-lan. In addition battles are staged between boars and elephants. Foreign ambassadors are invited as guests of the King to these festivities, which last ten days. I am unable to recall the ceremonies appropriate to the remaining months.

The above account by Zhou Daguan reveals useful information on Khmer custom during the time of the Angkor period. The Chinese New Year varies between January 21 and February 20. It is a historical fact that Zhou Daguan arrived in Angkor in autumn at the seventh Chinese moon, which corresponded to 1-29 August 1296. He stated that Cambodia celebrated the New Year on the tenth Chinese moon, which according to the calculation landed on the month of November.

What could be the reasons Khmers during the Angkor period celebrated the New Year in November? For obvious reason the first month of the year, which is Meakasé, usually fell in the month of November. It is therefore probable that ancient Khmers considered the first month of the year as the beginning of the new year. In addition to this, it is well proven that Khmers in the Angkor region during the Angkorian time had the capability to plant and harvest rice three or four times a year because of the water irrigation system and barays built around Angkor. Like during the time of Angkor, Cambodians nowadays have the capability to plant/grow/harvest rice three times in the wet season and one time in the dry season in the rain-fed lowland areas and/or floating rice areas. As shown in Figure 2, the month of November falls under the periods of medium wet and long wet seasons. The only viable dates in November for the New Year celebration that minimized the harvesting impact would be at the beginning of the month. For the medium wet season, the rice would not be ripe yet for harvesting; and for the long wet season, it would be just the beginning of the harvesting season.

When the calendar system was switched to the Buddhist calendar, the celebration of the new year in November was no longer applicable. Additionally, the celebration in November would cause some slight inconvenience for the people because it coincided with the beginning of the long wet harvesting season. The celebration in April was made to coincide with the Buddhist new year. Also, mid-April was the ideal time to celebrate because there was no planting or harvesting during this month.

Zhou Daguan said that people celebrated the Water Festival (*Bonn Om Touk)* on the sixth Chinese moon, which corresponded to the wet months of July-August. Nowadays, Cambodia celebrates the Water Festival on the full moon of either at the end of October or at the beginning of November. Angkor was an advanced society. Cambodian astronomy was as sophisticated as that of the Chinese. Zhou Daguan seemed to describe fireworks when he mentioned the rockets exploding in the sky. Cambodians must have used fireworks much earlier than Zhou Daguan arrived in Angkor. The first evidence of fireworks used in Europe did not appear until Marco Polo returned from China in the thirteenth century [Author's note: There is still a controversy on whether Marco Polo actually travelled to China and met Kublai Khan. Some historians believe that Marco Polo really existed and visited China because some of his descriptions were found to be true. On the other hands, some skeptics and archaeologists believed the story was written by Marco Polo's prison mate Rustichello. They believed Rustichello wrote the story based on Marco's tales that he picked up from travelers he met during his lifetime as a merchant. They said that some of Marco Polo's accounts could not be verified or seemed to be fabricated. Marco Polo never mentioned about the Great Wall of China, but most of all if he were such an important figure, then why was his name not mentioned in any Chinese Imperial Records?].

CHAPTER 4

THE FUNAN PERIOD
扶南
(1st CENTURY – CIRCA 540)

It must be emphasized, in the absence of any writing in a local language, that the identification of the language of Funan is not possible, but the indirect evidence of Tun-Sun, plus the evidence of the many Khmer inscriptions of the early 7ᵗʰ century, in what had obviously been Funan territory, strongly suggest that the population was Khmer, even if the port cities may have been full of other groups, in particular Austronasians. In the field of archaeology too, "Excavation work at Oc Eo shows no true discontinuity between Funan and pre-Angkorian levels, in ceramic and statuary traditions, or in stratigraphic sequences, which tends to favour the hypothesis of Mon-Khmer linguistic dominance in the area under Funan control (including probably the Thai-Malay Peninsula).

Funan Reviewed: Deconstructing the Ancients
Michael Vickery[5,p125]

THE MEANING OF FUNAN AND THE LOCATION OF ITS CAPITAL

According to Paul Pelliot,[24,p288] the Chinese name 扶南 for Funan was based on the dictionary of M. J. Bonet, which means "defended south." However, in the 3rd century Tso Sseu wrote it as 夫南 (pronounce Foonaan), but in the 7th century Yi-tsing wrote it as 跋南 (pronounce as Pa-naan). Based on these variations, Pelliot theorized that the Chinese transliterated the name of the country.

The name Funan recorded in 289 AD in the Chinese imperial dynastic history designated the empire in the Southeast Asia, centered near the basin of the Great Lake (Tonlé Sap) and the delta of the Mekong River. The Funan people were the original inhabitants of this region. In his book, *Histoire Ancienne des États Hindouisés d'Etrême-Orient,*[32] George Coedès mentioned that the Chinese pronunciation of two characters 扶南 (pronounce Funan, but Coedès wrote them as *b'ui-nam*), came from the pronunciation of the old Khmer word *bnam*, which is now *phnom* — thus suggesting that the Môn-Khmer language was already in use, ahead of the Sanskrit language. The word *Ba Phnom* means Father Mountain or Male Mountain in Khmer. A tenth century inscriptions considered Ba Phnom to be the Holy Mountain. The name Funan may have been derived from the word Ba Phnom. Based on the Chinese writing, there was another school of thought that *Nan or Nam* (南) could possibly mean "South" as in *Yueh Nam* (越南), in which the Chinese called Vietnam to indicate the Yueh people in the south (meaning south of China). Étienne Aymonier attempted in this regard by breaking down the word Funan to "Fu Nan" and suggested its meaning to be "Protected South." However, "Protected South" would be written differently as 護南. In his article *Sri Lanka-Cambodia Relations,*[2] Dr. Hema Goonatilake stated that the capital city of Funan was called *Phnom Ksach Sâ* (White Sand Mountain) that is presently located in Prey Veng in Cambodia.

The Chinese records and the archaeological finding at O Keo (but misspelled as Oc Eo by western scholars) indicated that Funan was already a maritime power before the heavy contacts and interactions with the Brahmans, around the early third century AD. The report by the Chinese envoy Kang Tai (康泰) was unambiguous about Funan being a maritime trader country.[10] He described that Funan already knew how to build large ships as long as fifty meters each, *with the capacity to carry seven hundred people and one thousand tons of supplies — the ship was so large that it required four sails to propel it.*[33,pp21-22] Fan Shih Man who was king of Funan from 205 to 225 AD vanquished and dominated the other kingdoms in the region with his large ships. Funan as a maritime power is stated by Vickery as follows:[5]

> *It is now a commonplace of Southeast Asian history that the great navigators of the time were neither Indian nor Chinese, but Southeast Asian, in particular the peoples speaking Austronasian languages. Their spread from the interior of Taiwan, through the Philippines and Indonesia, into the Polynesian islands of the pacific, and as far as Madagascar, as well as the Chamic languages of the mainland, prove that they possessed great boat-building and navigation skills in prehistoric times. In fact the Chinese texts of the Funan period are unanimous in saying that when traveling beyond the coast of what is now northern and central Vietnam, they had to take Southeast Asian ships...*
>
> *Subsequently a maritime history specialist confirmed that the very early large K'un-lun junks were Southeast Asian, and that they were 'enormous ships sewed together like those described later [emphasis added] in the Indian Ocean'; and that the 'existence of [Chinese] junks for the high seas is thus not probable until the 9th century, nor certain until the 12th century.'*

Because Funan had disappeared and had not left concrete remnants of great civilizations like China and India, the Western thinking tends to be prejudicial toward Southeast Asia. They could not fathom that Southeast Asians were capable of surpassing the Chinese and Indians in the arts and techniques of ship building.

After 540 AD, the word Funan disappeared from the imperial Chinese history and was replaced by the word *Po-nan* which seemed again to be possibly a Chinese transliteration of the Khmer word *Phnom* or *Ba Phnom.* According to George Coedès, *Vyadhapura* (city of hunters) was the ancient capital of Funan located at the foot of *Ba Phnom* (present-day Phnom Ksach Sâ), which was south of the confluence of the Mekong and Tonlé Sap Rivers (*Tonlé Chaktomouk*). It was on the eastern side of Mekong. Michael Vickery differed with George Coedès on the meaning and location of Vyadhapura. The capital of Funan was written in Chinese as Temu (特牧) that Coedès transcribed to be the old Khmer word for *dmak* or *dalmak (or Tomu),* which is the equivalent for the word *tromeak (ត្រមាក់)* in modern Khmer, meaning mahout or elephant driver. Thus, Coedès assigned a Sanskrit name *Vyadha* which means hunter. However, Vickery argued that the transcription should have been *d'ek-miuk,* where the first syllable had a Môn-Khmer origin that signified water (Teuk, ទឹក). As to the meaning of the second syllable Vickery could not come up with a satisfying answer. At this time in history, Funan would not have any knowledge of Sanskrit — much less naming its capital in Sanskrit — until it came into contact with the Indian Brahmans around the early third century. The name of the capital of Funan should not have been Sanskritized because it confused the readers and left the impression that Funan was fully Indianized. The name should have been left in its original Môn-Khmer form. As to the location of Vyadhapura, Vickery is not committed to either Ba Phnom (present-day Prey Veng province) or Angkor Borei (present-day Takeo province), but he seems to agree with Pelliot and Aymonier by favoring Angkor Borei (present-day Takeo province). This latter would have been located approximately fifty miles southwest of Ba Phnom, on the western side of the Tonlé Sap River. In his final conclusion, Vickery prefers to leave it to archaeology to pinpoint the exact location of Vyadhapura.[5; 34]

Because I am not an archaeologist, I would resolve the location from my background as an engineer and systems management point of view. According to historical records, when Chenla attacked Funan before its final collapse the Funan king fled to Nafuna — believed to be in the region of present-day Kampot. If Angkor Borei were the capital of Funan, then its distance to Nafuna would not be strategically far enough for the Funan king to feel safe. It would make more sense if Ba Phnom were the capital of Funan because its distance to Nafuna would not only have been farther away but the Funan king would have been separated by both the Mekong and Tonlé Sap Rivers from any pursuits by Chenla. Geographically, Chenla which was on the northeastern region with its capital near Vat Phu would have attacked Funan from the eastern side (where Ba Phnom was located) instead of from the western side (where Angkor Borei was located). Therefore, if Ba Phnom were considered to be the capital of Funan it would make more sense that the Funan king would flee across the Mekong River to Nafuna to put as much distance from Chenla and at the same time make it much more difficult for the Chenla army to reach him. Based on my analysis, I would favor Ba Phnom as the capital of Funan.

There is also the K.127 Inscription,[35] discovered in 1931 in Sambor by George Coedès, that tends to favor Ba Phnom as the location for Vyadhapura. The date Saka 605, which corresponded to 683 AD, indicated that the stele was created under the reign of Jayavarman I (657-693) whose capital was located in Vyadhapura according to George Coedès. However, Lawrence Palmer Briggs said that the original capital of Jayavarman I was in Isanapura (or Sambhupura; present-day Sambor in Kratié) but he moved it to Banteay Prey Nokor, east of the present-day city of Kampong Cham. The discovery of the K.127 Inscription may have solved two problems: 1) it tends to favor Ba Phnom as the location of Vyadhapura; and 2) it tends to support Briggs' claim that the capital of Jayavarman I was originally located in Sambor and then it moved farther south. Based on the discovery of the K.127 inscription in Sambor and on my analysis I described above, I believe that the capital of Jayavarman I was originally in Sambor as Briggs has indicated but it then moved to Vyadhapura (Ba Phnom in Prey Veng) instead of in Banteay Prey Nokor. The relocation of Isanapura to Banteay Prey Nokor is further elaborated in Chapter 5 under the reign of Jayavarman I. For lack of further archaeological evidences, I would side with Coedès and favor Ba Phnom as the capital of Funan. The map illustrating the Funan Empire is shown in Figure 11.[6; 16]

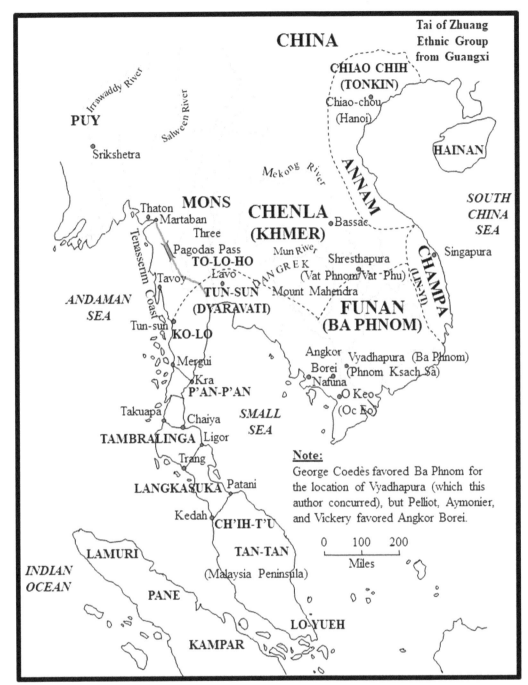

Figure 11. The Funan Empire and its Vassal State Chenla
(Angkor Borei is shown as a reference point only because the original ancient name is not known)
[Map adapted from References 6 & 16]

THE LUNAR DYNASTY

According to the legend, Kaundinya (name transcribed by Coedès), whom the Chinese called Hun Tien and the Khmer called Preah Thong, came from India and married the local princess Liu Yeh (Soma). They founded Funan in the first century from many settlements that existed along the Mekong River and created the Lunar Dynasty. Vickery doubted there was such a person named Kaundinya of Brahman origin because there is no evidence to show that "the initial conqueror came from India."

By 225, under the reign of Fan Shih Man, Funan conquered most of the neighboring states, including Chenla. Funan expanded its relationship with India under the reign of Fan Chan near the middle of the third century. The Chinese sources said that the first official contact between Funan and India did not occur until Fan Chan, the nephew of Fan Shih Man who usurped the throne from his cousin Fan Chin Sheng, sent his relative on a mission to India. It is said that the Indian prince was surprised to see an envoy of a king travelling so far away from his homeland. European scholars always believed that Southeast Asia was a backward society and that it was India that brought its civilization to this part of the world. There is no question that Southeast Asia owes a great debt of gratitude for India's significant role in the region, but Southeast Asia was far from being a backward society. Paul Cravath was correct when he said that "the early historians — for the most part, individuals in the colonial service of the Netherlands, Great Britain or France — tended to manifest what has been called a 'Euro-centric' bias from which we have only recently begun to free ourselves."[33,p2]

Subsequently, more exchanges between Funan and India occurred after the first contact initiated by Fan Chan. The infighting between the royal families provided opportunities for outsiders to take advantage of the turmoil in Funan. An Indian, believed to be from Kushan, in the name of Chandana came to Funan and seized power. He installed himself king of Funan in 357 AD. Another Indian, from the region of P'an-P'an (present-day Chumphon in Thailand) succeeded Chandana. He reigned under the name of Kaundinya. Because Coedès already assigned the name of Kaundinya to Hun Tien, he felt compelled to assign a roman number "II" to distinguish the new Kaundinya of the fifth century from the Hun Tien/Kaundinya of the first century. The new Kaundinya was known under the name of *Chiao Chen-ju* (僑陳如) in the Chinese chronicle. The indianization of Funan was completed under his reign. Kaundinya Jayavarman succeeded Kaundinya "II" in 478 AD and reigned until 514 AD. He was known under the Chinese name of *Chiao Chen-ju Che-li-pa-mo* (僑陳如闍耶跋摩). Rudravarman, the son of a concubine of Kaundinya Jayavarman, usurped the throne by killing his half-brother who was the legitimate heir. He reigned from 514 to 540 AD. He was called *Liutuobamo* (留陁跋摩) by the Chinese. The Funan Empire extended all the way to the Gulf of Tonkin on the East, to the Indian Ocean on the West, and down to the Malay Peninsula on the South. The genealogy of the Funan kings is shown in Figure 12.

The Hun Tien-Liu Yeh Bloodline

1   Hun Tien (混塡) **or Kaundinya – (Around 1st Century AD)**
    ហ៊ុន ទៀន / កៅណ្ឌិន្យ / ព្រះថោង

Transliterated Name: Kauṇḍinya (per Coedès)
Other Names: Preah Thong (per Khmer legend)
Born: Around 1st Century in Indraprashta, south of Delhi in India (according to legend)
Relationship: Founder of Funan and of the Lunar Dynasty; a man from the southern country called
    Jiao or Mofu (Chinese source); son of King Adityavamsa of Intapah (According to legend)
Capital: Temu (特牧); either Angkor Borei or Ba Phnom (Vyadhapura)
Genealogy: Figures 12 and 24

Historically, Hun Tien was considered the founder of Funan and of the Lunar dynasty. He was the first king of Funan. This belief was based on the work of the eminent French scholar George Coedès and French sinologist Paul Pelliot. It must be noted that a pre-Funan country existed prior to the arrival of Hun Tien where Soma was its princess. The knowledge about Hun Tien and his descendants, up to the reign of Fan Shih Man came mainly from the work conducted by Paul Pelliot. He collected the information from the Chinese archives and published his work called *Fou-Nan* in the *Bulletin de l'École Française d'Extrême-Orient* in 1903.[24]

The name of Hun Tien was recorded in the History of the Liang Dynasty called Liang Shu (梁書) in 636 AD. The Chinese chronicle, written by Yao Cha (姚察) and Yao Silian (姚思廉), mentioned that China sent two envoys named Kang Tai (康泰) and Zhu Ying (朱應) to Funan in the third century. It told the story of a foreigner named Hun Tien who came to Funan in the first century on a ship from the southern country called Jiao (徼) or Mofu. Vickery suggested that Jiao was a dialect used in Southeast Asia and transcribed to mean "foreigners and lands in tropical Asia."[5,p11] Most scholars identified the current Malay Peninsula as Mofu. Because the Chinese envoys were in Funan in the third century, they must have obtained the story of Hun Tien from their Funan contemporaries and wrote in the chronicle as the story was told to them. According to the Chinese source, Hun Tien married Liu Yeh (柳葉) near the end of the first century. The traditional meaning of Liu Yeh reported in most literature is willow leaf, but some scholars argue that this translation is incorrect because there are no willow trees in Cambodia. Because of the similarity of the Chinese characters between willow (柳) and coconut (椰), some scholars interpreted Liu Yeh to mean coconut leaf.

A note must be injected here concerning the union and origin of Hun Tien and Liu Yeh. According to one of the legends (there are many variants), Liu Yeh was sometimes replaced with Soma or Neang Neak. Rightly so, Vickery made a distinction between Liu Yeh, Soma, and Neang Neak. Liu Yeh is a historical name mentioned in the Chinese Imperial Records; Soma was mentioned as early as the 7th century in the Champa inscription where it discussed about Bhavapura of Chenla and also on the epigraphy at Angkor centuries later; and Neang Neak, mentioned as the daughter of the Naga (dragon/serpent) king, was created probably after the Angkor period. The celebrated Chinese writer, Ma Duanlin (馬端臨), who was famous for his publication of the Chinese encyclopedia in 1317, wrote that the king of P'an-P'an in the fifth century "reclines on a golden couch shaped like a dragon."[1,p52] Two observations can be made concerning this account: 1) P'an-P'an, located north of the Malay Peninsula between the Small Sea and Andaman Sea (near present-day Chumphon in Thailand), was the country of origin of Kaundinya "II" — it is also possible that it is the country of origin of Hun Tien because he came from the same region; and 2) the legend of Neang Neak as the daughter of the Naga king could possibly be based on the P'an-P'an's king.

The union between Hun Tien and Liu Yeh produced a son, but the Chinese chronicle did not mention his name. Hun Tien ruled over Funan, a kingdom consisting of many settlements along the Mekong River between the current Chau Doc district in Vietnam and the city of Phnom Penh in Cambodia. He gave seven of the settlements to his son to rule as his fiefdom. After Hun Tien died, his son succeeded him. There were no records on how long the father and son ruled over Funan.

Michael Vickery, an expert on Cambodia and Southeast Asia history, disputed the historical name of Hun Tien written in Chinese to its translated Sanskrit name Kaundinya. George Coedès deconstructed the Chinese words 混塡 (Hun Tien) to *Chiao Chen Ju,* thus rendering it to *Kaundinya* in Sanskrit. Michael Vickery eloquently argued that George Coedès' interpretation of the Chinese words 混塡 (Hun Tien or its variation such as Hun Chen, Yuen Zien, and Yuen Dien) to mean Kaundinya could not be correct because of his inconsistency in transcribing the next known descendants of Kaundinya.[2; 34] Coedès did not attempt to transcribe the remaining Kaundinya's descendants with the "Hun" name to a Sanskrit name. For example, he transcribed the Chinese name 混盤況 to Hun P'an Huang (or Yuen Buan Xiwang). Nowhere in the Chinese chronicles was the name of Kaundinya mentioned prior to the reign of Kaundinya "II" (beginning fifth century to 434 AD). Kaundinya "II" name was recorded in the Chinese chronicle as *Qiaochenru* (僑陳如). If Hun Tien (混塡) were Kaundinya as George Coedès had suggested, then why did the Chinese not write it as 僑陳如 as they had done for Kaundinya "II" ? Additionally, why would all the descendants after Hun Tien not named Kaundinya but chose to retain the same family and/or clan name "Hun" instead? Is it conceivable that Coedès transcribed the original/local name Hun Tien into a Sanskrit name, Kaundinya, with his preconceived inclination and belief to attribute India's greater and more direct roles for the foundation of Funan?

Michael Vickery suggested that "Hun" may be a Môn-Khmer or prehistoric Austronesian clan name that ruled over Funan prior to the great influx of Indian Brahmans. He further stated that the translated work of Paul Pelliot from the Chinese chronicles about Funan indicated that India did not come into direct contact with Funan until the early to mid-third century. It seemed that Funan was already an established kingdom by the time the Brahmans arrived.

If Kaundinya were not the Sanskrit name corresponding to the Chinese name Hun Tien, then Kaundinya "II" who reigned at the beginning of the fifth century that the Chinese called Qiaochenru (or Kiao-tchen-you) should have just been called Kaundinya.

Hun Tien/Kaundinya was the founder of the Lunar Dynasty. According to legend, Kaundinya was supposedly a son of the Intapah King named Adityavarman who ruled over a region north of India. It said that Kaundinya was banished from Indraprashta, the legendary city founded by Pandavas, the son of Pandu in the Indian epic Mahabharata. Even though it is a legend, however some of the places mentioned in Mahabharata were based on actual locations or regions of India. Indraprashta was considered to be the first Delhi city and its location was about twenty miles south of the nowadays city of Delhi in India. There is no basis or supporting document to attest that Hun Tien was a Brahman or even coming from India. George Coedès' logic or interpretation of rendering the name Hun Tien to a Sanskrit name Kaundinya was not persuasive and somewhat bias due to his belief that Cambodia [in this context it would be Funan] was founded by Brahmans. There is little to dispute that Hun Tien came from a country neighboring Funan. He and Liu Yeh may have even spoken the same language, either Austronasian or Môn-Khmer.

2   Hun P'an Huang (混盤況) – (Mid-2nd Century-202) ហ៊ុនប៉ាន់ហួង

Relationship: Unknown, but seemed to be related to Hun Tien
Capital: Temu (特牧); either Angkor Borei or Ba Phnom (Vyadhapura)
Genealogy: Figures 12 and 24

His name, Hun P'an Huang, reported in the Chinese chronicle seems to suggest he came from the same bloodline or clan of Hun Tien. Nothing much is known about him and his reign except that he lived longer than ninety years. According to the Chinese chronicle there was at least another ruler prior to Hun P'an Huang. It mentioned only that he was the son of Hun Tien but it did not give his name. It stated only that he succeeded his father and ruled over seven settlements but it did not specify the date of his reign.

3   Hun P'an P'an (混盤盤) – (202-205) ហ៊ុនប៉ាន់ប៉ាន់

Relationship: Second son of Hun Pan-Huang
Capital: Temu (特牧); either Angkor Borei or Ba Phnom (Vyadhapura)
Genealogy: Figures 12 and 24

The Chinese chronicle reported that Hun P'an P'an was the son of Hun P'an Huang. He must have been an old man when he succeeded his father because Hun P'an Huang was over ninety years old when he died. It may be one of the reasons that Hun P'an P'an reigned for only three years before he passed away. He was the last Funan ruler from the Hun clan. Nothing much is known about him.

The New Bloodlines

4   Fan Shih Man (范師蔓) – (205-225)[7, p23] ហ្វាន់ស៊ីម៉ាន់

Relationship: A General under Hun P'an-P'an
Capital: Temu (特牧); either Angkor Borei or Ba Phnom (Vyadhapura)
Genealogy: Figures 12 and 24

The Hun clan ended after the death of Hun P'an P'an. Because Hun P'an P'an reigned for only three years, he may not have enough time to set the foundation for his bloodlines to succeed him. How Fan Shih Man gained power was not known. The Chinese chronicle said that he was a general under Hun P'an-P'an. Being in charge of the army granted him a lot of power that allowed him to control the political events of the country. The Chinese chronicle did not mention how he became king. It mentioned only that he was a great general. It was under his reign that Funan became an empire. He extended the territory of Funan all the way to Chiao-chi (Tonkin) on the East, as far to the Andaman Sea on the West, and down to the Malay Peninsula on the South. The account from the Chinese chronicle mentioned the conquest of Fan Shih Man over his enemies as follows:[1]

> *Fan Shih-Man attacked and conquered the neighboring kingdoms. All recognized themselves his vassals. He took the title of Great King of Funan. Then he had great ships built and crossing the immense sea he attacked more than ten kingdoms, including... Tun-hsun. He extended his territory 5,000 or 6,000 li (1,250 or 1,500 miles). Then he wished to subdue the country of Chin-lin (believed to be Sovannaphoumea in the Thaton-Martaban region). But he fell ill.*

As a military man, he was a great organizer. It was believed that five kingdoms were vassals of Funan. As his health deteriorated, Fan Shih Man named his son Fan Chin Sheng to succeed him. According to sinologists and experts on Khmer civilization, like Georges Maspero and Louis Finot, they believed that the word *Fan* was probably a transliteration by the Chinese of the Sanskrit word *Varman*. Their interpretations that Fan could be Varman may be due to their acceptance of Paul Pelliot and George Coedès' thesis that the founder of Funan was an Indian. Fan could not possibly be Varman because this latter is always used as a suffix while Fan is always used as a prefix. Therefore, Fan cannot be Varman as suggested by the above prominent scholars. However, Vickery suggested that Fan could be *Poñ*.

5　Fan Chin Sheng (范金生) – (225~230)[2] ហ្វាន់ចិនស្តេង

Relationship: Son of Fan Shih Man
Capital: Temu (特牧); either Angkor Borei or Ba Phnom (Vyadhapura)
Genealogy: Figures 12 and 24

He succeeded his father, Fan Shih Man, after he became ill. Fan Chin Sheng's reign was short as his cousin Fan Chan sent his soldiers to kill him.

6　Fan Chan (范旃) – (230~243)[2] ហ្វាន់ច័ន្ធ

Relationship: Cousin of Fan Chin Sheng
Capital: Temu (特牧); either Angkor Borei or Ba Phnom (Vyadhapura)
Genealogy: Figures 12 and 24

He was the son of Fan Shih Man's sister. As a cousin of Fan Chin Sheng he was put in charge of two thousand soldiers to protect the king. With his mother's support, Fan Chan used his power to usurp the throne by ordering his soldiers to kill his cousin Chin Sheng who just became king. The first exchange of embassies between Funan and India happened during Fan Chan's reign. As the new king, Fan Chan sent a relative named Su Wu on a diplomatic mission to India. It took Su Wu more than a year to reach the mouth of the Ganges River where there resided a prince belonging to the Murunda dynasty that ruled over the Kushan region. In return the Indian prince sent an envoy named Cheng Sung with a present of four horses to accompany Su Wu back to Funan. The trip took over two years and when they arrived in Funan the kingdom had a new king.[24,p271,pp277-278,p292]

7   Fan Chang (范長) – (243~244)[2] ហ្វាន់ឆាង

Relationship: Son of Fan Shih Man
Capital: Temu (特牧); either Angkor Borei or Ba Phnom (Vyadhapura)
Genealogy: Figures 12 and 24

Fan Chang was just a little child when his father Fan Shih Man died in 225 and his brother, Fan Chin Sheng, was assassinated five years later. Because of the danger to his life, he was smuggled out of the palace to safety. He was raised among the people. He patiently waited for the right time to reclaim the throne that was rightfully his. At the age of twenty he recruited men who were still loyal to his brother to support his cause. With his recruits Fan Chang had his revenge by killing the usurper Fan Chan. However, his reign was short-lived as he, himself, was assassinated in turn.

8   Fan Xun (范尋) – (244-287)[2] ហ្វាន់ស៊ុន

Relationship: A General under Fan Chan
Capital: Temu (特牧); either Angkor Borei or Ba Phnom (Vyadhapura)
Genealogy: Figures 12 and 24

The cycle of assassinations never ceased. Fan Xun was a general under Fan Chan. Seizing on Fan Chang's youth and his lack of support within the government because he was raised outside the palace, Fan Xun mounted a coup and killed the new young king. This took place probably around 244 AD.

It was during his reign that two envoys of the Chinese Emperor Sun Chuan (孫權), Kang-Tai   (康泰) and Zhu Ying (朱應), arrived at the court of Funan between 245 and 250 AD.[3]   Their mission was to gather information about Funan. After returning to China, these two envoys published a book and a report of their mission. Zhu Ying, especially, wrote a report on Funan. Unfortunately, his original work was lost but it was quoted throughout the Chinese dynastic history. Zhu Ying mentioned of books written in a language similar to Indian scriptures that were preserved in the Funan libraries. The first known record about Funan and China exchanging embassies were mentioned in the Chinese dynastic history. It said that Funan sent an envoy offering some musicians and products to the Chinese Emperor in 243 AD. The following is a sample of the account found in the Chinese dynastic history about how prisoners were treated during the reign of Fan Xun.[6,p268]

> *He built belvederes and pavilions, where he was accustomed to take a walk. Morning and noon, he gave three or four audiences. Foreigners and subjects offered him presents of bananas, sugar cane, turtles, and birds.*
>
> *The law of the country is not to have prisons. The accused fasts and practices abstinences for three days. Then an axe is heated red and he is forced to carry it seven steps; or a gold ring or some eggs are thrown in boiling water and he must take them out. If he is guilty, the hand is burnt; if he is innocent, it is not. Also crocodiles are kept in the moats of the walls; and, outside of the gates, there are wild beasts in an enclosure. The accused are thrown to the wild beasts or to the crocodiles. If the wild beasts or the crocodiles do not eat them, they are considered innocent; at the end of three days, they are released.*

Some of these traditions or a variation of them are still being practiced today in Cambodia, such as the presumed guilty person sticking his finger in a boiling lead to prove his innocence. This practice was done for the purpose to have the accused confessed of his/her crimes before putting him/her through this cruel process. Either way, guilty or innocent the accused person would be burnt if he/she went through the process.

The influence of Indian culture and custom, mainly from the region situated between the Godaveri and Khrisna rivers, seemed to start its acceleration during this period. Evidence of Indian sculptures scattered throughout Funan and Java dated from this time period. Fan Xun had a long reign. It was believed that he died around 287.[2]

9 Sindhu Chandana (357-?) ហ៊ុន ទ្បៀន / សិន្ធុចន្ទ / ឈូចន្ទកាន់

Transliterated name: Sindhu Cănd
Other Names: Tianzhu Zhanta (天竺旃檀) or Chu Chan-Tan
Relationship: Usurper
Capital: Temu (特牧); either Angkor Borei or Ba Phnom (Vyadhapura)
Genealogy: Figures 12 and 24

There was a gap between the end of the reign of Fan Xun and the beginning of the reign of Chandana. There are no records of rulers during that period. The reign of Chu Chan-Tan was mentioned in the Chinese records during the time of the Chin dynasty. The records said that in 357 AD, a person named Chu Chan-Tan who called himself king was a usurper. Chu Chan-Tan was of Indian origin. His name was transcribed in Sanskrit as Chandana. Furthermore, according to Coedès, Chandana came from the royal title *Chandan* found among the Murunda dynasty that ruled over the kingdom of Kalinga in India from the first to the end of the fourth century AD. The dominance of the Muranda dynasty over Kalinga that ended around the end of the fourth century coincided around the arrival of Chandana in Funan. The open-up of Funan with India during the reign of Fan Chan near the middle of the third century through exchanges of embassies brought about the arrival of Chandana and other Indians of influence to Funan. It was believed that Chandana was either expelled or sent from Kushan to establish another kingdom under the umbrella of the Murunda dynasty.[6] However, Michael Vickery seemed to reject the thesis that Chu Chan-Tan was of Indian origin coming from Kushan. The Chinese emperor rejected the gift of tame elephants that Chu Chan-Tan offered because he had some doubts about Chu Chan-Tan's legitimacy as king of Funan. There were no records of how long Chu Chan-Tan's reign lasted.

10 Kaundinya "II" (Beginning 5th Century-434) កៅណ្ឌិន្យ "២"

Transliterated name: Kauṇḍinya
Other Name: K'iao-tch'en-jou or Chiao Chen-ju (僑陳如)
Relationship: Undetermined
Capital: Temu (特牧); either Angkor Borei or Ba Phnom (Vyadhapura)
Genealogy: Figures 12 and 24

Kaundinya "II" that the Chinese called Qiaochenru was an Indian Brahman from the region of P'an-P'an (盤盤), a small Hindu kingdom located in the southern tip of the Malay Peninsula around the third to the seventh century. He was believed to be a wise Brahman. His fame and wisdom had reached Funan. He probably drew his inspiration from Chandana, a foreigner of Indian origin like him, who succeeded in becoming king of Funan. He acceded to the throne around the beginning of the 5th century and assumed the name Kaundinya. Some scholars and experts on Cambodia history suggested that he chose the name Kaundinya to bring his legitimacy to the throne as a way to link his lineage to the first Kaundinya, the founder of the Funan kingdom. This theory has no merit because it was based on the assumption that Hun Tien was Kaundinya. There is no evidence to suggest that is the case except for the thesis put out by

George Coedès which does not seem totally convincing. A Chinese by the name of Liang-Shu related the story of how this Indian Brahman came to Funan:[36,p24]

> *One of his [Chandana's] successors, Chiao Chen-ju (Kaundinya) was originally a Brahman of India. A supernatural voice said to him: "You must go and reign in Funan." Kaundinya rejoiced in his heart. He reached P'an-p'an at the South. The people of Funan heard of him. The whole Kingdom rose with joy. They came to him and chose him King. He changed all the rules according to the customs of India.*

This period may be truly considered to be the beginning of the indianization of Funan. Historically speaking, this Brahman would be considered as the first Kaundinya. The historical name Hun Tien from the Chinese records should have been left in its original form and not translated to Kaundinya as Coedès had done. Kaundinya was just an interpretation by Coedès to render the local name Hun Tien (probably of Môn-Khmer origin) to sound as if it originated from India. Historical record suggested that many Indian Brahmans accompanied Kaundinya "II" for his trip to Funan. The country was completely indianized during the reign of Kaundinya "II", which suggested that the king had a lot of help to achieve this feat. Kaundinya "II" could not have done the job by himself without the help and knowledge of other Indian Brahmans. There were five main areas of changes that were systematically implemented in the Funan society during the reign of Kaundinya "II". They were the following:[6,p25] 1) The worship of Indian gods and linga was implemented in temples; 2) The Indian abugida system of writing based on the Pallava scripts was introduced at this time — the earlier system of writing in Funan during the second to third centuries mentioned in Chinese historical records by Zhu Ying was probably based on different Indian scripts used by the Kushan; 3) The utilization of the Saka era was introduced during this time, thus providing more accurate information on the history of Funan; 4) The utilization of the title *Varman* — Sanskrit word meaning Armor or Protector — was clearly introduced during this time; and 5) The legend of Soma as a Naga princess and the Lunar dynasty founded by Hun Tien were enhanced and reintroduced to the Funan society.

It was during his reign that a great influx of Indian immigrants came to Funan. Kaundinya "II" had a long and successful reign. He was estimated to pass away in 434 AD.

11   Srei Indravarman (434-477?) ស្រីឥន្ទ្រវរ្ម័ន

Transliterated name: Srī Īndravarmăn
Other Name: Chilituopamo (持梨陀跋摩)
Relationship: Undetermined
Capital: Temu (特牧); either Angkor Borei or Ba Phnom (Vyadhapura)
Genealogy: Figures 12 and 24

The Chinese historical records mentioned that a new king by the name of *Chilituobamo* or *Che-li-to-pa-mo* (持梨陀跋摩) succeeded Kaundinya "II". He sent embassies to China on two different occasions; the first one was sent in 434-435 AD which was followed by the second one in 438 AD. It is believed that Srei Indravarman was the new king. Because it was the first time that the word *Varman* was found in the Chinese records, scholars believed that this title started under the reign of Srei Indravarman. Not much else was known about him.

It must be noted that it was around this period that the Champa king named Fan Yang Mai II (or Pham Duong Mai II) turned against its protector Funan. After failing to reclaim the lost territory Chiao Chou (Tonkin) from China in 433 AD, Fan Yang Mai II decided to take his revenge on Funan in the mid-fifth century by attacking and then annexing Panduranga (present-day Pham Rang in Vietnam), one of the districts of Funan. Champa's animosity toward the Khmer may have started from that period of history.[6,p27]

The Last Funan Kings and Funan's Contribution for the Spread of Buddhism in China, Japan, Korea, and Vietnam

12 Kaundinya Jayavarman (478-514) កៅណ្ឌិន្យ ជ័យវរ្ម័ន

Transliterated name: Kauṇḍinya Jăyavarmăn
Other Name: Chiao Chen-ju Tue-ye-pa-mo (僑陳如闍耶跋摩)
Relationship: Undetermined
Capital: Temu (特牧); either Angkor Borei or Ba Phnom (Vyadhapura)
Genealogy: Figures 12 and 24

The date of Kaundinya Jayavarman's accession to the throne may have occurred earlier than 478 according to two different inscriptions. An inscription in Sanskrit found in the Mekong delta at *Prasat Pram Loveng* (K5, known in Vietnamese as Tháp Mười), dated by George Coedès to belong in the middle of the fifth century, indicated that Kaundinya Jayavarman had a son named Gunavarman. He seemed to be the crown prince because he was called "the moon of the family of Kaundinya."[6,p28] The inscription is now displayed at the Museum of Vietnamese History in Ho Chi Minh City (HCMC).[37; 38] Another inscription at *Neak Ta Dambang Dek* in southern Cambodia mentioned that Queen Kulaprabhavati was the principal wife of King Kaundinya Jayavarman. Coedès dated the inscriptions to be in the second half of the fifth century.[6,p28]

Chinese records indicated that Kaundinya Jayavarman had another son by the name of Fan Tang.[6,p28] A dissention between the father and son occurred prior to 478 which led Fan Tang to flee the country after a revolt. He took refuge in Lin-yi (Champa). Somehow he was able to seize the throne and became king of Champa. Nagasena (那伽仙), the celebrated Indian monk who was in the service of Kaundinya Jayavarman reported the news to the king after he arrived in Funan from his China mission. Nagasena picked up the news of Fan Tang seizing the throne of Champa after the ship he was travelling from Canton was wrecked at the shore of Lin-yi. Nagasena and his people arrived in Funan with great difficulty as they were robbed on their journey back home. On hearing the news that Fan Tang became king of Lin-yi, Kaundinya Jayavarman sent Nagasena back to China to lobby Emperor Wu Di (武帝, posthumous name — or personal name Xiao Yan 蕭衍) of the Liang dynasty to remove Fan Tang from the throne. Instead of listening to the Funan king, the Chinese emperor acknowledged Fan Tang's reign and granted him the title of "General Pacifier of the South, Commander-in-Chief of the Military affairs of the seashore, King of Lin-yi" in 491 AD.[6,p29] Fan Tang never received the official recognition because he was driven out of power before the Chinese envoy arrived in Lin-yi.

The above account in the Chinese dynastic history seemed to suggest that Kaundinya Jayavarman and his son Fan Tang had a major disagreement. Why would Kaundinya Jayavarman want his son removed from the throne of Lin-yi and be punished? What caused the revolt in Funan that led to Fan Tang fleeing the country? Could it be possible that Fan Tang organized the revolt and tried to seize the throne from his father? His plan may have fallen apart and the only option left for him was to flee the country. Fan Tang would not have been successful in seizing Lin-yi's throne if he did not have military support. Fan Tang may have used his soldiers who were participating in the failed coup against Kaundinya Jayavarman to overthrow the king of Champa.

Kaundinya Jayavarman died in 514 AD after his envoys arrived at the Chinese Imperial Court in the same year. By the end of his reign Funan was completely indianized.

Even though Brahmanism was fully established in Funan during the reign of Kaundinya Jayavarman, Buddhism also flourished in the country as well by the presence of a strong Buddhist center. Funan contributed to the development of Buddhism in China, Japan, Korea, and Vietnam. During this time, two monks from Funan named Mandrasena (or Mandra Thera) and Sanghavarman (or Sanghapala Thera) went to China to help in the translation of Buddhist documents that were later incorporated in the Chinese tripitaka. Mandrasena arrived in China in 503 AD. He started immediately to work on the translation of the *Mahāprajñāpāramitā Mañjuśrīparivarta Sūtra* (later classified under the name of *Saptaśatikā Prajñāpāramitā Sūtra*) into Chinese that is known as *Wenshushili Suoshuo Mohe Bore Boluomi Jing* (文殊師利所說摩訶般若波羅蜜經).[39] This text in Chinese was the catalyst that set up the Mahayana Buddhist foundation of the Tiantai school (天台宗) and Chan school (禪宗) in China; which in turn spread for the establishments of the Tendai-shū school in Japan and the Cheontoe school in Korea. The Mahayana Buddhism from China also spread to Vietnam. The Japanese Tendai-shū school combined the Chinese Taintai and Chan teachings. The word Zen (禪) came from the Chinese word Chan (or Dzyen), which in turn was originated from the Sanskrit word *dhyāna*. The meaning of this word can be interpreted as contemplation, meditation, thought, or reflection. Sanghavarman left Funan and arrived in China in 506 AD at the age of 46. Because of his deep knowledge in Buddhism, the Chinese emperor Wu Di assigned him to work with Mandrasena on the translation of Buddhist scripture *Vimutti Magga* (the Way of the Freedom). According to the Buddhist teaching, this scripture predated the *Visutthi Magga* (the Way of Purity).[40] Sanghavarman spoke many languages and was able to master the Chinese language better than Mandrasena. He was well respected in China and was known as the Tripitaka master. As his fame spread he also encountered detractors along the way. A Chinese monk by the name of Hui-Yi from the temple of Qi-Huan challenged Sanghavarman for a debate by accusing him of false Buddhism teaching. The debate took place at Nanjing. Sanghavarman was able to demonstrate his thorough understanding of the Buddhist canon and brought into evidence his interpretations of the Buddha's teaching. After an exhaustive debate Hui-Yi acknowledged Sanghavarman's masterful performance and accepted to follow his teaching.[39] Sanghavarman spent sixteen years in China, from 506 to 522 AD, translating holy books for the Chinese emperor. After he retired in 522 AD, he spent the next two years living in China before he passed away in 524 AD.[6,p29]

Until recently the majority of the work of Mandrasena and Sanghavarman in Chinese has never been translated into western languages. The translation from the Taishō Tripitaka[41] volume 8, number 232 is now available in English.[42] Funan, under the reign of Kaundinya Jayavarman, had thus contributed for the spread of Buddhism in China, Japan, Korea, and Vietnam. All Buddhism schools in the above countries had their origins from the great works of the Funan monks Mandrasena and Sanghavarman.

13   Rudravarman (514-540) ព្រះរាជបុត្រ

Transliterated name: Rudravarmăn
Other Names: Sarvabhauma – Lieou-to-pa-mo (留陁跋摩)
Relationship: Son of a concubine of Kaundinya Jayavarman
Capital: Temu (特牧); either Angkor Borei or Ba Phnom (Vyadhapura)
Genealogy: Figures 12 and 24

Rudravarman succeeded his father in 514 AD after he had reigned for 36 years. This seemed to suggest that Rudravarman was already advanced in age when he took over the throne.

Rudravarman was not the legitimate heir. Chinese records under the Liang dynasty in 502 AD mentioned that Rudravarman was the son of a concubine of Kaundinya Jayavarman. It said that Rudravarman killed his younger half-brother, the son of the legitimate Queen. The Chinese records did not give either the name of the queen or of her son. As mentioned earlier, the inscriptions at *Neak Ta Dambang Dek* identified Queen Kulaprabhavati as the principal wife of Kaundinya Jayavarman. The inscriptions at *Prasat Pram Loveng* mentioned Gunavarman as the son of Kaundinya Jayavarman and also seemed to suggest that he was the crown prince. George Coedès dated the inscriptions to be in 450 AD.

Furthermore, he speculated that Gunavarman could be the son of Queen Kulaprabhavati. If it were so, Gunavarman would have been at least 64 year old when Kaundinya Jayavarman died in 514 AD. If Rudravarman were assumed to be of the same generation as Gunavarman, then he would have been around 90 years old when he died in 540 AD.

Buddhism became even more prominent under the reign of Rudravarman. Six embassies during the years 517, 519, 520, 530, 535, and 539 AD were sent to the Imperial Court of China. The last Funan envoy mentioned to the Chinese Imperial Court in 539 AD that Funan possessed a twelve-foot long hair of the Buddha. The Chinese Emperor ordered his envoy to go to Funan to collect the Buddha's hair.

Rudravarman passed away in 540 AD and he was the last Funan king. Because he was a usurper, Rudravarman's death may have caused some chaos in Funan that ultimately brought about its downfall. Coedès indicated in the genealogy chart that Viravarman and Prithivindravarman were the sons of Rudravarman.[1; 32] Lawrence Palmer Briggs[6,p63] and Adhir Chakravarti[43,p19] differed with Coedès on this issue. Because neither Viravarman nor Prithivindravarman succeeded Rudravarman, Chakravarti theorized that they were their sons-in-law. While Chakravarti had Viravarman and Prithivindravarman as the husbands of Rudravarman's daughters, Briggs showed only Viravarman as the husband. Funan existed for a while as a vassal state of Chenla.

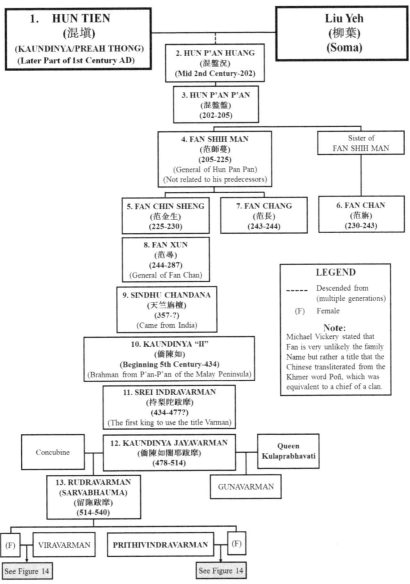

Figure 12. Genealogy of Funan Kings of the Lunar Dynasty (Later Part of 1st Century – 540)

CHAPTER 5

THE CHENLA PERIOD
真臘
(CIRCA 540 − 802)

The Khmer conquerors were not frontier barbarians unappreciative of the civilization of Funan, for they had long lived as a contiguous vassal subjects. Khmers had infiltrated southward into the lower Mekong Valley at all social levels extending from the peasant cultivators to the elite of the royal court. The Khmers had also been recipients of cultural influence both Buddhist and Hindu, coming from the Môns via the Menam Valley and the Korat plateau.

Southeast Asia – Its Historical Development
John F. Cady [16,p85]

THE MEANING OF CHENLA AND ITS RISE TO POWER

The existence of Chenla came through the meticulous record keeping by the Chinese. The name Chenla or Zhenla (真臘) was first encountered in the Annals of the Sui (Sui Shu, 隋書) that was compiled by Wei Zheng (魏徵) in 636 . Wei Zheng was Duke Wenzhen of Zheng (鄭文貞公) who served Emperor Taizong as Chancellor for 13 years during the Tang Dynasty. The chronicle mentioned that Chenla sent its embassy to China in 616. As the history of Cambodia later indicated, this was the year under the reign of Isanavarman or Yishenaxiandai (伊奢那先代) per Chinese record. There is a passage in the Chinese annals during the Sui Dynasty from 589 to 618 that mentioned Chenla, Chitrasena, and his son Isanavarman. It said that Chenla was located southwest of Lin-yi (Chinese name for Champa). It must be remembered that by this time, Chitrasena and Isanavarman had mostly conquered Funan. Therefore, Chenla as a whole would be considered west or southwest of Champa. The Chinese source did not give any supporting documents as to why the country was named Chenla. Georges Coedès believed the word Chenla was a Chinese translation of the word Kambuja. It was during this time that the Chinese stopped mentioning the name Funan and replaced it with the name *Po-nan,* which may be another Chinese way of saying Funan.

I have always wondered where the name Chenla came from. Coedès' explanation for the meaning of Chenla did not satisfy me. I would like to offer my own explanation and understanding on this subject. I believe that the name Chenla, which means pure wax in Chinese, was a literal translation of the Khmer words *Kramuon Soth (ក្រមួនសុទ្ធ).* An old Khmer province named *Kramuon Sâ (ក្រមួនស),* which means white wax, was located in the present-day Rach Gia in Vietnam. The province was named in this manner because it has an abundant of Melaleuca trees (Myrtaceae) which attracted a lot of bees during the blooming season to produce beeswax. The renowned port of O Keo (Oc Eo) during the Funan period was situated in the province of *Kramuon Sâ.* In its pure form, the natural color of the wax is golden yellowish, not white. Could it be possible that Chenla was the intended and correct translation by the Chinese of the Khmer words *Kramuon Soth* and over the centuries the name changed to *Kramuon Sâ?* It could also be possible that *Kramuon Sâ* was the original name of the province and the Chinese could not distinguish between the words *Sâ* (white) and *Soth* (pure) because both words sound very similar. From the Chinese reference point of view, a pure wax would make more sense than a white wax. If *Kramuon Sâ* were indeed the original name of the province, the Khmer people may have found a way to process the pure wax from its golden yellowish color to a white color that would be sought after and prized by traders who did commerce at the port of O Keo. The province of *Kramuon Sâ* was located well within the boundary of Water Chenla. White wax may be one of the items that were traded and exported out of Chenla through O Keo, one of the busiest ports in Southeast Asia in the ancient time. Therefore, the Chinese may have literally translate *Kramuon Soth* as Chenla to designate the country commonly known by Khmer as Kampuchea Krom.

From the legendary reign of Kambu Svāyambhuva to Śreshṭhavarmǎn (495-530), Chenla was still considered to be under the vassalage of Funan. The rise of Chenla's power coincided with the undefined line of successions and broken line of new rulers in Funan. The ascendancy of each new Funan ruler to the throne never went smoothly. Chenla took advantage of the instability in Funan and started to prepare for the conquest over its former master state. Chenla's power started to rise under Śrutavarmǎn (Protector of Vedas — Knowledge) who reigned from 435 to 495. He was credited for starting the chain of events that would ultimately free Chenla from Funan's domination. He was succeeded by his son, Sreshthavarman (Best Protector) from 495 to 530. Sreshthavarman established the Chenla capital, Śreshṭhapura, at the foot of the Vat Phnom Mountain (nowadays Vat Phu Temple/Mountain in Laos). Bhavavarman I (Protector of Shiva) succeeded Sreshthavarman from 550 to 590. He conquered Funan and claimed the throne as king of both Chenla and Funan. However, Chenla's domination of Funan was not fully complete at this time. His cousin Chitrasena[1,p68,note20] succeeded him and reigned under the name of Mahendravarmǎn (Protector of the Great Indra) from 590 to 611. The complete annexation of Funan took place under the reign of his son Īśānavarmǎn (611-640), but some of Funan's vassal states still sent tributes to China until 671 as a sign of independence from Chenla. The existence of Funan as a state seemed to disappear in 627. Chenla absorbed Funan and merged the two countries into a single empire. Jayavarman I succeeded his father, Isanavarman, and reigned from 640 to 681. Chinese records indicated that Chenla was divided into Upper Chenla or Land Chenla (Luzhenla — 陸真臘, also called Wendan — 文單, or Polou — 婆鏤) and Lower Chenla or Water Chenla (Shuizhenla — 水真臘) in 707 under the reign of Jayadevi (681-713 or 693-713). After the breakup, Land Chenla seemed to lose its significance and Water Chenla tended to dominate the politics of the region. The breakup of Chenla brought chaos and civil wars into the region. Mahipativarman was the last Water Chenla king.

The conquest of Chenla over Funan was chronicled in the New History of the Tang Dynasty (Xia Tang Shu — 新唐書). It was compiled by Ouyang Xiu (歐陽修) and Song Qi (宋祁) in 1060. According to the Khmer legend, Chenla was founded by a Brahman named Kambu Svayambhuva and a Chenla princess named Mera, an Apsara of great beauty and elegance during the period when Chenla was still a vassal state of

Funan. The Solar Dynasty was thus created. Dvaravati, which was a sister state of Chenla made its presence known at the Chinese Imperial court in 608 under the name of To-lo-ho.[6,p48]

During the Funan period, all inscriptions were written in Sanskrit. As the Chenla period took over, the inscriptions transitioned to a mixture of Sanskrit and Khmer scripts.[6,p43] The Chenla period lasted for about two and a half centuries, from 540 to 802.

The cult of linga, which was the worship of phallus in the form representation of Brahma, Vishnu, and Shiva, may have started earlier than the *Mukhalinga (Mukha = face; linga = phallus)* sandstone found at Vat Po Metrei in Takeo that dated to 7th-8th centuries.[44,p12] A representation of the Vat Po Metrei Mukhalinga is shown in Figure 13.

Figure 13. Representation of Mukhalinga Sandstone at Vat Po Metrei in Takeo, 0.83 m (Graphic based on Ref. 44)

According to Helen Ibbitson Jessup, this Mukhalinga was a symbol of "fertility and the life force" in the trimurti (three forms of deities) representations as follows: 1) the square section of the base was Brahma the creator looking in the four cardinal directions; 2) the octagonal mid-section was Vishnu the maintainer or preserver of the life force looking in all eight directions; and 3) the top round section was Shiva the destroyer or transformer of the life force. The Mukhalinga was substituted with a simple linga without a face during the Angkor period.

THE SOLAR DYNASTY

The Kambu-Mera Bloodline

[Kambu Svayambhuva កម្ពុស្វាយភ្កូម៌]

Transliterated Name: Kambu Svāyambhuva/Svāyabhūmi (self-creating)
Relationship: Founder of Chenla and the Solar Dynasty
Capital: Sreshthapura (at the foot of Vat Phu)
Genealogy: Figures 14 and 24

During this period, Chenla was still a vassal state of Funan. The original legend mentioned that the Hindu god Hara (Shiva), offered Mera as a gift to the great Brahman hermit Kambu Svayambhuva to be his wife. Mera was depicted as a beautiful *Apsara* with great elegance. Kambu was believed to come from Aryadesa, the kingdom located north of India.

In the Hindu and Buddhist mythology, Apsara is a female spirit with an exceptional beauty. She loves to entertain through music and dance. She is associated with the water and cloud spirit. Apsara is akin to the Greek mythology of a nymph that portrays her as a divine and beautiful spirit who loves to sing and dance and animates the nature.

George Coedès speculated that the name Mera may have been forged to make it appear as being of Khmer origin.[1,p66] Coedès added, "A line of kings was born from this couple Kambu-Mera."[1,p66] Coedès' statement implied that Mera was of Hindu origin like Kambu Svayambhuva. There is no evidence to support that Mera was of Hindu origin. To absolve Mera — the symbol for the origin of the Khmer civilization — of her Khmer identity is to insinuate that Khmer people may not have played any major roles for the advancement of the Khmer society.

Vickery recognizes George Coedès and Paul Pelliot as great synthesizers. He admires Coedès' talent as a writer who could link different historical events and tied them all together. To be able to achieve that feat required a great synthesizer mind and imagination. However, Vickery finds a major fault in Coedès because of his unwillingness to "pull back and state that some details were irreconcilable" as well as in both Coedès and Pelliot on the "wilder speculations about Indian influence." Vickery's criticism on these two great minds is as follows:[5,p104]

> *Although Pelliot was a better scientist that (sic) Coedès, they both viewed Funan, and Southeast Asia, through Indological spectacles; and suppositions based on what Indians were supposed to have done, or what Indian culture did, in Southeast Asia, came to them naturally whenever a strange detail required explanation.*

In contrast to Coedès and Pelliot, Dutch historians are more generous concerning the interactions between the Southeast Asian and Indian cultures. The Dutch archaeologist F.D.K. Bosch stated the following:[33,p5]

> *...the awakened Indian spirit fecundated the living matter of [Southeast Asian] society, thus procreating a new life that was predestined to develop into an independent organism in which foreign and native elements were to merge into an indissoluble entity.*

Kambu Svayambhuva was credited for founding the Chenla Solar dynasty probably around the first century AD. He was considered the first legendary king who ruled Chenla under the vassalage of Funan.

[Srutavarman (435-495) ស្រុតវរ្ម័ន]

Transliterated Name: Śrutavarmăn (whose armor was the Vedas)
Relationship: Descendant of Kambu Svayambhuva
Capital: Sreshthapura (at the foot of Vat Phu in present-day Laos)
Genealogy: Figure 14 and 24

There were no records indicating who succeeded the legendary King Kambu immediately. Srutavarman was the first known Chenla king on records who descended from the line of the Solar Dynasty according to the Ta Prohm inscriptions.[45] He took the initiative to liberate Chenla from the domination of Funan. Under his reign, Chenla attained some degree of independence from Funan. He reigned for sixty years as king of Chenla and passed away in 495. The genealogy is shown in Figure 14.

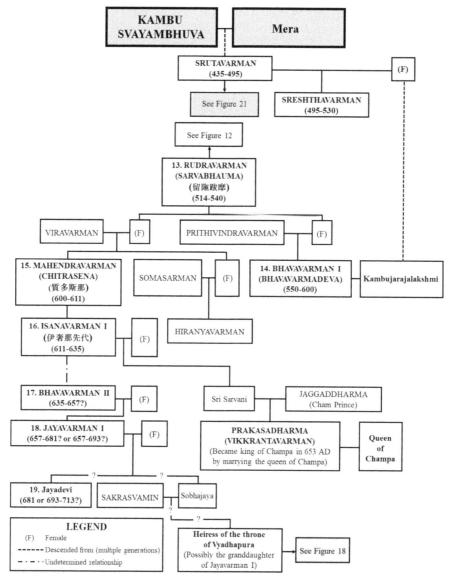

**Figure 14. Genealogy of Chenla Kings and Queens of the Solar Dynasty
before the Division to Upper and Lower Chenla in 707 AD**

[Sreshthavarman (495-530) ស្រេស្ឋហៃរ៉ែន]

Transliterated Name: Śreshṭhavarmăn
Relationship: Son of Srutavarman
Capital: Sreshthapura (at the foot of Vat Phu in present-day Laos)
Genealogy: Figures 14 and 24

He succeeded his father, Srutavarman, as king of Chenla. The Ta Prohm stone inscriptions mentioned that Shreshthavarman came from the line of great kings. The following are the original two inscriptions in Sanskrit and their English translations:[45,pp271,p284]

*āsid akhaṇḍamanudaṇḍadharāvanīndravandyo varaç çrutavatāṃ çrutavarmma-sūnuḥ
çrīçreṣṭhavarmanṛpatiç çucibhir yaçobhiç çreṣṭo vadātavasudhādharavaṃça-yoniḥ.*
*çrīkamvuvaṃçāmvarabhāskaro yo jāto jayādityapurodayādrau prāvodhayat prā-
ṇihṛdamvujāni tejonidhiç çreṣṭhapurādhirājaḥ.*

There was a king that the masters of the earth, carriers of the inviolable scepter of Manu, must venerate, excellent among the wise men, son of Srutavarman: Sri Sreshthavarman, the best of its glowing glory, originated from a brilliant family of kings.

Sun of this sky which is the family of Sri-Kambu, born in this mountain of the Levant, which is Jayādityapura, this treasury of splendor, supreme king of Sreshthapura, awoke the hearts of living beings like the lotus.

Coedès located the city of *Sreshthapura* to be at the foot of *Vat Phu* in present-day Laos. He reigned for 35 years and is believed to have died in 530. The genealogy is shown in Figure 14.

[Kambujarajalakshmi (Around 530 to 550-?) កម្ពុជរាជាលក្ស្មី]

Transliterated Name: Kambujarājalakshmī /Kambujarājālaksī
Relationship: Descendant from the line of the mother of Sreshthavarman
Capital: Sreshthapura (at the foot of Vat Phu in present-day Laos)
Genealogy: Figures 14 and 24

The Ta Prohm inscription mentions that Kambujarajalakshmi reigned in Chenla and that she came from the maternal side of the king, which in this case would mean King Sreshthavarman. It did not say whether she succeeded Sreshthavarman immediately or there was another king before her. It can be deduced that Kambujarajalakshmi started her reign between 530 and 550 based on the fact that she was the wife of Bhavavarman who succeeded Rudravarman as king of Funan around 550. The inscription does not indicate when she passed away. The following is the Ta Prohm inscription in Sanskrit and its translation in English:[45,pp272,p284]

Jātā tadīye navagītakīrtticandrollasanmātṛkulāmvurāçaurarāja lakṣmīr iva yā satīnām agresarī kamvujarājalakṣmiḥ.

Born in the maternal family of the king as well as in an Ocean where her glory shone tirelessly like a moon, Kambujarajalakshmi, the first exceptional woman among all the women, reigned.

THE UNIFICATION OF THE LUNAR AND SOLAR DYNASTIES

14   Bhavavarman I (550-600) ភវវរ្ម័ន (ទី១)[1,pp68-69]

Transliterated Name: Bhavavarmăn
Other Name: Bhavavarmadeva[6,p39]
Relationship: Son of Prithivindravarman and Grandson of Rudravarman
Capital: Bhavapura (near Sreshthapura and Vat Phu in present-day Laos)
Genealogy: Figures 14 and 24

The turning point in the history of Funan and Chenla started with the ascendancy of Bhavavarman I. The capital of Chenla, Bhavapura, was located north east of the Great Lake (Tonlé Sap). A seventh century inscription of *Ang Chumnik* mentioned that Bhavavarman I succeeded Rudravarman, the last known king of Funan. In the historical context of the genealogy of Khmer kings, the monarchy transitioned from the Funan Lunar Dynasty to the Solar Dynasty when Bhavavarman I ruled Chenla. Because Rudravarman was the Funan king from the Lunar Dynasty and Bhavavarman I was his grandson, how can he be considered a Chenla king from the Solar Dynasty? How can these two facts be reconciled? There were two clues that shed some light on this issue. The first clue was recorded on an inscription dating from the 10th century that George Coedès transcribed as follows:[1,p67] "The line of descent of Kambu unites the sun race, which it claimed as its own, with the moon race, that of Funan." Another clue came from the 12th century inscription of Ta Prohm that says Kambujarajalakshmi (fortune of the kings of the Kambujas) was a queen who ruled Chenla and that she descended from the maternal side of Sreshthavarman.[6,p39] Furthermore, it said that Bhavavarman I (also called Bhavavarmadeva) was her husband. The inscription in Sanskrit and its interpretation are shown below:[45,pp272-284]

> *bharttā bhuvo bhavapure bhavavarmmadevo vibhrājamānarucirañjitamaṇḍalo yaḥ pūrṇaḥ kalābhir avanīndrakulaprasūteḥ karttāmṛtāṃçur iva tāpaharaḥ (I) prajānām.*

> *The husband of the earth of Bhavapura, Bhavvarmadeva, whose glittering radiance illuminated the universe, poured into the arts [or: full of all kalā], soothing like the moon of the burns of creatures, was the progenitor of a lineage of kings.*

Briggs differed from Coedès concerning the father of Bhavavarman I. According to Briggs, Viravarman was the father of Bhavavarman I.[6,p40] On the other hand, Coedès said that Rudravarman had two sons, Prithivindravarman and Viravarman. In the genealogy chart, Coedès indicated that Bhavavarman I was the son of Prithivindravarman and his cousin Chitrasena was the son of Viravarman.[1] Briggs showed in the genealogy chart that Rudravarman had only a daughter and she was married to Prithivindravarman and his cousin Chitrasena was the son of Viravarman. Their union produced Bhavavarman I.[6,p63] Coedès also mentioned that Sārvabhauma was the grandfather of Bhavavarman I.[1,p66] He deconstructed the word Sarvabhauma to mean universal monarch, a title reserved for the king of Funan when he ruled over the other vassal states. This title may be the precursor to the Chakravatin title that means universal ruler. Coedès deduced that Rudravarman who ruled Funan and all its neighboring states, including Chenla, was the universal monarch mentioned as Sarvabhauma. I chose to use Coedès' genealogy chart of Rudravarman's descendants instead of the one produced by Briggs because it produced more details.

An epigraphic text mentioned that Kambujarajalakshmi was queen of Chenla but it never said directly that her husband Bhavavarman was king of Chenla. Bhavavarman I claimed his accession to the throne through his lineage as the grandson of Rudravarman, the last Funan king of the Lunar dynasty. After the death of Rudravarman, Funan was in turmoil and weak. On the other hand, Chenla became more powerful. Taking advantage of the weakness of Funan and coupled with the flood in 549 that destroyed parts of Funan,[46,p48] Bhavavarman I with his cousin Chitrasena, as head of the Chenla army, attacked Funan at the beginning of his reign.[1,p68,note20] The event seemed to suggest that Bhavavarman I and his cousin Chitrasena, who came from the Funan Lunar bloodline, may have some issues for the line of succession with the other princes of Funan. The inscriptions described the exploits of Bhavavarman I and Chitrasena by saying that they "pushed their conquest at least up to Kratié on the Mekong, to Buriram between the Mun River and the Dangrek Mountains, and to Mongkolborei west of the Great Lake."[1,p68] Chenla had gained the upper hand after ten years of battle with Funan. Because of Chenla's success, China decided to intervene. The fact that Chenla was her neighbor created a concern for China. Because of the strong resistance she encountered from Funan with no ending in sight, Chenla used the occasion to acquiesce to the Chinese demand for ending the war.[46,p48] By this time, Chenla had already gained much territory and seemed to be in charge of Funan. The role now seemed to be reversed. Chenla was now in charge, but the control over Funan was not totally complete. By conquering Funan, Bhavavarman I united the Lunar bloodline of Hun Tien-Soma with the Solar bloodline of Kambu-Mera. The Funan king who succeeded Rudravarman fled from Vyadhapura and took refuge in Nafuna, believed to be in the region of present-day Kampot.

After conquering Funan, Bhavavarman I reigned as king of both Funan and Chenla. He became king probably in 550. Because of his lineage, Bhavavarman I seemed to go out of his way to promote his claim as the descendant of Hun Tien-Soma Lunar dynasty. The inscription of *Hanchey* stated the following:[6,p41]

> *Born in the race of Soma (Hanchey - 15 A, stanza 3)...moon of the skies of the Lunar race (Hanchey - 15 B, stanza 3)...born in the pure, unbroken line of Kings* — *(Hanchey - 535, 3, No.12, stanza 19).*

Bhavavarman I was connected to the Solar Dynasty only through his wife, Queen Kambujarajalakshmi of Chenla. He and his successors made every attempt to preserve the legacy of Rudravarman, the last king of Funan, by inscribing the king's achievements with elaborate praises. Bhavavarman I was also influenced by the advice he received from the two ministers, Dharmadeva and Simhadeva, which he retained from Rudravarman. Bhavavarman I had a son who reigned for a short time in his place while he took the time off to retire in a monastery. The inscriptions showed that Shaivism was practiced during his reign. The commemoration of lingas was mentioned for the first time in Cambodian epigraphies. By conquering Funan, Bhavavarman I intended to replace Buddhism that was flourishing in Funan with Shaivism. Oddly enough, unlike his grandfather Rudravarman who was a Buddhist, Bhavavarman I was a Shaivist. The Buddhist Chinese pilgrim I-ching mentioned about the dire religious condition in Funan at the end of the seventh century. He wrote that in Funan "the law of the Buddha prospered and spread, but today a wicked king has completely destroyed it and there are no more monks."[1,pp67-68] Because the above event occurred during the reign of Bhavavarman I, the "wicked king" that I-ching mentioned must have been Bhavavarman I.

Bhavavarman I had a long reign. There are no inscriptions that clearly indicated the end of his reign but he was still alive in 598. The king rewarded his cousin Chitrasena for his loyal service with a vast territory. The king probably passed away around 600 because that was the year Chitrasena was coronated under the name of Mahendravaman.[1,p69] After the death of Bhavavarman I, his son was not chosen as his successor. The genealogy is shown in Figure 14.

15   Mahendravarman or Chitrasena (600-611) មហេន្ទ្រវរ្ម័ន ឬ ចិត្រាសេនា

Transliterated Name: Mahendravarmăn
Other Names: – or Tche-to-sseu-na (質多斯那)
Relationship: Son of Viravarman and cousin of Bhavarvarman I[1,p68]
Capital: Aninditapura/Baladityapura (present-day Sambor Prey Kuk)
Genealogy: Figures 14 and 24

Chitrasena was in charge of the Chenla army. He succeeded Bhavavarman I and reigned under the name of Mahendravarman. According to George Coedès, Chitrasena's accession to the throne occurred around 600.[1,p69] Bhavavarman I's son who reigned for a short time when his father retired to the monastery was not chosen as the new king. Chitrasena who already ruled over a vast domain that Bhavavarman I gave it to him probably felt he was entitled to succeed the king for his loyal service. Allowing Bhavavarman I's son to reign would divide the Chenla kingdom and thus weakening its new found power. Mahendravarman carried on Bhavavarman I's policy of total conquest over Funan and the rest of the neighboring states that his cousin had not had a chance to finish. He entered into a peace agreement with Champa.

The success of Mahendravarman's campaign over Funan and its neighboring states did not please China. The Chinese Emperor was troubled and wanted to stop Mahendravarman's progress. When Chenla was a vassal state of Funan, it did not pose a threat to China because Funan was far away and Chenla, that shared the northern border with China, was just a weak country. The moment Chenla took over Funan, the Chinese Emperor felt that Chenla was becoming too powerful.

The date of Mahendravarman's death was not known, but it is believed that he did not have a very long reign because he must have been quite advanced in age himself when he succeeded Bhavavarman I. The date of his death was arbitrarily set at 611 based on the Chinese texts which said that the king succeeding Chitrasena sent an embassy to China in 616-617. The genealogy is shown in Figure 14.

16   Isanavarman I (611-635)[1,p72; 6,p46] កសានវរ្ម័ន (ទី១)

Transliterated Name: Īśānavarmăn
Other Name: Yishenaxiandai (伊奢那先代)
Relationship: Son of Mahendravarman
Capital: Isanapura (Aninditapura/ Baladityapura — present-day Sambor Prey Kuk)
Genealogy: Figures 14 and 24

Isanavarman means "Protector of Lord Shiva." He inherited a vast territory when he succeeded his father, Mahendravarman, around 611. There were numerous inscriptions, as well as records from the Chinese Imperial dynasty covering the period of Isanavarman I's reign. The Chinese chronicle said that "Isanavarman inherited a kingdom extending from somewhere near the forks of the Mekong, up to beyond the basin of the lower Mun; and along the Tonlé Sap, south of the Great Lake; and that he extended his boundaries on the west, up to the upper valley of the Menam, then occupied by the Kingdom of Dvaravati; and to the north, up into what is now central Laos; and that he conquered and annexed Funan."[7,p51] The conquest of Chenla over Funan had reduced some former vassal kings to the status of lordships. The independent Baladityapura (or Aninditapura), whose descendants claimed to come from the line of Hun Tien/Kaundinya-Soma but separate from the line of Isanavarman, had been downgraded from the status of a kingdom to a state. Isanavarman had the status of the king of Baladityapura reduced to a simple Lord.

Writing on the reign of Isanavarman, the Chinese chronicle mentioned that it was customary for the new king who ascended the throne to mutilate and confine his brothers as described below by Ma Duanlin:[1,pp74-75]

Every three days the King goes solemnly to the audience-hall and sits on a bed made of five pieces of sandalwood and ornamental with seven kinds of precious stones. Above his bed is a pavilion of magnificent cloth, whose columns are of inlaid wood. The walls are ivory, mixed with flowers of gold. The ensemble of this bed and the pavilion form a sort of little palace, at the background of which is suspended, as at Ch'ih-t'u, a disk with rays of gold in the form of flames. A golden incense burner, which two men handle, is placed in front. The King wears a girdle of ki-pei cotton, dawn-red, which falls to his knees. He covers his head with a bonnet laden with gold and stones, with pendants of pearls. On his feet are sandals of leather and sometimes of ivory; in his ears, pendants of gold. His robe is always made of a very fine white cloth called pe-tre. When he appears bare-headed, no precious stones are noticed in his hair. The dress of the great officials is almost like that of the King. The great officers or ministers number five... There are many inferior officers.

Those who appear before the King touch the earth three times with the forehead, at the foot of the steps to the throne. If the King calls them and orders them to show their degrees, then they kneel, holding their hands on their shoulders. They go then to sit in a circle around the King, to deliberate on the affairs of the Kingdom. When the séance is finished, they kneel again, prostrate themselves and return. More than a thousand guards dressed with cuirasses and armed with lances are ranged at the foot of the steps of the throne, in the halls of the palace, at the doors and peristyle.

The sons of the queen, legitimate wife of the King, are alone eligible to the throne. The day when the new King is proclaimed, all the brothers are mutilated. A finger is cut off on one, a nose on another. Then their subsistence is provided for, each in a separate place, without ever calling any of them to any charge.

Contrary to the Chinese chronicle, there were no mentions found in any Khmer inscriptions about the kings mutilating or confining their siblings when they acceded to the throne prior to the reign of Isanavarman I. The Chinese chronicle seemed to indicate that Chenla may not be fully consolidated and in total control of its vassal states. It seemed that Isanavarman took the drastic measures described by the Chinese chronicles to prevent any uprising and claimants to the throne. Most of all, Isanavarman I feared that his second cousin — the son of Bhavavarman I — or the princes from the Baladityapura/Aninditapura Lunar dynasty would rebel against him.

Isanavarman I followed the tradition by retaining his predecessors' minister, Simhavira. He was the son of Dharmadeva who came from the famous and hereditary family of Adhyapura. Prior to the conquest of Funan, the capital of Chenla seemed to be centered near Vat Phu. The New History of the Tang Dynasty said that shortly after 627, Isanavarman I conquered Funan and annexed all its territories, but even then Funan still sent embassies to China as a form of protest. Funan, now reduced to a vassal state, had its capital Tomu (特牧) — that George Coedès identified as probably Ba Phnom — taken over by Chenla. The Chinese chronicle said that the former king of Funan who was now reduced to the rank of Lord was forced to relocate to the south at a new city called Na-fu-na.[24,p274] Coedès transcribed the name of this city to Naravaranagara, possibly Angkor Borei. Pelliot transcribed it as Navanagara, which fitted well with the Chinese transcription of Na-fu-na. Briggs, believes that Na-fu-na is closer to present-day Kampot,[6,p31] which is further south of Angkor Borei.

The conquest of Funan in the Vat Chakret inscription[47] seemed to describe that a monument or statue of Shiva-Vishnu was erected by a vassal state of Isanavarman I. It commemorated the victory of the lord of the three cities — Cakrankapura, Amoghapura, and Bhimapura (probably present-day Phimai in Thailand) — over the fourth city named Tamrapura from a rebel prince. The lord of the three cities was probably Isanavarman I, and the rebel prince from the fourth city was probably a Funan prince who descended from Rudravarman. Scholars have located Tamrapura to be Tomu, which Coedès assigned the name in Sanskrit as Vyadhapura or in Khmer as Ba Phnom. The Chinese chronicle mentioned a total of thirty important cities in Chenla and that each city had a governor in charge. Aninditipura was identified to be located north of the eastern end of the Great Lake (present–day Tonlé Sap). Étienne Aymonier identified Cakrankapura to be Chi Kreng located to the west of Aninditapura, in the province of present-day Siem Reap.[48; 49,p464] Georges Groslier located Amoghapura to be in the province of present-day Battambang.[50,pp359-372]

After the complete annexation of Funan, Isanavarman I decided to relocate the Chenla capital from Bhavapura to Aninditapura (Baladityapura) — a location that is close to the present city of Kampong Thom, near the village of Sambor Prey Kuk. This area contains many temples of the pre-Angkorian period. The capital was renamed to Isanapura, probably after the death of Isanavarman I. The territorial conquest by Isanavarman I extended all the way to the west to the Môn Kingdom of Dvaravati (Tun-Sun), bordering present-day Myanmar (Burma). Brahmanism flourished under Isanavarman I and the worship of Harihara, the merging of Shiva and Vishnu into one body, appeared in Cambodia for the first time. However, Henri Parmentier believed that the worship of Harihara had already happened during the Funan period. It must be noted that this combination of Shiva and Vishnu into one body occurred earlier in Pallava (south India) in the period preceding 450.[51,p 3,p114] Isanavarman I continued the policy of his father by maintaining a good and friendly relation with Champa, which led to his daughter marrying a Cham prince.

Based on the Cham inscriptions, Isanavarman I had a daughter named Sri Sarvani.[6,pp51-52] The Cham inscriptions shed some light on Sri Sarvani. It said that she married a Cham prince by the name of

Jaggaddharma and seemed to indicate they lived in Bhavapura, probably during the reign of Bhavavarman I. They had a son named Prakasadharma. Afterward, the family returned to Champa. In 653, Prince Prakasadharma married the queen of Champa. He then changed his name to Vikrantavarman and became king of Champa. He was the author of the Cham inscriptions.

Many of the inscriptions praised Isanavarman I as a great warrior, builder, and glorious monarch who ruled over three kings [they were probably the kings of Cakrankapura, Amoghapura, and Bhimapura which Isanavarman I had conquered]. Chenla reached its apogee during the reign of Isanavarman. Funan coins had been found in various places, but coins fabricated by Chenla had not been discovered until recently. Arlo Griffiths showed pictures of a gold coin (Figure 15) in his essay *Early Indic Inscriptions of Southeast Asia*[52,p57] that was discovered at Angkor Borei in Takeo. The inscription on the coin used old Khmer scripts dating from the pre-Angkor period. Because of his expertise in old Khmer, I enlisted the help of Sotheara Vong to decipher and interpret the inscriptions on the coin. The obverse side shows a picture of a deity sitting on a lotus flower with inscription saying "Srīśānavarman," which according to Sotheara Vong was the name of Isanavarman. The picture on the reverse side shows a galloping horse with the inscription saying "Kaṃśānap(ura)." The last scripts were effaced, but they could be interpreted as "ura" (ī:), which according to Claude Jacques would indicate Isanapura. Based on these inscriptions, the coin was minted during the period of Isanavarman. The coin is currently stored at the National Bank of Cambodia in Phnom Penh.

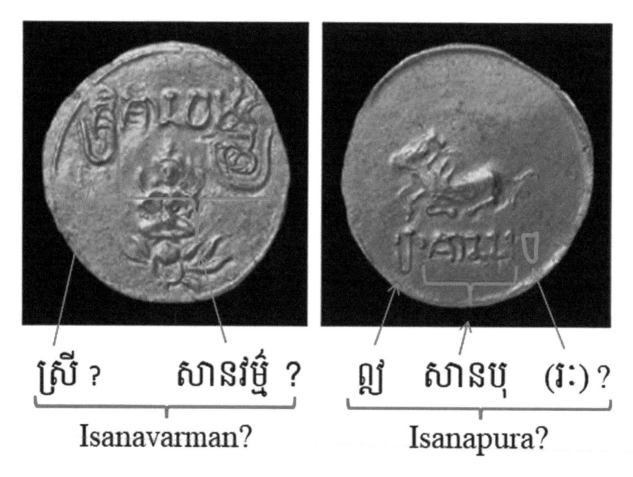

**Figure 15. Gold Coin Discovered at Angkor Borei Showing the Inscriptions
Saying "Srīśānavarman" (Isanavarman) on the Obverse Side and
"Kaṃśānap(ura)" (Isanapura) on the Reverse Side
(Photo Extracted from Arlo Griffiths' Essay in Ref. 52)**

The complete conquest over Funan occurred under Isanavarman I's reign, but he was still not in total control of Funan's former vassal states. Ma Duanlin mentioned that four states, Séng-kao, Wu-ling, Chia-cha, and Chiu-mi still sent embassies to China at least until 638.[53] According to Briggs,[6,p50] these four states were located north of the Dangrek Mountains in nowadays Central and Upper Laos. These states were not conquered and annexed into Chenla until 650-656. The end of Isanavarman I's reign was not certain but it was believed he passed away probably around 635. The genealogy is shown in Figure 14.

17 Bhavavarman II (635-at most 657) ភវវរ្ម័ន (ទី២)

Transliterated Name: Bhavavarmăn
Posthumous Name: Paramarudraloka[6,p114]
Relationship: Undetermined, but probably not related to his predecessors
Capital: Vyadhapura (According to Coedès); Angkor Borei (According to Briggs).
Genealogy: Figures 14 and 24

The relationship between Bhavavarman II and his predecessors is not known. The discovery of Bhavavarman II by George Coedès was purely by chance. Coedès found an inscription of unknown origin in a storehouse in Phnom Penh. The inscription, dated 639, mentioned a king named Bhavavarman. Prior to this finding, the genealogy of Khmer kings showed that Jayavarman I was the next king following Isanavarman I.

The origin of Bhavavarman II is unknown and there are no evidences to support him as the son, brother, or even approved successor of Isanavarman I according to Briggs. However, Coedès mentioned two inscriptions that said a son succeeded Bhavavarman. Because Bhavavarman I was succeeded by his cousin Chitrasena, this newfound Bhavavarman was called Bhavavarman II. Accordingly, Coedès concluded that the king who succeeded Bhavavarrman II, which was Jayavarman I, was his son.[1,p72] Briggs on the other hand said that Jayavarman I was connected to Isanavarman I but had no relationship to Bhavavarman II.[6,p63] How he came into power was a mystery. He was not served by the family of Adhyapura that traditionally served the new king. Was there a power struggle that he won over the loyalties of other Khmer elites due to Isanavarman I's daughter marrying a Cham prince? Did the marriage of Sri Sarvani, the daughter of Isanavarman I, to a Cham prince bring out the unrest in the country? Was it the reason why Sri Sarvani, the daughter of Isanavarman I, and her family left Chenla and returned to Champa to avoid any fallout from the power struggle?

There was an inscription of nine Sanskrit lines that Coedès found at Trapeang Meas in Kampong Chhnang giving eulogy to King Bhavavarman and mentioning that he came from the line of the Lunar dynasty. There were also inscriptions of Ponhea Hor in Takeo and Hanchey (on the Mekong above the fork) which Coedès considered to belong to the reign of Bhavavarman II. The French epigraphist Auguste Barth, one of the founders of *l'École Française d'Extrême-Orient* and expert in Hinduism and Sanskrit inscriptions on Cambodia, considered the Ponhea Hor and Hanchey inscriptions to be the oldest in Cambodia. The name of Bhavavarman could be detected on the Ponhea Hor inscriptions. However, some experts considered that the Hanchey inscriptions did not belong to the reign of Bhavavarman II but to that of Bhavavarman I instead. The reason scholars placed the inscription in the period of Bhavavarman I's reign because of its praise of the king's prowess and warlike powers. Bhavavarman II was never known to be such a person but Bhavavarman I was, because he fought over Funan and started to assert the control of Chenla over Funan. The same way as he took over the throne, the end of Bhavavarman II's reign was also a mystery. How his reign ended was not known. He probably passed away around 657 because Jayavarman I was believed to accede to the throne around this year. The genealogy is shown in Figure 14.

18   Jayavarman I (at least 652~693) ជ័យវរ្ម័ន (ទី៩)

Transliterated Name: Jăyavarmăn
Relationship: Son of Bhavavarman II[1,p72],but related to Isanavarman I[6,p63]
Capital: Vyadhapura (according to Coedès); moved from Isanapura to Banteay Prey Nokor
    (according to Briggs)
Genealogy: Figures 14 and 24

According to Vong Sotheara, Jayavarman I was already on the throne in 652. This date is earlier than the previously known date of 657. Vong Sotheara came up with this new date from his reading of the Ka 63 or K.1235 Inscription.[54] The inscription, written in Sanskrit, was discovered in 1997 at Vat Podhivong Loeu at the foot of the Bayang Mountain in the Kirivong district in Takéo. The inscription mentioned that Jayavarman I went to worship god Yajñapatīśvara in 574 Saka regularly (or 652 AD). Yajñapatīśvara was the Khmer name for Harihara, which is the combination of Vishnu as Hari and Shiva as Hara.

George Coedès determined that Jayavarman I was the son of Bhavavarman II after he had studied two inscriptions. Jayavarman I succeeded his father at Vyadhapura. After Jayavarman I acceded to the throne, he called on people who served under Isanavarman I to come back to serve him. Those were the people of the hereditary family of Adhyapura. Lawrence Palmer Briggs on the other hand would state only that Jayavarman I was connected to Isanavarman I and that the origin of Bhavavarman II was unknown. If Jayavarman I were the son of Bhavavarman II as Coedès had concluded, then why Jayavarman I did not continue to use the people who served his father, but switched to the people who served under Isanavarman I instead?

Many inscriptions of the reign of Jayavarman I tended to praise him as a great warrior and king. Most of the inscriptions are in Sanskrit and some of them are in Khmer. His conquest seemed to have reached the Upper Laos, all the way to Nan Chao in Yunnan.[16,p87] The inscription at Vat Phu attributed Jayavarman I for having invented new warfare system, such as the use of cavalry and a new way of checking and disciplining the charges of elephants. After praising him as a great warrior, another inscription mentioned that he was a man of peace. He was devoted to bring peace to the region. After he had pacified the country, he decided to lay aside his weapons. The inscriptions seem to indicate that he may have abandoned warfare too soon because Chenla was in turmoil near the end of his reign. Isanapura was not the capital anymore and he had to move it to Banteay Prey Nokor, east of the present-day city of Kampong Cham. Briggs believed that the capital was originally located at Isanapura because he considered Jayavarman I to be the son of Isanavaman I. Because there are no inscriptions located near the vicinity of Isanapura, but more of them are found from Angkor Borei to Banteay Prey Nokor instead, Briggs concluded that Jayavarman I had moved his capital probably to Banteay Prey Nokor.[1,p56] The relocation of the capital farther south of Isanapura seemed to indicate that he lost control of some vassal states in the north and that his kingdom was shrinking.

Due to the preponderance of inscriptions found on Jayavarman I − a total of nineteen inscriptions were attributed to his reign, more than any other king until the arrival of Yasovarman I − throughout the region, his reign must have been a long one. He did not have any male heir to succeed him. The inscriptions mentioned that Jayavarman I still reigned in 681, but beyond that date there is no certainty of when his reign ended. Two inscriptions that pertained to Jayavarman I were found to be dated in 685 and 693; but those were the dates after 681, the only known date with certainty of his latest reign. An assumption can therefore be made that Jayavarman I probably reigned until 693. Therefore, his reign could possibly last until 693, the date beyond the certainty date of 681. The long reign of Jayavarman I seemed to indicate that he was able to keep together the vast majority of the territory that he inherited. Signs of turmoil grew louder near the end of his reign because his enemies knew that he did not leave a male heir to succeed him. He had only a daughter, which probably gave reasons to the Chenla minor princes or the princes from the Chenla vassal states to take advantage of the situation to rebel against the Chenla central power.

One of the newly formed Solar Dynasty, recorded as Sambhupura and centered at the present-day Sambor (thence where its name came from) in the Kratié province, seemed to gain independence from Chenla. As it was customary during that time, Sambhupura was usually named after its founder — in this case it would be Sambhuvarman. However, there is no such person found in any inscriptions. The inscriptions recorded that the first ruler of Sambhupura was a female named Indrani. She married the son of Nripatindravarman of Aninditapura by the name of Pushkaraksha (Indraloka) He then became king of Sambhupura.[6,p58] The genealogy is shown in Figure 14.

It was during this period that an inscription of the number zero was carved on a stele discovered by George Coedès in 1931. The year Saka 605, corresponding to 683-684 AD, that was etched on the stele was the earliest unambiguous number zero ever discovered in the history of human civilization. A more detailed description of this finding is discussed in Book II under the reign of King Sisowath Monivong.

19   Jayadevi (~693-Post 713) ជ័យទេវី

Transliterated Name: Jăyadevī
Relationship: Daughter of Jayavarman I[1,p85]
Capital: Vyadhapura (according to Western Baray inscription); Baladityapura (according to the Chinese[1,p86]
Genealogy: Figures 14 and 24

The period after the death of Jayavarman I was very tumultuous. There seems to be some disagreements among historians about the relationship between Jayadevi and Jayavarman I. Pierre Dupont and Adhir Chakravarti differed on the translation of the Angkor Inscription that was found at the Western Baray, called K.904 (see Inscriptions at end of the book). While Dupont said that Princess Sobhajaya was the daughter of King Jayavarman I and Queen Jayadevi,[55,p19] Chakravarti said that she was only the daughter of Jayavarman I.[43,p51] Chakravarti added that the relationship of Jayadevi with Jayavarman I was not mentioned in the inscription. Sobhajaya married a Brahman named Sakrasvamin. According to Mahesh Kumar Sharan, Sakrasvamin was a Shaivite born in India in Madhya Desa.[56,p3] The region of Madhya Desa is believed to be located south of the Himalaya, north of Vindhya (present-day Madhya Pradesh), and west of Prayaga (present-day Allahabad). George Coedès, in his book *The Indianized State of Southeast Asia* also said that Sobhajaya was the daughter of Jayavarman I in the Angkor Inscription, but he also stated that Jayadevi was the daughter of Jayavarman I in another inscription.[1,p85; 32] He did not give the inscription number. Lawrence Palmer Briggs, who based his finding on Coedès was mistaken when he said that Jayadevi was the widow of Jayavarman I.[6,p57] It seems that both Dupont and Briggs may be mistaken about Jayadevi being the wife of Jayavarman I. If Coedès were correct, then Jayadevi and Sobhajaya were either sisters or half-sisters. The inscription said that Jayadevi complained about the dire situation in the country when she joined Sobhajaya in donations to the Siva Tripurantaka sanctuary that was built by Sobhajaya. In Indian mythology, Siva Tripurantaka is known as the destroyer of the Tripura state; located in north-east India.

Jayavarman I passed away without leaving any male heir. The inscription said that Jayadevi was queen of Vyadhapura in 713 but it did not specify when she acceded to the throne. The accession of Jayadevi implied that she succeeded Jayavarman I and that she was the older sister of Sobhajaya. The genealogy of the Chenla kings and queens before its breakup to the Upper and Lower Chenla is shown in Figure 14.

In the meantime, princes from the ancient Baladityapura/Aninditapura Lunar dynasty vied for power and tried to challenge Chenla as well as the newly formed Sambhupura Solar dynasty for supremacy. According to the Chinese, the division of Chenla into the Upper (or Land) and Lower (or Water) Chenla happened after 707. The map of the Chenla Empire before its breakup in 707 is shown in Figure 16.

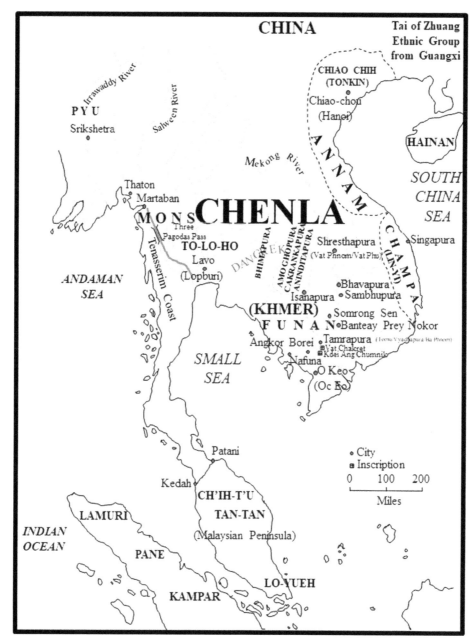

Figure 16. The Chenla Empire before the Breakup with Funan as its Vassal State (540-707)
(Map adapted from References 6 and 16)

THE DIVISION OF CHENLA (707-802)

The reign of Jayadevi was a troubled one. It marked the end of a united Chenla. According to the Tang Dynasty[57] — 唐代 (618-907), Chenla was divided into two states at the end of the Shenlong (神龍) period, which occurred after February 707. The Upper Chenla was also called Land Chenla or Luzhenla (陸真臘) — or Wendan (文單) or Polou (婆鏤). The Lower Chenla was also called Water Chenla or Shuizhenla (水真臘). Concerning Luzhenla, Paul Pelliot believed that Baria was the old region of ancient (kou or ku, 古) land (lou or lu, 陸) Zhenla.[24,p286] Pelliot said that Aymonier was intrigued on certain details that were mentioned in the Chinese texts about the countries P'o-li and Lang-ya-sieou. He was particularly interested about the name P'o-li as well as the name Ko-lo. Pelliot said there was an old text written by an Annamese author that mentioned Ba-loi and Co-luc. According to Pelliot, these names referred to Funan.

In any case, Louis Gabriel G. Aubaret who was the French counselor in Siam in the 1860s, combined the words "kou" and "lou" to form "ko-lo," that Étienne Aymonier interpreted as "Kouk Telok." As mentioned in history, Kok Thlok was the ancient or mythological name of Cambodia. Pelliot stated that the sino-annamese name Ba-loi corresponded to the Chinese name P'o-li. Aubaret found out that in another book the word "loi" was changed to "ria," which in this case would transform the word "Ba-loi" to "Baria." The map of the Upper and Lower Chenla is shown in Figure 17.

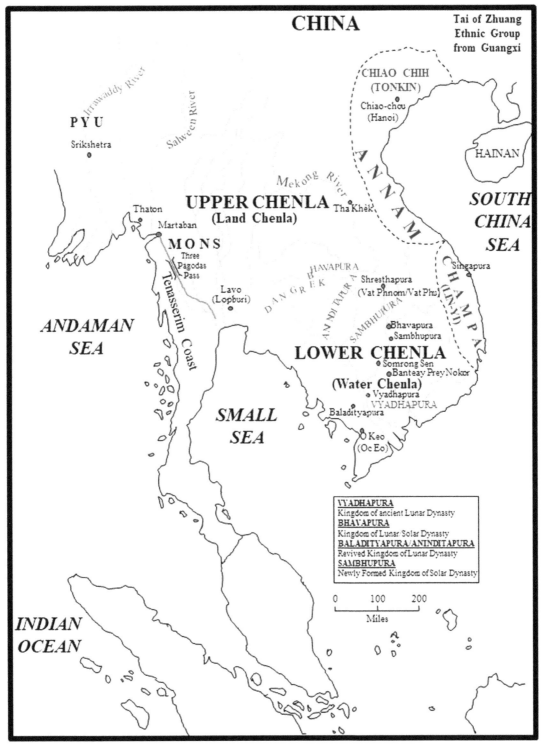

Figure 17. The Division of Chenla (707-802)
(Map by Kenneth So; adapted from References 6 and 16)

Land Chenla or Upper Chenla

The original capital of Chenla was in Shresthapura near Vat Phu of present-day Laos. After Chenla conquered Funan that included Sambhupura (centered at the present-day Sambor), Vyadhapura (Ba Phnom according to Coedès; located in present-day Phnom Ksach Sâ in Prey Veng province), and Baladityapura (present-day Angkor Borei), the capital was relocated and renamed to Bhavapura — about 100 miles south of Shresthapura — in honor of Bhavavarman I (550-600), considered to be the first Chenla king. The relocation of the capital was intended to place the new Chenla government at the central location of the kingdom. Land Chenla considered itself as the original homeland of the Khmers. After the breakup of Chenla in 707, Land Chenla sent its first embassy to China in 717. Five years later, in 722, Land Chenla and Champa joined forces to help Mai Hac De, the Tai-Yueh-Muong's chief of Nghe An (present-day Hanoi), in his revolt against the Chinese governor of Chiao-chou.[6,p59; 58,p164] After defeating the Chinese army, Mai Hac De proclaimed himself the "Black Emperor," but he did not have time to enjoy his reign because immediately afterward the Chinese sent a reinforcement to defeat and kill him.

Briggs mentioned[6,p59] that after the foundation of the Kingdom of Nan Chao (南詔), China had to defend itself numerous times against the forces of powerful Nan Chao rulers who also allied themselves with Tibetan rulers. China was under attack from the most powerful Nan Chao king named Kolofeng in 750, the year the Chenla embassy — the Chinese did not specify which Chenla — arrived at the Chinese Imperial Court. Even with several armies sent against him, the Chinese could not hold the cities against the attack of Kolofeng. China was courting Chenla for help in its war against Kolofeng. In 753, the Crown Prince of Land Chenla and twenty-six of his relatives were received with great honor by the Chinese Imperial Court. They joined the Chinese army in 754 to fight the battle against Nan Chao, but Kolofeng was still able to defeat the Chinese army handily.[6,p59] Concerning Nan Chao, the theory that the Tais originated from Nan Chao of the Yunnan province is no longer correct. The new finding[59] identified the Tais belonging to the Zhuang ethnic group with ninety percent of their population living in Guangxi, the Chinese province bordering the eastern side of Yunnan.

In 771, the heir of Land Chenla named Pomi (婆彌) and his wife arrived at the Chinese Imperial Court. They offered eleven elephants in tribute to the Chinese Emperor. On 13 December 771, Pomi received the title Kaifuyitongsansi (開府儀同三司) — "Palace Opener who enjoys the same honors as the three higher officers."[58] In 799, Land Chenla sent an envoy named Litouji (李頭及) to China. He was also received with great honor and a title from the Chinese Imperial court. That was the extent of relationship given by the Chinese about Land Chenla.

Water Chenla or Lower Chenla

China did not offer much information about Water Chenla because of its minimal contact with the country. There are no specific records of China receiving any embassies from Water Chenla. Most of the knowledge about Water Chenla came from the Khmer inscriptions and also from the tale given by an Arab seaman in the ninth century. Water Chenla included Sambhupura, Vyadhapura, and Baladityapura. The inscription of 713, in Sanskrit and Khmer, from West Baray mentioned about Queen Jayadevi making offerings to the Hindu god Shiva Tripurantaka. Apparently she was queen of Water Chenla at least until 713. The Prey Mien inscription dated in 726, in present-day Takeo, was written in Khmer. It commemorated Harihara but did not mention the name of the reigning king in that period. Two inscriptions from Kratié: the Preah Theat Preah Srei in Thbong Khmum, dated 770, and the Lobok Srot in Sambor, dated 781, mentioned a king named Jayavarman.[1,p94; 6,p60] Coedès called him Jayavarman I bis because he could not identify exactly who he was and also he wanted to avoid renumbering the Jayavarman kings during the Angkor period from I to IX.

As mentioned previously, troubles started near the end of Jayavarman I's reign and accentuated during the reign of his daughter Jayadevi. Two new dynasties vied for the position of leadership to replace Vyadhapura as the center of power. Nripatindravarman revived the old Lunar Dynasty of Baladityapura and reigned on the western strip of the Mekong delta. Balidityapura is believed to be Angkor Borei. On the eastern side of the Mekong River, a newly Solar Dynasty of Sambhupura was formed to rival the Lunar Dynasty of Baladityapura.

While his father Nripatindravarman reigned at Baladityapura, Pushkaraksha (also known as Indraloka by his posthumous name) became king of Sambhupura by marrying Princess Indrani who was heir to the kingdom of Sambhupura. In the meantime, the successor to Jayadevi of the kingdom of Vyadhapura — once the dominant force in the region — was left to reign only over a small area near the capital of Banteay Prey Nokor. Briggs believed that the alliance between Pushkaraksha and Indrani of Sambhupura in combination with Nripatindravarman controlling the southernmost region of Water Chenla may have precipitated the breakup of Chenla.[6,p64] After the death of his father sometimes after 716, Pushkaraksha relinquished the kingdom of Sambhapura to his son (possibly Sambhuvarman II) so that he could take over the more important Kingdom of Baladityapura. To complete the control of Water Chenla, Pushkaraksha's son (possibly Sambhuvarman II) married the heiress to the throne of Vyadhapura who was possibly the granddaughter of Jayadevi. They produced a son named Rajendravarman who succeeded his father around the middle of the eight century. Afterward, Rajendravarman married Nripatindradevi. The reign of Rajendravarman brought the kingdoms of Baladityapura, Sambhupura, and Vyadhapura into one umbrella. They produced a son named Mahipativarman who married Rajendradevi, the great-granddaughter of Yasomati and of the Brahman Agastya from Aryadesa of Northern India (see the Genealogy of the Kings of Cambodia in Ref. 1). According to Briggs Agastya "played a prominent part in the establishment of Aryan culture in South India and possibly in Java."[6,p105] Their union produced a daughter named Indradevi, who became the mother of the future King Yasovarman I. The proposed genealogy of the kings and queens of Land Chenla is shown in Figure 18.

Mahipativarman was a young king but his reign seemed to be short-lived. What could cause the king to die relatively young? The clue may be revealed in a story told by an Arab merchant named Sulayman that he picked up from the annals of the country of Zabag, believed to be Java, during his seafaring days in 851. The event must have occurred around the end of the eight century. The story was published by Abu Zayd Hasan in 916 and then translated later By G. Ferrand in French, which was further translated into English by M. Ferrand. The story which was reported by Paul Pelliot[60,pp127-128] and then by Lawrence Palmer Briggs[6,p67-68] in his book *The Ancient Khmer Empire*. It is necessary to understand this story in its full context because Mahipativarman's action led to the invasion of Chenla by Java, and subsequently to the accession of Jayavarman II and his rise to power.

The story mentioned that the population of the Khmer country in the 9th century outnumbered those of its neighbors. The Khmer king was young when he inherited the throne. One day the king said to his minister privately on a boat trip: "I wish to see before me, on a plate, the head of the Maharaja, King of Zabag." Realizing that the king's words would offend the Maharaja of Zabag it they reached his ears, the minister advised his king not to repeat his wish. Because of his youth and impetuous manner, the king did not heed his minister's advice and repeated his wish at his court in front of his ministers, generals, and noble families. As expected, the words of the Khmer king's wish had reached the Maharaja. He felt insulted and told his ministers he would teach the young Khmer king a lesson. The Maharaja instructed his minister to equip 1,000 vessels with arms and soldiers for a secret invasion of Chenla. As a diversionary tactics, the Maharaja announced openly that he would take a pleasure trip to the different islands in his kingdom. When the preparation was finished, the Maharaja set sail directly to the Khmer country. The vessels went up the river and reached the capital of Chenla without troubles. The battle was swift because the Khmers were caught by surprise. The Maharaja entered the royal palace, captured the Khmer king, and sit on the throne to show he was the master. As a punishment, the Maharaja had the Khmer king beheaded on put on a platter. The annals said that the Maharaja wanted only to punish the Khmer king and that he returned to Java without taking anything from the Khmer country. The Maharaja recognized the wisdom of the Khmer minister and entrusted him with the job to find a good and capable person to replace the fallen Khmer king.

Upon his return to Java, the Maharaja had the head of the Khmer king embalmed and put in a vase. He had the vase sent to the new Khmer king accompanied by a letter saying: "I have been prompted to act as I have done against your predecessor because of the hatred he manifested against us, and we have chastened him (to give a lesson) to those who wish to imitate him. We have applied to him the treatment he wished to apply to us. We think it wise to send you his head, for it is not necessary now to keep it here. We do not draw any glory from the victory we have won over him." The annals said that the standing of the Maharaja had increased when the news of the Khmer king reached India and China. As to " kings of the Khmers, every morning, on rising, turn the face in the direction of Zabag, incline themselves to the earth and humiliated themselves before the Maharaja to render him homage."

Because this was a critical period in the history of Cambodia, it is therefore necessary to analyze the above story from the Khmer point of views. Concerning this story, was it possible that the king mentioned his desire casually in private to his minister and never had any intention to follow it through? Did the advice from the minister precipitate the king's action into doing something irrational because his minister dared to give him advice against his wish instead of just listening to him? As a reminder, it must be pointed out that the story was written from the conqueror's point of view.

Did the Khmer king realize that his statement could be very offensive to the Maharaja of Zabag? The bombastic statement of the Khmer king would be interpreted by the Maharaja as a challenge to his dignity and his honor. If the Khmer king had made his wish known at his court in front of his dignitaries, then the Maharaja had no choice but to respond to the challenge to avoid being perceived as weak among his subjects and his neighbors. The world must be viewed in the context of its time period where honor and dignity trumped everything.

Since the story was published, many scholars have tried to determine the identity of the Khmer king and the location of Zabag. Briggs suggested that Zabag was located in Central Java and the Maharaja came from the Sailendra dynasty that practiced Mahayana Buddhism. Coedès said that the Maharaja was King Jayanasa of Srivijaya who reigned around 682.[1,pp82-83,p93] I believe that the Maharaja could not have been Jayanasa as Coedès suggested because during this time period the Khmer king would have been Jayavarman I, which did not fit the profile of a young king told in the story because by 681 or 693 Jayavarman I was already an old man. According to most scholars, the event was supposedly taken place near the end of the 8th century and not the 7th century. The existence of Srivijaya that became an ally with the Sailendra dynasty was made known only in 1912 after Coedès announced its discovery. The difficulty of identifying Srivijaya was due to the different countries calling Srivijaya by different names. The Chinese called it Sanfotsi or San Fo Qui; the Khmer called it Malayou; the Arab called it Zabag; and the Indian called it Yavadesh in Sanskrit and Javadeh in Pali. The Sailendra of Java and the Srivijaya of Sumatra were rivals. To alleviate Srivijaya's fear of the Sailendra's emerging power, the king of Sailendra proposed to form a marriage of alliance with the Srivijaya.

Because the story was written by the winner it requires some analyses to weed out the information. The main reason of Sailendra's conquest over Water Chenla may not be the insult that the Khmer king supposedly made to the Maharaja. It may actually have something to do with the Maharaja himself who was an expansionist warrior. Also, it was very unlikely that the Maharaja left Chenla empty handed and did not make any ravage to the country. On the contrary, the Sailendra's invasion of Annam in 767 and of Champa in 787 created a lot of damages to these two countries.

King Sanjaya (717-760) founded the Sailendra dynasty. According to the theory based on the Carita Parahyangan (Tale of Parahyangan) — that covered the Sunda Kingdom (located on the western part of Java) from 669 to 1579, prior to the pre-Islamic period — King Panangkaran (760-775) converted from Hinduism to Buddhism after he received the advice from his ailing father, King Sanjaya. His father wanted his son to embrace the more pacifist faith because he worried that the Shivaistic faith brought too much fear into people's lives.[61] The prominence of Buddhism in Sailendra pushed the practitioners of Hinduism into leaving east Java in mass exodus. In an ironic way, Buddhism did not pacify the Sailendra rulers but made them more warrior-like instead. Sailendra flexed its power by waging wars against Annam in 767 and Champa in 787. It must be noted that the military expansion did not start with Sailendra. It started under the Srivijaya dynasty before it formed an alliance with the Sailendra dynasty around 760. The Srivijaya kingdom controlled the "spice route traffic and local trade, charging a toll on passing ships." When Champa opened a port and started to attract traders in the 8th century, Srivijaya went into war with Champa because it posed a threat to Srivijaya's lucrative commerce. An unfinished inscription of 782 found at Ligor mentioned that Sailendra was ruled by a king named Vishnu who was also known by his ruthless name as "the killer of enemy heroes." This king was better known as Sangrama Dhananjaya or Dharanindra. The inscription praised him as the "supreme King of Kings" and "Chief of the Sailendra family."[6,p66] The text said that "King Vishnu bore the title of Maharaja to indicate that he was a descendant of the family of the Sailendras."[1,p89] King Dharanindra who reigned in Sailendra from 775 to 800 was probably the Maharaja mentioned in the story.

Who was the unfortunate Khmer king that the Maharaja decapitated? According to the story, the decapitation of the Khmer king occurred right at the beginning of the Sailendra invasion of Chenla, which happened probably after the invasion of Champa in 787. The Khmer king who reigned under a unified Water Chenla was Mahipativarman who succeeded his father Rajendravarman at Baladityapura, probably around the end of the 8th century. Mahipativarman would fit the profile of the young king mentioned in the story. The location of Baladityapura (Angkor Borei) that was close to the seashore would give credence to the surprise attack by the Maharaja forces. The other Chenla kings lived too far inland for the Maharaja to surprise them, let alone win the battle so easily. The Arab Sulayman did not witness the event or live during the time the story took place. He told the story through a second hand account.

After the death of Mahipativarman, the minister was left with the task of choosing a new king, supposedly without the interference from the Maharaja. This part of the story may just be an attempt by Java to show the benevolence nature of the Maharaja. During this period, Water Chenla was in great turmoil because the country was left without a ruler. Contrary to the Arab tale, Java seemed to have a hand in selecting a new king for Water Chenla. Historical records indicated that a Khmer prince, who would later become Jayavarman II, came to Chenla from Java probably around 800. He did not establish his reign as king of Chenla until 802. The origin and reign of Jayavarman II will be discussed in more details in the next chapter for the Angkor period.

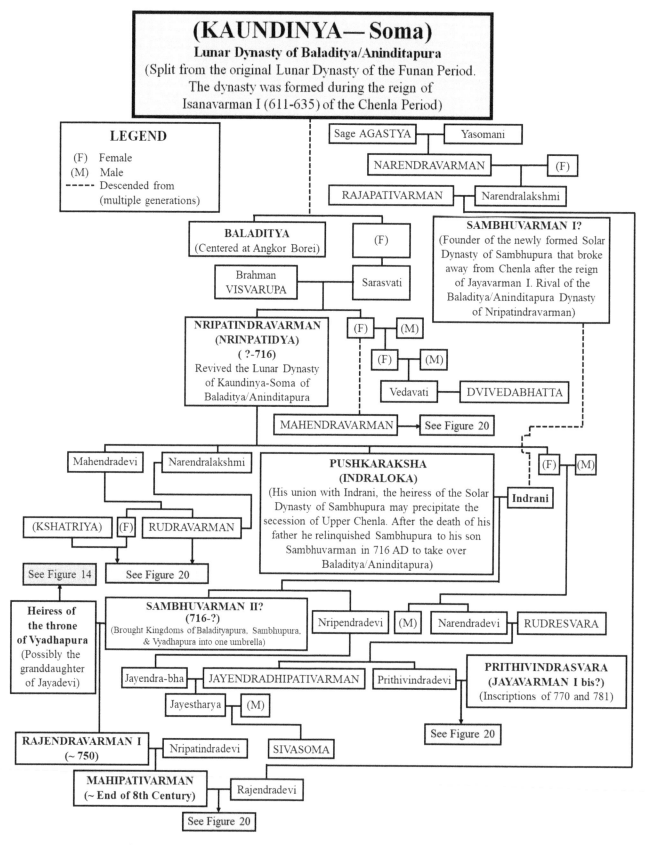

**Figure 18. Genealogy of the Land Chenla Kings and Queens
after the Division of Chenla (707-802)**

CHAPTER 6

THE ANGKOR PERIOD
(KAMBUJA PERIOD)
(802-1431)

But the monuments are there and no mere shutting of the eyes will dispose of them: Angkor Thom, a walled city within whose metropolitan area at one time must have lived more people than were to be found in the Rome of Augustus or the Carthage of Hannibal; and Angkor Vat, supreme architectural effort of this strange culture, not only the most grandiose temple of the group, but one of the most stupendous undertakings begun by man since the cornerstone was laid for the Tower of Babel.

Four Faces of Siva: The Mystery of Angkor
National Geographic, September 1920
Robert J. Casey [62,pp303-304]

Historians classified the Angkor period from the beginning of Jayavarman II's reign in 802 to the fall of Angkor in 1431. The period between Jayavarman Paramesvara or Jayavarman IX (1327~1368) and the fall of Angkor in 1431 was very confusing and uncertain. The Angkor Period contains three dynasties followed by a trouble period. The first dynasty started from Jayavarman II in 802 and ended under the reign of Harshavarman III in 1080. The second dynasty is specifically called the Mahidharapura dynasty. It brought in new bloodlines not related to any previous Angkor kings. The Mahidharapura dynasty started from Jayavarman VI in 1080 with Hiranyavarman as the progenitor and Suryavarman II as one of his descendants and one of the greatest Khmer kings. The dynasty ended with Dharanindravarman II in 1160. The third dynasty started with Yasovarman II, continued through Jayavarman VII — considered by historians to be the greatest Khmer kings — and ended with Jayavarman Paramesvara. The third dynasty had its lineage that could be traced all the way back to the following four dynasty branches: 1) Mahidharapura dynasty of King Hiranyavarman; 2) Lunar dynasty of Hun Tien-Liu Yeh; 3) Lunar dynasty of the Baladitya/Aninditapura; and 4) Solar dynasty of Kambu-Mera. The trouble period covered the rest of the Angkor period, from around 1368 to 1431.

During the Angkor period, the royal succession were divided into two systems, the matrilineal and patrilineal, that included the ambilateral descent system into the equation.

Michael Vickery stated in his paper called *Some Remarks on Early State Formation in Cambodia* that the ambilateral descent system set up a rule of succession where the nobility of higher descent and of the same generation would inherit the throne first before it would be passed down to the next generation.[63,p108] The system would break down if the reigning monarch decided not to abide by the understood rule and tradition, by passing down his throne to his son instead of to his brother or another person of the same generation with higher ranking than his son. The problem became particularly acute when Yasovarman I decided to pass down his throne to his son, Harshavarman I, who was still young at the time. Jayavarman IV, who traced his ancestry to the same one as that of his brother-in-law Yasovarman I — thus of the same generation — felt that he had been usurped when Harshavarman I, Yasovarman I's son, inherited the throne.

The Angkor period was the golden age of the Khmer civilization. For the Khmers to prosper, they must liberate themselves from the yoke of Java. Unsuspecting of Jayavarman II's cleverness and sense of nationalism, Java chose him as its puppet to rule over Water Chenla to replace the decapitated Khmer king. Jayavarman II plotted very carefully until the right time to declare his independence from Java in 802. He is credited as the founder of Angkor, and also for introducing the concept of Devaraja (God-King) as a universal monarch (Chakravatin). Grandiose projects started under Indravarman I (877-889) that left a lasting legacy for future Angkor kings to follow. Angkor grew and spread over a vast area. New grand scale projects were commissioned under each new king, such as the building of miles-long *Barays* (reservoirs), the construction of hundreds of miles of canals, and the erecting of monuments with stones without using mortar — an engineering ingenuity at the time. Angkor reached its architectural apogee under the reign of Suryavarman II (1113-1150) with the construction of Angkor Wat, one of the most magnificent architecture the world has ever known. Angkor Wat is not only the largest temple in the world, but it is also intricate in its design and beauty. Bayon is a complex monument with at least 50 massive towers of stone faces (only 37 remaining) built under the reign of Jayavarman VII. The enormous construction scale of Angkor that had not been rivaled since the time of the Great Pyramids of Egypt and the Great Wall of China could be achieved only with a lot of manpower, domesticated animals such as elephants, and skilled labors such as engineers, architects, astrologers, astronomers, mathematicians, sculptors, artists, and scribes. It must be reminded that the Great Wall of China that is estimated to be approximately 5,500 miles long is not a continuous wall, but it is rather made up of discontinuous walls, trenches, and hills built by different Chinese emperors under multiple dynasties.

The tale of the Arab merchant Sulayman in 851 provided a glimpse of the Khmer population during the Angkor period. His mention of the Khmer population that was more numerous than that of the neighboring countries attested to the manpower pool the Khmer kings could use to build the grandiose projects of Angkor. One can only wonder the splendor of Angkor as the center of knowledge and civilization in Southeast Asia. While London was still a small town with a population of only twenty thousand, Angkor was the most marvelous metropolis in Asia with a population close to one million[64,p34] bustling with energy and activities.

The magnificence of Angkor is undeniable. Unlike the pyramids of Egypt, the Great Wall of China, and the Taj Mahal of India that are in plain sight for people to see, Angkor was hidden in a remote Khmer jungle full of mystery for 500 years until it was rediscovered in 1860 by the French explorer Henri Mouhot. Angkor selfishly guarded its secrets for hundreds of years. The announcement of the existence of Angkor was such a revelation that the world was bewildered and asked the question of how could such a wonder have existed and been hidden for so long? The scale of Angkor spreading through an area of over 1,000 square kilometers could not even be matched by the pyramids of Egypt. Only the scale of the Great Wall of China can rival Angkor, but not in its architecture. The intricate carvings on the wall throughout Angkor cannot be equaled by anything found in the world. Paul Cravath, who studied the Apsara dancers on the bas-reliefs of Angkor, wrote a book called *Earth in Flower*[14] along with Kent Davis, the publisher of the book, who is also writing a book on the women of Angkor Wat indicate that over 1,800 carving Apsara figures adorn the wall of Angkor Wat. An image of Apsara on the wall of Angkor is shown in Figure 19.

Figure 19. Image of Apsara on the Wall of Angkor
(Photo by Kenneth So)

The awe-inspiring, emotional, and admiration of the splendor of Angkor is captured in the book "Angkor the Magnificent" by Helen Churchill Candee in 1922 as follows:[65,pp6-7]

Angkor was of the past. Cambodia existed as a quiet country of dark-skinned jungle-people and fishermen. Angkor left no history: it simply passed. Asia forgot it, and sleeping Europe had never known of it.

Thus it was when Cambodia with other countries of Indochina fell under the protection of France.

One day a French naturalist penetrated the jungle, as a boy fired with curiosity penetrates the forest on a farm. He came upon the towers of Angkor Vat. He who had found for days of travel nothing larger nor more recondite in construction than a bamboo hut, saw before him thrusting through the jungle the magnificent pile of architecture. In an ecstasy he sprang forward to meet marvel after marvel. It was unbelievable. He thought himself translated to some other planet. Such beauty, such grandeur, could not exist on earth unknown. He questioned the brown natives. They said the temples had always been there, the gods had built them for their own habitat, and proved it by legends.

The greatest expansion of Khmer territory occurred under the reign of Jayavarman VII. After the great achievements under Jayavarman VII, Angkor started into a declining period. The decadence of Angkor coincided with the birth of Ayutthaya in 1351 where their kings were descendants from the Khmer royal bloodlines of Suphanburi. Angkor had the misfortune of encountering one of the worst natural disasters since its existence. A thirty-year mega drought, from 1362 to 1392,[66] fell on Angkor and rendered the intricate canal networks that used to irrigate water for farming almost useless. Angkor that depended on the large reservoirs and canals to regulate the water for all year-round farming could no longer feed its growing population of one million people. The decadence of Angkor continued to get worse after the attack by Ayutthaya during the reign of Barommaracha II. In 1431, only eighty years after its foundation, Ayutthaya invaded and sacked Angkor.

THE FIRST ANGKOR DYNASTY (802-1080)

Historians credited Jayavarman II as the founder of Angkor. He meticulously and carefully plotted his way to unite the different Chenla kingdoms that were broken up by the Maharaja of Zabag at the end of the 8th century. Jayavarman II's greatness culminated in his declaration of independence on Mount Mahendra (Phnom Kulen) in 802 which started the emancipation of Kambuja from the yoke of Java. The genealogies of all the Khmer kings from Jayavarman II to the end of the first dynasty of the Angkor period are summarized in Figures 20, 21, and 22.

20   Jayavarman II (802-850) ជ័យវរ្ម័ន (ទី២)

Transliterated Name: Jăyavarmăn II
Posthumous Name: Paramasvera (The Supreme Lord)
Relationship: Son of Prithivindresvara and Prithivindradevi (posthumous names; sister of
    Jayendradhipativarman); possibly the son of Jayavarman I bis (according to Briggs[6,p69]
Religion: Shaivism?
Purohita: Sivakaivalya
Guru: Yogisvarapandita (descendant of the sacerdotal family of Bhas-svamini).
Capital: Started at Indrapura (Banteay Prey Nokor in the lower Mekong River, east of present-day
    Kompong Cham); moved to Hariharalaya (Roluos ruins about 15 km southeast of Siem Reap);
    then to Amarendrapura (present Angkor Thom region around Western Baray); then to
    Mahendraparvata (Mount Mahendra or Phnom Kulen); and finally returned to settle at
    Hariharalaya.
Genealogy: Figures 20 and 24

The reign of Jayavarman II was very unusual among the reigns of all the Khmer kings. In spite of his long reign, he did not leave any inscriptions that can be found as a testament to his legacy. Most of his achievements were described in the inscriptions of the 11th century found at Sdok Kak Thom inscription

K.235 dated 8 February 1053.[1,p97; 67,p1] The exact date of Jayavarman II's accession to the throne is not known, but it is believed that he was the person chosen by the Maharaja of Zabag (Central Java) to replace the decapitated Khmer king — believed to be most likely Mahipativarman, the Khmer king who ruled over Water Chenla at Baladityapura near the end of the 8th century. However, Claude Jacques[68] and Michael Vickery[69] seemed to contest that theory and believed Jayavarman II started his career at Vyadhapura, which would have been near Banteay Prey Nokor in present-day Kampong Cham.

The event of the decapitation of the Khmer king must have taken place right after the invasions of Chiao Chi (Tonkin) in 767 and of Champa in 787 by Sailendra.[1,p89; 19,p95] King Sanjaya who reigned in Dailendra from 717 to 760 was a Shaivite but he allowed his people to actively practice and promote Mahayana Buddhism. In his ailing years, Sanjaya encouraged his son Panangkaran who reigned from 760 to 775 to embrace Buddhism. Dharanindra who succeeded Panangkaran from 775 to 800 was the king who attacked Chiao Chi and Champa and most likely the one who beheaded the Khmer king. Coedès advanced an interesting theory about the Javanese Sailendra's invasion of Chenla. He pointed out that unlike the kings of Chenla who were Shaivites, the last kings of Funan — Kaundinya Jayavarman and his son Rudravarman — were Buddhists like the Javanese Sailendra.[19,p96] The invasion of Chenla may have something to do more with religion and the restoration of an old monarchy than the story of the offensive wish made by the Chenla king. The Sailendra king may have intended to restore the Khmer country to the practice of Buddhism like during the time of Rudravarman, the last king of Funan. Coedès went even further in his theory by linking the Sailendra king to Funan. He made an interesting argument that the Sailendra dynasty may be the reemergence of the old Funan dynasty. Funan, which was known as the "kings of mountain," lost its glory after it was conquered by Chenla. The Funan rulers and their supporters may have escaped to some of its former vassal states or to Java and then reemerged as the Sailendra dynasty. He stated the following:[1,pp88-89]

> *The name Sailendra, "king of the mountain," is an equivalent of (Siva) Girisa, and perhaps expresses an Indian adaptation of Indonesian beliefs which place the residences of gods on mountains… In any case, the appearance in the southern islands of Sailendras, with their imperial title maharaja, was, we can safely say, "an international event of major importance."*
>
> *I wonder if these "kings of the mountain" were not, in fact, attempting to revive the title of the ancient kings of Funan, who were zealous adherents of the linga Girisa and set themselves up as universal sovereigns. This hypothesis has gained some ground since J. G. de Casparis identified Naravarnagara, the last capital of Funan in the southern Indochinese Peninsula, with the variant Varanara in an inscription of the ninth century. This inscription mentions that the country Varanara was ruled by a king Bhujayottungadeva, who appears to have been the founder of the Sailendra dynasty in Java.*

Coedès' theory could be partly corroborated with the Chinese records that say sometimes after the conquest of Funan by the Chenla king, Mahendravarman (Chitrasena), the Funan king fled from Vyadhapura to Nafuna (identified to be in the Kampot region) to put his distance farther away from its Chenla conqueror.[6,p31] The descendants of the defeated Funan kingdom may have founded the Sailendra kingdom.

The history is not clear on the event that took place between the time of Mahipativarman's decapitation and the officially recorded year of Jayavarman II's accession to the throne in 802. It is possible that the Khmer country was left without a king during this period. The Khmer inscription mentions only that Jayavarman "came from Java to reign in the city of Indrapura" but does not specify the exact condition of his stay in Java or his return to Kambuja. The name Chenla was replaced by Kambuja or Kambujadesa around this period. It is not known whether Jayavarman II was in captivity or visiting Java voluntarily. Some scholars claimed that Jayavarman II was on a war campaign in Java. This theory does not seem probable considering that Kambuja had just been conquered by Java a few years earlier. I do not subscribe to this new theory and do not believe that Jayavarman II had the means and credentials yet to form an army in such a short time to mount a campaign against a powerful army of the Java king. Jayavarman II must have either been raised as Java's puppet king to take over the throne in Kambuja in the future or he voluntarily exiled himself to Java to escape the turmoil in Kambuja. The records did not indicate whom Jayavarman II visited in Java. The kings who ruled Srivijaya and Sailendra during that time were probably Samaratungga and Dharanindra, respectively. Both kings were Mahayanist Buddhists. During his stay in Java, did Jayavarman II also visit the Shaivite kingdom of Gresik? Gajayana, a son of King Devasimba who reigned at Kanjuruhan — with its capital located at Ho-ling (742-755) and then moved to Gresik, near present-day Surabaya in Indonesia — built an Agastya sanctuary at Dinaya, near present-day Malang in Indonesia.[1,p90; 6,p65,p69] The sanctuary was worshipped by the Java people.[1,p88] Coedès mentioned that both Gajayana and Devasimha were related in some capacity to King Sanjaya who ruled Sailendra from 717 to 760. The connection between Prince Gajayana of Gresik and Jayavarman II cannot be ignored. According to the genealogy of Khmer kings,[1; 6,p105] the sage Agastya was the great-grandfather of Rajendradevi, the wife of Mahipativarman — the Khmer king who was decapitated under the order of the Majaraha. Rajendradevi was the mother-in-law of Indravarman I, who was the nephew of Dharanindradevi — the wife of Jayavarman II.

The weakening of the Sailendra dynasty by 800 may have given the opportunity for Jayavarman II to return to Kambuja. His return probably took place around 800 (or possibly as far back as 790) because all evidence indicates that Jayavarman II began his reign in 802. It required Jayavarman II at least two years to pacify the country that was in great turmoil due to the absence of a strong and unified ruler. Jayavarman II started out very carefully by installing himself at Indrapura, near the region of Sambhupura where his family was believed to have come from. According to Briggs,[6,p81] based on the Digraphic Inscriptions [Khmer inscriptions from 889 at the start of the reign of Yasovarman were written in two alphabets of Indian origin, the southern Pallava scripts and the northern Nagari scripts], Jayavarman II was the great-grandson of Nripatindravarman — the king of Baladitya who restored the old kingdom of Baladityapura — from his maternal side. Briggs' statement must be amended to say that Jayavarman II was the great-great-grandson of Nripatindravarman on his maternal side and great-grandson by marriage from his wife's maternal side because he married Dharanindradevi, who was the great-granddaughter of Nripatindravarman. The inscriptions of Preah Theat Preah Srei dated 770 and Lobok Srot dated 781 that Coedès discovered (only after the inscription about Jayavarman II had been found first) in the ancient province of Thbong Khmum in Kratié and in the province of Sambor in Kratié, respectively, mention of a king named Jayavarman making a foundation for Vishnu.[6,p60] Coedès called this king Jayavarman I bis because he could not properly determine who he was since he came much later after Jayavarman I had passed away, and seemed to be too early to be assigned it to Jayavarman II. To avoid resequencing all the Jayavarman's names, Coedès assigned the name of Jayavarman I bis to this king. Some scholars speculated that Jayavarman I bis may be the father of Jayavarman II. The fact that Jayavarman II decided to choose Indrapura, which is located near Sambhupura in the province of Sambor in Kratié, as his first residence after his return from Java gives even more weight to the connection between him and Jayavarman I bis. If Jayavarman II were raised to be a Mahayana Buddhist by the Sailendra king, then the plan did not succeed. Jayavarman II's faith may have rekindled if he had visited the sanctuary of Agastya at Dinaya that Prince Gajayana of the kingdom of Gresik had founded to commemorate the sage Brahman, who was Jayavarman II's ancestor.

After his return from Java, Jayavarman II settled at Indrapura. Jayavarman II had many wives according to the 11th century inscriptions of Palhal[6,p83] and the Digraphic inscriptions of Phnom Sandak.[6,p90] His principal wife was Queen Dharanindradevi who ruled Dviradapura near present-day Longvek. She was the niece of Rudravarman from her maternal side and the aunt of Indravarman I from his paternal side. However, another 11th century inscription mentions that Hyang Pavitra of Haripura was the principal queen of Jayavarman II. The inscription provides more details by saying that she was the progenitor of Sivacarya, the *purohita* (Chief Priest) who served Jayavarman V, Udayadityavarman I, and Suryavarman I. It seems that Dharanindradevi was either the posthumous or official name of Queen Hyang Pavitra. Jayavarman II's other minor wives included Hyang Amrita (also called Nripendradevi), the younger sister of the Brahman scholar Sivakaivalya, whom Jayavarman II made him his *purohita*; Bhassvamini from the region of Vat Phu (she was the progenitor of Yogisvarapandita, the *guru* of Suryavarman I); and Kambujalakshmi, also called Praña (her mother named Pinsvangramavati was married to a Brahman named Kesavabhati). Briggs believed that Hyang Pavitra may be the same person as Dharanindradevi. Kambujalakshmi had three brothers with all three of them holding prominent positions. The first brother, Pranavasarva or Nripendravikrama was the chief of castes; the second brother, Sivatman, was in charge of the king's sleeping chamber; and the third brother, Vishnuvala (also called Lakshmindra), was in control of the king's private treasury. Kambujalakshmi is also thought to be the same person as Dharanindradevi because of her influence as a queen on Jayavarman II for having her three brothers served the king in important and trusted positions.

Chakravatin: The God-King

When Jayavarman II arrived in Indrapura, the country was still unruly. Therefore, he instructed his general Prithivinarendra to pacify the country. His chief priest, Sivakaivalya, and his brother Sivavinduka also accompanied Prithivinarendra on this mission. They were successful in putting down all kinds of resistance and made the districts under their control pay tribute to Jayavarman II. After having achieved his first goal, Jayavarman II continued to search for a more suitable and secured location for his capital. He moved to Hariharalaya, identified to be in Ruluos — approximately 15 km southeast of present-day Siem Reap. After staying there for a while he moved again and decided to settle at Amarendrapura, located at present-day Angkor Thom near West Baray. Again, Jayavarman II was not happy with Amarendrapura because he seemed to be looking for a place where he could symbolically liberate himself from Java's yoke. He seemed to have found a place that would suit all his needs. He founded his capital at Mount Mahendra (Phnom Kulen) that he called Mahendraparvata. Phnom Kulen is the source of the Siem Reap River. In order to liberate himself from Java, he called on a Brahman named Hiranyadama from Janapada, identified to be in the province of Mlu Prei.[6,p89] Hiranyadama's expertise in magic and sacred rituals was required to liberate Kambuja from Java and to establish Jayavarman II as the sole ruler. The ceremony would elevate Jayavarman II to be a Chakravatin. It essentially meant he was a world ruler, which was translated to mean God-King. Chakravatin literally means "wheel ruler" in the sense that the wheel is turning without being obstructed or impeded by anybody. The ceremony was performed on Mount Mahendra in 802. Hiranyadama taught Sivakaivalya, Jayavarman II's *purohita*, to perform the *Devaraja* ceremony. The inscription of Sdok Kak Thom[1,p99; 6,p89] mentions the following four sacred *sastras* required to perform the ceremony: *Siraccheda, Vinasikha, Sammoha,* and *Nayottora.* They represent the four mouths of Shiva. The first sastra, *Siraccheda,* was very symbolic. The ceremony called for the simulation of the decapitation in effigy of the king of Sailendra to liberate once and for all Kambuja from Java's subjugation. The sacred ceremony was a powerful symbol for Jayavarman II to send a message to Java and any potential enemies that he was the universal ruler and nobody else was above him. It was a strong statement of declaration of independence by Jayavarman II to Java. Only Sivakaivalya and his descendants were allowed to perform this sacred ceremony that was taught by Hiranyadama. It seemed that Jayavarman II established his residence at Mount Mahendra only to perform the sacred ceremony. The location of Mount Mahendra may have more to do with symbolism than anything else. Jayavarman II's choice of Mount Mahendra may symbolize the title of "Kings of the Mountain" from the old tradition that was attributed to Funan kings. After residing at Mount Mahendra for a period of time, Jayavarman may have figured out that it would not be a good strategic location to defend against potential Javanese invasion or any invasions from his enemies. He may be able to hold off his enemies for a while but not indefinitely. Staying at Mount Mahendra would be suicidal from a strategic standpoint. Finally, he decided to settle down and reestablished his capital at Hariharalaya probably for logistic reason. His settlement at Hariharalaya would allow him to take advantage of the fertile land and the natural resources of the Great Lake, and also to foresee any attacks from his enemies without being trapped if he were to stay at Mount Mahendra. In 2012, a team of scientists and archaelogists used laser light called LIDAR (Light Detection And Ranging) to survey the area around Angkor and discovered a large city near Phnom Kulen that experts believed to be Mahendraparvata.

Khy Phanra mentioned in his essay *Angkor: Essai de Lecture de la Civilisation et de l'Histoire* that the Khmer civilization of the Funan/Chenla/Angkor left the Mekong delta and moved farther inland because it could not sustainably maintain and master the region wetland.[70] Contrary to his thesis, I believe the Khmer civilization settled at Angkor, away from the Mekong delta for tactical reasons. Jayavarman II learned a lesson from the surprised and quick defeat of Water Chenla during the reign of Mahipativarman by the Sailendra Maharaja. After his return from Java, Jayavarman II wanted to avoid the same fate as his predecessor. The reason he moved so many times was because he was searching for a suitable remote area that could support the population of his kingdom before he could declare his independence from Java. The Angkor location was ideal for his settlement because it has the water resource needed to sustain and expand his kingdom, and remote enough to prevent any surprise attacks from his enemies, that included not only Java but also Champa. Angkor was strategically located because any attacks had to come from the Great Lake and Jayavarman II would be prepared for it. He would have the advantage over his enemies if they ever decided to attack his kingdom.

Unlike previous kings before him, Jayavarman II descended from another Solar Dynasty that was founded by Sambhuvarman in the 7th century during the reign of Jayavarman I. During this period Funan had disappeared and was completely annexed by Chenla. The newly formed Solar Dynasty of Sambhupura broke away from the original Solar Dynasty and settled around Sambor and Kratié. He was called the "guardian of the honor of the solar race of Sri Kambu." It is believed that Jayavarman II was the person who brought up the name Kambu and connected it to the founder of the Solar Dynasty. Under his reign, Jayavarman II introduced the concept of Devaraja as the universal monarch and according to Georges Maspero, he may have also started the ritual of *Preah Khan Reach* (Sacred Sword) that was used for the consecration of a new king when he ascended the throne.[6,p94] He also made the position of *purohita,* Chief Priest, to be hereditary and elevated it to be the most important position in the service of the monarch. In his book *Royal Succession in Ancient Cambodia,*[43,p59] Adhir Chakravarti mentioned that in addition to Jayavardhana (Jayavarman III), Jayavarman II had another son named Indrayudha. Jayavarman II passed away in 850 (but Claude Jacques stated that he dies around 835)[71,p21] and left the sacred sword, *Preah Khan Reach,* and a palladium to his son Jayavardhana, the future king Jayavarman III.

21   Jayavarman III (850-877) ជ័យវរ្ម័ន (ទី៣)

Transliterated Name: Jăyavarmăn III
Other Name: Jayavardhana[1,p103]
Posthumous Name: Vishnuloka
Relationship: Son of Jayavarman II and Dharanindradevi (Hyang Pavitra)
Religion: Vaishnavism (Vishnuism) based on the posthumous name
Purohita: Suksmavindu (nephew of Sivakaivalya)
Capital: Hariharalaya (Present-day Roluos, about 15 km southeast of Siem Reap)
Genealogy: Figures 20 and 24

Not much is known about Jayavarman III. He succeeded his father, Jayavarman II, at Hariharalya in 850 at the age of eighteen. Inscriptions said that he was a wise ruler and a great elephant hunter. He died in 877 while he tried to capture an elephant. The inscription said that he received a posthumous name of

Vishnuloka, which indicated that he was a Vishnu worshipper. His *purohita*, named Suksmavindu, was the nephew of Sivakaivalya — the chief priest of Jayavarman II. An epigraphy mentions that Jayavarman III had a valiant brother named Indrayudha who was captured by the king of Champa. Indrayudha did not succeed his brother. Adhir Chakravarti speculated that Indrayudha either died before his father Jayavarman II or was eliminated by his brother (or half-brother) Jayavarman III for the war of succession.[43,p59] He may also have died as a prisoner in Champa.

22 Indravarman I (877-889) កម្រ្តេង្វរ៉ែន (ទី១)

Transliterated Name: Īndravarmăn I
Posthumous Name: Isvaraloka
Relationship: Son of Prithivindravarman and Prithivindradevi (sister of Punnagavarman); nephew of Jayavarman II by marriage; son of Jayavarman III's maternal uncle, maternal great-grandson of Nripatindravarman
Religion: Shaivism
Purohita: Suksmavindu (nephew of Sivakaivalya)
Guru: Sivasoma (disciple of the renown and respected Hindu philosopher Shankaracharya)
Capital: Hariharalaya (Present-day Roluos, about 15 km southeast of Siem Reap)
Genealogy: Figures 20, 22, and 24

Indravarman I succeeded Jayavarman III in 877 and continued to reside at Hariharalaya. He was the paternal nephew of Queen Dharanindradevi, the principal wife of Jayavarman II. He was also the great-grandson of Nripatindravarman (the Water Chenla king from the kingdom of Baladityapura/Aninditapura.) from his mother's side but great-great-grandson from his father's side. He married Indradevi, the daughter of Rajendradevi and Mahipativarman — the Water Chenla king who was decapitated by the Maharaja of Zabag. Indradevi was the great-great-granddaughter from her mother's side of the sage Brahman Agastya from North India. Agastya played a prominent role in uncovering some of the most revered Hindu Vedic scriptures. Agastya who was from the north Aryadesa (India) is admired and honored in the south because he was credited for introducing the grammar to the Tamil people. A temple of worship was built in his honor by Prince Gajayana of the kingdom of Gresik in Java. The fact that Indravarman I married a direct descendant of one of the most literate Brahmans in the Hindu world suggests that Kambuja may have been attracting a lot of interest from learned men from India.

Indravarman I was credited for starting grandiose projects, which left a legacy for future kings of Angkor to follow. He was a king with a vision. In addition to his own knowledge, his understanding of the country's needs could possibly come from the good advice he may have received from the side of his wife's family. The inscriptions do not say whether Indradevi's maternal grandparents (Rajapativarman and Narendralakshmi) came to Kambuja, but it is not improbable to assume that they may have followed their daughter Rajendradevi (Indradevi's mother) when she married Mahipativarman. Rajapativarman would have undoubtedly received good trainings from Agastya, the grandfather of his wife, who was one of the most respected and learned Brahmans in India. It is therefore possible that Indradevi's grandfather would have been used for advice by Indravarman I. During his reign, Indravarman I realized that enormous amount of water during the monsoon season went to waste. He commissioned the building of a large reservoir (Indratataka/Baray of Hariharalaya located in Lolei, north of Bakong and Preah Ko) and an irrigation network to regulate water for rice planting and harvesting. With a large reservoir, water could be discharged in the dry season to feed the rice fields. His ingenuity allowed the Khmer people to plant and harvest rice three or four times per year. The canals could be used for dual purposes. It was used for water irrigation as mentioned above, but it was also used to transport laterite stones from Phnom Kulen to construct monuments. The transition from the use of bricks to laterite stones to build monuments seemed to coincide with this period. The inscription at Preah Ko, the shrine Indravarman I built for his parents, said that the reservoir was 800 meters wide by 3,800 meters long. It was the largest reservoir of its time. He also built Bakong, his state and memorial shrine housing a linga dedicating to Shiva. Bakong was the first Khmer architecture depicting *Nagas* as a symbol to protect the temple, where gods reside separately from the human world. His *guru* (spiritual teacher), Sivasoma, was credited for helping Indravarman I in the resumption of epigraphic tradition that was absent during the reigns of Jayavarman II and III. Sivasoma was a disciple of the renown and respected Hindu philosopher Shankaracharya (788-820) who was influential in his teaching to restore the Advaita Vedanta (sub-school of Vedenta, the philosophy for the goal of the Vedas) and Dharma to its original purity form in India. It seemed that a great deal of knowledge was passed down from India to Kambuja during this period. Sivasoma took Vamasiva under his tutelage. As a guru, Sivasoma eclipsed the *purohita* Suksmavindu who continued to serve Indravarman I in the same capacity as he had served Jayavarman III. Briggs mentioned that Sivasoma was the second cousin of Jayavarman II but he did not specify how he was related to the king, while Coedès showed in the genealogy on his book *The Indianized States of Southeast Asia*[1] that he was the grandson of Jayendradhipativarman, the brother of Jayavarman II's mother. If it were so, then it would place Sivasoma in the same generation as Indravarman I. It could be possible that Sivasoma was Indravarman I's guru but in my opinion it is unlikely that the king would choose somebody of his age as his guru. The likely scenario is more probable to place Sivasoma in the same generation as Jayavarman II as proposed by Vickery in his paper *Some Remarks on Early State Formation in Cambodia*.[63] Based on epigraphy and more detail research, Vickery proposed two alternative lineages of Sivasoma, with one placing Sivasoma as the older brother of Jyestharya and son of Jayendravallabha and Jayendradhipativarman, the brother of Jayavarman II's mother (Prithivindradevi); and the other still placing Sivasoma as the son of Jayendradhipativarman, but with Jayendravallabha as the sister of Jayendradhipativarman and Jayestharya as her daughter. I believe the first scenario is the most likely one. The proposed partial genealogy of Indravarman I and Sivasoma is shown in Figure 20 and the complete genealogy shown in Figure 24.

The process of unification under Indravarman I showed successful results. The Khmer territory under his reign extended from Moat Chrouk (Chau Doc or present-day An Giang province in South Vietnam) in the south; to present-day Ubon in Thailand in the north; and to the plateau of present-day Korat in Thailand in the west.[1,p111; 19,p97] Because of Sivasoma's royal lineage (he was Jayavarman II's cousin) and position as the guru to the king, he dominated the purohita's position held by Suksmavindu. The king passed away in 889 and received the posthumous name of Isvaraloka. He was credited for the re-unification of Kambuja. A group of inscriptions dated 879 at Preah Ko in Roluos, is one of the earliest epigraphies found in Cambodia. They are classified as belonging to the Kambuja period.[6,p61]

23   Yasovarman I (889~900) យសោវរ្ម័ន (ទី ៩)

Transliterated Name: Yasovarmăn I
Other Name: Yasovardhana[1,p111; 19,p98]
Posthumous Name: Paramasivaloka[1,p108,p114]
Relationship: Son of Indravarman I and Indradevi (Hyang Narendra)
Religion: Shaivism
Purohita: Suksmavindu (nephew of Sivakaivalya)
Guru: Vamasiva (disciple of Sivasoma)
Capital: Started at Hariharalaya (Present-day Roluos, about 15 km southeast of Siem Reap) and then
    moved to Yasodharapura (Present-day Phnom Bakheng)
Genealogy: Figures 20 and 24

The death of Yasovarman I is a point of contention among historians. While the accession of Yasomarman I is well determined, his death on the other hand cannot be pinpointed with great certainty. Before he succeeded his father in 889, Yasovarman I was known under the name of Yasovardhana. He was the son of Indravarman I and Indradevi. Oddly enough, Yasovarman I did not claim his throne through the lineage side of his father, Indravarman I, nor through Jayavarman II — the founder of the Angkor/Kambuja Dynasty — who was the husband of his grand aunt. All the inscriptions about Yasovarman I show that efforts were made to connect him through his maternal's side as the great-great-great-grandson of the sage Agastya; and through his grandfather, Mahipativarman (the son of Rajendravarman) — the king who consolidated his power over all the independent states and reigned as the uncontested ruler over Water Chenla. The reason that Yasovarman I did not claim his reign through Indravarman I may be due to the fact that his father did not designate him as his heir. Claude Jacques mentioned that Indravarman I chose his son from another wife to succeed him.[71,p25] It seemed that the fight of succession took place right after the death of Indravarman I, which Yasovarman I came out as the victor. It may be for this reason that Yasovarman I left Hariharalaya and founded Yasodharapura, mentioned throughout the inscriptions as Vnam Kantal (Central Mountain). For a long time scholars thought that Vnam Kantal was Bayon. It was not until 1930, after the work of Victor Goloubev, that Vnam Kantal was correctly identified as Phnom Bakheng. The word Bakheng may be broken down into *Ba* and *Kheng*. The word *Ba* could possibly mean male while the word *Kheng* could mean dignified, elegant, or majestic. Therefore, *Phnom Bakheng* could mean the elegant (dignified or majestic) male mountain (or hill). The name of Bakheng appeared for the first time on the 16th century inscriptions (K.285 and K.465) that mention the restoration work performed on Buddhist statues. The statues were erected on Phnom Bakheng.

Yasovarman I's claim to the throne seems to reinforce the Khmer adoption of the matrilineal form of succession (or in this case he was forced to do so) and also of trying to reach to the farthest and highest ancestor rankings in the royal lineage. It also suggests that Agastya's descendants may have played an important role in Yasovarman I's life. The capital started out at Hariharalaya but subsequently moved to Yasodharapura. Yasovarman I chose Phnom Bakheng, situated on a natural hill, to represent Mount Meru — the sacred mountain in Hindu cosmology — that he called Yasodharagiri. The proximity of the mountain to the Siem Reap River reflected the sacred Ganges River, worshipped by the Hindus.

Vamasiva, the disciple of Sivasoma, became the guru of Yasovarman I. He did not get the coveted position of purohita probably because he was not from the lineage of Sivakaivalya, the first chief priest who served Jayavarman II; or he never fully learned the ritual of Devaraja that was passed down the line to the descendants of Sivakaivalya. The position of purohita was proclaimed hereditary by Jayavarman II according to the wish of the Brahman Hiranyadama, who taught the sacred Devaraja ceremony to Sivakaivalya. The intent of Hiranyadama was to secure the knowledge of the sacred and powerful magic of the Devaraja ritual and prevent it from falling into the wrong hand. Therefore, to safeguard its secrecy, only the descendants of Sivakaivalya were allowed to learn and perform the ritual.

It was during Yasovarman I's reign that two languages using two different scripts appeared side by side on all inscriptions for the first time, but it seemed that they were used only during the early years of his reign. They are called Digraphic Inscriptions. In addition to the common Khmer language using the Pallava scripts, Sanskrit inscriptions based on the Indian Nagari scripts were also written. According to twelve Digraphic Inscriptions founded throughout Kambuja, Yasovarman I was very active in the first year of his reign. Simultaneously, he commissioned the construction of monasteries called Yasodharasrama and the digging of an enormous reservoir called Yasodharatataka, commonly known as East Baray [located east of Angkor Thom. It is presently dried]. He understood that people needed resting places during their pilgrimages. During his reign he had 100 Ashrams (monasteries) built throughout the kingdom. He also understood the wisdom of water preservation by following the footsteps of his predecessor, Indravarman I. The size of Yasodhataka, 1,830 meters wide by 7,150 meters long,[72,p161] even surpasses that of Indrataka (Lolei Baray). Yasovarman I tried to accommodate the different faiths practiced by the people. He had three different monasteries built south of East Baray — the Brahmasrama (for devotees to Brahma), the Vaisnavasrama (for devotees to Vishnu), and the Saugatasrama (for devotees to Buddha) — to take care of the needs of the people.

There are no inscriptions in existence that gives a panegyric about the life of a Khmer king with such praise and profusion than those of Yasovarman I. His prowess, intelligence, good looks, and strength were unrivalled and even "made his creator jealous." Those were the praises adorning and attributed to Yasovarman I. Probably because of these extraordinary praises earlier historians incorrectly assigned some Angkorian monuments, such as Bayon and Angkor Thom, to the work of Yasovarman I. After discounting all the accolades, Yasovarman I is still considered by historians as one of the greatest Khmer kings. The stele of Lolei of 893 and the inscription of Baksei Chamkrong of 947 say that the Khmer territory extended all the way to the borders of China and Môn kingdom in Thaton.[6,p113] Based on these epigraphies, Georges Maspero drew a map of the Khmer Empire extending to present-day China's Yunnan province to the north, to present-day Myanmar's Shan state to the northwest, and to present-day Thailand's Chumphon province (old P'an-P'an in Malaysian Peninsula) to the southwest.

As mentioned earlier, there are disagreements among historians about the date of the death of Yasovarman I. Lawrence Palmer Briggs said the exact date of the death of Yasovarman I could not be determined. From the Phimeanakas inscription (K. 291) and from another inscription that was not dated, Briggs came to believe that Yasovarman I died before 910.[6,p113] George Coedès was more specific by stating that Yasovarman I died in 900.[1,p114] It seemed he based his assessment on one inscription dated in 902 that mentioned a decree had been issued by Paramasivaloka, which in this case was the posthumous name of Yasovarman I.[1,p312] Sotheara Vong who had studied Saveros Pou's book, *Nouvelles des Inscriptions du Cambodge II,* had written a paper in Cambodian (សិលាចារឹកអក្សរ K.1051 និងរជ្ជព្រះបាទហសិរ្ឞ ទី១ សព្វថ្ងៃរក្សាទុកនៅវត្តសម្ដេចក្នុងភូមិសាស្ត្រស្រុកសង្ខែខេត្តបាត់ដំបង) on this subject. He disagreed with Saveros Pou's year of Saka 877, which corresponded to 955/956 AD, as the date of the death of Yasovarman. Sotheara Vong said that Saveros Pou misinterpreted the date given in the inscription. According to him, the date should have been read as Saka 821, which would correspond to 899/900 AD. It must be noted that due to the Cambodian New Year occurring in November during that period, the conversion from the Saka year to the Christian year could not be pinpointed with certainty without additional information such as the month and date. In the same paper, Sotheara Vong mentioned that Claude Jacques provided a different date and said that the death of Yasovarman I occurred in 912 AD. With all the above information, I believe that the death of Yasovarman I was probably around 900 AD based on his posthumous name that appeared on the inscription dated Saka 823 (902 AD).

Yasovarman I left two young sons, Sri Rudraloka and Sri Paramarudraloka (posthumous names), when he passed away. The period after his death was marked by instability with infighting between princes. In his relatively short reign, Yasovarman I had achieved great accomplishments. He originally built the temple of Preah Vihear with light material, which led to its completion in stone by his successors. The setting of Preah Vihear was ideal for a Khmer monarch who dedicated the temple for Shiva because of its spectacular location sitting atop of a high cliff over 500 meters above the lower ground.

[Jayasimhavarman (900-912?) ជ័យសិម្ហវរ្ម័ន]

Transliterated Name: Jayăsimhavarmăn
Other Name: Future Jayavarman IV
Relationship: Son of Mahendradevi and Brother-in-law of Yasovarman I
Genealogy: Figures 20, 22, and 24

The inscription at Vat Chakret (K.60 and K.61)[6,pp114-115] mentions of a Prince named Jayasimhavarman, which was believed to be the husband of Jayadevi — the younger sister of Yasovarman I. Because the sons of Yasovarman I were too young to reign, their uncle Jayasimhavarman was believed to be acting as a regent after the death of their parent. It seems he was the regent taking care of the country from 900 to probably 912, because the inscription mentions that Harshavarman I (the oldest son of Yasovarman I) "made a donation in 912 in the ancient capital of Funan."[1,p114] This statement seems to say that the oldest son of Yasovarman I was already reigning under the name of Harshavarman I in 912.

24   Harshavarman I (as late as 912-925?) ហឝាវរ្ម័ន (ទី១)

Transliterated Name: Hasāvarmăn I
Posthumous Name: Rudralola[1,p116]
Relationship: Eldest son of Yasovarman I
Religion: Shaivism
Purohita: Kumarasvamin (nephew of Vamasiva but he never received the title purohita)
Capital: Yasodharapura (Present-day Phnom Bakheng)
Genealogy: 20, 22, and 24

Not much is known about Harshavarman I, but he was portrayed as being strong and skillful in the art of weaponry. It seems that Yasovarman I may have died too soon, leaving his eldest son too young to reign. His uncle, Jayasimhavarman (most likely future king Jayavarman IV) — husband of Jayadevi, the younger sister of Yasovarman I — acted as a regent in the early years of Harshavarman I until he became king probably around 912. The nephew of Vamasiva, Kumarasvamin, conducted the Devaraja ritual for Harshavarman I. Like his uncle, he did not get the coveted position of *purohita* (Chief Priest). The inscription indicates that the king's uncle, believed to be Jayasimhavarman (the name was not specifically mentioned), rebelled against him in 921. He moved to Chok Gargyar to reign under the name of Jayavarman IV in opposition to his nephew Harshavarman I who was reigning in 922 at Yasodharapura. Harshavarman I was estimated to pass away around 925. There are no records on the cause and exact date of his death. Harshavarman I's death is a mystery because he was still a young king in 923. His legacy includes the temple of Baksei Chamkrong that he built to house statues of his ancestors. He received the posthumous name Rudraloka.

25   Isanavarman II (925?-928) ឥសានវរ្ម័ន (ទី២)

Transliterated Name: Īsānavarmăn II
Posthumous Name: Paramarudraloka[1,p116]
Relationship: Younger son of Yasovarman I and younger brother of Harshavarman I
Religion: Shaivism
Purohita: Kumarasvamin (nephew of Vamasiva but he never received the title purohita)
Capital: Yasodharapura (Present-day Phnom Bakheng)
Genealogy: 20, 22, and 24

Isanavarman II succeeded his older brother, Harshavarman I, probably around 925. There are no records indicating the exact date of his accession but the inscription shows that he was still reigning in 925. Like his older brother, he was depicted and praised as beautiful with extraordinary talents. His reign was short-lived and seemed to last only until 928. He received the posthumous name Paramarudraloka.

26   Jayavarman IV (928-941) ជ័យវរ្ម័ន (ទី៤)

Transliterated Name: Jayăvarmăn IV
Other Name: Jayasimhavarman
Posthumous Name: Paramasivapada[1,p115; 6,p122]
Relationship: Son of Mahendradevi and Brother-in-law of Yasovarman I
Religion: Shaivism

Purohita: Isanamurti (never received the title of purohita)
Capital: Chok Gargyar (also called Lingapura) – located near Koh Ker[6,p117]
Genealogy: Figures 22 and 24

The relationships between Jayavarman IV and Rajendravarman II, which will be expounded in subsequent sections, are very ambiguous. Even great minds like Louis Finot, George Coedès, and many other scholars were confounded. Coedès attempted to solve this ambiguity by theorizing that Jayavarman IV and Rajendravarman II were half-brothers, having the same mother by different fathers.[6,p123; 73.1,pp135-137] With the information from Lawrence Palmer Briggs,[6] George Coedès,[1, 19, 32, 74] and Adhir Chakravarti,[43] I pieced together the lineage and relationship of Jayavarman IV with his ancestors and successors.

The inscription at Baksei Chamkrong (K.286, Stanza 35)[6,p123] mentioned that Jayavarman IV married one of the sisters of Yasovarman I.[6,p116,p123] Coedès mentioned that he founded a city called Chok Gargyar in 921,[19,pp98-99] located near Koh Ker and about 100 miles north east of Angkor, and then crowned himself king. According to Aymonier, Gargyar was an ancient name of the Koki tree which had been corrupted to Koh Ker. Officially, Koh Ker is spelled កោះកេរ្ដិ៍ in Khmer, which means heritage island. Because there are no islands in the area, I suggest that Koh Ker was possibly intended to mean "to dig and repair" which would have been written កាស់រិក in Khmer. The inscription of Prè Rup says that Jayadevi was the wife of Jayavarman IV.[6,p116] Jayavarman IV had a son with Jayadevi named Harshavarman II and according to the Prasat Bayang inscription he succeeded his father in 941.[6,p123] The Prasat Kok Chak inscription said that Jayavarman IV and Rajendravarman II "belonged to the same race,"[43,p62,p74] which implied they inherited their thrones through their maternal line. Harshavarman II and Rajendravarman II were historically believed to be brothers[43,p63] until the discovery of the Prè Rup inscription confirmed it otherwise because it said that Jayadevi and Mahendradevi were sisters. From the above inscriptions and information I interpreted that Jayavarman IV and Rajendravarman II were half-brothers, having the same mother but different fathers. Also, Jayavarman IV was the uncle of Rajendravarman II by his marriage to Jayadevi. Because Harshavarman II was the son of Jayavarman IV and Jayadevi, the younger sister of Mahendradevi, it would make him the cousin of Rajendravarman II.

The inscription of Vat Chakret dated 912, after the death of Yasovarman I, reveals some interesting clues. The inscription mentions of a prince named Sri Jayasinhavarman. Abel Bergaigne, the French epigraphist and founder of the Indianist school at the French university of Sorbonne, studied the Vat Chakret inscriptions (K.60 and K.61) and determined that the work was not commissioned by a king because it was sloppy with many incorrect spellings. His study seems to suggest that Prince Jayasinhavarman was in control of the country after the death of Yasovarman I and that the king's two sons were probably too young to rule the kingdom. It is believed that Jayasinhavarman was the name of Jayavarman IV before he rebelled against his nephew, Harshavarman I, in 921 to found his own city named Chok Gargyar, also known as Lingapura. Isanamurti performed the Devaraja ritual for Jayavarman IV but like his counterpart, Kumarasvamin who served Harshavarman I and Isanavarman II, never received the title of *purohita*. Jayavarman IV outlasted his two nephews.

The rebellion of Jayavarman IV against Harshavarman I to found his own capital and crown himself king is an interesting case that portrays the rule and tradition of the ambilateral descent system. The accession of Harshavarman I may conform to the patrilineal system but it violated the rule and tradition of the ambilateral descent system that prescribed the successor to the previous monarch should be the person of the same generation and of the highest ranking within the royal lineage. This rule is similar to a tribe electing the elder in the group as its leader and not necessarily having the son replacing the father after he had died to be the leader of the tribe. The inscription says indirectly that Jayavarman (IV) was married to Jayadevi, the younger sister of Yasovarman (I) and Mahendradevi. Supposedly, the three of them were the children of Indravarman I. Because Jayavarman IV was the brother-in-law of Yasovarman

I, he was therefore of the same generation as the king himself. Furthermore, the inscription says that Rajendravarman (II) was the elder brother of Jayavarman (IV) of the same mother, but not necessarily of the same father. The inscription also says that Mahendradevi, the elder sister of Jayadevi and Yasovarman (I), was the mother of Rajendravarman. Therefore, Jayavarman IV was at the same time the husband of Jayadevi and also her nephew. This kind of relationship was not unique in Khmer royalty. A lineage line can therefore be constructed based on the above information and also on previous information from the inscriptions. I propose that Jayavarman IV and Rajendravarman II had the same mother, Mahendradevi, but different fathers. The proposed genealogy is shown in Figure 20 with the complete genealogy shown in Figure 24. The lineage of Jayavarman IV from his maternal side places him in the same category as that of Yasovarman I. Therefore, Jayavarman IV would be ranked higher than Harshavarman I, his nephew and son of Yasovarman I. In the eyes of Jayavarman IV, he would consider Harshavarman I a usurper. His breakaway from Harshavarman I and Isanavarman II would be considered legitimate according to the rule and tradition of the ambilateral descent system.

The early death of Harshavarman I and Isanavarman II, raised the question among historians whether Jayavarman IV had anything to do with it. Jayavarman IV died in 941 and was given a posthumous name Paramasivapada.

27 Harshavarman II (941-944) ហសាវរ្ម័ន (ទី២)

Transliterated Name: Hasāvarmǎn II
Posthumous Name: Vrahmaloka (K.393)[1,p115; 6,p122; 75,p11]
Relationship: Son of Jayavarman IV and Jayadevi
Religion: Shaivism
Purohita: Atmasiva (nephew of Isanamurti)
Capital: Chok Gargyar
Genealogy: Figures 20, 22, and 24

Harshavarman II was the son of Jayavarman IV and Jayadevi, the younger sister of Yasovarman I.[6,p123] The inscription of Prasat Bayang dated 941 praises both Harshavarman II and his father Jayavarman IV. It also indicates that Harshavarman II succeeded his father in 941. It seems that Atmasiva, the nephew of Isanamurti, was awarded the position of *purohita* that his uncle never received. The accession of Harshavarman II violated the rule and tradition of the ambilateral descent system. The king had a short reign. He died in 944 and received the posthumous name of Vrahmaloka. The inscription of the Nom Van temple (K.393) of present-day Nakhon Ratchasima in Thailand mentions the posthumous name and title of Harshavarman II as *Kāla vrah samtacc nai vrahmaloka*.[75,p11] The proposed genealogy of the Khmer kings during the Angkor period from Jayavarman II to Harshavarman II is shown in Figure 20 with the complete genealogy shown in Figure 24.

28 Rajendravarman II (944-968) រាជិន្ទ្រាវរ្ម័ន (ទី២)

Transliterated Name: Rājindrāvarmǎn II
Posthumous Name: Shivaloka[6,p124,p133]
Relationship: Son of Mahendravarman and Mahendradevi; Half-Brother of Jayavarman IV; and Cousin of Harshavarman II; married to Narendradevi and Prana.
Religion: Shaivism
Purohita: Atmasiva (nephew of Isanamurti)
Guru: Yajnavaraha (grandson of Harshavarman I)
Capital: Moved from Chok Gargyar back to Yasodharapura[6,p124]
Genealogy: Figures 20, 21, 22, and 24

The inscription of Prè Rup (Stele 37) mentioned that Rajendravarman II was the son of Mahendravarman and Mahendradevi, the elder sister of Yasovarman I and Jayadevi, and that he acceded to the throne in 944.[6,p123; 73.2] Rajendravarman II's genealogy can be traced directly to Nripatindravarman of the revived Lunar Dynasty of Kaundinya-Soma of Baladitya-Aninditapura from his mother's side. From his father's side, it shows that Rajendravaman II's lineage could also be linked to the same revived Lunar Dynasty of Kaundinya-Soma of Baladitya-Aninditapura but from a different route. Some historians said that because Mahendradevi was the elder sister of Jayadevi, therefore her husband Mahendravarman should have been the next in line to succeed Yasovarman I instead of Jayavarman IV. Neither Mahendravarman nor Rajendravarman II seemed to contest the reigns of Jayavarman IV and his son Harshavarman II. The inscription of Prè Rup mentions that Rajendravarman II had made a sacrifice,[43,p63] probably to avoid a civil war. If the matrilineal rule were applied for the line of succession, Mahendravarman would be ranked ahead of Jayavarman IV because his wife Mahendradevi was the elder sister of Jayadevi (the wife of Jayavarman IV). If the ambilateral descent system were applied, Mahendravarman who was of the same generation as Yasovarman I would rank higher than Jayavarman IV for one reason; but for another reason, Jayavarman IV who was the son of Mahendradevi (with a different husband) would make him the stepson of Mahendravarman. However, a case could be made for Jayavarman IV succeeding Yasovarman I because he was not only the son of Mahendradevi but also the husband of Jayadevi, both the sisters of Yasovarman I.

Rajendravarman II's accession to the throne seemed to encounter some challenges, possibly from Harshavarman I's son-in-law, Damodara. On the other hand, Damodara's eldest son Yajnavaraha played a bigger role during the last year of Rajendravarman II's reign. He founded the temple called Tribhuvanamahesvara located at Banteay Srei. The inscription calls him *Vrah Guru* (the highest rank accorded to a teacher in the service of the king). Atmasiva continued to serve the new king in the same position as *purohita*.

As soon as he ascended the throne, Rajendravarman II moved the capital from Chok Gargyar (Koh Ker) back to Yasodharapura. It is my conjecture that the reason Rajendravarman II moved his capital from Chok Gargyar back to Yasodharapura was probably his way to infer that he did not inherit the throne through his half-brother (of the same mother), Jayavarman IV, but rather through his maternal side that had a direct lineage to Yasovarman I and Indravarman I. Because he was an admirer of Yasovarman I, Rajendravarman II's decision to move his capital back to Yasodharapura was also his way to pay homage to his uncle. After he returned to Yasodharapura, he started to restore the capital to its glory day with decorations of gold and precious stones.[6,p124; 7,p106]

In 960, Rajendravarman II waged a war with Champa and destroyed its capital. The Cham inscription of Po Nagar (present-day Nha Trang in Vietnam) says that after the invasion of Champa, the Khmer took the golden statue of the Hindu goddess Bhagavati from the temple of Po Nagar to Kambuja.[6,p126] The temple was erected to commemorate Lady Yan Po Nagar, the founder of the Cham kingdom, who came to be identified by later Cham generation as Bhagavati.

An observation can be made that Jayavarman IV applied the patrilineal rule for the accession of his son. If the ambilateral descent system were applied, Rajendravarman II would have been the next king in line after Jayavarman IV because he would be considered of the same generation as Jayavarman IV and would have ranked ahead of Harshavarman II, the son of Jayavarman IV. Because Harshavarman II's reign was short, a case could be made of the possibility of foul play which paved the way for Rajendravarman II early accession to the throne.

It was under his reign that the name of Yasodharapura was mentioned for the first time. To commemorate the work that Yasovarman I had started, Rajendravarman II resumed the building of the Preah Vihear temple. He completed the Court II except for the library section.[6,p130] He was assassinated in 968, on the same year that Banteay Srei (Female Citadel) was consecrated. He received the posthumous name of Sivaloka.

29   Jayavarman V (968-1001) ជ័យវរ្ម័ន (ទី៥)

Transliterated Name: Jayăvarmăn V
Posthumous Name: Paramaviraloka
Relationship: Son of Rajendravarman II and Narendradevi[6,p134]
Religion: Shaivism
Purohita: Atmasiva (nephew of Isanamurti); Sivacarya succeeded his grand uncle Atmasiva
Guru: Yajnavaraha (grandson of Harshavarman I)
Capital: Yasodharapura (Present-day Phnom Bakheng)
Genealogy: Figures 21 and 24

When Jayavarman V succeeded his father in 968 he was still very young. The inscription mentions that he completed his study under the tutelage of *Vrah Guru* in 974, six years after he became king, thus implying he was probably still a teenager when he acceded to the throne. *Vrah Guru* is believed to be Yajnavaraha, the grandson of Harshavarman I. Atmasiva continued to serve Jayavarman V in the same capacity (*purohita*) as he had done for Jayendravarman II. The hereditary rights of the sacerdotal families for *purohita, hotar, and guru* kept on growing. Those families became more and more influential in the affairs of the state. Sivacarya succeeded Atmasiva, his grand uncle, as *purohita.* Jayavarman V married a princess who descended from Srutavarman of the Solar Dynasty of Kambu-Mera. Jayavarman V had a younger sister named Indralakshmi that he gave in marriage to a Brahman born in northern India on the banks of the Yamuna (the largest tributary river of the Ganges) named Divakarabhatta (Divakara). The marriage of Indralakshmi to the Brahman reinforced the tie that already existed between Kambuja and India. Divakarabhatta contributed to the constructions of many Shaivite monuments. Jayavarman V died in 1001 and did not leave any heirs to the throne. He received the posthumous name Paramaviraloka.

30   Udayadityavarman I (1001-1002) ឧទយាទិត្យាវរ្ម័ន (ទី១)

Transliterated Name: Udayādityāvarmăn I
Other Name: Jayayudhavarman
Relationship: Nephew of Rajapativarman I and Jayavarman V's wife[6,p144]
Religion: Shaivism
Purohita: Sivacarya (grandnephew of Atmasiva)
Capital: Yasodharapura (Present-day Phnom Bakheng)
Genealogy: Figures 21 and 24

Udayadityavarman I succeeded Jayavarman V in 1001. Sivacarya still performed his duty of *purohita.* Udayadityavarman I was the nephew of Jayavarman V's wife. Divakarabhatta, the husband of Indralakshmi — the younger sister of Jayavarman V — would have been the person to succeed Jayavarman V if the rule of matrilineal were upheld. The reason Divakarabhatta was not chosen to succeed Jayavarman V may be due to the fact he was not of the Angkorian royal bloodline. Udayadityavarman I was only connected to Jayavarman V through his aunt (Jayavarman V's wife), who was the younger sister of his mother. Considering the above lineage, the legitimacy of his reign is questionable. However, Udayadityavarman I's reign at Angkor lasted only a few months before he was overthrown by Jayaviravarman.

Fratricidal War and Ambiguous Origins

The legitimacy of Udayadityavarman I's accession to the throne was questionable. It may be for this reason that his reign was challenged, which caused his downfall. For Udayadityavarman I to lose his reign so soon after he had been king for only a few months suggests that he may not have much support among the officials and dignitaries in his kingdom. Trudy Jacobsen, in her book *Lost Goddesses: the denial of female power in Cambodia history,*[76,p52] mentions that Udayadityavarman I and Jayaviravarman were brothers.

Khmer inscriptions at a later date indicate that Suryavarman I became king of Angkor in 1002 but he was still not fully in control of the country because Jayaviravarman, his foe, was reigning at Ruluos until at least 1006. Finally, Suryavarman I ruled supreme in 1011 after he had put down all his enemies.[1,pp134-135]

The period between Udayadityavarman I and Suryavarman I is ambiguous because of some confusing and contradicting inscriptions describing the events that led to Suryavarman I as the uncontested ruler of Angkor. Adding to the ambiguity are the Chronicles of Chiang Mai, written in Pali, which further confounded historians of the events that took place in Kambuja in the 11th century.

The Khmer inscriptions of Preah Khan of Kampong Svay, Prasat Ampil, and Bos Preah Nang say that Suryavarman I acceded to the throne in 1002. However, the inscription of Tuol Prasat (Kompong Svay) says that Jayaviravarman also acceded to the throne in 1002. From 1002 to 1006, both Suryavarman I and Jayaviravarman issued inscriptions related to their reigns, but after 1007 only inscriptions from Suryavarman I could be found. Because two kings reigned in Angkor at the same time, this led scholars like Aymonier, Finot, and Leclère into believing that Jayaviravarman and Suryavarman I are the same person. If this were the case, then why would they use two different names in the inscriptions? Later scholars like Coedès debunked the theory that Jayaviravarman and Suryavarman I are the same person. Unlike Jayaviravarman who claimed to descent from the Solar Dynasty, Suryavarman I claimed his ancestry descended from the Lunar Dynasty. All inscriptions related to Jayaviravarman were only found in the Angkor vicinity while those of Suryavarman I, especially of the early years, were scattered from north-east to north-west of the country. The above evidence suggests that Jayaviravarman and Suryavarman I were antagonists. The Sdok Kak Thom and Preah Khan of Kampong Svay inscriptions which mentioned Suryavarman I waging a war and triumphing over his enemies further reinforced the belief that he was the enemy of Jayaviravarman. The inscription of Tep Pranam says that Suryavarman I was the ruler of the Angkor region in 1005 and that of Prasat Trapeang Run mentions Jayaviravarman as the king of the Roluos region in 1006. Taking all the above inscriptions into account, it seems that Jayaviravarman had toppled Udayadityavarman I in 1002 and reigned at Angkor. However, his reign at Angkor seems to be short-lived because soon after, on the same year, Suryavarman I fought and chased Jayaviravarman from Angkor. In his defeat, Jayaviravarman moved to Roluos and still waged a war against Suryavarman I, at least until 1006. After a hard fought war, Suryavarman I came out the victor and ruled as the "uncontested master" in 1011. Coedès mentioned that three kings were "reigning simultaneously" based on his study of *the Khmer epigraphy of the first ten years of the eleventh century.*[1,p134] He could not provide a clear relationship between those three kings, but he stated that they were foes. It is a certainty that Suryavarman I was fighting Jayaviravarman at least until 1006. What is unclear was what happened to Udayadityavarman I after he was defeated by Jayaviravarman in 1002. The above epigraphy seems to suggest that Udayadityavarman I may be still alive and may be the third king fighting a war, probably against Suryavarman I, because being the king of Angkor was the prize. This may explain why it took Suryavarman I until 1011 to subdue all his enemies because he had to fight a war on two fronts.

The Chronicles of Chiang Mai which was written five hundred years after the occurrence of the events must be used cautiously; only as a supporting and not as a leading document. Georges Coedès wisely cautioned against relying too heavily on the Chronicles of Chiang Mai for historical facts.[1,p137] Adhir Chakravarti even stated that the *Chamadevivamsa* of the Siam Annals is "the least trustworthy of all these texts."[43,p68] The chronicles were composed from the 15th to the 16th centuries in Pali in three parts:[1,p136] the *Chamadevivamsa* (early 15th century); the *Jinakalamali* (completed in 1516); and finally the *Mulasasana.* The following is the account mentioned in the *Chamadevivamsa* text:[1,p136]

A king of Haripunjaya (Lamphun) named Atrasataka (var. Trabaka, Baka) went to attack Lavo (Lopburi), where Ucch'itthachakkavatti (var. Ucch'itta-, Uchhitta-) reigned. At the moment when the two sovereigns were preparing for battle, a king of Siridhammanagara (Ligor) named Sujita (var. Jivaka, Vararaja) arrived off Lavo with a considerable army and fleet. Confronted by his third depredator, the two adversaries fled in the direction of Haripunjaya. Ucch'ittha arrived first, proclaimed himself king there, and married the wife of his adversary, who withdrew by boat to the south. Sujita, the king of Ligor, established himself as master at Lavo. At the end of three years, his successor, or perhaps his son, Kamboraja, went to attack Ucch'ittha again at Haripunjaya, but he was defeated and had to return to his capital.

Chakravarti, based on Coedès' study, mentioned that the above event could be corroborated in the *Song-Che* account that was recorded in 1001 by King To-siu-ki who reigned at Tan-lieou-mei (written as Tan-mei-lieou), a country from the Malay Peninsula. Coedès thinks that To-siu-ki could possibly be the Chinese transcription of Sujita — a variant of Jivaka — which is corrupted from its original name Javaka, thus denoting the Malay origin of the word. Furthermore, he suggested that Ucc'itthachakkavatti could be the Pali name attributing to Udayadityavarman I; that Sujita could be Jayaviravarman; and Kamboraja could be Suryavarman I. Chakravarti suggested that the Chronicles of Chiang Mai could be accepted if a correction on the story could be made by substituting Lavo (Lopburi) with Angkor, believing that the author of the Chronicles may have the two cities mixed up. Chakravarti interpreted that because Udayadityavarman I (Ucc'itthachakkavatti) was not the legitimate heir, King Atrasataka from Lamphun of the Môn Kingdom of Haripunjaya took the opportunity to challenge his reign by attacking him. While Atrasataka and Udayadityavarman I were preparing for war, the Ligor King Sujita from Siridhammanagara Kingdom (Tambralinga) of the Malay Peninsula arrived at Angkor with his army and his impressive military fleet. After seeing the new invader with such an overwhelming force, Atrasataka and Udayadityavarman I fled to Haripunjaya, but Udayadityavarman I arrived there first. He married Atrasataka's wife and declared himself king. Sujita took over Angkor and reigned under the name of Jayaviravarman. Kamboraja, that Coedès identified as Suryavarman I, succeeded his father Jayaviravarman three years later. Suryavarman I failed to defeat Udayadityavarman I at Haripunjaya.

The above *Chamadevivamsa* text from the Chronicles of Chiang Mai cannot be considered as factual events. Coedès made a poignant remark that the names of Sujita and Kamboraja are not repeated in the *Jinakalamali* and the *Mulasasana* texts, which rendered the account in the *Chamadevivamsa* suspect. Furthermore, the texts were written five hundred years after the events had supposedly occurred, which makes the account even less reliable. The *Chamadevivamsa* text seems to be an attempt by a later chronicler trying to reconstruct past historical events that were probably based on oral accounts. The chronicle seems to mirror some of the historical events depicted in the Khmer epigraphy of the 11th century, but had facts mixed up. If Lavo (Lopburi) were substituted for Angkor that Chakravarti had suggested, and then comparing the Khmer epigraphy with the *Chamadevivamsa* text, the results would yield the following account: 1) Jayaviravarman attacked Udayadityavarman I at Angkor vs. Atrasataka (of Haripunjaya) attacked Ucch'itthachakkavatti at Angkor; 2) Suryavarman I attacked Jayaviravarman at Angkor vs. Sujita (of Siridhammanagara/Tambralinga) attacked Atrasatak and Ucch'itthachakkavatti at Angkor; 3) Suryavarman I occupied Angkor and took the wife of his rival (Jayaviravarman) as his queen[43,p69] vs. Ucch'itthachakkavatti fled to Haripunjaya and married the wife of his adversary (Atrasataka); 4) Suryavarman I became king of Angkor vs. Sujita became king of Angkor; 5) Suryavarman I reigned for forty-eight years at Angkor vs. Sujita reigned for three years at Angkor; and 6) Udayadityavarman II succeeded Suryavarman I at Angkor vs. Kamboraja succeeded Sujita at Angkor. In summary, if Lavo were substituted for Angkor, Ucch'itthachakkavatti for Udayadityavarman I, Sujita for Jayaviravarman, and Kamboraja for Suryavarman I as suggested by Coedès and Chakravarti, the version of the Chiangmai Chronicle would turn out as follows:

A king of Haripunjaya (Lamphun) named Atrasataka (var. Trabaka, Baka) went to attack Angkor, where Udayadityavarman I reigned. At the moment when the two sovereigns were preparing for battle, a king of Siridhammanagara (Ligor) named Jayaviravarman arrived off Angkor with a considerable army and fleet. Confronted by his third depredator, the two adversaries fled in the direction of Haripunjaya. Udayadityavarman I arrived first, proclaimed himself king there, and married the wife of his adversary, who withdrew by boat to the south. Jayaviravarman, the king of Ligor, established himself as master at Angkor. At the end of three years, his successor, or perhaps his son, Suryavarman I, went to attack Udayadityavarman I again at Haripunjaya, but he was defeated and had to return to his capital.

As noted above, the story does not match with the historical events mentioned in the Khmer epigraphy. The Khmer epigraphy says that Suryavarman I married the wife of Jayaviravarman while the Chiang Mai Chronicle says that Udayadityavarman I married the wife of Atrasataka. The Khmer inscription says that Suryavarman I reigned supreme at Angkor while the Chronicle says that Jayaviravarman established himself as master at Angkor. The Khmer inscription mentions that Suryavarman I did not have any heirs while the chronicle says that Suryavarman I was the son of Jayaviravarman.

31 Jayaviravarman (1002-1002/1011) ជ័យវិរ្យវរ្ម័ន

Transliterated Name: Jayăviravarmăn
Other Name: Narapativiravarman
Relationship: Brother of Udayadityavarman I; married to Viralakshmi.
Religion: Shaivism
Purohita: Sivacarya (grandnephew of Atmasiva)
Guru: Yogisvarapandita (descendant of the sacerdotal family of Bhas-svamini)
Capital: Yasodharapura (Present-day Phnom Bakheng)
Genealogy: Figures 21 and 24

From the chronology of the events, based on the inscriptions, it seems that Jayaviravarman contested the legitimacy of Udayadityavarman I as soon as he acceded to the throne in 1001. A few months after the accession of Udayadityavarman I, Jayaviravarman overthrew the king and proclaimed himself king of Angkor in 1002. The origin of Jayaviravarman has remained a mystery for a long time. Previous historians were not able to determine the exact origin of Jayaviravarman. Even Coedès was not able to unlock this mystery. Briggs remained silent on this issue. Chakravarti gave the origin of Jayaviravarman, but he utterly failed on this subject. Not only was he wrong when he said that Jayaviravarman was the "Sujita/To-siu-ki who had come from Siridhammanagara (Ligor, Malay Peninsula),"[43,p69] but he ignored his own warning when he based his finding solely on the Pali texts of the *Camadevivamsa* that he said to be "the least trustworthy of all the texts." Finally, Trudy Jacobsen was able to demonstrate in her book, *Lost Goddesses: the denial of female power in Cambodia history*,[76,p52] that Jayaviravarman was in fact the older brother of Udayadityavarman I. The following is an extract of her analysis:

There is, therefore, an excellent reason for attributing the identity of Jayamahesvari to Mahendradevi ... We may go one step further and identify Jayamahesvari as the kanlong kamraten an Anve Tonlé ...
The tradition of immortalizing royal women from this family continued for the next two generations. In 979 Jayavarman V directed three dignitaries and an elite religious instructor to donate their land along the river to other elite persons so that they could establish villages and erect images of deities and members of their families. The persons whose images were erected were Rajapativarman, a general and brother-in-law of Jayavarman V; an unnamed ten kamraten

an, mother of Narapativiravarman and Jayayudhavarman, the commissioners of the images; and a ten Tvan, who was the mother of the ten Kamraten an, Rajapativarman, and Jayavarman V's wife. K. 356 mentions these people, but adds that Narapativiravarman was the elder brother of Udayadityavarman I (1001-1002). It seems clear that Jayayudhavarman was Udayadityavarman I. Following the end of Udayadityavarman I's reign, a king named Jayaviravarman appeared. He issued an inscription in the year of his accession asserting the rights of the kanlong kamraten an Anve Tonlé to a piece of land under dispute. Jayaviravarman was none other than Udayadityavarman I's elder brother, Narapativiravarman.

The overthrow of Udayadityavarman I by Jayaviravarman was therefore a fratricidal war. It seems that Jayaviravarman (Narapativiravarman) was jealous of his younger brother, Udayadityavarman I, for acceding to the throne ahead of him. This may explain the swiftness of Jayaviravarman's victory over Udayadityavarman I because the latter may not expect his own brother to betray him. Based on Jacobsen's finding, it seems that Jayayudhavarman was the birth name of Udayadityavarman I before he became king and Narapativiravarman was the birth name of Jayaviravarman before his accession to the throne. In summary, Jayayudhavarman succeeded Jayavarman V and reigned under the name of Udayadityavarman I. Soon after Udayadityavarman I's accession, Narapativiravarman overthrew his younger brother and reigned under the name of Jayaviravarman. It seems he took this name after he married Viralakshmi (the wealth and prosperity of Vira) because Jayaviravarman means "the victorious Vira protector". He may have married Viralakshmi to legitimize his reign because the inscription of Prasat Khna says that she was a relative of Harshavarman from her maternal side.

Jayaviravarman retained the *purohita* and other hereditary sacerdotal families who served under Udayadityavarman I. Jayaviravarman was able to reign at Angkor for a very short time before he himself was toppled by Suryavarman I in 1002. After his defeat, Jayaviravarman went to Roluos to establish his capital and continued to wage a battle against Suryavarman I for another eight years. He finally succumbed to Suryavarman I in 1010. The Prasat Ben inscription says that Sri Narapatindralakshmi was the queen and legal wife of Jayaviravarman.

32 Suryavarman I (1002-1050) សុរិយាវរ្ម័ន (ទី១)

Transliterated Name: Suriyāvarmăn I

Other Name: Sri Suryavarmadeva

Posthumous Name: Nirvanapada[1,p135]

Relationship: Son of Jivaka; married to Viralakshmi (Widow of Jayaviravarman; sister of Narapatindravarman; descendant of Harshavarman I and Isanavarman II).

Religion: Shaivism and then changed to Buddhism based on his posthumous name.

Purohita: Sivacarya; Sadasiva succeeded his uncle Sivacarya who passed away. However, Sadasiva was the last purohita from the family line of Sivakaivalya. Suryavarman I relieved Sadavisa from his purohita duty and offered him to marry the sister of Queen Viralakshmi with an accompanying title *kamsteng Sri Jayendrapandita.*

Guru: Yogisvarapandita (descendant of the sacerdotal family of Bhas-svamini)

Capital: Started at Yasodharapura (Present-day Phnom Bakheng), moved to Phimeanakas (outside the boundary of Yasodharapura), then settled at present site of Bayon.

Genealogy: Figures 20, 21, 22, and 24

Jayaviravarman's reign in 1002 at Angkor, after having toppled Udayadityavarman I, was very brief because the inscriptions say that Suryavarman I also reigned at Angkor in 1002. This seems to indicate that Suryavarman I attacked Jayaviravarman immediately after his defeat of Udayadityavarman I, and that it could even be a surprise attack because of how quickly he was able to defeat Jayaviravarman.

Jayaviravarman waged a war with Suryavarman I for eight more years, thus suggesting that he had a strong army, which gives even more credence to the 1002 surprise attack against his brother Udayadityavarman I. After an exhausting war, Suryavarman I finally defeated Jayaviravarman and became the uncontested ruler of Kambuja in 1011. Some other inscriptions confirmed only that Jayaviravarman reigned at Roluos until at least 1006. Suryavarman I's defeat of Jayaviravarman had been partly helped by people who favored Buddhism. The path to Buddhism had been eased by the policies and favoritism implemented by Rajendravarman II and Jayavarman V, even though both of them were Shaivites. Both kings were annoyed by the ever expanding control that the hereditary sacerdotal Shaivic families had on the country. To counterbalance their power, Rajendravarman II and Jayavarman V appointed people of Vishnuic and Buddhic backgrounds in positions of importance. It may be for this reason that Suryavarman I was very lenient to Buddhism, which the people of Buddhist faith returned the favors by supporting him.

Oath of Loyalty

To secure the loyalties from his ministers and all officials, Suryavarman I asked them to take the oath of allegiance to him. The oath, with a total of eight inscriptions, is engraved on the pillars of the Gopura at the entrance of the Royal Palace. It contains a long list of 4,000 names of dignitaries. The following is the content of the oath translated by Coedès and reported by Briggs:[6,p151]

> *In 933c [A.D. 1011], ... August-September ... This is the oath which, we, belonging to the body of tamvrac [lector] of the first (second, third, or fourth) category, swear, all, without exception, cutting our hands, offering our lives and our devotion gratefully, without fault, to H.M. Sri Suryavarmadeva, who has been in complete enjoyment of sovereignty since 924c [A.D. 1002], in the presence of the sacred fire, of the holy jewel, the Brahmans and the acaryas. We will not revere another king, we shall never be hostile (to our king), and will not be accomplices of any enemy, we will not try to harm him in any way. All actions which are the fruit of our thankful devotion to H.M. Sri Suryavarmadeva, we pledge ourselves to perform them. If there is war, we promise to fight and to risk life, with all our soul, in devotion towards our King. If there is no war and we die by suicide or sudden death, may we obtain the recompense of people devoted to their masters. If our existence remains at the service of His Majesty up to our death, we will perform our task with devotion to the King, whatever may be the time and circumstances of our death. If His Majesty orders us to go far away, to obtain information in any matter, we will try to learn the thing in detail and each of us to keep this promise in whatever concerns us. If all of us who are here in person do not keep this oath with regard to His Majesty, may He still reign long, we ask that He inflict on us royal punishment of all sorts. If we hide ourselves in order not to keep this oath strictly, may we be reborn in the thirty-second hell as long as the sun and the moon shall last. If we fulfill this promise without fault, may His Majesty give orders for the maintenance of the pious foundations of our country and for the sustenance of our families, because we are devoted to our master, His Majesty, Suryavarmadeva, who has enjoyed complete sovereignty since 924 saka (A.D. 1002); and may we obtain the recompense of people devoted to our masters, in this and the other world.*

Purported Evidence of Suryavarman I being of Malay Origin Not Credible

There is no concrete evidence showing that Suryavarman I was of Malay origin as reported by Leclère, Briggs, Chakravarti, Cady, and many other scholars. His Malay origin was solely based on the Chronicles of Chiang Mai that were written in the 15th to the 16th century and of the Song-Che account in 1011 from the country of the Malay Peninsula which I demonstrated earlier about their unreliabilities. Even Coedès who studied these texts very carefully did not endorse the truthfulness of these accounts. His suggestion about Kamboraja — mentioned in the chronicles as the successor or son of the Malay king named Sujita

— as Suryavarman I, was only a wild hypothesis. Coedès even made a comment that the chronicles could be imaginary.[1,p137] The confusion and erroneous origin of Suryavarman I may have been perpetrated by Leclère when he stated that Suryavarman I was Jayaviravarman[7,p109] and by Briggs when he said that Suryavarman I was "a son of the king of Tambralinga … named Sujitaraja,"[6,p159] which is a variant of Jivaka as indicated in the genealogy tree of Suryavarman I.[6,p156] Adhir Chakravarti and John Cady committed the same mistake by repeating that Suryavarman I was from Tambralinga, probably basing their findings on Leclère and Briggs.

As mentioned by Jacobsen, based on the epigraphy inscription, Suryavarman I courted Viralakshmi by offering her "a tiara, earrings, clothes of gold, and all sorts of finery, and he also offered a covered palanquin of gold" to win her heart. Furthermore, he offered her older brother to retain the family title of Narapatindravarman and accorded the title of Prince of Vanapura to her younger brother Bhuvanaditya. Suryavarman I intended to gain the hand of Viralakshmi in marriage to legitimize his reign because of her clear lineage to Harshavarman I and Isanavarman II, which went through Yasovarman I and all the way to Indravarman I.

The origin of Suryavarman I is not as well-defined as that of Viralakshmi. His claims depicted in the inscriptions of Takeo dated 1002, of Vat Thipdei B dated 1005, of Preah Vihea dated 1028, and of Prasat Khna dated 1041 are vague. The above mentioned inscriptions say that he came from the lineage of Indravarman I's maternal side and that his queen, Viralakshmi, included Harshavarman I and Isanavarman II.[6,p148] None of the inscriptions mention the parents of Suryavarman I. Various attempts to trace the ancestry of Suryavarman I had been made by previous scholars like Leclère, Coedès, Briggs, Chakravarti, and Jacobsen. I have gathered and pieced the collective works of the above mentioned scholars to come up with the genealogy of the Khmer Kings from Rajendravarman II to Suryavarman I, with the result shown in Figure 21. The proposed genealogy of Suryavarman I and Viralakshmi shown in Figure 22, traces their ancestries all the way to Indravarman I.

Sacerdotal Families in the Service of the King

The inscriptions of Sdok Kak Thom, Vat Thipadei B, and Ta Keo B indicate that Suryavarman I retained the services of the hereditary sacerdotal families and high functionary officials who had served Jayaviravarman. His *guru* was Yogisvarapandita. The Sdok Kak Thom inscription says that Sivacarya kept his *purohita* position but died in the early years of Suryavarman I's reign. Sivacarya's nephew named Sadasiva inherited the *purohita* position from the line of Sivakaivalya. However, Suryavarman I relieved Sadavisa from his *purohita* duty and offered him to marry the sister of Queen Viralakshmi with an accompanying title *kamsteng Sri Jayendrapandita*. Sri means luminous. Even though he gave up his *purohita* position, the king still retained him as his spiritual master. Sadavisa was the last *purohita* from the family line of Sivakaivalya that was founded under the reign of Jayavarman II. It seems the drastic move by Suryavarman I to divest the house of Sivakaivalya from the hereditary position of *purohita* was calculated. He probably felt that the house of Sivakaivalya was becoming too powerful as the sole decision maker to be invested with the right to perform the Deveraja ceremony, thus legitimizing the king's accession to the throne. Suryavarman I wanted to strip down the power that the house of Sivakaivalya had a hold of the monarchy. There were no reasons given in the inscriptions as to why Suryavarman I reformed the system for the function of *purohita*.

Preah Vihear

Evidence by the numerous inscriptions found west of the Great Lake (Tonlé Sap) indicates that Suryavarman I expanded his kingdom westward of Angkor. He occupied the lower Menam in the kingdom of Lavo (present-day Lopburi in Thailand) and seemed to have the Môn kingdom of Dvaravati under his subjugation. Suryavarman I is known for his passion for trying to improve on existing monuments by rebuilding and adding new sections, especially to those monuments located on top of mountains such as

Prasat Neak Buos, Vat Phu, and Preah Vihear. Suryavarman I was credited for the construction of Preah Vihear, but the temple of Court I/Gopura I was originally started by Yasovarman I with light material in dedication to Shiva. Rajendravarman II added the stone construction of Court II/Gopura II. Suryavarman I completed the temple, probably in 1026, by expanding it to include Court III/Gopura III, Gopura IV, and Gopura V. The temple is perched on the top of a triangular promontory of the Dangrek mountain range. The triangular promontory, with its tip pointing south, stretches 150 meters in length and expands to 160 meters at its base. At the tip of the promontory sits the sanctuary with its Court I and Gopura I at an elevation of 525 meters above the plain. An outline of Phnom Kulen, located approximately 100 kilometers southward, can be discerned on a clear day. Court II and Gopura II are adjacent to Court I. Leading to Court III and Gopura III is a causeway, including some steps, slowly steeping down with ten markers on each side and a rampant adorning with a seven-headed naga. After a few steps down leaving Court III, another causeway — called the Small Pavement — of 150 meters long with 35 markers on each side descends gradually to reach Gopura IV. On the north end of the gopura are four steps of stair going down to meet another causeway, called the Main Pavement. On the eastern side of the causeway is attached a stair leading to a large pond called Srah Song. The causeway, with 65 markers on each side and 244 meters in length, descends to connect with Gopura V. A 10-meter wide stair of 400 steps is attached on the east side to the Gopura V. Immediately on the north end of Gopura V, a steep stair descends to merge with a wide causeway that is adorned on each side by a big rampant naga with its tail and head raised up to meet another steep stairway. The end of the stairway leads to a large open area connecting to the plain. The graphical depiction of the temple of Preah Vihear sitting on the top of the promontory of Phnom Dangrek is shown in Figure 23.

Capitals under Suryavarman I
At the beginning of his reign, Suryavarman I used Yasodharapura as his capital. Afterward, he moved his capital to Phimeanakas (located within the enclosure of the future site of Angkor Thom), originally built by Jayavarman V, located just on the outskirt of the wall of Yasodharapura. Near the end of his reign, he built a new capital on the location where Bayon now stands (the monument temple was not built yet at this time). It was also suggested by Coedès that Suryavarman I may have built Preah Khan of Kampong Svay, also known by the local name as Prasat Bakan that contains the pyramid-temple Preah Damrei. Coedès suggested that this pyramid-temple could be the Hemasringgagiri. Preah Khan of Kampong Svay is located about 100 km east of Angkor in the Preah Vihear province. Suryavarman I is credited for the digging of West Baray, also known by its modern name *Baray Teuk Thla* (Reservoir of clear water), that is considered to be the largest reservoir with a dimension of 2.2 x 8.0 km. It is located immediately west of the future site of Angkor Thom. Suryavarman I's reign was marked by peace and prosperity. He died in 1050 and received the posthumous name of Nirvanapada. His posthumous name, which means host of nirvana, leaves no doubt of his Buddhist affiliation and tolerance toward Buddhism. He had a son named Viravardhana. Suryavarman I is considered as one of the greatest Khmer kings.

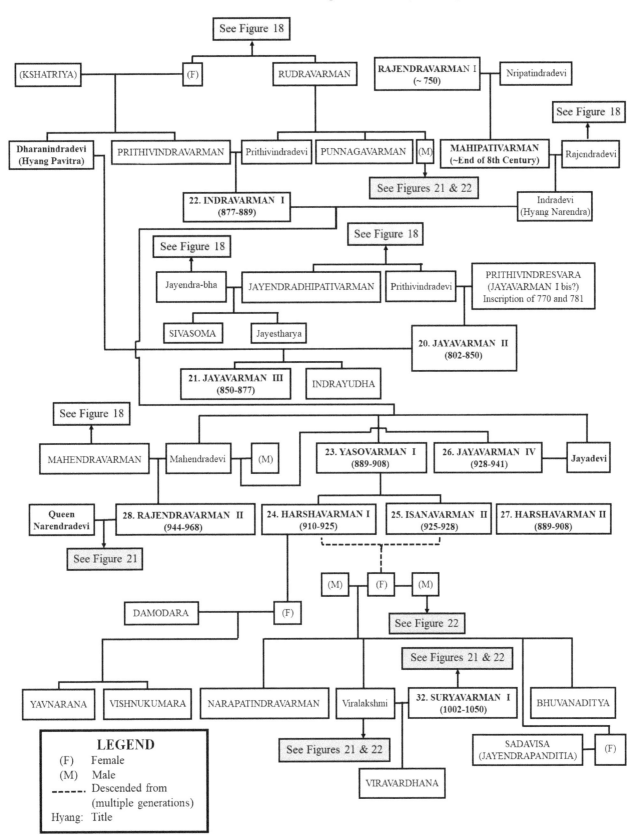

**Figure 20. Genealogy of the Khmer Kings during the First Angkor Dynasty
(From Jayavarman II (802) to Harshavarman III (1080) – Part 1)**

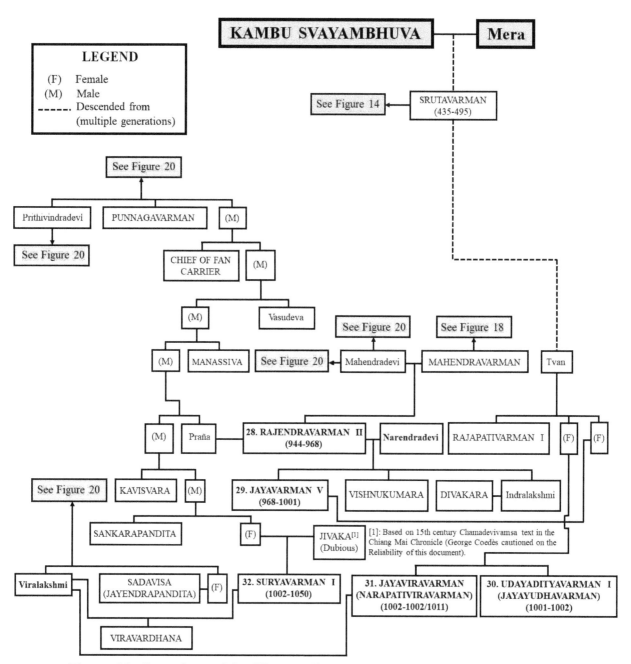

**Figure 21. Genealogy of the Khmer Kings during the First Angkor Dynasty
(From Jayavarman II (802) to Harshavarman III (1080) – Part 2)**

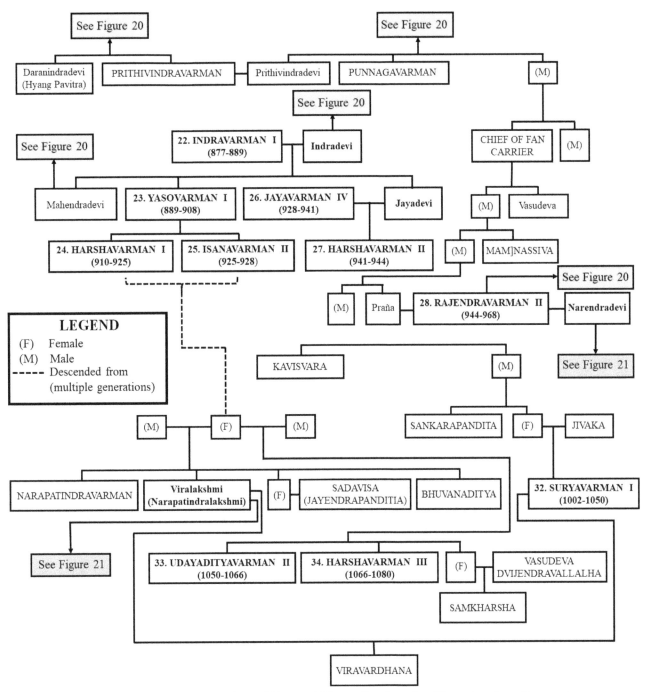

Figure 22. Genealogy of the Khmer Kings during the First Angkor Dynasty (From Jayavarman II (802) to Harshavarman III (1080) – Part 3)

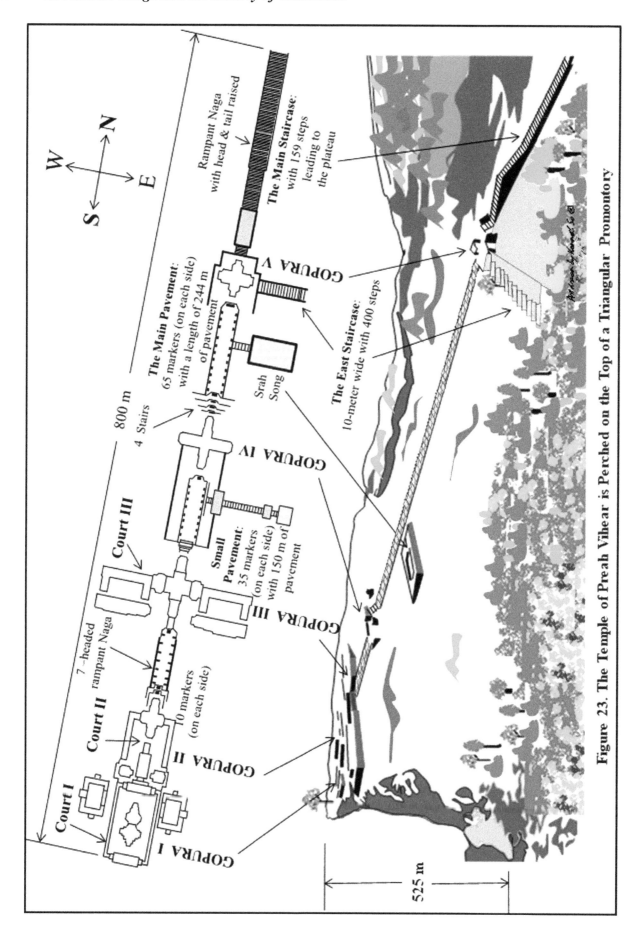

Figure 23. The Temple of Preah Vihear is Perched on the Top of a Triangular Promontory

33   Udayadityavarman II (1050-1066) ឧទយាទិត្យាវរ្ម័ន (ទី២)

Transliterated Name: Udayādityāvarmăn II
Capital: Yasodharapura
Relationship: Half-brother of Viralakshmi, the wife of Suryavarman I (based on Chakravarti)
Religion: Shaivism
Purohita: Sankarapandita (from a new family line of Saptadevakula that had a common ancestry
   with Harsharvarman III).
Guru: Vagindrapandita (died young; he was related to Sri Jayendrapandita, the brother-in-law of
   Suryavarman I); Sri Jayendrapandita who was the last purohita from the family of Sivakaivalya
   serving under Suryavarman I replaced Vagindrapandita.
Genealogy: Figures 22 and 24

There are no direct records describing the relationship between Udayadityavarman II and
Suryavarman I. The succession seemed to be smooth, thus indicating that the new king was close to his
predecessor. Maspero speculated that Suryavarman I was the grandfather or grand-uncle of
Udayadityavarman II. On the other hand, Coedès believed that Udayadityavarman II was the son of
Suryavarman I. Both men did not provide any evidence to support their beliefs, but they probably based
their assumptions on the smooth transition between the two monarchs and also on the support given by
the high officials for Udayadityavarman II's accession. According to the Prasat Ben inscription,[43;p77]
Suryavarman I and Narapatindralakshmi (Viralakshmi) had a son named Viravardhana. If they had a son,
why did Viravardhana not succeed his father?

Up to now, Maspero, Coedès, Briggs, and other historians were not able to explain the true relationship
between Suryavarman I and Udayadityavarman II. On the other hand, Chakravarti[43] was able to
demonstrate convincingly the probable relationship between these two kings, based on some indirect
evidence. The Prasat Preah Kset inscription dated 1067 mentions that Samkharsha, the son of
Dvijendravallalha, came from the region of Madhyadesa in India. The location of Madhyadesa was
somewhere in northern India near the Himalaya, corresponding probably to present-day Allahabad in Uttar
Pradesh, India. It must be pointed out that the Môn-Khmer people originally came from the "upper bend
of the Mekong River,"[16] probably from the region of Meghalaya that is near present-day Bangladesh and
south of the Himalaya. Furthermore, it says that Samkharsha was the nephew of Udayadityavarman II and
Viralakshmi. He was given a royal title of *Kamrateng Añ Aso Madhyadesa.* This inscription and other
inscriptions from different temples reveal enough information for one to draw the relationship of the above
royalties. The fact that Samkharsha was the nephew of both Udayadityavarman II and Viralakhsmi
indicated that these two persons were closely related either as siblings or cousins. The inscription mentions
that Viralakhsmi had only two brothers, Narapatindravarman and Bhuvanaditya, and an unnamed sister
who was married to Sadavisa. The other inscription mentions that Udayadityavarman II had a younger
brother named Harshavarman III and an unnamed sister who was married to Vasudeva Dvijendravalllha,
the father of Samkharsha. An assumption can then be made that Viralakshmi was probably half-sister of
Udayadityavarman II. Therefore, an argument can be made that Suryavarman I was the half-brother-in-
law of Udayadityavarman II. The proposed genealogy of Viralakshmi, Suryavarman I, Udayadityavarman
II, and Harshavarman III is shown in Figure 22. Based on the above finding, Chakravarti said the claim
by Udayadityavarman II "appears more like an attempt at *post facto* legitimization of what was really
usurpation of power by Udayadityavarman II, possibly by overthrowing Viravardhana, the son of
Suryavarman I." The above conclusion is farther from the truth if Udayadityavarman II were indeed the
half-brother-in-law of Suryavarman I. If the ambilateral descent system of succession were applied, then
Udayadityavarman II was in his right to succeed Suryavarman I instead of his son, Viravardhana. As a
half-brother-in-law, Uddayadityavarman II would be of the same generation as Suryavarman I. Because

he came from the same lineage as Viralakhsmi, Udayadityavarman II would rank higher than Viravadhana. Therefore, the accession of Udayadityavarman II was proper according to the ambilateral descent system. It may be the reason why his accession to the throne seemed to go smoothly.

According to the inscription, Udayadityavarman II was a person with great beauty. He was a seducer of women, but it also says that he was a great warrior and a king with wisdom. The Cham inscription dated 1056 suggested that his reign was a troubled one. It mentioned that a Cham prince named Yuvaraja Mahasenapati, son of King Jaya Paramesvarman, defeated the Khmers probably around 1050. They ravaged the city of Sambhupura. In the southern part of Kambuja, another rebellion took place in 1051 under the leadership of a man named Aravindhahrada probably with the support of the Chams. Udayadityavarman II sent several generals to quash the rebellion but they were unsuccessful until Senapati Sangrama, the great Khmer general whose ancestors served the Khmer kings since the time of Jayavarman II, led the army himself and went down to defeat the rebel Aravindhahrad who fled and took refuge in Champa.[6,pp168-169]

The inscription indicates that the position of *purohita* was given to a new family. Sankarapandita, from the family of Saptadevakula, became the new *purohita* under the reign of Udayadityavarman II. Two more important persons in the service of the king are mentioned in the inscription. The highest title to a non-royal family member and to a Brahman, *dhuli jeng vrah kamrateng añ,* was granted to Vagindrapandita who was related to *kamsteng Sri* Jayendrapandita (or Sadavisa, brother-in-law of Suryavarman I) from his paternal side. Vagindrapandita was the king's *guru. Dhuli* means dust and *jeng* means feet. *Vrah kamrateng añ* is a title that was equivalent to a Lord. Therefore, the title would translate approximately to "The dust of the feet of the Lord." Unfortunately, Vagindrapandita died young, in the early years of Udayadityavarman II's reign. *Kamsteng Sri* Jayendrapandita replaced Vagindrapandita, but with an upgraded professional title of *Vrah Guru* and a personal title of *vrah kamrateng añ Sri Jayendrapandita.* He seemed to also inherit Vagindrapandita's title of *dhuli jeng vrah kamrateng añ* according to the inscription of Sdok Kak Thom.[6,pp169-170] *Vrah Guru* parted his knowledge by teaching the king "sciences, grammar, law and all the other *sastras.*" The inscription at Sok Kak Thom discovered in 1052 in Bhadraniketana — currently located in present-day Thailand on the eastern side, close to Cambodia and about 20 km south of Ta Phaya in Sra Kaew province — reveals that the temple was built to commemorate the house of Sivakaivalya, the founder who performed the cult of Devaraja under the reign of Jayavarman II. It also commemorates Jayendrapandita by the presence of two lingas; the first linga called *kamrateng jagat Sivalinga* that Jayendrapantida founded himself, and the second linga called *Sarva Jayendraparamesvara* that Udayadityavarman II founded for his *Vrah Guru* who had taught him so much. Afterward, the house of Sivakaivalya disappeared and was never mentioned again in any Khmer inscriptions. When the temple of Baphuon was built in honor of the king, it was Sankarapandita that the king called on to be the architect. The temple was decorated with gold and it was an advanced concept in architecture compared to previous temples. Its pyramid-temple, known as the Baphuon style, served as the model for future temples to imitate.

Udayadityavarman II's total embrace of the cult of Devaraja with his Shaivite faith was in contrast to Suryavarman I who seemed to be only half-committed to the cult. It seemed that Udayadityavarman II was trying to reverse the influence of Buddhism that was gaining under the reign of Suryavarman I. The inscription of Prasat Preah Khset reveals that the revolt of Kamvau in 1067, which was crushed by Sangrama — he came from the line of family that served the kings faithfully since Jayavarman II — may have something to do with religion. Could it possibly be that the king's policy toward Buddhism was less tolerant than that under the reign of Suryavarman I? Because the inscription says that Udayadityavarman II was still living in 1067, it therefore suggests that the king may have abdicated in 1066 to allow his younger brother, Harshavarman III, to succeed him. Udayadityavarman II is credited for completing the construction of West Baray that Suryavarman I started. West Meboun sits on an island in the center of the Baray.

34   Harshavarman III (1066-1080) ហសាវរ្ម័ន (ទី៣)

Transliterated Name: Hasāvarmăn III
Posthumous Name: Sadasivapada[6,p178]
Relationship: Brother of Udayadityavarman II; Descendant of Harshavarman I and Isanavarman II.
Religion: Shaivism
Purohita: Sankarapandita (from a new family line of Saptadevakula that had a common ancestry
    with Harsharvarman III)
Capital: Yasodharapura
Genealogy: Figures 22 and 24

Harshavarman III succeeded his brother, Udayadityavarman II, in 1066 while he was still alive. The Prasat Preah Khset inscription seems to suggest that Udayadityavarman II abdicated in favor of his younger brother. The reason of his abdication was not given. The inscription never mentions whether Udayadityavarman II had any children. Sankarapandita continued to serve Harshavarman III in the same capacity as *purohita.* The inscription of Longvek indicates that Harshavarman III was a man of peace. The inscription of Palhal[6,p91; 77] traces the ancestry of Harsharvarman III to Punnagavarman — the founder of the house of Saptedevakula — who was the ancestor of the *purohita,* Sankarapandita, and uncle of Indravarman I. It may be for this reason that Suryavarman I made a move to relieve Sadasiva from his *purohita* position and let his half-brother-in-law, Harshavarman II, handle the situation of whom he wanted to take over the Chief Brahman position. Suryavarman I's tactical move was to break up the power of the sacerdotal house of Sivakaivalya and transfer it to the House of Saptedevakula which shared the same ancestry line with his wife Viralakshmi who was the half-sister of Udayadityavarman II and Harshavarman III. In addition to being the uncle of Indravarman I, Punnagavarman was also connected to the maternal side of Jayavarman II.

Harshavarman III wanted peace but never found it. It is not clear how he died, but it is almost a certainty that his reign ended with people revolting against his government, probably because of religious differences. According to Coedès, the reign of Harshavarman III ended in 1080. He received the posthumous name of Sadasivapada. The proposed genealogy of Harshavarman III is shown in Figure 22. The proposed genealogy of all the Khmer kings from Hun Tien-Liu Yeh (Kaundinya-Soma) to the end of the first dynasty in the Angkor period is shown in Figure 24.

THE SECOND ANGKOR/MAHIDHARAPURA DYNASTY (1080-1160)

Bloodline not Related to the Lunar or Solar Dynasty

The capital of Mahidharapura was located north of the Dangkrek Mountain in the upper Mun valley somewhere near present-day Phimai in Thailand. It was ruled by Hiranyavarman, a vassal king of Chenla from Kshitindragrama. The location of Kshitindragrama is undetermined but it is believed to be probably in the same vicinity of Phimai. Khmer inscriptions have mentioned the name of Mahidharapura many times in the past. Geographically, Mahidharapura which was located beyond the boundary of Water Chenla would suggest that their rulers were vassalages of the Land Chenla kings. History seems to stop mentioning Land Chenla as Water Chenla gained strength and expanded to absorb Land Chenla and its vassal states to become the Angkor Empire. The Angkor period from Jayavarman II to Harshavarman III was ruled by the royal bloodlines of Water Chenla. The Angkor period after Harshavarman III, starting from Jayavarman VI to Dharanindravarman II, was ruled by the Mahidharapura dynasty that has no connections with the bloodlines of previous Angkor kings.

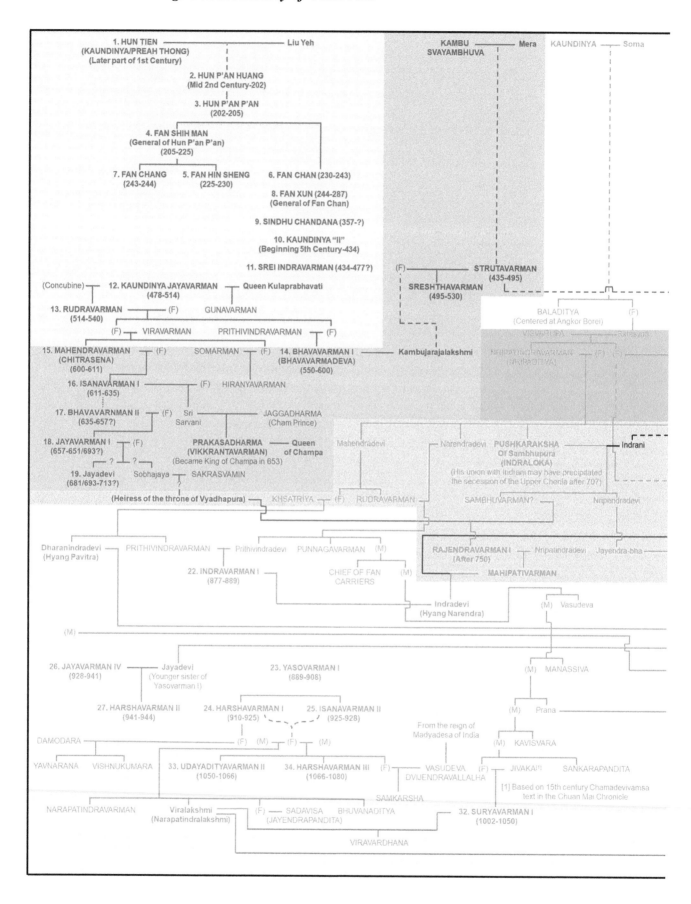

LEGEND

——— (Blue) Lunar Dynasty of Hun Tien-Liu Yeh (Kaundinya/Soma)
——— (Red) Solar Dynasty of Kambu-Mera
——— (Green) Lunar Dynasty of Baladitya/Aninditapuraformed during the reign of
 Isanavarman I of the Chenla Period
——— (Black) Solar Dynasty of Sambhapura formed during the Chenla Period
 and centered at Sambor/Kratie
——— (Brown) Descendants of the Indian sage Agastya from North India
 Funan Period (1st Century-540)
 Chenla Period prior to the breakup (540-707)
 Ancient Kingdom of Baladitya centered around Angkor Borei
 Revived ancient Kingdom of Baladitya after the death of
 Jayavarman I
 Water/Lower Chenla Period (707-802)
 Angkor Period (802-1431) – Figure shown up to 1080
 Agastya Bloodline
 Female (F) Male (M)
= = = = Descended from (multiple generation)

.... Undetermined Relationship

Figure 24.
Genealogy of Khmer Kings
for the Funan, Chenla, and
End of the First Angkor Dynasty
(Based on References 1, 6, 7, & 43)

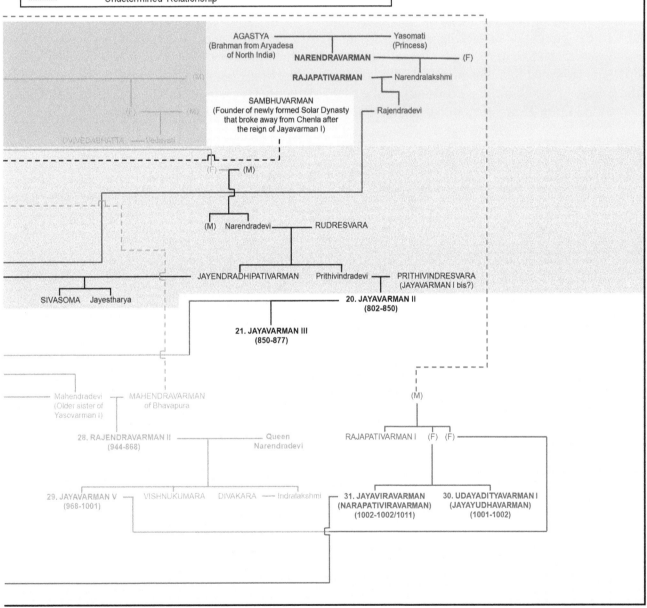

[Hiranyavarman ហិរនិយាវ័រ្ម័ន]

>Transliterated Name: Hiraniyāvarmăn II
>Capital: Mahidharapura (near present-day Phimai in Thailand)
>Genealogy: Figures 25, 26, and 48

Hiranyavarman was a vassal king of Chenla who ruled over Mahidharapura. To his credit, Hiranyavarman never claimed that he descended from the bloodline of Suryavaman I or any lines from the other Angkor kings. He had no relationship with the Lunar or Solar dynasties. His wife was named Hiranyalakshmi. Both Coedès[1] and Briggs[6] mentioned that they had at least four children, a daughter and three sons. They did not give the name of the daughter but they indicated Dharanindravarman I was the first son, followed by Jayavarman VI as the second son, and Yuvaraja as the youngest son. Chakravarti, after an extensive research, differed slightly on the order and genders of Hiranyavarman and Hiranyalakshmi's children.[43] He determined that they had six children. He placed Dharanindravarman I as the elder son, followed by Jayavarman VI, Yuvaraja, an unnamed daughter who was the grandmother of Suryavarman II, another unnamed daughter, and the youngest daughter named Dharanindralakshmi who was the grandmother of Dharanindravarman II. All the above three scholars also mentioned that Hiranyavarman had an unnamed wife who was the great grandmother of Suryavarman II. While Coedès and Briggs indicated that this unnamed wife had a son with Hiranyavarman, Chakravarti did not commit to the gender of the child. The genealogy of the Mahidharapura Dynasty according to Coedès and Briggs is shown in Figure 25 and the one according to Chakravarti is shown in Figure 26.

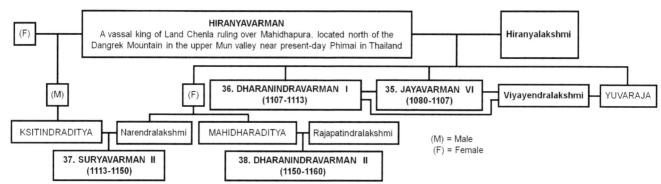

Figure 25. Genealogy of the Mahidharapura Dynasty (1107-1160)
Based on Coedès[1], Briggs[6], Leclère[7], and Chakravarti[43]

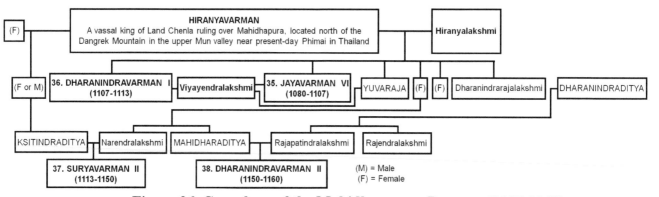

Figure 26. Genealogy of the Mahidharapura Dynasty (1107-1160)
Based on Adhir Chakravarti[43]

35   Jayavarman VI (1080-1107) ជ័យវរ្ម័ន (ទី៦)

Transliterated Name: Jayăvarmăn VI
Other Name: Jayavarmadeva[7,p179; 45,p285]
Relationship: Son of Hiranyavarman and Hiranyalakshmi; married to Viyajendralakshmi.
Religion: Vaishnavism (or Vishnuism)
Purohita: Bhupendrapandita I and Bhupendrapandita II?
Guru: Divikara (title of Divakarapandita).
Temples[78]: Phimai (in present-day Nakhon Ratchasima, Thailand)
Capital: Yasodharapura and then Mahidharapura
Posthumous Name: Paramakaivalyapada[6,p183]
Genealogy: Figures 25, 26, and 48

The end of the reign of Harshavarman III was a tumultuous one. The inscriptions do not provide the reason for the people's revolt against the government of Harshavarman III, but most scholars believed it was caused by religion. From my point of view it could possibly also be caused by the sacerdotal family of Sivakaivalya whose last *purohita*, Sadasiva, was permanently removed from his position by Suryavarman I. It was very likely that the descendants of Sadasiva were not happy with Suryavarman I's successor, Udayadityavarman II, whose first action after he became king was to award the powerful and influential hereditary position of *purohita* to Sankarapandita, whose lineage belonged to the family of Saptedevakula that traced its ancestry all the way back to Punnagavarman, where Harshavarman III and Udayadityavarman II shared a common bloodline. Considering the above internal struggle between the sacerdotal families of Sivakaivalya and Saptedevakula, it is therefore possible that the descendants of Sadasiva may have secretly played a role in the revolt.

The accession of Jayavarman VI could be a little bit due to providence, a little bit to luck, and a little bit to planning. The providence brought Jayavarman VI and a young, ambitious, and brilliant Brahman named Divakara together when they were young. The luck was caused by the turmoil at the end of the reign of Harshavarman III, thus providing a great opportunity for the young ambitious prince from Mahidharapura to take advantage of the unruly situation in Angkor. The end of Harshavarman III's reign left many claimants to the throne of Angkor. Jayavarman VI took advantage of the chaos to establish order. Without wasting time, Jayavarman VI led the pack and proclaimed himself, king in the north, probably within the region of his ancestral home. The inscription on the door pillar of the Prè Rup temple mentioned that Jayavarman VI became king in 1080. The Khmer and Sanskrit inscriptions on the door pillar of the Nom Van monastery (Ratnapura) dated 1082 (near present-day Korat) dealt about the royal order from King Jayavarman (VI) who instructed high civil servants, as well as religious dignitaries, to take great care of the monastery. He addressed his royal order specifically to the following high officials: 1) Lakshmindravarman, the author of the inscription; 2) Bhupendravarman, probably the author of two unpublished inscriptions and he was also believed to be the Brahman in charge of the "post of inspector of religious establishments and arbiter of disputes among the nobilities in religious as well as in civil matters," known also under the name of Bhupendrapandita; 3) Rajendravarman, a general who was in charge of the central army; 4) Kavindralaya, the Preceptor in charge of the monastic orders; and 5) the following *bhagavans* (chaplains/purohitas): Yogisvarapandita, Vagindrapandita, Sivagupta, and Nirvana.[6,p179] The suffix "varman" for the above high official names suggests that they were of the *shatrya* (royalty) class. To have such support from important families, Jayavarman VI must have planned well for the takeover of the Angkor throne. The task of assembling these supporters must have been given to Divakara, a brilliant tactician, who had remained very loyal to Jayavarman VI. It must be understood that the religious order was very important in ancient time. They formed the elite groups that helped the king rule his kingdom. Without the full support of these elites groups the king would not be able to run the country and maintain peace. Because Jayavarman VI came from the upper Mun valley near present-day Phimai, one of his priorities seemed to be building and restoring some of the temples in the region. Parmentier considered Phimai, Nom Van, and Phnom Rung (all located in present-day Thailand), that were built under the reign of Suryavarman I, to be temples having true Khmer architecture.

The coronation of Jayavarman VI was performed by Divikara, who had been elevated to the position of *Vrah Guru* with the accompanied title of Divakarapandita. The inscription of Ta Prohm, which was written a century later, seems to indicate that Jayavarman VI was crowned in Yasodharapura but later moved his residency back to Mahidharapura. The Phnom Sandak inscription mentions that Sri Vijayendralakshmi was to become the wife of Yuvaraja, the younger brother of Jayavarman VI. However, by 1096 Yuvaraja was dying and to preserve the love within the family, he handed his wife to Jayavarman VI and asked his brother to marry her.

Jayavarman VI was considered the founder of Vat Phu (located in present-day Laos), originally named *Vrah Thkval* (Preah Thkal means the Elevated God). He had the temple erected in 1102 to honor the god Sri Bhadresvara, one of the names for Shiva.[14,pp192-195] He did not live to see the completion of the temple because the construction was not finished until 1139, which was 37 years later during the reign of the future king Suryavarman II. Throughout his reign, Jayavarman VI was in constant struggle with Harshavarman III's claimants. He had a long reign and passed away in 1107, but before his death he asked his older brother, Dharanindravarman I, to take Vijayendralakshmi as his wife to preserve the harmony within the family. Scholars have been searching for the reasons that caused the crown prince and the two kings, all brothers, to marry Vijayendralakshmi successively after each one had died. The inscription of Phnom Sandak says that Vijayendralakshmi came from Amalakasthala, the same place of origin of the sacerdotal family of Bhas-svamini whose descendant included Yogisvarapandita, the *guru* of Suryavarman I. There is no revelation of her descending from any royal families. Therefore, the probable explanation may be that Suryavarman I considered marrying into a sacerdotal family and having the support of the clan to be more important during this trouble period than marrying into a royal family. The genealogy is shown in Figures 25, 26, and 48. The Ta Prohm inscriptions in Sanskrit and their translations in English below provide some specific information about Jayavarman VI:[45,p272,p285]

Çrīmadyaçodharapure dhigatādhirājyo raja jitārivisaro jayavarmmadevaḥ āvāridheḥ pratidiçan nicakhāna kīrttistambhān mahidharāpurābhijanāspado yaḥ.

tadbhāgimeyo vinayorjitaç çrīmahīdharāditya iti pratītaḥ çrīsūryyavarmmāvanipāla mātṛjaghan-yajo yo vijitārivarggaḥ.

Having obtained the supreme royalty in the holy city of Yasodharapura, and after having conquered the mass of the enemies, King Jayavarmadeva whose family lived at Mahidharapura planted pillars of glory in all directions, up to the sea.

The son of his sister, powerful by his conduct, named Sri Mahidharaditya, conqueror of the troops of his enemies, was the brother of the mother of King Sri Suryavarman.

36 Dharanindravarman I (1107-1113) ធរណីន្រ្ទវរ្ម័ន (ទី ៩)

Transliterated Name: Dharaṇindravarmăn I
Posthumous Name: Paramanishkalapada
Relationship: Son of Hiranyavarman and Hiranyalakshmi; Older brother of Jayavarman VI; married to Viyajendralakshmi, the widow of Jayavarman VI.
Religion: Vaishnavism (or Vishnuism)
Guru: Divikara (title of Divakarapandita)
Capital: Mahidharapura
Genealogy: Figures 25, 26, and 48

Jayavarman VI died before his older brother, Dharanindravarman I, by six years. When Dharanindravarman I succeeded Jayavarman VI in 1107 he was already of old age. The consecration was conducted by Jayavarman VI's *Vrah Guru,* Divakarapandita. The inscription indicates that Dharanindravarman I was reluctant to take over the throne as it said he was "without having desired royalty." He was a religious person who sought only peace. It was probably for this reason that presumably Jayavarman VI named his younger brother Yuvaraja to be the Crown Prince. The inscription mentions that Yuvaraja was still alive at least until 1096, but unfortunately he died before both of his brothers. Before Jayavarman VI died, he gave away his wife, Vijayendralakshmi, to his older brother. Both, Dharanindravarman I and Vijayendralakhmi must have been of old age by then. The king reigned for six years until he was overthrown by his maternal grandnephew, Suryavarman II, in 1113. The inscription of Prasat Chrung mentions only that Dharanindravarman I was defeated. The other inscription that mentions of Suryavarman II killing his enemy king did not name the king. Therefore, no definitive conclusion can be made that Dharanindravarman I's died by the hand of his own grandnephew. He could have simply died of old age after Suryavarman II had defeated him. After his death, Dharanindravarman I was given a posthumous name of Paramanishkalapada. The genealogy is shown in Figures 25, 26, and 48.

The Great King

37   Suryavarman II (1113-1150) សុរិយាវរ្ម័ន (ទី២)

Transliterated Name: Suriyāvarmăn II
Posthumous Name: Paramavishnuloka
Relationship: Son of Ksitindraditya and Narendralakshmi; Great-grandson of Hiranyavarman, the king of Land Chenla ruling over Mahidharapura and progenitor of the new dynasty; Grandnephew of Jayavarman VI and Dharanindravarman I
Religion: Vaishnavism (Vishnuism)
Guru: Divikara (title of Divikarapandita)
Temples:[78] Angkor Wat, Thommanon, (early 12th century), Banteay Samrè (1st half of 12th century), Phnom Rung (in present-day Buriram, Thailand), Boeung Mealea (Garland Pong, mid-12th century), Chao Say Tevoda (end of Suryavarman's reign)
Capital: Yasodharapura
Genealogy: Figures 25, 26, and 48

Suryavarman II gained the throne of Angkor through force by defeating his maternal great-uncle, the feeble and peaceful Dharanindravarman I, and successor of Jayavarman VI. As mentioned earlier, Jayavarman VI and Dharanindravarman I did not find peace during their reigns. They constantly had to do battles with the descendants of Harshavarman III. It may be for this reason that Jayavarman VI remained at Yasodharapura only briefly before moving back to Mahidharapura, the hometown of his ancestors, after he had defeated Harshavarman III. It was only after getting rid of Dharanindravarman I that Suryavarman II went on to defeat the successor of Harshavarman III. Coedès who found the name of Nripatindravarman on the unfinished inscription of Prè Rup believed that this person may be the successor of Harshavarman III.[6,p187,note8] According to Adhir Chakravarti, Harshavarman III's successor was his son whom he designated as Harshavarman IV, the father of Jayarajacudamani.[43,p88] If Chakravarti were correct, then Nripatindravarman and Harshavarman IV could be the same person.

Even though Suryavarman II was known as a warlike king, the inscriptions during his reign seem to be relatively mute on any of his battles against the neighbors, except for some scenes on the Angkor Wat bas-reliefs showing him leading his troops into battle. The battles that took place against the Chams and Dai Viets were found on the Cham inscription of My Son and from the Vietnamese documents. The Khmer inscriptions of Suryavaman II's exploits pertain mostly to previous Khmer Angkor kings.

Prior to him becoming king, Suryavarman II seemed to lament his family serving two masters; suggesting in this case that one of them was Dharanindravarman I and the other probably Nripatindravarman. Being young and ambitious, Suryavarman II decided to get rid of his two masters. The battles of Suryavarman II over Dharanindravarman I and his success in unifying the country were translated by Coedès from the inscriptions of Prasat Chrung and Vat Phu. The inscription of Prasat Chrung describes the quick battle that Suryavarman II delivered over Dharanindravarman I: "After a battle that lasted one day, King Sri Dharanindravarman was stripped of his defenseless kingdom by Sri Suryavarman." The inscription of Vat Phu mentions that Suryavarman II became king by unifying the two kingdoms.

The inscription of Ban Theat probably describes the killing of Nripatindravarman because it mentioned the person that Suryavarman II had killed as his enemy.[1,p159; 6,p187] It would seem unlikely that Suryavarman II would have called his great-uncle, Dharanindravarman I, his enemy; especially, by the violent way he slew him like an animal. As the successor of Harshavarman III, Nripatindravarman was assumed to be also practicing Shaivism which was the competing religion to Vaishnavism that was practiced by Suryavarman II. The name of Suryavarman II's enemy king was not mentioned, but it was probably meant for Harshavarman III's successor, believed to be his son named Nripindravarman[6,p187,note8] who was also believed to be Harshavarman IV according to Chakravarti.[43,p88] The following was the translation of the Ban Theat inscription by Finot:[1,p159,note80]

> *Releasing the ocean of his armies on the field of combat, he [Suryavarman II] gave terrible battle; leaping on the head of the elephant of the enemy king, he slew him, just as Garuda swooping down from the top of a mountain kills a serpent.*

Suryavarman II became king in 1113 after he had unified the kingdom, but his coronation did not take place until six years later.[1,p187] The ceremony was performed by *Vrah Guru* Divakarapandita, who by now was an old man. Cambodia which had interrupted its diplomatic relations with China since the time of Jayavarman II decided to renew its relationship with the Sung Dynasty by sending its ambassadors to China three years after Suryavarman II became king. Four years later, in 1120, Suryavarman II himself went to China to establish a personal relationship with the Chinese Emperor. Scholars have been able to reconstruct the early history of Cambodia because of the diplomatic relations that Funan and Chenla had with China, which the Chinese envoys had carefully recorded in the Chinese Imperial annals. The interruption of the diplomatic relations with China during the Angkor period left a big void in Cambodia history. Fortunately, this void was filled up by the abundant inscriptions produced by the Angkor kings, which enabled scholars to continue writing the history of Cambodia uninterrupted. Ironically, the resumption of the diplomatic relations with China coincided with fewer inscriptions produced by the Khmer kings. In 1317, the celebrated Chinese writer, Ma Duanlin (馬端臨), wrote the following account on the resumption of the diplomatic relations between China and Cambodia:[6,p189; 79,pp485-488]

> *Under the Sung dynasty, at the twelfth moon of the sixteenth year ching-ho (A.D. 1116), the king of Chenla sent as ambassadors, two great dignitaries of the kingdom. ... They came with a suite of 14 persons. They were given court clothes and then ... [one of the ambassadors] said to the Emperor: "From afar, the nations of the south and west have their regards fixed on the changes of fortune which operate on the fate of the peoples by the sacred institutions of the Empire. Scarcely have we arrived to contemplate anear your glory than we are already filled with your benefits. Although we have yet not been able to prove our great attachment nor demonstrate our gratitude, we solicit permission to appear at the Imperial disposition with the clothes you have given us." The Emperor gave them all they asked and ordered that all the details of their reception should be recorded in the official annals. The following year (1117), at the third moon, these foreigners took*

their leave and returned to Chenla. The second year suan-ho (1120), new envoys of the same country arrived again. Their king received investiture with honors equal to those accorded to the king of Chen-Ching [Champa]. The third year kien-yuen (1128), the Emperor conferred high dignities on the king of Chenla ..., who was recognized great vassal of the Empire. Some difficulties relative to the affairs of commerce were then examined and regulated (1136-1147).

Suryavarman II was a great builder of monuments, a religious reformer, and also a great warrior. However, from the Cham inscriptions and Vietnamese documents it does not seem that he was such a great war tactician. Cambodia had seen the greatest expansion of its territory under the leadership of Suryavarman II, but it came at a great price. The moment he consolidated his power in Cambodia, Suryavarman II went on to fight wars with Champa and with the relatively new but well-disciplined kingdom of Dai Viet, that had gained its independence from China in 939.[1,p159-160] From 1123 to 1124 Suryavarman II constantly provoked Champa. He led an unsuccessful war against Dai Viet in 1128 even though he had 20,000 men under his command. Unfazed by the unsuccessful attempt to invade Nghe-an (north central coast of present-day Vietnam), Suryavarman II assembled a fleet of 700 vessels strong to attack Thanh-hoa (south of present-day Hanoi). He was able to get Champa to join him in the war against Dai Viet in 1132. Under the command of Duong Anh-nhe, the provinces of Nghe-an and Thanh-hoa joined forces to drive away the threatening armies of Cambodia and Champa. During that time, Champa was ruled by a weak king, Harivarman V (1113-1139), who would not dare standing up against the powerful Khmer king. Because he did not have a son, Harivarman V decided in 1133 to adopt a prince, who was born in 1106 and whose origin was not mentioned, as a Yuvaraja to be his heir. Near the end of the king's reign, the Yuvaraja started to exert more and more control on the policy of Champa, which drew the ire and jealousy of legitimate heirs. In 1136, the Yuvaraja who was acting on behalf of Harivarman V decided to switch his allegiance and sided with the Dai Viet king, Ly Than-tong. Suryavarman II continued to fight Dai Viet until 1138 without Champa's assistance. In 1139 the Yuvaraja succeeded Harivarman V and reigned under the name of Jaya Indravarman III. Suryavarman II had not forgotten about Jaya Indravarman III's un-cooperation during his war against Dai Viet in 1138. Because of that betrayal, Suryavarman II took his wrath on Jaya Indravarman III by invading Champa and seized its capital, Vijaya (Binh Dinh province in present-day Vietnam). After the Khmer invasion, Jaya Indravarman III had disappeared. He may have been killed by Suryavarman II. The event happened around 1145.

After the defeat of Champa, Rudravarman IV, who was the legitimate claimant to the throne, rallied his people and proclaimed himself king of Champa in Panduranga (south of Champa) in 1145. He died shortly afterward, in 1147. Sivanandana, who had been in exile since the reigns of Harivarman V and Jaya Indravarman III, succeeded his father, Rudravarman IV, under the name of Jaya Harivarman I. Immediately after Jaya Harivarman I became king, Suryavarman II sent a mixed army composed of Khmers and Chams to fight the new Champa king in 1148. The mixed Khmer army was under the command of the Khmer general Senapati Sankara. Jaya Harivarman I fought Senapati Sankara at Rajapura (Chakling in present-day Phan Rang in Vietnam). The mixed Khmer army was totally defeated in 1148. On his second campaign, Suryavarman II sent a stronger army to fight the Champa king at Virapura, but again the Khmer army was defeated. To show that he was still master of the Chams, Suryavarman II proclaimed his brother-in-law Harideva as the king of Champa at Vijaya. Jaya Harivarman I counteracted immediately by taking his troops north and got the upper hand by seizing Vijaya. He met Harideva head on at Mahisa and completely defeated the Khmer army in 1149. He killed Harideva and all his officers. It was a total victory for the Cham king and a crushing defeat for Suryavarman II, who for a while thought he was invincible. Jaya Harivarman I was consecrated king at Vijaya in 1149. He was considered one of the greatest Champa kings. Was the defeat of the Khmer army caused by the use of Cham recruits? Suryavarman II may have made a blunder by incorporating the Chams in the Khmer army. It would not be surprising that some of those Cham soldiers in the Khmer army would act as spies for Champa.

Suryavarman II did not learn his lesson even after the total defeat of the Khmer army by the weaker Cham forces. He seemed to love war because in 1150 he resumed his war against Dai Viet. The outcome of his campaign against Dai Viet proved this time to be even worse than the one he conducted earlier. Without consideration of the weather situation, Suryavarman II sent his forces against Dai Viet in the months of September and October, which was a rainy season. The Khmer forces were not only exhausted after having crossed the Wu-men Mountains to Dai Viet, but they also caught fever on their way to Nghe-an. They were so weak when they arrived at Nghe-an that they had to withdraw their troops and return to Cambodia without conducting any battles. It must be remembered that the above battle descriptions were written by the winners, which one could assume may have been embellished to a certain extent.

Coedès mentioned of other battles taken place in the west that were recorded in the chronicles of the upper Menam.[1,p161] According to Coedès, the battles may or may not take place during the reign of Suryavarman II because he considered the chronology of the events somewhat unreliable. However, it was a piece of historical data that is worth mentioning. The chronicles mentioned of the battles around 1150 between the Khmers of Lavo (also spelled Louvo and mentioned as Lo-ho in the Chinese chronicles located in present-day Lopburi in Thailand) and the Môns of Haripunjaya (present-day Lamphun in Thailand). When Suryavarman I came into power he exerted his control over Lavo and installed a vassal Khmer "king" or governor to run the place. The chronicles then mention that in 1150 a king by the name of Adityaraja, whose origin was unknown, came down to challenge the Khmers. This is probably where Coedès considered the unreliability of the chronology of the event. The reign of Suryavarman I occurred from 1002 to 1050. If the battle took place in 1150, it would fall under the reign of Suryavarman II. Either the chronicle had the two kings mixed up or the era mixed up by a century. The Khmers fought Adityaraja and chased him all the way to Haripunjaya, but were unable to dislodge him from the city. Finally the Khmers signed an agreement with Adityaraja with the settlement of a Khmer village named Kambojagama, located southeast of Haripunjaya. Because the agreement was not preapproved by the Khmer king, it became null and void. The Khmers had to conduct another campaign against Adityaraja, but this time it ended in failure.

History has shown Suryavarman II to be a great warrior, but the Cham inscriptions and the Annam documents seem to say otherwise. His campaigns against Champa and Dai Viet ended up in failures with the loss of a lot of lives. The campaign against Haripunjaya in the west, which may or may not be associated with Suryavarman II, also ended up in another failure. It may be for these reasons that no definitive war exploits by Suryavarman II were found on the Khmer inscriptions. Nevertheless, according to the *History of the Sung* by the Chinese, Suryavarman II was still able to preserve a large Khmer Empire during his reign. The Chinese history recorded the following:[1,p161-162]

> *Chenla (Cambodia) was bordered by the southern frontiers of Chan-ch'eng (Champa) in the north, by the sea to the east, by P'u-kan (the kingdom of Pagan) in the west, and by Chia-lo-his (Grahi, in the region of Chaiya and of the bay of Bandon on the east coast of the Malay Peninsula) in the south.*

As a builder, Suryavarman II had no equal except the future king Jayavarman VII. Suryavarman II is credited for the additions or constructions of the following temples: 1) Vrah Thkval (or Vat Phnom in Khmer, Vat Phu in Lao in present-day Laos); 2) Preah Pithu, located inside Angkor Thom; 3) Thommanon, located a short distance from Angkor Thom's Victory Gate (built at the beginning of the king's reign); 4) Chao Say Tevoda, located across the road from Thommanon (built towards the end of the king's reign); 5) Banteay Samrè, located near East Baray (architecture similar to Phimai); 6) Prasat Bakan (Preah Khan of Kampong Svay or Bakan Svay Rolay), located 100 km east of Angkor in the Preah Vihear province; and 7) Angkor Wat.

Preah Khan of Kampong Svay was an ancient city covering approximately five kilometers square. It was suggested by Coedès that this city may have been built by Suryavarman I before 1006 and that he used it as his capital during his early reign. It has a large baray (2,987 m by 518 m) that supplied water for the residents. The reservoir is presently dried. Preah Khan of Kampong Svay served as a royal residence for Suryavarman II and future king Jayavarman VII. Preah Khan of Kampong Svay produced a lot of beautiful Khmer arts, where the famous head of Jayavarman VII is now displayed at the National Museum in Phnom Penh. Fortunately or unfortunately, depending on one's point of view, many of those arts were taken by Louis Delaporte to France and are now displayed at the Musée Guimet in Paris.

Angkor Wat and its Bas-Reliefs

The greatest achievement by Suryavarman II was the construction of Angkor Wat (see Figure 27), which stands as a testimony to his genius. Angkor is a corruption of the Khmer word *Nokor* that was derived from the Sanskrit word *Nagara,* which means city or capital. Wat, which means temple in Khmer, also came from the Sanskrit word *Vatika*, which means hut or site of a house). Therefore, Angkor Wat means Temple City. Angkor Wat was not the original name of this great monument. It was a name given by French scholars who borrowed it from Gabriel Quiroga de San Antonio who had seen Angkor in 1604. He described it as "a temple with five towers," which he called "Angor [*sic*]."[80,p90]

There is a correlation between Vat Phu and Angkor Wat, both temples built and/or completed by Suryavarman II. According to Briggs, many scholars believe that the name *Vrah Prang* found at Vat Phu was attributed to Angkor Wat.[6,p194] The inscription of Vat Phu mentioned that the combination of the image of Shiva and Vishnu, known under the Angkor period as Sangkara-Narayana, was erected at Vrah Prang in 1122, which corresponded to the time when Angkor Wat was being built. Vrah Prang means Holy Tower or Holy Pyramid in Khmer. Vrah Prang may be the earliest name for Angkor Wat. Afterward, the name of Vrah Vishnuloka, which means "The Holy Abode of Vishnu," appeared on inscriptions. Scholars believe that this name pertains to Angkor Wat. I believe that the word "Angkor" may have come from the combination of the words "Ang Nokor," where "Ang" indicates "king" and "Nokor" indicates "city." Over the years, the words may have been combined to form "Angnokor" and then shortened to "Angkor."

Figure 27. View of Angkor Wat from the Main Entrance

The exact date for the construction of Angkor Wat is not known but it is believed it started soon after Suryavarman II became king and consolidated his power. It took approximately thirty two years to complete the temple. Divakarapandita who was the guru of Suryavarman II was elevated to the title of *Dhuli Jeng Vrah Guru* (it literally means the dust of the feet of the guru) between 1119 and 1121.[6,p188] It was the highest title accorded to a person not of royal bloodline. He was the third person to have received such a lofty title. The first title was granted to Vagindrapandita, the guru of King Udayadityavarman II; and the second one was granted to Sri Jayendrapandita who was Udayadityavarman II's purohita, but he had to abandon this title when he was awarded the royal title *vrah kamrateng añ* [*vrah kamrateng añ* could be translated as my Master, which was equivalent to My Lord] after marrying the younger sister of the king's wife. Suryavarman II put Divakarapandita to be in charge of the construction of Angkor Wat. Later in time Divakarapandita received another honor that was of a divine nature. It was the first time that a Khmer monarch ever accorded such a lofty honor to a living person. Unlike previous Khmer monuments that were dedicated to Shiva and faced east, Angkor Wat faced west. For a long time scholars have searched for the reasons of this phenomenon. The bas-reliefs of Angkor Wat are covered with scenes from the Mahabharata and Ramayana epic stories. In the Mahabharata, Krishna was the incarnation of Vishnu while in the Ramayana, Rama was the embodiment of Vishnu of a semi-devine nature. Because Angkor Wat was adorned with the battle scenes from the Mahabharata and Ramayana epic stories as well as from the Baghavata Purana texts, it can be safely said that the temple was built to honor Vishnu. Suryavarman II, himself, believed he was the reincarnation of Vishnu by having his image merged with Vishnu like that of Harihara, where Shiva and Vishnu merged into one body. The implication is clear. Shiva was no longer relevant because Suryavarman II replaced him and merged with Vishnu.

Angkor Wat was built in dedication to the "Preserver of the Universe," an epithet reserved for Vishnu. The floor plan of Angkor Wat and its galleries with the descriptions of the bas-reliefs is shown in Figure 28. The main entrance to Angkor Wat starts from the west side. The bas-reliefs cover all the four sides of the Angkor murals. They illustrate the scenes based on the Indian epic stories of the Ramayana and Mahabharata; of the Bhagavata Purana from the Indian sacred book; and of Suryavarman II's life as a monarch warrior. Thomas S. Maxwell stated in his book *Of Gods, Kings, and Men: The Reliefs of Angkor Wat*[81] that the bas-reliefs was laid out according to the sequence of the cosmic scale of the Hindu yuga periods, namely Kali (shortest period), Dvapara (twice the period of Kali), Treta (Three times the period of Kali), and Krita or Satya (the longest and four times the period of Kali). He said that the scenes depicted on the East Gallery would correspond to the Krita (Satya) yuga because it belonged to the adobe of the gods where lived Vishnu; the scenes on the North Gallery corresponded to the Treta yuga, which measured in cosmic scale because it still belonged to the adobe of the gods where Vishnu and his avatar Krishna battled out against demons; the scenes on West Gallery that depict battles between demons and the semi-devine humans such as Rama and Krishna belonged to the Dvapara yuga; and the final scenes on the South Gallery belonged to the mortals, which is the present-time where the world is in decadence. However, Maxwell said that the proper way to view the bas-reliefs was to start from the South Wing of the West Gallery and then move counterclockwise until one arrived at the North Wing of the West Gallery. The reason given by Maxwell to view the bas-reliefs this way is the following:[81,p13]

> *They were not intended to constitute a detailed exposition of some unchanging theological system — the element of permanent continuity is provided by the yuga time-frame that starts in the east — but they were intended to represent the declaration of faith and the mission statement of a powerful Vaishnava ruler who believed in war as his kshatriya duty, and in Vishnu as his warrior examplar. And it was to experience this personal statement concerning the king that the reliefs had to be read in a sequence starting in the west. The visitor to the temple in this case turned right in front of the main entrance, passing the depiction of Krishna, with whom the Kali Yuga – that is the present – begins, and then encounters the king and the theme of mortality along the south wall.*

On the Third Enclosureproviding the cosmic background to Suryavarman's deeds in the here and now.

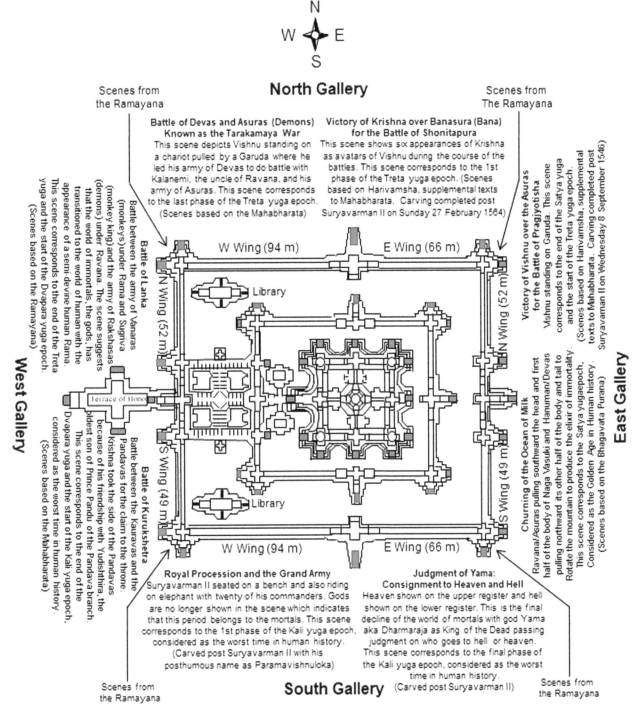

Figure 28. Floor Plan of Angkor Wat Bas-Reliefs Carved on the Third Enclosure

In my opinion, we would understand the story of the god and human relationship better if we were to view the bas-reliefs from the South Wing of the East Gallery and then going counter-clockwise until we reach the end of the East Wing of the South Gallery. The story has to start with the scene of the Churning of the Ocean of Milk where Vishnu and his avatars cooperated with the demons to produce amrita, the elixir of immortality. It was from this point forward that the world of conflicts developed between the gods and demons. This period was called the Krita or Satya yuga, which according to the Hindu was *the first age of truth* and considered as the "Golden Age" for humanity. As we progress through the bas-relief scenes, we start to slowly realize the imperfection of the world through the many wars conducted by Vishnu and his avatars against the demons. Vishnu realized that even with his mighty power he could not stop the force of evil because the cosmic power is greater than him as the world kept on decaying until it reached the Kali yuga, which according to the Hindu is the present time and it is the worst period in human history. However, at the end of the scenes of the bas-reliefs there is a salvation for good people as the Judge of the Dead, Yama aka Dharmaraja, is the final arbiter of who goes to hell and who goes to heaven. At the end of the Kali yuga, the four yuga cycles are repeated. It is for this reason that I prefer to start the viewing of the bas-reliefs from the South Wing of the East Gallery because it tells the story in a more coherent way. Viewing the scenes in this fashion would provide us a fuller appreciation of the genius of Divakarapandita. The depicted scenes of the bas-reliefs could not have been carved without a thorough understanding of the Ramayana, Mahabharata, and Bhagavata Purana stories. In this case, Divakarapandita had a great influence in the carving of the bas-reliefs.

Churning of the Ocean of Milk (East Gallery, South Wing)

The bas-relief is 49 meters long. The scene was based on the Bhagavata Purana sacred texts instead of that of the Mahabharata. In the Purana texts, Vishnu played a central role directing the churning of the ocean while in the Mahabharata it was Indra who was in charge with the occasional interferences from Vishnu and Brahma.

The scene depicts the cooperation between the *devas* (gods) and the *asuras* (inhabitants of the underworld, demons) to produce amrita, the elixir of immortality. Unable to extract the elixir on their own, the *asuras* requested Vishnu's help. On the advice of Vishnu, the *devas* formed an alliance with the *asuras* to extract amrita from the ocean.

The scene starts on the south side with a multi-headed Ravana (antagonist of Rama) holding the head of the *naga* Vasuki and his team of 92 *asuras* pulling the body of the *naga* in one direction (southward). In the center, a four-armed Vishnu stands on Mount Mandara directing the churning operation, with the giant tortoise Kurma (the second avatar of Vishnu) supporting the mountain on its back to prevent it from sinking. The body of the *naga* is coiled one loop around the mountain. On the north side, a team of 88 *devas* pull the other half of the body of the *naga* with Hanuman (monkey god) grabbing its tail to pull it in the opposite direction (northward). The back and forth pulling motions by the *devas* and *asuras* rotate Mount Mandara into producing amrita, the elixir of immortality. The rotation back and forth of Mount Mandara was so destructive that it disturbed the ocean floor which shred and killed fish and many animals living in the ocean as portrayed in the bas-relief. A carving of another *naga* is shown at the bottom of the bas-relief. In the Mahabharata this *naga* was called Ananta (meaning eternal/infinite), the brother of Vasuki. As Mount Mandara rotates, the movement creates the mountain to sink into the ocean and it requires the help of the giant tortoise to support the mountain on its back to make it stay afloat. Traditionally, the north side is viewed as belonging to heaven and the south side as belonging to hell or the underworld. Placing the *devas* on the north side and the *asuras* on the south side was within the traditional belief.

This bas-relief corresponds to the Krita or Satya yuga epoch, which was considered as the "Golden Age" period. As a background, Thomas S. Maxwell described the story of the Churning of Ocean of Milk from the Mahabharata, which the Purana texts subsequently modified, as follows:[81,pp20-24]

The epic formulates the story as follows. 1: The gods assemble on Mount Meru, axis of the worlds, to discuss ways and means of acquiring the amrita, so that they might become immortal. To assist them, Vishnu advises Brahma that both the gods and the demons together should churn the ocean, after all the precious stones and healing herbs of the natural world have been added to it to create the mixture – a kind of cosmic soup – from which amrita can be extracted. 2: But the gods are unequal to the task of uprooting Mandara, the mountain that is to serve them as the churning rod, so at the request of Vishnu and Brahma the Serpent King named Ananta ("Endless"), who lies at the very bottom of the world, performs this feat for them. 3: Gods and demons then ask the Turtle King, Akupara, and the king of gods, Indra, to provide the lower and upper supports for the mountain, and the ocean itself agrees to be churned on condition that it also receives a share of the amrita. 4: A second Serpent King, Vasuki, the brother of Ananta, is used as the rope to cause the mountain to revolve, the demons taking up positions at his head, the gods at his tail. 5: As they heave alternately on the serpent, both teams are covered with flowers shaken from the mountain. Fire and smoke emitted from the serpent's mouth in the course of the churning form storm clouds over the demons, but the ensuing downpour cools the gods, who are weakening. 6: The churning process is destructive: at the foot of the mountain, aquatic creatures in the ocean and in the underworld are destroyed by its violent rotation, while above, the creatures inhabiting its slopes perish as the whole mountain is engulfed in flame when the trees on its slopes fall and catch fire. 7: The juice of all the sap and molten gold flowing down from the burning mountain is charged with the power of the amrita which will change the gods into immortals, but as it enters the sea, it only turns the water into milk which, as the churning continues, becomes butter; there is still no sign of the drink of immortality. 8: At this, the exhausted gods protest to Brahma and declare that only with Vishnu's help can the amrita now be obtained. Accordingly, Vishnu confers the extra strength which the protagonists need to continue the churning. 9: As this proceeds with renewed vigour, the treasures at last begin to appear: the moon, the goddesses Lakshmi and Sura, the white horse called Uccaihsravas, the jewel named Kaustubha and, finally, the long-awaited amrita, contained in a pot held by Dhanvantari, the physician of the gods. 10: The demons struggle violently among themselves for their separate portions of the magical drink, but here Vishnu again intervenes, transforming himself into a deceptive female shape of such seductiveness that the bemused demons give up the amrita. Vishnu presents the potion thus won to the gods, who drink it.

Victory of Vishnu over the Asuras: Battle of Pragiyotisha (East Gallery, North Wing)

The bas-relief is 52 meters long. George Coedès who had studied this bas-relief in great details believed that the scene was based on the Harivamsha Purana, the supplemental texts of the Mahabharata due to the clue given by the fallen four demons thrown out of the elephants. These four demons that Coedès identified as Asuras Muru, Nisunda, Hayagriva, and Pancanada were the characters mentioned in the Harivamsha Purana texts. This bas-relief was carved under the reign of Ang Chan I and completed on Wednesday 8 September 1546 as indicated in the inscription[81,p178] and translated below by George Coedès,[81,p34] except as indicated in brackets which were the notes I added for clarification:

Inscription:

brah pāda mahāvisṇuloka thve bvuṃ dān srac nau phen byar luḥ thleṅ raja brah pāda stac brah rājaoṅkāra parmmarājādhirāja rāmādhipati parmmacakrabartt[i]raja pre brah mahīdhara nā rājasilpi punaḥ chalk phen niyāy anu...kumluṅ aṭasaka maminakṣatra buddhabāra purṇṇami bhadrapadda.

Translation:

His Majesty Mahavishnuloka [my note: posthumous name of Suryavaman II; also called Paramavishnuloka] had not yet completed two panels [my note: phen byar]; when His Majesty Brah Rajaonkara Paramarajadhiraja Ramadhipati Paramachakravartiraja [my note: Ang Chan I] ascended the throne, he charged Brah Mahidhara, of the royal artisans [my note: rājasilpi], with sculpting a narrative on the panels [my note: punaḥ chalk phen niyāy]... in the 8th Saka [my note: aṣṭasaka] year (of the decade) [my note: Ardaksak, 1467 Saka], year of the Horse [my note: maminakṣatra], Wednesday [my note: buddhabāra], full moon [my note: purṇṇami] of Bhadrapada [my note: September].

The panel shows a battle scene of soldiers marching in unison and the leaders of the armies riding on horses, lions, elephants, or on chariots pulled by horses or mythical animals. In one scene, it shows a four-armed Vishnu, incarnated as Krishna, standing on the shoulders of a *Garuda* (a mythological bird that is half human and half bird) with the *asuras* converging on both sides. Coedès believed this scene represents the Battle of Prāgiyotiṣa,[81,p34] believed to be the modern city Brahmaputra in Assam located in northeast of India.[81,p38] This scene is believed to have taken place at the end of Satya yuga and the start of the Treta yuga epoch.

It was reported that Ang Chan I noticed the incompletion of the two panels, namely the North Wing of the East Gallery and the East Wing of the North Gallery (to be discussed next), during his campaign fighting the Ayutthayan army of King Ramathibodi II in the Angkor region in 1525. After he had defeated the Ayutthayan army, Ang Chan I ordered his architects and sculptors to complete the work that had already been sketched on the two panels.[81,p41] Years later when Ang Chan I came back to Angkor to check on the work on the panels, it was said that he was surprised to discover Bayon that was hidden in the jungle since the fall of Angkor, which was about 200 years earlier.[81,p37]

Victory of Krishna over Banasura: Battle of Shonitapura (North Gallery, East Wing)

The bas-relief is 66 meters long. As mentioned previously, this section was believed to have already been sketched under the reign of Suryavarman II but left unfinished. This scene is a continuation of the previous panel that was carved on the North Wing of the East Gallery. Again it was based on Harivamsha Purana texts. The work was commissioned by Ang Chan I and completed on Sunday 27 February 1564 as indicated in the inscription[81,p178] and translated below by George Coedès,[81,p34] except as noted in brackets which were the notes I added for clarification:

Inscription:
vraḥ pāda mahāviṣṇuloka thve bvuṃ dān saṃrac nau phdāṅ byar thlen raja vraḥ pāda saṃtec vraḥ rājaoṅkāra parmmarājādhirāja ta parmmapavitra oy chlāk niyāy osā saṃrac nā luḥ ekacatva-raaṣṭapañcasaka kurnakṣatra pūrṇṇamī phalguṇa ādityabāra saṃrac nu rppyaṅ bhnāk tai byar mum ru vreṅ.

Translation:
His Majesty Mahavishnuloka had not yet completed two panels; when His Majesty Brah Rajaonkara Paramarajadhiraja Paramapavitra ascended the throne, he had a narrative sculpted [my note: oy chlāk niyāy]. One strove to finish it [my note: osā saṃrac] in 1-4-8-5 Saka [my note: eka-catvara-aṣṭa-pañca saka], year of the Pig, full moon of Phalguna, Sunday [my note: ādityabāra]. The two galleries and balustrades were solidly completed (?) as in the past.

The bas-relief depicts the Battle of Shonitapura between Krishna and Bana. There are six carvings of Krishna incarnated as Vishnu showing him some times with four arms and other times with eight arms. After witnessing Bana's rigorous meditations and serious devotion to learning, Shiva agreed to adopt Bana as his son and fulfill his desire to have 1,000 arms. Bana became an invincible warrior. His one-thousand arms made him so powerful that he defeated all his enemies which left him no opponents to fight against. The battle of Shonitapura started when Bana punished Aniruddha by tying him up magically with snakes because he dared courting his daughter Usha without his blessing. Krishna mounted a campaign to fight

Bana when he learned that his grandson Aniruddha had been punished in this horrible fashion. Shiva stepped in to defend his adopted son Bana when he heard that Krishna was leading his army to come to Shonitapura. The battle between the two great deities would be a disastrous for the world of Hinduism if it were allowed to happen. In turn, Brahma stepped in and told Shiva that he and Krishna were made from the same god and asked him to withdraw himself from the conflict. For his respect to Brahma, Shiva agreed not to interfere in the battle between Krishna and Bana. Even with his one-thousand arms Bana was no match against Krishna as he threw his serrated disk, the Sudarshana Chakra, which spun forcefully and severed all Bana's arms except four of them. With Bana defeated, Krishna freed Aniruddha from the magical snakes that bound him. The opening scene in the bas-relief shows the Garuda in anger because he was not able to cross the mighty flame that Bana set up to hold off his enemies from entering into Shonitapura. In another scene it shows Krishna standing on a pig, probably to symbolize that the carving was done in the year of the Pig. There are a couple of scenes showing an eight-armed Krishna standing on the shoulders of a *Garuda* fighting Bana and his army. In one scene Bana is shown with multiple arms, to represent the 1,000 arms cited in Harivamsha/ Mahabharata, standing on a chariot that is supposedly pulled by two mythical animals. It is in this scene that Bana was supposed to have his arms cut off by Krishna's flying disk; but the sculptor who followed the original sketch did not want to disturb anything and to show him maimed. Showing Bana with his one-thousand arms attached to his body was on one hand an aesthetic expression by the artist, but on the other hand it was to showcase the power that Bana possessed which in the end still succumbed to Krishna who was even more powerful. The scene at the end of the panel shows Krishna paying respect to Shiva by offering him flowers from his left three hands while retaining weapons in his right three hands. It was probably to symbolize that Krishna made a peace offering to Shiva but he was still very guarded and prepared to fight again because he had just cut off the arms of Bana. Shonitapura is believed to be located in present-day Bangladesh. This scene is believed to have taken place in the first phase of the Treta yuga epoch.

Vishnu and his Army of Devas Fighting against Kalanemi and his Army of Asuras: The Tarakamaya War (North Gallery, West Wing)

The bas-relief is 94 meters long. This scene is based on the Mahabharata. It depicts some of the most important gods in the Hindu mythology. Michael Freeman and Claude Jacques[72,p65] and Thomas S. Maxwell[81,p64] described them as follows,[72] where Lokapalas denote Guardians of the Directions of Space who helped Vishnu fight Kalanemi and his army of Asuras:

Kubera (Lokapala): God of Wealth and ruler of the north; riding on a Yaksha (located 27m from the start of the panel)

Agni (Lokapala): God of Fire and ruler of the south-east; riding in a chariot pulled by a rhinoceros (located at 33m)

Skanda: God of War and son of Shiva; riding on a peacock (located at 37m)

Indra (Lokapala): God of Vedic and ruler of the east; riding on the elephant Airavata (located at 44m)

Vishnu: One of the Supreme Trinity Gods in Hinduism (Brahma and Shiva are the other two gods); riding on Garuda (located at 54m)

Kalanemi: Depicted with multi-headed (a tower of seven visible heads stacked up in two rows of three, one face frontal ang two in profile, with one more at the apex; riding in a horse-drawn chariot (located at 60m)

Yama (Lokapala): Judge and King of the Dead who ruled the south; riding on a chariot pulled by black water-buffalos (located at 63m)

Shiva as Ishana (Lokapala): God of the north-east; riding in a chariot pulled by two bulls Nandi (located at 67m)

Brahma: One of the Supreme Trinity Gods in Hinduism; riding on hamsa, a mythological bird (located at 71m)

Surya (Locapala): The Sun God and ruler of the south-west; riding in a chariot pulled by horses (located at 76m)

Vayu (Locapala): God of the Winds and ruler of the north-east; riding in a chariot pulled by a horse (located between Surya and Varuna)

Varuna (Locapala): God of the Ocean and ruler of the west; riding on a 5-headed naga (located at 86m)

The positioning of the soldiers in the battle scenes indicates that the army of Kalanemi came from the west to fight the army of Vishnu that came from the east. The army of Vishnu and his Devas can be identified by the pointed helmets they wore on their heads and facing west while those of Kalanemi can be seen as wearing top-flatted helmets and facing east.

The bas-relief depicts the battle scene at the crucial moment of the Tarakamaya War where Kalanemi, riding in his drawned-horse chariot, charges through the carnage toward Vishnu who stands on the shoulders of his Garuda and ready to draw his arrows. The Tarakamaya War pitted the manipulator of space against the manipulator of Time. This scene is believed to have taken place in the second phase of the Treta yuga epoch. As a background of the war, Thomas S. Maxwell described it this way:[81,p64]

> *Hostilities opened with an awesome exchange of deceptive appearance between Vihnu and one of the Asura leaders named maya, both of whom were famed as Lords of Illusion (Mayapati, Mayeshvara). But the decisive phase of the battle, which is subject of the Angkor Wat relief, began when another leader of the demons, Kalanemi (Rim of the Wheel of Time), commanded the attack on Vishnu. As embodiment of the cutting edge of time (Kala, which also means Death), his strategy was to rob Vishnu of the dimension that he ruled, which was space – Vishnu is a Spacemaker (as Trivikrama) and the Pervader of All Space (Sarvadigvyapin) – and then move in to destroy him. This the demon sought to achieve by slaying the Lokapalas, Guardians of the Directions of Space, who were present on the battlefield in the form of gods fighting on Vishnu's side. In the Hindu scheme there are eight such Lokapalas, each of whom rules over one of the four cardinal or intermediate directions, and they are all represented in the army of Vishnu in the Angkor Wat relief.*

Battle of Lanka: Rama and Ravana (West Gallery, North Wing)

The bas-relief is 52 meters long. The scene is based on the Ramayana. Like in the previous panel, the craftsmanship is excellent. The scene depicts Rama and the Monkey King, Sugriva, leading the army of Vanaras (monkeys) into battle with Ravana, the king of Lanka, and his army of Rakshasas (demons) to rescue Sita, Rama's wife. Rama stands on the shoulders of Hanuman (Monkey God) pulling his bow and arrow as he was ready to strike on his enemy. The above scene depicts the second battle between Rama and Ravana. As told in the Ramayana, Rama had defeated Ravana once but he spared his life and let him go. Even though Ravana lost his first battle he still wanted to fight Rama again to revenge his son Indrajit after he had been killed by Rama's brother Lakshmana. It was based on this background that the bas-relief was told and sculpted. This time period was the transitional phase of the yuga epoch where the realm of the gods descends to earth in the form of the semi-devine figure of Rama. This scene is believed to have taken place at the end of the Treta yuga and the start of the Dvapara yuga epoch.

What makes the Ramayana story so endearing and enduring is the human nature of Rama. He has his foible like a human that people can identify with, but he also has an almost god-like strength that people aspire to have.

Battle of Kurukshetra (West Gallery, South Wing)

The bas-relief is 49 meters long. The scenes are based on the Mahabharata. They depict the battle between the two cousins, the Kauravas and the Pandavas, to claim the throne of Hastinapura of the Kuru Kingdom.

Dhritarashtra and his younger brother, Prince Pandu, descended from the Kuru King Shantanu. Pandu was chosen to succeed his father because Dhritarashtra, who was born blind, was disqualified to be king.

One day on a hunting trip Pandu fatally shot Rishi Kindama because he mistakenly took the sage and his wife as a deer while they were copulating in a forest. Because Pandu was not remorseful for his action, the dying sage put a spell on him. Kindama cursed Pandu to have the same fate as him, which was to have Pandu die the moment he had sexual intercourse with any of his wives. As a result of him not able to produce heirs, Pandu decided to abdicate the throne and sought refuge in the forest to atone for his sin and to live the life of non-sexual contact. However, he did not go to the forest alone as he was accompanied by his two wives, Kunti (daughter of Shurasena, a Yadava ruler of Mathura that is believed to be located in present-day Uttar Pradesh) and Madri (Princess of the Madra kingdom, believed to be located between Northeast Iran and Punjab-Haryana, India). Because Dhritarashtra could not be king, he acted as a regent during Pandu's absence from Hastinapura.

Pandu's curse provided an opportunity for the sage Durvasa to intervene in this tragic affair. As is told in the Mahabharata, Durvasa was born as a result of Shiva's raging argument with Brahma. Shiva carried his anger home and made life untenable for his wife Parvati to live with. As a result of his anger and frustration, he visited the wife of the sage Ati, Anasuya, and deposited his magical potion on her to produce a son; and as a result Durvasa was born. Durvasa came to Kunti's rescue by enabling her to produce three sons through the intervention of three different gods as follows: Yudhishthira (meaning "one who is steadfast even during war") by Yama, the God of Dharma/Righteousness; Bhima (meaning "of terrible might") by Vayu, the God of Winds; and Arjuna (meaning "of stainless deeds") by Indra, the God of Vedic. During their living in the forest, Kunti and Madri became very close. As a compassionate person, Kunti shared the good news with Madri on how she was able to conceive. With the same blessing, Madri produced a twin named Nakula (meaning "the charming one") and Sahadeva (meaning "equal to a thousand gods") by Ashvins, the God of Medecine. Forgetful of the curse as well as unable to control his urge, Pandu decided one day to have sexual intercourse with Madri. As expected, Pandu died. Felt with great remorse Madri committed Sati by immolating herself on her husband's funeral pyre. Kunti was left alone to raise all the five children by her own.

Dhritarashtra's wife, Gandhari, wanted to have 100 sons. Her wishes were granted by Vyasa (meaning the "Compiler"), the great sage who wrote the story of the Mahabharata. Duryodhana (meaning "unconquerable warrior") was Dhritarashtra and Gandhari's first born but he was younger than his cousin Yudhishthira, the son of Dhritarashtra's younger brother Pandu. During this time Dhritarashtra had not heard of the whereabouts of his brother until one day he found out that Kunti was alive with five sons. He invited them back home. Duryodhana who felt threatened by Yudhishthira as claimant to the throne because he was not only his senior but also the son of Pandu, the deceased king of the Kuru Kingdom, refused to acknowledge Yudhishthira as kin. However, due to pressure from the people Dhritarashtra bowed to the public opinion and recognized Yudhishthira as heir, but he divided the kingdom into two territories. Dhritarashtra kept half of the kingdom for his son Duryodhana to rule at Hastinapura; the other half of the kingdom was given to Yudhishthira to rule at Indraprastha. From that moment on the Kuru Kingdom branched out into the old Kaurava branch and the newly created Pandava branch. Duryodhana who was not happy about the split of the Kuru Kingdom wanted to reunite the two territories under his rule. Yudhisthira himself may have also felt cheated because the Kuru Kingdom should have been for him alone to rule. Duryodhana proposed to Yudhisthira a game of dice to settle the dispute. Encouraged by Draupadi (his shared-wife with the other four brothers; which she also had five sons, one from each husband) to take on Duryodhana's challenge, Yudhisthira agreed to gamble his kingdom away. Unaware that the dices had been tempered by Shakuni, Duryodhana's maternal uncle who owned a pair of magic dices, Yudhisthira agreed to play the game and threw the dices to determine the outcome of the challenge. As expected, Yudhisthira lost the challenge and the Pandavas along with Draupadi became enslaved. Not being satisfied for having Draupadi enslaved, Duryodhana and his brothers humiliated her further by trying to disrobe her for fun. Draupadi prayed Vishnu to save her from the humiliation. As Duryodhana was unwinding Draupadi's clothe her prayer was answered because the clothe was getting longer to the point that Duryodhana became exhausted and stopped. As a gesture of goodwill and compassionate uncle, Dhritarashtra ordered that everything that belonged to the Pandavas be returned to them. Learning of his father's kind gesture Duryodhana protested and demanded that one final game of dice be played. The stakes were that the loser and his clan would agree to be self-exiled for 12 years and another year in hiding so that nobody could find them. If they were to be found in their last year of hiding, then the cycle of self-exiled would be repeated. Because the dices had been manipulated, the Pandavas lost the bet again. Thirteen years had passed and the Pandavas returned to Hastinapura to reclaim Indraprastha. As expected, Duryodhana refused to hand over the other half of the kingdom to the Pandavas. The Pandavas asked Krishna to intervene to settle the dispute so that the war could be prevented but Duryodhana would hear none of it. It was for this reason that the Pandavas declared war to the Kauravas, which culminated into the Battle of Kurukshetra that lasted 18 days.

The beginning scene of the bas-relief depicts the dying Bhishma, the eighth son of King Shantanu and uncle of Yudhisthira and Duryodhana, shot by hundreds of arrows. This scene was set as a reference point in the Battle of Kurukshetra because that moment occurred on the 10th day of the battle. Even as he was dying in the battlefield of Burukshetra, Bhishma still gathered enough strength to preach about goodness and about conducting oneself the right way; before he died he handed over his Vishnu Sahasranama (a list of 1,000 names of Vishnu) to Yudhisthira. To the west next to the dying Bhishma, sit the Pandava's five brothers respectfully praying for Bhishma's soul. As a background for the story of the Mahabharata, Bhishma was against the war but because he had sworn to his father to serve the Kuru King he had therefore no choice but to defend Duryodhana. On the first day before the battle started, Bhishma gave a blessing to Yudhisthira. Krishna was the charioteer for Arjuna, which was the most important position in a battle because in ancient time victories or defeats depended on the skill of the charioteers. Unlike the other bas-reliefs where Vishnu and his avatars played the central roles, the Battle of Kurukshetra relegated the roles played by gods as diminishing to indicate that the Dvapura yuga was ending and the Kali yuga had entered.

Royal Procession and the Grand Army (South Gallery, West Wing)

The bas-relief is 94 meters long. This bas-relief has a historical significance because it is based on Suryavarman II's life as a monarch. It was completed after Suryavarman II's had passed away because he was represented by his posthumous name of Paramavishnuloka. The bas-relief was probably completed by his immediate successor. It starts with two registers but then merge to a single one. The upper register shows an idealized representation, not a portrait, of Suryavarman II seating on a royal bench with numerous number of parasols to indicate his ranking order as a king (see Figure 29). His figure was carved proportionally larger than his subjects, again in keeping with his rank as the king. On the lower register, Aymonier identified Rajendravarman — the General of the Army of the Center as mentioned on the Nom Van inscription — on an elephant accompanied by the other nineteen commanders with the number of parasols indicating their ranking positions. Small names were inscribed on the bas-relief. Coedès also identified another important minister, Sri Virendradhipativarman, mentioned on the Chok Vakula inscription. The carving also shows the troops of Lavo under the command of Jayasinhavarman and of the Tai mercenary soldiers under the command of their chiefs. The significance of this bas-relief is important because it is the first time that the Tai was depicted on Khmer murals. It also established the time frame of the Tai appearance in Cambodia. This scene is taken place during the first phase of the Kali yuga epoch.

Figure 29. Bas-Relief Depiction of Paramavishnuloka, Posthumous Name of Suryavarman II (1113-1150), at the Angkor Wat, South Gallery, West Wing

Yama Judgment: Consignment to Heaven and Hell (South Gallery, East Wing)

The bas-relief is 66 meters long. The scenes were carved post Suryavarman II. It depicts Yama, the Lord of Death but also called King of Dharma or Dharmaraja in Buddhism, consigning good people to heaven and bad people to hell. Yama, the first human who died in the history of mankind, had the privilege to rule the world of the departed.

The scene in the bas-relief took place in the final phase of the Kali yuga epoch. The bas-relief started with two rows of good people processing harmoniously forward, but suddenly a third row emerged at the bottom. The split shows horses with their riders on the second row stepping on the heads of the sinners on the bottom row. These sinners were shown with leashes passing through their nostrils. They were dragged forward by their handlers. At one point of the scene on the bottom row, we notice two dogs attacking the sinners and according to the Hindu mythology these two dogs belonged to Yama. The contrast between the two upper rows and the bottom row is very striking. The two upper rows showed good people worshipping and/or carrying their leaders on palanquins accompanied by great numbers of parasols. As to the bottom row, the scene showed the sinners suffering and desperately marching forward. In one scene it showed an elephant breaking the bodies of the sinners in halves with his mouth and trump. Along the procession, the sinners were either beaten by their handlers or harassed by wild animals. At about 18 meters from the start of the panel, the scene showed Yama with 18 arms sitting majestically on a buffalo. Sixteen of his eighteen arms held in each hand a sword or baton as a sign of authority. It seems that Yama relegated the judgment for the afterlife to Dharma and Chitragupta who sit next to each other, which can be recognized on the second row at about 22 meters from the start of the panel. Chitragupta, who was conceived out of Brahma's body and mind, was known as the person who kept meticulous records of everybody from birth to death. It was for his thorough knowledge of every human being's life that Yama assigned Chitragupta to decide on his behalf who went to hell and who went to heaven. The scene showed Chitragupta passing judgment on the sinners and afterward had them thrown to hell through an opening on the floor in the second row. It was from this moment forward that the second and third row merged to form a single top row.

The scene of the top row started the entry into heaven, which according to the Hindu mythology had 37 levels. The first scene into heaven showed, according to scholars, Suryavarman II as Paramavishnuloka sitting in a palace surrounded by Devas. In contrast to this heavenly scene, the bottom scene showed the image of hell with its guardians/demons stroking the fire with long poles to keep it burning stronger. The Hindu mythology says there are 32 levels of hell. As mentioned by Michael Freeman and Claude Jacques,[72,p62] the different hell levels are shown in the following scenes:

3rd Hell (Vaitarani): At 5 meters from the scene of the opening floor of the second row, the demons
    pull out the tongues of the damned with long pincers.
6th Hell (Nirucchvasa): The slow roasting of the damned.
9th Hell (Taptalaksamaya): The burning lake.
10th Hell (Ashthibhanga): The bone smashing of the damned.
11th Hell (Krakacchela): The gluttons are sawn in halves.
12th Hell (Puyapurnahrada): Bodies of the damned (stealers of strong liquor, seducers others'
    wives, sinners intention by being near wives of scholars) torn to pieces.
23th Hell (Kalasutra): Demons roasted the damned.
29th Hell (Cita): The frozen hell showing the damned shivered.
32nd Hell (Maharaurava): Near the end of the panel, the damned are standing on pieces of stone
    with their hands tied to the frames and their bodies nailed to them.

According to the Hindu cosmology, the four yuga cycles will repeat, starting with the Krita or Satya yuga, after the Kali yuga runs its course. The Kali yuga epoch is considered to be the worst time in human history. In this panel, gods retreated from the central role and let human take over because this epoch is considered to belong to the realm of the human being.

Angkor Wat in Relation to Space and Time

Eleanor Mannikka who had studied Angkor Wat in details for twenty years had discovered that the temple was carefully designed according to the Hindu law of cosmology and that the bas-reliefs, especially those on the east side, were built to synchronize with the astronomical event of the sun. She wrote a book called *Angkor Wat: Time, Space, and Kingship*[82] that was solely dedicated to the architecture of Angkor, its bas-reliefs, and its relationship to the Hindu Laws of Manu that discussed the *yuga* epoch or era according to the Hindu cosmology.

Mannikka based her work on Guy Nafilyan, from the École Française d'Etrême-Orient, who spent two years in the field surveying and measuring the dimensions of Angkor Wat in the early 1960s. Mannikka measured the distance of the bridge over the moat and determined it to be 617 feet in length. The surveys did not reveal anything extraordinary until Mannikka changed the measurements to the cubit units. Through trials and errors, she was able to equate a cubit unit to 0.43545 meter (or 1.4286 ft). Khmer in ancient times used hattha (ហត្ថ) as a measuring unit. Traditionally, a hattha is the distance from the point of the elbow to the tip of the middle finger or approximately 0.5 meter as a general rule. Mannikka's discovery is significant because it determined the exact measurement of a hattha, which in this case corresponds to 0.43545 m or 1.4286 ft. After converting the measurements of Angkor Wat to the cubit units, Mannikka was astounded to find that the pathway to Angkor Wat was laid out precisely according to the Hindu law of cosmology; and the alignment and construction of the temple was associated with the sunlight direction during the equinox and solstice seasonal changes of the earth toward the sun. Through her measurement conversions, Mannikka[82,p50] determined that the length of the main bridge crossing the western moat was approximately 432 cubits [(617 ft)/(3.28084 ft/m)x(1 cubit/0.43545 m) = 432 cubits or hatthas]; the length of the causeway from the end of the bridge to the western tip of the cruciform was 864 cubits (1,234 ft); the length from the middle of the bridge to the doorway of the third enclosure (first gallery) was 1,296 cubits (1,851 ft); and the length from the beginning of the bridge to the entrance of the second gallery was 1,728 cubits (2,469 ft). Mannikka noticed that those four numbers corresponded to the following four *yuga* periods in Hindu cosmology (multiplied by a factor of 1,000): 1) *Kali* (432,000 years); 2) *Dvapara* (864,000 years); 3) *Treta* (1,296,000 years); and *Krita* or *Satya* (1,728,000 years).

It is my contention that the measurements Mannikka assigned for the *Tretya yuga* and *Krita (Satya) yuga* are inconsistent with the distance of the Angkor Wat pathway shown in the satellite image. The explanation given above by Mannikka merits to be reexamined. Based on the aerial view of Angkor Wat by Google Earth, Mannikka's calculation was short by a considerable distance, especially for the *Satya yuga*. Figure 30 shows the comparison between Mannikka's depiction of the four *yuga* distances in relation to Angkor Wat[82,p50] and those proposed by me.

The relative scale shown in Mannikka's book,[82,p50] replicated and transferred in Figure 30, does not correspond to that shown in the aerial view of Angkor Wat provided by Google Earth. The following is the explanation extracted from Mannikka's book for the four *yuga* periods related to the distances of Angkor Wat:[82,p49-51]

> *Kali yuga: Our own time period, is the worst of all. During the kali yuga the human life span is the shortest ever; and famine are common; morality and ethics are all but lost…When the two halves of the span of the western entrance bridge are measured in cubits, together they equal 431.07 cubits, or very close to a total that may symbolize the 432,000 years in a kali yuga. In this type of correspondence, each cubit would be a "module" for 1000 years. Space then becomes a symbol for time, and we would consequently leave our own era behind on the bridge before entering the temple.*
>
> *Dvapara yuga: From the end of the bridge on the east, at the point where the first step up to the western entrance begins, to the point at which the naga balustrade around the central galleries of Angkor Wat intersects the causeway (864.83 cubits).*
>
> *Tretya yuga: From the center of the bridge to the doorway into the third gallery (1292.02 cubits).*
>
> *Krta yuga: From the first step up to the bridge to the last step out of the threshold of the second gallery, facing the upper elevation of the temple (1725.89 cubits).*

I propose an alternative explanation for the four *yuga* periods in relation to the Angkor Wat architecture. Angkor Wat, a city temple, was built to represent Mount Meru, considered to be the holiest mountains where all Hindu gods reside. It is considered to be the center of the universe that is used as the basis of architectural foundations for all Hindu temples. Mount Meru is considered the equivalent of Mount Olympus in the Greek mythology. The focal point for Angkor Wat is the central tower where Suryavarman II was laid to rest [note: the Vishnu image placed in the central tower had disappeared a long time ago due to politics in religion. It was later replaced with statues of the Buddha], which symbolized that he joined the Hindu gods in his afterlife. In order to join the Hindu gods, one must travel through the four cycles of the *yuga* periods. If one crosses the bridge, the person would have travelled through the *Kali* period, considered in the Hindu cosmology to be the worst or decadence period in human history. According to the Hindu religion, the present-day civilization would fall under the *Kali* period where spirituality is found lacking and degenerate into chaos. This is considered the Dark Age with no morality and the relationship between people and God is at the farthest distance that is almost unreachable.

After the bridge, as one continues to walk along the causeway in the east direction toward the central tower, one would have covered the *Dvapara* period (twice the distance of the *Kali* period) after reaching the western end of the cruciform. At this point, the person has not entered the third enclosure which is considered the holy boundary surrounding the main complex of Angkor Wat. The *Tretya* period (three times the distance of the Kali period) would require the person to travel westward back to the beginning of the bridge probably as a way to purify his body, mind, and soul before proceeding to the *Satya* or *Krta* period, which was the final stage of the yuga cycle. Finally, to reach Mount Meru where all the Hindu gods reside, the person would have to cover the *Satya* period (four times the distance of the Kali period), considered to be the golden age in the Hindu cosmology. The person would have to start from the beginning of the bridge with a new purified self by traversing the length of the *Satya* period before entering the central tower to join the abode of the Gods. The representative *yuga* periods in relation to the Angkor Wat distances are depicted in both Figures 30 and 31.

In his book, *Lost Star of Myth and Time*,[83,pp71-75] Graham Hancock provided more details about the Kali yuga, Dvapara yuga, Treta yuga, and Satya yuga. Each yuga period went through 360 degrees cycle. Therefore, the four yuga periods of 432,000 years for Kali; 864,000 years for Dvapara; 1,296,000 years for Tretya; and 1,728,000 years for Sataya would correspond to earth years of 1,200 [432,000/360 = 1,200], of 2,400, of 3,600, and of 4,800, respectively. The Hindu cyclical yuga periods of Kali, Dvapara, Tretya, and Sataya are analogous to the Greek concept of the Iron Age, Bronzed Age, Silver Age, and Golden Age, respectively.

Concerning the Bas-relief of the Churning of the Sea of Milk (East Gallery, South Wing), Mannikka could not be correct when she said that the 91 southern asuras corresponded to the number of days from the fall equinox (September 23) to winter solstice (December 22); and the 88 northern devas corresponded to the number of days from spring equinox (March 21) to summer solstice (June 21).[82,p17] Mannikka was incorrect for three reasons: 1) the number of days from September 23 to December 22 is 90 and not 91; 2) the number of days from March 21 to June 21 is 92 and not 88; and 3) Mannikka was using the dates for the equinoxes and solstices of the 20th century rather than those for the 12th century. Jean Meeus wrote a book called *Astronomical Algorithms*[84] and Ken Slate wrote codes based on the book to calculate the dates of equinox and solstice occurrences.[85] According to Ken Slate's calculation, the spring equinox, fall equinox, summer solstice, and winter solstice during the time of Suryavarman II (1113-1150) occurred on 14-15 March, 16 September, 15 June, and 14 December, respectively. Therefore, during the Angkor Wat period the numbers of days from the fall equinox (September 16) to the winter solstice (December 14) were 94 days; and from the spring equinox (March 14) to the summer solstice (June 15) were 93 days.

One may have wondered why the stairs leading to the top of the central tower were built in such a steep fashion. I believe the reason for this unusual construction may have something to do with the limitation of the distance imposed by the *yuga* periods. Because of the amount of distance available to build the stairs to the top of the central tower (there must be a reason why the top must be at a certain height), the architects of Angkor Wat had no choice but to make the stairs steep. Would there be a relationship between the number of stairs and the Hindu cosmology? Divakarapandita who was in charge of overseeing the construction of Angkor Wat and his team of architects must have been well educated in the arts and sciences of mathematics, astronomy, and Hindu literature. Mannikka summarized her great admiration for the architects of Angkor Wat in her book as follows:[82,pix] "The architects of Angkor Wat were brilliant and well educated — true sages whose knowledge ranged from architecture to Sanskrit poetry to astronomy to religious rituals. They were extraordinary human beings for any society, in any era."

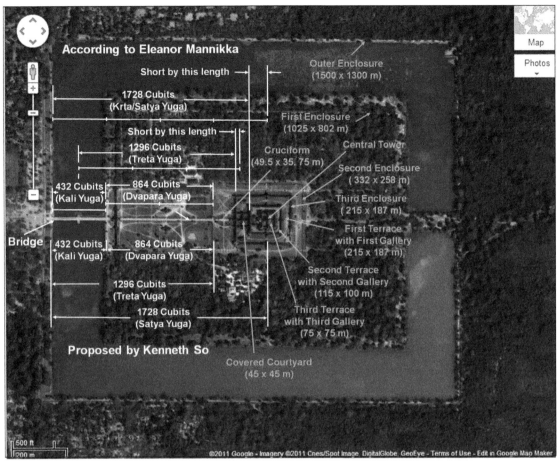

**Figure 30. Comparing Eleanor Mannikka and Kenneth So's Proposed Measurement
of Angkor Wat in Relation to the Yuga Eras in the Hindu Cosmology
(Map Courtesy of Google Earth)**

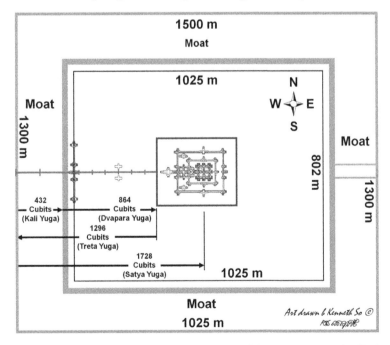

**Figure 31. An Alternative Measurement of Angkor Wat in Relation to
the Yuga Periods in the Hindu Cosmology Proposed by Kenneth So**

Angkor Wat in Relation to the Precession

As attested later by Zhou Daguan who visited Angkor from August 1296 to June-July 1297, the Brahmans were well educated and well versed in the fields of literature, mathematics, astronomy, cosmology, physics, and architecture. Divakarapandita was Jayavarman VII's *Vrah Guru* who was in charge of overseeing the construction of Angkor Wat. In addition to Angkor Wat being built in accordance to the Hindu law of cosmology mentioned previously, the British writer and investigative journalist Graham Hancock also noticed the relationship between the temples and the precession of the equinoxes.[86] In the early second century BC, the Greek mathematician and astronomer Hipparchus noticed that the positions of the stars in the sky had shifted from measurements recorded earlier by his peers. He realized that the displacement of the stars was caused by the wobbling of the earth at its axis. The wobbling generated a slow conical motion which is known as precession. Modern calculations predict that it would take 25,290 years to complete one cycle of precession. It would require 72 years for the precession to move by one degree (25,290 years/360 degrees = 72 years per degree). Hancock noticed that the causeway of Angkor Wat from the bridge at the outer moat leading to the temple was 3/4 degrees off from its axial west-east direction. By multiplying 0.75 with 72 one would obtain the number 54. This number is significant because it was found everywhere at Angkor. There were 54 asuras and 54 devas on each side of the road-bridge at the gate of Angkor Thom, with a total of five road-bridges. Mannikka made some interesting observations concerning the number 54 used for the construction of Angkor Wat. She theorized that the bas-relief of the Churning Sea of Milk was placed on the East Gallery to position between the oscillations of the sun-moon movement.[82,pp34-36] She observed that the number 54 coincided with the average of the sun maximum north-south arc (49 degrees) and the moon maximum north-south arc (59 degrees). As it will be shown later, the number 54 was again duplicated for the number of face-tower of Lokesvara at Bayon and Banteay Chhmar. In addition to the correlation between the number 54 and the celestial mechanics, the 3/4 degree offset to the west-east axial line for the construction of the causeway would give about one day of warning before the appearance of the spring equinox.

The complexity, beauty, architecture, bas-reliefs, and enormous size of Angkor Wat is unmatched by any past and future Khmer monuments. Parmentier described the beauty and decorations of Angkor Wat with the following perfect expression:[6,p109]

> *The great temple of Angkor Wat is remarkable, not only for its architectural arrangement, but also by the perfect subordination of the sculpture to the composition of the ensemble; the decoration is almost everywhere treated as embroidery, in order not to draw the eye and, by the variety and intensity of the shades, breaks the unity of the simple wall. And also the ornament is everywhere, even at the most invisible corner; one feels there is an homage to the god more than an attraction for the pilgrim. This decorative minuteness is pushed to the extreme; if one is struck by the work and the formidable expense represented by the 10 kilometers of border in chiseled sandstone of the moats, one is none the less stupefied when one thinks of the execution of the 10,000 ridge-crests which were aligned on all the ridges, so delicate that not a single entire specimen has come down to us.*

As a monarch, Suryavarman II was also considered as one of the greatest religious reformers. The religion in the Angkor period started out as Shaivic, but by the time Suryavarman II took over it became

Vishnuic with a lot of tolerance for Buddhic practice. The switch from Shaivism to Vishnuism and Buddhism did not occur abruptly. The syncretism (combination of different forms of belief or practice) was gradual as the road was paved since the time of Suryavarman I, who started to inject pro Vishnuism and Buddhism elements into his administration to counterbalance the powerful influence of the Shaivic sacerdotal families.

There was a debate among scholars on whether to classify Angkor Wat a mausoleum or a temple. Jean Przyluski[7,p204] considered Angkor Wat a mausoleum based on its location away from Yasodharapura (it was customary not to build a tomb in an area among the living), on the main entrance facing west (the direction of sunset to end the day), and on the arrangements of the bas-reliefs going counter-clockwise (as in *prasavya* moving from left to right, a religious ceremony practiced by the Hindu for the dead). George Coedès did acknowledge some funerary characters of the monument, but he countered that the arrangement of the bas-reliefs moving from left to right was mainly for practical reason for the sculptors (and probably for the viewers who read from left to right). He claimed that the decoration and architecture of the monument was consistent with the tradition for the construction of a temple. Coedès believed that Angkor Wat was originally built as a temple in dedication to Vishnu but served as Suryavarman II's resting place after his death. Therefore, he suggested a compromise by calling Angkor Wat a funerary temple.

Considering the importance of Suryavarman II in the history of Cambodia and his dominant personality, it is rather peculiar that nothing was said about the last few years of his reign. The last inscription about him was in 1145. It is not a doubt that he still lived until at least 1150 based on the Cham inscriptions and Vietnamese documents. His disastrous campaigns against the Cham in 1148 and 1149 and against the Dai Viet in 1150 may have resulted in two consequences: 1) Suryavarman II may have given orders to Divakarapandita who overviewed the construction of Angkor to not mention anything about the failed campaigns against his enemies that occurred near the end of his reign; 2) A revolution may have taken place and Suryavarman II may have either been retired or killed by his cousin, Dharanindravarman II, who succeeded him.[6,p204] Suryavarman II received the posthumous name Paramavishnuloka, which means the supreme abode of Vishnu. According to Coedès, the favoritism of Vishnu over Shiva coincided with the modern Vishnuism movement that was led by Ramanuja in India in the twelfth century. Divakarapandita and Bhupendrapandita I and II who had served Suryavarman II faithfully also passed away sometime during that period.

Scholars have identified the legendary name Preah Ket Mealy to be associated with Paramavishnuloka.[6,p203] This name may have been created much later, possibly in the 16th century around the time when Ang Chan I commissioned to have then unfinished bas-reliefs on the North Wing of the East Gallery and East Wing of the North Gallery completed on September 1546 and February 1564, respectively.[81,p34]

The exact date of Suryavarman II's death is not known, but it can be placed around 1150. According to Khin Sok, Bakou (Brahman in charge of conducting rituals for Khmer kings) originated under the reign of Preah Ket Mealea[87,p195] but I believe the tradition may have started much earlier under the reign of Jayavarman II when the Chief Brahman Sivakaivalya performed the Devaraja ceremony on mount Mahendra in 802.

After studying one hundred and forty stanzas, dated from the period of Suryavarman II, that show almost perfect execution with high quality of craftsmanship, Aymonier attributed to Suryavarman II for the "renaissance in letters and studies" that had been in decline since the reign of Udayadityavarman II.[14] The genealogies are shown in Figures 25, 26, and 48.

The bas-relief of the *Royal Procession and the Grand Army* (South Gallery, West Wing) was not completed during the lifetime of Suryavarman II but probably after his death based on his posthumous name Paramavishnuloka, which means Highest World of Vishnu, shown on the bas-relief.

Recent Discovery of Structures Around Angkor Wat

Until recently, scholars and archeologists have not been aware of the complexity of urban areas around Angkor Wat or Greater Angkor. In 2012, archeologist Damian Evans and his colleagues used a laser technology known as Light Detection and Ranging (LIDAR) to map an area of 370-km^2 around Angkor from a helicopter. LIDAR enabled Evans and his team to determine the contours of dwelling and structures around Angkor Wat which would have been impossible to see with the naked eye. To the surprise of Evans and his team, the results showed new structures that were unknown to scholars and archeologists prior to the LIDAR survey. The urban areas around Angkor Wat were quite sophisticated and extended beyond the boundaries that scholars had thought. Bruce Bower from the Science News wrote the article, "Lasers unveil secrets and mysteries of Angkor Wat," concerning this finding.[88] The scale of the cities near Angkor was so enormous that Veronica Walker said, "Cambodia could have been the largest empire on Earth in the 12th century."[88] While the medieval London was still relatively a small city with an estimated of 30,000 inhabitants, scholars have said that the population around Angkor was anywhere between 750,000 to a million people. The Ta Prohm inscription mentioned that 3,000 tons of rice were produced by 66,000 farmers per year to feed themselves and the additional 12,640 people who worked to maintain the temples.[64,p34] Furthermore, the Angkor inscription mentioned that 300,000 laborers and 6,000 elephants were used for the construction of Angkor Wat. Considering the scale of the project, it should not be not a surprise that LIDAR had discovered unknown structures around Angkor.

LIDAR, which is not a new technology, has been in used since the 1960s for measuring pollutants in the environment. Until only recently that scholars have recognized the great benefits for the LIDAR application in the field of archaeology.

The application of LIDAR for the Angkor study has generated new insights into the understanding of Angkor and its surrounding. Roland Fletcher, the archaeologist from the University of Sydney who conducted the Greater Angkor Project enthusiastically said:[88] "Researchers have driven and walked over many of these new discoveries for a century." After working on this project for a long time, Roland Fletcher was still in awe of what he had already discovered and what he expect to discover farther down the line. He exclaimed that "there was nothing like Greater Angkor until the advent of 19th century industrial cities." As Bruce Bower, the author of the article "Lasers unveil secrets and mysteries of Angkor Wat," wrote: [88] "Cities of around 1 million people arose in China by the ninth century, but those metropolises covered one-half or less the area of Greater Angkor. Spread-out cities in the mold of Greater Angkor became more common in the 1800s as trains and cars made long-distance travel easier. But discoveries at Greater Angkor shatter a long-standing assumption that urban sprawl was impossible without mechanical forms of transportation, he says."

38   Dharanindravarman II (1150-1160) ធរណីន្រ្ទវរ្ម័ន (ទី២)

Transliterated Name: Dharaṇindravarmăn II
Other Name: Jayavarmesvara[1,p222]
Posthumous Name: Paramanishkalapada[6,p205]
Relationship: Son of Mahidharaditya and Rajapatindralakshmin; Cousin of Suryavarman II.
Religion: Mahayana Buddhism
Capital: Undetermined
Genealogy: Figures 25, 26, and 48

Dharanindravarman II succeeded Suryavarman II, probably around 1150. He was the cousin of Suryavarman II. Mahidharaditya was the father of Dharanindravarman II and the younger brother of Narendralakshmi, the mother of Suryavarman II. Dharanindravarman II's mother, Rajapatindralakshmi, was the daughter of Dharanindraditiya and Dharanindrarajalakshmi — the younger sister of Jayavarman VI. Dharanindravarman II was married to Chudamani. The Ta Prohm inscription mentioned that Dharanindravarman II was a fervent Buddhist and that Jayarajacudamani (according to Coedès, the first two syllables — Jaya and raja — were later added to her name under the reign of Jayavarman VII) was the daughter of a king named Harshavarman.

In the genealogy tree at the end of his book *The Indianized State of Southeast Asia,*[1] Coedès showed Harshavarman III to be the father of Chudamani. Briggs reproduced the same genealogy in his book *The Ancient Khmer Empire.*[6,p186] Without going through elaboration, Chakravarti discounted Harshavarman III as the father of Chudamani and assigned Harshavarman IV as her father instead.[43,p88] Based on my calculation below, I can say that both hypotheses have their own merit.

The Ta Prohm inscription mentioned that Jayavarman VII's sons were soon to become men when Dharanindravarman II died in 1160.[6,p205] The inscription implies that the oldest son of Jayavarman VII was probably around 17 years old (if one considers manhood starting at eighteen). If we assume Jayavarman VII had his first child at 18 years of age, then we can deduce that Jayavarman VII was at least 35 years old when his father died [17 + 18 = 35]. Therefore, Jayavarman VII would have been born around 1125 [1160 – 35 = 1125; also see Ref. 1, p. 169 and Ref. 6, p 209]. Harshavarman III died in 1080. If Chudamani were his daughter, then she would have to be born no later than 1081. If this were the case, then Chudamani would have been 44 years old when Jayavarman VII was born [1125 – 1081 = 44]. Assuming that the maximum childbearing age for a woman is between 55 years old, then the earliest date for Chudamani's birth was in 1070 [1125 – 1070 = 55]. On the other extreme of the assumption, if the minimum childbearing age for a woman is 10 years old, then Chudamani would have to be born in 1115 [1125 – 10 = 1115]. If this were the case, then it is possible that Chudamani could be the granddaughter of Harshavarman III and daughter of Harshavarman IV.

According to Coedès, Harshavarman IV was probably Nripatindravaman I that Suryavarman II had defeated and whose name is mentioned on the inscription of Ban Theat. The union between Dharanindravarman II, from the Mahidharapura dynasty, and Chudamani, from the Baladitya dynasty and Agastya ancestry, produced Jayavarman VII, one of the greatest Khmer kings. Dharanindravarman II did not leave any inscriptions about his reign or any of his achievements. Most of what is known about Dharanindravarman II came from the inscriptions dating during the reign of Jayavarman VII and also from the Champa documents.

Kambuja, under the reign of Dharanindravarman II had a strong political, cultural, as well as religious relationship with Sri Lanka. The Sri Lanka chronicle *Culavamsa* reports that at the request of Dharanindravarman II, King Parakramabahu I (1153-1186) sent his daughter to Kambuja to be the bride of Jayavarman VII but the convoy carrying the princess was captured by the Burmese.[89] Burma was not only contesting Kambuja in the area of trades but also in its relationship with Sri Lanka. Because Dharanindravarman II was a fervent Buddhist, he wanted to strengthen his relationship with Sri Lanka to spread Buddhism in Kambuja. It must be remembered that prior to Dharanindravarman II, Funan was at one time a strong center for Mahayana Buddhism in spite of Brahmanism being the state religion. Chenla, under the reign of Kaundinya Jayavarman (478-514), sent two Buddhist monks, Sanghapala (or Sanghavarman) and Mandra (or Mandrasena), to China to help in the translation of Tripitaka into Chinese. Chenla contributed for the spread of the Mahayana Buddhism to China, Korea, Japan, and Vietnam.

About this time, a major event took place in India that had a strong repercussion in Sri Lanka. The stronghold of Hinayana Buddhism in southern India could not coexist with Brahmanism. The Hinayanists were forced to leave India and settle in Sri Lanka. Recognizing the merits of Hinayanism, King Parakramabahu I called a council to reform the Sinhalese Buddhism. As a result, Sri Lanka became the major learning center for Hinayana Buddhism. Monks from different part of Southeast Asia, like the Môns from Lavo and Pagan came to Sri Lanka to study the new religious system. While Pagan adopted Hinayana Buddhism, Kambuja was still holding on to the tradition of Mahayana Buddhism and did not adopt Hinayanism until sometimes in the middle of the thirteen century.

The exact date of Dharanindravarman II's death is not known, but it is believed he passed away around 1160. He was given a posthumous name of Paramanishkalapada. The genealogy is shown in Figures, 25, 26, and 48.

THE THIRD ANGKOR DYNASTY (1160-1368)

The Merging of the Mahidharapura Dynasty with the Old Lunar and Solar Dynasties

Dharanindravarman II, the father of the future king Jayavarman VII, was the last king from the Mahidharapura dynasty. He had no connection with the Lunar and Solar dynasties of the Funan and Chenla empires. A new bloodline emerged in the third Angkor period as a result of Dharanindravarman II's marriage with Chudamani, the daughter of Harshavarman III (according to Briggs and Coedès) or Harshavarman IV (according to Chakravarti), who traced her lineage to the old Lunar and Solar dynasties. Dharanindravarman II and Chudamani are considered the progenitors of the Third Angkor Dynasty.

39   Yasovarman II (1160-1165) យសោវរ្ម័ន (ទី២)

Transliterated Name: Yasovarmăn II
Other Name: Sri Yasovarmadeva[6,p206]
Relationship: Related to Dharanindravarman II or Jayarajacudamani (Chudamani); possibly a
    brother or cousin of Jayavarman VII.
Religion: Mahayana Buddhism
Temples:[78] Beng Mealea, Chao Say Tevoda, Banteay Samrè, Bakong
Capital: Yasodharapura (possibly Banteay Chhmar)
Genealogy: Figure 32

Jayavarman VII should have succeeded his father Dharanindravarman II, but it was Yasovarman II who acceded to the throne instead. The circumstance of how he came to power is not clear. Originally, historians thought that Jayavarman VII was the person who immediately succeeded his father. They based their conclusion chiefly on the Ta Prohm inscription that showed Jayavarman VII succeeding Dharanindravarman II. The inscription did not mention any kings between Dharanindravarman II and Jayavarman VII. Until Coedès studied the work of Aymonier on previously inedited inscriptions of the Prasat Chrung that he realized there were two other kings reigning between Dharanindravarman II and Jayavarman VII. Why was there a discrepancy between the inscriptions? The reason was probably due to the fact that the Ta Prohm inscription was intended only as a genealogy of Jayavarman VII and not as a list of Khmer kings.

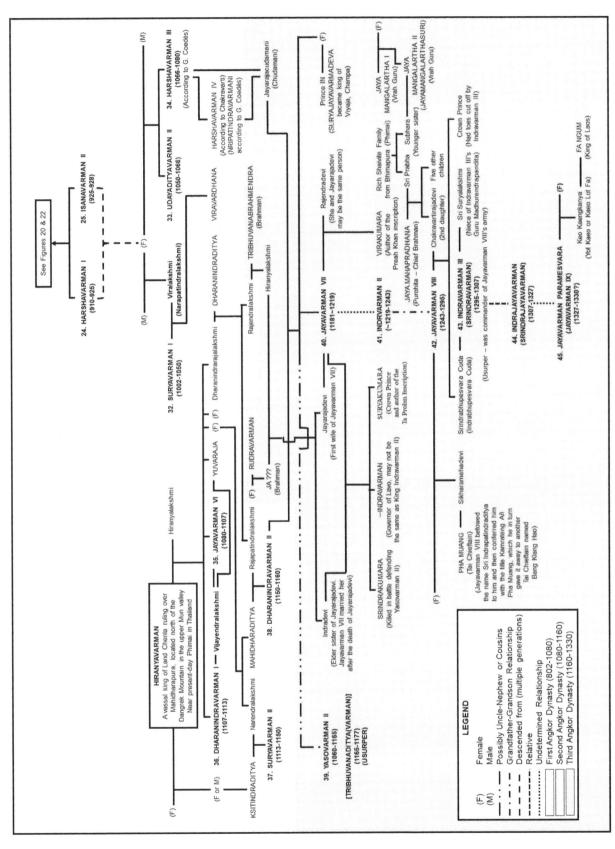

Figure 32. Genealogy of the First, Second, and Third Angkor Dynasties

[Including Harshavarman III (1st Dynasty), Suryavarman II (2nd Dynasty), and Jayavarman VII (3rd Dynasty)]

When Dharanindravarman II died in 1160, Jayavarman VII was at least thirty five years old according to Briggs[6,p205] and Coedès[1,p169] and had children who were to become men. Yasovarman II seemed to be a close relative of the family for the fact that Jayavarman VII did not protest his accession to the throne. According to the inscription of Banteay Chhmar, Jayavarman VII also had his son fighting to defend King Yasovarman II against the revolt of Bharata Rahu (Bharata and Rahu, according to Claude Jacques[90,p20]) depicted on the bas-relief of Banteay Chhmar as an *asura* (demon) swallowing the sun and the moon during the eclipse. Yasovarman II's accession to the throne may be partly due to happenstance on one hand, and on the rule of the ambilateral descent system on the other hand. Jayavarman VII was on his way to Champa to fight a war when he received the news of the death of his father.[6,p207] It was due to the absence of Jayavarman VII from Cambodia that gave Yasovarman II the opportunity to succeed Dharanindravarman II. Scholars have not been able to definitely clarify the relationship between Yasovarman II and Jayavarman VII. Briggs and Cocdès have only been able to suggest that Yasovarman II was a close relative to Jayavarman VII and possibly a cousin. If Yasovarman II were the cousin of Jayavarman VII whose father he succeeded — Jayavarman VII might not have much choice on this matter because he was away from the country — but he might not so willingly allow his son, Crown Prince Samtac Srindrakumara, to fight to defend the king against his enemy. Srindrakumara was risking his life fighting Bharata Rahu, mentioned on the Banteay Chhmar inscription (or Daitya Rahu mentioned in the Prasat Chrung inscription), who led the revolt against Yasovarman II. During the battle, the anak Sanjak (probably equivalent to a royal bodyguard) Arjuna and anak Sanjak Sri Dharadevapura lost their lives protecting Srindrakumara. In another event in a campaign against Champa, two other Sanjaks — Sri Deva and Sri Vardhana — sacrificed their lives to protect Srindrakumara per the inscription K.227.[90,p20] The two Sanjaks were of Cham origins from Vijaya. The inscription mentioned that the statues of the four fallen heroes were erected in their honor in the four corners at Banteay Chhmar; and that of "Kamrateng jagat Sri-Srindradeva" placed in the middle of the temple.[6,p206] Briggs deduced that the above statue of the prince could only be Srindrakumara, the son of Jayavarman VII. The revolt and battle with Rahu from the Banteay Chhmar inscription was translated by Coedès in 1928 as follows:[6,p206]

> *When Bharata Rahu manifested his spirit of treason against the King Sri Yasovarmadeva to take possession of the holy (royal) palace, all the troop of the capital ... fled. The Prince engaged in combat. The anak Sanjak Arjuna and the anak Sanjak Sri Dharadevapura fought to defend the Santac. They fell before (him). The Prince struck the nose of Bharata Rahu and upset him, In the meantime, order was given to award the title of Vrah Kamraten añ Sri Nirpasinhavarma to the anak Sanjak Devapura, son of the anak Sanjak (Arjuna and (sic — should be or) Sri Dharadevapura) and to erect their statues; as to all the members of their families, the Prince accorded them riches and dignities.*

In his book, *Banteay Chhmar, Garrison-Temple of the Khmer Empire*, Peter Sharrock provided an updated and longer version of the K.227 inscription by Claude Jacques.[90,p20] Instead of one person named Bharata Rahu as translated by George Coedès, Claude Jacques translated as Bharata and Rahu which indicated two persons.

Concerning Yasovarman II's origin, an argument can be made that he might belong on the side of Chudamani's lineage instead of that of Jayavarman VII's father. An inference can be made that Yasovarman II may be from the same bloodline as Yasovarman I when Yasovarman II rendered homage to Yasovarman I by taking on his name when he became king. Chudamani shared the same lineage with Yasovarman I that had its origin from the Lunar Dynasty of the Baladitya/Aninditapura. If Yasovarman II were to belong on the side of Chudamani's lineage, then he may possibly be her brother, which would make him the uncle of Jayavarman VII. If this were the case, then the rule of the ambilateral descent system would apply because he would be of the same generation as Dharanindravarman II and of higher ranking than Jayavarman VII. It may be for this reason that Jayavarman VII had not protested against the accession of Yasovarman II.

The reign of Yasovarman II lasted only five years. According to the inscriptions of Prasat Chrung and Phimeanakas,[6,p207] Yasovarman II was overthrown and killed in 1165 by an ambitious high-ranking officer of the court named Tribhuvanaditya. He usurped the throne and ruled under the name of Tribhuvanadityavarman. The genealogy is shown in Figure 32.

The Usurpation of Power and the Cham Invasion

[Tribhuvanadityavarman (1165-1177) ត្រិភុវណ្ឌាឌិត្យាវ្រ្មិន]

Transliterated Name: Trībhuvanadityavarmăn VI
Other Names: Tribhuvanaditya, Tribhuvanadityadeva[6,pp206-207]
Relationship: High official of Yasovarman II
Capital: Yasodharapura

The Betrayal of Yasovarman II's High Official

Before his usurpation, Tribhuvanadityavarman was a high official who served Yasovarman II under the name of Tribhuvanaditya. He revolted against the king in 1165. Jayavarman VII was in Champa when he heard the news of the revolt.[6,p207] He disengaged himself from the campaign against Champa and decided to return to Cambodia to come to the rescue of Yasovarman II. He was too late because by the time he arrived in Cambodia Tribhuvanaditya already seized the throne and killed the king. He enthroned himself and reigned under the name of Tribhuvanadityavarman. Instead of rushing into a war against Tribhuvanadityavarman, Jayavarman VII decided to wait and take a more careful approach to regain the throne that was rightfully his. Concurrently of what happened in Cambodia, a similar event took place in Champa in 1166. A rebel named Ong Vatuv revolted against his king, Jaya Harivarman I. He seized the throne of Champa in 1166-1167. He reigned under the name of Jaya Indravarman (IV) Ong Vatuv. Was the overthrow of the king of Champa a mere coincidence or was Ong Vatuv emboldened by the event in Cambodia a year earlier when Tribhuvanaditya successfully mounted a military coup and killed Yasovarman II?

The Cham Invasion (1177)

While Tribhuvanadityavarman was enjoying his reign, Jaya Indravarman (IV) Ong Vatuv was preparing his invasion of Cambodia. The Cham king seized on the illegitimacy of Tribhuvanadityavarman's reign, and probably also counted on the unhappiness of the Khmer people, to launch an attack on Cambodia. First, the Champa king came into a peace agreement with the Dai Viet in 1170. Second, he enlisted a high Chinese official as his war strategist. It was by chance that the Chinese man ended up in Champa as a result of a shipwrecked in 1171. The Chinese man would play a prominent role in the Champa's invasion of Cambodia. In its first attempt, the Chinese man advised Jaya Indravarman IV to abandon the use of elephants and replace them with men equipped with crossbows riding on horsebacks to attack Cambodia. The first campaign by land ended up in a complete failure. Undaunted, the Champa king conducted a second invasion of Cambodia in 1177. This time with a well-armed fleet, Champa attacked Angkor from the sea through the Great Lake. Under the guidance from the same Chinese man, the Cham fleet arrived at the Mekong delta, went up to the Great Lake, and took Angkor by surprise. The Cham killed Tribhuvanadityavarman and pillaged the city. The Cham left Angkor in ruin.

The Anarchy Period (1177-1181)

With Tribhuvanadityavarman slain and Jayavarman VII, the true heir to the throne away from Angkor, Cambodia fell into a period of anarchy for four years, from 1177 to 1181. The Cham had ransacked Angkor and left it completely in ruin. Cambodia had never been so thoroughly vanquished since the conquest by the Maharaja of Zabag (from Central Java) around 790. The last time Cambodia was destroyed, the country had it rebuilt with a stronger leader. The aftermath of the maharaja's invasion of Cambodia brought about the emergence of Jayavarman II. He proved himself not only to be a dominant and smart leader, but he also unified the country that was in chaos and made it even more powerful than Java. The destruction of Angkor, would again bring about a new leader that would define the Khmer Empire.

The Apogee of the Khmer Empire and the Edification of Temples

40   Jayavarman VII (1181-1219) ជ័យវរ្ម័ន (ទី៧)

Transliterated Name: Jayăvarmăn VII
Other Name: Jayavarmadeva[6,p179; 45,p285]
Posthumous Name: Mahaparamasaugata[1,p172]
Born: No later than 1125 (according to Coedès[1,p169])/Death: 1219
Relationship: Son of Dharanindravarman II and Chudamani; married to Jayarajadevi (1st wife), Indradevi (2nd wife and older sister of Jayarajadevi), and Rajendradevi (3rd wife or possibly the same person as Jayarajadevi).
Religion: Mahayana Buddhism
Purohita: Hrishikesa (title: Jaya Mahapradhana)
Guru: Jaya Mangalartha
Temples:[78] Ta Prohm, Preah Khan, Angkor Thom, Bayon, Royal Palace, Elephant Terrace, Jayatataka or Baray of Preah Khan, Neak Pean, Srah Srang, Ta Nei, Ta Som, Ta Prohm Kel, Hospital Chapel, Prasat Chrung, Krol Kô, Banteay Chhmar
Capital: Started at Preah Khan of Kampong Svay during his exile, then moved to Angkor and founded Angkor Thom after he became king.
Genealogy: Figure 32

Figure 33. Statue of Jayavarman VII Sitting in a Virasana Position

The most famous statue of Jayavarman VII is shown in Figure 33. It shows him sitting in a Virasana position with the right leg resting on the left leg like the pose used by the Buddha. This is in contrast to the adamantine position where both legs are entwined. The Virasana position is also called the Hero Pose, where *Vira* means "warrior" and *Asana* means "as of" or "resembling." The statue clearly portrays Jayavarman VII as a true Buddhist practitioner because it shows him as a simple man without crown or jewelry in contrast to Suryavarman II who was a Vishnuist. The statue was found at Krol Romeas, located in the outer skirts of the western wall of Angkor Thom at the border of East Baray. The statue is presently displayed at the Phnom Penh National Museum.

Jayavarman VII was the son of Dharanindravarman II. They came from the same line of Suryavarman II and Jayavarman VI of the Second Angkor Dynasty or the Mahidharapura Dynasty. His father's bloodline did not belong to either the Solar or Lunar Dynasty. On the other hand, his mother Chudamani (Jayarajacudamani) came from the same line as Yasovarman I of the First Angkor Dynasty that had its origin from the Lunar Dynasty of Baladitya/Aninditapura. The dynasty was founded by Kambu Svayambhuva. According to Coedès and Briggs, Chudamani was the daughter of Harshavarman III but Chakravarti assigned her to be the daughter of Harshavarman IV (see section on Dharanindravarman II), the son of Harshavarman III.

The inscriptions tell us that Jayavarman VII became a Buddhist through the influence of his father who was a fervent Buddhist. Jayavarman VII married quite young. His first and principal wife, Jayarajadevi, was the daughter of Hiranyalakshmi and great grandniece of Jayavarman VI from her maternal side. Both Jayavarman VII and Jayarajadevi were Buddhist devotees (of the Mahayana branch). A brief description of Jayarajadevi's personality and nature of her character was revealed on the Phimeanakas inscription. It mentioned of her "asceticism, her virtuous conduct, her tears, her likeness to Sita, found by her husband and then separated from him, her body thinned by observances, her religion, her devotion to him, her joy at his ultimate return."[6,p205] By comparing her to Sita, the faithful wife of Rama, and describing her of practicing asceticism, the short inscription above provides the readers a glimpse of an almost sainthood-like personality of Jayarajadevi. Like Sita, Jayarajadevi was also separated from her husband but still she was very devoted to him.

Jayavarman VII would have succeeded his father Dharanindravarman II had he not been away from the country conducting a campaign against Champa at Vijaya (present-day Phan Rang or Binh Dinh in Vietnam.[1,p169; 6,p207] Yasovarman II, believed to be a close relative of Jayavarman VII — either a cousin according to Coedès and Briggs or possibly an uncle from Jayavarman VII's maternal side according to my analysis — did not waste his time waiting for Jayavarman VII to come back to Angkor as he took over the throne immediately after the death of Dharanindravarman II. Jayavarman VII did not seem to object, or he may not have much choice in this matter due to the fact he was away from Angkor, to contest Yasovarman II's accession to the throne. Instead of coming back to Angkor he prolonged his stay in Champa, probably in the Cambodia-Champa region. However, he hastily returned to Cambodia after receiving the news of the revolt and treachery of Yasovarman II's high official named Tribhuvanaditya in 1165. By the time he arrived in Cambodia Tribhuvanaditya had already killed Yasovarman II, consolidated his power, and crowned himself king of Angkor under the name of Tribhuvanadityavarman. With the army under his command from the aborted Champa campaign, Jayavarman VII could have gone to war against Tribhuvanadityavarman and would probably come out victorious, but he decided to avoid a civil war that would have spilled too much blood. What were the reasons for him not to engage in a battle against Tribhuvanadityavarman? Could it be that that Jayarajadevi and their children were being held hostages at Angkor? Another possibility could be that Jayavarman VII did not want to see more Khmer blood spilling so soon after so much suffering already. Another consideration could be that after witnessing how Tribhuvanaditya was able to defeat a reigning king, Yasovarman II — in spite of the help from Jayarajadevi and Jayavarman VII's son in support of the king — Jayavarman VII probably thought that a civil war would be too costly and long lasting and therefore decided to wait for the right opportunity to mount a campaign against the usurper. However, I believe that the circumstance to attack Tribhuvanadityavarman was not favorable yet for Jayavarman VII because Champa was ready to launch a major offensive against Angkor. If Jayavarman VII were going to conduct a campaign against Tribhuvanadityavarman, then he would have to fight a battle on two fronts because he would have to fight Jaya Indravarman (IV) Ong Vatuv of Champa also. Being a great war tactician, Jayavarman VII chose the wisest path by letting Tribhuvanadityavarman and Jaya Indravarman (IV) on Vatuv slug out each other. Jayavarman VII expected that the winner would come out weaker after the war. During his waiting period, Jayavarman VII decided to establish his residency at Preah Khan of Kampong Svay (located about 100 km east of Angkor in present-day province of Preah Vihear). Jayavarman VII used this period to reflect and chart his future.

Jayavarman VII probably did not expect the war between Tribhuvanadityavarman and Jaya Indravarman (IV) on Vatuv to drag on for so long. Twelve years after he usurped the throne, Tribhuvanadityavarman was killed and Angkor fell to Champa. In 1177, Angkor was sacked, pillaged, and destroyed. Anarchy and confusion became widespread and the chaos extended all the way to the fringe of the Khmer Empire. King Adityaraja of the Môn kingdom of Haripunjaya (present-day Lamphun in Thailand) seized on this occasion to try to reconquer the former Môn kingdom of Lavo from the Khmer Empire. It took Jayavarman VII four years of battles, from 1177 to 1181, to retake Angkor and get rid of the Cham's occupation of Cambodia. It could have been the end of Khmer grandeur if it were not for Jayavarman VII's skills as a great warrior and also, as fate would have it, his longevity that enabled him to achieve great accomplishments. The inscriptions of Jayavarman VII defeating the Chams are very limited, but the one of Ta Prohm seems to indicate that a major naval battle took place and that Jayavarman VII came out victorious. The scenes of the naval battle were depicted on the bas-reliefs of Bayon and Banteay Chhmar. After conquering the Chams, Jayavarman VII was crowned king in 1181. He was already of advanced age by the time he became king because he was born no later than 1125 according to Coedès.[1,p167]

Jayavarman VII's job was not finished after he acceded to the throne because some parts of the country were still in turmoil. He had to put down the revolt that took place at Malyang (southern region of present-day Battambang) in 1182. The My Son inscription[1,p170] mentioned that Jayavarman VII appointed a young exiled Cham prince, named Sri Vidyanandana, to conduct the campaign against Malyang. The young Cham prince was undoubtedly related to the late Champa king, Jaya Harivarman I, that the rebel Ong Vatuv killed around 1166-1167. After killing his king, Ong Vatuv enthroned himself and reigned under the name Jaya Indravarman (IV) Ong Vatuv. The My Son inscription did not offer any clues as to how Vidyanandana escaped from Champa and took refuge in Cambodia. It mentioned only that he was a refugee prince from Champa. The following is the transcription of the My Son inscription:[1,p170]

When he was in the prime of youth, in saka 1104 (1182 AD), Prince Vidyānandana went to Cambodia. The king of Cambodia, seeing that he had all the thirty-three marks [of the fated man], took an interest in him and taught him, like a prince, all the sciences and military skills. While he was living in Cambodia, a city in this kingdom named Malyang, which was inhabited by a throng of wicked men over whom the Cambodians had established their mastery, revolted against the king of Cambodia. This king, seeing that the prince was well versed in military science, charged him with leading the Cambodian troops to take the city of Malyang. He complied completely with the wishes of the king of Cambodia. This king, seeing his valor, conferred on him the high rank of Yuvarāja and gave him all the possessions and good things that could be found in the kingdom of Cambodia.

It must be noted that the rank of Yuvaraja that Jayavarman VII conferred on Vidyanandana described in the above My Son inscription was for the Yuvaraja of Champa and not of Cambodia. It is a mystery as to why Jayavarman VII put so much trust in this young Cham prince by teaching him all the art of warfare. After putting down the revolt at Malyang, Jayavarman VII turned his second campaign eight years later against Champa, a country that had created so much destruction and misery to Angkor. Again he entrusted his campaign to this tested young Cham prince. Vidyanandana was happy to oblige because not only would he be able to avenge the death of Jaya Harivarman I, but he believed that Jayavarman VII would reward him for his success and install him as king of Champa once he had beaten Jaya Indravarman (IV) Ong Vatuv, the usurper, who had caused so much misery to Angkor. Before embarking on a campaign against Champa, Jayavarman VII had secured the neutrality of the Dai Viet emperor Ly Cao-tông in 1190. The inscription of Po Nagar (present-day Nha Trang in Vietnam) mentioned that Jayavarman VII "took the capital of Champa and carried off all the lingas."[1,p170] The battle took place at Chakling (present-day Phan Rang in Vietnam).[7,p121] Vidyanandana moved swiftly, took the capital Vijaya, captured Jaya Indravarman (IV) Ong Vatuv and transported him back to Cambodia as prisoner. The battle at Vijaya, translated from the My Son inscription said the following:[6,p215]

> *In 1112 saka [A.D. 1190], King Sri Jaya Indravarman Ong Vatuv made war against the King of Kambujadesa. The latter sent the Prince [Vidyanandana] at the head of the troops of the Kambuja to take Vijaya and defeat the king. He captured the king and had him conducted to Kambujadesa by the Kambuja troops. He proclaimed Suryajayavarmadeva Prince In, brother-in-law of the king of Kambujadesa, as king of the city of Vijaya.*

According to Ma Duanlin, the famous author of the 1317 Chinese encyclopedia, Prince Vidyanandana took the name Suryavarmadeva after he had vanquished the Champa king. The following was Ma Duanlin's account:[6,pp215-216]

> *The king of Chenla [Kambujadesa] descended, in his turn, on the Chen Ching [Champa] at the head of a large army, exterminated the inhabitants, seized the king in his palace, led him into captivity after having killed his counselors and ministers and put an officer of Chenla in his place on the throne of Chen Ching.*

I believe Ma Duanlin may have confused either Prince In (brother-in-law of Jayavarman VII) or Prince Vidyanandana (Cham prince adopted by Jayavarman VII) with Jayavarman VII when he said "king of Chenla." According to the My Son inscription, Jayavarman VII chose his brother-in-law Prince In to occupy the vacant throne of Champa instead of installing Vidyanandana as the new king to replace Jaya Indravarman (IV) Ong Vatuv. Prince In reigned at Champa under the name of Suryajayavarmadesa. For Vidyanandana's exploit, Jayavarman VII rewarded him with the southern part of Champa, Panduranga (Rajapura, near present-day Phan Rang in Vietnam). Vidyanandana reigned as king under the name of Suryavarmadeva. Based on the meaning of the two names, it indicated that Prince In was of higher ranking than Vidyanandana. The reign of Suryajayavarmadeva did not go well. The Cham people revolted against Suryajayavarmadeva; because he was a Khmer, they considered him a foreigner. Suryajayavarmadeva could not control the situation, therefore he decided to abandon Viyaja and flee to Cambodia. Seizing on this opportunity, a Cham prince named Rashupati took over the vacant Vijaya throne and reigned under the name of Jaya Indravarmadesa or Jaya Indravarman V. Without giving the Cham king time to establish his reign, Jayavarman VII decided to release the former Cham king Jaya Indravarman (IV) Ong Vatuv to go back to Champa to help Vidyanandana-Suryavarmadeva fight the new Cham king. Why did Jayavarman VII release his former enemy to join Vidyanandana-Suryavarmadeva in the battle against Rashupati? Perhaps Jayavarman VII feared that Vidyanandana-Suryavarmadeva had become too powerful and it was in his intention all along to divide Champa into two parts. The battle was swift and Rashupati was killed. Seizing on his ambition to be the sole ruler of Champa, Vidyanandana-Suryavarmadeva killed Jaya Indravarman (IV) Ong Vatuv in a battle to control Champa. This event took place in 1192. The event was described on the My Son inscription as follows:[6,p216]

> *In ... 1114 saka (A.D. 1192) the king of Cambodia sent Jaya Indravarman IV (Ong Vatuv) to help the prince (Vidyananda) reconquer Champa. They met at Rajapura, took Vijaya, defeated and killed Jaya Indravarman V (Rashputi) and ruled over Vijaya. Then Jaya Indravarman IV fled from the Cambodians and went to Amaravati where he raised a revolt and invaded Vijaya; but the prince defeated him and put him to death. Henceforth, the prince ruled without opposition.*

Jayavarman VII felt betrayed by Vidyanandana-Suryavarmadeva. It seemed that Jayavarman VII's hunch was correct about the ambition of the young Cham prince that he raised as a warrior. Jayavarman VII did not make Vidyanandana-Suryavarmadeva to be the sole ruler of Champa because he wanted to restrain his power. Jayavarman VII probably felt uneasy about this young ambitious king. He may have felt that he had taught Vidyanandana-Suryavarmadeva too well in the art of warfare, and that he may pose a danger for Cambodia in the future. Considering that he was already advanced in age, probably around sixty seven years old, Jayavarman VII may have felt he would not be around to stop Vidyanandana-Suryavarmadeva if the young Cham king ever intended to expand his kingdom at the expense of Cambodia. It was therefore in Jayavarman VII's design to split Champa into two kingdoms to clip some of Vidyanandana-Suryavarmadeva's power.

With his success, Vidyanandana-Suryavarmadeva became the uncontested king of all Champa. Afterward, Jayavarman VII tried without success to control Vidyanandana-Suryavarmadeva. He had grown to be too independent and seemed to no longer fear Jayavarman VII. To punish the young Cham king for his disobedience, Jayavarman VII sent an army to Champa but it was immediately defeated. He sent another army in 1194 but it was defeated again. Patiently, Jayavarman VII took another young Cham prince named Angsaraja of Turai-vijaya under his tutelage. He raised him at Angkor and like what he had done previously for Vidyanandana, he promoted this young prince to the rank of Yuvaraja (of Champa). Angsaraja was the elder son of the Cham king Jaya Harshavarman II (1162-1163) and grandson of the Cham king named Jaya Harivarman I that Jaya Indravarman (IV) Ong Vatuv had killed and usurped the throne. By nurturing Angsaraja to become a warrior, Jayavarman VII may have been thinking for the future of someday toppling Vidyanandana-Suryavarmadeva and replacing him with a more obedient Cham king. It took another eleven years before Jayavarman VII was able to bring down Vidyanandana-Suryavarmadeva. It was the Cham's king paternal uncle, Yuvaraja Ong Dhanapatigrama (or Managahna Ong Dhanapati), working under the service of Jayavarman VII who deposed Vidyanandana-Suryavarmadeva in 1203. According to the Annamese documents translated by Maspero,[91,p166,note8] Vidyanandana-Suryavarmadeva and his family escaped to Dai Viet with over two hundred boats. He arrived at Co-la (present-day northern Annam) and asked for an asylum. The emperor of Annam may have instructed the governor of Nghe-an (north central coast of present-day Vietnam) to get rid of this troublesome and unwanted Cham king. Realizing the plot against his life was taking place and believing that he may be trapped at Nghe-an, Vidyanandana-Suryavarmadeva concocted an escape plan. He invited the governor to come on board to his vessel and instructed his boats to be burned away. In the confusion, the Cham king escaped to sea and then disappeared completely from history.

From 1203 to 1220, Champa became the province of Cambodia. Jayavarman VII sent Yuvaraja Angsaraja to serve the government of Yuvaraja Ong Dhanapatigrama in Champa. In 1207, Jayavarman VII entrusted Yuvaraja Angsaraja with the command of a Khmer army composed of Burmese and Siamese recruits on a campaign against Dai Viet. No regular Cambodian soldiers were used for this campaign. This may be Jayavarman VII's strategy to provide Angsaraja with some experience on the battlefield without involving unnecessary killing of Khmer soldiers. He would become king of Champa in 1226 and reigned under the name of Jaya Paramesvaravarman II.[1,p171]

The Khmer Empire was already extensive in 1178 but it had expanded to its greatest size under Jayavarman VII. After putting down the revolts in Cambodia, Jayavarman VII consolidated and expanded his power by conquering and controlling other territories on the fringe of the Khmer Empire. The boundaries of the Khmer Empire in 1178 were described by Ling-wai Tai-ta[1,p181; 6,p208; 92] to extend to Chan-ch'eng (Champa) on the north; to the sea on the east; to P'u-kan (Pagan, present-day Burma/Myanmar) on the west; to Kia-lo-hi or Chia-lo-hsi (Grahi, a vassal state of San-fo-t'si aka Srivijava) on the south; to Chen-li-fu (Chanthaburi) on the near-west; to Teng-liu-mei (Tambralinga) on the west and southwest of Chen-li-fu; to Po-ssu-lan (has not been identified with certainty but Ma Duanlin said that it shared the same border with Chen-li-fu on the southeast that Hirth and Rockhill[6,p209] identified as Pa-sseu-li, the region mentioned by Zhou Daguan); to Lo-ho (Lavo) on the west; to San-lo (unidentified but Hirth and Rockhill believed it to be Sien-lo, a name the Chinese called the Siam people); and to Ma-lo-wen (Malyang in the Khmer inscription or Mou-liang as described by Zhou Daguan, which is south of present-day Battambang). In 1225, Chao Ju-kua published in his annals *Chu-fan-chih* the above names that he borrowed from Ling-wai Tai-ta but added six other vassal states. Those states included the Wa or Karen country, believed to be in the northern part of present-day Laos, and unidentifiable states Lu-yang, T'un-li-fu, Wa-li, Ai-p'eng, and Tu-huai-sun.[1,p181] The unrecognized states listed above are however believed to be small Tai states located in the upper Mekong River. The estimated boundary of the Khmer Empire under Jayavarman VII is shown in Figure 34.

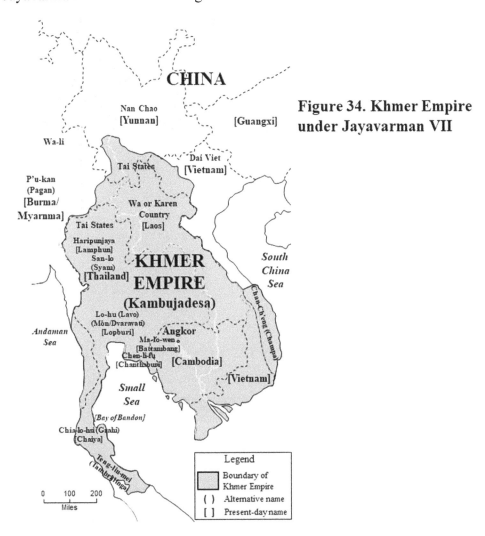

Figure 34. Khmer Empire under Jayavarman VII

In addition to being a great warrior, Jayavarman VII was also a great builder and a king who had great compassion for his people. As soon as he acceded to the throne and put down the revolt, Jayavarman VII embarked on a humanitarian project and on a mission to rebuild the capital that was destroyed by the Cham. It was the most intense period of building activity in the history of the Khmer civilization, probably also of the world. Jayavarman VII was probably sensing his mortality and he may have wanted to honor his parents and accomplish all the good deeds before he departed the world. That may explain the reasons why he built Ta Prohm to honor his mother; Preah Khan to honor his father; and the hospitals and resting houses to ease the pain and suffering of the people according to the Buddhist principles.

The following temples and projects were built or completed by Jayavarman VII: Banteay Kdei, Preah Khan, Ta Prohm, Jayatataka (Pond of Victory or Pond of Jayavarman VII) or Baray of Preah Khan, Neak Pean, Ta Som, Ta Nei, Banteay Chhmar, Angkor Thom, Prasat Chrung, Bayon, Elephant Terrace, Ta Prohm Kel, the Royal Palace, Phimeanakas, Baphuon, Hospital Chapels and resting areas, Krol Ko, Srah Srang, and possibly Preah Khan of Kampong Svay. Banteay Kdei seems to be the first temple built and dedicated as a funerary temple. Some of the major works of Jayavarman VII are summarized below:

Ta Prohm

It is a funerary temple dedicated to the mother of Jayavarman VII, Jayarajacudamani. The temple is similar to Banteay Kdei but on a bigger scale. A carving of his mother to the likeness of the mother of the Buddha known as Prajnaparamita (Perfection of Wisdom) adorned the temple.[6,p229] The name of the temple was originally called Rajavihara (The royal temple or royal monastery). Suryakumara was the author of the Ta Prohm inscription that was dated in 1186. He was mentioned as the Crown Prince.

Preah Khan

It is a funerary temple dedicated to the father of Jayavarman VII, Dharanindravarman II. In addition to being a funerary temple, Preah Khan (Figure 35) also served as a learning center with its own university and library (Figure 35) that had more than 1,000 teachers working. Based on the inscription referencing to the site as a "lake of blood," scholars believed that the temple was built on a ground where a major battle took place, which in this case would be the victory of Jayavarman VII over the Chams. This was originally the holy city that Jayavarman VII built. He named it Nagara Jayasri (Luminous or Fortunate City of Victory). This place is synonymous with *Preah Khan Reach* (or Sacred Sword) as the Holy Palladium of the Khmer monarchy. The Preah Khan inscription says that Jayasri was holier than the Indian holy city of Prayaga (present-day Allahabad) because it was surrounded by three bodies of waters (Baray) that were blessed and sanctified by three holy waters while Prayaga was only sanctified by two holy bodies of waters. The Jayatataka (Baray of Preah Khan, immediately east of Preah Khan) was dedicated to Bodhisattva Avalokitésvara (Buddhahood-like being for Mahayana Buddhism), the East Baray (immediately south of Preah Khan and east of Angkor Thom) was dedicated to Shiva, and the West Baray (immediately west of Angkor Thom) was dedicated to Vishnu. The holy city of Prayaga, located in Uttar Pradesh and considered to be the second oldest city in India, was renamed to Allahabad (Settled by the God in Persian) by the Mughal emperor Akbar the Great (1556-1605). It is considered a holy city because it was built at the confluence of the two holiest rivers in India, the Ganges and Yamuna.

A statue of Dharanindravarman II sculpted in the likeness of a Bodhisattva Avalokitésvara (enlightenment-being with the compassion of the Buddha) adorned the temple. Crown Prince Virakumara, the son of Jayavarman VII and Rajendradevi, was the author of the Preah Khan inscription dated 1191. The Preah Khan inscription mentioned that Jayavarman VII gave a name Jayabuddhamahanatha[6,p229] to twenty-three statues scattered in religious monuments all over the Khmer empire. The meaning of the word Jayabuddhamahanatha can be broken down as follows: 1) *Jayabuddha* would mean Jayavarman VII in glory to Buddha; and 2) *Mahanatha* would mean the great savior. Jayabuddhamahanatha's name is found in the following cities in present-day Thailand: Lopburi, Suphan Ratburi, Phetchaburi, and Mulang

Sing. It was the recognition of the name of Jayabuddhamahanatha on the statues that enabled scholars to identify the monuments in Thailand to belong to the period of Jayavarman VII.

Preah Khan Temple   Preah Khan Library

Figure 35. The Temple and Library of Preah Khan

Angkor Thom

It is undoubtedly the largest city in ancient Cambodia and one of the largest cities in the ancient world. Angkor Thom is enclosed by a square periphery wall with each side measuring approximately 3 km and in turn surrounded by a moat. The entrances to Angkor Thom are guarded by four gates located on the four cardinal points and an additional gate called the Victory Gate located on the west side. All four external gates are similar, but the completely renovated South Gate shows the splendor and magnificent architecture of the Bayon art. The gates were built in the form of towers with the entrances wide and tall enough to accommodate elephants and war equipment to pass through. On the top of each entrance gate sits an impressive figure with three giant faces looking in all three cardinal directions to indicate he was the guardian of the city. There are statues of 54 asuras (demon) and 54 devas (god) on each side of the road-bridge leading to the entrance to the gate. These statues are also found on the other four gates. At the center of Angkor Thom sits the magnificent Bayon, the State Temple and pride of Jayavarman VII. The Royal Palace and its court are only a short distance away from Bayon. Phimeanakas, Baphuon, the Elephant Terrace, and many other monuments are located inside Angkor Thom. The general view of Angkor Thom in relation to Angkor Wat and other monuments in Angkor is shown in Figure 36.

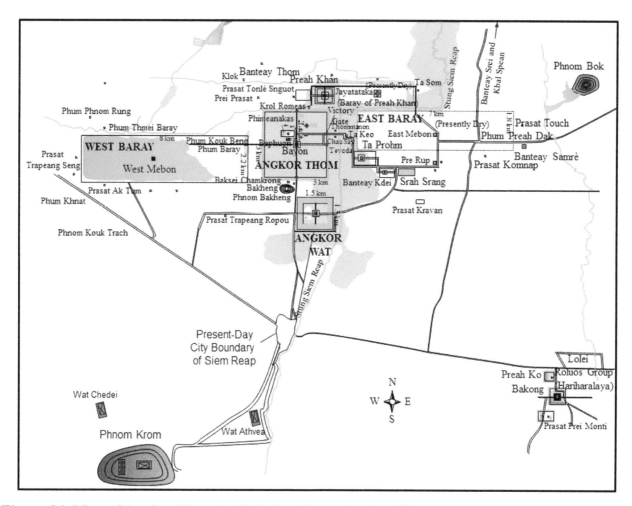

Figure 36. Map of Angkor Thom in Relationship to Angkor Wat and Other Angkor Monuments

Bayon

The construction of Bayon started probably around 1200. It is a very complex monument and it was used as the State Temple for Jayavarman VII and also for his successors. The temple is like a mountain full of duplicated four-faced towers. There are 37 towers still standing, out of the 50 or more towers estimated by Paul Mus.[6,p230; 78,p78] According to the APSARA (Authorité pour la Protection du Site et l'Aménagement de la Région d'Angkor) Authority, there would be 54 towers. I believe the original number of the four-faced towers represents the age of Jayavarman VII at the time of his accession to the throne. Coedès and Briggs believed that Jayavarman VII was born before 1130[6,p209] but Coedès later revised it to no later than 1125.[1,p169] The inscription said that Jayavarman VII was crowned king in 1181.[1,p170] Assuming that he was born between 1125 and 1130, then the age of Jayavarman VII would be between 51 and 56 when he became king. I believe 54 was the original number of towers because it matches the estimated total number of towers at Banteay Chhmar that have similar features.[93]

Either by coincidence or by design, the number 54 was also used for the construction of Angkor Wat such as the 54 Asuras and 54 Devas on the road-bridge at the gates of Angkor Thom, the average north-south solar-moon arc of 54° between winter and summer solstice; and the main Angkor Wat causeway axis offset by 0.75° which corresponds to 54 years of precession (it requires 25,920 years for a precession to complete a cycle of 360°).

Each face-tower was assembled with stones to represent a giant head of Bodhisattva Avalokitésvara Samantamukha (enlightenment-being with the compassion of the Buddha who has faces in all directions) or Lokésvara with the four faces looking in all the four cardinal directions. It must be understood that Mahayana Buddhism, as opposed to Hinayana Buddhism, was practiced under the period of Jayavarman VII's reign. The Mahayanists believe in enlightened beings (Bodhisattva Avalokitésvara) that reach Buddhahood but postpone entering nirvana in order to help more human beings to achieve enlightenment. The concept is opposed to Hinayana Buddhism that believes a being cannot postpone his fate in entering nirvana once he reaches the enlightenment stage. The faces of Lokésvara were a symbol saying that Buddhism was now replacing Brahmanism. The faces clearly represent Jayavarman VII. The temple monument is not comparable to anything existed in the world because the architecture is so unique and so revolutionary. It is called the Bayon architecture that is departed from previous Khmer architecture. After Jayavarman VII, Bayon had been vandalized and gone through many transformations due to religious differences, changing from Buddhism to Brahmanism and then reverting back to Buddhism.

Jayatataka or Baray of Preah Khan with Neak Pean

Jayatataka (Pond or reservoir of Jaya, which in this case means Jayavarman VII), also called Baray of Preah Khan, is located immediately east of Preah Khan and is approximately 3,500 meters in length by 900 meters in width. The Baray was built in dedication to the Buddha but later changed to Bodhisattva Avalokitésvara. Again, this was due to the belief concept differences between Hinayana Buddhism and Mahayana Buddhism. The floor plan of Neak Pean is shown in Figure 37.

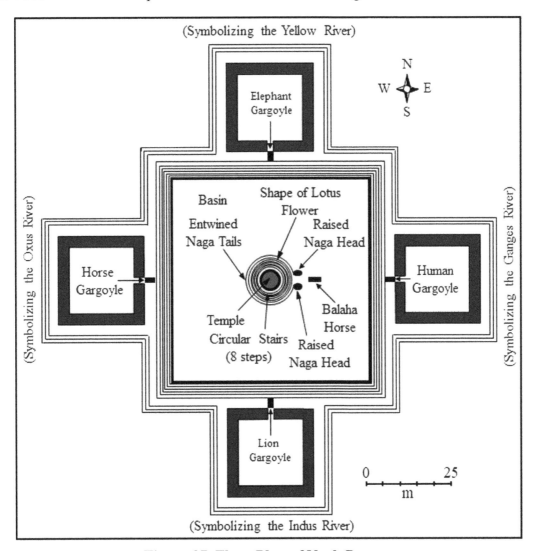

Figure 37. Floor Plan of Neak Pean

A square basin with each side measuring 70 meters was constructed in the middle of the Baray. An elevated circular base of 14 meters in diameter supporting the temple sits in the middle of the basin. The temple was in turn built on the top of eight circular steps. Two serpents attached to the circular bottom step with their tails entwined face the west side while their heads are raised fanwise on the east side to offer a gateway to the temple. The temple is named Neak Pean which means entwined or coiled serpents (or naga). The upper step was built specifically in the form of a lotus flower to represent Buddhism. The water in the basin is fed through four gargoyles represented on the north by the head of an elephant; on the west by the head of a horse; on the south by the head of a lion; and on the east by the head of a human. Coedès interpreted that the water in the basin represented the mythical lake Anavatapta, which means "heat-free", in the cosmological view of Buddhism. According to the legend, the lake has a miraculous power to soothe and calm down the tormented human souls that are full of fires. The lake, supposedly identified as Lake Manasarovar is located in the Himalayas, specifically at the bottom of Mount Kailash. The lake is the source of water that feeds the four great rivers of the world, namely Ganges in the east, the Indus in the south, Oxus in the west, and Huang He (Yellow River) in the north.[94] The four gargoyles are the representations of the four great rivers.

Banteay Chhmar

The meaning of Banteay Chhmar can be interpreted in two different ways, depending on how it is written in Khmer. The word *chhmar,* as in ឆ្មារ, means small/narrow/fine/slim; while the word *chhma,* as in ឆ្មា, means cat. The most popular translation for Banteay Chhmar is the "Citadel of the Cats," but it is sometime referred as the "Narrow or Small Citadel" to contrast with Angkor Thom which means "Large City." The Banteay Chhmar complex functioned both as a funerary temple and also as an outpost for defense purposes, thus came the name Banteay which means citadel or fortress. However, Michael Vickery believed that the word "banteay" was added later because he said that such word had never been found in any Angkor inscriptions.[95] Not only the word "banteay" was not found in the Angkor period, but Vickery said that according to Coedès the original name of the monument was unknown. The citadel is located at the foot of the Dangrek Mountains at about 100 miles northwest of Angkor, close to the present-day Cambodia-Thailand border. The citadel is presently in disrepair but in its heyday it must have rivaled in size and grandeur to Preah Khan and some other great Khmer monuments. It is considered to be the fourth largest temple of the Angkor period of the Bayon style.[93] The citadel is elongated in east-west direction with the outer wall measuring approximately 1,700 x 2,200 meter. It was enclosed by a moat with a width of 63 meter. Within the citadel there was a second wall about 690 x 770 meters surrounded by a moat approximately 50 meters wide. In the center of the second enclosure wall sits the main temple (40 x 170 meters) with a wall about 190 x 250 meters in length, covering 538 meters of bas-reliefs (Bayon covers only 315 meters). There were four causeways in the outer wall with Asuras (demons) pulling nagas similarly to those at the entrance of Angkor Thom. There was a Baray measuring approximately 800 x 1,700 meters on the east side of the citadel. Half of the Baray is dry (western section) and the other half is wet (eastern section). The center of the Baray stands a basin that is now empty of water. An artificial island supporting a Mebon similar to that of Preah Khan was built in the middle of the basin. Figure 38 shows the floor plan of the citadel of Banteay Chhmar and its Baray, based on my interpretation of the description given by George Groslier,[96] of the work done by Dr. Olivier Cunin,[93] and of the statement given in the "Action Plan for Banteay Chhmar 2014."[97]

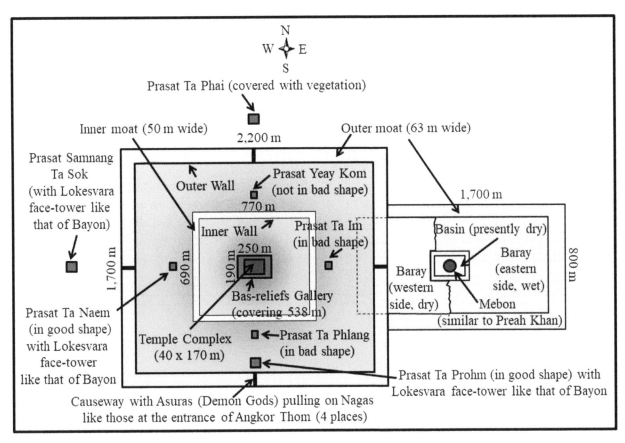

Figure 38. General Floor Plan of Banteay Chhmar
(Map based on References 95, 96, and 97)

It is believed that the funerary temple was built to honor the son of Jayavarman VII, Crown Prince Samtac Srindrakumara, who lost his life between 1160 and 1165 in defending King Yasovarman II against either Bharata Rahu or Tribhuvanaditya.[6,p206,p235] The K.227 inscription, displayed at the National Museum in Phnom Penh, mentioned the names of Sanjaks (probably equivalent to a royal bodyguard) Arjuna and Sri Dharadevapura who sacrificed their lives to protect the Crown Prince on one occasion; and then of Sanjaks Sri Deva and Sri Vardhana who sacrificed their lives to protect the same Crown Prince on another occasion. The statue of Srindrakumara was erected at the central temple while those of the four Sanjaks stood at the four corners of the temple.[6,p206] The temple of Banteay Chhmar published by Georges Groslier in 1937.[96] The three dimensional conceptualization of the Banteay Chhmar temple based on the floor plan layout of Georges Groslier was proposed by Dr. Olivier Cunin in Reference 93. Groslier estimated that 55 towers were built,[6] but according to John F. Cady[16] 56 towers were erected. It is my belief that 54 towers were built because this number would have corresponded to the number of face-towers at Bayon and also to those of the Asuras as well as Devas on the road-bridge at the gates of Angkor Thom. As mentioned earlier in the Bayon section, I believe the number of face-towers represented the age of Jayavarman VII when he acceded to the throne and also, either by design or coincidence, the number 54 was applied to the construction of temples found at Angkor.

The Banteay Chhmar complex, which was built in the Bayon style, is important and very significant for the understanding of the architectural style during the Bayon period. Unlike Bayon that was vandalized and transformed from Buddhism to Shivaism and then back to Buddhism, depending on the kings who succeeded Jayavarman VII, Banteay Chhmar was untouched by the religious upheaval and politics of the time because it was located far away from Angkor Thom where the seat of power occurred. For this reason, the Banteay Chhmar architecture was maintained in its pure Bayon style.

Srah Srang

Srah Srang is interpreted to mean "Royal Bath" or more correctly "Royal Bath Lake" (Srah = lake; Srang = bath for king or monks). The lake was originally dug during the reign of King Rajendravarman II (944-968) under the supervision of the chief architect Kavindrarimathana. The inscription dating in that period says that the "water has been stored for the benefit of all creatures." Jayavarman VII made some improvement around 1200 by adding a terrace on the western side. Srah Srang is still in use today and its size is approximately 350 x 700 meters. It is one of the most serene scenes in Angkor.

Grouping of the Main Temples near Angkor Wat

By pure coincidence, if we combined the main temples built under the reign of Jayavarman VII with those of his predecessors, with Angkor Wat as the starting base for the layout, an amazing pattern emerged showing that the grouping of the temples at Angkor — Angkor Wat, Bayon, Preah Khan, Ta Prohm, Banteay Kdei, Prasat Kravan, Pre Rup. East Mebon, and Ta Som — coincided with the constellation of Draco. This grouping of temples against the Draco constellation as seen from the earth in 10500 BC is shown in Figure 39.

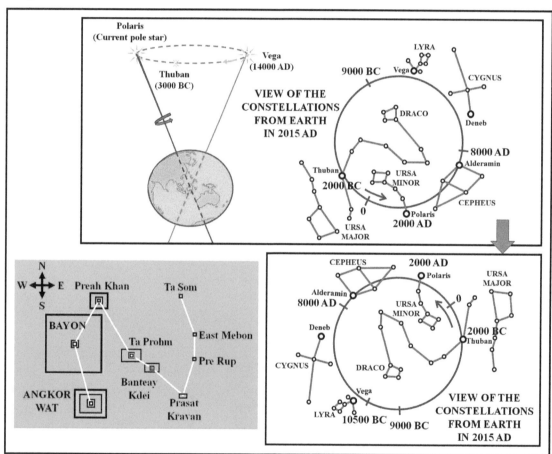

Figure 39. Grouping Pattern of the Major Angkor Temples Shows Remarkable Resemblance to the View of the Draco Constellation (Map of the Constellation, Courtesy of Alex Whitaker)

Jayavarman VII and his Duties as a Buddhist King

As a Buddhist practitioner, Jayavarman VII did not neglect the suffering of his people. The Preah Khan inscription mentioned that 121 rest houses were built approximately every fifteen kilometers throughout the empire. There were 57 rest houses from Angkor to the capital of Champa, Vijaya; 17 from Angkor to Phimai (scholars have found eight of them); 46 in the other cities that have not been identified yet; and one at Phnom Chisor. Realizing the lack of public facilities to care for his people, he commissioned the construction of 102 hospitals. Approximately over 30 locations where the hospitals were built have been identified as of today.

Most of what is learned about Jayavarman VII came from the Phimeanakas inscription. It described Jayavarman VII as a very energetic person with a strong belief in Buddhism (Mahayana) that he inherited from his father, Dharanindravarman II, and reinforced it by his marriage with Jayarajadevi and Indradevi. Physically, Jayavarman VII had a powerful build with a charismatic face. He was portrayed on the bas-reliefs at Angkor and on three other statues, with the most famous one showing him sitting in a Virasana position (Figure 33). The statue shows Jayavarman VII in a blissful state and completely absorbed in meditation. The statue is about 1.38 m in height. Oddly, his arms are missing from the statue. Had the statue been vandalized or desecrated? If it were so, then why is the head not also missing? If the arms were originally attached to the body, then the hands would be resting on his laps based on the position of the body and on other similar statues. If the statue were desecrated and the arms were later removed, then why would his laps remain clean and not show any traces of hands attached to the laps? Was the sculptor instructed to render the statue with the arms missing or was it the freedom of expression on the part of the sculptor to portray Jayavarman VII in this fashion? Additionally, it is somewhat perplexing that the statue portrayed him semi-naked with only a loincloth covering his entire body. The statue seems to suggest that Jayavarman VII had attained enlightenment and abandoned all earthly possession. The image is in tune with the Buddhism philosophy that Jayavarman VII embraced. Prior to this, under the Brahmanism period, most of the statues would show the persons or deities in their complete forms. The body parts that are missing on some of the statues were mainly due to vandalism or caused by the casualties of wars. There are two other statues of Jayavarman VII, one is kept in Bangkok, Thailand, and the other one is a bust displayed at the Musée Guimet in Paris, France.

Jayarajadevi and Indradevi

It is well-known that Jayarajadevi was the principal wife of Jayavarman VII, but the inscription of Preah Khan dated 1191 mentioned that Rajendradevi was also his principal wife.[6,p209] Coedès mentioned that Jayavarman VII had a proclivity of attaching his name to things that he loved the most such as attaching the prefix Jayaraja to his mother's birth name Chudamani to make it Jayarajacudamani, as indicated on the Ta Prohm inscription. As for Jayarajadevi, her name may have been simply Devi or with another prefix attached to Devi. Briggs believed that Jayarajadevi and Rajendradevi may have been the same person.[6,p209] Coedès did not offer any opinion on this matter. It is possible that Rajendradevi may be the birth name of Jayarajadevi and when she became Jayavarman VII's wife, the syllable Rajendra was dropped and replaced with Jayaraja to become Jayarajadevi. The first syllable, Jaya, was meant to indicate she was the wife of Jayavarman VII and the second syllable, raja, was meant to give her the royal rank of a monarch's wife. When Jayarajadevi passed away, Jayavarman VII married her older sister Indradevi and elevated her to the queen position. Her name was preserved in its original form as Indradevi probably on purpose. Jayavarman VII could not drop the syllable Indra and replaced it with Jayaraja as he had done for Rajendradevi because to do so would duplicate the name of his first and principal wife Jayarajadevi. However, he could have added Jayaraja to Indradevi to make it Jayarajaindradevi but to do so would imply that she was of higher rank than Jayarajadevi because of the additional epithet of the word Indra in the name. Indradevi was not only talented but also very literate who "surpassed in her knowledge the knowledge of philosophers." It was unusual and extraordinary to have such a literate woman in ancient Cambodia, but it was not totally surprising because her father and grandfather who were Brahmans may have parted their knowledge/teaching to Indradevi. She was so well versed in the scripture that Jayavarman VII appointed her to be in charge of teaching Buddhism to women at the monastery in which Jayarajadevi was one of her students. Indradevi was not married to Jayavarman VII yet because Jayarajadevi was still alive. Indradevi was the author of the Phimeanakas inscription that was written flawlessly in Sanskrit. The images of Jayarajadevi and Indradevi are represented on the wall in Preah Khan as shown in Figure 40. The statue shown in Figure 41 is displayed in the Musée Guimet in Paris. The museum identified the statue to be possibly representing Jayarajadevi due to its resemblance of the prayerful term of Prajñāpāramitā or Tārā.

**Figure 40. Carving of Jayarajadevi (Left) and Indradevi (Right)
on the Wall of Preah Khan (Photo by Kenneth So)**

**Figure 41. Presumed Statue of Jayarajadevi — Based on its Resemblance
of the Prayerful Term of Prajñāpāramitā or Tārā (Musée Guimet)**

Jayavarman VII's Sons

Jayavarman VII had at least four sons according to the inscriptions and possibly another one (or two) son based on the Burmese Glass Palace Chronicle and Sri Lanka historical data. The four known sons from the Khmer inscriptions are: 1) Samtac Srindrakumara who died between 1160 and 1167 defending Yasovarman II against his enemies (a monument at Banteay Chhmar was erected in his honor); 2) -indravarman (the prefix of his name seems to be missing but Coedès believed it was Nripatindravarman[6,p238] who was governor at Lavo (present-day Lopburi in Thailand) between 1160 and 1165; 3) Suryakumara, mentioned as Crown Prince on the inscription, who was the main author of the inscription of Ta Prohm that was carved around 1186; and 4) Virakumara, the author in charge of the 1191 Preah Khan inscription that specifically mentioned him as the son of Rajendradevi. The first three sons are attributed to Jayarajadevi. The other son (possibly two sons) of Jayavarman VII mentioned in the Burmese and Sri Lanka chronicles are discussed below.

Buddhism in the form of Mahayana flourished under Jayavarman VII. The Burmese Glass Palace Chronicle and the Kalyani Inscriptions in Burma mention that in 1182 a monk named Tamalinda and son of a Khmer king returned to Burma with four monks from four other countries after he had stayed in Sri Lanka to study the Tripitaka. Coedès identified Tamalinda to be the son of Jayavarman VII[89] but he did not specify whom his mother was. Why did Tamalinda return to Burma instead of going back to Kambuja after his study in Sri Lanka? Why did he enter monkhood instead of becoming a politician or a warrior like Jayavarman VII's other sons? His knowledge of Tripitaka would have been greatly helpful to Kambuja as the country tried to recapture its glory day as one of the Buddhist learning centers in Southeast Asia. Considering that Jayavarman VII built Preah Khan to be the learning center with over 1,000 teachers ready to part their knowledge to new students, it is somewhat perplexing that Tamalinda did not go back to Kambuja to serve his father. Did Tamalinda feel he was not one of Jayavarman VII's favorite sons and therefore decided to enter monkhood and made a conscious decision to stay away from his father? Could it be possible that Tamalinda preferred Burma because of his religious differences with Jayavarman VII? Sri Lanka had a religious reform shifting from Mahayana to Hinayana Buddhism around the middle of the twelfth century while Kambuja was still embracing Mahayana Buddhism during Jayavarman VII.

Contrary to some scholars who believed that Buddhism spread from Thailand to Cambodia, Michael Wright claimed it came from Sri Lanka to Cambodia first through Tambralinga (Present-day Nakhon Sri Thammarat) and firmly established its foundation under the reign of Jayavarman VII.[89] Afterward, Buddhism spread from Cambodia to the north and west, corresponding to present-day Laos and Thailand. Concurrently with Buddhism, anything that came out of Angkor was to be emulated because of its prestige. The cult of Devaraja of divine right and the magic and sacred Khmer scripts, *Aksar Moul* (known as *Khom* scripts in Thai), were later adopted by the kings and monks in Thailand. Khom is a Môn word for Khmer. As evidence, Michael Wright brought up the fact that the Pali language was written in Khmer scripts and used for centuries in the Angkor period. He argued that if Buddhism had found its foothold first in Thailand, then Pali would not have been written in Khmer but in Thai or Sinhala scripts. Furthermore, he said that the Emerald Buddha, the Thai national treasure and symbol of the palladium of Thai society, was brought from Sri Lanka to Angkor, moved to Laos, and ended up in Thailand.

The Chronicle of the Emerald Buddha (Preah Keo Morakot)

The Chronicle of the Emerald Buddha is divided into two periods. The first part of the chronicle talks about the origin of the Emerald Buddha that dated back to around the first century AD. The second part talks about the displacement of the Emerald Buddha that took place probably around the 12th to the 15th centuries. The Chronicle of the Emerald Buddha was originally written in Pali and then translated into the Chieng Mai dialect on a palm leaf manuscript.[98] Camille Notton, a young French diplomat trained in Thai language, stumbled upon the manuscript when he was assigned to work in Chieng Mai in 1916. He translated the manuscript into French and then into English in 1932.

The chronicle is a mixture of fable and fact-based events. The first section of the manuscript mentions that monk Nagasena at Wat Asokarem in Pataliputra (present-day Patna in India), with the help of Indra and Vishnu, created four statues of the Buddha as follows:[98]

> *"Phra Ken Chan Deng (Budhha-Heart-Sandal-Red, which was made by King Pasena), Prah Bang (Buddha-Part; so-called because as it is said in the chronicle of The Phra Bang, everybody among human beings and angels contributed a small quantity of gold, silver, and copper for casting the statue), Phra Keo Amarakata (Buddha-Crystal-Smaragd [Emerald]), Phra Che Kham (Budda-Pure-Gold)..."*

The manuscript mentioned five statues but failed to identify the fifth one. As a devoted Buddhist monk, Nagasena believed that the statues of the Buddha would help spread Buddhism and give prominence to the following countries: Lankadvipa (Sri Lanka), Ramalakka, Dvaravati, Chiang Mai, and Lan Xang (Laos).

The second section said that because of the civil war, the king of Pataliputra sent the Emerald Buddha to the king of Lankadvipa for safe keeping. The chronicle said that the king of Pataliputra and his successors never came back to Sri Lanka to retrieve the Emerald Buddha. For two hundred years the statue remained in Sri Lanka and as a result the country flourished and became the center of Buddhism. The chronicle continued and said that because of their dissatisfaction of the Buddhist scriptures from India, Burma sent their monks to Sri Lanka to have them translate the Tripitaka. The account reported by Eric Roeder is as follows:[98]

> *"Finishing their tasks in Lanka the monks made arrangements for their return to Pagan. Two boats set off for the return voyage, one carrying scriptures written by Sri Lankans, and the other carrying teachings for the people of Pagan as well as the image of the Emerald Buddha. As fate would have it, the boat carrying the Emerald Buddha never arrived in Pagan.*

Camille Notton who translated the Chronicle of the Emerald Buddha could not determine who its author was and when the chronicle was written. I will attempt to differentiate facts from fictions, but before doing so it is necessary to report the rest of the story from the chronicle. Eric Roeder reported the following events described in the chronicle:[98]

> *"Anuruddha flew back to Pagan, weary with the length of time it was taking for the boat carrying the scriptures (Tripitaka) and the Emerald Buddha to arrive in his kingdom... Upon his arrival, Anuruddha received word that the long missing boat had arrived in Indrapatha Nagara (Angkor)... The newly-arrived treasures came into the hands of Indrapatha, but this ruler of Angkor ignored Anuruddha's demand to return both the Tripitaka and the Emerald Buddha to Burma. Angered by the news that the king of Angkor refused to return the treasured items, Anuruddha flew through the air to Angkor to scare Indrapatha and his associates. Anuruddha flew around Indrapatha and his men, slashing their necks with his sword. While bleeding, the men were not seriously wounded and Indrapatha, fearing Anuruddha's powers, relinquished control of the Tripitaka. Yet the Pagan King Anuruddha, perhaps in his haste to leave Angkor, took only the boat containing the Tripitaka, leaving behind the statue of the Emerald Buddha."*

It must be noted that Anawratha, and not Anuruddha, was the historical Pegan king. Anuruddha (the son of Sukkhodona who was the brother of King Suddhodana, the father of Siddhartha Gautama Buddha) who was a disciple and cousin of Gautama Buddha could not have existed at the Angkor period described in the chronicle. Furthermore, Anuruddha who realized arahantship (attained high spiritual knowledge) and espoused the teaching of the Buddha of non-violence would not use a sword to slash people's necks, which was completely contrary to the Buddha's teaching. It is also not believable that the king of Sri Lanka would give away the Emerald Buddha without reason to Burma.

I believe the Chronicle of The Emerald Buddha was written by Pagan scribes who tried to justify the action of the Burmese king (probably King Sithu I) for the kidnapping of the Sinhalese princess. The princess was sent as a bride to Jayavarman VII by King Parakramabahu I of Sri Lanka at the request of the Khmer king Dharanindravarman II. The name of King Anawratha, the founder of the Pagan Empire that appears in the chronicle was credited for the unification of the Irrawaddy valley. He ruled the Pagan Empire from 1044 to 1078. He established contacts with Sri Lanka and introduced Theravada Buddhism to Burma. Kambuja, under the reign of Dharanindravarman II, was practicing Mahayana Buddhism. By sending a princess to be the bride of Jayavarman VII, King Parakramabahu I was probably expecting to convert Kambuja to Theravada Buddhism like it had done a few decades earlier, around the middle of the 12th century. As a result of this new alliance, the king of Burma probably felt threatened by Kambuja as the leader of Therevada Buddhism in Southeast Asia, the role that Burma had been playing until this time. It may be for this reason that Burma tried to disrupt the alliance between Sri Lanka and Kambuja. The chronicle says that one boat was carrying the Tripitaka and the other one the Emerald Buddha. I believe that King Parakramabahu I may have sent the princess in one boat, a copy of the Tripitaka in another boat to be used as new scriptures for Theravada Buddhism, and the Emerald Buddha as a gift for the marriage either in the same boat or in another boat. At least an extra boat had been sent by the king of Sri Lanka to accompany the voyage of her daughter to Angkor.

Dorothy Fickle, the author of the book *Images of the Buddha in Thailand,* [99] who has studied the craftsmanship of the images of the Buddha in Sri Lanka has come up with an observation that the Buddha is depicted with a Virasana position. Can it be a coincidence that the famous statue of Jayavarman VII is also shown in a Virasana position like the statue of the Emerald Buddha? I believe that the image of the Emerald Buddha may have influenced the craftsmanship for the statue of the famous Jayavarman VII's Virasana pose. I also believe that Burma was targeting only to kidnap the Sinhalese princess to disrupt the alliance between Sri Lanka and Kambuja but was aware of the other two treasures, the Tripitaka and the Emerald Buddha, only after the ships arrived at Ligor (present-day Nakhon Si Thammarat in Thailand) and then continued its way to Angkor. A film called *Emerald Buddha, Seat of the Center of Earth,* directed in 1995 by Timor Somogyi of the Films for the Humanities & Sciences Department of Princeton University implies that a ship carrying a princess and the Emerald Buddha arrived at Ligor.

The Chronicle of the Emerald Buddha is one source of information, but there is another one called the Luang Prabang Chronicle that is equally important but with slightly less mythology injected into the story. In general, the Luang Prabang Chronicle is similar to the Chronicle of the Emerald Buddha. Instead of Anuruddha flying, the Luang Prabang Chronicle says that he disguised himself as a merchant on a Chinese boat and tried to steal the Emerald Buddha from Angkor, but was not successful in his attempt. It says that only after a violent storm at Angkor (the Chronicle of the Emerald Budhha mentions of a great flood at Angkor during the reign of King Dharmasoka or Thommasoka) that the Emerald Budhha was removed and sent to the north and kept at Ayutthaya by two Khmer monks who betrayed the king. This story will be further discussed in the reign of Thommasoka near the end of the chapter and in Chapter 8 under *The Origin of the Thai.*

Khmer Prince Becoming King of Sri Lanka

In addition to the strong relationship between Sri Lanka and Cambodia that was brought up earlier under the reign of Dharanindravarman II, Mendis Rohanadeera — a prominent and well respected Sri Lanka archaeology and history professor on Buddhism — identified the Sri Lanka king, Kirti Sri Nissankamalla (1187-1196), to be a Khmer prince from a state neighboring Lavo of the Dvaravati Kingdom (present-day Singpuri/Lopburi in Thailand), which was a Khmer territory under Jayavarman VII's empire[89]. Furthermore, Rohanadeera said that the Sinhala king Parakramabahu I sent his niece in marriage to the Khmer prince when he was still in Singpuri. This may be a second attempt by the Sri Lanka king to form an alliance with the Khmer Empire that had been thwarted by Burma when this latter kidnapped a Sinhala princess that King Parakramabahu I sent to be the bride of Jayavarman VII at the request of his father, King Dharanindravarman II. As mentioned earlier, Burma did not want Kambuja to form an alliance with Sri Lanka because this latter which was recognized as the "Holy Land of Buddhism" would place the Khmer Empire in a prominent role to help spread Buddhism. In addition to being rivals in religion, Burma was also in trade rivalry with Kambuja. Burma made every attempt to disrupt commerce activities between Sri Lanka and Kambuja as well as to other countries.[89]

Burma's belligerences resulted in the confiscations of elephants, money, and ships that Sri Lanka used to do commerce with other countries. The aggressive actions of Burma angered King Parakramabhatu I. The Sri Lanka king ordered retaliation by sending his fleet of ships to invade Burma, which they defeated the Burmese army and destroyed many villages.

Concerning the Khmer prince, could he be -indravarman, the governor of Lavo (Lopburi) and son of Jayavarman VII? A strong case can be made that the Sri Lanka king Kirti Sri Nissankamalla is indeed -indravavarman. Srindrakumara who was killed during the battle defending Yasovarman II could not have been the Sri Lanka king. Because Kirti Sri Nissankamalla's reign started in 1187, it would also preclude Virakumara (the other son of Jayavarman VII) as the Sri Lanka king for the fact that his duty as king of Sri Lanka would not permit him to spend inordinate amount of time on the Preah Khan inscription that was dated in 1191. It would only leave Suryakumara and -indravarman (the two remaining sons of Jayavarman VII) as the probable candidates for the Sri Lanka king. Suryakumara was the author of the 1186 Ta Prohm inscription which occurred one year before the Khmer prince acceded to the throne of Sri Lanka, but because he was the crown prince of Kambuja it would also exclude him as the king of Sri Lanka. Therefore, the only person left was -indravarman, the governor of Lavo, whom the Culavamsa chronicle of Sri Lanka mentions as the Khmer prince of Singpuri who succeeded King Parakramabahu I in 1187.

King Nissankamalla of Sri Lanka left an inscription that mentions the existence of a Khmer residential quarter called *Kambojavasala* in Polonnaruwa (ancient capital city of Sri Lanka). The inscription indicated that there was a special quarter reserved for Khmers in Sri Lanka whose inhabitants included monks, ambassadors, as well as soldiers. Furthermore, the inscription said that the king took care of the Khmer inhabitants by providing them with clothing, gold, and necessary items for living.

The full implementation of Buddhism by Jayavarman VII was paved by Suryavarman I and Dharanindravarman II who had made the religion flourish alongside Shaivism and more acceptable to the officials. Even though Buddhism had replaced Brahmanism under Jayavarman VII, the official ceremony was still being handled by Brahmans. It was a tradition that had existed over many centuries and became part of the Khmer monarchy's culture. A Brahman named Jaya Mangalartha became Jayavarman VII's guru. An inscription at Angkor Thom mentioned that a Brahman scholar named Hrishikesa became Jayavarman VII's chief priest (*purohita*) and that the king gave him the title Jaya Mahapradhana.[1,p173] George Coedès stated that Hrishikesa (Jaya Mahapradhana) came from Narapatidesa, a region believed to be located in Burma. The inscription said that Hrishikesa who "having learned that Cambodia was full of eminent experts on the Veda, came here to manifest his knowledge."

The date of Jayavarman VII's death is somewhat of a mystery, especially for a major monarch that historians considered to be the greatest Khmer king. Based on Annam and Champa chronicles during the period of 1216 to 1218 and on the study by George Coedès' students, Jayavarman VII's reign is believed to last until his death around 1219.

One of the theories espoused by some scholars concerning the collapse of the Khmer Empire was attributed to Cambodia adopting Buddhism as its religion. This theory does not seem to have any merits for the following reasons: 1) Why did the Khmer Empire reach its apogee during the reign of Jayavarman VII who abandoned Brahmanism for Buddhism?; 2) Why did Thailand, which embraced Buddhism, continue to grow and expand?; and 3) Kublai Khan embraced Buddhism and continued to see the Mongol territory expanded after Genghis Khan. The theory for the collapse of the Khmer Empire will be discussed in subsequent chapters. The genealogy is shown in Figure 32.

The Decline of the Khmer Empire

41   Indravarman II (1219-1243) ឥន្ទ្រវរ្ម័ន (ទី២)

Transliterated Name: Īndravarmăn II
Other Name: Sri Indravarman[6,p238]

Relationship: Undetermined (He may or may not be (Nripat)–indravarman, the son of Jayavarman
   VII who was the governor of Lavo).
Religion: Brahmanism (Mahayana or Theravada Buddhism according to my opinion)
Purohita: Hrishikesa (title of Jaya Mahapradhana)
Guru: Jaya Mangalartha
Temples:[78] Prasat Suor Prat, Ta Prohm, Banteay Kdei, Ta Som, Ta Nei
Capital: Angkor Thom
Genealogy: Figure 32

Indravarman II's reign was very obscure and there was almost nothing written about him, except for
one inscription mentioning that he died in 1243. Because he succeeded Jayavarman VII, historians tend
to consider him as his son. However, there are no definite proofs or inscriptions that indicate he was the
son of Jayavarman VII. The inscription at Angkor mentioned that "-indravarman", a name with missing
scripts, as the governor of Lavo (present-day Lopburi in Thailand) and son of Jayavarman VII. George
Coedès believed "Nripat" was the missing prefix, which would render the prince name to be
Nripatindravarman.[6,p238] There is no certainty to confirm whether Indravarman II was indeed the same
person shown in the inscription as -indravarman. As I have demonstrated earlier, if -indravarman were
indeed King Kirti Sri Nissankamalla of Sri Lanka, then Indravarman II is not the son of Jayavarman VII.
A question must then be raised as to why Suryakumara, who was designated as the crown prince, was not
chosen to succeed Jayavarman VII? The inscription is silent on this subject. Was there a power struggle
between Jayavarman VII's sons and other claimants to the throne of Angkor?

Claude Jacques talked about this subject in his paper called *Les Derniers Siècles d'Angkor*[100] but he
did not provide any explanations why Indravarman II was chosen as the successor to Jayavarman VII.
According to George Coedès who had studied the inscription, he did not believe that Indravarman II was
the son of Jayavarman VII. If that were the case, would Claude Jacques not find the above situation
somewhat irregular and suspicious? Claude Jacques put forth a theory that Indravarman II who succeeded
Jayavarman VII contributed to the completion of some of the monuments that were not finished under the
reign of his predecessor. The "great reform" of the "Bayon art" should also be credited to Indravarman
II.[100,pp372-373] Furthermore, he theorized that the absence of inscription about Indravarman II could be due
to his successor (presumably Jayavarman VIII) erasing all traces of his achievements. His theory is one
explanation concerning the vandalism and erasing of all traces of Buddhism pertaining to the periods of
Jayavarman VII and Indravarman II, but I find his conjecture to be inconsistent for at least two reasons:
1) if Indravarman II's successor made every effort to erase all traces of his achievements why would he
still leave the name of Indravarman II as the king who succeeded Jayavarman VII?; 2) why did the
successor still leave the inscription of Indravarman II's guru and chief priest, Jaya Mangalartha and Jaya
Mahapradhana, known as the Mangalartha inscription intact?

I propose a different theory which I shall explain below. For Indravarman II who inherited a great
empire and who had a long reign, it is expected that there would be at least inscriptions mentioning some
of his accomplishments during his ruling period. The absence of information about Indravarman II led
historians to speculate that he may be the legendary Leper King (Sdach Komluong) mentioned throughout
Cambodia history.

Zhou Daguan, the Chinese envoy who visited Angkor during the reign of King Indravarman III in
1296, mentioned that one of the Khmer kings contracted leprosy.[27,p35; 60,p162] Using the process of
elimination, the identity of the Leper King could be determined with some certainty. The Leper King
period was supposed to occur in the 13th century between the reign of Jayavarman VII and Indravarman
III. There were four kings reigning during this period, namely Jayavarman VII, Indravarman II,
Jayavarman VIII, and Indravarman III. Indravarman III could be excluded as the Leper King because
Zhou Daguan specifically said that the Leper King pertained to a king in the past and not during his visit

to Angkor. Because a great deal of information is known about Jayavarman VII, there is no reason to believe he was the Leper King either. It would leave either Indravarman II or Jayavarman VIII as the probable Leper King. Based on his long reign and the Ayutthaya chronicle that provides ample information about the Khmer king, Jayavarman VIII could also be eliminated as the king who contracted leprosy, which leaves only Indravarman II as the very likely Leper King. If Indravarman II were indeed to contract leprosy, then it is understandable that he would stay out of the public eyes, spend his remaining years in seclusion and in obscurity, and forbid scribes to mention about his reign except to say he was the king who succeeded Jayavarman VII.

There is evidence of a Khmer king leaving Angkor in the 12th-13th centuries to India to seek the cure for the leprosy that he contracted. The orientalist and indologist French scholar named Sylvain Lévi who was particularly known for his work on the dictionary of Buddhism, cited the *Telugu* manuscript that is housed at the University of Madras library (one of the three oldest universities in India) telling a story of a Khmer leper king who was cured of his disease in his pilgrimage to India.[6,p232] Furthermore, there was a story in the Sri Lanka tradition mentioning that there was a group of Khmer warriors living in the capital of Sri Lanka in the 12th-13th centuries. Nowadays, there is a bronze statue of Lokésvara of Khmer origin displayed in the Museum of Colombo in Sri Lanka to represent a foreign king who was cured of leprosy.[6,p232] Who was this Lokésvara personality? The fact that a foreign (Khmer) king went to Sri Lanka to search for the cure of leprosy supports the eminent scholar Professor Mendis Rohanadeera's finding that the Sri Lanka king Kirti Sri Nissakamalla was a Khmer prince from Singburi.[89] If King Kirti Sri Nissakamalla were -indravarman, the son of Jayavarman VII, it would then be sensible on the part of Indravarman II to seek help from the king of Sri Lanka who may be one of his kin and compatriots. It would also support my theory that in addition of Indravarman II being a Leper King, he may also be a Buddhist instead of a Shaivite as believed by many historians.

I concur with Claude Jacques that Indravarman II was a Buddhist but I do not agree with him when he said that it was Jayavarman VIII who erased all Indravarman II's achievements because he was a Shaivite. I believe the effacement of Buddhist traces from monuments was perpetrated by Jayavarman VIII's guru Jaya Mangalartha and chief priest Jaya Mahapradhana, which I will explain below. Etienne Aymonier theorized that King Yasovarman I who reigned from 889 to 908 was the Leper King but he did not elaborate further.[60,p162] I do not agree with Aymonier because the inscriptions pertaining to Yasovarman I profusely praised him as intelligent, strong, and good looking that would make his creator jealous. Additionally, he was too far removed from the time of when the Leper King was supposed to occur. Scholars even considered Yasovarman I as one of the greatest Khmer kings.

The statue of the Hindu god Yama — Lord of the Death — that was built during the time period of Jayavarman VII was incorrectly identified to be the Leper King. The statue shows Yama with a moustache sitting with one leg folded and the other one raised. The current statue of the Leper King located in the northwest corner of the Royal Square at Angkor Thom is only a replica of the original one that is now displayed at the National Museum in Phnom Penh, Cambodia. In the late 1950s, the French scholar and conservator of the temples of Angkor Bernard Philippe Groslier, saw marks around the neck of the Leper King statue and realized immediately that thieves tried to cut off its head to sell it in the black market. He had a replica made to replace the statue and had the original shipped to the national museum in Phnom Penh.[101,p585] The Leper King is also known by the name of Dharmaraja according to the inscription found on the base of the original statue. The legend of the Leper King assigned to the statue may have been falsely started because of moss and lichen growing on the statue, rendering it to be discolored as resembling a person contracting leprosy. Afterward, it probably grew into a legend which would confound with the historical fact of the real king contracting leprosy.

The Jaya Mangalartha inscription indicates that both Jaya Mangalartha and Jaya Mahapradhana who served Jayavarman VII were retained as the guru and chief priest of Indravarman II, respectively. The inscription calls the king by the name of Sri Indravarman. Scholars have suggested — based on the evidence that the statues of Buddha or the sculptures of Lokésvara at Bayon were destroyed or allowed to be vandalized and replaced with those of Shiva — that Indravarman II may not be a Buddhist but rather a Shaivite. However, I would suggest that the destruction of Buddhism symbols after the death of Jayavarman VII may not be given under the order of Indravarman II but under the orders of Jaya Mangalartha and Jaya Mahapradhana instead.

If Indravarman II were indeed the Leper King and coupled with the evidence of the bronze statue of Lokésvara in Sri Lanka as mentioned above, then one can surmise that he was a Buddhist king. Could it be possible that Indravarman II left Angkor and went to India and Sri Lanka to seek treatment for the cure of his leprosy as cited in the *Telugu* manuscript above? If that were the case, then it would explain the absence of inscription concerning his reign. The affairs of the state would then be handled by his guru and chief priest during his absence from Angkor. Because of their Shaivite faith, Jaya Mangalartha and Jaya Mahapradhana would undo Jayavarman VII's work by reverting Buddhism back to Shaivism. How could Jaya Mangalartha spend more time on the inscription about his family than that of the king unless this latter was absent from Cambodia. Another speculation could be advanced concerning the Crown Prince Suryakumara not succeeding Jayavarman VII. Undoubtedly, Suryakumara would be a fervent Buddhist like his father. The guru and the chief priest had probably all along planned to revert Buddhism back to Shaivism after the death of Jayavarman VII. If Suryakumara were allowed to succeed his father, then their plan would all fall apart. Therefore, it would be in their best interest to manipulate the outcome of the person to succeed Jayavarman VII. Because the inscription was silent during this period and Indravarman II who seemed to be a puppet king and whose origin is undetermined, one can suggest that the scheme conducted by Jaya Mangalartha and Jaya Mahapradhana was successful.

The lack of information on Suryakumara and Virakumara who spent their time producing inscriptions on Ta Prohm and Preah Khan seems very odd. Was there a conspiracy to remove the children of Jayavarman VII from succeeding him? Were these two princes, children and direct heirs of Jayavarman VII, murdered to make room for Indravarman II who could be easily manipulated?

Immediately after the death of Jayavarman VII, the Khmer Empire started to lose the grips on its vassal states. Cambodia decided to leave Champa around 1220. Prince Angsaraja of Turai-vijaya that Jayavarman VII had raised at the court of Angkor became king of Champa in 1226 under the name of Jaya Paramesvaravarman II.[1,p171,p182] The emergence of the Tai states, most of them former vassal states of the Khmer Empire, started to pose real threats to Cambodia. Tambralinga, the Khmer vassal state in the Malaysian Peninsula, regained its independence from Cambodia in 1230 or earlier.[6,pp238-239] King Sri Dharmaraja Chandrabhanu who descended from the Padmavamsa dynasty was the ruler of Tambralinga. He played an important role in the emergence of the future kingdom of Ayutthaya. The genealogy of Indravarman II is shown in Figure 32.

42   Jayavarman VIII (1243-1295) ជ័យវរ្ម័ន (ទី៨)

Transliterated Name: Jayăvarmăn VIII
Other Name: God of Chao Muang Sri Sodharapura
Posthumous Name: Paramesvarapada[6,p244]
Relationship: Probably the grandson of Indravarman II; married to Chakravartirajadevi.
Religion: Reported in literature as Brahmanism, but it is debatable.
Purohita: Hrishikesa (title: Jaya Mahapradhana); Vidyesavid (grandnephew of Sarvajnamuni, a prominent Brahman from the family of Aryadesa) succeeded Jaya Mahapradhana.
Guru: Jaya Mangalartha; Jaya Mangalartha II (uncle of Jayavarman VIII by marriage) replaced his father Jaya Mangalartha.
Temples[16]: Bapuon, Terrace of the Leper King, Preah Pithu,
Capital: Angkor Thom (Sri Sodharapura which is a corrupted name of Sri Yasodharapura)
Genealogy: Figure 32

Jayavarman VIII succeeded Indravavarman II in 1243 but because of the lack of inscriptions or information concerning these two kings, no definite conclusion can be made about their relationships. The succession which seemed to be normal would therefore indicate that these two kings were related. Because of his long reign that lasted over fifty years, thus suggesting he acceded to the throne at a young age, Jayavarman VIII is believed to be the grandson of his predecessor. Both Jaya Mangalartha and Jaya Mahapradhana retained their positions as guru and chief priest of Jayavarman VIII, respectively. By this time they must have been of advanced ages themselves. They both exerted great influence on the young king.

After the death of Indravarman II, Jaya Mahapradhana went on his pilgrimage to Bhimapura (Present-day Phimai in Thailand) in 1165 saka (1243 AD) to pray for the resting soul of the king.[6,p238] By this time he was about sixty years old. He took the opportunity to marry Sri Prabha, a young girl from a rich Shaivite family. They produced six children. They gave their second daughter in marriage to the king. She was known as Queen Chakravartirajadevi, which means the supreme queen goddess.[6,p240] They produced two children, one boy and one girl with the latter one named Sri Srindrabhupesvara Cuda.[6,p251] The mother of the queen had a younger sister named Subhadra who married a Brahman named Jaya Mangalarthasuri whose epithet is "Prince of Professors." He is the son of Jaya Mangalartha and historians differentiate him from his father by calling him Jaya Mangalartha II. The fact that Jaya Mahapradhana had his second daughter (Chakravartirajadevi) married Jayavarman VIII and the younger sister of his wife (Subhadra) married into the family of Jaya Mangalartha would give even more credence to the conspiracy theory that I raised earlier concerning the accession of Indravarman II. It was also very likely that Jaya Mahapradhana and Jaya Mangalartha (I and II) played a big part in the choice of the young king to succeed Indravarman II. In this manner they would exert their influence on the young king and continued to ensure that Shaivism remained strong after their deaths.

The Jaya Mangalartha family was so influential that the king built a temple in Angkor Thom that he sanctified as the Temple of Mangalartha. According to Briggs, the temple was named to honor Jaya Mangalartha II,[6,p243] but I believe it was dedicated to the family of Mangalartha. By this time, Mangalartha II had replaced his father who had passed away as Jayavarman VIII's guru. In 1295, the king erected a statue of his guru and another one of the guru's mother at the temple. It must be noted that Jaya Mangalartha II was not only Jayavarman VIII's guru but he was also his uncle by marriage. As a consequence, Jaya Mangalartha II's mother was the grandaunt of the king by marriage. The king honored these two people by giving deity's names to their statues. They were called Sri Jaya Trivikrama-Mahanathha and Sri Jaya Trivikrama-Devesvari.[6,p243] George Coedès mentioned that by this time Jaya Mangalartha II was over one hundred years old[1,p212] but Briggs believed the inscription was probably meant for Jaya Mangalartha, the father, because Jaya Mangalartha II could not have been born before 1243.

To help sustain the temple, Jayavarman VIII provided three villages with slaves to care for the temple. The temple required a priest to run it. Therefore, to secure the uninterrupted functioning of the temple Jayavarman VIII issued a proclamation that the position of the chief priest would be hereditary with the female becoming the chief priest if the male line became extinct.[6,p243]

To keep Brahmanism as the dominant religion, Jayavarman VIII (probably with the influence and recommendation of his guru and chief priest) called on Vidyesavid and Madhurendrapandita (or Madhurendrasuri) to join his court. Vidyesavid was given the title of royal *hotar* (chief priest). According to the inscription of Angkor Wat — post Jayavarman VII's reign — Vidyesavid came from a prominent Brahman family of Aryadesa (northern India), whose granduncle Sarvajnamuni built a temple in Madhya Desa.[1,p212; 6,p243] The Brahman Sakrasvamin who was the brother-in-law of Queen Jayadevi, daughter of Jayavarman I, came from Madhya Desa.[58,p3] The region of Madhya Desa is believed to be located south of the Himalaya, north of Vindhya (present-day Madhya Pradesh), and west of Prayaga (present-day Allahabad). Prior to coming to Angkor and becoming Jayavarman VII's royal *hotar*, Vidyesavid was the priest at the temple that his granduncle built. His knowledge in astronomy and his wisdom reached Jayavarman VIII.[6,p243] The inscription at Banteay Srei mentions that Madhurendrapandita was the descendant of Jayavarman V's guru, the person in charge of building Banteay Srei. He was given a post as "administrator and dispenser of the royal favor."

The reign of Jayavarman VIII fell under turbulent times with the rise of Sukhothai, the emergence of Ayutthaya, and the conquest of the Mongols throughout the world. George Coedès mentioned that under the reign of Kublai Khan, the Mongol sent a small army to Cambodia in 1283 via Champa.[19,p193] To keep Cambodia out of Mongol's complete domination, Jayavarman VIII acknowledged his vassalage by sending tribute to Kublai Khan. The Khmer Empire lost the Tai states which made up mostly of present-day Thailand during this time period. An analysis of the rise of Sukhothai and Ayutthaya will be discussed in depth in Chapter 8 under *The Origin of the Thai*.

As I was doing my research on Jayavarman VIII and Zhou Daguan I came upon an old article in Radio Free Asia (RFA), dated 27 April 2010, that said a team of Cambodian researchers from the Royal Academy of Cambodia had discovered an ethnic group with a population of more than 1,000 living in Xishuangbanna at the southern tip of the Yunnan province in China.[102] Dr. Sum Chhum Bun who led the team believed that these people were the descendants of two Khmer families of mahout (elephant trainer) that the Khmer king sent to China to take care of the elephants [that were given as a gift to the Chinese emperor]. Dr. Sum Chhum Bun added that the Khmer king *sent two more families to cook for the Chinese emperor* (ដើមបុរ៉ុង) after he found out the emperor was fond of Khmer cuisine. He said that this event took place near the end of the 13th century, which in this case would have been Emperor Chenzong (aka Timur Khan) who ruled China from 1295 to 1307. The Cambodian team said that this ethnic people remembered some ancient Khmer words and were also able to speak them. If Dr. Sum Chhum Bun were correct concerning the time period, then the Khmer king would have been Jayavarman VIII. It is very possible that the Khmer had introduced noodles to China by these Khmer cooks because the best known Khmer staple food called *Num Banhchok* (នំបញ្ចុក) was made of noodles.

God of Chao Muang Sri Sodharapura

The Vat Mahadhatu inscription of Sukhothai that is currently preserved at the National Library of Thailand in Bangkok mentioned that the God (phi fā) of Chao Muang Sri Sodharapura bestowed the title of *Kamratēng Añ Phā Muang Sri Indrapatīndrāditya* to the Tai Chieftain Pho Khun Pha Muang Chao of Muang Rat[103,p5] and also gave the sword *Jaiyasrī* and his daughter named Nang Sikharamahadevi in marriage to the Tai chieftain.[103,pp7-8; 41,p195] Sri Sradharajaculamuni Sri Rattanalankadipa Mahasami pen chao, the grandson of Pha Muang, was the author of the Vat Mahadhatu inscription.[103,p3] The Tai chieftain of the small principality of Muang Rat was located in the eastern territory of Sukhothai,[103,p5] probably in present-day Uttaradit in Thailand. The word muang has no direct equivalency in modern vocabulary. Muang is above the primary unit of a village and could be a conglomeration of villages. Some scholars translated muang as realm.

Who was the God of Chao Muang Sri Sodharapura? Coedès found the clue to the meaning of Sri Sodharapura. In a 17th century document, he found a letter from the king of Cambodia addressed to the king of Japan where Cambodia was written as *Kambujādhipati Srīyasodhara brah Mahānagara Indraprastha Rastharājadhānī*.[103,pp8-9] According to Coedès, Sri Sodharapura was the corrupted name of Sri Yasodharapura, the ancient name of Angkor Thom. Sriyasodharapura was changed to Sriy-Sodharapura, then to Sri Sodharapura. Subsequently, Khmer monarchs after the Angkor period adopted the above name to designate their capitals. Coedès discovered that King Mahanibbhana (Nippean Bat) reigned at Sri Sodararajadhani (Catummukha Mangala Sakalakambujadhipati Srisodhara Pavaras Indapattapuri Rattharajasima Mahanagara), which was spelled Siri Sandhara in Pali and Srei Santhor in Khmer.[103,p8] Therefore, the God of Chao Muang Sri Sodharapura mentioned on the Vat Mahadhatu inscription dated no later than 1357 [based on the Nagara Jum inscription dated 1357 of the year of the

Rooster which mentions the Vat Mahadhatu inscription that is presently preserved at the National Library of Thailand in Bangkok] was identified by historians as none other than Jayavarman VIII.

It seems that Jayavarman VIII recognized the emergence of Pha Muang as a strong Tai chieftain and wanted to secure his loyalty. By conferring on Pha Muang the Angkorian title equivalent to a king (or vice-king) and making an alliance with him by giving his daughter in marriage, Jayavarman VIII would expect to calm down the rebellion that was fomented on the fringe of Khmer territory in the northwest region. Pha Muang's Pali name was recorded as Rocaraja.[6,p240] It seems the effort that Jayavarman VIII invested on Pha Muang to secure his loyalty did not pay off because a few years later, around 1247,[104,p41] he joined forces with a Tai chieftain by the name of Bang Klang Hao to rebel against the Khmer king. Bang Klang Hao was the chieftain of Muang Bang Yang located in the neighboring area of Sukhothai. Contrary to Pha Muang, Bang Klang Hao did not pledge his allegiance to the Khmer king. The Khmer may have been taken by surprise with Pha Muang's betrayal as the combined forces of the rebels defeated the Khmer outpost controlled by the Khmer general named Khlon Lamphong (the bold Khom) at Sri Satchanalai (present-day Sawankhalok in Thailand). The rebel army entered Sri Satchanalai in victory. Upon occupying the city, Pha Muang decided (probably under a threat) to give his title of *Kamratēng Añ Sri Indrapatīndrāditya* and the *Jaiyasrī* sword (sword of victory) to Bang Klang Hao.[103,p7]

The coronation of Bang Klang Hao as king of Sukhothai took place post 1247, probably around 1253. He is known by his short name Sri Indraditya. Coedès could not determine the exact date of Sri Indraditya's enthronement but he estimated to be in 1220, which seems to be erroneous.[1,p196] The analysis of this victory and of Ram Khamhaeng, the second son of Sri Indraditya, who played a prominent role in the rise of Sukhothai will be discussed more thoroughly in Chapter 8 reserved for *The Origin of the Thai*.

The reign of Jayavarman VIII was marked by defeats and the loss of Khmer territory to the Tai warlords. His reign coincided with the attempt of territorial expansion in Southeast Asia by the Mongols under the reign of Kublai Khan. The conquest of the Mongols on Nan Chao benefitted in the emergence of the Tai states in the Menam valley that were under the control of the Khmer Empire at the time. The occupation of Nan Chao by the army of Kublai Khan in 1253-1254 forced the Tai residents to migrate toward the Menam valley. The new Tai refugees included hardened warriors who had experience fighting the Mongols. This new influx of Tais from Nan Chao contributed in replenishing the Tai chieftains like Mangrai and Ram Khamhaeng with soldiers and weaponry. Even though the Mongols were not as successful in occupying and controlling Southeast Asia as they had done in Eurasia, their policies had benefitted the Tai states in the Menam valley at the expense of Cambodia. The Mongols' conquest of Southeast Asia did not meet with the same success as they had accomplished in Eurasia because of the condition of the terrain. Unlike Eurasia that is covered with plains, Southeast Asia terrain is covered with dense tropical forest that is not amenable for cavalry warfare where the Mongols excelled at. Emboldened by the lack of the Mongols' success, the Khmer king refused to submit to Kublai Khan's rule. To punish the Khmers and countries opposing his rule, Kublai Khan encouraged the Tai to conduct raids and warfare against their neighbors. According to Camille Sainson,[105] Kublai Khan ordered the governor of Yunnan in 1268 to invade Champa (Chen Cheng) and Cambodia (Chenla). Finally, the Mongol general-in-chief Su-Wu (Sugatu) conquered Champa in 1282 but failed to subjugate Cambodia. Zhou Daguan mentioned that the Angkor court even imprisoned the two Chinese military envoys (one carrying the Standard of the Tiger and the other the golden tablet) that Su-Wu sent to Cambodia.[6,p242; 27,pxviii-xix] According to Pelliot, Kublai Khan who became the Chinese Emperor and founded the Yuan Chinese dynasty never received homage from Cambodia until his death in 1294.[6,p242]

By 1295 Jayavarman VIII was an old man and probably infirm also. It may be for this reason that his trusted general Srindravarman who was in charge of the army and also a lover of his daughter Srindrabhupesvera Cuda mounted a coup d'état to take over the throne. Jayavarman VIII was forced to abdicate and he passed away probably in 1296 or shortly after. By this time, the Khmer Empire had lost most of the territory covered by present-day Thailand. Lavo seemed to be still part of the Khmer territory. Jayavarman VIII received the posthumous name Paramesvarapada. The genealogy is shown in Figure 32.

43 Indravarman III (~1295 or early 1296-1307) កិន្រ្ទវ៉ិន (ទី៣)

Transliterated Name: Īndravarmăn III
Other Name: Sri Srindravarman[6,p251; 19,p195]
Title: Vrah Pāda Kamrateṅ Añ Śrī Srīndravarmadeva (K.754[75,p9])
Relationship: Son-in-Law and General of Jayavarman VIII; married to Srindrabhupesvara (1st wife and daughter of Jayavarman VIII and Chakravartirajadevi) and Sri Suryalakshmi (2nd wife)
Religion: Theravada/Hinayana Buddhism
Purohita: Vidyesavid; Name effaced, but it was believed to be Vidyesadhimant who succeeded Vidyesavid
Guru: Madhurendrapadita (uncle of Sri Suryalakshmi); descendant of *Vrah Guru* Yajnavaraha (grandson of Harshavarman I)
Capital: Angkor Thom
Genealogy: Figure 32

This is an important period in Khmer history because a great deal of information concerning Khmer custom, tradition, and way of life were provided by Zhou Daguan during his stay in Angkor. Zhou Daguan was the Chinese envoy who accompanied the Chinese ambassador that the government of Timur Khan (the Chinese called him Cheng Song or Chengzong) — the son of Kublai Khan — sent to Angkor. Zhou Daguan stayed at Angkor for almost one year from August 1296 to July 1297.

Srindravarman was the name of Indravarman III before he acceded to the throne. He was entrusted with the command of King Jayavarman VIII's army. He was purported to be of Samrè's origin. The Samrè people were the inhabitants of the southern and eastern regions of Angkor. They were fierce and able warriors from where most of the kings' armies were recruited. It may be of his Samrè origin that he preferred Theravada Buddhism over Brahmanism. According to the Vat Kok Khpous (also called Kok Svay Chek near Siem Reap) inscription in Pali dated 1309, Indravarman III offered a village as a gift to a Hinayanist chief monk in 1308.

Srindravarman was the lover of Princess Srindrabhupesvera Cuda, the cherished daughter of King Jayavarman VIII. As he was in command of the king's army, he also had big ambitions. He had served Jayavarman VIII faithfully but as the king was getting very old and infirm, Srindravarman realized that the moment was perfect and the best opportune time for him to seize power. He had the princess steal the *Preah Khan Reach* (Royal Sacred Sword) from her father and bring it to him. It was Jayavarman II that started the tradition of the *Preah Khan Reach* as the palladium of the Khmer monarchy. A monarch would not be considered legitimate if he reigned without the possession of the Royal Sacred Sword. Upon learning that his sister had stolen the *Preah Khan Reach*, the crown prince — the name was not given — prepared a counter-offensive to resist the take-over by Srindravarman. Because of his position as the general of the king's army, Srindravarman had the upper hand by making the first move and had the crown prince arrested. Srindravarman had the crown prince's toes cut off and then had him incarcerated. In the old tradition, when a prince had his toes cut off, this would prevent him from qualifying for the throne because he would be considered as not possessing all the qualities to be king.[6,p244] Zhou Daguan had mentioned that criminals with toes cut off would not be allowed to cross the gates and enter into the city.[60,p142] The above account was also reported by Zhou Daguan as follows:[27,p72]

The present ruler is the son-in-law of his predecessor, who, devoted as he was to his daughter, gave her the chance to steal the golden sword (of office) and give it to her husband, thus depriving her brother of the succession. This brother strove to stir the soldiery to revolt, but the prince, hearing of this, cut off his brother-in-law's toes and threw him into a dark dungeon.

By golden sword Zhou Daguan must have meant *Preah Khan Reach* where its sheath was made out of gold. The *Preah Khan Reach* was the symbol of the Khmer palladium where its function was used for the Khmer king's coronations from the time of Jayavarman II until the 20th century.

Historical documents seem to suggest that Srindravarman forced the old and feeble king to abdicate. Having everything under his control, Srindravarman married the princess to legitimize his reign. He was crowned king by the Chief Brahman Vidyesavid (according to the Angkor Wat inscription and reigned under the name Indravarman III[6,p251]). A few years later he married Sri Suryalakshmi, the niece of his guru Madhurendrapadita.[6,p251] Sri Suryalakshmi is the elder daughter of Madhurendrapandita's sister. The event seems to suggest there was a conspiracy and agreement between Indravarman III and his guru as well as with his chief priest. It must be remembered that the coronation of a king could not be considered official without the full sacred ceremony conducted by the Chief Brahman. According to the inscription of Banteay Srei, Madhurendrapandita was a descendant of *Vrah Guru* Yajnavaraha (grandson of Harshavarman I) who was the guru of Jayavarman V.[6,p243]

As will be discussed later, I suggest that the story of the legendary Ta Trasâk Paêm may be a distortion of the above historical event and the Khmer chroniclers used it to fill the gap of the genealogy of the Khmer kings during the uncertainty period between Jayavarman Paramesvara and Nippean Bat.

Chief Brahman Vidyesavid passed away during the reign of Indravarman III. The king appointed another Brahman to take his place. His name from the Angkor Wat inscription is effaced, but it is believed to be the eminent Brahman named Vidyesadhimant.

The first year of Indravarman III's reign coincided with the arrival of Zhou Daguan. He wrote a report of his trip after he returned to China that the Chinese historian T'ao Tsing-i included in his collection of notes and essays famously known as *Shuo-fu* (說郛). The report was first translated into French by Jean-Pierre Abel-Rémusat in 1819 called *Description du royaume de Cambodge par un voyageur Chinois qui a visité cette contrée à la fin du XIII siècle; précédé d'une notice chronologique sur le même pays extradite des annals de la Chine,* then by Paul Pelliot in 1902 called *Mémoires sur les coutumes du Cambodge, par Tcheou Ta-kouan,*[60] and then into English by J. Gilman d'Arcy Paul called *The Customs of Cambodia.*[27]

Zhou Daguan (週達觀) was a native of Wenzhou (温州) in the province of Zhejiang (浙江). He left the port-city Wenzhou on the 20th day of the second month of the year ping-shen (丙申), which corresponded to 24 March 1296. He sailed in the direction ping-wei (丁未), which signified south-southwest. He arrived at Tchen-ch'eng (占城) on 18 April 1296. Tchen-ch'eng was the Chinese appellation for Champa. From Tchen-ch'eng it took him about 15 days (approximately on 3 May 1296) to arrive in Chen-pu (真蒲), identified as Baria (present-day Ba Ria-Vaung Tau in Vietnam). From there, he headed in the direction kun-shen (坤申), which signified south-west-quarter-west. He then sailed through the Sea of K'un-lun (崑崙), corresponding to Koh Tralach (កោះត្រឡាច) that is presently called Con Son, and arrived at the mouth of the river (Mekong delta). He entered at the fourth mouth of the river, which would have been Mé Sâ (មេស) but is presently called My Tho, because the other entrances were not accessible. From the entrance of the fourth mouth, it took him 15 days to arrive in Ch'a-nan (査南), which suggested the place to be Kompong Chhnang. From there he switched to small boats from the rest of the journey. He arrived ten days later at Fo-hsuen (佛村), which literally means village of the Buddha. Zhou Daguan must have mistranslated the name Pursat (ពោធិ៍សាត់) which signified drifting banyan tree, for bodhisattva (ពោធិសត្ត) which signified Buddha. From Fo-hsuen he crossed the fresh water sea (淡洋), which would be Tonlé Sap, and arrived at Kan-p'ang hsui (干傍取) on 1-29 August 1296. Zhou Daguan said that Kan-p'ang hsui was located 5 li (about 20 km) from the city, which in this case would mean Angkor Thom. Etienne Aymonier proposed Kan-p'ang hsui to signify Kampong Chei, which meant port of victory.

Paul Pelliot translated the account of Zhou Daguan's journey from Wenzhou to Angkor,[60,pp127-140] which Lawrence Palmer Briggs reported it in his book *The Ancient Khmer Empire* as follows:[6,p244]

Of the many mouths one can enter only by the fourth. All the others are encumbered with sand banks, which large ships cannot cross. Whichever way one looks, he sees only rattans, old trees, yellow sands, white rushes. At first glance, it is not easy to locate the true mouth. Even mariners find it difficult. From the mouth one can, with a favorable current, in fifteen days reach at the north a country called Ch'a-nan. Here, one changes to a smaller boat and in ten days, with favorable current, passing via Pan-lu-suen, "half-way village," and Fo-hsuen, "village of the Buddha," and crossing the fresh water sea, one arrives at Kan-p'ang hsui, 50 li from the city.

Some of the names described in his voyage could be easily identified with modern towns. Other names could also be deduced based on his descriptions and the route of his itinerary. Undoubtedly, *Ch'a-nan* is Kompong Chhnang. *Fo-hsuen* described as "village of the Buddha" could be deduced as Pursat. The Khmer legend said that the province of Pursat (ពោធិ៍សាត់, Pôsat) was named after a drifted banyan tree (ពោធិ៍ រសាត់, Pôrosat).

According to the legend, after seeing a banyan tree floating up a river people rescued it and planted it for good luck. When Zhou Daguan arrived at Pôsat he must have confounded the name for Pothisat (ពោធិសត្វ, Boddhisattva) and translated it as the village of the Buddha. Another case that could be made about the Chinese's misinterpretation of the name Pôsat for the village of the Buddha was when the Chinese recorded the name as *P'u-t'i-sa* in the chronicle *Shu-yi Chou-tzu lu*[106,p52] during the Yung-lo period (1403-1424). In this case, the Chinese transliterated the name of the city instead of describing it as Zhou Daguan had done. Could it be that the original name of Pursat was indeed Pothisat?

Solang and Beling Uk have given their interpretation on this subject and stated that the village of the Buddha could not have been Pursat as believed by George Coedès and other historians. Their disagreements are based on the fact that Pôsat does not signify Buddha and that Pursat is located 25 km inland.[107,ppv-vi] Solang and Beling Uk are correct concerning Pursat located inland for a dry season but the town is much closer to Tonle Sap for a wet season. When Zhou Daguan was traveling through Tonle Sap to Angkor, it was during the month of August which was during the peak of the wet season. During that time of the year, Tonle Sap would expand about six times its normal size from 2,700 square km to about 16,000 square km. The edge of the lake would be much closer to the city outskirt.

From *Fo-hsuen* Zhou Daguan crossed the fresh water sea, which is the lake of Tonlé Sap, and arrived at the port of Angkor. I have interpreted the itinerary of Zhou Daguan, which is shown in Figure 42.

Pelliot found it perplexing that Zhou Daguan never called Angkor Thom by its proper name. During his stay in Angkor, Zhou Daguan never mentioned the word Angkor but only "the city," "the walled city," or "the capital city."

Angkor Thom was not the original name of the city but a name assigned by the French. The Chronicle of the Emerald Buddha that was translated into the Chieng Mai dialect and believed to be written around the 12th to the 15th century called Angkor Thom by the name Indrapatha Nagara.[98] The Vat Mahadhatu inscription of Sukhothai dated no later than 1357 and is now preserved at the National Library of Thailand in Bangkok mentioned of a Khmer king from Sri Sodharapura.[103,p5] George Coedès identified Sri Sodharapura as a corrupted name of Sri Yasodharapura, which was the ancient name of Angkor Thom. From the 2/k.125 Fragment that Michael Vickery discovered in the National Library of Thailand in Bangkok in 1971 and estimated to be written around the 14th to 15th centuries, the Ayutthayan called Angkor Thom by the name of Preah Nokor Luong.[108,p11] The Cambodian chronicles called Angkor Thom by the name Eyntapath Moha Nokor, which Adhémard Leclère deconstructed to mean City of Indra of the Great Kingdom.[7,p196] The name Eyntapath (ឥន្ទបត្ត) was stamped on coins used under the reign of King

Ang Duong. If the name of Angkor were called Eyntapath or Preah Nokor Luong which signifies Holy City of the King, then Zhou Daguan may have decided to just call it "the city" for simplicity.

Zhou Daguan spoke of Indravarman III as not being afraid to venture outside the palace and walked on the streets. This may be due to the fact that he came from a commoner background and as a general who was used to venture outside. Zhou Daguan recorded the dates of different festivals that Khmer people celebrated throughout the year (see Chapter 3 on Khmer Traditional Calendar). He mentioned of Khmer men who understood astronomy and knew how to calculate the moon and sun eclipses. He also gave a brief description of the way Khmer calendar was calculated. From his description, Angkor was still a rich city with gold covering some of the monument such as the towers of Bayon and Phimeanakas, the window frames of the council hall, and the tower Neak Pean. The houses of the nobles had verandas and lead tiles. He estimated the number of concubines and women who attended the palace to be between 3,000 and 5,000. He admitted he did not quite understand the religious practices in Kambuja (he still called the country Chenla, but the inhabitants called themselves Kambuja) but said that there were three main religions, which were *Pan-ch'i, Ch'u-ku,* and *Pa-ssu-wei.*

Zhou Daguan's account about the three religions that he observed in Angkor was translated in French by Paul Pelliot[60,pp148-151] and then translated in English by J, Gilman d'Arcy Paul.[27,p1]

Zhou Daguan was a little perplexed about what the *Pan-ch'i* (斑詰) religion was as he said: "I am unable to say what inherited creed lies back of them, as they have no school or seminary for training. It is equally difficult to find out what are their sacred books. I have only observed that they dress like men of the people, except that all their lives they wear around the neck a white thread that marks them as men of learning. The pan-ch'i often rises to high position." Zhou Daguan seemed to describe the *Bakous,* the Brahman priests who are still performing their function in the service to the king to the present day. The white ribbon is called *upavita.* It is understandable that Zhou Daguan could not figure out the sacred book the *Pan-ch'i* read or the school they were trained because the knowledge the Brahman priests possessed could be passed down only through hereditary lineage. Outsiders are not allowed to learn the sacred rituals performed by the *Bakous* that were passed down by Sivakaivalya, the Chief Brahman of Jayavarman II.

The *Ch'u-ku* (苧姑) that Zhou Daguan mentioned as having their heads shaved, wearing yellow clothing with their right shoulders exposed, and walking barefoot was definitely the description of Hinayanist monks. The term *Ch'u-ku* may have been borrowed from the Siamese word *chao-ku* or *jao-gu,* which means "my lord." Vickery who quoted Geoff Wade said that the Chinese scribes and translators were more familiar with the *Hsien* (Thai) terms as the Chinese residents in Ayutthaya drafted diplomatic and trade letters on behalf of the rulers of Ayutthaya to the Chinese court.[75,p39] Zhou Daguan said that the worship of the Buddha in Chenla was universal.

The description of *Pa-zhong-wei* (八忠惟) given by Zhou Daguan is harder to figure out. He said that they wore a piece of red or white cloth on their heads and worshipped an altar-stone. They did not congregate with people and did not drink wine. Because of his unfamiliarity with the customs and religion in Kambuja, he called them Taoists. Paul Pelliot and Finot believed they belonged to the Shaivite faith called Pashupata that was referred in the epic of Mahabharata. The Pashupata movement was especially influential between the 7th and 14th centuries.

The Chinese products that were most sought after were described by Zhou Daguan as the following:[6,p248] "gold, silver, silks (especially colored); then some tin, lacquer plates, mercury, vermillion, blue porcelain, paper, sulfur, saltpeter, santal, iris root, musk, hemp cloth, umbrellas, iron pots, copper plates, oils, sieves, wooden combs, needles, mats."

Historians tend to depict that Angkor was in its downfall and the country was collapsing. Based on Zhou Daguan's testimony, Kambuja but especially Angkor was still rich, full of vigor, and strength. Briggs stated the following:[6,p250]

Although the thirteenth century seems to have been one of reaction and weak government, the Memoirs of Chou Ta-Kuan and the few inscriptions of the thirteenth and fourteenth centuries do not picture a decadent Cambodia. They describe a Cambodia wealthy and prosperous, in the full tide of its magnificence. They tell us that the country was recently ravaged by the Siamese, but they hint that this was due to the weakness of an aged king and that a vigorous young ruler was now keeping the enemy at a distance. To be sure, the territory of the Khmer Empire had been greatly reduced; but the lost territory consisted mainly of vassal states, peopled chiefly by non-Khmers. Kabujadesa proper was still intact.

The 1309 inscription of Vat Kok Khpous written partly in Pali, Sanskrit, and Khmer mentions that Indravarman III abdicated in 1307 in favor of the Yuvaraja. According to Coedès, he abdicated in favor of his brother-in-law and then entered into monkhood.[19,p195] The inscription says that one year after his abdication Indravarman III offered a village named Sirindaratanagama to the chief monk Mahathera Siri Sirindamoli. According to Hema Goonatilake, Mahathera is a title that is related to the Sinhala Buddhism. The Sanskrit inscription says that afterward, King Sri Srindravarman (Indravarman III) ordered a monastery built and a statue of the Buddha erected. He then assigned four villages to be in charge for the maintenance of the monastery.[6,p252; 90]

There are no definite records on what Indravarman III did after his abdication. Because he was still young at the time of his abdication, Coedès suggested that Indravarman III probably retired at the monastery and devoted the remaining of his life to the study of Theravada Buddhism.[6,p252] Because Indravarman III abdicated relatively young a question was raised as to what was his reasoning? Did he have a guilty conscience by forcing his predecessor who was his father-in-law to abdicate? If he were to retire at the monastery was it to atone for his sin? The genealogy is shown in Figure 32. The inscriptions and chronicles do not mention that Indravarman III had any offsprings. The Yuvaraja that Indravarman III chose to succeed him was a relative, believed to be his brother-in-law, but no definite relationship could be traced.

Indravarman III must be the unnamed king mentioned in the Cambodian legend whose reign occurred during the time the Chinese envoy visited Angkor. The legend says that two more kings, Preah Allasa Reach and Preah Volék Reach, succeeded the above king but I could not place them anywhere to fit the chronology under the Khmer king genealogy.

44 Indrajayavarman (1307-1327) ក្រុន្ធជ័យវ៉ែន

Transliterated Name: Īndrajayāvarmăn
Other Name: Srindrajayavarman (Mangalartha inscription)[6,p252; 19,p195]
Relationship: Possibly the brother-in-law of Indravarman III[19,p195]
Religion: Therevada/Hinayana Buddhism (K.144[75,p10])
Capital: Angkor Thom (Srindrajayapura)
Genealogy: Figure 32

A Khmer legend mentions that there was a great flood in Angkor in the early fourteenth century which occurred during the reign of a king named Preah Sénéka.[19,p130] Could this legendary king be Indrajayavarman? The inscriptions of Mangalartha temple (dated post 1243), of Vat Kok Khpous (dated 1309), of Angkor Wat (dated post 1327), and of Bayon (dated post 1327) did not provide any useful information about the reign of Indrajayavarman. The inscription of Angkor casually mentions that a Brahman from a prominent family, probably Vidyesadhimant, became the royal *hotar* of King Srindrajayavarman.[6,p253] The relationship between Indrajayavarman and Indravarman III was not defined, except that Indravarman III chose him as the Yuvaraja. However, some historians believed he was the king's brother-in-law. The genealogy is shown in Figure 32.

45   Jayavarman Paramesvara (1327~1368: at least 1353 and at most 1371)
ជ័យវរ្ម័នបរមេស្វារៈ (Bayon inscription[6,p252])

Transliterated Name: Jayăvarmăn Paramesvara
Other Names: Jayavarmadiparamesvara,[6,p252] based on Angkor Wat inscription; Parasmathakema-
raja,[6,p254] based on Laotian chronicle; Jayavarman IX[6,p252]
Religion: Theravada/Hinayana Buddhism
Relationship: Undetermined
Capital: Angkor Thom
Genealogy: Figure 32

Historical records during this period are sparse and unclear. The undated Bayon inscription mentioned that Jayavarman Paramesvara acceded to the throne of Angkor in 1327. Another inscription at Angkor Wat mentioned his name as Sri Jayavarmadiparamesvara three times. He was the last Khmer king inscribed on monuments and temples during the Angkor period. There was no mention of how long his reign lasted, but it was believed to be a long one that lasted at least to 1353. Briggs mentioned that even though the name of Jayavarman Paramesvara was used during the king's lifetime, it would be more appropriate to assign it for a posthumous name. Therefore, he called him Jayavarman IX. The relationship between Jayavarman Paramesvara and his predecessor is undetermined.

The reconstruction of the events during this period is based on the combination of the Khmer inscriptions at Angkor Wat, the Chinese Imperial Records, and the Laotian Chronicles related to the reign of Fa Ngum.

According to the Laotian Chronicles,[6,p256] there was a Khmer king named Parathakemaraja who reigned at Angkor from 1330 to at least 1353. Briggs believed this king to be none other than Jayavarman Paramesvara,[7,p254] the father-in-law of Fa Ngum. By this time, the Hinayana Buddhism introduced from Sri Lanka had taken a very firm hold in Kambuja and had already spread to the masses.

George Coedès who quoted Louis Finot said that the origin of the Lao kingdom, known as Lan Xang, could be traced back to Thao Tavang, the last of the Thao among the Laotian chiefs that included fifteen Khun titles, six Thao titles, and multiple Phraya titles.[104,pp223-224] Thao Tavang was the father of Phraya Lang, the progenitor of all the Phrayas from Laos. The history of Laos started with Phraya Lang. According to the Laotian Chronicles, Phraya Lang was exiled to the mountains because he was such a bad ruler. Phraya Khamphong was called to replace his father Phraya Lang. He reigned at Muang Sawa (Present-day Luang Prabang) under the name of Phraya Suvarna Khamphong. When his son was born, Suvarna Khamphong sent a message to his exiled father asking him what name he would like to give to his grandson. His father answered angrily: "Phi Fa Pha," which means "May heaven strikes you down."[104,p224] Instead, Suvarna Khamphong named his son Phi Fa (Spirit of Heaven) who is also known by Phraya Fa Ngiew, the father of the future Phraya Fa Ngum who was credited for the foundation of Lan Xang.

It seems that banishment always followed the new Laotian royal families. Based on the Laotian Chronicles, Paul Le Boulanger mentioned in his book *Histoire du Laos Français*,[109,pp41-46] that King Suvarna Khamphong of Muang Sawa banished his son Fa Ngiew and grandson Fa Ngum (son of Fa Ngiew) to Angkor in the 1320s. The chronicles said that Fa Ngiew was caught having an affair with one of his father's concubines.

If Fa Ngum and his father came to Angkor in 1327 during the first year of Jayavarman Paramesvara's reign, then Fa Ngum would have been eleven years old because the chronicles said he was born in 1316. Jayavarman Paramesvara assigned a Theravada Buddhist monk named Maha Pasaman Chao (also known as Preah Mahasamana) to be the teacher of Fa Ngum. Jayavarman Paramesvara gave away his daughter, Princess Keo Kaengkanya (also called Yot Kaeo or Kaeo Lot Fa by the Laotian), in marriage to Fa Ngum when he reached the age of sixteen.[19,p172] Believing in Fa Ngum's leadership, Jayavarman Paramesvara decided to help his son-in-law and Fa Ngiew to take over the throne of Muang Sawa. The exact date is not known, but it is believed to be probably in 1350 that Jayavarman Paramesvara provided Fa Ngiew and Fa Ngum an army of 10,000 soldiers for their battle at Muang Sawa. They marched toward Muang Sawa and defeated the army of King Suvarna Khamphong, but Fa Ngiew died during the siege of the capital. It was reported that instead of surrendering to his grandson in dishonor, the king committed suicide by hanging himself. Three years later in 1353, Fa Ngum continued in his conquest by taking over Wiangchan (present-day Vientiane) with ease. Coedès said that Fa Ngum seized Wiangchan using a method of deception by leaving "a stock of gold and silver arrows. Afterward, he feigned retreat and then pounced on his adversaries when they left their ranks to gather up the precious metal."[104,pp224-225] After his defeat of Wiangchan Fa Ngum returned to Muang Sawa or Chiangdong-Chiangthong (present-day Luang Prabang) where his coronation took place in 1353.[19,p173]

Under Fa Ngum a consolidation of Tai states was formed and a new independent Laotian kingdom called Lan Xang (million elephants) was created in 1353. Fa Ngum's campaign against Dai Viet was more of a challenge but he was finally able to negotiate with the king on the demarcation of the borders between the two countries. Fa Ngum's prowess was so great that most of the Tai states recognized his suzerainty over them. Briggs mentioned that even Lan Na under the reign of King Sam Phaya, and Ayutthaya under the reign of Ramathibodi submitted to Fa Ngum's suzerainty by paying him yearly tributes. The king of Ayutthaya offered Fa Ngum one of his daughters in marriage.[6,p254; 104,p225] The rise of the kingdom of Lan Xang coincided with the weakening of Sukhothai.

The accession of Fa Ngum to the throne of Lan Xang brought a new religious era to the country. The Sinhala Theravada Buddhism from Cambodia was introduced into Laos at the request of Queen Keo Kaengkanya after she witnessed the practice of animism where people of Lan Xang were performing rituals of animal sacrifices. Shortly after he became king, Fa Ngum sent his Khmer guru Preah Mahasamana to Cambodia requesting Jayavarman Paramesvara for help in implementing Buddhism in Lan Xang. Based on the 1602 inscription at Wat Keo (named after Queen Keo Kaengkanya) in Luang Prabang, the Khmer king (presumably Jayavarman Paramesvara) sent a team of 20 Buddhist monks to Laos. The team included three other experts in Buddhism scriptures namely Norasing, Norasan Noray, and Noradet. The team was under the leadership of three Sinhala monks who were presumably residing in Cambodia. The three Sinhala monks who headed the team were two brothers of Mahadeva Lanka and the other one was Maha Nandipanna.[89] The team carried a copy of the Tripitaka (three baskets of the Buddha's teaching that contain *Sutta Pitaka, Vinaya Pitaka,* and *Abhidharma Pitaka*) and a golden statue of Buddha called Preah Bang (called Phra Bang by the Laotian) that was mentioned earlier in the Chronicle of the Emerald Buddha.

According to the chronicle, Phra Bang was created by an Indian monk Nagasena in the first century AD. Scholars and experts in artifacts dismissed the first century date and provenance of the statue by suggesting that the feature of Phra Bang was of Khmer origin and not of India's or Sri Lanka's. The statue could have been created under the reign of Jayavarman Paramesvara for the purpose of introducing Theravada Buddhism into Laos. The capital city of Luang Prabang was named after the statue of Phra Bang which is presently housed at the Haw Phra Bang temple within the Royal Palace ground in Luang Prabang. Phra Bang is considered the palladium of Laos.

The Cambodian chronicles, but not the Ayutthayan chronicle, mentioned that Angkor was occupied by Siam in 1351, which would then fall under the reign of Jayavarman Paramesvara. The belief that Ayutthaya occupied Angkor in 1351 has been put in doubt by Briggs as well as by Vickery. Briggs argued that the occupation of Angkor in 1351 did not occur for the following reasons:[6,p253]

(1) *The Annals of Ayuthia, of which several recensions have found, do not mention such a conquest.*
(2) *The Chinese, who had intimate relations with Cambodia after 1370, give no hint of that country's previous subjection to Ayuthia and speak of its riches.*

(3)   Nothing is said in the Chronicles of the spoils of the temples at this time, which would have been great.

(4)   The Annals of Laos indicate that the king who was on the throne of Cambodia in 1330 was there in 1353.

(5)   According to the official Liste Chronique, the five kings mentioned in the Cambodian Chronicles reigned twenty-seven years, from 1382 to 1409, which, when the chronology is corrected means 1405 to 1432.

I concur with Briggs and Vickery's assessments and I would like to add one more criterion concerning the doubtfulness of Siam's occupation of Angkor in 1351. It is unfathomable to think that Ramathibodi (U-Thong) who submitted Ayutthaya to Fa Ngum's suzerainty would dare to invade Angkor that was ruled by Jayavarman Paramesvara, the mentor and father-in-law of Fa Ngum. U-Thong, the founder of Ayutthaya in 1351 and a Khmero-Thai from Lopburi, who married a Khmer princess from Suphanburi will be discussed more thoroughly in the Chapter 8 under *The Origin of the Thai*.

Based on the Laotian chronicles, Parathakemaraja believed to be Jayavarman Paramesvara (assigned as Jayavarman IX by Briggs) was still alive in 1353. There are no records showing the end of Jayavarman Paramesvara's reign or the date of his death. He is the last Khmer king whose name is mentioned on the epigraphy during the Angkor period. The genealogy of Jayavarman Paramesvara is shown in Figure 32.

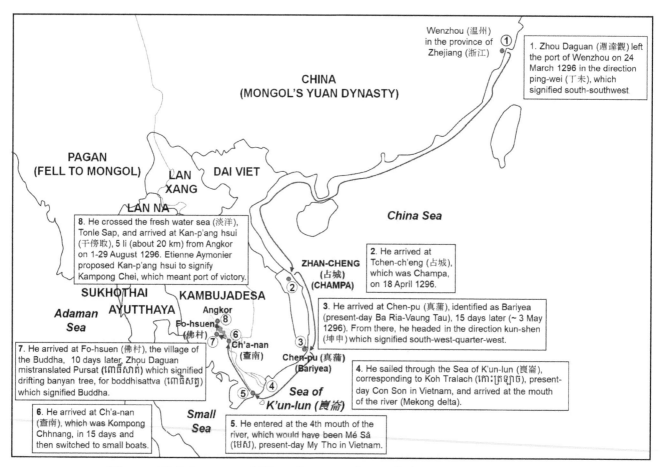

**Figure 42. Itinerary of Zhou Daguan from China to Angkor in 1296
(Map created, based on References 1, 27, and 60)**

THE AMBIGUOUS PERIOD OF THE MID 14TH-15TH CENTURIES

A tradition of South East Asian historical studies has been, when practicable, to consult Chinese records as a cross-check on other sources. Thus Briggs found support in Rémusat's translations of Ming documents to reinforce his arguments that Angkor was not in fact captured before 1430. He observed that the Chinese records were significantly silent on the subject of Thai-Khmer warfare in this period.

But Rémusat in 1829 misunderstood one important expression in the Ming-shih, which Mayers in 1875 rendered correctly [W. F. Mayers, "Chinese explorations of the Indian Ocean during the fifteenth century. III", The China Review, 4 (1875), 64.]. The expression indicates that the Khmer king was not living in Angkor at least from 1371 to 1373. The precision seems to provide a basis for reconstructing the chronology of this period in Khmer history and also for interpreting the dating systems used in the earliest published Khmer records relating to the reigns of Nippean Bat and his successors from about the middle of the fourteenth century to the beginning of the sixteenth century. An analysis of the Khmer records, controlled by the Chinese records, suggests that the Khmer information is susceptible to correction if the sequence of reigns is removed from an artificially contrived framework in time, based on the tradition that Nippean Bat began his reign a few years before the foundation of Ayudhyā in 1350 by Rāmādhipati, and if the major preoccupations of the Khmer chroniclers are identified. Their chronologies do not seem to have been carelessly constructed.

The Khmer King at Basan (1371-3) and the Translation of the Cambodian Chronology during the Fourteenth and Fifteenth Centuries
O. W. Wolters [106,p45]

The timeline in the mid 14-15th centuries from Jayavarman Paramesvera (Jayavarman IX) to Ponhea Yat is very ambiguous. Even prominent scholars on Cambodia and Thai histories diverge in their conclusions concerning the above period. The ambiguity is mainly due to the lack of epigraphies as Khmer no longer built grandiose monuments to record their achievements; to the lack of Chinese records to cover the events in Cambodia, especially after the accession of Samdach Chao P'ing-ya (Thsan-lieï-tchao-phing-ya) in 1405; to the interpretation of the transliterated names the Chinese gave to the Khmer kings; and to the loss of Khmer records caused by wars with Champa and Ayutthaya. The Cambodian chronicles of the 18th century and subsequent ones covering the above period were based on the *Ang Eng Fragment (AEF)* of 1796. The *AEF* must be studied with caution due to the fact that the document had to be submitted to King Rama I (1782-1809) of Siam for approval first before it could be officially released.[106,p54] The document was reported in animal years without specifying their numerical years in Cula, Saka, Buddhist, or Christian era. These omissions led to different interpretations by historians on the reigns of the Khmer kings. The *Nong Chronicle (NC)* — Nong's Royal Chronicle of Cambodia — was produced in 1818[110,p108] by Ang Chan II's official, Oknha Vongsa Sarapech Nong, after the *AEF*. Again the document reported the years only in animal signs. Adding to the ambiguity, the *NC* differed in certain areas from the *AEF*. The list (herein called *The List* per Wolters' appellation[106,p54] of the Khmer kings, based on the *AEF* and *NC*, was compiled in the 19th century by Doudart De Lagrée.

There are disagreements among eminent scholars on the date of Nippean Bat and Ponhea Yat's accessions. The Chinese imperial annals Ming Shi-lu *(MSL)* mentioned that *Samdach Chao P'ing-ya* (參烈超平牙) succeeded his father *Samdach P'o-p'i-ya* (參烈婆毘牙) in 1405.[106,p50] Lawrence Palmer Briggs stated that Jean Moura who was the French Resident General in Cambodia from 20 February 1868 to 10 March 1870 was mistaken when he identified *Samdach Chao P'ing-ya* as Ponhea Yat. Briggs identified P'ing-ya as Nippean Bat but he had to amend the Cambodian chronicles and shift Nippean Bat's accession to 1405.[6,p256] He assigned 1432 as the year of Ponhea Yat's accession to correlate with the fall of Angkor in 1431 under the reign of King Ramathibodi II that was mentioned in the Luang Praseut *(LP)* Chronicle.[104,p 59] Mak Phoeun, on the other hand, totally ignored the *MSL* and based his study solely on the Cambodian chronicles. He assigned 1346 as the year for Nippean Bat's accession and 1373/4 as the year when Ponhea Yat started his reign.[110,pp150-152] On the other hand, Adhémard Leclère said that Nippean Bat and Ponhea Yat acceded to the throne in 1340 and 1384, respectively.[7,pp195-216] Khin Sok based his finding on various historical documents as well as on the Cambodian chronicles. He assigned the accession of Nippean Bat to occur either in 1340[29,p28] or in 1394[29,p10] and that of Ponhea Yat to occur in 1417.[29,p65] Michael Vickery has not indicated the date of Nippean Bat's accession but he has stated that the dates of Ponhea Yat's revolt, capture, and escape from the Ayutthayan army occurred in 1442, 1443, and 1444, respectively.[75,p44] Oliver William Wolters discussed the reigns of Nippean Bat and Ponhea Yat that were given in the *AE* Fragment, *NC*, *The List*, the *MSL*, and the *Kuo-Ch'üeh* as well as the dates of his own proposal. George Coedès combined both the *MSL* and the Cambodian chronicles to come up with 1346 as the year for Nippean Bat's accession and 1405 as the year for Ponhea Yat's accession.[1,pp236-237] The reigns of Nippean Bat and Ponhea Yat as discussed above are summarized in Table 9 below.

Table 9. Reigns of Nippean Bat and Ponhea Yat Extracted from Various Sources

Khmer Kings	George Coedès [1]	Adhémard Leclère [7]	Lawrence Palmer Briggs [6]	Michael Vickery [75]	Mak Phoeun [110]	Khin Sok [29]	Oliver William Wolters [106]		
							Ang Eng Fragment	Nong Chronicle	The List (Records compiled by Doudard De Lagrée)
Nippean Bat	1346-1351 (p. 236)	1340-1346 (p. 195)	1405- (p. 256)	N/A	1346-1351/2 (p. 150)	1394- (per Vatta Kok Kăk Chronicle, p. 10) 1340- (per J. Moura, p. 28)	1346-1351 (p. 56)	1346-1353 (p. 56)	1382-1386 (p. 56)
Ponhea Yat	-1431- (p. 237)	1384-1431 (p. 216)	1432- (p. 256)	-1442, 1443, 1444- (Ponhea Yat's revolt, capture, & escape from Ayutthaya, p. 44)	1373/4-1433/4 (p. 152)	1417-1463 (Accession, p. 65 & Abdication, p. 34)	Non-Committal (pp. 62-63)	1373-1433 (p. 67)	1402-1433 (p. 67)
								1389-1404 (p. 72)	

Chronology of Khmer Kings by Adhémard Leclère

The events reported below are extracted from Adhémard Leclère's book *Histoire du Cambodge*.[7] The majority of the story in his book was mostly based on his examination of the Cambodian chronicle and on his study of various sources he collected from pagodas and interviews. George Coedès believed that Adhémard Leclère based his writing on the *copie P58* that was completed in 1909.[29,p20,p30]

For the benefit of the readers, the names of the Cambodian kings and the dates of the events are faithfully reproduced to avoid any confusion. When clarification is needed, I will inject my own understanding that is enclosed in italic brackets. The words Ayutthaya/Ayutthayan and Siam/Siamese will be used interchangeably in this section to denote the same thing. Based on my research, which is discussed more thoroughly in Chapter 8 under *The Origin of the Thai*, the war between Ayutthaya and Cambodia in the mid-14th century could essentially be categorized as a civil war because the Ayutthayan kings were descendants of the Khmer royal bloodline from Suphanburi, an earlier province of the Khmer Empire.

According to Coedès the founder of Ayutthaya, U-Thong, belonged to a family of Môn or Khmer origin.[19,p146] Professor Wilaiwan Khanittanan from Thammasat University, Department of Linguistic, said that U-Thong married a Khmer princess from Suphanburi.[111,p378] After he consolidated his power he reigned as King Ramathibodi. According to David K. Wyatt, Pha-ngua was the brother-in-law of Ramathibodi and older brother of the queen. He became king of Ayutthaya and reigned under the name of Borommaracha.[104,p54,p56] The Ayutthayan kings of Khmer royal bloodlines from Si Saowaphak and possibly to King Narai (1656-1688) could be traced all the way back to Ramathibodi and Borommaracha.

The uncertainty of the Ayutthayan kings of Khmer royal lineage after King Si Saowaphak is due to the dubious origin of King Song Tham. He claimed to be the son of a concubine of Si Saowaphak's father, King Ekathotsarot. The Khmer royal bloodline did not just remain in Ayutthaya but it also moved to Cambodia. According to a lost chronicle of Ayutthaya that Michael Vickery discovered in the National Library of Thailand in Bangkok in 1971 which he called *2/k.125 Fragment*,[108] there is a mention of Cau Yāt (Chau Ponhea Yat) as being the son of Brah Rām Cau (King Ramaracha of Ayutthaya). Intharacha (1409-1424) sent his second cousin Ramaracha into exile to Caturmukh (Phnom Penh) after he usurped the throne from him.[108,p11]

To provide a background for comparison with my proposal of the timeline during the ambiguous period that I will discuss later, I am presenting Adhémard Leclère's timeline for the reign of Ta Chey (also known as Ta Trasâk Paêm) to the reign of Préah Srey-Sauryopéar (also called Chauponhéa Yéat) that was discussed in his book *Histoire du Cambodge*. I preserve the spellings used by Leclère and try to remain as faithfully as possible to the flow of the account described in Leclère's book. Whenever appropriate, I will insert my own comments in brackets for clarification.

Ta Chey (Ta Trasâk Paêm)

According to the Cambodian chronicles as well as to the legend, Ta Chey who was the gardener of sweet cucumbers field (thus called Ta Trasâk Paêm as in grandpa of sweet cucumbers) killed the king by mistake when the latter sneaked into the garden at night to pick up some cucumbers. Ta Chey was chosen by the high dignitaries of the kingdom to replace the king that he had accidentally killed. He married the daughter of the deceased king and produced two children from their union, Nippean Bat and Sithean Reachea. Nipean Bat succeeded his father after he passed away in 1340. The story of Ta Trasâk Paêm is discussed more thoroughly in the section about the legendary kings.

Préah Nipéan-bat(1340-1346)

He was the son of Ta Chey. He started his reign in 1340 at Eyntapath Moha Nokor [from the Sanskrit Indraprastha Maha Nagara] that Adhémard Leclère deconstructed to mean it as the City of Indra of the Great Kingdom.[7,p196] In other words, it was the name for Angkor Thom. He reigned under the style name of *Brhat Pada Samdach brhat Parama Nirnava Pada*. His reign lasted five years before he passed away in 1346.

Préah Sithéant-réachéa(1346-1347)

He succeeded his brother Nipéan-bat in 1346 but passed away six months later. Nothing much is known about him.

Préah-srey Lompongsa-réach (1347-1353)

He succeeded his father Sithéant-réachéa in 1347. He reigned under the style name of *Brhat Samdach Brhat Rajagga Braht Parama Ramakangsa Rajadhiraja (Preah Bat Samdach Sdach Preah Reach ongka Preah Borom Lompongsa* Reacheathireach.[7,p196] He promoted his younger brother Préah Srey-Sauryotey to the rank of Uparaja (or Yuvaraja, Vice-King). The chronicle says that the king of Ayuthhaya [which would have been U-Thong/Ramathibodi if this event occurred in 1351] formed an army with two corps to launch an attack against Cambodia. The first corps with 5,000 soldiers was placed under the command of his grandson Sisavath and the second corps with 10,000 soldiers was placed under the command of his son Rama-Suon [according to the Ayutthayan chronicle, Ramesuan was thirty years old when he succeeded his father Ramathibodi in 1369 before he was overthrown in 1370 by his uncle Pha-Ngua who took the reigning name of Borommaracha].[104,p56] The above event described in the Cambodian chronicles would be improbable because Ramesuan would have been eight years old [1347-(1369-30) = 8] at the beginning of the reign of Lompongsa-réach or fourteen years old [1353-(1369-30) = 14] during the siege of Angkor that took place in 1353 [end of Lompongsa-réach's reign]. After learning that the Siam king was preparing his army to invade Cambodia, King Lompongsa-réach gave order to his brother, Uparaja Sauryotey, to form an army of 20,000 soldiers to counteract Siam. Caught by surprise with the swift Khmer response, the army corps of Sisavath was defeated. The Siam prince was killed during the battle. Outnumbered by the Khmer army, Rama-Suon retreated to Ayutthaya. After learning of the Siamese defeat and the death of his grandson, the Siam king reacted by forming a stronger army that comprised of three corps. The king placed the army under the command of his brother-in-law named Preah Barom Reach [Borommaracha]. The chronicle said that the three corps were each placed under the command of the three sons of Rama-Suon named Chau Basath, Chau Baat, and Chau Kâmbâng Pisey. The Cambodian chronicle continued and said that after the defeat of the Siam army Lompongsa-réach sent the soldiers back home to their families because he believed Siam would not dare going to war with the Khmers again. He misjudged the resolve of the Siam king. The Siam army crossed Cambodia's frontier toward Angkor. One more time Lompongsa-réach had to raise an army to fight Siam. He called on his nephew Sauryovongs to recruit men all over Cambodia to form an army that could defend against the Siamese invasion. After three days of march the Siam army arrived at the walled-city of Angkor Thom with Rama-Suon's troops positioning on the north side, Chau Basath's troops guarding the east side, Chau Baat's troops camping on the south side, and Chau Kâmbâng Pisey's troops installing on the west side. They launched an attack but were unable to take Angkor Thom. The Khmers gave a valliant effort defending the city. They fought from December to March [1352 to 1353]. After eight months on his mission to recruit men to form an army, Sauryovongs finally arrived at Angkor Thom with his troops. As his troops approached Angkor Thom they were surprised by an attack from the Siam army. Sauryovongs and his army were defeated and the prince escaped to Laos, either to Luang Prabang or Vientiane. After learning of the disappearance of Sauryovongs, the rest of the new recruits left Angkor and fled back to their hometowns. Even without reinforcement from Sauryovongs' army, Angkor Thom was able to withstand the attack from the enemies. The siege of Angkor Thom lasted more than a year. Finally, Lompongsa-réach succumbed to illness and died four years after he became king. The Cambodian chronicle records the date of his death to be in 1353.

Obaréach Srey-Sauryotey (1353)

He never had an opportunity to be crowned king after the death of his brother Srey Lompongsa-réach in 1353. He remained the Uparaja who was virtually prisoner within the compound of Angkor Thom as the city was still under siege. The long siege of Angkor Thom brought deaths, diseases, and even some despairs to the high officials as well as to the people who lived in the city. Even with low morale, the Khmers were able to push and send the Siamese into the moat surrounding the walls of Angkor Thom with every thrusting assault. The Siamese were unable to bring down Angkor Thom until one day the gate on the east side was broken, which allowed the Siamese to penetrate the city. Sauryotey and his small troops fought valiantly but they were outnumbered by the Siamese forces and finally he was killed in the battle. With the enemies in the city, thousands of Khmer people gathered to protect the sons of Lompongsa-réach, Borom-Rama (Paramaraja) and Thommasoka (Dhammasokaraja). The Bakous [Brahmans] and Prohm Borohet [Brahmapurohita, Chief Brahman] who were in charge for the safekeeping of Préah-khant (Royal Sacred Sword) and Lompêng-chey (Spear of Victory or Spear of Ta Chey), the palladium of the Khmer monarchy, carried those treasures and stayed close to the two princes. They escaped Angkor Thom with the help of the people who bravely thrusted themselves in front of the Siamese soldiers. The unselfish act of courage of the Khmer people allowed the Khmer princes and high dignitaries to escape with the Royal Sacred Sword and Spear. Their sacrifices were an act of national unity in defense against the enemies. They were victorious in defeat.

The occupation of Angkor by Three Ayutthayan Princes from 1353 to 1357

The Cambodian chronicle says the Siam king [no name was given but it must have been Ramathibodi] placed his son Chau Basath to rule Angkor with his two other sons, Chau Baat and Chau Kâmbâng Pisey, in charge of helping his brother govern the country. An army of 10,000 Ayutthayan soldiers were placed around Angkor. The Ayutthayan king instructed the rest of his soldiers to bring back to Ayutthaya all the Khmer riches such as royal jewelry, royal chariots, silver, gold, and precious stones as well as horses, elephants, and 90,000 prisoners out of the population of 100,000 inhabitants. The chronicles say that Chau Basath died after three years of reign and his brother Chau Baat succeeded him but died three months later of cholera. The last remaining brother, Chau Kâmbâng Pisey, took over the throne but disappeared after a battle against the Khmers who tried to take back Angkor [according to the Ayutthayan chronicle, the above period would fall under the reign of Ramathibodi who reigned in Ayutthaya from 1351 to 1369. There are no records in the Ayutthayan chronicle of Ramathibodi having three sons with the above names. On the other hand, Intharacha who reigned in Ayutthaya from 1409 to 1424 had three sons whose youngest one succeeded him in 1424 under the name of Borommaracha II. The two older brothers of Borommaracha II fought each other in a battle on elephant-back to claim the throne and they both died in the duel].

Srey-Sauryovongs (1357-1366)

He was the son of Sauryotey, nephew of Lomponsa-réach, and grandson of Nipéan-bat. He returned from Laos with a strong army he raised with the help of Khmer governors from the provinces that had not fallen to the occupation of Ayutthaya. With his army he retook the 90,000 Khmer prisoners back from Siam and chased the enemies out of Angkor. He acceded to the throne in 1357 and reigned under the style name of *Preah Bat Samdach Preah Reach Ongka Preah Srey Saryovong Reacheathireach (Brhat Pada Samdach Brhat Raja Angga Brhat Çry Suryavamsa Rajadhiraja).* The Cambodian chronicle says that under Sauryovongs' reign the Khmer frontier extended to Daung Nay [Rejected Coconut; present-day Dong Nai in Vietnam] on the western side of Champa's border; to Neang Rong Angk Reach [present-day Buriram in Thailand] on the southeast of Nokor Reach Seima [present-day Korat in Thailand]; to the sea on the west [present-day Gulf of Siam]; and to Snam Khsach Koukhan [somewhere in present-day Laos] on the north.[7,p207] The royal family gathered around Sauryovongs with Prohm Borohet [Chief Brahman] and the Bakous carrying the Préah-khant and the royal regalia as a sign of the Khmer king's return to reign at Angkor again. The king elevated his nephew (no name was cited) to the rank of Uparaja. Afterward, the king sent an army to protect Neang Rong [present-day Buriram in Thailand] to guard against future invasion of Khmer territory from Ayutthaya. Skirmishes between Cambodia and Ayutthaya started with this latter invading Cambodia and taking hundreds of Khmer people as prisoners to Ayutthaya. The Khmer governor of the province [the name was not given but the chronicle said that the province had a maritime border] retaliated by going into Ayutthaya and taking some of their people back to Cambodia. The incidence escalated into a major conflict. The Ayutthayan governor raised an army of 2,000 men and crossed the frontier of Cambodia. Learning of the incident, Sauryovongs called on his generals to raise an army of 50,000 men from the provinces of Treang [present-day Takeo], Bassac [Long Xuyen located in the southern section of present-day An Giang province in Vietnam], Preah Trapeang [sacred pond; present-day Tra Vinh in Vietnam], Au-Maul or Srok Trang [Palm Tree Country; part of present-day Soc Trang in Vietnam], Kramuon Sar [White Wax; present-day Rach Gia in Vietnam], Teuk Khmao [Black Water; present-day Ca Mau in Vietnam], Peam [Confluence; present-day Ha Tien in Vietnam], Kampot, and Kompong Som.[7,p208] The General-in-Chief was assigned to help the Treang governor and the general who spearheaded the troop was assigned to support the Bassac governor. The Siameses were crushed in the first battle. Cambodian went on to retake Mongkol Borei, Chanborei [present-day Chanthaburi in Thailand], and Neang Rong [present-day Buriram in Thailand].

After the Khmer conquest, the king of Ayutthaya [it would have been Ramathibodi according to the Ayutthayan chronicle] retaliated by taking the command of his army and called on his general Pichey

Darong to lead the battle against Cambodia. He retook the provinces that the Khmer had conquered. The Cambodian Uparaja was killed in the course of the battle. After learning of the Khmer defeat King Sauryovongs formed a new army and led the troops to fight the Siamese. Outnumbered by the new Khmer army, the Siamese withdrew their force but the Khmers pursued them to their frontier. The Siamese army was in disarray during the Khmer pursuit, leaving prisoners and armaments on the field. Cambodia found peace and prosperity for a few years. The Khmer kingdom extended as far as the old Khmer provinces of Baschimborei [present-day Prachinburi in Thailand] to the west, Nokor Reach Seima [present-day Korat in Thailand] to the northwest, Snam Khsach [Laos?] to the north, the Koukhan country [Laos?] to the northeast, Baria/Daung Nay [Open Country Plain-Rejected Coconut; present-day Ba Ria-Vaung Tau/Dong Nai in Vietnam] to the southeast, and the sea shore to the south.[7,p210] King Sauryovongs died of illness in 1366.

Préah Borom Rama (1366-1373)

He succeeded Sauryovongs in 1366. He was the son of Lompongsa-réach and cousin of Sauryovongs. He died of sickness in 1373 after seven years of reign.[7,p210] It was reported that within the lifetime of Borom Rama, the Ayutthayan king Ramathibodi passed away in 1369 and that he was succeeded by his son Rama-Suon who reigned less than a year before he was overthrown by his uncle Préah Barom-Réachéa [Borommaracha], the brother of Ramathibodi's wife. The new Ayutthayan king was a warlike king who fought with the smaller kingdoms north of Ayutthaya.

Préah Thommasoka (1373-1394)

He succeeded his older brother Borom Rama in 1373. He reigned under the style name of *Preah Bat Samdach Sdach Preah Reach Ang Preah Thommasoka Reacheathireach.* The Cambodian chronicle reported that after nine years of reign, Thommasoka received news from Ayutthaya that the Siam king Baromma réachéa [Borommaracha] had died [according to the Ayutthayan chronicle, he died in 1388 and not in 1382 (1373 + 9)] and that he was succeeded by his son Thong-lam [also Thong Lan or Thong Chan], but this latter was on the throne for only a week before he was killed by Rama-Suon [Ramesuan] — the son of Uthong [Ramathibodi] that Baromma réachéa had usurped the throne in 1369. Rama-Suon passed away in 1388 [according to the Ayutthayan chronicle he died in 1395[104,p56]], six years after his reign. He was succeeded by his son Samphya Chant who reigned under the name Barom réachéa [Siam King Ramaracha].

The Cambodian chronicle says that the new Ayutthayan king wanted to enlarge his kingdom. He appointed his son Preah Eyntréa-reachea [Nakhon In who later became King Intharacha (1409-1424)] as the Commander in Chief to attack Cambodia in December 1384. Learning of Ayutthaya's plan, Thommasoka formed four corps and placed them under the commands of Ponhéa Kêv [Bañā Kaev], Ponhéa Tey [Bañā Daiy], Chauponhéa Yéat [of royal lineage], and Samdach Chauhvéa Tôlaha [Prime Minister] to defend against the Siam attack. Unable to take Eyntapath [Angkor] after seven months of siege, the Siam commander decided to resort to deceit. With the blessing of the Siam king, six Siamese soldiers were chosen by the Siam commander to be whipped fifty times outside the Angkor rampart in full view of Khmer soldiers and commanders. At nighttime the six Siamese soldiers came to the Angkor gate and asked for protection, claiming that they had deserted from the Siam army. They told the guards they were being unfairly punished and wanted to avenge their sufferings by offering their services to the Khmer king. While the six soldiers were taken to be presented to the Khmer king, news broke out that the commander of the Siamese army had cut off the head of the soldier who let the six prisoners escape and planted it on a bamboo pole for everybody to see. The wounds on the six soldiers were so severe that two of them died. The death of the two Siamese soldiers and the decapitated soldier gave even more credibility that the whippings were real and that the desertion of the six Siamese soldiers were genuine. The surviving four soldiers were taken care of and assigned to take duties with the Khmer army. They fought against the Siamese army on many occasions. The four soldiers started to gain the trust of the Khmer generals.

The chronicle says that during the course of the siege two of the Khmer generals, Ponhéa Kêv and Ponhéa Tey, betrayed the Khmer king by opening the gate to let the Siamese army in the city [the four Siamese soldiers must have been able to convince these two generals that the Siamese victory was imminent]. The four Siamese soldiers were instantaneously killed by the Khmers but harms had already been done. The Siam soldiers rushed inside the city and killed Thommasoka in the course of the battle in 1394. Many Khmer high dignitaries were captured and taken prisoners to Ayutthaya. A large number of the population was able to escape including Chauponhéa Yéat and Prohm Borohet (Chief Brahman) who took the Préah-khant (Sacred Sword), the Lompêng-chey (Spear of Ta-Chey or Spear of Victory), and the Emerald Buddha with them to safety.

Interreign (1394-1401)

The Ayutthaya king [Ramaracha] proclaimed his son Ponhéa Prék king of Cambodia. He reigned under the name of Préah-Eyntréa-réachéa [Intharacha] in 1394 [according to the Ayutthayan chronicle Intharacha was not the son of Ramaracha but that of Borommaracha, which would make him second cousin of Ramaracha]. While surveying the city the Ayutthaya king noticed a large bull called Préah Kô (nandi) by the people. He asked an old Cambodian man for what purpose was the bull statue served? The old man answered that the statue was built during the time when Cambodia was powerful and the purpose was to hide the Préah Trey-bey-dak (Tripitaka) in its belly. The old man continued and said that people worshipped the statue as a Préah Phnaul [Sacred Foreseer] for the kingdom. When the Ayutthaya king left Angkor to return to Ayutthaya, he took with him the statue of Préah Kô and all its content within its belly, all the statues of Buddha that were made of gold and silver, all the priests and people who knew the law of dharma, Ponhéa Kêv and Ponhéa Tey who betrayed Cambodia, and about 70,000 Khmer inhabitants. As to Eyntréa-réachea he was able to locate the Préah-khant [the story seems to contradict the earlier one when it said that Chauponhéa Yéat and the Chief Brahman were able to escape and secure the Préah-khant and Lompêng-Chay from the Ayutthayan invading forces] and other royal regalia without which a king's reign could not be considerate legitimate. Fearing that the royal regalia would be stolen from him, Eyntréa-réachéa was thinking of sending the sacred items to Ayutthaya for safekeeping but a powerful storm erupted on that night pounding with incessant and loud thundering sounds that lasted all night until the next day. Eyntréa-réachéa was troubled by the event because he believed it may be a sign from heaven forewarning the removal of sacred items from Eyntapath. He had a dream that one of the Cambodian kings of the past stayed on top of him and warned him of dire consequences if he removed the sacred items from Eyntapath and sent them to Ayutthaya [this account could not have been known unless Eyntréa-réachea relayed his fear to somebody]. Finally, Eyntréa-réachéa decided against removing the sacred regalia out of Eyntapath. The Cambodia chronicle does not specify how long Eyntréa-réachéa reigned at Eyntapath and the reason of him leaving the city. The chronicle recorded that Eyntréa-réachéa was invited to become king of Ayutthaya after his brother, Phyéa Rama, who succeeded his father Rama-Suon in 1375 was overthrown by his own prime minister in 1380 [according to the Ayutthayan chronicle, Ramaracha was overthrown by his Chief Minister who allied himself with Nakhon In (the younger brother of Thong Chan who reigned only for a week before he was killed by Ramaracha's father). The Chief Minister invited Nakhon In to become king. He reigned under the name of Intharacha. Therefore, based on the Ayutthayan chronicle, Intharacha (Eyntréa-réachéa) would be the second cousin of Ramaracha (Phyéa Rama) and not his brother as stated in the Cambodian chronicle.].

Préah Srey Sauryovongs (1401-1417)

He was chosen by high dignitaries to become king from 1401 to 1417. He was the son of Sauryotey. The chronicle says that Sauryovongs reigned for sixteen years and died in 1417 at the age of 59. He had a son named Chau Ponhéa Yéat who was seventeen years old when he died.

Préah Barommasoka (1417)

He succeeded his uncle Sauryovongs in 1417. He was twenty nine years old when he acceded to the throne. The chronicle says that Eyntapath was again taken by the Siamese in 1420 and that Barommasoka died during the siege at the age of thirty two. He had reigned for about three years. Upon his death the city fell to the Siameses. Adhémard Leclère believed that the Cambodian chroniclers had confused the dates and events of the two reigns above and he considered them to be fictitious.

Préah Srey-Sauryopéar or Chauponhéa Yéat (1394-1431)

Leclère had him reigned from 1384 to 1431, but I believe it was a printing error; I also believe Leclère meant to say 1394 instead of 1384, which was the year that corresponded to the end of Thommasoka's reign. Chauponhéa Yéat was able to escape Angkor after the Siamese invasion. Sauryopéar recruited people all over the country to form an army and finally he was able to retake Angkor in 1384. He was officially crowned king in 1396 under the style name of *Préah Bat Sâmdach Sdac Préah Ongka Oéah Barom Réachéathiréach Ramathipadey Préah Srey-Sauryopéar Thommik Moha Réachéathiréach Préah barom Néath Barom Baupit.* He reigned for 47 years where he spent 17 years at Angkor, less than one year at Basan, and 30 years at Chatomoukh [Phnom Penh]. He abdicated in 1431 in favor of his oldest son Préah Noréay-réachéa and took the title Préah Moha-obayoréach Bârom Baupit.

Legendary Khmer Kings between Jayavarman Paramesvara and Ponhea Yat

There are many versions of the legends and contradictions among them abounded. One of the legends that provide specific names of the kings (no dates are given) who reigned after the historical king Jayavarman Paramesvara (Jayavarman IX) is presented in the order below:[6,p256; 7,pp140-141]

1. *Unnamed King:* He succeeded Jayavarman Paramesvara. Adhémard Leclère stipulated that he may be the king who reigned during the period that the Chinese sent its ambassador to visit Cambodia in 1296. It is my contention that Leclère erred in his stipulation because Jayavarman Paramesvara started his reign in 1327; **2.** *Preah Allasa Reach:* He was the son of the above unnamed king; **3.** *Preah Volék Reach:* He was the brother of Allasa; **4.** *Preah Sénaka Reach:* He was the younger brother of the above two kings. It was reported that a great flood occurred during the period of his reign; **5.** *Preah Sihanu Reach:* He was the son of Sénaka. He was killed by Ta Chey who is also known as Ta Trasâk Paêm (Grandpa of Sweet Cucumbers); **6.** *Ta Chey (Ta Trasâk Paêm):* Ta Chey killed King Sihanu by accident when he sneaked into the sweet cucumber garden at night. Afterward, he was chosen by the high officials of the kingdom to succeed the king that he had killed. He married the king's daughter, Chant Vara Vattey, who became Queen Srey Chantoreach. They had two sons, Preah Borom Nippean Bat and Preah Sithean Reachea. He reigned for seventeen years and died at the age of seventy. He is considered to be the progenitor of the present-day royal families;

Ta Trasâk Paêm Version Circulated Among the Masses

According to the Khmer legend, there was a gardener named Ta Chey living around the 14th century. It is believed he was of Samrè origin.[7,p30] Because he was famous for his skill of producing sweet cucumbers, he was given the nickname Ta Trasâk Paêm (Grandpa of sweet cucumbers). The legend said that one day he offered some of his sweet cucumbers to King Preah Sihanu Reach, which in this case would fall under the period of Jayavarman Paramesvara. The king loved the cucumbers so much that he ordered Ta Trasâk Paêm to save them solely for his own consumption. Ta Trasâk Paêm mentioned to the king that thieves loved to steal his cucumbers at night time the moment they became ripe. The king then gave Ta Trasâk Paêm a spear as a permission to kill whoever would trespass his garden to steal his cucumbers. Because he was craving for sweet cucumbers, the king went to visit the garden one night with two bodyguards, believed to be females. The use of female bodyguards to protect the monarch can be corroborated by the account described by Zhou Daguan who wrote the following:[27,p72]

> *When the King leaves his palace, the procession is headed by the soldiery; then come the flags, the banners, the music. Girls of the palace, three or five hundred in number, gaily dressed, with flowers in their hair and tapers in their hands, are massed together in a separate column. The tapers are lighted even in broad daylight. Then came girls carrying gold and silver vessels from the palace and a whole galaxy of ornaments, of very special design, the uses of which were strange to me. Then came still more girls, the bodyguard of the palace, holding shields and lances.*

As the king entered the garden, Ta Trasâk Paêm took the monarch for a thief because he could not recognize him in the dark. Like the king had instructed him a few days earlier to kill whoever tried to steal the cucumbers, Ta Trasâk Paêm threw the spear that he had in his hand at the intruder, which killed the king instantly. Upon hearing of the king's tragic death, all the dignitaries and high officials of the kingdom gathered to discuss on what to do and whom to choose to succeed the deceased king. The high officials found no fault on the part of the gardener because he was following the king's order to kill the intruder who tried to steal the sweet cucumbers with the royal spear as the king had instructed. Because he was using the royal spear to kill the king, the high officials felt that it was a sign from heaven acknowledging the gardener as a man of merits. The king had no male heir. Therefore, all the dignitaries offered the gardener the throne. Afterwards, Ta Trasâk Paêm married the king's daughter, Chant Vara Vattey, to legitimize his reign.

According to the legend, King Preah Sihanu Reach was the father of Princess Chant Vara Vattey. Ta Trasâk Paêm reigned under the style name *Preah Bat Samdach Preah Borom Moha Baupit Thormik Moha Reacheathireach (Brhat Parama Maha Bhupati Dharmika Maha Rajadhiraja)* with his queen Chant Vara Vattey taking the reigning name of Srey Chantoreach.[7,p131] They produced two sons, Preah Borom Nipean Bat and Preah Sithean Reachea. It is believed that the Royal Spear of Victory (or Spear of Ta Chey) among the royal regalia was the spear that Ta Trasâk Paêm used to kill the king.

Ta Trasâk Paêm Version Remembered by the Samrè Tribe

Before I start the story of Ta Trasâk Paêm I need to clarify the meaning of the word Samrè first. Baradat said that the name Samrè was to signify "the tattooed."[112,p1] The word samrè came from the word srè which means rice field. The field is tattooed with furrows and bunds when it is ploughed. The following is a summarized version of Ta Trasâk Paêm that I translated from the paper that R. Baradat wrote in 1941.[112] The legend was collected by Étienne Aymonier and Jean Moura from the descendants of the Samrè tribe that inhabited in the forest and near Phnom Kulen.

According to the Samrè tribe, Ta Trasâk Paêm was a man of merit from birth because he was born out of a miracle. In a village called Srah lived a young woman named Rèn who owned a rice field near Trapeang Touk (boat pond). One day a hermit appeared and fell in love with Rèn. Feeling very passionate about Rèn, the hermit impregnated the young woman at a distance. Out of this "miracle" a boy was born. Rèn named him Pou. As a boy, Pou was very skilled in games but he was shunned by the other boys as they mocked him of having no father and of being a bastard. Pou complained to his mother and she told him that his father is a hermit living on a mountain with eight faces, which according to Baradat is Phnom Kulen. When he became of age Pou asked his mother permission to leave home to search for his father. It took Pou seven years and he finally met an old hermit living in a forest. After Pou said he came from the village Srah and looked for his anchorite father, the hermit knew right away that Pou is his son. The hermit did not reveal his identity but he asked Pou to stay with him for seven days to rest first before he continued further on his search. Before he departed, the hermit gave Pou some sweet cucumber seeds to take back home with him. When he arrived home Pou told his mother he saw a beautiful woman named Rik and that he wanted to marry her. Pou and Rik built their new life together at Phnom Chamkar. They cleared the land and planted the cucumber seeds that the hermit gave Pou. The special seeds produced the most beautiful and fragrance cucumbers ever. Proud of their achievement, Pou and Rik carefully transported the cucumbers to Angkor Thom to offer them to the king. The king was so pleased after he tasted the sweet cucumbers. The king told Pou to grow the cucumbers exclusively for him. The king gave Pou a spear named Snèng Krabei (Buffalo horns) to guard his garden with the permission to kill anybody who tried to steal the cucumbers. The spear handle was made out of a pha-ao wood and the spear blade was made out of iron with serrated edge like pineapple leaves and shaped like the horns of a buffalo.

One season there was too much rain and as a result Pou's garden failed to produce enough cucumbers for the king's consumption. One day the king craved for the cucumbers. He left his palace with a few bodyguards but it was total darkness by the time they arrived at Phnom Chamkar. They used the stars of the crocodile [which would be the constellation of the Ursa Major] to guide them to Pou's garden. Without alerting of his arrival, the king and his bodyguards slipped into the garden to pick the cucumbers. Thinking they were thieves trying to steal the fame sweet cucumbers, Pou threw his spear which wounded the king mortally. The king asked his bodyguards to remove him from the garden and forbid them to punish Pou. The king said that Pou was only doing his duty as he had been ordered by him. The bodyguards transported the king back to Angkor Thom, but as he was dying the king instructed his bodyguards not to enter Angkor Thom but to bury him in an unmarked grave like a common criminal. After the king died and as the bodyguards passed Bampenh Reach/Kamping Reach (បំពេញរាជ្យ/កំពីងរាជ; meaning accessing the throne/santol fruit or Sandoricum koetjape) and Reachea Dak (រាជាធាក់; meaning fallen king/throne, located near Preah Khan) they decided to reverse course and buried the deceased king outside Angkor Thom as they had been instructed. Because the deceased king did not have any heir, the high dignitaries decided to have the sacred white elephant with the long tusks named Damrei Chey (Victory elephant) to choose the new king. High officials, princes, and people in Angkor Thom lined up in the streets but the elephant did not choose any of them. As the elephant kept on walking he suddenly came to a stop and shuddered at the sight of Pou who stood just outside the gate of Angkor Thom. The elephant knelt down and with his trump he embraced and picked up Pou to put him on his back. The sacred elephant had chosen Pou as the new king to rule Angkor. The high dignitaries and princes were not happy of the elephant's choice but there was nothing they could do about it because the event was witnessed by the people. That was the story told by descendants of the Samrè tribe that lived in the village of Srah Daun Rik (Pond of Lady Rik) about how Ta Trasâk Paêm became king.

No historical documents or evidence can be found to support the story of Ta Trasâk Paêm. The story of a gardener who grew sweet cucumbers is not uniquely Khmer. A similar story which formed the foundation of the Pagan kingdom in 1044 is also told in Burma. The two stories are too similar to be a coincidence. This is typical of a historical contamination case where one country borrowed the legend of another country and adapted it to fit its own purpose. It seems that the story of Ta Trasâk Paêm may have originated from Burma. The story of Ta Trasâk Paêm reminisces of the story of Ṣrindravarman (Indravarman III) who usurped the throne and married the daughter of the deposed king Jayavarman VIII. Both Ta Trasâk Paêm and Srindravarman were of humble backgrounds coming from the Samrè ethnic group located in the northern region of Siem Reap, near Phnom Kulen. It is my contention that the historical event of Indravarman III's usurpation of the throne and his marriage to the king's daughter was distorted through oral history to end up in the form of the legend of Ta Trasâk Paêm. Ponhea Yat's chroniclers who tried to reconstruct the chronology between the last recorded reign of the king of Angkor (Jayavarman Paramesvara) and Nippean Bat may have combined historical events with the Pagan legend to fill the gap in the Khmer history. The chroniclers would not have a comprehensive understanding of the Khmer historical events of that period without the possession of the Chinese and Laotian records at the time of their attempt to reconstruct the history. According to Adhémard Leclère there was an oral tradition that was passed down through generations about Ta Trasâk Paêm reigning for seventeen years.[7,p141] He died at the age of seventy and he was succeeded by his brother Ta Suos who reigned for twenty years under the name of Preah Meak Reachea. The son of Ta Trasâk Paêm, Nippean Bat, succeeded his uncle Ta Suos afterward.

Ta Suos

He was the brother of Ta Chey. He is also known under the name of Preah Jaya or Preah Phaya. He reigned for twenty years under the name of Preah Meak Reachea.

The Chinese Imperial Annals Ming Shi-Lu (明實錄)

The study of Southeast Asia between 1368 and 1644 cannot be complete without consulting with the Chinese imperial annals *Ming Shi-lu (MSL)* — (明實錄). The *MSL* is a compilation of events, which the Chinese called "Ming Real/True Records," that occurred under the Ming dynasty. The records are over 400,000 pages. The annals covered 13 out of 15 reigns. The first omission from the list covered the era of Jiànwén (建文) under the reign of Zhū Yǔnwén (朱允炆) from 1398 to 1402 (he was the second emperor from the Ming Dynasty). The reason for this omission was caused by Zhū Yǔnwén's uncle, Zhū Di (朱棣), who usurped the throne from his nephew and reigned from 1402 to 1424 under the name of Yǒnglè (永樂). He had all the records pertaining to Jiànwén erased. Not even a grave of the Jiànwén era can be found. The other omission from the list was the name of the last Ming emperor Zhū Yóujiǎn (朱由檢), known as the era of Chóngzhēn (崇禎) that lasted from 1627 to 1644. The reason for the omission was due to the fact that there were no Ming officials to compile the records, therefore all the records were not considered truthful. It is unfortunate that the records during the reign of the Jiànwén Emperor were erased because it could have shed some more light on Khmer history during this period.

Events Related to Cambodia

In 1819 the French sinologist Jean-Pierre Abel-Rémusat translated the *MSL* period pertaining to Cambodia which he published under the title *Description du royaume de Cambodge par un voyageur Chinois qui a visité cette contrée à la fin du XIIIᵉ siècle*.[113] Most historians who wrote about Cambodia during this period used his work for references. George Coedès quoted Rémusat in his book *The Indianized States of Southeast Asia*.[1] Oliver William Wolters' analysis of the *MSL* called *The Khmer King at Basan (1371-3) and the Restoration of the Cambodian Chronology during the Fourteenth and Fifteenth Centuries*[106] was based on both Rémusat's work and on the microfilm records of the *Hung-kê* located in the Beijing National Library. The translation of the *MSL* was "edited by the Institute of History and Philology, Academia Sinica, Taipeh." Wolters also used the *Kuo-ch'üeh* version of T'an Ch'ien as a cross-check against the *MSL*. The information shown in Tables 10a and 10b about the Chinese emperors and Khmer kings during the Ming period was extracted from the works of Coedès,[1; 32] Wolters,[106] and Rémusat.[113]

The first mention of the Khmer ruler was in 1368. The *MSL* mentioned that Hou-eul-na (Hu-êrh-na), king of Tchin-la (Chenla), sent an envoy named Naï-ye-ki to submit a letter and tributes near the beginning of the reign of Houng-wou (Hóngwǔ 洪武). He was the first emperor of the Ming Dynasty. He reigned from 23 January 1368 to 24 June 1398. On the eighth moon of the third year of the reign of Hóngwǔ (12 September 1370), the Chinese envoy named Kouo-tching (Kuo Chèng) arrived in Chenla with gifts to announce the accession of Hóngwǔ to the Khmer monarch. On the eleventh moon of the fourth year of the Hóngwǔ's reign (14 December 1371), the Khmer envoy arrived in China with a letter and tributes for the Chinese emperor. The royal style name of the Khmer king was recorded in Chinese as 真臘國巴山王忽兒

那 (Chenla Guo Pa-shan Wang Hu-êrh-na). Wolters translated the style name to Chen-la (Cambodia) Kingdom Pa-shan King Hu-êrh-na while I translated it to Chenla Country Pa-shan King Hu-êrh-na. Wolters who was professor of Southeast Asian History at Cornell University indicated that *Hu-êrh-na* was the name of the *Pa-shan* king of the country of Chenla. He said that *Pa-shan* was a direct transliteration of the word *Basan* (present-day Srei Santhor), the capital that the future King Ponhea Yat had established to get away from Ayutthaya after Angkor was attacked in 1431. On the other hand in his Working Paper Series No. 27, *Cambodia and Its Neighbors in the 15ᵗʰ Century,*[75] and in his paper *The 2/k.125 Fragment, a Lost Chronicle of Ayutthaya,*[108] Michael Vickery argued that *Hu-êrh-na* was the title and not the name of the king and that *Pa-shan* was Ba Phnom because *shan* in Chinese means mountain. I am rather in agreement with Wolters concerning his explanation for *Pa-shan*. If *Pa-shan* were *Ba Phnom* as Vickery had suggested, then why would the Chinese translate only the word *Phnom* to *Shan* and ignore to also translate the word *Ba*, which according to Vickery the word pā "in Khmer is a common initial component of place names and is considered to mean 'male' or the 'male principle'."[108,p 64]

The *MSL* mentioned that another mission from Chenla arrived in China with a tribute on the sixth year of the reign of Hóngwǔ, which Wolters recorded as 7 November 1373. In return, China offered a Ming imperial calendar and gifts to the Chenla king. The Cambodian mission arrived in China on the same day as that of the Ayutthayan. Rémusat mentioned that another tribute was presented by the Khmer king with the royal style name *Thsan-tha-kan-wou-tche-the-tha-tchi* (Samdach Kambujadhirāja) to the Chinese emperor on the twelfth year of the reign of Hóngwǔ, which in this case would have been in 1379. Wolters reported the name in Chinese as 真臘國王參答甘武持達志 (Chen-la Guo-wang Shen-da Gan-wu-chi-da-zhi) which he translated as Samdach Kambujadhirāja of Cambodia, but I translated it as Chenla King Samdach Kambujadesa. Based on his analysis, Wolters believed that the year 1379 of the Cambodian mission arriving in China was incorrectly assigned because he said that the *MSL* mentioned only the twelfth year of the Hóngwǔ but not the mission itself. Wolters used the *Kuo-ch'üeh* as a cross-check and came up with a different date, which was 6 January 1378. The king mentioned above was no longer described as *Pa-shan king of Chenla* but rather *Samdach of Kambujadesa (Cambodia).* It is customary for the Chinese to use the word Chenla or Kambujadesa to designate ancient Cambodia. They usually reserved the word Kambuja for the inhabitants of Cambodia. In the royal style name above, the Chinese used Chenla and Kambujadesa in the same sentence. Was it a way for the Chinese to emphasize that Chenla was now becoming Kambujadesa? The *MSL* seemed to say that the same Samdach presented another tribute to the Chinese emperor on 12 November 1380. On the sixteenth year of the reign of Hóngwǔ, that Wolters assigned as 14 October 1383, China sent a mission to Cambodia to "seal documents of mutual confirmation" which enabled China to implement the China policies on the Chinese citizens living in Cambodia.

Based on the above information Wolters deduced that the first Cambodian ruler, *Chenla Country Pa-shan King Hu-êrh-na,* was the same person as the second Cambodian ruler, *Chenla King Samdach Kambujadesa*. He said that *Hu-êrh-na* reigned at Basan for a short time, at least from 1371 to 1373, and then returned to reign at Angkor for the rest of his life. Wolters argument has some merits. According to David K. Wyatt, Ramathibodi (1351-1369) and his son Ramesuan (1369 for the first reign) conducted a war with Angkor without any outcome.[104,p59] If this were the case, then it is possible that *Hu-êrh-na* may have moved to Basan temporarily and left his generals to be in charge of defending Angkor against the attack of the Ayutthayan army. It may be for this reason that the Chinese called *Hu-êrh-na* the *Chenla Country Pa-shan King* during the above period. Angkor may have found some peace during the period of Borommaracha I from 1370 to 1388 because the Ayutthayan king was more concerned about ruling his country than conducting a war with Angkor after he had overthrown his nephew Ramesuan in 1369. Without the threat of Ayutthaya *Hu-êrh-na* returned to Angkor and it may be for this reason that this time China called him *Chen-la King Samdach Kambujadesa.*

An observation can be made concerning the Khmer and Ayutthayan missions that arrived in China at the same time on 7 November 1373 to pay tributes to the Chinese emperor. It seems that both countries were competing to gain favors from China. For *Hu-êrh-na,* he wanted the Chinese emperor to acknowledge him as the Khmer king over all of Cambodia after he had left Angkor temporarily to Basan. For the king of Ayutthaya (King Borommaracha I), he would want the Chinese emperor to accept him as the ruler of Ayutthaya, especially after he usurped the throne from his nephew Ramesuan.

The *MSL* continued that on the nineteenth year of the reign of Hóngwǔ, which Wolters assigned as October 1386, the Chinese emperor sent two envoys named Liu Min (Lieou-min) and T'ang Ching (Thang-king) to present china vases as gifts to the Khmer king. His name was not mentioned. The *MSL* mentioned the style name of the Cambodian king on the following year, saying that the Chinese emperor received gifts in elephants and perfume from *Thsan-lieï-phao-pi-sie-kan-phou-tche* on the twentieth year of the reign of Hóngwǔ, which Wolters assigned to be on 7 September 1387. Wolters reproduced the style name in Chinese as 參烈寶毘邪甘菩者, which he transliterated it to *Samdach Pao-p'i-yeh Kambuja.* Wolters used *Pao-p'i-yeh* instead of *Phao-pi-sie* but failed to change the Chinese words accordingly from 寶毘邪 to 保毘耶 per the *Kuo-ch'üeh* version.[106,p49] I believe that the name *Phao-pi-sie* or *Pao-p'i-yeh* was an attempt by the Chinese to transliterate the Khmer words *Chao Ponhea* which was a title that was equivalent to a king. Wolters believed that *Pao-p'i-yeh* was a new ruler. It can therefore be assumed that *Hu-êrh-na* reigned at least until 1383 and that *Pao-p'i-yeh* reigned at least from 1386. More tributes from Cambodia were sent to China from 1388 to 1404 but there were no Chinese records between 1386 and 1402 because Emperor Yǒnglè, a usurper, had all the records destroyed to remove any traces of his predecessor's reign. The next Cambodian ruler to appear in the *MSL* was recorded as Thsan-lieï-pho-pi-ya. The *MSL* mentioned that the Chenla king sent a mission with a tribute to China on the second year of the reign of Young-lo (Yǒnglè 永樂). Yǒnglè reigned from 17 July 1402 to 12 August 1424. Wolters said that the Cambodian mission arrived in China in September 1404. He provided the style name of the Cambodian king in Chinese as 婆毘牙 (P'o-p'i-ya), with his full interpretation as *Samdach P'o-p'i-ya.* I interpreted the style name as *Samdach Chao Ponhea.* The Cambodian king passed away either near the end of 1404 or at the beginning of 1405. On the third year of the reign of Yǒnglè, China sent a high-ranking official named Wang-tseu to assist on the funeral of the Cambodian king and then two other officials named Wang-tsoung and P'i-tsïn to help in the accession of the son who succeeded his father to the throne. The *MSL* recorded the style name of the new king as *Thsan-lieï-tchao-phing-ya,* which I interpreted as *Samdach Chao Ponhea.* Wolters said that the Chinese mission arrived in Cambodia on 10 August 1405 and he provided the name of the new king in Chinese as 平牙, with his full interpretation as *Samdach Chao P'ing-ya.*

Wolters argued that *Pao-p'i-yeh* and *P'o-p'i-ya* were two different persons based on his reasoning that the Chinese scribes "took the trouble to select different characters for the first syllable of these two names and also for *P'ing-ya.*"[106,p50] I believe that *Pao-p'i-yeh* and *P'o-p'i-ya* were the same person based on the reasoning that the Chinese scribes transliterated the Cambodian sound of the names with an approximation of the Chinese spelling. The Chinese spelled *Samdach* in two different ways (Samdach [Kambujadesa]: 參答 [甘武持達志] and Samdach [Pao-p'i-ya]: 參烈 [婆毘牙]). Again, they spelled Kambuja in two different ways (Kambuja[desa]: 甘武持[達志] and Kambuja: 甘菩者). I believe that *Pao-p'i-yeh* and *P'o-p'i-ya* were an attempt by the Chinese to transliterate the Khmer words *Chao Ponhea* (*Pao* or *P'o* = *Chao* and *p'i-yeh* or *p'i-ya* = *Ponhea*). Wolters himself made a remark that the *Kuo-ch'üeh* version spelled *P'o-p'i-ya* in two different ways; he spelled one way as 婆毘牙 and the other way he spelled it as 婆毘才, which rendered it to *P'o-p'i-ts'ai.*[106,p50] It seems that the title/style/epithet *Chao,* a word of Thai origin, was introduced to Cambodia around this period.

The *MSL/Kuo-ch'üeh* mentioned that between 1371 and 1404 Cambodia sent ten missions to China on the following dates:[106,pp48-50] 14 December 1371, 7 November 1373, 6 January 1378 (according to Ref. 107, p. 48, but 1379 according to Ref. 114, p. 29), 12 November 1380, 14 October 1383, 7 September

1387, 15 October 1388, 1389, 1390, and 1404. After P'ing-ya became king he sent more missions to China and the last one was recorded to occur in 1419.

Table 10a. Names and Royal Styles of Khmer Kings Mentioned in the Chinese History of the Ming Dynasty (Ming Shih-lu)

Translated/Interpreted Name	Transliterated Name	Chinese Name	Date	Source	Author's Comments
Name not mentioned	Hou-eul-na		1368	Jean-Pierre Abel-Rémusat (Ref. 113, p. 28)	Hou-eul-na, king of Chenla, sent an envoy named Naï-ye-ki to submit a letter and tributes near the beginning of the reign of Houng-wou (Hóngwǔ 洪武). He was the first emperor of the Ming Dynasty. He reigned from 23 January 1368 to 24 June 1398.
Name not mentioned	Name not mentioned		12 Sep 1370	Jean-Pierre Abel-Rémusat (Ref. 113, p. 26)	Kouo-tching arrived in Chenla with gifts from China on the eighth moon of the 3rd year of the reign of Houng-wou.
Name not mentioned	Name not mentioned		12 Sep 1370	Oliver William Wolters (Ref. 106, p. 47)	China envoy Kuo Chêng was sent to Cambodia to announce the accession of the first Chinese Emperor of the Ming Dynasty.
	Hu-êrh-na		1370	George Coedès (Ref. 1, p. 236)	Hu-êrh-na sent tribute in 1370 to the Ming Emperor.
	Hou-eul-na of Pa-Chan		14 Dec 1371	Jean-Pierre Abel-Rémusat (Ref. 113, p. 26)	On the 11th moon of the 4th year (of the Houng-wou's reign), the Basan (Pa-chan) or ruler of the kingdom named Hou-eul-na sent an embassador with a letter and tributes to China.
Chen-la (Cambodia) Kingdom Pa-shan King Hu-êrh-na (Wolters' translation) Chenla Country Pa-shan King Hu-êrh-na (author's translation)	Chenla Guo Pa-shan Wang Hu-êrh-na	真臘國口山王忽兒那	14 Dec 1371	Oliver William Wolters (Ref. 106, p. 47)	The Khmer envoys arrived in China with tributes for the emperor.
Name not mentioned	Name not mentioned		1373	Jean-Pierre Abel-Rémusat (Ref. 113, p. 29)	Tribute from Chenla arrived in China on the 6th year of the reign of Houng-wou. China gave a Ming imperial calendar and gifts to the Chenla king in return.
	Hu-êrh-na (Pa-shan king)		7 Nov 1973	Oliver William Wolters (Ref. 106, p. 48)	Cambodian mission arrived in China.
Chenla Kambujadhirāja (author's translation)	Thsan-tha-kan-wou-tche-the-tha-tchi		1379	Jean-Pierre Abel-Rémusat (Ref. 113, p. 29)	Chenla sent tributes to Houng-wu on his 12th year of reign.
Samdach Kambujadhirāja of Cambodia (Wolters' translation) Chenla King Samdach Kambujadesa (author's translation)	Chenla Guo-wang Shen-da Gan-wu-chi-da-zhi	真臘國王參答甘武特達志	6 Jan 1378	Oliver William Wolters (Ref. 106, p. 48)	Kambuja presented tribute to China.
Samdach Kambujā-dhirāja (Coedès translation)	Thsan-tha-kan-wou-tche-the-tha-tchi		1379	George Coedès (Ref. 1, p. 236)	Name of the Kambuja king mentioned.
Name not mentioned	Name not mentioned		1380	Jean-Pierre Abel-Rémusat (Ref. 113, p. 29)	Chenla sent tributes to Houng-wou on his 13th year of reign.
	Samdach Kambujadhirāja		12 Nov 1380	Oliver William Wolters (Ref. 106, p. 49)	Envoys from Kambuja presented tribute to China.
Name not mentioned	Name not mentioned		1383	Jean-Pierre Abel-Rémusat (Ref. 113, p. 29)	With consent of Chenla China sent inspectors to control Chinese citizens in Chenla on the 16th year of the reign of Houng-wou.
Name not mentioned	Name not mentioned		Oct 1383	Oliver William Wolters (Ref. 106, p. 49)	Chinese mission to Cambodia to seal "documents of mutual confirmation."
Name not mentioned	Name not mentioned		1386	Jean-Pierre Abel-Rémusat (Ref. 113, p. 30)	China officers named Lieou-min, Thang-king, and a few others were sent on the 19th year of reign of Houng-wou to present china vases to the king of Chenla.
Name not mentioned	Name not mentioned		Oct 1386	Oliver William Wolters (Ref. 106, p. 49)	China sent envoys named Liu Min and T'ang Ching to Cambodia.
Samdach Chao Ponhea Kambuja (author's translation)	Thsan-lieï-phao-pi-sie-kan-phou-tche		1387	Jean-Pierre Abel-Rémusat (Ref. 113, p. 30)	China received tributes in elephants and perfumes from Chenla on the 20th year of reign of Houng-wou.
Samdach Chao Ponhea Kambuja (aithor's translation)	Samdach Pao-p'i-yeh Kambuja	參烈寶毗邪甘蒲者	7 Sep 1387	Oliver William Wolters (Ref. 106, p. 49)	China envoys Liu Min and T'ang Ching received by new Cambodian king.
Samdach Chao Ponhea Kambuja (aithor's translation)	Tsan-lie Pao-p'il-sie Kan-p'u-che		1387	George Coedès (Ref. 1, p. 236)	The history of the Ming mentioned the name of the Kambuja king.

Table 10b. Names and Royal Styles of Khmer Kings Mentioned in the Chinese History of the Ming Dynasty (Ming Shih-lu)

Translated/interpreted Name	Transliterated Name	Chinese Name	Date	Source	Author's Comments
Name not mentioned	Name not mentioned		1388, 1389	Jean-Pierre Abel-Rémusat (Ref. 113, pp. 30-31)	Chela king sent tributes to Houng-wou (Hung-wu) on the 21st and 22nd years of his reign.
Chao Ponhea (Author's translation)	Pao-p'i-yeh		15 Oct 1388, 1389	Oliver William Wolters (Ref. 106, p. 49)	Khmer kings sent tributes to China in 1388 and 1389.
Name not mentioned	Name not mentioned		1390	Jean-Pierre Abel-Rémusat (Ref. 113, p. 31)	Chenla sent tributes to China on the 23rd year of the reign of Houng-wou.
Name not mentioned	Name not mentioned		1390	Oliver William Wolters (Ref. 106, p. 50)	Last Khmer mission sent during the Houng-wou period.
Name not mentioned	Name not mentioned		1403	Jean-Pierre Abel-Rémusat (Ref. 113, p. 31)	On the first year of his reign, Young-lo (Yŏngle 永樂) sent envoys named Tsiang-pin-hing and Wang-tchhou to Chenla. Young-lo reigned from 17 July 1402 to 12 August 1424.
Name not mentioned	Name not mentioned		15 Sep 1403	Oliver William Wolters (Ref. 106, p. 51)	China envoys, Chiang P'in-hsing and Wing Ch'iu, were sent to Cambodia and Champa to announce the accession of Young-lo.
Samdach Chao Ponhea (Author's translation)	Thsan-lieï-pho-pi-ya		1404	Jean-Pierre Abel-Rémusat (Ref. 113, p. 32)	Chenla king sent tributes to China on the 2nd year of the reign of Young-lo..
Chao Ponhea (Author's translation)	P'o-p'i-ya	婆毘牙	Sep 1404	Oliver William Wolters (Ref. 106, p. 52)	Cambodian mission arrived in China.
Samdach Chao Ponhea (Coedès' translation)	Th'san-lie-P'o-p'i-ya		1404	George Coedès (Ref. 1, p. 237)	Name of Khmer king mentioned in the History of the Ming.
Samdach Chao Ponhea (Author's translation)	Thsan-lieï-tchao-phing-ya		1405	Jean-Pierre Abel-Rémusat (Ref. 113, p. 33)	On the 3rd year of the reign of Young-lo, China sent a high ranking official named Wang-tseu to assist on the funeral of the Chenla king; and two other officials named Wang-tsoung and P'i-tsin to help in the accession of the son who succeeded his father to the throne.
Samdach Chao P'ing-ya (Wolters' translation)	:P'ing-ya	平牙	10 Aug 1405	Oliver William Wolters (Ref. 106, pp. 49 & 52)	Cambodia envoys arrived in China to announce the death of P'o-p'i-ya..
Chao Ponhea Yat (Coedès' interpretation)	Ts'an-lie Chao-p'ing-ya		1405	George Coedès (Ref. 1, p. 237)	The History of the Ming reported the announcement of the death of P'o-p'i-ya and the succession of his son.
Name not mentioned	Name not mentioned		1408	Jean-Pierre Abel-Rémusat (Ref. 113, p. 34)	China received tributes from Chenla on the 6th year of the reign of Young-lo.
Name not mentioned	Name not mentioned		1414	Jean-Pierre Abel-Rémusat (Ref. 113, p. 34)	China received tributes from Chenla on the 12th year of the reign of Young-lo. The envoys from Chenla complained to the Chinese Emperor about the Cochinchinese (Champa) preventing them from delivering the tributes to China.
Name not mentioned	Name not mentioned		1417	Jean-Pierre Abel-Rémusat (Ref. 113, p. 34)	China received tributes from Chenla on the 15th year of the reign of Young-lo.
Samdach Chao Ponhea (Author's translation)	Thsan-lieï-tchao-phing-ya		1419	Jean-Pierre Abel-Rémusat (Ref. 113, p. 34)	China received a golden letter and tributes from Cherla on the 17th year of the reign of Young-lo.
Name not mentioned	Name not mentioned		1426-1435	Jean-Pierre Abel-Rémusat (Ref. 113, p. 34)	China received Chenla envoys during the reign of Siouan-te (Xuāndé 宣德). He reigned from 27 June 1426 to 31 January 1435. After that there were no more tributes sent by Chenla.
Name not mentioned	Name not mentioned		1452	Jean-Pierre Abel-Rémusat (Ref. 113, p. 34)	China received tributes from Chenla on the 3rd year of the reign of Emperor King-thaï (Jingtai 景泰). He reigned from 22 September 1449 to 1 February 1457.
Chao Ponhea (Author's translation)	P'ing-ya		23 Dec 1408, 23 Feb 1414, 3 Aug 1417, 5 Apr 1419	Oliver William Wolters (Ref. 106, p. 53)	The ming source said that P'ing-ya sent more missions to China.

Reconstruction of Lost Records

As stated earlier, the accessions of Nippean Bat and Ponhea Yat have not been commonly agreed by historians. Refer to Table 9 for a summary of their reigns. Based on all available information, I will attempt to establish the chronology of the reigns of the Khmer kings from Paramesvara to Ponhea Yat and also to define the most probable dates for the accessions of Nippean Bat and Ponhea Yat.

Who was *Thsan-lieï-tchao-phing-ya* that was mentioned in the *MSL*[114,p33] as the eldest son who succeeded his father *Thsan-lieï-pho-pi-ya* in 1405? According to the Cambodian legend, Nippean Bat was the eldest son who succeeded his father *Ta Chey*, also known as *Ta Trasâk Paêm*, during the uncertainty period after the reign of Jayavarman Paramesvara.

As mentioned earlier, Lawrence Palmer Briggs reported that Jean Moura attributed the reign of Nippean Bat to occur in 1405 and that of Ponhea Yat in 1432. Moura said that because of the records lost during the wars with Champa in 1421 and also with Ayutthaya in 1431, Ponhea Yat commissioned his ministers to determine the chronology of events prior to his reign as soon as he became king. From their memories, Khmer chroniclers were able to go back only 27 years into the past. The year 1405 would be obtained when 27 years were subtracted from 1432, which in this case would correlate well with the date mentioned in the *MSL* as the year when *P'ing-ya* succeeded his father *P'o-p'i-ya*.

In his study of the Cambodian chronicles, Moura accounted for six Khmer kings between Nippean Bat and Ponhea Yat[6,p255] as follows: Sithean Reachea (1409-1409), Lompong Reachea (1409-1416), Soriyotei (1416-1416), Soriyovong (1416-1425), Borom Reachea (1425-1429), and Thommasoka (1429-1431). I would amend Borom Reachea to Borom Reamea (Paramarāma) based on George Coedès' work. Briggs differed from Moura on the number of kings during this period. He mentioned that there were only four reigning kings.

I have determined that there were officially four kings between the reigns of Nippean Bat and Ponhea Yat, but six reigns if one were to include Sithean Reachea (1409-1409) and Soriyotei (1416-1416). Sithean Reachea succeeded his brother Nippean Bat after his death but he died six months later without being officially proclaimed king. Soriyotei was Uparaja (Vice-King) when he succeeded his brother Lompong Reachea but he had never been consecrated. There is also the evidence of the *2/k.125 Fragment (Baiisavatar kru1i sri ayudhaya, No. 2/n. 125)* that Michael Vickery discovered in the National Library of Thailand in Bangkok in 1971 — even though the provenance of the *Fragment* was not dated, but by all indication it seems to predate the Ayutthayan and Cambodian chronicles — that seems to support Ponhea Yat as the king after the fall of Angkor in 1431. The document seems to preclude Ponhea Yat as the king before 1431.

The consensus is that Ponhea Yat had a long reign and that he established his capital at Basan in 1432 and then moved it to Chaktomouk (Phnom Penh) a year later due to flood, which would have been in 1432/1433, and remained there for thirty years until he abdicated in 1463.

Various Sources Concerning the Timeline for the Uncertainty Period (from Jayavarman Paramesvara to Thommasoka)

After an exhaustive search, I have compiled a comprehensive list of the ruling periods by the Khmer and Ayutthayan kings. The list is shown in Table 11.

The timeline documented in the *Histoire du Cambodge* by Adhémard Leclère[7,pp195-223] has many contradictions when compared to the events reported in the Ayutthayan chronicles documented by David K. Wyatt in his book *Short History of Thailand*.[104] During the 15th century, the Ayutthayan chronicles mentioned that Angkor fell to Ayutthaya specifically only in 1431 under the reign of Borommaracha II. Wyatt said that "Borommaracha II resumed the struggle against Angkor that had been pursued, but not concluded, by Ramathibodi and Ramesuan."[104,p59] Based on the Ayutthayan chronicles, the attack of Angkor under the reign of Lompong Reachea between 1347 and 1353 described in the Cambodian chronicles seems to be improbable.

Table 11. Correlation between Khmer and Ayutthayan Kings in the 14th and 15th Centuries

Cambodian Legend Extracted from Histoire du Cambodge (Adhémard Leclère – Ref. 7. pp. 140-141)	Lawrence Palmer Briggs The Ancient Khmer Empire (Ref. 6, p. 256)	Adhémard Leclère Histoire du Cambodge (Ref. 7, pp. 195-223)	George Coedès The Indianized States of Southeast Asia (Ref. 1, pp. 236-237)	David K. Wyatt Thailand: A Short Story (Ref. 104, pp. 50-85)	Wilaiwan Khanittanan Khmero-Thai: The Great Change in the History of the Thai Language of the Chao Praya Basin (Ref. 111, pp. 375-379)	Jean-Pierre Abel-Rémusat Description du Royaume du Cambodge (Ref. 113, pp. 25-34)	O. W. Wolters The Khmer King at Basan (1371-73) and the Restoration of the Cambodian Chronology during the 14th and 15th Centuries (Ref. 106, pp. 44-54)	Michael Vickery Cambodia and its Neighbors in the 15th Century (Ref. 75, p. 20)
Leclère summarized the reigns of the legendary Khmer Kings as follows: 1. King reigning during Chinese envoy's visit to Angkor in 1296.	Jayavarman Paramesvara (1327-) [Bayon inscription] Jayavarmadiparamesvara (1327-) [Angkor inscription] Parasmathakemaraja (-1330-1353-) [Laotian Annals]	Nipéan-bat (1340-1346) [Son of néay Chey] Sithean-réachéa (1346) [Brother of Nipéan-bat] Srey Lompongsa-reach (1347-1351) [Eldest son of Nipéant-bat]	Nirvānapada or Nippean Bat (1346-1351)					
2. King who succeeded the above king. 3. Allasa (Son of previous king) 4. Volék (Brother of Allasa) 5. Sénéka (Brother of Allasa and Volék) 6. Sihanu (Son of Sénéka) 7. Ta Chey (Killed Sihanu and married his daughter) 8. Ta Suos (Brother of Ta Chey) 9. Nippean Bat (Son of Ta Chey. Accession in 1340)		Srey-Sauryotey (1353) [Brother of Srey Lompongsa-reach] Siam's Occupation of Angkor (1353-1357) [Ruled by Chau Basath, Chau Baat, and Chau Kambang-Pisey] Srey-Sauryovongs (1357-1366) [Son of Srey-Sauryotey] Barom-Rama (1366-1373) [Son of Srey Lompongsa-reach] Thommasoka (1373-1394) [Younger brother of Barom-Rama] Sim's Occupation Of Angkor (1394) [Ayutthayan Prince Ponhe Prêk reigned at Angkor under the name Of Eyntréa-réachéa] Préah Srey Sauryovongs (1401-1417) [Son of Srey-Sauryotey. He died at the age of 43. Leclère believed that the Khmer chroniclers may have been confused with the reign of the previous king with the same name. Srey Sauryovongs.] Préah Barommasoka (1417-1421) [Nephew of Srey Sauryovongs. Leclère also believed this king to be fictitious.] Préah Srey-Sauryopéar or Chauponhéa Yéat (1384-1431) [Son of Préah Srey Sauryovongs. He was 17 when his father died in 1417]	Lompong-rājā or Lampong Reachea (1351-1352) Occupation of Angkor By Ramathibodi (1352-1357) [Son of Nirvānapada] Sūryavaṃśa Rājādirājā or Soriyovong (1357-1377) [Coedès said he was Hou-eul-na and brother of Lompong Reachea; but in my opinion I believe he was the son of Soryoti (brother of Lompong Reachea) And grandson of Nippean Bat.] Ts'an-ta Kan-wu-che-ch'e-ta-che or Samdach Kambujādhirāja (1377-1380) [Coedès said he was King Paramarāma (Borom Reamea) and son of Lompong Reachea.] Ts'an-lie Pao-p'i-sie Kan-p'u-che or Samdach Chao Ponhea Kambuja (1380-1393) [Coedès said he was Dhammāsokarājādhirājā (Thommasoka) who succeeded his brother Borom Reamea. He was killed by the Ayutthayan invaders. King Ramesuan put his son Indarājā (Intharacha) on the throne of Angkor, but it was assassinated almost immediately.]	U-Thong or Ramathibodi (1351-1369) Ramesuan (1st Reign: 1369-1370) [Son of Ramathibodi] Boronmaracha (1370-1388) [Brother-in-law of U-Thong] Thong Chan/Lan (1388) [Son of Boronmaracha] Ramesuan (2nd Reign: 1388-1395) [Son of Ramathibodi] Ramaracha (1395-1409) [Son of Ramesuan] Intharacha or Nakhon In (1409-1424) [He was the son of Boronmaracha] Boronmaracha II (1424-1448) [Youngest son of Intharacha]	U-Thong or Ramathibodi (1351-) [He was a Khmero-Thai prince from Lavo (Lopburi) who married a Khmer princess from Suphanburi. Both provinces were under the Khmer jurisdiction prior to local warlords' rebellion against Angkor. U-Thong founded Ayutthaya in 1351. His son, Ramesuan, born of his Khmer princess from Suphanburi was sent to govern Lopburi. The royal vocabulary "Raja-sap", borrowed from the Khmer was created by King Boromtraolokanat (Trailok) and promulgated into law in 1461.]	Hou-eul-na (at least 1371-at most 1379) Thsan-tha-kan-wou-tche-the-tha-tchi (at least 1379-at most 1387) Thsan-lieï-phao-psie-kan-phou-tche (at least 1387-at most 1404) Thsan-lieï-pho-pi-ya (at least 1404-1405) Thsan-lieï-tchao-phing-ya (1405-at least 1419) [He was the son of Thsan-lieï-pho-pi-ya]	Chen-la Country Pa-shan King Hu-êrh-na (at least 1371-at least 1378) Chen-la King Samtac Kambujadesa (at least 1378-at least 1383) Samtac Pao-p'i-yeh Kambuja (at least 1383/at most1387-at most 1404) Samtac P'o-p'i-ya Kambuja (at least 1404-1405) Samtac Chao P'ing-ya (1405-at least 1419) [Son of P'o-p'i-ya]	Vickery referenced the Ming Shi-lu records and the following four Ayutthayan Chronicles: 1. Luang Praseut (dated 1680 and considered to be the most reliable) 2. Long Chronicle (dated 1795 and contained the most details about Ayutthaya's relation with Cambodia from the 14th to the 15th centuries) 3. Van Vliet-Sangitiyavangs (dated early 19th century. Related to events of the first mid-17th century) 4. Two Fragments (discovered in the 1930s. Very detailed and related to events of the 15th century. Agreed with Luang Praseut Chronicle)

According to Wyatt, Ramesuan was 30 years old when his uncle Ramathibodi overthrew him from power in 1370.[104,p56] From 1347 to 1353 Ramesuan would have been between seven and thirteen years old (if Ramesuan were 30 years old in 1370, then he would have to be born in 1340). He would not have been given the command of 10,000 soldiers by his father Ramathibodi to attack Angkor at such an early age. The occupation of Angkor from 1353 to 1357 by the sons of Ramathibodi — Chau Basaths, Chau Baat, and Chau Kâmbâng Pisey — is never mentioned in the Ayutthayan chronicle. There are no records of Ramathibodi having three sons. The overthrow of Ramaracha by his Chief Minister occurred in 1395 and not earlier as has been suggested by Leclère. Intharacha who was offered the throne by the Chief Minister was second cousin of Ramaracha and not his brother as the Cambodian chronicles had reported.

In his book, Leclère mentioned of a story that was passed down through oral tradition of a gardener named Ta Trasâk Paêm (grandpa of sweet cucumbers) who had been selected by the high officials of the kingdom to replace the king that he had accidentally killed,[7,p141] supposedly King Jayavarman Paramesvara (within the context and timeline of the legend). To fully legitimize his reign Ta Trasâk Paêm married the daughter of the deceased king. They produced two children by the names of Nippean Bat and Sithean Reachea. Ta Trasâk Paêm reigned for seventeen years. He was succeeded by his brother Ta Suos who reigned for twenty years under the name of Preah Meak Reachea. Nippean Bat succeeded his uncle Ta Suos after his death.

The timeline proposed in *The Indianized States of Southeast Asia* by G. Coedès[1,pp236-237] seems sensible but does not seem to correlate well with the Laotian and Ayutthayan chronicles. Coedès mentioned that Ramathibodi laid a siege at Angkor as early as 1352 where Lampong-rāja (Lompong Reachea), the son of Nirvānapada (Nippean Bat), was reigning. The inscriptions at Angkor Wat and Bayon mention that Jayavarman Paramesvara acceded to the throne in 1327 but do not provide any clue to how long his reign lasted. On the other hand, the Laotian chronicle specifically mentions that Parathakemarāja — which most scholars agree to be Jayavarman Paramesvara — reigned at least until 1353. As mentioned earlier, Jayavarman Paramesvara was the father-in-law of Fa Ngum, considered to be the founder of the Laotian kingdom, known as Lan Xang. In this context, the Laotian chronicle can be considered to be more reliable than the Cambodian chronicles in this trouble period.

If the Laotian chronicle could be used as the basis to gauge the ruling period of Jayavarman Paramesvara, it is improbable that Ramathibodi would dare attacking Angkor in 1352 for the fact that Fa Ngum had invaded Ayutthaya and that Ramathibodi had accepted the Laotian sovereignty. As a sign of submission, Ramathibodi gave his daughter in marriage to Fa Ngum as well as paying tribute to the Laotian king.[6,p254]

Coedès mentioned that Angkor was taken in 1353 on the basis of the Annals of Ayutthaya, but according to scholars no such thing is ever mentioned in the Ayutthayan chronicle. Sūryavaṃśa Rājādhirāja (Soriyovong) succeeded Lompong Reachea and Coedès believed he may be the king that the *MSL* called Hu-êrh-na who sent tributes to the Chinese emperor in 1370. Coedès believed that he reigned for twenty years. He was succeeded by his nephew Paramarāma (Borom Reamea), son of Lompong Reachea. Coedès believed he was the king that the *MSL* called King *Ts'an-ta Kan-wu-che-ch'e-ta-che* (Samdach Kambujādhirāja) in 1379. Borom Reamea was succeeded in 1380 by his brother Dhammāsokarājādhirāja (Thommasoka) and Coedès believed he was the king that the *MSL* called Ts'an-lie Pao-p'i-sie Kan-p'u-che in 1387. Basing his finding on the Annals of Ayutthaya, Coedès seemed to be mistaken again when he said that Angkor was taken by Ramesuan in 1394 and that King Thommasoka was killed in the battle. He said that Ramesuan placed his son Indarāja [Intharacha] on the throne of Angkor but he was assassinated soon after [no date is given]. Coedès' account seems to be erroneous because Intharacha usurped the throne from his second cousin Ramaracha in 1409. As David K. Wyatt indicated, Intharacha was the son of Borommaracha and not of Ramaracha. The *MSL* mentions that a king named *Ts'an-lie P'o-p'i-ya*, which Coedès could not identify, reigned at Angkor in 1404 and that he was succeeded in 1405 after his death by his son Ts'an-lie Chao-p'ing-ya that Coedès identified as Chau

Ponhea Yat. According to Coedès, Ponhea Yat took the name of Sūryavarman upon his accession and reigned at Angkor for twenty six years before he decided to abandon it in 1431 because of the difficulty to defend the city against the attack by Ayutthaya. Ponhea Yat moved his capital to Basan (present-day Srei Santhor) for one year before settling down permanently at Chaktomouk (Phnom Penh).

The timeline reported in the *Essai de Tableau Chronologique des Rois du Cambodge de la Période Post-Angkorienne* by Mak Phoeun[110,pp150-152] does not seem to take into account the events mentioned in the *MSL*. Mak Phoeun seems to be basing the reigns of the Khmer kings only on the Cambodian chronicles. He started with Param Nibbānapad (Parâm Nippean Bât) who reigned from 1346 to 1351/2, followed by Siddhānarājā (Setthean Reachea) reigning from 1351 to 1352; Param Lambaṅsarājā (Parâm Lompong Reachea) from 1351/2 to 1353/5; Cau Pā Sāt (Chau Ba Sat) from 1353/4 to 1355/6; Cau Pā Āt (Chau Ba At) from 1355/6 to 1357/8; Cau Ktum Paṅ Bīsī (Chau Kdom Bâng Pisei) from 1357 to 1358; Srī Suriyovaṅs (Srei Soriyovong) from 1357/8 to 1366/7; Paramarāmā (Parâm Reamea) from 1366/7 to 1370/1; Dhammāsokarāj (Thoamea Sokarach) from 1370/1 to 1373/4; Indarājā/Bañā Braek (Entareachea/Ponhea Prèk) from 1373 to 1374; and Paramarājā I/Cau Bañā Yāt (Parâm Reachea I/Chau Ponhea Yat) from 1373/4 to 1433/4.

The timeline proposed in *The Khmer King at Basan (1371-3) and the Restoration of the Cambodian Chronology during the Fourteenth and Fifteenth Centuries* by O. W. Wolters[106,p73] neglects to take into account the occupation of Angkor in 1431 by Ayutthaya. He proposed the following timeline: 1) From the first occupation of Angkor by Ayutthaya to the accession of Ponhea Yat: 1369-1389; 2) Ponhea Yat: 1389-1404; 3) Noreay: 1404-1428; 4) Srey: 1429-1443; Accession of Dharmarājādhirājā: 1444.

The timeline suggested in *The Ancient Khmer Empire* by Lawrence Palmer Briggs[6] seems to be sensible but it does not correlate well with the *MSL* for the period of Nippean Bat's reign. Briggs suggested two different timelines. The first timeline is based on the combination of the Sankrit inscriptions, the Laotian annals, the Chinese dynastic history Ming Shi-lu (*MSL*), and the Cambodian annals. The second timeline is based on the Cambodian chronicles. The first suggested timeline is as follows: 1) Jayavarman Paramesvara (-1330-1353-) from the Sanskrit inscription or Paramathakemarājā (1327-?) from the Laotian annals; 2) Hou-eul-na (-1371-) from the *MSL;* 3) Samtac Prah Phaya (-1404) from the *MSL;* 4) Samtac Chao Phaya/Phing-ya (1405-?) from the *MSL* or Nippean Bat (1405-?) from the Cambodian annals. The second suggested timeline is as follows: 1) Samtac Chao Phaya Phing-ya/Nippean Bat (1405-1409); 2) Lampong or Lampang Paramarājā (1409-1416); 3) Sorijovong or Sorijong or Lambang (1416-1425); 4) Barom Racha or Gamkhat Rāmadhapati (1425-1429); 5) Thommo-Soccorach or Dharmasoka (1429-14310; 6) Ponhea Yat or Gam Yat (1432-?).

Fortunately, the events between Jayavarman Paramesvara and Sithean Reachea were recorded in the *MSL*. Even though the names (or style names) of the Khmer kings were not mentioned in a manner that could be easily identified and correlated with existing names mentioned in the Cambodian chronicles, they nevertheless provided valuable information during this period of Khmer history.

It is first necessary to resolve the identity of *Samdach Chao P'ing-ya* (參烈超平牙) who succeeded his father *Samdach P'o-p'i-ya* (參烈婆毘牙) in 1405 as mentioned in the *MSL* before any timeline can be established during this uncertainty period. Based on the examination and study of documents written by prominent scholars, I am convinced that the most sensible date of Ponhea Yat's accession to the throne was in 1432 as mentioned by Jean Moura and Lawrence Palmer Briggs. The discovery of the document called *Baiisavatar kru1i sri ayudhaya, No. 2/n. 125* in the National Library of Thailand in Bangkok in 1971 by Michael Vickery[108] would seem to preclude Ponhea Yat acceding to the throne before 1432. The document had remained hidden until Vickery discovered it, probably because it was written in Thai scripts that were difficult to read and understand which would consequently hinder the interest of most scholars. The document was not dated and its provenance was not mentioned, but by all indication it seemed that it predated the Ayutthayan and Cambodian chronicles. Vickery wrote a paper called *The 2/k.125 Fragment, A Lost Chronicle of Ayutthaya*[108] to reveal and explain the meaning of the texts in the document.

Vickery's paper has bridged the gap of understanding during the period of the fall of Angkor. The events mentioned in the *2/k.125 Fragment* will be discussed more thoroughly in subsequent sections, especially under the reigns of Thommasoka and Ponhea Yat and also under the interreign period of the Ayutthaya occupation of Angkor in 1431.

The Cambodian chronicles indicated that Ponhea Yat was the king who reigned after Thommasoka and that he was of royal blood who served the king during the period when Angkor was attacked by Ayutthaya. It was during the reign of Thommasoka that Angkor fell to Ayutthaya. Unlike the Cambodian chronicles that mentioned the fall of Angkor in many occasions, the Ayutthayan chronicles on the other hand mentioned that Angkor fell only in 1431. Considering the above chronology and coupled with the fact that Ponhea Yat's chronologers and high officials could go back only twenty seven years into the past to recollect events prior to his reign, the most sensible timeline would be to suggest that Ponhea Yat became king in 1432. If 27 years were subtracted from 1432, the result would be 1405 which would correspond to the year P'ing-ya succeeded his father P'o-p'i-ya. In this case, it would suggest that Nippean Bat would be P'ing-ya that was mentioned in the *MSL*. There are two versions of the story in the Cambodian chronicles. One story mentioned that Nippean Bat succeeded his father Ta Chey (Ta Trasâk Paêm) while another story mentioned that he succeeded his uncle Ta Suos (Preah Meak Reachea). As I have discussed earlier, Jayavarman Paramesvara reigned from 1327 to at least 1353 and at most 1368 (the year of the first Cambodian king, Houl-eu-na or Hu-êrh-na, to appear in the *MSL*). According to the Cambodian legend/story, Ta Chey and Ta Suos had reigned for a combined 37 years. If this number were subtracted from 1405 (the year of Nippean Bat/P'ing-ya's accession) then Ta Chey would have started his reign in 1368. I am aware of the unreliability of the Cambodian story/legend, but in this case Cambodian chronologers and/or historians who were unaware of the Chinese records in the *MSL* may have created the story/legend to fill in the gap of the historical events between the reigns of Jayavarman Paramesvara and Nippean Bat. I will assume 1368 as the end of the reign of Jayavarman Paramesvara and the beginning of the reign of Hu-êrh-na. According to Wilaiwan Khanittanan, King Ramathibodi of Ayutthaya sent his son (probably Ramesuan) and his brother-in-law (probably Pha-Ngua who later became King Borommaracha) on a campaign against Angkor and won the battle in 1369.[111,p375] Ayutthaya had won the battle but had never occupied Angkor. Could it be possible that Ramathibodi seized on the opportunity of the death of Jayavarman Paramesvara, the father-in-law of King Fa Ngum of Lan Xang (Ramathibodi had accepted the suzerainty of Fa Ngum over Ayutthaya), to attack Angkor? The event seemed to correspond to the hypothesis suggested by Oliver William Wolters about the Khmer king *Hu-êrh-na* reigning at Basan to stay away from Angkor because it was under attack from the Ayutthayan army.

If Ta Chey had reigned for 17 years, Ta Suos would have succeeded his brother in 1385 and he would have passed away in 1405 after 20 years of reign. As discussed earlier, I considered *Chenla Country Pa-shan King Hu-êrh-na* and *Chenla King Samtac Kambujadesa* mentioned in the *MSL* to be the same person. In this case, the historical Cambodian king Hu-êrh-na mentioned in the *MSL* would correspond to the legendary king Ta Chey who is popularly known as Ta Trasâk Paêm. As has been stated earlier, I believe that *Samdach Pao-p'i-yeh Kambuja* and *Samdach P'o-p'i-ya* to be the same person, where the Chinese would transliterate *Chao* with *Pao* or *P'o* and *Ponhea* with *p'i-yeh* or *p'i-ya*. This king mentioned in the *MSL* would correspond to the legendary king Ta Suos who reigned under the name of Preah Meak Reachea or Preah Phaya. As mentioned earlier, *Pao* or *P'o* was probably the Chinese transliteration of the Khmer word *Chao* but it could possibly also mean *Preah;* and *p'i-yeh, p'i-.ya,* or *p'ing-ya* that I believe was the Chinese transliteration of the Khmer word *Ponhea* could also be interpreted as *phaya*.

The *MSL* specifically mentioned that *Samdach Chao P'ing-ya* succeeded his father *Samdach P'o-p'i ya* in 1405. According to the Cambodian chronicles and legend when Ta Suos or Preah Phaya acceded to the throne under the name Preah Meak Reachea, Nippean Bat would have been at the most sixteen years old if one assumes he were born a year after the union between Ta Trasâk Paêm and Chant Vara Vattey. It is conceivable that Ta Suos took advantage of Nippean Bat's youth and inexperience to usurp the throne from his nephew or that he decided to apply the rule of ambilateral descent system to claim his right to the throne. Because he was not only older than Nippean Bat but he was also the brother of Ta Trasâk Paêm, thus of the same generation, Ta Suos would feel he was the legitimate heir to the throne. If P'ing-ya were Nippean Bat, then how could one explain the discrepancy between the *MSL* and the legend reported in the Cambodian chronicles when it said that Nippean Bat succeeded Ta Suos instead of Ta Trasâk Paêm? I believe that the Chinese who witnessed the coronation of *P'ing-ya* may have erroneously think that the new king was the son of his predecessor because it was in the Chinese tradition to have the son succeeding his father, which was not necessarily true for the case in Cambodia. Nothing much is known about the reign of Ta Suos. The Chinese information on *Po-p'i-ya* is weak. This is due to the records that were erased on the order of the Chinese Emperor Yônglé. There is another discrepancy that needs to be explained concerning the duration of the reign of *P'ing-ya* as compared to Nippean Bat. The *MSL* said that China still received tributes from *P'ing-ya* as late as 1419. How could this be possible since Nippean Bat reigned only for four years according to the Cambodian chronicles? Because I believe that *P'ing-ya* was a style name and not the personal name of Khmer kings, I contend that the *P'ing-ya* who succeeded *P'o-p'i-ya* in 1405 was not the same person who sent a tribute to China in 1419.

Concerning the story of Ta Chey (Ta Trasâk Paêm) and his brother Ta Suos (Preah Meak Reachea) who had a combined reign of 37 years, it is my contention that the Cambodian chroniclers under the reign of Ponhea Yat or some future chroniclers created this story to fill in the gap of the missing Khmer history between the period of Jayavarman Paramesvara and Nippean Bat. It seems that the duration of the combined reign of these two brothers are too convenient for this story to be factual. The timeline from the start of the reign of Jayavarman Paramesvara to the fall of Angkor is proposed in Figures 43 and 44.

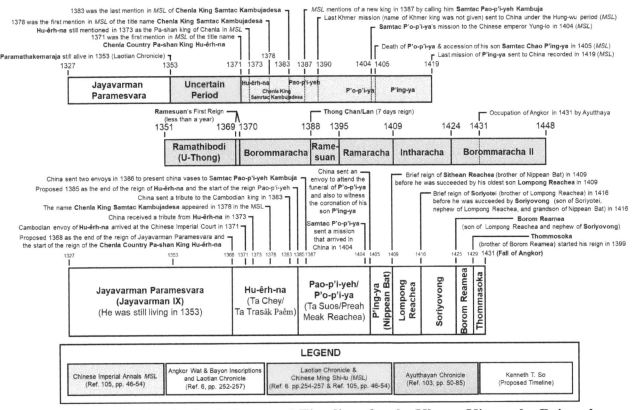

Figure 43. The Author's Proposed Timelines for the Khmer Kings who Reigned during the Uncertainty Period from 1327 to 1431

The timeline was carefully considered based on the Angkor Wat and Bayon inscriptions combined with the Laotian chronicle, the Ayutthayan chronicles, the Cambodian chronicles, and the Chinese records in the *MSL*. Because of the lack of information during the reign of Nippean Bat and also of the uncertainty of events that took place during this period, I will take the traditional approach suggested by Jean Moura and L. P. Briggs concerning the chronology from Nippean Bat to Ponhea Yat but has to amend Borom Reachea with Borom Reamea according to George Coedès' study.

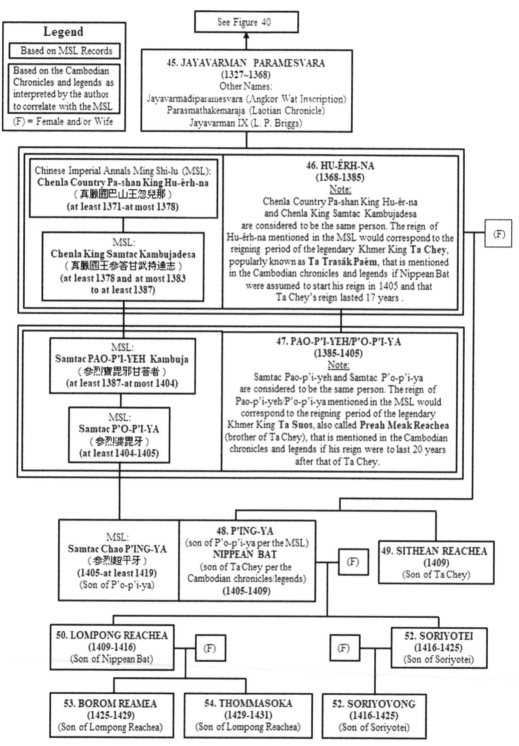

Figure 44. Genealogy of Khmer Kings Proposed by the Author during the Uncertainty Period from Jayavarman Paramesvara to Thommasoka

46 **Chenla Country Pa-shan King Hu-êrh-na** (真臘國巴山王忽兒那) ហ៊ូវេរណា

and/or **Chenla King Samdach Kambujadesa** (真臘國王參答甘武持達志) – **(1368-1385)**

Relationship: Undetermined according to the *MSL* but the timeline of Hu-êrh-na's reign would correlate well with that of the legendary Ta Trasâk Paêm (Ta Chey) as mentioned in the Cambodian chronicles.

Religion: Assumed Theravada/Hinayana Buddhism

Capital: Angkor Thom (1368-1371), Basan (1371–1373), Angkor Thom (1373-1385)

Genealogy: Figures 44, 45, and Appendix 3

It is obvious that the name Houl-eul-na recorded in the *MSL* in 1368[113,p28] and that of *Chen-la Guo Pa-shan Wang Hu-êrh-na* (真臘國巴山王忽兒那) recorded in 1371[106,p47] were of the same Khmer king. The style name in Chinese literally means *Chen-la Country Pa-shan King Hu-êrh-na*. The word *Pa-shan* was an attempt by the Chinese to transliterate the Khmer word Basan (present-day Srei Santhor). The name *Hu-êrh-na* could not be identified with any historical name in the Khmer epigraphies or chronicles. Michael Vickery believes that Hu-êrh-na was an attempt by the Chinese to transliterate the Khmer word *ka-ru-na.* This word is a form of etiquette used by commoners to address the kings.

The *MSL* did not mention the date of the accession of Hu-êrh-na, supposedly the king who succeeded Jayavarman Paramesvara, and the Cambodian epigraphies did not provide the end of the reign of Jayavarman Paramesvara either. The Laotian chronicle mentioned that Jayavarman Paramesvara was still alive in 1353. Based on the earlier discussion it can be deduced that Hu-êrh-na's reign started at least from 1368. The *MSL* did not specifically mention the end of Hu-êrh-na's reign but only the style name of the next Khmer king that took place in 1378. The *MSL* mentioned that a tribute sent by the Cambodian king *Chen-la Guo-wang Shen-da Gan-wu-chi-da-zhi* (真臘國王參答甘武持達志), which literally means *Chen-la King Samdach Kambujadesa,*[106,p48] was received at the Chinese Imperial Court on 6 January 1378. Based on the style name, this new king was no longer reigning at Basan but rather at Angkor because he was the king of Kambuja and not of Basan as mentioned previously in the *MSL*.

According to Wilaiwan Khanittanan, Ramathibodi sent his son (believed to be Ramesuan) and his brother-in-law (believed to be Pha-Ngua) on a campaign against Angkor. They won the battle in 1369 but had never remained to occupy Angkor.[111,p375] If this were true, then Ramathibodi may have seized on the opportunity of the death of Jayavarman Paramesvara to attack Angkor. If this were the case, then the hypothesis advanced by O. W. Wolters about *Hu-êrh-na* reigning temporarily at Basan to avoid the attack by the Ayutthayan army could not be discarded. Borommaracha I was known as a warrior king who did not hesitate to grab power from his nephew Ramesuan after this latter succeeded his father U-Thong/Ramathibodi in 1369. The account of the above event will be discussed in length in Chapter 8 under *The Origin of the Thai.*

I believe that *Chen-la Country Pa-shan King Hu-êrh-na* and *Chen-la King Samdach Kambujadesa* are the same king. Based on the *MSL,* the reign of Hu-êrh-na would last no longer than 1387 due to the fact that the style name of a new king appeared on the scene during that year. As discussed earlier, I estimated that the reign of Hu-êrh-na would end around 1385. If the Cambodian chronicles were amended and moved the year of Ta Chey's accession to 1368, then he would have passed away in 1385 after seventeen years of reign.

47 **Samdach Pao-p'i-yeh Kambuja** (參烈寶毘邪甘菩者) or

Samdach P'o-p'i-ya (參烈婆毘牙) – **(1385-1405)** ប៉ៅពីយេ / ពោពីយ៉ា

Relationship: Undetermined according to the *MSL* but the timeline of the reign of Pao-p'i-yeh/P'o-p'i-ya would correlate well with that of the legendary Ta Suos (Preah Meak Reachea or Preah Phaya) as mentioned in the Cambodian chronicles

Religion: Assumed Theravada/Hinayana Buddhism
Capital: Angkor Thom (Eyntapath Moha Nokor)
Genealogy: Figures 44, 45, and Appendix 3

The *MSL* recorded that the Chinese emperor sent his emissaries Liu Min and T'ang Ching in October 1386 and that they arrived in Cambodia on 7 September 1387 to present china vases to a Khmer king by the name of *Samdach Pao-p'i-yeh Kambuja* (參烈寶毘邪甘菩者[106,p49]). As discussed earlier, I estimated that the reign of Pao-p'i-yeh started around 1385. The *MSL* did not mention how Pao-p'i-yeh was related to his predecessors, but the legendary part of the Cambodian chronicles mentioned that Ta Suos succeeded his brother Ta Trasâk Paêm during this uncertainty period and reigned under the name of Preah Meak Reachea. He was also known as Preah Phaya. George Coedès, according to Vickery in his Working Paper Series No.27,[75,p39] believed that Pao-p'i-yeh was not a name but rather a title by suggesting that *Pao-p'i* corresponded to *bo bañā*.

More missions were exchanged between Cambodia and China after 1387 but the name of the Cambodian king was not cited until 1404 when the *MSL* mentioned that China received a tribute from the Cambodian king named *Samdach P'o-p'i-ya* (參烈婆毘牙). The Chinese information on P'o-p'i-ya is weak. This is due to the records that were erased on the order of the Chinese Emperor Zhū Yŏnglè (朱永樂) after he usurped the throne from his nephew Zhū Jiànwén (朱建文) in 1402. The name of P'o-p'i-ya appeared for the first time in 1404 when the *MSL* mentioned that *Samtac P'o-p'i-ya*[106,p50] (參烈婆毘牙) sent a Cambodia mission to China to pay respect for the accession of the Chinese Emperor Yong-lè. As discussed earlier, I believed that *P'o-p'i-ya* and *Pao-p'i-yeh* were the same person unlike O. W. Wolters who believed that *P'o-p'i-ya* was a new king. The *MSL* mentioned that *P'o-p'i-ya* passed away either in late 1404 or early 1405.

The above period correlates well with the Cambodian chronicles mentioning that Ta Suos succeeded his brother Ta Chey and reigned for 20 years. If the Cambodian chronicles were amended and moved the year of Ta Suos' accession to 1385, then his reign would have ended in 1405. Ramaracha reigned in Ayuthhaya during this period. His relationship to the Cambodian kings will be discussed under the reigns of Thommasoka and Ponhea Yat.

48 Samdach Chao P'ing-ya (參烈超平牙) or Nippean Bat — (1405-1409) សម្ដេចចៅពិង្យ៉ា / និព្ពានបទ

Transliterated Name: Nibbānapad
Other Names: Param Nibbānapad, Mahanibbhana[103,p8]
Posthumous Name: Preah Bat Samdach Preah Borom Nipean Bat[7,p195]
Reign Title: Brhat Pada Samdach brhat Parama Nirnava Pada[7,p195]
Relationship: P'ing-ya was the son of Pao-p'i-ya according to the MSL, but Nippean Bat was the son of Ta Trasâk Paêm according to the legend in the Cambodian chronicles
Religion: Theravada/Hinayana Buddhism
Capital: Angkor Thom (Eyntapath Moha Nokor from the Sanskrit Indraprastha Maha Nagara — City of Indra of the Great Kingdom[7,p196])
Genealogy: Figures 44, 45, and Appendix 3

The *MSL* mentioned that China sent a high-ranking official named Wang-sen to attend the funeral of *Samdach P'o-p'i-ya* (參烈婆毘牙) and two other officials named Wang-tsoung and P'i-tsin to witness the coronation of his son *Samdach Chao P'ing-ya* (參烈超平牙) in 1405.[113,p33]

As discussed earlier, I attributed the style name *Samdach Chao P'ing-ya* to correspond to Nippean Bat who succeeded his uncle Ta Suos according to one legend but to his father Ta Trasâk Paêm according to another legend. According to the timeline I laid out, it would be more appropriate to have Nippean Bat succeeding his uncle Ta Suos. As explained earlier, I believed that the Chinese may have erroneously reported that *P'ing-ya* was the son of his predecessor *P'o-p'i-ya* as it was the custom in China.

Nothing much is known about Nippean Bat except what was written in the Cambodian chronicles. The legendary part of the chronicles that is considered to be part of Cambodian history mentioned that Nippean Bat had a younger brother named Sithean Reachea. They were both the sons of Ta Trasâk Paêm and Chant Vara Vattey [she was supposedly the daughter of Jayavarman Paramesvara according to the chronology of the Cambodian chronicles but the daughter of King Sihanu Reach according to the legend] who became Queen Srey Chantoreach. Nippean Bat had two sons, Lompong Reachea and Soriyotei. Depending on the Cambodian chronicles, Nippean Bat's reign lasted between four and six years. Jean Moura and L. P. Briggs determined that Nippean Bat reigned for four years.

The year 1409 corresponded to the time when Nakhon In who reigned under the name of Intharacha usurped the throne of Ayutthaya from his second cousin Ramaracha. According to David K. Wyatt, Ramaracha was sent into exile but he did not specify the location. Michael Vickery who based his finding on the Luang Praseut *(LP)* Chronicle said Ramaracha was sent to govern a location called *Padāgūcām*. He deconstructed the word to *prāp jhām* which means "put down the Cham," an area known as the Cham River in the 19th century and is now identified as the *Chaktomouk River (Caturmukh)*. The relationship between Ramaracha and Cambodian kings will be discussed under the reigns of Thommasoka and Ponhea Yat.

49   Sithean Reachea (1409) សិទ្ធានរាជា

Transliterated Name: Siddhānarājā
Title: Non-consecrated king
Relationship: Younger brother of Nippean Bat
Religion: Theravada/Hinayana Buddhism
Capital: Angkor Thom (Eyntapath Moha Nokor)
Genealogy: 53 and 54

With amendments and adjustments of the dates to the Cambodian chronicles, it was determined that Sithean Reachea succeeded his brother Nippean Bat in 1409. His reign was short because he passed away six months later without having been consecrated. In this case the ambilateral descent system was applied for the line of succession. Sithean Reachea who was of the same generation as Nippean Bat and of higher ranking than his nephew Lompong Reachea (Nippean Bat's son) would therefore inherit the throne first before it would be passed down to the next generation. Not much is known about Sithean Reachea because of his short reign.

50   Lompong Reachea (1409-1416) លំពង្សរាជា

Transliterated Name: Laṃbaṅsarājā
Other Names: Paramarājādhirāja, Param Laṃbaṅsarājā, Lampang Paramaraja, Lāmbăn
Reign Title: Brhat Samdach Brhat Rajagga Braht Parama Ramakangsa Rajadhiraja (Preah Bat Samdach Sdach Preah Reach ongka Preah Borom Lompongsa Reachea-thireach[7,p196]
Relationship: Eldest son of Nippean Bat
Religion: Theravada/Hinayana Buddhism
Capital: Angkor Thom (Eyntapath Moha Nokor)
Genealogy: 53 and 54

Moura determined that the reign of Lompong Reachea lasted seven years. The Cambodian chronicles said that Lompong Reachea reigned under the style name of *Preah Bat Samdach Sdach Preah Reach Ongka Barom Lompongsa Reacheathireach.*[7,p196] He promoted his younger brother Preah Soriyotei to the rank of Uparaja. With an amendment and adjustment to the dates of the Cambodian chronicles, it was determined that Lompong Reachea reigned from 1409 to 1416.

The *MSL* mentioned that in 1414 Cambodia had difficulties delivering tributes to China because of the constant attacks by the Cham.[113,p34] As a result of Cambodia's complaint, China sent an envoy to warn Ngauk Klaung Vijaya of Champa [he succeeded his father Simhavarman in 1400, which the Vietnamese calls La Khai] to stop the hostilities and be a good neighbor with Cambodia.[106,p53; 113,p34] At the beginning of his reign, Ngauk Klaung Vijaya took the name Virabhadravarman and when he was crowned in 1432 he changed his name to Indravarman. He is known under the name of Chang-pa-ti-lai (Champadhiraja) in the *MSL*. The Cham inscription at Biên-hoa described the victory of the above king over Cambodia in 1421.[1,p238]

The reign of Lompong Reachea fell under the period where Intharacha usurped the throne of Ayutthaya from his second cousin Ramaracha in 1409.

51   Soriyotei (1416) សូរិយោទ័យ

Transliterated Name: Suriyodăy
Other Names: Srī Suriyodăy
Regence Title: Uparaja/Yuvaraja
Relationship: Younger brother of Lompong Reachea
Religion: Theravada/Hinayana Buddhism
Capital: Angkor Thom (Eyntapath Moha Nokor)
Genealogy: Figures 51, 52, and Appendix 3

With an amendment and adjustment to the dates of the Cambodian chronicles, it was determined that Soriyotei succeeded his older brother Lompong Reachea in 1416. His reign was brief because he died within the same year as an Uparaja. Nothing much is known about him.

52   Soriyovong (1416-1425) សូរិយោវង្ស

Transliterated Name: Suriyovaṅs
Other Names: Srī Suriyovaṅs, Sorijovong, Sorijong, Lambang
Reign Title: Brhat Pada Samdach Braht Raja Angga Braht Çry Suryavamsa Rajadhiraja (Preah Bat
    Samdach Preah Reach Ang Preah Srey Soryovongs Reacheathireach[7,p207])
Relationship: Son of Soriyotei and grandson of Nippean Bat
Religion: Theravada/Hinayana Buddhism
Capital: Angkor Thom (Eyntapath Moha Nokor)
Genealogy: Figures 51, 52, and Appendix 3

With amendments and adjustments of the dates to the Cambodian chronicles, it was determined that Soriyovong succeeded his father Soriyotei in 1416. He reigned under the style name of *Preah Bat Samdach Preah Reach Ongka Preah Srey Saryovong Reacheathireach (Brhat Pada Samdach Brhat Raja Angga Brhat Çry Suryavamsa Rajadhiraja)*. The Cambodian chronicles said that under his reign the Khmer kingdom extended as far as Baschimborei (present-day Prachinburi in Thailand) to the west, Nokor Reach Seima (present-day Korat in Thailand) to the northwest, Snam Khsach (Laos?) to the north, the Koukhan country (Laos?) to the northeast, Baria/Daung Nay (open country plain-rejected coconut; present-day Ba Ria-Vaung Tau/Dong Nai in Vietnam) to the southeast, and the sea shore to the south.[7,p210] King Soriyovong died of illness in 1425 after nine years of reign.

53   Borom Reamea (1425-1429) បរមរាមា

Transliterated Name: Paramarāmā
Relationship: Eldest son of Lompong Reachea
Religion: Theravada/Hinayana Buddhism
Capital: Angkor Thom (Eyntapath Moha Nokor)
Genealogy: Figures 44, 45, and Appendix 3

Adhémard Leclère,[7,p210], Mak Phoeun,[110,p151] and George Coedès[1,p236] said that Borom Reamea (Paramarāma) succeeded Soriyovong while L. P. Briggs[6,p256] said it was Borom Reachea. I believe that assigning the name of Borom Reamea as the successor to Soriyovong may be more appropriate. He was the oldest son of Lompong Reachea. With amendments and adjustments of the dates to the Cambodian chronicles, it was determined that Borom Reamea reigned in 1425. He died of sickness in 1429 after four years of reign. His reign corresponded to the period when Borommaracha II became king of Ayutthaya from 1424 to 1448. It was during his reign that Borommaracha II aggressively decided to attack Angkor.

54   Thommasoka (1429-1431) ធម្មាសោក

Transliterated Name: Dhammāsokarāj
Other Names: Dhammāsokarāj, Thommo-Soccorach, Dharmasoka
Reign Title: Preah Bat Samdach Sdach Preah Reach Ang Preah Thommasoka Reacheathireach
Relationship: Son of Lompong Reachea and younger brother of Borom Reamea
Religion: Theravada/Hinayana Buddhism
Capital: Angkor Thom (Eyntapath Moha Nokor from the Sanskrit Indraprastha Maha Nagara — City
    of Indra of the Great Kingdom[7,p196])
Genealogy: Figures 44, 45, and Appendix 3

With amendments and adjustments of the dates to the Cambodian chronicles, it was determined that Thommasoka succeeded his older brother Borom Reamea in 1429. He reigned under the style name of *Preah Bat Samdach Sdach Preah Reach Ang Preah ThommasokaReacheathireach.*

Borommaracha II who ruled Ayutthaya from 1424 to 1448 sensed the decline of the Khmer empire and probably took advantage of the defeat of Soriyovong by the Cham in 1421 to press his attack on Angkor. The Ayutthaya chronicles said that Borommaracha II mounted an attack against Cambodia and he finally succeeded in taking Angkor in 1431.[104,p59] Borommaracha II installed his son to rule Angkor very briefly before abandoning it.

The Cambodian chronicles described the attack of Angkor by Ayutthaya but the timeline must be amended to fit the historical event described in the *LP* Chronicle as well as in the *2/k.125 Fragment* that Michael Vickery discovered in the National Library of Thailand in Bangkok in 1971.[108] Learning of Ayutthaya's plan to attack Angkor, Thommasoka formed four corps and placed them under the commands of Ponhéa Kêv (Bañā Kaev per *LP* and *2/k.125*), Ponhéa Tey (Bañā Dai per *LP* and *2/k.125*), Chauponhéa Yéat of royal lineage (Cau Yāt per *2/k.125*), and Samdach Chauhvéa Tôlaha (Prime Minister). As told in the Cambodian chronicles, the Ayutthayan commander devised a mischievous plan to take Angkor after he had failed through seven months of siege of the city. He picked six soldiers and had them forcefully whipped outside the Angkor rampart in full view of Khmer soldiers and commanders. Apparently through the order of the Ayutthayan commander, the six soldiers were allowed to escape in the night. They presented themselves at the gate of Angkor and asked for protection from the Khmer commanders. They offered their services to the Khmer king and said they wanted to take revenge on Ayutthaya for causing them so much suffering. To make the desertion of the six soldiers more believable, the Ayutthayan commander displayed a decapitated head of the soldier who was responsible for letting the six prisoners escape. He had the head planted on a bamboo pole for everybody to view. The wounds on the six soldiers were so severe that two of them died. The death of the two soldiers and the head of decapitated soldier gave even more credibility that the whippings of the six soldiers were real and that their desertions were genuine. The surviving four soldiers were assigned to fight alongside the Khmer soldiers against the Ayutthayan army. The ploy of the Ayutthayan commander seemed to work as the four soldiers started to gain the trust of the Khmer generals. The Cambodian chronicles said that during the course of the siege two of the Khmer generals, Ponhéa Kêv and Ponhéa Tey, betrayed the Khmer king by opening the gate to let the Ayutthayan soldiers in the city. The four deserters must have been able to convince these two generals that the Ayutthayan victory was imminent. The Cambodian chronicles reported that the four deserters were instantaneously killed by the Khmers but harms had already been done. The Ayutthayan soldiers rushed inside the city and killed Thommasoka in the course of the battle in 1431. Many Khmer high dignitaries were captured and taken prisoners to Ayutthaya. A large number of the population was able to escape including Chau Ponhea Yat and Prohm Borohoet (Chief Brahman) who took the *Preah Khan Reach* (Sacred Sword), the Lompêng Chey (Spear of Ta-Chey or Spear of Victory), and the Emerald Buddha with them to safety. This account in the Cambodian chronicles about saving the royal regalia from the invading army of Ayutthaya seems to contradict with the story told in the *LP* Chronicle as well as in the *2/k.125 Fragment*. Vickery who had studied the Thai documents as well as the Cambodian documents carefully made the following comments:[108,p55]

> *The structure of the story in 2/k.125 – conquest of Angkor by King Paramarājādhirāj, the placing of his son Nagar Indr on the Angkorean throne, the involvement of two individuals, Bañā Kaev and Bañā Day, the removal of valuable objects to Ayutthaya – shows that it is to that extent the same story as recorded in LP in A.D. 1431 and the long Ayutthayan chronicles in 1421. Subsequent events, however, including mention of Yāt and his reconquest, are missing from all Ayutthayan chronicles, which have nothing more about Cambodia for another century.*

The discovery of the *2/k.125 Fragment* is significant because it corroborates with the *LP* Chronicle and to a certain extent with the Cambodian chronicles also. The provenance and date of the *Fragment* was not stated, but Vickery determined that it predated the Ayutthayan and *LP* Chronicle as well as the Cambodian chronicles of Ang Eng and Nong. He based his finding on the utilization of the official ranks mentioned in the *2/k.125 Fragment*. Vickery had observed that the ranks of *khun* mentioned in the story (which predated the accession of Borommatrailokanat, 1448-1488) had been elevated by two echelons to *braḥ* by the end of the fifteenth century for the following four major ministers:[108,p54]

Minister of the Capital: from *khun mo'aṅ* to *braḥ nagarpāt*
Minister of the Palace: from *khun văṅ* to *braḥ dharrmādhikarṇ*
Minister of Fields: from *khun nā* to *braḥ kṣetrā*
Minister of the Treasury: from *khun glàṅ* to *braḥ koṣādhipati*

Based on the above ranking system and some of the errors of the animal signs assigned to the Cula years that will be discussed below, it is very likely that the story in the *2/k.125 Fragment* was written after the reign of Borommaracha II and probably near the end of the fifteenth century. Based on his first hand examination of the *2/k.125 Fragment*, Vickery stated that it was not an original document but a copy from an earlier manuscript. Considering the details given in the story and the time it was supposedly written, the *2/k.125 Fragment* could be considered as a credible source of information. According to my analysis, the *Fragment* had to be written after Ponhea Yat decreed to rename *Prāp Jhām to* Chaktomouk in 1433[29,p69] due to the fact the *Fragment* specifically mentioned that Braḥ Rām Cau (Ramaracha) was sent into exile by the king of Ayutthaya to Caturmukh (Chaktomouk).

The Ayutthayan chronicles must have omitted the reconquest of Angkor by Ponhea Yat that was reported in the Cambodian chronicles as well as in the *2/k.125 Fragment* deliberately. The Cambodian chronicles did not provide the origin of Chau Ponhea Yat as it only said he was of royal blood fighting for Thommasoka against Ayutthaya. The origin of Chau Ponhea Yat will be elaborated in Chapter 10 during the post Angkor period.

THE FALL OF ANGKOR

The Ayutthayan Rule (1431-1432)

The *LP* chronicle mentioned that after taking Angkor in 1431, Borommaracha II installed his son Braḥ Nakhon In on the throne of Angkor but his reign lasted only one year.[75,p44] After the conquest of Angkor, Borommaracha II returned to Ayutthaya but he did not go back empty handed. They looted the palace and took the royal regalia back to Ayutthaya.[104,p59] Undoubtedly the Ayutthayans took Cambodian intellectuals, engineers, craftsmen, artists, as well as laborers back with them to Ayutthaya. Miriam T. Stark wrote the following passage about the looting of Angkor after the Thai invasion in 1431-1432:[115,p164]

> *By the ninth century AD, a clearly Khmer identity emerged in the Tonle Sap region that was expressed through both militarism and art. When the Thai army sacked the capital of Angkor in AD 1432, they conquered a distinctly Khmer kingdom. In taking the royal Khmer court back to the Chao Phraya region, the Thais appropriated distinctly Khmer traditions of statecraft, music, and art that reflected a well-developed ethnic and historic identity.*

The *2/k.125 Fragment* also mentioned that the Ayutthayan king installed his son on the throne of Angkor. It said that the "King's son, Cau Bañā Braḥ Nagar Indr, was ruling in Braḥ Nagar Hluoṅ."[108,p9,p11] The king mentioned above was referred to Samtec Braḥ Paramarājādhirāj Cau. With some explanations, this story seems to correlate well with the *LP* Chronicle.

Samtec Braḥ Paramarājādhirāj Cau and Cau Bañā Braḥ Nagar Indr

The Ayutthayan king, Samtec Braḥ Paramarājādhirāj Cau, mentioned in the *2/k.125 Fragment* referred to Borommaracha II (name recorded in the *LP* Chronicle). Cau Bañā Braḥ Nagar Indr mentioned in the *2/k.125 Fragment* referred to Nakhon In (name recorded in the *LP* Chronicle). There seems to be some misinterpretation and/or confusion concerning the association of Nakhon In with Intharacha (names recorded in the *LP* Chronicle). Firstly, Nakhon In was the son of Borommaracha I and not of Borommaracha II but because the Roman number was only added in the modern text for easy reference, this may create some confusion and misinterpretation. Secondly, Intharacha was the name before Nakhon In became king, but there is another Intharacha which the modern text called Intharacha II. He was the grandson of Borommaracha, which the modern text called Borommaracha II. Scholars may have confounded King Intharacha II for King Nakon In (whose name was Intharacha before he changed it to Nakhon In after he became king) and erroneously attributed him, Nakhon In, as the son of Borommaracha II. Because of the mixture and duplication of names, I believe that the Cau Bañā Braḥ Nagar Indr mentioned in the *2/k.125 Fragment* was intended to mean Intharacha II and that his father Samtec Braḥ Paramarājādhirāj Cau was intended to mean his grandfather Borommaracha II. According to the *LP* Chronicle, Intharacha II ruled as regent under the name Borommaracha III from 1463 to 1488 and then as King Intharacha II from 1488 to 1491. Braḥ Nagar Hluoṅ was the name for Angkor Thom. According to the Cambodian chronicles Ponhea Prék was the son that Borommaracha II placed on the throne of Angkor. Ponhea Prék reigned at Angkor under the name of Preah Eyntrea Reachea (or Intharacha in Thai). The Ayutthayan prince reigned at Angkor very briefly, probably for less than a year, before he abandoned it and returned to Ayutthaya.[104,p59]

The *2/k.125 Fragment* did not specifically mention the fall of Angkor in 1431 but it gave some reference points that can be used to deduce the approximate date that Samtac Brah Paramarājādhirāj Cau (Borommaracha II) installed his son, Cau Bañā Brah Nagar Indr on the throne of Angkor. There are two clues in the story that can be used to determine when the events took place. The first clue in *2/k.125 Fragment* mentioned that prior to Cau Bañā Brah Nagar Indr occupying the throne of Angkor, King Bañā Rām of Hansāvati (Môn kingdom) passed away and he was succeeded by Bañā Baro.[108,p9] According to Vickery, the Môn chronicle Rājādhirāj said that Brah Cau Baro succeeded King Sudodharmarājādhirāj in 803 Cula. This year would correspond to AD 1441/1442. I have found another source that differed from the Môn chronicle Rājādhirāj and it seems to correlate better with the timeline of the events described in the *2/k.125 Fragment*. Donald M. Stadner wrote in the SOAS Bulletin of Burma Research, Volume 6 (2008) that King [Sudharma] Rajadhiraj [of Hanthawati] reigned from 1384 to 1420.[116,p30] This statement indicates that the events in the story occurred after 1420 but no later than 1448, the end of the reign of Borommaracha II. The second clue, extracted from Vickery's translation said the following:[108,p15,p17]

> *...Much later it was known that Cau Yāt had probably escaped, and Nāy Dharrmarāj, Nāy Ñi Jāṅ Dòṅ, Nāy Prajā, Nāy Dòṅ Tret Saṅsār, and Nāy Ñibbkāy agreed to the Khmer fleeing from Brah Nagar Hluoṅ to go to stay with Cau Yāt. He organized them as left, right, forward, and rear. [Cula] era 845, Year of the Pig, fifth of the decade, Cau Bañā Kaev and Bañā Dai, of the tribe of mahā barrg, whom the King had brought from Brah Nagar Hluoṅ, were discussing with Jīy Prajā, the astrologer, about committing treason against Samtec Brah Paramarājādhirāj Cau, and promised one another that in accordance with his wish, they would let Jīy Prajā, the astrologer, rule the kingdom of Ayutthaya and would send Bañā Kaev and Bañā Dai, and the regalia which had ben taken, back to Brah Nagar Hluoṅ.*

The above story provides a lot of useful information. An analysis on some of the key elements in the story is required to determine the timeline of the event that took place. [Cula] era 845, Year of the Pig, fifth of the decade provides a reference point for the story. Major personalities in the story could be found in the *LP* Chronicle as well as in the Cambodian chronicles.

Clue for the Fall of Angkor Mentioned in the 2/k.125 Fragment

The statement [Cula] era 845, Year of the Pig, fifth of the decade is erroneous for at least two reasons: 1) Cula 845 did not correspond to the Year of the Pig but to the Year of the Hare; and 2) Cula 845 would correspond to AD 1483/1484, which would fall outside the period of the event that took place. The event took place under the reign of Samtec Brah Paramarājādhirāj Cau, better known as Borommaracha II who reigned from 1424 to 1448. [Cula] 845 can therefore be excluded from the event. It leaves only Year of the Pig and/or fifth of the decade as the viable solution to fit the event. Fifth of the decade means Pagnjasak (Pagnja = 5; and Sak = era), which is a manner of counting the 10-year cycle that is used in the lunisolar calendar system (see Chapter 3 for a better understanding on how the lunisolar calendar is calculated).

There are only four Cula options as shown below that would satisfy either Year of the Pig or fifth of the decade within the event time frame:

1) Cula 785, Year of the Hare, fifth year of the decade (Pagnjasak) = AD 1423/1424
2) Cula 793, Year of the Pig, third year of the decade (Treysak) = AD 1431/1432
3) Cula 795, Year of the Ox, fifth year of the decade (Pagnjasak) = AD 1433/1434
4) Cula 805, Year of Pig, fifth year of the decade (Pagnjasak) = AD 1443/1444

Based on the above four options, Cula 793, Year of the Pig, third year of the decade (Treysak) which corresponded to AD 1431/1432 is the only year that would correlate with the *LP* Chronicle concerning the fall of Angkor in 1431.

Vickery came to a different conclusion concerning the event that took place in the *2/k.125 Fragment.* He Chose Cula 805 because he based his information on the Môn chronicle Rājādhiāj which stated that King Sudodharmarājādhirāj passed away in Cula 803, which would correspond to AD 1441/1442. He chose Cula 805 because that was the Year of the Pig and fifth year of the decade mentioned in the *2/k.125 Fragment.* He discarded Cula 845 because he recognized that it was outside the event timeline. He stated that Bañā Yāt's resistance against Ayutthaya lasted at least 12 years (1443-1431 = 12) instead of one year that is commonly believed by historians. There is no clear evidence that Angkor had been occupied by Ayutthaya longer than one year.

The statement "[Cula] era 846, Rat Year, second month, Samtec Braḥ Paramarājādhirāj Cau sent up for Bañā Jaliaṅ, Mahā Dhamarāja, Bañā Rāmarāj, and Bañā Saen Tāv" in the *2/k.125 Fragment* could not be correct.[108,p45] Cula 846 was not a Rat year but a Dragon year that corresponded to AD 1484/1485. These years were outside the timeline of the event that was described in the *2/k.125 Fragment.* The Rat year that fell under the reign of Borommaracha II (1424-1448) would either be AD 1432/1433 (Cula 794) or AD 1444/1445 (Cula 806). I believe that the event took place in AD 1432/1433 because it would correlate well with the year that Ponhea Yat was fighting against Ayutthaya to reconquer Angkor.

Because the animal signs and the Cula years for the events mentioned in the *2/k.125 Fragment* did not properly match, I believe that the scribe(s) who copied the *2/k.125 Fragment* from another manuscript must have either made a mistake during his copy or added the Cula years into the Fragment incorrectly. It was in the Khmer tradition as well as in the Thai and Lao traditions to report the events that occurred in history in animal years/signs by using some reference points that seemed to be obvious during the time that the scribes wrote the stories, but they became less obvious to the readers after many generations later.

Bañā Kaev and Bañā Dai

King Paramarājādhirāj (Borommaracha II) took Bañā Kaev and Bañā Dai with him to Ayutthaya. As mentioned earlier they were the Khmer generals appointed by Thommasoka to defend Angkor Thom, but they betrayed the Khmer king by siding with Ayutthaya. The *LP* Chronicle said that "they appear as prisoners taken to Angkor along with a number of images"[75,p47] but this statement seems to be in contradiction with the story described in the *2/k.125 Fragment* as reproduced above. The *2/k.125 Fragment* did not mention them as prisoner but only that they were brought back from Angkor by King Borommaracha II. It did not seem they were prisoners but guests of the Ayutthayan king. If they were prisoners they would not have the means to prepare a coup against Borommaracha II and the opportunity to discuss and convince the Ayutthayan Court astrologer Jīy Prajāto join in their plan to overthrow the king. Why would the astrologer of the king listen to two helpless prisoners? If their plan succeeded they would install the astrologer as the new king of Ayutthaya. It seems that Bañā Kaev and Bañā Dai may have had remorse and wanted to return the Cambodian regalia back to Angkor. The only way they could accomplish their objective was to topple Borommaracha II.

Vickery identified the above two Bañās as of Pear origin. The Pears are concentrated mostly on the western region of Cambodia. The above two personalities are mentioned in the Cambodian document of the 19th century but not in the *AE* Fragment of 1796. Their plan to topple the king failed. Borommaracha II had Bañā Kaev, Bañā Dai, Jīy Prajā, and all the astrologers of the royal court of Ayutthaya arrested and impaled. As a symbol of warning to any potential betrayers of the Ayutthayan crown, Borommaracha II had their bodies exposed in plain sight for people to view.[108,p21] Borommaracha II wanted to spare the life of Bañā Kaev's son, Cau Kaev Fā, but this latter wished to be executed because he did not want to live in shame and be known as the "son of the astrologer."[108,p23]

The *LP* Chronicle as well the Cambodian chronicles never mentioned the professions of Bañā Kaev and *Bañā Dai* but the *2/k.125 Fragment* unequivocally stated that Bañā Kaev was an astrologer like Jīy Prajā, the Ayutthayan Court astrologer. This may explain why Bañā Kaev was able to convince Jīy Prajā and the other Ayutthayan astrologers to join him and Bañā Dai (who may also be an astrologer) in their plan to topple Borommaracha II.

The discovery of the *2/k.125 Fragment* by Michael Vickery was very significant because it contributed to the understanding of Khmer history during that tumultuous period. Michael Vickery was brilliant in his interpretation and explanation of the Fragment, but there are some areas in his paper that need to be exploited further. My explanation and analysis concerning some inconsistencies between the *2/k.125 Fragment* and Ayutthayan/Cambodian chronicles are covered in the next chapter under the reign of Ponhea Yat. Based on my understanding and analysis of the *2/k.125 Fragment* in combination with the Ayutthayan and Cambodian Chronicles, a genealogy tree for Khmer kings from Jayavarman Paramesvara to Ponhea Yat could be generated. It is shown in Figure 45. The genealogy of the Khmer kings from Jayavarman Paramesvara (Angkor period) to Chey Chetha I (Longvek period) is shown in Appendix 3.

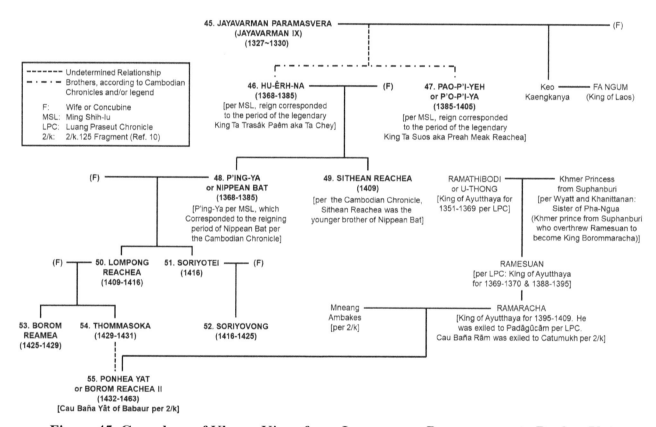

Figure 45. Genealogy of Khmer Kings from Jayavarman Paramesvara to Ponhea Yat

CHAPTER 7

REASONS FOR THE COLLAPSE OF ANGKOR

It is the custom of historians in writing of the train of events which began with the siege, capture and sack of Angkor by the Siamese and ended in the removal of the capital to the other side of the kingdom, to call this train of events the fall of Angkor. Hitherto, there has been no essential agreement on the date. Some writers have believed the Siamese — as we may now call the Tai of Sukhotai and Ayuthia — captured Angkor more than once during the last century and a half of its existence as capital. This writer believes it may now be considered as established that Angkor was captured but once during that period and that the date of the siege and capture was 1430-1431 and that of the abandonment of Angkor Thom as capital took place in 1432.

The Ancient Khmer Empire
Lawrence Palmer Briggs [6,p257]

It would be misguided to think that the people during the Funan, Chenla, and Angkor periods enthusiastically embraced Brahmanism as their religion. The cult of Devaraja with the monarch as the universal ruler was created under the auspice of Brahmanism. The religion was used as a tool for the kings, Brahmans, and families of the upper class to control people of the lower class. Concerning the religion, the inscriptions during the above periods never ceased to mention the cult of Devaraja and the worship of linga that were the core belief of Brahmanism. These practices were mainly reserved for the kings, Brahmans, and noble families but not for people of low stature. Sanskrit, the language of high learning used in Brahmanism to perform sacred rituals and official functions was controlled by the Brahmans, the kings, and people of the upper class. The language was considered sacred and beyond the reach of commoners. There were no Brahmans assigned to teach Sanskrit or Brahmanism to the people at the local level. People during the above periods were more familiar with the animistic practices of worshiping spirits and dead ancestors than Vishnu or Shiva. Buddhism had briefly found its voice during the above periods but did not endure because of the control exercised by the Brahman priests to preserve Brahmanism. Their resistance to share their knowledge had kept them in power for centuries. Brahman priests started to lose their grips under the reign of Suryavarman I when he appointed people of Vishnuic and Buddhic backgrounds to positions of equal importance to balance out the influence of Brahmans who had been controlling Cambodia since the time of Jayavarman II. Probably sensing the ever increasing influence of Brahmans, Suryavarman I decided to divest the house of Sivakaivalya that produced the hereditary position of purohitas (Chief Brahmans) since the reign of Jayavarman II to remove some of its power. The people of lower stature had always had an affinity for Buddhism. It was Dharanindravarman II who started Buddhism but it was Jayavarman VII who firmly implemented it as the state religion. But after Jayavarman VII, Buddhism was temporarily displaced by Brahmanism until it found its renaissance under future kings who sponsored and embraced Buddhism again. With the state-sponsored, Buddhism was diffused to the masses without hindrance and it became the religion embraced by the common people. Under Buddhism, temples were built throughout the country and not just concentrated only in the Angkor area. The temples were served as worship and learning centers under the guidance and teaching of monks. Pali and Khmer languages were taught to commoners. Reading and writing were no longer reserved for the privilege of the upper class families.

The collapse of Angkor was not caused by one single event but rather by an accumulation of events over the centuries that finally led to its demise. Most historians attributed the fall of Angkor to the conversion from Brahmanism to Buddhism that left the Khmer empire in a state of weakness, but I would argue it was the other way around. Brahmanism was the religion that was needed when it was introduced to Funan and Chenla. The indigenous people who were not literate and not well organized needed a central authority to manage and bind all the different groups scattered in the region together. Brahmanism fit the system very well in the early period. The knowledge that the Brahmans brought from India was concentrated only on the upper class that ruled the country effectively. They guarded their knowledge within their inner circle and did not share it with the masses. The Khmer empire became endangered after the constant arrival of the Tais who escaped the persecution by the Chinese and the Mongols. The new Tais were more warrior-like and their settlement among the more established Tais in the region resulted in competition for new leadership positions within the Tai community. The Tais were well aware of the Khmer dominance in the region but it was less of a threat when compared to that of the Mongols. They knew that the Khmers possessed secret and sacred knowledge and held on to it for centuries. The knowledge that the Khmers held were not shared with the common people. When the Thais of Sukhothai and Ayutthaya — whose ancestries had a lot in common with the Khmers — invaded Angkor and took the learned men and all secrets with them, Cambodia was left without intellectuals and the people who remained did not have any knowledge on how to administer and grow the country. The knowledge had shifted from Angkor to Ayutthaya. If Cambodia had converted to Buddhism earlier with monks parting their knowledge to the masses around the country, Cambodia would not have been left in the dark after the Thai invasion of Angkor. The collapse of Angkor was caused by a combination of the following phenomena:

1. Too slow to convert from Brahmanism to Buddhism. The power and knowledge were concentrated only among the Brahmans, the khsatryas (families of royal lineages), and the nobles instead of sharing them with the masses. The secrets of Cambodia's power disappeared when the Thais of Khmer ancestries invaded Angkor and took the Brahmans and all the intellectuals with them back to Ayutthaya. If Buddhism had been implemented earlier, the knowledge of Khmer ingenuity would have been preserved among the masses even after Angkor had fallen. The government which reverted to Brahmanism did not have the support of the people after they had experienced Buddhism, a more tolerant and compassionate religion, under the reign of Jayavarman VII. If war were to break out with Ayutthaya, which practiced Buddhism, Angkor would have a hard time for the full allegiance of the Khmer people to defend the country.

2. Psychology played a powerful role in the demise of the Khmer civilization. People in ancient times were very superstitious and clang on to traditions without reservation. When the Thais took the Emerald Buddha — the symbol of power, protection, security, and prosperity — from Angkor during the reign of Thommasoka, the Khmer people as well as the Khsatryas and high dignitaries

were left in a sense of despair, believing they were no longer being protected by their gods against the enemies.

3. Credible evidences show that Jayavarman VII's son, -indravarman (not to be confused with Indravarman II who succeeded Jayavarman VII), left his governorship at Lopburi to become king of Sri Lanka. As a result, other Khmer princes may have fought among themselves for the claim of the vacant governorship position of Lopburi. A new figure emerged during that time. An obscure Khmer-Thai leader named U-Thong from Lopburi consolidated his power by marrying a Khmer princess from Suphanburi. He reigned as king of the newly founded kingdom of Ayutthaya and challenged Angkor for supremacy. Ayutthaya became a strong rival of Angkor.

4. The combination of unusually strong monsoon seasons and two periods of long droughts, one from 1345 to 1365 and the other from 1401 to 1425,[66,p1048] had thrown havoc to the proper *functioning of the Angkor canals. Angkor Thom was no longer able to feed its population estimated to be close to one million inhabitants. The abandonment of Angkor in 1432 shortly after the end of the second drought season was probably necessary. That may be the reason also why the Thai could not remain at Angkor after it was invaded.*

5. The location for the foundation of Angkor was chosen mainly for strategic reason. Jayavarman II had to find a location for his capital that not only could be defensible but also had to be remote enough to prevent any surprise attacks from his enemies, especially from Java. It was probably due to its location that the Khmer empire was able to expend and exert its influence in Southeast Asia. Angkor was centrally located as the capital for the Khmer empire but as its empire contracted and diminished in influence, its location was no longer viable for the emerging trade and commerce that required a seaport to do business. The politics of the region had changed. Angkor had to compete in commerce and prestige against Ayutthaya where its capital was located close to the sea. That was one of the reasons that Angkor was abandoned and the capital of Cambodia was relocated to Chaktomouk in present-day Phnom Penh.

6. The Mongol's conquest of the world had an indirect impact on the fall of Angkor. To escape the Mongols the Tais from southern China moved southward to settle around the Chao Praya valleys. Their skills as hardened warriors had emboldened the Tais who had settled in the valleys in earlier centuries to even be more warrior-like. At the beginning they were fighting among themselves. Lan Na fought Sukhothai and this latter in turn fought Ayutthaya to vie for supremacy. Ayutthaya came out victorious but its prestige was still limited because it had not conquered Angkor yet. Ayutthaya emerged as a power in the region after it had defeated the Khmer. The center of power had shifted from Angkor to Ayutthaya.

7. The combination of the rise of Ayutthaya under the war-like king Borommaracha II and the emergence of Champa as a powerhouse under the leadership of Binasuor (called Chê Bông Nga by the Vietnamese and Ngo-ta Ngo-che by the Chinese[1,p237]), had cumulated in the defeat of Indrajayavarman in 1321 by the Cham which weakened Angkor for the perfect timing of the invasion of Angkor in 1431 at the hand of Borommaracha II.

8. The shrinkage of Cambodia territories resulted in the loss of population to form a big army and also in the loss of opportunities for the capture of more elephants to use for warfare.

9. The common people would not object to the construction of the barays (reservoirs) because they were worthwhile projects that allowed them to grow rice all year-round. However, when they were called upon or were forced to build temples, especially the big projects like Angkor Wat and Bayon, that provided no benefit to them it was understandable they may have some bitterness toward the elite class. The Angkor inscription mentioned that 300,000 laborers and 6,000 elephants were used for the construction of Angkor Wat. The use of this magnitude of resources would undoubtedly sap the strength of the kingdom and the rancor of the people for generations. As a result, people were less inclined to defend the country against the Ayutthayans that Khmer people viewed as essentially of the same background and culture.

The latest studies conducted by the research teams of Brendan M. Buckley[117] and Mary Beth Day[66] validated the theory that Angkor may have been abandoned because it could no longer support its inhabitants due to a combination of unusually strong monsoon seasons and extended period of droughts lasting for decades. It was discovered that Angkor was not a regular city but rather a "hydraulic city" full of canals covering an area of nearly 1,000 square kilometers. During the monsoon season, instead of allowing water to go to waste the Khmer engineers captured it by diverting most of the water to large barays such as the East and West Barays as well as to smaller barays for storage. The water was managed for farming after the monsoon season through its release from the barays to the different canals. With this ingenuity and through proper management of the water, Angkor was able to support its population of 750,000 (or as high as one million) in the 14th and 15th centuries while the population of London numbered only 30,000 in the medieval time. The Ta Prohm inscription mentioned that 66,000 farmers were laboring to produce 3,000 tons of rice per year to feed themselves and the 12,640 people who were working and maintaining the temple.[64,p34] If Preah Khan, Angkor Wat, and Bayon were included in the equation, it would require around 300,000 farmers to produce 12,000 tons of rice per year to support the population of Angkor Thom.

The teams of Brendan M. Buckley and Mary Beth Day were able to determine that Angkor went through cycles of unusually high monsoon seasons followed by two periods of mega-droughts in 1345-1365 and 1401-1425.[66,p1048] They came with the above conclusion after they had studied the ring-width of the 979-year po mu trees (Fokienia hodginsii cypress tree) that grew from 1030 to 2008 in Vietnam[117] and the core soil sample of the West Baray lake bed.[66] In his paper, Buckley made the following statement:

> *What our study demonstrates, however, is that decades of weakened summer monsson rainfall, punctuated by abrupt and extreme wet episodes that likely brought severe flooding that damaged flood-control infrastructure, must now be considered an additional, important, and significant stressor occurring during a period of decline.*

It can therefore be concluded with certainty that in addition to the wars and political events, the abnormal weather cycles in the mid-14th century and early 15th century disrupted the proper functioning of the canals in the Angkor region and ultimately contributed to the abandonment of Angkor Thom.

CHAPTER 8

ဖြ:နုံမြၚၚ္သုဉ္ဉကြလောယ်နဋ္ဋ ဖြ:နုံမြၚၚ္သုဉ္ဉကြလောယ်နဋ္ဋ

THE ORIGIN OF THE THAI

Indeed, the people who brought the core elements of the contemporary Thai identity to what is now Thailand did not arrive in the central portion of the Indochina peninsula until about a thousand years ago; for them we had best reserve the word Tai, a term used to denote the various Tai peoples in general, peoples sharing a common linguistic and cultural identity that in historic times has become differentiated into a large number of separate but related identities. The modern Thai may or may not descend from the late-arriving Tai but may instead descend from the region's still earlier Mon or Khmer inhabitants or the much later Chinese or Indian immigrants. Only over many centuries has a "Thai" culture, a civilization and identity, evolved as the product of interaction between Tai indigenous and immigrant cultures.

Thailand, a Short History
David K. Wyatt [104,p1]

As a former outpost of Lopburi, which was a study center for Khmer civilization (Kasetsiri 1976: 85), at the beginning, Ayutthaya must have used Khmer as the language of wider communication in the same manner as Lopburi. The Khmer language, especially the written one, was then regarded as being holy and had magical power. People paid special respect to written materials which happened to be mostly about religion and kings. The Thais of Ayutthaya, formerly under the Khmer control, could also speak Khmer besides their own language... Though Thai historians do not agree on where King U-Thong came from, they all agree that he married a Khmer Princess and that Ayutthaya inherited all the Khmer administrative system and culture... When King U-Thong founded Ayutthaya in 1351 A.D., he was actually a Khmero-Thai or Khmer-speaking Thai. At least he must have been educated as a Khmer leader because he became king in the Khmer tradition — a god-king.

Khmero-Thai: The Great Change in the History
of the Thai Language of the Chao Phraya Basin
Wilaiwan Khanittanan [111,pp 376- 378]
Department of Linguistic, Faculty of Liberal Arts
Thammasat University

THE TAI MIGRATION AND STATES FORMATION

A full understanding of the history of Cambodia from the Angkor period to the present time cannot be accomplished without taking into consideration the events that shaped the Tai world, whose people contributed to the foundation of the present-day Thai society. The history of Cambodia during this time period is intricately linked to the history of Thailand like a Siamese twin. Where did the Thai people come from and how did they manage to grow in influence in Southeast Asia? This section and the subsequent ones trace the evolution of the Tai people through their migration from China to Southeast Asia, resulting in the foundations of the kingdoms of Lan Na, Sukhothai, and Ayutthaya, which then merged to form Siam, and then Thailand.

One of the major events that took place in Southeast Asia in the thirteen century was the consolidation and emergence of the Tai people that started their migration from southern China in the first millennium AD, steadily spreading to uplands of northern Southeast Asia, and finally moving down to the plains for more inhabitable and farming spaces due to population growth and also to the demand for manual labor. According to numerous studies, the origin of the Tai people that dated back to the early centuries AD are now generally accepted as emerging from the extreme southeastern region of the present-day Guangxi province in China.

The Tai people are identified as belonging to the Zhuang ethnic group where approximately 90% of its entire population in China is presently living in Guangxi, which represents about 32% of the Guangxi population.[59; 118] As the Tai population continued to grow and coupled with the Imperial China's hegemonic policy in the early centuries AD toward its southern neighbors, the Tai people began to disperse and migrate southward to avoid China's persecution. As a result, the Tais began to diverge and develop their own linguistic dialects differentiated through five distinguishable groups. The first Tai group that remained in southern China like the Zhuang people living in Guangxi, Guizhou, and Yunnan still retained its original language. The second Tai group like the White, Black, and Red Tais was split from the original group and migrated from the first to the fourth century to the northern region of Annam. This new community developed its own identity and dialect. The third Tai group was again split from the second group to migrate down farther to Muang Then, located in the present-day Dien Bien Phu region around the fourth to the eighth century. The fourth and fifth groups were split from the third group around the eight to the tenth century. The fourth group continued farther south and settled near present-day Luang Prabang in Laos. The fifth group continued south-west and settled near present-day Chiang Saen in northern Thailand, bordering Laos and Burma. From the tenth century onward this fifth group continued its migration farther south to found the Lan Na, Sukhothai, and Ayutthaya kingdoms. The map of their migration routes is shown in Figure 46. Over centuries of separation, the above five groups developed their own distinct cultures and traditions. The first and second groups adopted the Chinese and Vietnamese culture. The third, fourth, and fifth groups developed their own languages that are all similar, but still distinct, and are spoken in northern Laos, Thailand, Burma (Shan state), known collectively as the Isan region. The early settlements of the Tai people were mainly on hillsides away from the indigenous Southeast Asian population who resided on the plains. Even though the Tai population was expanded over a large territory spanning from present-day northern Laos to northern Thailand and all the way to Burma, there exists one common theme that still relates the Tai world through the legend of Khun Borom.

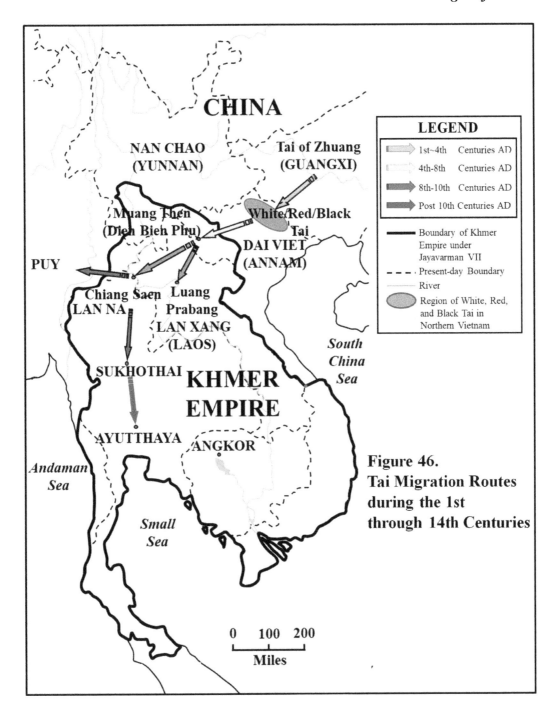

**Figure 46.
Tai Migration Routes
during the 1st
through 14th Centuries**

The Legend of Khun Borom

The Laotians considered Khun Borom Rachathirath to be the founder of the Tai world. The legend implies that the Tais emanated from Laos and spread to the other regions, but this is contrary to historical facts. Through their belief, the Laotians considered Laos to be the center of the Tai civilization. The Khun Borom legend told of gods sending a flood to kill all humans as a punishment for their ingratitude and then repopulating the earth with three village chiefs and a buffalo that the gods sent back to earth. The new population was divided into the dark-skinned and light-skinned groups where the Lao people emerged from the latter group. With the guidance and help from the gods, the three chiefs taught the Tai, identified as the Lao in the legend, on how to cultivate rice and build houses. As the population continued to grow and needed further guidance, the chief of the gods sent his own son, Khun Borom, to rule the earth for twenty five years. He set out governing rules and implemented moral laws. Khun Borom produced seven sons and appointed each one of them to rule over the Tai world of Luang Prabang (present-day Laos), Siang Khwang (present-day Tran-ninh plateau in Vietnam), Lavo-Ayutthaya (present-day Thailand), Chiang Mai (present-day Thailand), Sipsong Pan Na (present-day southern Yunnan in China), Hangsavati (the Môn state of Pegu in present-day Myanmar/Burma), and in Nghe-an (north central coast of present-day Vietnam).[104,p9] Until recently, Nan Zhao (Nan Chao) which was located in present-day Yunnan in China was erroneously considered to be the birthplace of the Tai people. New studies revealed the Tais to be linguistically and culturally different from the Nan Zhao people. Even though it is considered a legend, the Chinese nevertheless identify Khun Borom to be the historical figure Piloko (皮羅閣). This identification is now considered to be historically inaccurate because Piloko was of Nan Zhao origin. History credited Piloko for bringing the six Zhoas tribes [Mengshe (蒙舍), Mengsui (蒙巂), Langqiong (浪穹), Dengtan (□□), Shilang (施浪), and Yuexi (越析)] into a unified kingdom called Nan Zhao (南詔) in 737 with the support of the Tang dynasty.[119] The Chinese Imperial court recognized Piloko as the "Prince of Yunnan." Nan Zhao, which developed into a strong kingdom, played a key role in the evolution of the Tai world. Nan Zhao's rise in power, from the eight to the tenth centuries, and its war against China and Southeast Asia prevented China from having easy access and communication to the region south of its border. If it were not for Nan Zhao fighting the powerful Imperial China, the Tai may have been completely absorbed into a greater China and the present-day Tai world in Southeast Asia may have never existed as it is now.

China's Alliance with Chenla to Fight against the Tai

During this period, an important development took place between China, Nan Zhao, and Chenla. A historical background needs to be injected during this period on the relationship between China and Chenla. The original capital of Chenla was in Shresthapura near Vat Phu of present-day Laos. After Chenla conquered Funan — which included Sambhupura, Vyadhapura, and Baladityapura — the capital was relocated and renamed to Bhavapura. The new capital was about 100 miles south of Shresthapura and it was renamed in honor of Bhavavarman I (550-600), considered to be the first Chenla king. The relocation of the capital was intended to place the new Chenla government at the central location of the kingdom. Land Chenla (or Upper Chenla) considered itself as the original homeland of the Khmers. After the breakup of Chenla in 707, Land Chenla sent its first embassy to China in 717. China was ruled by the 7th Emperor Xuan Zong (玄宗) of Tang from 712 to 756. Five years later, in 722, Wendan (Land Chenla as called by the Chinese) and Champa joined forces to help Mai Hac De, the Tai-Yueh-Muong's chief of Nghe-an (north central coast of present-day Vietnam), in his revolt against the Chinese governor of Chiao-chou (present-day Hanoi).[6,p59; 58,p164] After defeating the Chinese army, Mai Hac De proclaimed himself the "Black Emperor," but he did not have time to enjoy his reign because immediately afterward the Chinese sent a reinforcement to defeat and killed him.

Under the reign of Piloko, Nan Zhao was on good term with China but after his death the relation between the two countries deteriorated. Lawrence P. Briggs[6,p59] and David K. Wyatt[104,p11] mentioned that after Piloko, China had to defend itself numerous times against the forces of new Nan Zhao (南詔) rulers who allied themselves with Tibetans. In 750, China was under attack from the most powerful Nan Zhao king named Kolofeng, the son of Piloko. That was the year the Chenla embassy — the Chinese did not specify which Chenla, but it was probably Land Chenla — arrived at the Chinese Imperial Court. Concerning the naming of their descendants, Wyatt mentioned that the Nan Zhao people followed a strict pattern of traceability, a pattern not found among the Tai people.[104,p12] He said that "the chao of Nan Zhao followed the patronymic linkage system in choosing their names, the first syllable of each ruler's name being the same as the last syllable of his father's name thus, Pi-lo-ko, Ko-lo-feng, Feng-chia-I, I-mou-hsun, and so on, a pattern common among the Lolo and other Tibeto-Burman groups but unknown among the Tai. Moreover, the lists of Nan Zhao words mentioned in the *Man Shu* are identifiable as Lolo and untraceable as Tai. No Tai legend or chronicle mentions Nan Zhao or any of its rulers, but nineteenth-century Lolo chiefs in central Yunnan traced their ancestry back to Nan Zhao ruling house." *Man Shu* is an account written in 860s AD by a Chinese official of the Imperial Court under the reign of Emperor Yi Zong (懿宗) of Tang (859-873) about the well-discipline kingdom of Nan Zhao.

Kolofeng was determined to defeat the Chinese who occupied his kingdom. The Chinese could not hold the cities against the persistent attacks by Kolofeng in spite of additional enforcement of Chinese armies. China courted Chenla for help in its war against Kolofeng. In 753, the Crown Prince of Wendan (Land Chenla) and twenty six of his relatives were received with great honor by the Chinese Imperial Court. They joined the Chinese army in 754 to fight the battle against Nan Zhao, but Kolofeng was still able to defeat the Chinese army handily.[6,p59] In 771, the heir of Wendan named Pomi (婆彌) and his wife arrived at the Chinese Imperial Court of the Emperor Dai Zong (代宗) of Tang (762-779). They offered eleven elephants in tribute to the Chinese Emperor. On 13 December 771, Pomi received the title Kaifuyitongsansi (開府儀同三司) — "Palace Opener who enjoys the same honors as the three higher officers."[58] In 799, Wendan sent an envoy named Litouji (李頭及) to China. He was also received with great honor and a title from the Chinese Imperial court. That was the extent of relationship given by the Chinese about Wendan.

During the above period, between the sixth and the ninth centuries, the Môn kingdom of Dvaravati was located in present-day central and northeastern Thailand. The kingdom flourished as the Buddhist center where scholars and monks were trained to teach and study Buddhism. The Tais who settled in the northern region of present-day Thailand would very likely come into contact with the Dvaravati civilization, which was extended as far as Haripunjaya (present-day Lamphun in Thailand). The Dvaravati kingdom founded a colony at Lavo (present-day Lopburi). Afterward, Lavo grew and transformed into a kingdom, which ultimately surpassed and replaced Dvaravati as the Môn kingdom. Dvaravati and Lavo went into a decline after the ninth century because the Khmers, after Jayavarman II, started to emerge as an empire and encroached on the Môn territory. Under the reign of Suryavarman I (1002-1050), the Khmer conquered Dvaravati and made it a vassal state of Angkor. During the expansion of the Khmer Empire, the Môn and the Tai became part of the Khmer population. The Tai soldiers (mentioned as Syam on the inscription) marching in unison are still seen on the bas-reliefs of Angkor Wat (South Gallery, West Wing) under Suryavarman II's watching eyes at the royal procession. As previously mentioned, the Khmer Empire saw its greatest expansion during the reign of Jayavarman VII (1181-1219). The son of Jayavarman VII, -indravarman, was the governor of Lavo (Lopburi). After the death of Jayavarman VII, Angkor started to lose its grip on its vassal states. The Tai of Sukhothai seized on the opportunity to wrestle its independence from the Khmer Empire.

The Emergence of Lan Na

Early Tai chronicles mention that before the existence of Lan Na there was a principality ruled by a Tai prince named Phang in the tenth century. Its frontier extended to Annam on the east, to Nan Zhao on the North, to the upper Salween region of the Shan state on the west, and to Lavarattha on the south.[106,pp25-26] According to Wyatt, Lavarattha was Haripunjaya (present-day Lamphun). This statement may not be accurate because there was no single kingdom of that size that had ever existed under a single Tai ruler in the early period of the tenth century. On the other hand, there were small provinces ruled by various warlords. The chronicles said that the principality was attacked by a Khom ruler from Umangasela (located at headwaters of the Ping River in Chiang Mai). In this case the principality (as opposed to kingdom) may just be a limited size of territory around Chiang Mai. Khom is a Môn word to designate Khmer. At the beginning of the tenth century, Angkor was ruled by the powerful Yasovarman I (889-908). Jayavarman V (965-1001), not known as a strong king, ruled Angkor by the end of the tenth century. After the defeat of Phang, the Khmer ruler sent the Tai prince to Lawa (near present-day Mae Sai and Chiang Saen in Thailand) to become the chief of the village. He was required to pay tributes in gold annually to the Khmer ruler. Prince Phang produced two sons. The first born was named Suffering Prince and the second born was named Phrom, also known as Brahmakumara. This name, Brahmakumara, suggests he was of Khmer or Môn origin and not of Tai. After he became an adult about two decades later, Prince Phrom led a revolt and chased the Khmer back to the frontier of Lavarattha. He seized on the opportunity of Khmer civil war to accomplish the above feat. The above event must have taken place during the war between the three Khmer kings (Udayadityavarman, Jayaviravarman, and Suryavarman I) who vied for supremacy to rule Angkor. Afterward, Prince Phrom reinstated his father as the ruler of Chiang Saen. He went on to found his own city called Wiang Chaiprakan in present-day Fang in the northern part of Chiang Mai in Thailand. The Tai legend mentions that sometimes around 1017 an army from the west invaded Fang, forcing Prince Phrom to flee farther to the south to found his new principality in the region of Kamphaeng Phet, located near the boundary of the Khmer Empire. Over the centuries intermarriages took place between the descendants of Prince Phrom and the different indigenous rulers spreading throughout the region. The legend seems to indicate that Prince Phrom's ruling covered only a limited territory and did not extend beyond Kamphaeng Phet.

The emergence of the Tai world coincided with the tumultuous time of the Khmer Empire and the loss of its control in the far western region of Angkor. During this time, a new kingdom called Lan Na emerged. Historians considered Mangrai to be the founder of the Lan Na Kingdom with Chiang Mai as its capital. According to the chronicles of Chiang Mai, around the middle of the twelfth century, a descendant of Prince Phang by the name of Khun Chuang ruled Chiang Saen. He was considered to be the progenitor of the ruling house of Lan Na. Mangrai was born in Chiang Saen in 1238 whose mother was the daughter of the ruler of Chiang Hung (present-day Jinghong in China). He succeeded his father Lao Meng as the ruler of Chiang Saen in 1259 when he was twenty one years old. When he took over the reign, Mangrai realized that the Tai were lacking in unity with principalities in the region fighting each other. He was determined to bring peace to the region through force. He conquered each principality, one by one, and brought them into submissions under his rule. He moved his capital to Fang around 1274, the town founded by his ancestor Prince Phrom. In 1276 Mangrai became friend with King Ngam Muang of Phayao/Chiang Rai, the kingdom that he originally planned to invade. Phayao was located about fifty miles southeast of Fang. Earlier in his youth during his study at Lopburi, at the age of sixteen, Mangrai made a lasting friendship with a young prince named Phra Ruang (popularly known as Ram Khamhaeng). By fate, Mangrai was called to mediate a dispute between King Ngam Muang and Prince Ram Khamhaeng on the matter of the prince trying to seduce the wife of the king. After having settled the dispute, a bond of friendship between these three men was formed.[104,p35] An alliance between the ruling houses of Chiang Saen (Mangrai), Phayao/Chiang Rai (Ngam Muang), and Sukhothai (Ram Khamhaeng) was born to unite the Tai world.

During his reign, Mangrai plotted to overthrow the rich kingdom of Haripunjaya (Mon Kingdom located in the Ping Valley in northwestern of present-day Thailand), which he succeeded easily through deceits. Mangrai placed a spy inside the palace. At opportune time the spy open the gate for Mangrai to overthrow and kill the king. Mangrai climbed on the throne of Haripunjaya on 23 April 1281. His satisfaction was not complete until he conquered Pegu (Môn capital in lower part of present-day Burma/Myanmar) in 1289 and then formed an alliance with the king by marrying his daughter. As his power increased, Mangrai was able to demand from the Pagan-Ava kingdom to deliver to him five hundred families of "goldsmiths, silversmiths, and coppersmiths" without going to war and shed any blood. After all his successes, Mangrai decided to move his capital to Chiang Mai on 27 March 1292, but the construction of his residency did not start until 19 April 1296 due to the war with the Mongols. During this period, China was occupied by the Mongols. Mangrai's rise in power gave the Mongols a concern. The Mongols attacked and occupied Chiang Hung in 1290. The ruler was Mangrai's second cousin. Mangrai came to the rescue of Chiang Hung and retook the city. The Mongol's campaign against Mangrai resulted in failure with the war ended in 1312 only after it had been resolved through diplomacy. The success of Mangrai in the battlefields did not translate into his success over his family life. Probably being impatient to succeed his father, Mangrai's oldest son tried to seize the throne by force. He failed in his attempt and was killed during the coup.[104,p38] No date was given as to when this event occurred, but it was probably around 1312.

By 1312, Mangrai was about seventy four years old. According to Wyatt, he had already sent his third and youngest son Khun Khrua to govern the principality of Muang Nai located on the eastern Shan states.[1,p226; 104,p38] He appointed his second and favorite son Jayasangrama or better known as Khun Kham to govern Chiang Rai. Khun Kham succeeded his father at Chiang Mai after his death in 1317. Only after a few months of reign, Khun Kham abdicated in favor of his son Saen Phu and appointed his other two sons as rulers of Muang Fang and Chiang Khong. Khun Kham returned to Chiang Rai to retire. However, Khun Khrua, the youngest son of Mangrai and brother of Khun Kham, challenged the accession of his nephew Saen Phu. Caught by surprise about their uncle's aggressive claim to the throne, Saen Phu and his brother Nam Thuem (prince of Chiang Khong) fled to Chiang Rai to seek their father's protection. The event that ensued after Khun Khrua was somewhat confusing according to Coedès.[1,p226] Coedès said that Nam Thuem was able to drive Khun Khrua out of Haripunjaya; and on the order of his father he put his older brother Saen Phu back on the throne of Chiang Mai. The event occurred between 1322 and 1324.

Khun Kham was getting old and ailing. Being a dutiful son, Saen Phu abdicated in favor of his son Kham Fu so that he could spend full time in Chiang Rai to take care of his ailing father. Khun Kham finally passed away between 1325 and 1327. After the death of his father, Saen Phu regained the throne of Chiang Mai and between 1325 and 1328 he founded a city that bore his name called Chiang Saen. His son Kham Fu succeeded him after he passed away in 1334. Kham Fu's reign was a short one because he died a few years later after he acceded to the throne. He was succeeded by his son Pha Yu around 1337.

When Mangrai died he left a lasting legacy by allowing Buddhism to prosper in his kingdom. He was respectful of the Môn culture and was the sponsor of many Buddhist monasteries.

Based on George Coedès and David K. Wyatt, the chronology of the kings of Lan Na of the Mangrai Dynasty[1,p226; 103,pp310-311] and of the kings of Chiang Mai[104,p311] can be summarized as follows:

Kings of Lan Na
Mangrai: 1259-1317

Khun Kham or Jayasangrama/Cheyyasongkhram [son of Mangrai]: 1317-1318 (abdicated in favor of his son Saen Phu after a few months on the throne).

Saen Phu [son of Khun Kham]: 1318-1319 (fled to Chiang Rai for his father's protection after his uncle challenged his accession).

Khun Khrua [younger brother of Khun Kham]: 1319-1322 (he challenged his nephew's accession and took over the throne).

Nam Thuem/Saen Phu [Nam Thuem was the younger brother of Saen Phu]: 1322-1324 (Nam Thuem fought back and after driving away his uncle Khun Khrua out of Haripunjaya he handed the throne back to his older brother. Saen Phu abdicated in favor of his son Kham Fu to take care of his ailing father Khun Kham).

Kham Fu [son of Saen Phu]: 1324-1325/1327.

Saen Phu: 1325/1328-1334 (he regained the throne after his father Khun Kham passed away between 1325 and 1327).

Kham Phu [son of Saen Phu]: 1334~1337.

Pha Yu [son of Kham Phu]: ~1337 or 1345-1355.

Ku Na: ~1355 or 1367-1385.

Saen Muang Ma [son of Ku Na]: 1385-1401.

Sam Fang Kaen [son of Saen Muang Ma]: 1401-1441.

Tilokaracha [sixth son of Sam Fang Kaen]: 19 May 1442-27 May 1487.

Yot Chiang Rai [grandson of Tilokaracha]: 1487-18 July 1495.

Muang Kaeo [son of Yot Chiang Rai]: 1495-7 February 1526.
Ket Chettharat [younger brother of Muang Kaeo]: 1526-1538 (1st reign).
Chai [son of Ket Chettharat]: 1538-1543.
Ket Chettharat [brother of Muang Kaeo and father of Chai]: 1543-1545 (2nd reign).
Jiraprabha/Chiraprapha [Queen]: 25 June 1545-1546.
Jayajestha/Chaiyasetthathirat/Setthathirat: 17 July 1546-20 August 1547 (he was also king of Lan Xang, ancient for Laos).
Interreign Period: 1547-1551.
Phra Mekutawisutthiwong: 9 May 1551-1564 (Burmese occupation of Lan Na in 1558).
Wisutthithewi/Visuddhadevi [Queen]: 1564-1578 (under the suzerainty of Burma).
Tharrawaddy Prince: 1578-1607 (under Burmese rule).
Two sons of Tharrawaddy Prince: 1607-1613 (under Burmese rule).
Thadoyaw: 1613-1615.
Si Song Muang: 1615-1631.
Phraya Thipphanet: 1631-1659.
Ruler of Phrae: 1659-1672.
Ingsemang: 1672-1675 (under Burmese rule).
Chephutarai: 1675-1707 (under Burmese rule).
Mangraenara: 1707-1727 (under Burmese rule).
Thep Sing: 1727 (a rebel).
Ong Kham: 1727-1759.
Chan: 1759-1761.
Khi Hut: 27 April 1761-1762.
Abhayagamani: 1766-1768 (under Burmese rule).
Moyagamani: 1768-1771 (under Burmese rule).
Revolt of Lan Na: 1771-1774.

Kings of Chiang Mai
Kavila; 1775-1816 (King of Lamphun from 1775 to 1781).
Thammalangka: 1816-1821.
Kham Fan: 1822-1825.
Phutthawong: 1826-1846.
Mahawong: 1846-1854.
Kavilorot: 1856-1870.
Intanon: 1871-1897.
Suriyawong: 1901-1911.
In Kaeo: 1911-1939.

THE FOUNDATION OF SUKHOTHAI

The Angkorian rules and system of government were more sophisticated than any types of systems found in Southeast Asia during the period of the Khmer Empire. The exposure of the Tai people for the last few centuries under the Angkorian rules had prepared the Tai elites very well to challenge the influence and power of the Khmer Empire that had been diminishing after the death of Jayavarman VII. By the middle of the thirteenth century, a web of political connections had been formed among the Tai princes of Suphanburi, Phetburi, Chainat, Phitsanulok, and Nakhon Si Thammarat, with this latter playing an important role in the expansion and diffusion of Theravada Buddhism imported from Sri Lanka to the Tai world as well as to the Khmer Empire. The population of Nakhon Si Thammarat was an amalgam of indigenous people, traders, Tai, Môn, and Khmer. The centuries old contact with the Khmer Empire provided the Sukhothai elites an advantage of ruling over the new Tai arrivals and indigenous people. Wyatt perfectly stated the following about the Tai elites:[104,pp40-41]

> *Their experience in the relatively more developed, complex, sophisticated environment shaped by centuries of Angkorean Khmer rule and influence gave this Tai elite of the Chao-phraya valley and the upper peninsula a distinctive culture, different in some critical respects from that of their cousins to the north who ultimately became known as Lao or Shans. They seem to have been accustomed to relatively more complex, hierarchical social and political organization than the Tai Yuan or Lao. To their native animistic religion, they added a considerable body of Indian Brahmanical beliefs and practices, particularly associated with the rituals of rites of passage and domestic crises. These Tai — who may have had Mon or Khmer origins — historically have been referred to as Siamese, a local variant on the word Syam of the Cham, Khmer, and Pagan inscriptions. The term takes on political significance when one of their states, Sukhothai, is referred to in Chinese sources toward the end of the thirteenth century as Siem, that is, Siam.*

There are some debates on the exact date of the reign of Sri Indraditya, acknowledged among historians as the founder of Sukhothai, as well as on the names of his successors and their accessions to the thrones. The traditional history shows the chronology of the reigns of Sukhothai kings as follows:[104,p309]

Sri Indraditya: 1239?-1259? (First king of Sukhothai)
Ban Müang: 1259?-1279? (Oldest son of Sri Indraditya)
Ram Khamhaeng [Phra Ruang]: 1279?-1298 (Youngest son of Sri Indraditya)
Lö Thai [Lerthai, Leotai]: 1298-1346/47 (Son of Ram Khamhaeng)
Ngua Nam Thom: 1346/7 (Cousin of Lö Thai & son of Ban Müang)
Mahathammaracha I [Lüthai, Lithai]: 1346/7-1368/74? (Son of Lö Thai)
Mahathammaracha II: 1368/74-1398 (Son of Mahathammaracha I)
Mahathammaracha III [Sai Lüthai]: 1398-1419 (Son of Mahathammaracha II)
Mahathammaracha IV [Borommapan]: 1419-1438 (Son of Mahathammaracha III)

The information available on Sukhothai deals mostly during its period of sovereignty but provides little details about its origin. I have pieced together the origin of Sukhothai from the studies by Paul Petitthuguenin[15], Eric Roeder,[98] George Coedès,[103; 120; 121] David K. Wyatt,[104] Wilaiwan Khanittanan,[111] Michael Vickery,[122] and Piriya Krairiksh.[122; 123] The studies by the above mentioned authors were mostly based on the pioneering works established by previous scholars and on the local epigraphies of the region such as the pillar of Nagara Jum at Vat Mahadhatu; on the historical Pali texts of the 16th century; on the Siamese Northern Annals; on the Ram Khamhaeng Inscription; and on the Chinese Dynastic Annals *Ming Shi-lu (MSL)*. I recognize that additional details are needed to shed some more light on the relationship between Sukhothai and Cambodia. The names of the Sukhothai kings extracted from the above studies are reported below for the purpose of correlating them with those mentioned in the traditional Sukhothai chronology.

The foundation of Sukhothai started with a Muang Rat lord. The location of Muang Rat could not be exactly determined, but Coedès believed it was located in the Eastern territory of Sukhothai in 1359. I believe it is probably in present-day Uttaradit in Thailand.

It is useful to repeat what was said under Jayavarman VIII about Pha Muang. The Vat Mahadhatu inscription of Sukhothai that is currently preserved at the National Library of Thailand in Bangkok mentions that the God (phi fā) of Chao Muang Sri Sodharapura bestowed the title of *Kamratēng Añ Phā Muang Sri Indrapatīndrādiatya* to the Tai Chieftain Pho Khun Pha Muang Chao of Muang Rat;[103,p5] and that this same God of Sri Sodharapura also gave the sword *Jaiyasrī* and his daughter named Nang Skharamahadevi in marriage to the Tai chieftain.[1,p195; 103,pp7-8] This Tai Chieftain may also be of Khmer background. Sri Sradharajaculamani, the grandson of Pha Muang, was the author of the Vat Mahadhatu (or Mahathat) inscription.[103,p3]

Who was the God of Chao Muang Sri Sodharapura? According to George Coedès, Sri Sodharapura was the corrupted name of Sri Yasodharapura, the ancient name of Angkor Thom. Sriyasodharapura was changed to Sriy-Sodharapura, then to Sri Sodharapura. Subsequently, Khmer monarchs after the Angkor period adopted the above name to designate their capitals.[103,p8] The God of Chao Muang Sri Sodharapura mentioned on the Vat Mahadhatu inscription, dated no later than 1357, was identified by historians to be Jayavarman VIII. The Vat Mahadhatu inscription is mentioned in the Nagara Jum inscription — which was dated 1357 of the year of the Rooster — and it is presently preserved at the National Library of Thailand in Bangkok. The word God was used because Khmer kings were considered God-King (Devaraja) in the tradition established by Jayavarman II in 802.

By making an alliance with Pha Muang and giving him a lofty title equivalent to an Uparaja (Vice King), as well as giving away his daughter in marriage, Jayavarman VIII was expecting that his son-in-law would use the prestige of his power to calm down the rebellion that was fomenting on the far end of the northeastern region of the Khmer Empire. Instead, Pha Muang betrayed Jayavarman VIII a few years later, around 1247, by joining forces with a Tai chieftain by the name of Bang Klang Hao to rebel against the Khmer king.[104,p41] Bang Klang Hao was the chieftain of Muang Bang Yang located in the neighboring area of Sukhothai. Jayavarman VIII may have been taken by surprise by Pha Muang's betrayal as the combined forces of the rebels defeated the Khmer outpost controlled by the Khmer general named Khlon Lamphong (known as the bold Khom) at Sri Satchanalai (present-day Sawankhalok in Thailand). The rebel army entered Sri Satchanalai in victory. Upon occupying the city, Pha Muang unexpectedly decided to relinquish his title of *Kamratēng Añ Sri Indrapatīndrāditya* and bestow it to Bang Klang Hao; and at the same time he handed over the *Jaiyasrī* sword (sword of victory) to him.[103,p7] The coronation of Bang Klang Hao as king of Sukhothai that took place after 1247, probably around 1253, was an act of rebellion as well as of defiance against the Khmer Empire.

Coedès mentioned that the coronation of Bang Klang Hao was consecrated by Pho Khun Pha Muang as follows:[103,p7]

> *Afterwards Phō Khun Phā Mu'ang consecrated (abhisheka) Phō Khun Bāng Klāng Thāo as Chao Mu'ang Sukhodaya, and conferred his own name on his ally, that is to say the name of Śrī Indrapatīndrāditya, with the title of Kamratēng Añ Phā Mu'ang.*

Bang Klang Hao is better known by his short name as Sri Indraditya. The Nagara Jum Inscription (dated Saka 1279 or 1357 AD) that is stored at the National Library of Thailand in Bangkok, where its origin is believed to have come from Vat Mahadhatu (also known as Wat Yai) of Sukhothai, says that Sri Indraditya had a son named Pho Khun Ramaraja.[103,p10]

One of the most important steles during the Sukhothai period was found at Savankalok (popularly known as the Ram Khamhaeng Stele). The stele was dated by Aymonier to have been engraved around 1292. The inscription was translated by Father Schmidt and reported by Paul Petithuguenin in his paper called *A Propos des Origines et de l'Histoire Ancienne du Siam*.[15,p9] In the inscription, Phra Ruang provided the details and origin of his life. He mentioned that his father was "Sri Indra Ditya," his mother was Nang Suong, and one of his brothers was Ban or Muang. He said that his name Rama Kamhang came from his battle against the governor of Chod, an ally of Pegu (capital of present-day Myarnma), when he demonstrated his skills as a fearless warrior who put his enemies to flight at the age of nineteen. He said that after the death of his father, he served his older brother Ban faithfully and that in turn he would succeed him. He was estimated to have been born between 1240 and 1250. A passage in the Northern

Annals said that Phra Ruang was born in the year of the Pig, which in this case would have corresponded to 1240. Petithuguenin assigned the year of the Pig to correspond to 1251, which is one year outside the estimated assumed year for the birth of Phra Ruang. He was estimated to have acceded to the throne between 1275 and 1280. If the Ram Khamhaeng Inscription were used as the basis for the Sukhothai history, then it could be said that Phra Ruang acceded to the throne in 1200 Saka, which would correspond to 1278/1279 in the year of the Tiger. The inscription on Side 3 and Lines 10-27 (Appendix 4) said that Ram Khamhaeng had planted palm trees fourteen years prior to 1214 Saka in the year of the Dragon. The inscription would therefore imply that Ram Khamhaeng acceded to the throne in 1200 Saka. According to the Northern Annals, Phra Ruang married a daughter of the Chinese Emperor and a son named Phra Suchak was born out of their union.[15,p10] According to Aymonier, Phra Ruang died in 1324 at the age of 73 after fifty years of reign.[15,p10] If this were the case, then Phra Ruang would have acceded to the throne in 1274 at the age of 23 and he would have been born in 1251, which would correspond to the year of the Pig as had been described in the Northern Annals. A passage in the Northern Annals said that towards the end of his reign Phra Ruang became very eccentric with no manner or concern for etiquette.

Petitthuguenin mentioned that the next two successors of Phra Ruang were based on the Nakhon Yum inscription that Aymonier had translated. Phra Ya Sua Thai succeeded his father Phra Ruang and reigned from 1324 to 1340. Phra Ya Sua Thai was the same person named Phuak Soucharat in the Northern Annals. Phuak Soucharat was also known as Phra Suchak, the grandson of the Chinese Emperor mentioned earlier.[15,p10] During his reign he called on Chinese engineers to help fortifying the city and strengthening the army. The Northern Annals attributed the introduction of firearms and canons to this king. He died during the battle against the Malaysians. His son Phraya Hri Daya Raja succeeded him and reigned from 1340 to 1357.[15,p11] Not much is known about him.

Based on the Nakhon Yum and Khmer inscriptions of Sukhothai, as well as on other epigraphies, Sri Surija Vans'a Rama Maha Dharma Radjadhiraja succeeded his father Phraya Hri Daya Raja and reigned from 1357 to 1388.[15,p11] He was very literate and well versed in cosmology. He was credited for reforming the calendar system and was believed to be responsible for introducing the Chula Sakarach to Sukhothai. He sent over thirty elephants to China in 1387, one year before his death.

Mahadharmarajadhiraja succeeded his predecessor from 1388 to 1415. Aymonier established his reign from the inscription of Vat Boramanivet that originally came from Sukhothai.[15,p12] Not much is known about him.

From the *MSL*, Aymonier attributed the transliterated name Sanlai Polomo Datahtirai to Samtac Parama Rajadhiraja, the Sukhothai king who reigned from 1415 to 1453. He was believed to be the adopted son of Mahadharmarajadhiraja.

Concerning the identity of Brañā Rāmarāja mentioned earlier, Coedès determined from the Nagara Jum Inscription that he was Phra Ruang (or more popularly known as Ram Khamhaeng). The inscription said that Brañā Lu'daiyarāja (better known as King Lithai of Sukhothai or Mahathammracha I) was the son of Brañā Lu'daiya (better known as King Lerthai or Leotai of Sukhothai) and grandson of Brañā Rāmarāja, and that he acceded to the throne of Sukhothai in 1279 Saka in the year of the Rooster (1357/58 AD) under the style name Śrī Sūryavaṃśa Mahādharmarājādhirāja.[120,p14] Phra Ruang had an older brother named Ban that Petithuguenin identified as Phya Sri Thama So Karat. Based on his finding, Petithuguenin believed that Sri Indraditya reigned in Sukhothai from about 1250 to 1270.[15,p8] The Ram Khamhaeng Inscription said that Ban succeeded his father and reigned from about 1270 to 1275.

The chronology of the Sukhothai dynasty as reported by Wyatt can be summarized as follows:[104,p309]

Sri Indraditya: ~1247-1270, but 1239?-1259?

Other name includes Bang Klang Hao. He usurped the title *Kamratēng Añ Phā Muang Sri Indrapatīndrādiya* that Jayavarman VIII bestowed on the Tai Chieftain Pho Khun Pha Muang Chao of Muang Rat. In order to legitimize his reign, Bang Klang Hao had Pho Khun Pha Muang perform the consecration ceremony to complete the coronation process. The Northern Annals mentioned in one of its passage that Sri Indraditya became very eccentric and that he had no concern for etiquette near the end of his reign.

Ban Muang: 1270-1275, but 1259?-1279? per Wyatt

Other name includes Phaya Sri Thama So Karat. He was the oldest son of Sri Indraditya.

Ram Khamhaeng: 1275-1324, but 1279?-1298 per Wyatt

Other names include Phra Muang and Braña Rāmarāja. He was the younger brother of Ban Muang and son of Sri Indraditya. He married a daughter of the Chinese Emperor and produced a son named Phra Suchak.

Braña Lu'aidaiya: 1324-1340, but 1298-1346/47 per Wyatt

Other names include Lö Thai, Lerthai, Phra Ya Sua Thai, Phuak Soucharat, and Phra Suchak. He was the son of Ram Khamhaeng and grandson of the Chinese Emperor.

Braña Lu'daiyarāja: 1340-1357, but 1346/7-1368/74? per Wyatt

Other names include Mahathammaracha I, Lüthai, *Lithai*, Phraya Hri Daya Raja, and Sūryavaṃśa Mahadharmarājadhirāja. He was the son of Braña Lu'aidaiya.

Mahahammaracha II: 1357-1388, but 1368/74-1398? per Wyatt

Other name includes Sri Surija Vans'a Rama Dharma Radjadhirāja. He was the son of Braña Lu'daiyarāja.

Mahathammaracha III: 1388-1415, but 1398-1419 per Wyatt

Other names include Sai Lüthai and Mahadharmarājadhirāja. He was the son of Leuthai.

Mahathammaracha IV: 1415-1453, but 1419-1438 per Wyatt

Other names include Borommapan, and Samtac Parama Radjadhirāja. He was the adopted son of Mahathammaracha III.

Upon the death of Mahathammaracha IV in 1438 (according to Wyatt[104,p58]), Sukhothai was absorbed into the Kingdom of Ayutthaya under the reign of King Borommaracha II. It was under the Sukhothai period that the Thai scripts were invented, which ultimately replaced the Khmer scripts that were still in use even under the reign of King Lüthai (or Braña Lu'daiyarāja).

The Controversy of the Ram Khamhaeng Inscription

It is an indisputable fact that the Khmer language was being practiced during the early Sukhothai period until at least under the reign of King Lithai. During the first quarter of 1907 Crown Prince Maha Vajiravudh, before he became King Rama VI, surveyed the cities of Kamphaeng Phet, Sawankhalok, Sukhothai, and Phitsanulok. Upon returning to Bangkok he published a paper in 1908 about his finding to set up the ground work for other scholars to use. In his own words he said he published the paper "in the hope that it would give an opportunity for specialist in archaeology to further their deliberations and to make hypotheses on statements pertaining to the cities of Sukhothai, Sawankhalok and Kamphaeng Phet."[124,p11] Vajiravudh had even corrected the name of Wat Takon (as in sediments; other people called it Wat Ta Kuan as in grandpa Kuan), located in the Sukhothai Historical Park in Thailand, to the Khmer name Wat Trakuan (an aquatic plant of the bindweed kind, popularly used in Southeast Asia). He corrected the name based on his understanding that the Khmer language was still used and in vogue in the times of King Lithai. [124,p13]

According to Lucien Fournereau (he was the architect who overviewed the archaeology department at the Musée Guimet in Paris), the Ram Khamhaeng stele that is housed at the National Museum in Bangkok was believed to have been discovered in 1834 by Prince-monk Mongkut in Wat Mahathat (Wat Mahadhatu, also called Wat Yai) along with the inscription (Inscription IV) of King Lithai that was written in the Khmer language.[124,p24] Specifically, in the official communication with the French Ambassador Charles de Montigny in 1856, King Mongkut enlisted the French government's help for the translation of the Ram Khamhaeng stele that he said he found in Sukhothai.[125] The stele was written in ancient Thai scripts giving a panegyric of Ram Khamhaeng's origin as well as of his reign. The invention of the Thai scripts was attributed to King Ram Khamhaeng. The genuine origin of the Ram Khamhaeng stele had never been in doubt; until recently, when prominent scholars like Michael Vickery, Michael Wright, and Piriya Krairiksh as well as the Lecturer Polachan Wankwan questioned the authenticity of the Inscription, which created a controversy and forced other scholars to examine and study the stele more carefully. Because the early history of Thailand is based on the Ram Khamhaeng Inscription and because of the great respect historians have for King Mongkut, scholars are very reluctant to question the integrity of the Inscription and disturb the fairy tale of Camelot-like of the Sukhothai period. It calls upon scholars like Michael Vickery, Michael Wright, and Piriya Krairiksh to stir the debate about the authenticity of the Ram Khamhaeng Inscription. These eminent scholars presented their cases through academic papers and argued that the Inscription was not produced in the thirteenth century. Based on the arguments presented by the above scholars, some people suspected and speculated that the Inscription was probably the creation of the erudite Prince-monk Mongkut.

In his paper *The Ram Khamhaeng Inscription: A Piltdown Skull of Southeast Asian History?*,[122] Michael Vickery pointed out some anomalies that were not consistent with Sukhothai corpus period such as "(1) the placement of all vowel signs on the line, a feature unknown to any Indic script of Southeast Asia or in any of the major scripts of India, (2) a complete modern tone-marking system, not found again until the 17th or 18th century after very gradual and tentative developments, and (3) certain vowel signs common to modern standard Thai, but not used in the 14th century Sukhothai corpus."

Michael Wright was also critical of the Ram Khamhaeng Inscription in his paper *A Pious Fable, Reconsidering the Inscription I Controversy: A 'Demonic' View.*[125] He pointed out some inconsistencies and raised many good questions.

The most convincing arguments against the authenticity of the Ram Khamhaeng Inscription were probably demonstrated by Piriya Krairiksh in his paper *Towards a Revised History of Sukhothai Art: A Reassessment of the Inscription of King Ram Khamhaeng.*[122] Based on his expertise as an art historian, Krairiksh took a different approach in his arguments by demonstrating that: 1) The vocabulary and meaning used on the stone inscription were not consistent with other Sukhothai inscription; 2) Current archaeological research could not support many of the monuments and locations mentioned in the stone inscription; 3) Many of the vocabularies used in the stone inscription were suspiciously borrowed from inscriptions used during the Sukhothai era; and 4) Many of the vocabularies used in the stone inscription were conspicuously similar to the vocabulary used in literature during the Ayutthaya and Bangkok era.

After Vickery, Wright, and Krairiksh presented their academic papers, the other scholars came out in force to give their counter-arguments in support of the Ram Khamhaeng Inscription. The matter is still unresolved to the present-day. The academic papers concerning the Ram Khamhaeng Inscription were assembled by James R. Chamberlain and published in a book called *The Ram Khamhaeng Controversy* in 1991.[122]

Because I am not an expert on ancient Thai language like Vickery or an authority on the Thai arts like Krairiksh, I will use a different approach in my assessment of the Ram Khamhaeng Inscription. I will use my logical engineering approach and systems management skills that I developed and practiced as a rocket scientist engineer to determine the incongruity of the passages in the Inscription. The following are my assessment of the Ram Khamhaeng Inscription (see Appendix 4 for the English translation of the Inscription):

1. **[Face 1/Lines 1-18]**: The inscription was written in the first person as if Ram Khamhaeng himself wrote it. But for the rest of the inscriptions (Face 1/Lines 18-35 and Faces 2-4), the sentences were all switched to the third person as if somebody else wrote it. This seems somewhat odd.

2. **[Face 1/Lines 18-35 and Face 2/Lines 1-8]:** Considering that another war with Angkor may still occur even after Ram Khamhaeng's father Sri Indraditya had won the battle against the Khmer Empire; and added to this threat was the fact that the emerging Kingdom of Ayutthaya wanted to conquer Sukhothai, it is somewhat hard to believe that King Ram Khamhaeng was so benevolent as not to levy any taxes against his subjects to fill in his coffer in preparation for a war. It is also hard to believe that King Ram Khamhaeng would respond to a ringing bell that was hung at the palace gate and came down to spend the time to take care of all the individual cases of his subjects personally. Because Ram Khamhaeng was the king of Sukhothai with all the wealth and power over his subjects, it is somewhat puzzling that the Inscription emphasized that the king did not get angry at someone else's wealth. What purpose did it serve to make that statement in the Inscription? Was it to praise that Ram Khamhaeng was a true Buddhist that he was not envious of people?

3. **[Face 4/Lines 4-8]:** The sentence in Line 4 started with "In 1207 Saka, a Year of the Boar." The Boar year for 1207 Saka is incorrect because this Saka year corresponded to the animal year of the Rooster. The year of the Boar would be 1209 Saka instead. If the inscriptions were written by Ram Khamhaeng during his time period, how could he have made such a mistake? On the other hand, the year of the Goat assigned for 1205 Saka in Face 4/Lines 8-11 was correct. What was Ram Khamhaeng's purpose of "inventing" new Thai scripts if he were going to bury them and enclosed them in cetiya (stupa)? It does not seem logical that after all the efforts to come up with new Thai scripts Ram Khamhaeng decided to hide them from view. The account in this passage is very similar to that of the discovery of the Emerald Buddha (see the discussion below in the section "The Reappearance of the Emerald Buddha") by the monks in Chiang Rai who found the statue hidden in a cetiya. Could it be a pure coincidence that Prince-monk Mongkut discovered the *RK* Inscription and that the passage in the Inscription just happens to mirror the tale of the discovery of the Emerald Buddha?

4. **[Face 4/Lines 11-27]:** The sentence that said "King Ram Khamhaeng was sovereign over all the Tai. He was the teacher who taught all the Tai to understand merit and the Dharma rightly" was not truthful. How could Ram Khamhaeng make such a claim when in his youth, as Prince Phra Ruang, he was seducing the wife of King Ngam Muang of Phayao/Chiang Rai[104,p35]. It was due to the intervention of Mangrai that the dispute between Phra Ruang and Ngam Muang was resolved. As the teacher of Dharma how could he justify his action when he said he captured men and women and turned them to his father after he raided a town or village? Raiding a town, which implied killing people, was not an act that could be equated to Dharma. Historians go out of their way to ignore or dismiss the bad quality of Ram Khamhaeng described in the Northern Annals that mentioned he was a player who ignored etiquette near the end of his reign.[15,p10] The sainthood-like personality description of Ram Khamhaeng seems to be somewhat fabricated. The above panegyric statement seems to describe Mongkut because of his knowledge in Dharma. It must be remembered that Mongkut spent 27 years as a monk before he became king.

5. If the Thai scripts were invented by Ram Khamhaeng and used during his times, then why would his grandson King Lithai be still using the Khmer language throughout his reign? The case for the Inscription created after or during King Lithai's lifetime could be made.

6. Even if King Ram Khamhaeng were the author of the new Thai scripts, it would be wrong and incorrect to say that he had invented the scripts. It is obvious that the Thai scripts were based on the Khmer scripts. In his examination of the Thai scripts and after an exhaustive comparison with

the other scripts, Cornelius Beach Bradley concluded that they were borrowed and modified from the Khmer scripts. He said "a strict examination was therefore made into the positive evidence in favor of the theory of a Cambodian origin of Siamese writing."[126,p6] The comparison of the Thai scripts with the Khmer and other scripts in the region is shown in Figure 47.

7. The stele inscription over one meter tall that is standing in front of the uposathagara (ordination hall) of Wat Chiang Man in the province of Chiang Mai was dated to have been carved in 1581 AD. The inscription mentioned that Chiang Mai was founded on 12 April 1839 B.E. (1296 AD). It said that King Mangrai commissioned for the building of the uposathagara and that the Burmese ruler Phaya Saen Luang had the place restored in 2114 B.E. (1571 AD). The inscription, shown in Figure 48, is of Thai Yuan language inscribed in Thai Yuan scripts. It is obvious that the Thai Yuan scripts resemble more with the Khmer scripts than the *RK* scripts. If the Ram Khamhaeng scripts were invented before these Thai Yuan scripts, why would the scripts not resemble each other?

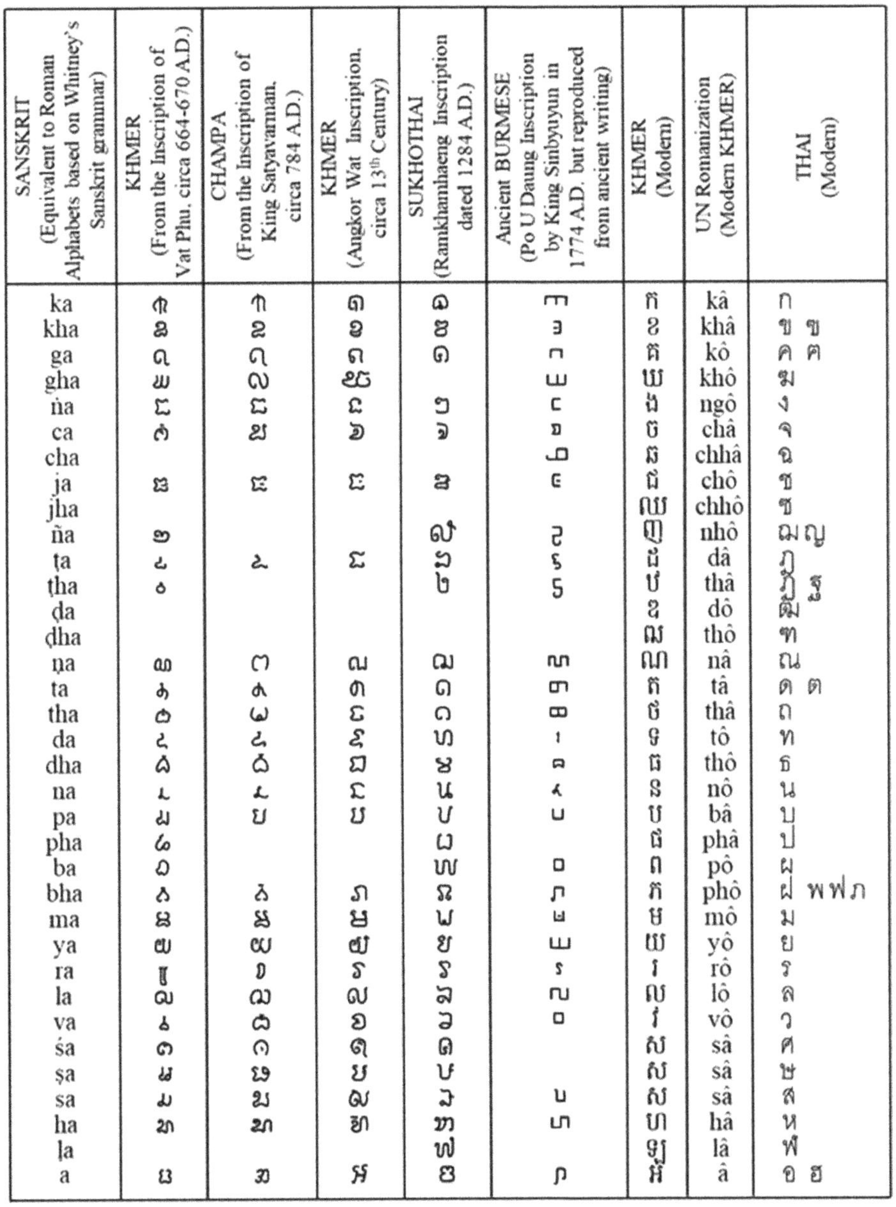

SANSKRIT (Equivalent to Roman Alphabets based on Whitney's Sanskrit grammar)	KHMER (From the Inscription of Vat Phu, circa 664-670 A.D.)	CHAMPA (From the Inscription of King Satyavarman, circa 784 A.D.)	KHMER (Angkor Wat Inscription, circa 13th Century)	SUKHOTHAI (Ramkhamhaeng Inscription dated 1284 A.D.)	Ancient BURMESE (Po U Daung Inscription by King Sinbyuyun in 1774 A.D. but reproduced from ancient writing)	KHMER (Modern)	UN Romanization (Modern KHMER)	THAI (Modern)
ka							kâ	ก
kha							khâ	ข ฃ
ga							kô	ค ฅ
gha							khô	ฆ
ṅa							ngô	ง
ca							châ	จ
cha							chhâ	ฉ
ja							chô	ช
jha							chhô	ฌ
ña							nhô	ญ ญ
ṭa							dâ	ฎ ฏ
ṭha							thâ	ฐ
ḍa							dô	ฑ
ḍha							thô	ฒ
ṇa							nâ	ณ
ta							tâ	ด ต
tha							thâ	ถ
da							tô	ท
dha							thô	ธ
na							nô	น
pa							bâ	บ
pha							phâ	ป
ba							pô	ผ
bha							phô	พ ฟ ภ
ma							mô	ม
ya							yô	ย
ra							rô	ร
la							lô	ล
va							vô	ว
śa							sâ	ศ
ṣa							sâ	ษ
sa							sâ	ส
ha							hâ	ห
ḷa							lâ	ฬ
a							â	อ ฮ

Figure 47. Comparison of Khmer, Thai, Cham, and Burmese Scripts (Figure based on Cornelius Beach Bradley's Study[126])

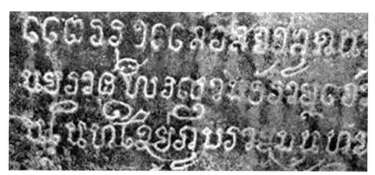

Figure 48. Inscription of Wat Chiang Man in Chiang Mai (dated 1581)

Cornelius Beach Bradley who wrote a paper called *The Proximate Source of the Siamese Alphabet*[126] stated that the Khmer scripts had not only evolved but that the Thai scripts, speech, and art were borrowed from the Khmer. The following is the quote from his academic paper:[126,p11]

> *Cambodia culture was Brahmanical and Indian throughout. Cambodian writing retains its distinctive Sanskrit features to the present day. Historically, the shape of the Cambodian letters — originally Indian — underwent gradual change, until in the thirteenth century A.D., they are found to approximate very nearly the Sukhothai letters in, scribed a little later. The close cultural contact between the two peoples suggested by the epigraphy, is strongly corroborated and extended by consideration of the very large borrowings from Cambodia found in Siamese speech, ceremonial, art, and government.*

Based on the above questions that I raised, a case can be made to discredit the authenticity of the Ram Khamhaeng Inscription.

The Reappearance of the Emerald Buddha

As reported earlier in Chapter 6 under the reign of Jayavarman VII, the Emerald Buddha was mentioned in the Luang Prabang Chronicle as well as in the Chronicle of the Emerald Buddha. The Luang Prabang Chronicle said that the Emerald Buddha was removed from Angkor by two monks who betrayed the Khmer king, Thommasoka, who reigned from 1373 to 1394. They took the Emerald Buddha to the north. This tale seems to corroborate with the Chronicle of Chiang Mai saying that the Emerald Buddha stayed in Chiang Rai during the reign of Saen Muang Ma from 1385 to 1401 (but from 1388 to 1411 according to Eric Roeder[98]).

The following account of the Emerald Buddha is mainly extracted from Eric Roeder's *The Origin and Significance of the Emerald Buddha*[98] and David K. Wyatt's *A Short History of Thailand.*[104]

According to the chronicle, the Emerald Buddha was hidden from view until its discovery in 1436. In that year, lightning struck down a cetiya (stupa) in Chiang Rai which opened up the stupa to reveal a statue of the Buddha. At the time, monks at the temple did not pay too much attention to the statue because it was covered with stucco plaster exposing only a portion of the body with gold leaf, which was ordinary because it was customary to apply gold leaf on the statue of the Buddha. Believing it was an ordinary statue, the monks stored it in the temple among the other statues. After a few months the plaster covering the statue started to come off. The chief monk of the temple noticed that it was not an ordinary statue because beneath the plaster he saw that the statue was made up of crystal with beautiful green color. Intrigue, he started to remove the plaster covering the statue and beneath it he saw a one-piece green crystal Buddha with its entire splendor. Words spread throughout Chiang Rai and people started to flock to the temple to venerate and pay homage to the statue of the Buddha. The statue was called *Phra Keo Morakat* that is now popularly known as the Emerald Buddha.

Why was the Emerald Buddha buried in the stupa? I believe that the Khmer king who succeeded Thommasoka — in this case it would have been King Ponhea Yat — may be still looking for the Emerald Buddha after it was stolen from Angkor by the two monks. Because the Emerald Buddha was a wedding gift from the Sri Lanka King Parakramabahu to Jayavarman VII, Ponhea Yat may feel it was very important to recover this treasure. The two monks, believed to be of Môn origins, who stole the Emerald Buddha may feel it would be prudent to hide the statue to allow time to pass. As memory faded away and people forgot about the origin of the statue, the two monks would then retrieve the Emerald Buddha from the stupa to expose it for the world to see. Because the statue had been hidden in the stupa for about forty years, it was very likely that the two monks had died before they had time to remove it from the stupa. With the two monks dead, the knowledge of the existence and whereabouts of the Emerald Buddha were also lost. If it were not for the lightning striking the stupa, the Emerald Buddha may have been hidden forever from view and its existence would have been the stuff of legend.

Upon hearing of the discovery of the Emerald Buddha, King Sam Fang Kaen ordered that the statue be sent to Chiang Mai. By some strange phenomenon, on two different occasions, the elephants that were used to transport the statue refused to go in the direction of Chiang Mai but ran towards the direction of Lampang instead. Being superstitious, Sam Fang Kaen decided not to challenge the supernatural power and allowed the Emerald Buddha to be transported to Lampang. The statue remained in a temple in Lampang — posteriorly named Wat Phra Keo — for thirty two years until King Tilokaracha ordered the Emerald Buddha to be moved to Chiang Mai in 1468. The statue stayed at Chiang Mai for public viewing and worshipping until 1551. For the lack of a male successor to rule the Kingdom of Chiang Mai, high-ranking officials and religious leaders chose the 15-year old Chao Chaiyaset as their new king. Chao Chaiyaset was the son of King Phothisan of Lan Xang and Princess Nang Yotkham, the daughter of the previous king of Chiang Mai. Chao Chaiyaset extended his name to Chao Chaiyasetthathirat but he is also known as Setthathirat. King Phothisan passed away shortly after his son became king of Chiang Mai. Because he suspected that he may be prevented from returning to Chiang Mai after attending his father's funeral, Setthathirat decided to take the Emerald Buddha with him to Luang Prabang by explaining that it was an opportunity for him to spread merits to his relatives. His stay in Luang Prabang stretched to three years, which annoyed the high-ranking officials and religious people in Chiang Mai. Impatient of waiting for the king's return, the Chiang Mai officials decided to choose Mekuti (or Mae Ku), a monk and distant relative of Setthathirat, to rule the kingdom. The high officials tried to have the Emerald Buddha returned to Chiang Mai but to no avail. After staying twelve years in Luang Prabang, the Emerald Buddha moved along with the king when Setthathirat changed his residency to Vientiane in 1563. The Emerald Buddha remained in Vientiane for 215 years until Chao Phaya Chakri, the military commander of King Taksin, conquered Vientiane in 1778 and took the statue to Thonburi. The Emerald Buddha (Phra Kaew Morakot) is now housed at Wat Phra Kaew in the compound of the Grand Palace in Bangkok.

THE FOUNDATION OF AYUTTHAYA AND MODERN THAILAND

Ayutthaya which formed the foundation of modern Thailand can be broken down into different dynasties within the following periods: 1) the Ayutthaya Period included the U-Thong, Suphannaphum, Prasat Thong, and Ban Phlu Luang dynasties; 2) the Thonburi or Taksin Period; and 3) the Bangkok Period which is ruled by the Chakri dynasty. Tables 12a-12f list the names of the Thai kings accompanied by references and a short summary of their activities during the above periods.

Table 12a. Kings of Ayutthaya (1351-1448)

Reign Name	Other Name	Reign Period	Relationship	Provenance/ Clan	Comments (unless noted, all indicated pages are from Reference 104)
KINGS OF AYUTTHAYA (U-Thong/Ramathibodi Dynasty of Lopburi-Suphanburi)					
Ramathibodi	U-Thong	1351-1369	First king of Ayutthaya	Lopburi	A Khmer-Thai from Lopburi. He married a Khmer princess from Suphanburi (Ref. 111, pp. 378-379). Conducted war against Angkor with no outcome (p. 59).
Ramesuan	Rama-suon	1369-1370	Oldest son of Ramathibodi	Lopburi & Khmer Royal Blood of Suphanburi	Overthrew by his uncle Pha-ngua (who became Borommaracha), the brother of his mother. Continued war against Angkor with no outcome (p. 59).
KINGS OF AYUTTHAYA (Pha-ngua/Borommaracha Dynasty of Suphanburi)					
Borommaracha I	Pha-ngua	1370-1388	Ramathibodi's brother-in-law	Khmer Royal Blood of Suphanburi	Usurped the throne from his nephew Ramesuan (p. 56). He was a Khmer prince and brother of Ramathibodi's wife from Suphanburi (Ref. 111, pp. 378-379).
Thong Chan	Thong Lan	1388	Son of Borommaracha I		He was was 17 years old when he succeeded his father Borommaracha. He reigned only for a week before he was killed by Ramesuan (p. 56).
KINGS OF AYUTTHAYA (U-Thong/Ramathibodi Dynasty of Lopburi-Suphanburi)					
Ramesuan	Rama-suon	1388-1395	Oldest son of Ramathibodi	Lopburi and Khmer Royal Blood of Suphanburi	Second reign of Ramesuan. He killed his cousin Thong Chan, the son of Borommaracha, to reclaim the throne (p. 56).
Ramaracha	Cau bañā rām	1395-1409	Son of Ramesuan		He was 21 years old when he succeeded his father. He appointed Thong Chan's younger brother, Nakhon In, to govern Suphanburi which was the ancestral province of his father Pha-ngua/ Borommaracha.
KINGS OF AYUTTHAYA (Pha-ngua/Borommaracha Dynasty of Suphanburi)					
Intharacha	Nakhon In	1409-1424	Younger brother of Thong Chan and youngest son of Borommaracha I	Khmer Royal Blood of Suphanburi	He formed an alliance with Ramaracha's chief minister and overthrew the king. Ramaracha was exiled to padāgūcām, identified by Michael Vickery as Chaktomouk (p. 57; Ref. 45, p. 11; Ref. 75, p. 48).
Borommaracha II	Samtec Prah Paramarājā-dhirāj Cau	1424-1448	Son of Intharacha		Borommaracha II was not expected to succeed his father because he had two older brothers with more claim to the throne. To settle their dispute, the two older brothers fought each other on elephant-back to claim the throne but they both died in the duel. By default, Borommaracha II became king. He installed his 7-year old son Ramesuan II to rule at Sukhothai as viceroy after the death of King Mahatthammaracha IV in 1438 (p. 59). With a reinforced army he was able to take Angkor in 1430-1431 (p. 59). He put his son Cau Bañā Brah Nagar Undr to rule Angkor but he died of illness and was replaced by his brother Bañā Brack (Ref. 108, pp. 27 & 56). Angkor was looted and abandoned. The Khmer king left Angkor to set a new capital at Basan in 1431/1432. In 1442 Borommaracha II conducted a war with Lan Na with no outcome until his death in 1448 (Ref. 104, p. 59 & Ref. 127, p. 12).
Borommatrai-lokanat	Ramesuan II, Trailok	1448-1463	Son of Boromma-racha II		He reigned in Ayutthaya from 1448 to 1463. He continued to pursue the war against Lan Na (Chiang Mai) that his father had started in 1442 (p. 59).
		1463-1488			He moved his capital from Ayutthaya to Phitsanulok in 1463 to be closer to the frontier of Lan Na so that he could conduct the war more effectively (p. 67). He left his son to act as regent in Ayutthaya. He abdicated in 1465 (but on pp. 66-67, it said he abdicated in 1464) to enter monkhood but left the order after 8 months to resume his reign (Ref. 127, p. 13).

Table 12b. Kings of Ayutthaya (1448-1569)

KINGS OF AYUTTHAYA (Pha-ngua/Borommaracha Dynasty of Suphanburi)					
Reign Name	Other Name	Reign Period	Relationship	Provenance/ Clan	Comments (unless noted, all indicated pages are from Reference 104)
Borommaracha III (Regent)	Intharacha II	1463-1488	Son of Borommatrai-lokanat	Khmer Royal Blood of Suphanburi	When Trailok moved the capital to Phitsanulok, he left his son Borommaracha III to rule Ayutthaya as a regent under the name of Borommaracha III (p. 67)
Intharacha II	Boromma-Racha III	1488-1491	Same person as Boromma-racha III		He succeeded his father Borommatrailokanat in 1488 and changed his regent name Borommaracha III to rule as King Intharacha II (p. 73). He died in 1491 (Ref. 127, p. 14).
Ramathibodi II	Jethādhirāj	1491-1529	Elder brother of Boromma-racha III/ Intharacha II		He was the older brother of Borommaracha III (Ref. 127, p. 14). In 1526, he appointed his eldest son as viceroy (Uparaja) to govern Phitsanulok (p. 76).
Borommaracha IV	No Phutthangkur	1529-1533	Son of Ramathibodi II		He succeeded his father in 1529 (Ref. 127, p. 15). He died of smallpox in 1533 (p. 76).
Ratsada	Ratsadathirat	1533-1534	Son of Boromma-Racha IV		He was 5 years old when he succeeded his father. He was overthrown and then killed by his half-brother Chairacha. He reigned only for five months (p. 76).
Chairacha	Jeyarāyā-dhirāj	1534-1547	Half-brother of Ratsada and son of Boromma-racha IV		He usurped the throne by killing his half-brother Ratsada. Nevertheless, Chairacha was remembered as a good and wise king. He employed 120 Portuguese mercenaries to protect him (p. 76). He died in 1547 (Ref. 127, p. 16).
Yot Fa		1547-1548	Oldest son of Chairacha and Lady Si Sudachan		His mother, Lady Si Sudachan, was the concubine of Chairacha. Yot Fa was 11 years old when he aceeded to thr throne. There was an earthquake at the time (127, p. 16). His mother acted as regent. She had a daughter with a minor palace official. She was determined to make him king. She would execute anybody who dared to contest her. Finally, she had her own son, the young king Yot Fa, poisoned. He died in July 1548. Her lover, with the title of Khun Woravongsa, was placed on the throne (p. 78).
Khun Woravongsa	Woravong-sathirat, Khun Jinarāj, Bun Si	Jun 1548-Jul 1548	Lover of Si Sudachan (mother of Yot Fa)	Unknown	He was put on the throne by Lay Sudachan (King Yot Fa's mother). Khun Woravongsa's reign lasted only six weeks (he was called Khun Jinarāj per Ref. 127, p. 17), The nobles revolted against the usurper and killed him. They called on Prince Thianracha, Yot Fa's half-brother, to leave the monkhood and come to reign as king of Ayutthaya (p. 78).
Chakraphat	Thianracha, Thienrājā-dhirāj	Jul 1548-Jun 1569	Son of Ramathibodi II and younger brother of Boromma-racha IV	Khmer Royal Blood of Suphanburi	Brief war with Cambodia in 1549, which lasted only a few months (p. 78). Pegu (Burma) attacked Ayutthaya in 1549 and captured Chakkraphat's eldest son Ramesuan (p. 79). The queen and her daughter died during the attack (Ref. 127, p.17). The war with Cambodia resumed in 1555-1556. Siam attacked Longvek by land and sea with an army of 30,000 men in 1556 (Ref. 127, p. 18), but the king's chief commander Phraya Ong Savankalok died.
Mahin	Mahintha-thirat	Jan 1569-Aug 1569	Son of Chakkraphat		Ineffective king. Ayuttahaya fell to the Burmese on 8 August 1569 (p. 82 and Ref. 127, p. 20). Mahin was taken prisoner to Burma (Ref. 127, p.20).

Table 12c. Kings of Ayutthaya (1569-1656)

KINGS OF AYUTTHAYA (Pha-ngua/Borommaracha Dynasty of Suphanburi)					
Reign Name	Other Name	Reign Period	Relationship	Provenance/ Clan	Comments (unless noted, all indicated pages are from Reference 104)
Maha Thammaracha	Sanphet I, Khun Phiren Tharathep	Aug 1569-Jun 1590 1569-1579(1)	Son-in-law of Chakkraphat	Khmer Royal Blood of Suphanburi	He was put on the throne by the Burmese (p. 87). He was Viceroy of Phitsanulok (p. 80). His mother was a relative of Chairacha and his father a descendant of Sukhothai kings (p. 80). The war with Cambodia resumed in 1575, 1578, and 1581 with Cambodia finally conquering Prachinburi in 1581 (Ref. 127, p. 21). (1) Khin Sok (Ref. 29, p. 338) said that the official Annals of Siam recorded the death of Maha Thammaracha to be in Cula 942 (1579 AD) but George Coedès placed his death in 1590.
Naresuan	Sanphet II, Naret, Black Prince	Jun 1590-25 Apr 1605 1579(1)-1606	Son of Maha Thammaracha		He was born in 1555. His mother was the daughter of Chakkraphat and she was the chief queen of Maha Thammaracha (p. 88). He made his younger brother Ekathotsarot a junior co-ruler (p. 88). Naresuan died at the age of fifty on 25 April 1605 after a bou
Ekathotsarot	Sanphet III, White Prince	25 Apr 1605-1610	Son of Maha Thammaracha and brother of Naresuan		He inherited a glorious kingdom from his brother.
Si Saowaphak	Sanphet IV	1610	Son of Ekathotsarat		He was killed by a monk named Phra Phimontham (p. 92).
KINGS OF AYUTTHAYA (Uncertain Dynasty of Suphanburi)					
Song Tham	Intharacha III, Phra Phimontham	1610-13 Dec 1628	He was a monk and purpoted to be the son of Ekathotsarot's concubine	Possibly descended from Khmer Royal blood of Suphanburi	He usurped the throne by killing Si Saowaphak (p. 92). His reign name translates to "The Just King" (p. 92).
Chettha	Chettha-kuman	13 Dec 1628-Aug 1629	Oldest son of Sing Tham		He was 15 years old when he succeeded his father (p. 93). Song Tham's purpoted cousin, Si Worawong, advocated for Chettha to be the next king. He was rewarded with the position of Kalahom (minister of defense). He concocted a plan to have the younger brother of Song Tham, Si Sin, and many others killed. Later on, he killed Chettha in August 1629.
Athittayawong		Aug 1629-Sep 1629	Younger brother of Chettha and son of Song Tham		Si Worawong killed Athittayawong in September 1629 (p.93).
KINGS OF AYUTTHAYA (Prasat Thong Dynasty)					
Prasat Thong	Si Worawong, Suriyawong	Sep 1629-Aug 1656	Purpoted to be the cousin of Song Tham through his mother and as the illegitimate son of Ekahotsarot	Possibly descended from Khmer Royal blood of Suphanburi	Si Worawong was a usurper. He Disposed of all the claimants to the throne. He reigned under the name Prasat Thong, which means golden palace (p. 93).
Sanpet VI	Chao Fa Chai (Chai)	7-8 Aug 1656	Oldest son of Prasat Thong		He wax deposed by his uncle Suthammaracha and his half-brother, Prince Narai (p. 93).

Table 12d. Kings of Ayutthaya (1656-1758)

					KINGS OF AYUTTHAYA (Prasat Thong Dynasty)
Reign Name	**Other Name**	**Reign Period**	**Relationship**	**Provenance/ Clan**	**Comments (unless noted, all indicated pages are from Reference 104)**
Suthammaracha		8 Aug 1656-26 Oct 1656	Younger brother of Prasat Thong	Possibly descended from Khmer Royal blood of Suphanburi	With the help of Narai, Suthammaracha overthrew Chai and crowned himself king (p. 93).
Ramathibodi III	Narai	26 Oct 1656-11 Jul 1688	Younger half-brother of Chai and son of Prasat Thong		He deposed Suthammaracha and took the throne for himself (p. 93). Jesuit priests tried to convert him to catholicism (pp. 97-101).
Phra Petracha		11 Jul 1688-1703	Dubious claim as cousin to Narai and as having blood lineage to previous kings	Suphanburi	He was a usurper. His rise to power was due to his mother being the wet nurse to Narai and that he was raised as Narai's foster brother (p. 102). Narai has two brothers, Aphaiphot and Noi, and an adoptive son named Mom Pi (p. 103). Phetracha and his son Sorasak fabricated a story to implicate all the three princes in the Makasarese revolt (p. 93). Phetracha who was made co-regent during Narai's illness seized on the opportunity to arrest Phaulkon, the Greek advisor and trusted friend of Narai, and then had him killed on trumped up charge of treason. He had Mom Pi murdered. Soon after Narai passed away, Sorasak killed Aphaithot and Noi (p. 103). Phetracha took Narai's sister and daughter as his wives to secure his legitimacy (p. 108). He had two sons with them. Phra Khwan and Trat Noi (p. 108). He made his son Sorasak Uparaja (p. 108). The father and son were ruthless toward everybody. As Phra Khwan grew older, Sorasak had the prince killed because he felt that the prince would displace him in the line of succession. Phetracha was furious upon learning of Sorasak's action. To punish Sorasak, Phetracha made his nephew Phichaisurin his heir (p. 109).
Suriyenthara-thibodi	Sanphet VIII, Sua, Sorasak	1703-1709	Oldest son of Phetracha		Prince Phichaisurin who was made heir would not dare to contest Sorasak for the throne (p. 109). Sorasak was better known as King Sua (King Tiger) for his ruthless behavior toward people around him. He had two sons, Princes Phet and Phon, and named both of them Uparaja but he did not trust either of them (p. 109).
Phumintharacha	Surinda, Phet, Thai Sa	1709-Jan 1733	Oldest son of Suriyenthara-thibodi		He was popularly called King Thai Sa. His reign was relatively peaceful (p. 109). Cambodia was a vassal to Ayutthaya (p. 109). He sent mahatthai Phraya Chakri in 1720 to reinstall Srei Thommo Reachea II to the throne of Cambodia (p. 109; and Ref. 7, p. 371). He made his younger brother Prince Phon who served him faithfully, Uparaja. He had three sons Naren, Aphai, and paramet born of the same mother. His preference was to have his second son, Aphai, his successor.
Borommakot	Phon, Borommat-hammikarat	Jan 1733-13 Apr 1758	Youngest brother of Phumintha-racha		He revolted against his brother's decision to make Aphai king. After the death of his brother he conducted a battle against the royal guards and with the help of Khun Chamnan they took the royal palace (p. 110). He reformed the system of government to prevent one individual from acquiring too much power (pp. 110-111).
Uthumphon	Doc Duea	13 Apr 1758-May 1758	Son of Borommakot & half-brother of Uparaja Senaphithak who was flogged to death		The death of Borommakot's eldest son and heir to the throne, Uparaja Senaphithak (he was flogged to death for having an affair with one of his father's concubine), left an unclear line of succession to the throne. After Uthumphon acceded to the throne, his older half-brother Anurakmontri/Ekkathat rebelled against the king. After a reign of 10 days he abdicated in favor of his older half-brother Anurakmontri (p. 115).

Table 12e. Kings of Ayutthaya (1758-1767) and of Siam (1767-1925)

KINGS OF AYUTTHAYA (Prasat Thong Dynasty)					
Reign Name	**Other Name**	**Reign Period**	**Relationship**	**Provenance/ Clan**	**Comments (unless noted, all indicated pages are from Reference 104)**
Borommaracha V	Suriyamarin, Anurak-montri, Ekkathat	May 1758-7 Apr 1767	Older half-brother of Uthumphon	Suphanburi	He took over the throne after Uthumphon abdicated after only 10 days of reign. He reigned as Borommaracha but he is better known as Suriyamarin, the name of his palace (p. 115).
KINGS OF SIAM (Thonburi Court)					
Taksin		Late 1767-6 Apr 1782	Son of a Chinese father and a Siamese mother. He proclaimed himself King of Siam.	Ayutthaya	He was the son of a Chinese father and Siamese mother (p. 123). He was adopted by a noble family in Ayutthaya (p. 123). He became governor of the province of Tak (where his Name came from). He led his army to fight the Burmese who surrounded Ayutthaya. He used his prowess and seized on the power vacuum caused by the Burmese invasion to proclaim himself king of Ayutthaya. The Burmese had decimated most of the Ayutthayan royal families. According to the Thai chronicles he annexed the Khmer provinces of Battambang and Siem Reap (p. 124), but it was not so according to the Cambodian chronicles. As Taksin was accused of being crazy, General Chakri seized the throne and put the king to death (p. 128). It is now believed that Taksin's eccentric and strange behaviors may have been attributed to dementia.
KINGS OF SIAM (Bangkok Court of the Chakri Dynasty)					
Ramathibodi	Rama I, Chakri, Thong Duang, Buddaha Yodfa, Chulaloke,	7 Apr 1782-7 Sep 1809	First king of Rattanakosin, son of Thongdee and Doaroeung	Unspecified	He usurped the throne from taksin. He put his predecessor, King Taksin, to deth and took over the throne (p. 128). He killed all Taksin's children except his grandson. Chakri's daughter had a son with Taksin.
Phra Phuthaloetla	Rama II, Buddha Loetla, Nabhalai,	7 Sep 1809-21 Jul 1824	Son of Rama I and Queen Aamarinda		He was born in 1768. By the time he succeeded his father at the age of 41 he was already experienced in the affairs of the state. He enlisted members of the Bunnag family of Persian ancestry to help him govern the country.
Phra Nangklao	Rama III, Chetsada-bodin	21 Jul 1824-3 Apr 1851	Son of Rama II and consort Sri Sulalai (daughter of governor of Nonthaburi)		His reign was controversial. He was born in 1788 and older than Mongkut who was born in 1804, but because he was the son of A concubine he was not chosen as heir to the throne. He acceded To the throne because Monkut, the legitimate son of Rama II and Queen Sri Suriyendra, was in the monkhood when his father died.
Mongkut	Rama IV, Vajirayan	3 Apr 1851-1 Oct 1868	Half-brother of Rama III; son of Rama II and Queen Sri Suriyendra (the daughter of Rama I's sister)	Bangkok	He spent 27 years as a monk before he acceded to the throne at the age of 47. He was an erudite man when he left the monkhood and it served him well as a king. It is believed by some scholars that he was the inventor of the Ram Kamhaeng stele.
Chulalongkorn	Rama V	1 Oct 1868-23 Oct 1910	Son of Rama IV and Queen Debsirinda		He adopted the rule of successions from the European monarchies. He was also credited for modernizing the country.
Vajiravudh	Rama VI	23 Oct 1910-26 Nov 1925	Son of Rama V and Queen Saovabha Bongsri		He was not popular and spent extravagantly for his second coronation. At his deathbed he named his half-brother, Prince Prajadhipok, to succeed him (p. 221).

Table 12f. Kings of Siam (1925-1935/1946) and of Thailand (1935/1946-Present)

Reign Name	Other Name	Reign Period	Relationship	Provenance/ Clan	Comments (unless noted, all indicated pages are from Reference 104)
KINGS OF SIAM (Bangkok Court of the Chakri Dynasty)					
Prajadhipok	Rama VII	26 Nov 1925-2 Mar 1935	Younger brother of Rama VI	Bangkok	A coup d'état by the People's Party on 24 June 1932, where Phibunsongkram was one of the leaders, stripped the king much of his power which led to his abdication on 2 March 1935.
KINGS OF SIAM/THAILAND (Bangkok Court of the Chakri Dynasty)					
Ananda Mahidol	Rama VIII	2 Mar 1935-9 Jun 1946	Nephew of Rama VII and grandson of Rama V	Bangkok	He was chosen to replace Prajadhipok. He died by gunshot on 9 June 1946. His autopsy by 20 doctors (16 Thai, 2 British, 1 Indian, and 1 US) concluded that the death was as follows: regicide (16 doctors), accident (2 doctors), and suicide (2 doctors) - (Ref. 130).
KINGS OF THAILAND (Bangkok Court of the Chakri Dynasty)					
Bhumibol Adulyadej	Rama IX	9 Jun 1946-13 Oct 2016	Younger brother of Rama VIII and grandson of Rama V	Bangkok	Bhumibol acceded to the throne after the death of his older brother, King Ananda. After a long bout of illness, King Bhumibol passed away at the Siriraj Hospital in Bangkok on 13 October 2016. He was the longest reigning monarch of the Chakri Dynasty.
Maha Vajiraongkorn	Rama X	1 Dec 2016-Present	Oldest son of Rama IX and Sirikit Kitiyakara		Vajiralongkorn's private life as a prince was scandalous and very controversial. He succeeded his father and was crowned king on 1 December 2016 at the age of 64.

The Ayutthaya Period of the U-Thong, Suphannaphum, and Prasat Thong dynasties was predominated by the royal lineage of Khmer descents. Historians credited the foundation of Ayutthaya in 1351 to U-Thong. As the Tai world gained in strength and numbers of population, new leaders with great ambitions emerged to form kingdoms of their own. The northern parts of the region were dominated by powerful warlords like Mangrai of the Lan Na Kingdom; and Sri Indraditya of the Sukhothai Kingdom who wrestled his independence from Angkor. The successes of these two warlords may have provided an incentive for U-Thong about a century later to challenge the authority of Angkor that had a firm control of Lopburi up to about 1290. Lopburi was an extension of Angkor that had its own cultural and administrative operation almost independent of the central power of Angkor. It must be remembered that Jayavarman VII sent his son –indravarman (the prefix of his name was missing and according to Coedès he was not the same person as Indravarman II who succeeded Jayavarman VII) to govern Lopburi (known as Lavo at the time) between 1160 and 1165. As the power of Angkor over Lopburi waned, a new leader in the name of U-Thong emerged to lead the population against Angkor.

The U-Thong and Suphanburi Dynasties and their Connections to Khmer Royal Bloodlines

The origin of U-Thong is still debatable. Some scholars said he was a wealthy Chinese merchant, but George Coedès believed he "may have belonged to a family of Môn or Khmer origins"[19,p146] and John F. Cady said he was a Môn leader of Dvaravati origin.[16,p59] U-Thong consolidated his power as the new leader in the region by marrying the sister of Prince Pha-ngua of Suphanburi.[104,p54] Suphanburi was the center seat of power of Prince Pha-ngua's family. Professor Wilaiwan Khanittanan of the Department of Linguistic at the Thammasat University said that Thai historians may not agree on the origin of U-Thong but they all agreed that U-Thong's wife was a Khmer princess.[111,p378]

In his academic paper *Khmero-Thai: the Great Change in the History of the Thai Language of the Chao Phraya Basin,*[111] Willaiwan Khanittanan made the following statement:

> *Though Thai historians do not agree on where King U-Thong came from, they all agree that he married a Khmer Princess and that Ayutthaya inherited all the Khmer administrative system and culture.*

... Acquiring Khmer must have been "a must" for all minority leaders and elites at the time. There was evidence that three princes from the north who later became kings — Ramkhamhaeng, Mengrai, and Ngam-muang — went for their education at Lavo or Lopburi at the same time. This city was earlier an outpost of the Khmer capital and a study center for Khmer civilization such as Buddhism and Hinduism (Kasetsiri 1976:85).

When King U-Thong founded Ayutthaya in 1351 A.D. he was actually a Khmero-Thai or Khmer-speaking Thai. At least he must have been educated as a Khmer leader because he became king in the Khmer tradition — a god-king. He sent eight Brahmins in Benares to perform his accession ceremony. After the ceremony he was given the name Ramathibodi and ruled as a god-king (Testimony of the people from the old capital 1973:59). He sent Ramesuan, his son born of his Khmer wife, to rule Lopburi, the city traditionally assigned to future king. King U-Thong and later kings were successful in establishing Ayutthaya as the center of the empire, replacing Angkor Thom, the Khmer center. Lopburi became Ayutthaya's major city instead of the Khmers'. People of other cities looked, then, to Ayutthaya as the center of learning. Theravada Buddhism prospered and Brahmins also became indispensable to the capital from the very beginning.

U-Thong who founded Ayutthaya in 1351 reigned as King Ramathibodi until 1369. He was succeeded by his son Ramesuan who had to step down after a short reign after his uncle Pha-Ngua challenged him for the throne. Pha-Ngua was a Khmer āāāāince from Suphanburi and also the brother of U-Thong's wife. Pha-Ngua reigned as King Boromaracha from 1370 to 1388. He was succeeded by his 17-year-old son Thong Chan/Lan but it was only for a week because Ramesuan took over the throne by killing his cousin. Ramesuan's second reign lasted from 1388 to 1395. He was succeeded by his 21-year-old son Ramaracha. As a gesture of reconciliation, Ramaracha offered the Suphanburi governorship to his uncle Nakhon In, the younger brother of Thong Chan/Lan that his father had killed. Ramaracha reigned from 1395 to 1409 until he was overthrown by his own Chief Minister.

In the chronicle of Ayutthaya written by Prince Vasuki (aka Somdet Phra Paramanujit) in 1840 and revised by Dr. Dan Beach Bradley under the tutelage of King Mongkut in 1865, it said that Somdet Phra Ram (Ramaracha) was very angry at his Minister's behavior and he wanted to arrest him. Fearing for his life, the Minister went to Somdet Phra Indraraja (Intharacha aka Nakhon In) and handed the prince the scepter that he stole from Ramaracha. With his loyal army, the Minister overthrew Ramaracha.[127,pp10-1] After he was deposed, the Chief Minister invited Nakhon In to become king and Ramaracha was sent into exile to *Padāgūcām*.[127,p11] The Luang Praseut (LP) Chronicle confirmed the same story.

Michael Vickery broke down the word *Padāgūcām* to *prāp jhām*, which means to put down the Cham where in the 19th century the Chaktomouk River was known as the Cham River.[108, 128]

Nakhon In reigned as King Intharacha from 1409 to 1424. Intharacha had three sons. He died without appointing an heir. As a consequence, two of his oldest sons claimed the throne. They decided to fight a duel on elephant-back to settle their dispute, but they were both killed in the battle. As fate would have it, the youngest brother was left as the sole claimant to the throne. He reigned as Borommaracha II from 1424 to 1448. He put his 7-year-old son Ramesuan (II) to rule at Sukhothai as Viceroy after the death of King Mahathammaracha IV in 1438. The Ayutthaya chronicle said that Somdet Paramaraja (aka Borommaracha II) conquered Nakhong Luang (Angkor) in 1431.[127,p11] He put his grandson Phra Nakhon Indr (aka Cau Bañā Brah Nagar Indr) to rule Angkor and ordered Phraya Keo and Phraya Thai to remove all the statues of the Buddha and bring them to Ayutthaya.[127,p11] According to the *2/k.125 Fragment*, the Ayutthayan prince died of illness and was immediately replaced by his younger brother Bañā Braek.[108,p21] Angkor was looted and abandoned after one year. The Khmer king who succeeded Thommasoka, Ponhea Yat, left Angkor to set a new capital at Basan in 1431/32.

In 1442 Borommaracha II conducted a campaign against Lan Na but by the time of his death the war had not been concluded. He was succeeded by his son Borommatrailokanat, also known as Trailok for short but also Ramesuan II. He reigned from 1448 to 1463 in Ayutthaya. Because of the war against Lan Na, Trailok decided to move his seat of power to Phitsanulok in 1463 to be closer to the Lan Na border. He left his son Borommaracha III to rule as Regent in Ayutthaya from 1463 to 1488. Trailok abdicated in 1465 (827 Cula, year of the Rooster) to enter monkhood but left the order eight month later;[127,p13] but according to Wyatt he said that Trailok abdicated in 1464.[104,pp66-67] He continued his reign until his death in 1488.

Borommaracha III succeeded his father Borommatrailokanat and reigned as Intharacha II in Ayutthaya from 1488 to 1491. He was succeeded by his younger brother Ramathibodi II from 1491 to 1529. He appointed his eldest son No Phutthamgkun as Viceroy of Phitsanulok in 1526. After his death, Ramathibodi II was succeeded by his son No Phutthamgkum who reigned as King Borommaracha IV in 1529, but his reign lasted only four years because he died of smallpox in 1533. His son Ratsada was only five years old when he acceded to the throne. His reign lasted only five months before he was assassinated by his half-brother Chairacha in 1534. In spite of his usurpation to power, Chairacha is remembered as a good and wise king. He employed 120 Portuguese mercenaries for protection. He reigned from 1534 to 1547.

Chairacha was succeeded by his 11-year-old son Yot Fa, but because of his young age his mother Lady Si Sudachan acted as the Regent on his behalf. She ruled with an ironclad and would execute any officials who dared to contest her rule. She had an affair with a minor palace official and bore him a daughter. She committed one of the most heinous crimes a mother could do. She poisoned her own son so she could put her lover on the throne. The young King Yot Fa died in July 1548. Lady Si Sudachan accomplished her goal by installing her lover Woravongsa (the Ayutthayan chronicle called him Khun Jinaraj) on the throne in 1548, but his reign was short-lived because six weeks later the nobles revolted and killed the usurper. The nobles asked Yot Fa's half-brother, Thianracha, to leave the monkhood and took over the throne. He reigned as King Chakkraphat from July 1548 to June 1569. He had a brief war with Pegu (Burma) and Cambodia in 1549 and another one where he attacked Cambodia in 1556.[127,pl] One of the confusions about the attack of Longvek may stem from the fact that the Prince Vasukri used the name Lavëk (Longvek) to indicate Cambodia. He did not make any distinction between Lavëk, the city, and Lavëk, the country. As a result of this ambiguity, some historians erroneously said that Longvek had been attacked as early as 1555. Even Wyatt believed that Longvek was attacked during that time when he said "In 1555-56, a strong land and naval expedition was sent against Lawæk to ensure Khmer submission on Ayutthaya's vulnerable eastern flank."[104,p79]

Chakkraphat was succeeded by his son Mahin in 1569, but his reign was cut short the same year after the Burmese invaded Ayutthaya. According to the chronicle, Ayutthaya fell in 931 Cula, in the year of the Snake, on Sunday the 11th (day) of the 9th (decade) on a waxing moon[127,p20] [note: for 931 Cula, year of the Snake, it could not have been the 9th decade but rather the 1st decade). The Burmese who occupied Ayutthaya decided to put Chakkraphat's son-in-law, Maha Thammaracha (Somdet Mahadharmarajadhiraj), on the throne of Ayutthaya in August 1569. When the Burmese king left Ayutthaya, he took Mahin to Burma with him. Maha Thammaracha reigned until June 1590.

Naresuan succeeded his father Maha Thammaracha who died on 25 April 1605 after he fell ill. Naresuan was credited for bringing Ayutthaya into greatness. It was under his reign that two Persian merchant brothers, Sheikh Ahmad and Muhamad Sa-id, came to Siam. They were natives of Qom in Iran. They would establish one of the most powerful noble families in Thailand. After the death of Naresuan, his son Ekathosarot inherited a glorious kingdom from his father and reigned from 25 April 1605 to 1610. He was succeeded by his son Si Saowaphak but because of his incompetence he was deposed by a monk named Phra Phimontham who claimed to be the illegitimate son of Ekathotsarot. He acceded to the throne under the name of Song Tham in 1610. After having succeeded in business, Sheik Ahmad would serve in the government of King Song Tham. He was put in charge of monitoring the commerce with the West. The king would add another responsibility by appointing him to the position of Minister of Islamic Affairs.

He rose in rank to become Phra Khlang (Minister of Treasury) and finally to Samuha Nayok (Prime Minister). When Song Tham passed away on 13 December 1628, Phraya Si Worawong who claimed to be the cousin of Song Tham advocated for the 15-year-old Chettha to succeed his father Song Tham. After he acceded to the throne, Si Worawong was rewarded with the position of Kalahom (Minister of Defense). With his new found power Si Worawong concocted a plan to eliminate all the potential successors to Chettha. He had the younger brother of Song Tham, Si Sin, and many others killed. After getting rid of all his rivals, Si Worawong committed treason by killing Chettha in August 1629. Athittayawong succeeded his older brother Chettha but his reign was very short because he was killed by Si Worawong in September 1629. The U-Thong and Suphannaphum dynasties that carried the Khmer royal lineage of Suphanburi ended with death of Athittayawong.

The Prasat Thong Dynasty

After eliminating all his rivals, Si Worawong grabbed the throne for himself in September 1629 which started the era of the Prasat Thong Dynasty (Golden Palace Dynasty). He reigned under the name of Prasat Thong. His claim as being the cousin of Song Tham and son of Ekathotsarot was dubious. In his distrust of the nobles, Prasat Thong devised a plan to curb their powers. He split the control of the provinces into two distinct functions. The Northern provinces were given to the Kalahom (Minister of Defense) to be in charge while the Southern provinces were to be fallen under the jurisdiction of the Mahatthai (Minister of the Interior). He passed away in August 1656. An immediate turmoil followed the death of Prasat Thong. Because of two other potential claimants to the throne (Prasat Thong's brother Suthammaracha and Prasat Thong's other son Narai), Prasat Thong's oldest son Chao Fa Chai made the first move with his men by seizing the throne. Unhappy with his half-brother's move, Narai and his uncle Suthammaracha plotted to remove Chai from the throne. They immediately deposed Chai and executed him on 8 August 1656.

Suthammaracha climbed to the throne and appointed Narai as the Uparaja. After he became king, Suthammaracha wanted to kidnap Narai's sister, Princess Ratcha Kanlayani, by having his soldiers surrounding her house. The princess escaped and asked her brother Narai for protection. Narai was very upset at his uncle's behavior and decided to enlist the Japanese and Persian mercenaries to overthrow the king. They stormed the palace and captured the king at the rear of the palace as he was fleeing for safety. Suthammaracha was executed on 26 October 1656 at Wat Khok Phraya.

After the execution of Suthammaracha, Narai took the throne on the same day and reigned under the name Ramathibodi III. According to *The Diary of Kosa Pan,*[129,p7] Narai was born in 1632 and he was crowned under the name "Sommedethia Phra Naareyya Raachaattirat Chaadi Souriawongsa." Furthermore, it said that after he became king he was called "Sommedethia Phra Maahaa Kresatratti Raacha Thian Phou Ya." Kosa Pan was the first Siam ambassador known by the name Ok-phra Wisut Sunthon that was sent by King Narai in 1686 to establish a diplomatic relation with Louis XIV of France. Kosa Pan was the younger brother of Kosa Thibodi who served King Narai for 15 years as Phra Khlang until his death in 1683. According to Dirk Van der Cruysse, King Narai had the same wet-nurse as Kosa Pan and Kosa Thibodi.[129,p.11]

In addition to his sister Ratcha Kanlayani , Narai had two brothers named Aphaithot and Noi and an adoptive son named Mom Pi. After he became king, Narai brought his foster brother Phethracha — his mother was Narai's wet-nurse — to be his trusted counselor. Being a dubious person, Pethracha and his son Sorasak fabricated a story to implicate all the three princes in the Makasarese revolt. The revolt started with a small group of the same name that banded together with Cham princes to burn down Ayutthaya with the purpose to place one of Narai's younger brothers on the throne; but this group put a condition that the person to be put on the throne must convert to the Islam faith. In March 1688, Narai fell gravely ill and his health started to deteriorate. From his palace in his Lopburi palace, Narai convened a meeting with his closest advisor Constantine Phaulkon, his adoptive son Mom Pi, and his foster brother Phethracha to plan for his succession. Narai chose his daughter Yothathep to succeed him. The three men mentioned above were to act as regents until Yothathep chose a partner to reign with her. Preferably, Narai would want to see his daughter married either Phetracha or Mom Pi. However, Phetracha did not want to let fate decide for him. He seized on this opportunity to eliminate all potential rivals to attain his ambition. He had Constantine Phaulkon, the trusted close friend and advisor to Narai, executed on 5 June 1688 on trumped up charge of treason. Phaulkon was a Greek adventurer employed by the English East India Company in 1678. Within two years living in Ayutthaya he was able to speak Thai fluently. He entered into the service of Narai and became an interpreter for the ministry of Phra Khlang (Treasury). His rapid ascension in the Narai government to an equivalent rank of Chancellor may have made a lot of enemies; and consequently threatened the Muslim community that had great influence with the Phra Khlang prior to the arrival of Phaulkon. Having achieved his first goal, Phetracha had Mom Pi murdered. After a long illness, Narai finally died on 11 July 1688. Narai wanted to modernize Ayutthaya and was willing to employ foreigners in his administration. He was friendly to French Jesuit priests. They even wanted to convert him to Christianity. His death marked the end of the Prasat Thong Dynasty.

The Ban Phlu Luang Dynasty

Phetracha was a usurper. He started the Ban Phlu Luang Dynasty, which was named after his birthplace of Baan Phu Luang in the province of Nakhon Ratchasima.

According to the *Phongsawadan Krung Kao,* as reported by Dir Van der Cruysse,[129,p28] Phetracha and Kosa Pan were half-brother. Furthermore, he said that Kosa Pan — even though he had been to France and admired its greatness — he espoused Phetracha's policy of anti-westerners. Phetracha rewarded Kosa Pan with the position of Phra Khlang that was held by his older brother with a title of "Phraya Kosathibodi". Kosa Pan was against "the occupation by a French expeditionary force of Bangkok and Mergui, the two Siamese strongholds." [129,p30]

Without wasting time, Sorasak had Aphaitot and Noi killed. In order to secure the royal bloodline and legitimize his accession to the throne, Phetracha took Narai's sister (Ratcha Kanlayani?) and daughter (Sudawadi aka Yothathep) as his wives. He had two sons with them, Phra Khwan and Trat Noi. He elevated his son Sorasak to the position of Uparaja. As Prince Khwan grew older, Sorasak became insecure because he felt that his younger half-brother, who was of royal blood, would displace him in the line of succession to the throne. He had the prince killed. Phetracha was so furious when he learned of what Sorasak had done, that on his deathbed he chose his nephew Phichaisurin heir to the throne to punish for Sorasak's evil action.

Terror was the mode of operation under the reign of Phetracha. Even Kosa Pan, once a loyal follower of Phetracha, did not escape the atrocity handed out by Phetracha and his son Sorasak. The following is the account of the atrocious death of Kosa Pan in August 1700 that was described by Gabriel Braud in his letter to the directors of the Foreign Missions in Paris:[129,pp31-32]

He died two months ago, from whiplashes as much as from distress at being continually mistreated. For since royal anger cut off the end of his nose with a blow of a sabre four years previously, he only suffered persecution on the part of the court for which he was, one believes, somewhat suspect. An older daughter of his, and two or three sons, with his wives and concubines, were all arrested and tortured. His effects were seized two or three days before his death, and rumour at the court had it that out of despair, to end things, he plunged a knife into his chest...The body of the Barcalon [phra khlang] was taken at night to a pagoda to be interred without ceremony and deprived of the honour of their ordinary rites, which is to burn the body in a magnificent pyre. This was the sad end of the famous ambassador to France.

Phetracha did not trust Westerners. When he passed away in 1703 he had greatly reversed the course of Westerners' influence and his action may even have prevented the colonization of Ayutthaya by either the French or the British.

After the death of the Phetracha, Phichaisurin ceded his right to the throne to Sorasak because he was so scared of him. Sorasak acceded to the throne in 1703 under the name of Suriyentharathibodi. He was called King Sua (Tiger King) because he was so vulgar and ruthless in his behaviors. He had no manners and treated people around him viciously. He had two sons, Phet and Phon, that he did not trust but he still made both of them Uparajas anyway. His reign was short, lasted only six years as he passed away in 1709.

King Sua was succeeded by his oldest son Phet who reigned under the name of Phumintharacha, but he is more popularly known as Thai Sa (Backyard Pond) because of his fondness for the silver barb that he liked to fish in his backyard pond. His reign seemed to be relatively peaceful within the country but he had a war with Vietnam in his dispute to install a Khmer king on the throne. King Thai Sa dispatched Chao Phraya Chakri to fight the Vietnamese in Cambodia because he wanted to install Srei Thommo Reachea II (Ang Nou) at the Oudong throne in Cambodia. Phon, who had served his brother faithfully, was rewarded the position of Uparaja. Thai Sa's action came into conflict with the fact that he had three sons — Naren, Aphai, and Paramet — of which any of them could potentially be the heir to the throne. Thai Sa's problem was compounded with his own wish to see his second son, Aphai, succeed him. Thai Sa passed away in January 1733. Before he died, Thai Sa made it known that he would give the throne to his son Aphai. Because he was awarded the position of Uparaja, Phon felt he should be in line to succeed his brother. After Thai Sa passed away, Phon revolted against his nephew. With about four thousand of his supporters, Phon launched an attack against more than twenty thousand of the palace royal guards protecting his nephew. Phon was on the verge of defeat until he was rescued by Khun Chamnan Channarong, one of the leading Front Palace officials. Chamnan Channarong led Phon's forces to victory.

Phon, the brother of Thai Da, acceded to the throne in January 1733 under the name of Borommakot. He rewarded Khun Chamnan for his invaluable support with the title of Chao Phraya Chamnanborirak and he put him in charge of the Phra Khlang ministry. In order to prevent the other princes from holding too much power, Borommakot divided the departments — that were mostly occupied by princes — into thirteen smaller departments. Chamnan came from the line of the Persian Sheik Ahmad who had served previous Ayutthayan kings. Borommakot rewarded Chamnan's son, Sawang, to the position of Mahatthai after the death of the previous holder of this office, Chao Phraya Aphaimontri. To secure an heir to the throne, Borommakot made his oldest son Senaphithak the Uparaja. The king's plan fell apart when Senaphithak was flogged to death for his indiscretion of carrying an affair with one of his father's concubines. After the death of his oldest son, Borommakot decided to appoint his third son Uthumphon (the youngest half-brother of Senaphithak) to the Front Palace, which indicated he would be the favorite as heir to succeed him. Borommakot skipped his second son Anurakmontri (also known as Ekkathat and older half-brother of Uthumphon) as heir-apparent. When Borommakot passed away on 13 April 1758, he left the throne without a clear instruction to designate which son he wanted to succeed him. The officials elected Uthumphon king.

Unhappy with the election of his younger brother Uthumphon as king by the high officials, Anurakmontri rebelled and a battle erupted at the royal palace. After only about two weeks on the throne Uthumphon abdicated in favor of his older brother and then entered into monkhood. Anurakmontri acceded to the throne in May 1758 under the name of Borommaracha (V).

In 1760, the Burmese army invaded Ayutthaya but its leader died during the campaign and the army returned to Burma. Another invasion took place seven years later and this time Ayutthaya fell to the Burmese army. Borommaracha V died in 7 April 1767. Borommakot, who became a monk, was captured by the Burmese and died in 1796 in the Mandalay region. The death of both Borommakot and Borommaracha V closed the chapter on the Ban Phlu Luang Dynasty.

King of Thonbury

The Burmese invasion had devastated Ayutthaya and wiped out all the Ayutthayan royal families. With this vacuum emerged a new leader. A young governor named Sin from the province of Tak led his troops to attack the Burmese army at Chanthaburi, which he retook it in 1767. His prowess brought hope and courage back to the Ayutthayan people. People started to call him Taksin by combining his name with his province. Within a very short time he was able to liberate Ayutthaya from the Burmese army. Taksin decided not to return to Ayutthaya but chose to make Thonburi the seat of his power. Because the royal families were decimated, Taksin proclaimed himself king, probably sometime near the end of 1767.

Once in control of his country, Taksin started to expand his power beyond Ayutthaya into Lan Na, Laos, and Cambodia. In 1778 Taksin sent an army that was led by Chao Phraya Chakri, with the support of 20,000 Khmer soldiers supplied by Ang Non II (Srei Chey Cheth III), to Laos. Chakri marched into Vientiane, looted the city, and took the Emerald Buddha that had stayed in that country for 227 years to Thonburi. In the meantime in Cambodia, Samdech Chaovea Mohareach Mou betrayed his king Ang Non II. With the help of the Annamese army, Mou captured Ang Non II and had him killed. Unhappy with Mou's betrayal of his vassal Khmer king, Taksin sent Chakri to invade Cambodia in 1782 in the objective to install Yomareach Bèn — the Khmer high-ranking official loyal to Ang Non II — as its caretaker. The success of Taksin over his neighbors may have inflated his ego. It was reported that he became very eccentric as he considered himself to be the living Buddha and demanded that monks bowed to him. As the revolt broke out, Chakri came back to Thonburi to depose Taksin on 6 April 1782.[104,p128] He was executed without trial and the end of his reign was recorded to occur on 7 April 1782.[87,p47,note78] It is now believed that Taksin's behaviors may have been caused by dementia.

The Chakri Dynasty and the Emergence of Modern Thailand

The death of Taksin would bring about a new dynasty, called the Chakri Dynasty. When Chakri deposed Taksin, he did not only execute the king without trial but he also killed all his children with the exception of his grandson.

One of Chakri's daughters produced a son with Taksin. Chakri, whose birth name was Thong Duang, acceded to the throne on 7 April 1782 under the name Ramathibodi. However, he is more popularly known as Rama I. He was given a posthumous name Phra Phutthayotfa or Buddha Yodfa Chulaloke. The Chakri Dynasty is only briefly discussed in this section because there will be more opportunities to discuss on this subject in Chapters 10, 11, and 12 from the Post Angkor Period to the Colonial Period where the conflicts between Cambodia and Siam are more prevalent.

Chakri moved the seat of his power to the other side of the river to break off with the Taksin period. The new capital that he intended to build was located in the village of Bang Makok (ບຶ່ງໝາກ, pond of fruit Makok). The name was shortened to Bangkok. Rama I passed away on 7 September 1809. He was succeeded by his son Phen din-Khlang who reigned under the name Phra Phutthaloetla or Buddha Loetha Nabhalai, but he is popularly known as Rama II. By the time he succeeded his father he was forty-one years old, but his age gave him an advantage because he was well experienced in the affairs of the state. He enlisted members of the Bunnag family of Persian ancestry to help him govern the country. He passed away on 21 July 1824. Mongkut would have succeeded Rama II if it were not for the unexpected death of his father after he had entered into monkhood.

The officials decided to choose the illegitimate son of Rama II and older half-brother of Mongkut, Chetsadabodin, to be the third Rama king. He reigned under the name Phra Nangklao. There were speculations that Rama II was poisoned and that Mongkut remained as a monk because of the fear that he might be assassinated if he were to come out of monkhood. If Mongkut were to come out of the order, he would pose a threat to Rama III's reign. Nangklao died on 3 April 1851.

After spending twenty-seven years as a monk, Mongkut came out of the order and was chosen as King Rama IV to succeed Nangklao. His years as a monk prepared him well to take over the throne. He had studied Latin, English, science, and mathematics when he was a monk. He was an erudite scholar and became a reformist by creating another branch of Buddhism called Thammayut. He is believed by some scholars to be the inventor of the Ram Khamhaeng Inscription. Mongkut passed away on 1 October 1868. He is one of the most revered kings of the Chakri Dynasty.

Chulalongkorn who is also known as Rama V succeeded his father on 1 October 1868. He adopted a clear rule of successions that he borrowed from the European monarchies. He is also credited for modernizing the country. He passed away on 23 October 1910. Chulalongkorn and Mongkut were portrayed in the movie the King and I.

Vajaravudh acceded to the throne after the death of his father. He is also known as Rama VI. He was not a popular king and his extravagant spending on his second coronation was criticized by the people. At his deathbed, Vajaravudh named his half-brother Prajadhipok as his successor which he acceded to the throne on 16 November 1925 as Rama VII.

Prajadhipok's reign was in turmoil. A coup d'état by the People's Party (Khana Ratsadorn) on 24 June 1932, led by Pridi Banomyong and Luang Phibunsongkhram (his rank and title, but his birth name was Plaek Khittasangkha[104,p241]), stripped Prajadhipok much of his power which led to his abdication on 2 March 1935. The abdication of Prajadhipok ended the era of absolute monarchy and started the era of constitutional monarchy.

The National Assembly proclaimed Ananda Mahidol, who was only nine years old and living in Switzerland at the time, as the new king to replace Prajadhipok. He is recorded as Rama VIII. Phibunsongkhram became prime minister on 26 December 1938. He controlled the country by holding the two most powerful cabinet positions, the defense and interior ministries.[104,p242] In a political move to make Siam a larger country, Phibunsongkhram proclaimed in 1939 that Siam would be renamed to Thailand as a way to include Tai people living outside of Siam.[104,p243] As World War II approached, Phibunsongkhram became more militaristic and broke rank with Pridi. This latter was stripped of his ministerial post and was sidelined to act as Regent to the powerless King Ananda. Phibunsongkhram abandoned all democratic values and ruled Thailand with an iron fist. When World War II ended, Phibunsongkhram and his supporters were arrested and the power shifted to the Free Thai Movement Party. With the war ended, Pridi called on King Ananda to return home.

King Ananda came back to Thailand in December 1945 and Pridi resigned as Regent. Khuang Apaiwongs' Democrat Party contested in an election against Pridi's People's Party. The parties that supported Pridi won the majority of the seats but the Assembly voted to elect Apaiwongs prime minister. Apaiwongs did not keep his position too long as he resigned in March 1946 because of the lack of support for his policies from the Assembly. Pridi was elected by the Assembly to replace Apaiwongs. Six months after King Ananda came back from Switzerland, in June 1946, he was found dead on his bed of a gun shot in the head in the Grand Palace. The initial pronouncement of his death was determined to be caused by an accident, but after the autopsy composed of a team of twenty doctors (16 Thai, 2 British, 1 Indian, and 1 US), the report issued that the following opinions for the cause of the king's death:[130] 1) a regicide based on the conclusion of 16 doctors; 2) an accident based on the conclusion of 2 doctors; and 3) a suicide based on the conclusion of 3 doctors.

After the death of King Ananda, Bhumibol Adulyadej who was born on 5 December 1927 was chosen to succeed his brother. He acceded to the throne in June 1946. He is also known as Rama IX. Thailand was modernized and became a prosperous country under his reign. After 70 years of reign, King Bhumibol passed away on 13 October 2016 at the Siriraj Hospital in Bangkok, Thailand. He was the longest reigning king under the Chakri Dynasty. Under the Thai constitution, Bhumibol's oldest son Vajiralongkorn was invited to succeed his father. The crown prince asked to properly mourn the passing of his father before acceding to the throne. Vajiralongkorn who was born on 28 July 1952 was crowned King of Thailand and styled as Rama X. He was 64 years old.

CHAPTER 9

ព្រះមហាក្សត្រខ្មែរនិងប្រវត្តិសាស្ត្រកម្ពុជា

POST ANGKOR TO LONGVEK PERIOD
(INCLUDING AYUTTHAYA'S OCCUPATION)
(1432-1594/1595)

Finally the sack of Angkor ended the period of Classical Khmer civilization, beyond hope of restoration. This it did by two means: (a) It carried off the last remnant of the intelligentsia at a time when it could not be replaced. The theocracy was Indian in origin and was no doubt declining in numbers and influence. It had lost all contact with its source of inspiration in India, owing to the influx of Mohammedanism there. The loss of revenue in Cambodia had, doubtless, diminished its ranks. While it is true that no great monuments had been constructed for two centuries and no Sanskrit inscription carved for a hundred years, the monuments still remained in their care, villages and slaves were still assigned to their maintenance, and there was always a hope — or a dread — of return to power and wealth and of a government of their old faith. With the disappearance of this class and the removal of the capital of Angkor, the temples were soon abandoned, the old religions all but disappeared, Sanskrit was forgotten. (b) The frequent Siamese raids and the sack of Angkor, joined with the growing desire for an escape from their conditions, led the survivors to establish a new capital far from Angkor with its temples and other monuments to serve as reminders of their glorious but burdensome past and inspirations and models for a possible return to their former greatness.

The Ancient Khmer Empire
Lawrence Palmer Briggs [6,p259]

THE PRE-LONGVEK PERIOD (1432-1525)

55   Ponhea Yat or Borom Reachea II (1432-1463) ពញាយ៉ាត ឬ បរមរាជា (ទី២)

Transliterated Name: Bañā Yāt

Other Names: Cau Yat, Chau Ponhea Yat, Paramaraja II

Style Name: Preah Bat Samdach Sdach Preah Reach Ang Preah Borom Reacheathireach Reameathipadey Preah Srey Soriyopor Thommik Moha Reacheathireach Preah Boromneat Borom Baupit[7,p218]

Accession: 1432

Abdication: 1463

Deceased: 1467

Relationship: Undetermined according to the Cambodian chronicles; son of Srei Soriyovong according to Khin Sok; but son of Ramaracha of Ayutthaya (Cau Bañā Rām) according to the 2/k.125 Fragment discovered by Michael Vickery.

Mother: Ambakes

Wives: Srei Srangiem (sons: Neareay Reachea; Thommo Reachea); Mneang Chan (son: Srei Reachea)

Religion: Theravada/Hinayana Buddhism

Capital: Angkor, Basan (present-day Srei Santhor), Chaktomouk (Phnom Penh)

Genealogy: Figures 51, 52, and Appendix 3

The Origin of Ponhea Yat

The origin of Ponhea Yat is an enigma and has never been fully revealed, but based on information I pieced together I will show who he was and where he came from. Ponhea Yat is the progenitor of post-Angkorian kings.

After Ponhea Yat defeated the Ayutthayan army and reclaimed Angkor, he asked his ministers and astrologers to reconstruct the genealogy of the Khmer kings but the ancestry and origin of Ponhea Yat himself was not satisfactorily revealed in the chronicle. Adhémard Leclère was not committed to the exact relationship between Ponhea Yat and his predecessors, except to say that he was of royal lineage.[7,p212] Mak Phoeun also said that the relationship between Ponhea Yat and his ancestors could not be specified.[110,p152] Khin Sok was more precise in his description of the relationship between Ponhea Yat and his ancestors. He said that Ponhea Yat succeeded Parama Sokarāja (presumably Thommasoka), whom he shared the same great-grandfather.[29,p65] He specifically said that Ponhea Yat was the son of Srī Sūriyovaṅsa XXXII, where the Roman number indicates the order of all the Khmer reigning kings but not necessarily the name of the king himself.[29,p235] The order of the reigning kings included the legendary Khmer king Ta Trasâk Paêm. If the above lineage were considered, then it would put Ta Trasâk Paêm as the great-grandfather of Ponhea Yat and Thommasoka. I believe that including Ta Trasâk Paêm among the Khmer kings has jeopardized the sequencing order of the reigns of historical Khmer monarchs. If that were the case, then Ponhea Yat had to be either the son of Soriyovong (Srī Sūriyovaṅsa) or grandson of Sithean Reachea. The Cambodian chronicles never mentioned that Sithean Reachea had a son or Soriyovong had a son who became king. Assigning Ponhea Yat's accession through the lineage of the existence of the legendary Ta Trasâk Paêm is suspect.

The origin of Ponhea Yat can be found in the *2/k.125 Fragment.* In order to fully grasp the understanding of the relationship between Ponhea Yat and previous Khmer kings, it is necessary to go back to the foundation of Ayutthaya. As discussed in Chapter 6 under Chronology of *Khmer Kings by Adhémard Leclère*, and in Chapter 8 under *The U-Thong and Suphanburi Dynasties and their Connections to Khmer Royal Bloodlines*, the kings of Ayutthaya from Ramasuan to Si Saowaphak (possibly all the way to King Narai) were all descendants from the Khmer royal bloodline of Suphanburi.

Prior to the foundation of Ayutthaya by U-Thong who reigned as King Ramathibodi, Suphanburi and Lopburi were Khmer provinces under the control of Angkor. Lopburi which was an extension of Angkor had its own cultural and administrative operation almost independent of the central power of Angkor. Lopburi was almost equaled in prestige to Angkor because it was recognized as a study center for Khmer civilization which included Buddhism and Hinduism. In their early years, Ram Khamhaeng of Sukhothai, Mangrai of the ruling houses of Chiang Saen, and Ngam Muang of Phayao/Chiang Rai went to Lopburi for their education. One of Jayavarman VII's sons, believed to be -indravarman that Coedès assigned as Nripatindravarman, was the governor of Lopburi. U-Thong was a Khmero-Thai from Lopburi. He married a Khmer princess from Suphanburi. It seemed that U-Thong married the Khmer princess to legitimize his reign as king and to challenge Angkor for supremacy in the region. His brother-in-law, Pha-ngua, was a Khmer prince from Suphanburi and brother of the Khmer princess. Ramesuan succeeded his father Ramathibodi in 1369, but he was toppled by his uncle Pha-ngua after a short reign.

After conducting a coup to remove his nephew Ramesuan, Pha-ngua took over the throne and reigned under the name Borommaracha (I) from 1370 to 1388. He was succeeded by his son, Thong Chan, but his reign lasted only a week before he was killed by his cousin, the former king Ramesuan.

After regaining his throne Ramesuan reigned until his death in 1395. Ramaracha succeeded his father Ramesuan. While Ramaracha was still reigning, Nakhon In (son of Borommaracha (I) and younger brother of Thong Chan) formed an alliance with Ramaracha's Chief Minister to overthrow his second cousin from the throne. Nakhon In reigned as Intharacha from 1409 to 1424. According to the *LP* Chronicle, Intharacha sent Ramaracha into exile to a place called *Padāgūcām*.[108,p56] Like the *LP* Chronicle, the *2/k.125 Fragment* said that Braḥ Rām Cau (Ramaracha) was sent into exile, but it specified the place as Chaktomouk. However, the text implied that it was Samtac Braḥ Paramarājādhirāj Cau (Borommaracha II) and not his father Intharacha, as recorded in the *LP* Chronicle, who sent Braḥ Rām Cau (Ramaracha) into exile. Michael Vickery identified *Padāgūcām* to be *Chaktomouk* (present-day Phnom Penh), as explained in Chapter 9 under *The U-Thong and Suphanburi Dynasties and their Connections to Khmer Royal Bloodlines*. Because the *2/k.125 Fragment* specifically mentioned the name Chaktomouk, which existed only after Ponhea Yat decreed in 1433 to rename *Prāp Jhām* to this new name,[29,p69] it can therefore be concluded that the *Fragment* was written after 1433. Borommaracha (II) succeeded his father Intharacha in 1424 and reigned until 1448.

Borommaracha (II) was succeeded by his son Trailok, who reigned under the name of Borommatrailokanat from 1448 to 1463 in Ayutthaya and from 1463 to 1488 in Phitsanulok. While Borommatrailokanat moved his seat of power from Ayutthaya to Phitsanulok to conduct a campaign against Lan Na, he put his son Intharacha (not King Intharacha who was his grandfather) in charge to rule as regent in Ayutthaya under the name of Borommaracha (III) from 1463 to 1488. Borommaracha (III) changed his name to Intharacha (II) when he reigned as king from 1488 to 1491 after the death of his father. It must be remembered that the Roman numbers were added in modern text to avoid confusions for the king's names. Samtac Braḥ Paramarājādhirāj Cau, referred in the ancient text, corresponds to Borommaracha (II) in the modern text. Bañā Braek, in the ancient text, corresponds to Intharacha (II) in the modern text. It must be remembered that Intharacha (II) was his original name before his father assigned him the name Borommaracha (III) when he became regent. When Borommaracha (III) became king he decided to switch back to his original name Intharacha (II) as his reigning name. It must be reminded that before Intharacha (I) became king, he was called Nakhon In. For later chroniclers, Intharacha (I) could easily be confused with Intharacha (II), and this latter in turn could be confounded for Nakhon In. Because of the duplication of names, it was very easy for future chroniclers to get confused and mix up the names of the kings and their order of reigns in the process. In the context of the event that took place, Cau Bañā Braek would indicate Intharacha (II).

The *2/k.125 Fragment* said that Cau Yāt was the son of Braḥ Rām Cau.[108,p11] The implication is clear. Ponhea Yat was the son of Ramaracha. In subsequent passage, the name of Cau Yāt's mother was mentioned as Naṅ Āmbakes.[108,p15] Cau Yāt was later consecrated to become Cau Bañā Yāt of Babaur.[108,p35] Babaur (present-day Baribaur) was located on the west side of the Tonlé Sap River, approximately 20 miles northwest of Kompong Chhnang. Because Ramaracha became Borommaracha II's enemy, Ramaracha's son, Cau Yāt, took side and supported King Thommasoka against the Ayutthaya's attack on Angkor. It must be remembered that Cau Yāt came from the Suphanburi line of U-Thong/Ramathibodi, and that Samtac Braḥ Paramarājādhirāj Cau came from the Suphanburi line of Pha-ngua/Borommaracha I. Cau Yāt, who came from the Khmer royal bloodline of Suphanburi of his great grandmother's side, was probably also related to the Angkor Khmer kings. His exact relationship to Thommasoka could not be determined, but it must be a close one for the Khmer king to trust him with the command of an army to fight against the Ayutthayan forces.

After Samtac Braḥ Paramarājādhirāj Cau conquered Braḥ Naga Hluoṅ (Angkor Thom), he placed his son Cau Bañā Braḥ Nagar Indr (It will be shown later that this Ayutthayan prince was the older brother of Bañā Braek, the future king Intharacha II, identified in the *LP* Chronicle as the grandson of Borommaracha II) on the throne of Angkor.[108,p9,p11] The author of the *2/k.125 Fragment* must have been confused concerning the reigning sequences and names of the kings during the ruling periods of Borommatrailokanat and Intharacha (II). While Borommatrailokanat reigned at Phisanulok during his campaign against Lan Na (Chiang Mai), he let his son Intharacha (II) rule as regent in Ayutthaya. Because Intharacha (II) was ruling in Ayutthaya, I believe the chronicler of the *2/k.125 Fragment* may have been mistaken about Intharacha (II) as being the son of Borommaracha (II). Adding to this confusion was the duplicate names of Intharacha (II) and Intharacha (I), with this latter being the son of Borommaracha (I).

Because of duplicating names which rendered the story very difficult to follow, I have developed a genealogy tree, shown in Figure 49, to help the readers understand the confusing relationships between the royal families.

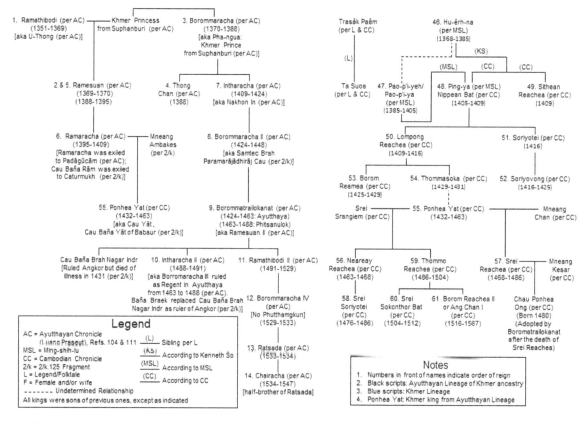

Figure 49. Relationships between Ayutthayan and Khmer Kings Discussed in the Luang Praseut Chronicle, Cambodian Chronicles, Chinese Dynastic Annals Ming-Shi-lu, and 2/k.125 Fragment of the National Library of Thailand in Bangkok

The *2/k.125 Fragment* said that Ayutthaya moved 150,000 soldiers that were supported by 100 elephants and 1000 horses to Angkor. They went on to attack Cau Yāt and his *mahā barrg* supporters in Chaktomouk.[108,p11] Vickery identified *barrg* as *Péars* or *Porrs* (man of color). The *Péars* were descendants of the *Samrès*, who were fierce warriors. Historically, the *Péars* were very loyal to Khmer kings. The *Péars* were awarded a portion of the land in the western part of Cambodia to use for their hunting ground. In the course of the battle between the Ayutthayan and Cau Yāt forces, Cau Yāt and many of his supporters were captured at Chaktomouk. After the defeat of Cau Yāt, Cau Bañā Braḥ Nagar Indr returned to Angkor. He became very ill during his trip and died after hc arrived at Angkor. The *2/k.125 Fragment* said that the Ayutthayan king was told of the death of his son (as mentioned earlier, the chronicler was mistaken. Cau Bañā Braḥ Nagar Indr was the grandson of Borommaracha II). After consultation with his ministers and generals (all the *dāv bañā*), the king put Bañā Braek (Ponhea Prék), the younger brother of the deceased prince, on the throne of Angkor.[108,p27,p56] In the Cambodian chronicles, the older brother of Bañā Braek that the Ayutthayan king put on the throne of Angkor was never mentioned. According to Adhémard Leclère, Ponhea Prék reigned at Angkor under the name Preah Eyntrea Reachea.[7,p213] This name corresponds to Intharacha (II) in the *LP* Chronicle.

The Escape of Ponhea Yat and the Defeat of the Ayutthayan Army

After receiving the news of Cau Yāt's capture, Samtac Braḥ Paramarājādhirāj Cau issued a royal order to bring the prince from Chaktomouk to Ayutthaya. Cau Yāt was warned of the king's plan by Mae Nāṅ Debdharaṇi (Mneang Tep Thoroni, which means "Venerable Lady of the Earth") and Mae Nāṅ Gaṅgā (Mneang Kongkea, which means "Lady of the Water/River") in a letter they hid in a betel leaf.[108,p13] Vickery identified Tep Thoroni as a title given to a queen of Sukhothai. It must be remembered that Intharacha (the father of Samtac Braḥ Paramarājādhirāj Cau/Borommaracha II) intervened in the Sukhothai internal affair by selecting a new king (Mahathammaracha IV) to replace the previous king, Mahathammaracha III, who was deceased in 1419.[104,p58] In this context, Sukhothai may not be totally in good term with Ayutthaya. Mneang Tep Thoroni may possibly be the wife of the deceased king Mahathammaracha III and she may not approve of the new Sukhothai king that Ayutthaya had selected to replace her husband. It was possibly in her interest to see Cau Yāt escape and took arms against Ayutthaya. Cau Yāt was put on a boat without being shackled, possibly as a respect of him being a prince or as not to raise any suspicion that he was taken prisoner bounding for Ayutthaya. Khun Nagar Jaiy was responsible for transporting and taking care of Cau Yāt until he arrived in Ayutthaya. Cau Yāt waited until nighttime, under the cover of darkness, to slip out of the boat into the water and swam away to safety. He went to meet Khun Blāpblājaīy, a friend of his parents, for protection. According to Vickery, Khun Blāpblājǎy was also mentioned in the *Ang Eng Fragment* as the protector of Ponhea Yat.[108,p15] It was during the exchange of information and questions with Khun Blāpblājǎy that Cau Yāt revealed Braḥ Rām and Nāṅ Āmbakes were his parents. Khun Blāpblājǎy sent Cau Yāt to meet the *barrg* tribe. By all indication, it seemed that Khun Blāpblājaīy was a powerful man and well connected. An agreement was made to have Cau Yāt in control of the Cheung Prey region (located approximately 50 miles north of Phnom Penh in present-day Kampong Cham). With the help of the *barrg* tribe and his chief supporters, Cau Yāt was able to mount successful attacks against the Ayutthayan forces and defeat them at Chaktomouk (Phnom Penh), Longvek, Pursat, and Braḥ Nagar Hluoṅ (Angkor Thom).[108,p33,p35,p41] The *2/k.125 Fragment* mentioned the following names and/or regions of Cau Yāt's supporter:[108,p37] *Ni Jāṅ Dòṅ, Pā Viset, Hmu'n Treṭ Saṅsār, Hmu'n Ṇarā*, governor of *bejrindr* (undetermined place), *mo'aṅ Lovek, mo'aṅ Kompong baisrī* (undetermined place), *mo'aṅ Trapeang blaṅ* (Trapeang Phlong, located at the present-day border between Cambodia and Vietnam in the Parrot's Beak region), *mo'aṅ Babaur* (located on the west side of the Tonlé Sap River at about 20 miles north west of Kompong Chnang), *mo'aṅ koe* (undetermined place), and *mo'aṅ katò* (undetermined place).

Pā Viset must have been an astrologer/Brahman priest based on the fact that he performed the consecration ceremony on Cau Yāt to become Cau Baña Yāt of Babaur. The ceremony elevated the prince to a higher position, equivalent to a king.[108,p35] The account in the *2/k.125 Fragment* stopped at the defeat of the Ayutthayan army by the forces of Cau Yāt. The remaining small portion of the story continued with the battle between Ayutthaya and Sukhothai.

The Aftermath of the Ayutthayan Defeat and the Relocation of the Khmer Capital to Basan

The *LP* Chronicle mentioned about the occupation of Angkor in 1431 and its abandonment one year later. According to David K. Wyatt, the *LP* Chronicle never talked about the defeat of the Ayutthayan army at the hand of Ponhea Yat. It seems that the omission of this historical event was intentional.

Wyatt gave the following brief description of the Ayutthayan occupation, looting, and subsequent abandonment of Angkor:[104,p5]

> *Finally in 1431-1432, Borommaracha II sent a major expedition against Angkor that succeeded in taking the city. The capital was looted – and Borommaracha's son was briefly installed as the vassal ruler of the state, comparable in status to Mahathammaracha IV of Sukhothai. Soon the city was abandoned, and the heir of the last Angkorean king fled to found a new kingdom in the region of Phnom Penh far to the east.*

The last Angkorian king mentioned above by Wyatt was intended to signify Ponhea Yat. It is not accurate to say that Ponhea Yat fled "to found a new kingdom" because the kingdom had never disappeared. When Ponhea Yat left Angkor to Basan, he was still king of Cambodia without only the control of Angkor. It was Ponhea Prèk, the son of Borommaracha II, and the Ayutthayan army's turn to flee Angkor when Ponhea Yat defeated the Ayutthayan army a year later. It was for different reasons that Ponhea Yat decided to abandon Angkor after the defeat of the Ayutthayan army, which I had elaborated in Chapter 7.

Before the discovery of the *2/k.125 Fragment,* the story of Ponhea Yat's conquest over Ponhea Prék and the Ayutthayan army in Angkor was mostly revealed through oral accounts and Cambodian chronicles. According to Khin Sok, Ponhea Yat took the widow of Indarājā (Eyntrea Reachea/Intharacha) named Srī Srañīem (ស្រីស្រង់ឹម) as his secondary wife.[29,p65] Srī Srañīem (Srei Srangiem) could not have been the widow of Ponhea Prék/Eyntrea Reachea because he later became King Intharacha (II) of Ayutthaya. Srei Srangiem had to be the widow of Cau Baña Braḥ Nagar Indr (Chau Ponhea Preah Nokor Eyntrea), the older brother of Ponhea Prék, who first reigned at Angkor before he died of illness. With the consultation of his ministers, Ponhea Yat made a decision to leave Angkor to Basan. One of the reasons for his departure was stated that it would be hard to defend Angkor against another Ayutthayan invasion for lack of resources and inhabitants.

The war with Ayutthaya had brought tremendous distresses and miseries to the Cambodian people living in the Angkor region. The war with Ayutthaya had scared people and it would be hard to convince the citizens around Angkor to remain in place without the full commitment of the government to defend the region from another Ayutthaya's invasion. It was probably due to the hardship of the aftermath of the war, in combination with the reasons discussed in Chapter 7, that Ponhea Yat decided to move his capital to Basan (present day Srei Santhor located approximately 30 km north east of Phnom Penh). It was very possible that Ponhea Yat chose Basan as his new capital because of his familiarity with this region during his resistance and fight against the Ayutthayan army, and most of all it was centrally located. It must be reminded that the southeastern part of Cambodia, now commonly known as Kampuchea Krom, was still a Cambodian territory before the Vietnamese annexed it in the 18th century. The king and his ministers left Angkor in 1431 AD. It was probably in Basan that his secondary wife, Srei Srangiem, gave birth to a son named Braḥ Nrāyaṇarājā (នារាយណ៍រាជា, Noreay Reachea). The Cambodian chronicles said that he was born in the year of the Pig of the third decade,[29,p65] which according to my calculation would correspond to 792/793 Cula or 1431/1432 AD. Ponhea Yat and his government remained at Basan for over a year, and because of floods that made life untenable and governing the country very difficult, Ponhea Yat decided to relocate his capital one more time.

The Relocation of the Khmer Capital to Phnom Penh

The Cambodian chronicles said that Ponhea Yat left Basan to Chaktomouk in 1978 of the Buddhist era, 1356 Saka, 796 Cula, in the year of the Tiger of the sixth the decade, in the month of Bisākha, on Tuesday of the ninth day of the waxing moon,[29,pp67-68] which according to my calculation would have corresponded to 18 May 1434.

Upon arriving in Chaktomouk, the king commissioned his ministers to prepare the terrain for major construction projects to make the city more livable. Canals were built to divert the flow of water to the royal palace. River bank levels were raised to prevent flooding, ponds were dug, new market areas were constructed, and the Phnom Penh hill that had not been upkept was renovated. Ponhea Yat decreed that the four confluent rivers called *Prāp Jhām (ព្រាបឈាម)* be renamed *Tonlé Chaktomouk Bopear (ទន្លេចតុមុខបុព្ផា)*.[29,p69] *Prāp* means "to put down" or "to conquer." According to Michael Vickery, *Prāp Jhām* means "to put down the Cham" because the area was known as the *Cham River*. He demonstrated that the word *padāgūcām* (the location where King Intharacha of Ayutthaya sent his second cousin King Ramaracha and father of Ponhea Yat into exile after he had overthrown him), mentioned in the *LP* Chronicle, came from the words *Prāp Jhām*. Chaktomouk became synonymous with Phnom Penh.

When Ponhea Yat moved to Phnom Penh, the Sri Lankan monks who served the king in Angkor and Basan also followed him throughout his displacements. During his reign in Phnom Penh, Ponhea Yat left a lasting legacy by establishing five Buddhist learning centers (wats). It seemed that two Sri Lanka monks, Buddhaghosa Maha Thera (ពុទ្ធឃោសាមហាថេរៈ) and Assajita Maha Thera (អស្សជិតៈមហាថេរៈ), had a lot of influences on King Ponhea Yat. Hema Goonatilake reported that after the death of Buddhaghosa, the king built Wat Buddhaghosachar in his memory.[89] This pagoda is now better known as Wat Chen Dom Dek (pagoda of the Chinese iron worker). Similarly, after the death of Assajita, the king built a new pagoda called Wat Bodhilom in his honor. This pagoda is now better known as Wat Unnalom. The king built three other pagodas — Wat Koh, Wat Dhammalankara, and Wat Lanka. The original Wat Koh — not the present one by the same name currently standing in Phnom Penh — had disappeared with only a Bodhi tree remaining. Wat Dhammalankara had also disappeared. Ponhea Yat built Wat Lanka in honor of Sri Lanka to house the monks from Sri Lanka, and also to use it as the library to keep the Tripitaka (known as the three "baskets" of Buddha's teaching that includes a *Sutra Pitaka,* a *Vinaya Pitaka,* and an *Abhidharma Pitaka*). Goonatilake mentioned that according to the royal chronicles, after the five wats were built, King Ponhea Yat moved the golden statue of the Buddha, that was brought from Sri Lanka and housed at Wat Pheam Phlom (near present-day *Phsar Chah,* old market), to Wat Unnalom. There was a royal procession for the ceremony with Ponhea Yat carrying the statue of the Buddha himself. He enshrined the statue at Wat Unnalom and called it *Preah Sokhalin.* The statue has disappeared from Wat Unnalom and its whereabouts is unknown.

A few year later after the king had settled in Phnom Penh, his secondary wives Mneang Chan (ម្នាងច័ន្ទ) gave birth to a son named Srī Rājā (ស្រីរាជា, Srei Reachea) in 1439/1440 (year of the Goat of the first decade). Srei Srangiem gave birth to a second son named Bañā Dhamma, also known as Thommo Reachea (ធម្មរាជា), in 1441/1442 (year of the Rooster of the third decade). Ponhea Yat abdicated in 1463 in favor of his first born son Neareay Reachea. According to Khin Sok,[29,p73] Ponhea Yat passed away four years later in 1467 (year of the Dog of the eighth decade, in the month of Pisak, on the fifth day of the waning moon). Khin Sok said that he died at the age of seventy, based on his reign starting in 1417. I believe that assigning 1417 as the starting year of Ponhea Yat's reign is incorrect, because during that time Angkor was still ruled by Soriyovong. Ponhea Yat was cremated and his ashes entombed in the stupa (cetiya) located in the north-west of Phnom Daun Penh (present-day Wat Phnom). The genealogy of Ponhea Yat is shown in Figure 50. It was during his reign that the prefixes *Chau Ponhea*, which came from Ayutthaya, were introduced to Cambodia. Prior to this period there were no Khmer monarchs utilizing these prefixes.

The name Phnom Penh was not originally meant for the capital, but for the land that Lady Penh built into a mound to honor and preserve the statues of the "Buddha" that she found in the trunk of a Koki (តើ) tree floating on the river. According to the legend, Lady Penh was a rich and pious widow living at the confluent and effluent of two great rivers. Nowadays, they are called the Mekong/Tonlé Sap for the confluent rivers and Mekong/Bassac for the effluent rivers. One year during a great flooding season, Lady Penh saw a trunk of a Koki tree floating and swirling in the river near the bank of her house. She called on the neighbors to help her pull the tree trunk out of the river. In the trunk, Lady Penh found a bronze statue of a four-faced "Buddha" and a stone statue of a long-haired "Buddha" holding a club in one hand and a conch in another hand.[29,p70] I believe the two statues represented Brahma and not Buddha, because Brahma was always portrayed with four faces to represent the four Vedic scriptures in the Hindu religion. He was also seen with four hands, each one holding different instruments such as a club, a conch, a serrated disc, and beads. According to the legend, the hill was completed in 1372 and the local people named it Phnom Daun Penh (the hill of grandma Penh) in honor of Lady Penh. The name was later shortened to Phnom Penh.

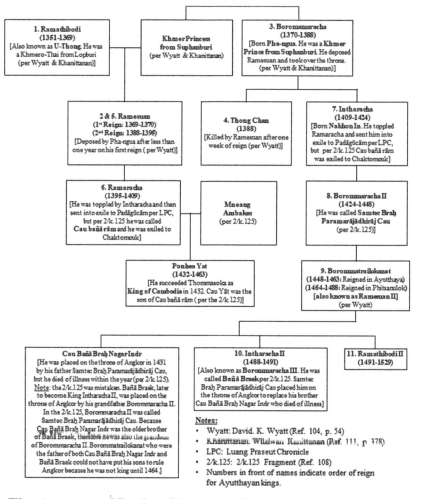

Figure 50. The Ancestry of Ponhea Yat According to the Luang Praseut Chronicle and the 2/k.125 Fragment Discovered by Michael Vickery in the National Library of Thailand in Bangkok in 1971

At the time, King Ponhea Yat founded his capital city near the hill of Daun Penh in 1434. The confluent and effluent of the Mekong/Tonlé Sap/Bassac Rivers were called Prap Chheam (ប្រាបឈាម, which means "covering with blood of the defeated enemy") or Prap Cham (defeated Cham), but the king issued a royal order to rename the rivers Tonlé Chaktomouk (it literally means "four-faced river"). The rivers were renamed because the Mekong River met the Tonlé Sap River and then separated again into two separate rivers, Mekong River and Tonlé Bassac River. It was such a coincidence that the statue of the four-faced "Buddha" was found at Chaktomouk. Realizing that the hill of Daun Penh was in disrepair, Ponhea Yat ordered the provincial governor, Chao Ponhea Decho (of present-day Samrong Tong province), to have the holes around the hill filled up and the banks at the river rose to prevent flooding. A pond was formed as a result of the soil removed from the area. The pond was called Boeung Decho. A Grand Market, now known as Phsar Thmei (New Market), was built by the French in the 1930s after the water was drained from the pond. Ponhea Yat ordered Oknha Phlong to build a canal to supply the Royal Palace with water from the river. The canal was called Prèk Oknha Phlong (the Stream of Oknha Phlong). In its place now stands the garden from east to west facing the Phnom Penh train station.

56   Neareay Reachea I (1463-1468) នារាយណ៍រាជា

Transliterated Name: Nārāy(ṇ) Rājā I
Other Names: Narayanaraja, Noreay Reameathipadey, Chao Ponhea Gamkhat
Style Name: Preah Bat Samdach Sdach Preah Reach Ongka Preah Neareay Reacheathireach Reameathipadey[7,p223]
Accession: 1463
Born: Circa 1431-1432/Deceased: 1468 (Died of illness)
Relationship: Eldest son of Ponhea Yat
Mother: Srei Srangiem (Ayutthayan)
Mother: Srei Srangiem (Ayutthayan)
Capital: Phnom Penh
Genealogy: Appendix 3

Neareay Reachea I was the oldest son of Ponhea Yat and Srei Srangiem. As mentioned earlier, Srei Srangiem was the widow of Cau Bañā Braḥ Nagar Indr (Chau Ponhea Preah Nokor Eynt) — the oldest son of Samtec Braḥ Paramarājādhirāj Cau (Borommaracha II). Braḥ Nagar Indr who was placed on the throne of Angkor in 1431 by his grandfather Borommaracha II died of illness within a year of his reign at Angkor. He was succeeded by his younger brother, Indarājā (Ponhea Prèk = Eyntrea Reachea), who was also known as Borommaracha III when he was a regent but changed it to Intharacha (II) when he became king.

According to the Cambodian Chronicle, Neareay Reachea I succeeded Ponhea Yat in 1463 at the age of 33.[29,p73] If Neareay Reachea I were born in 1432, as was mentioned earlier in the chronicles,[29,p65] he would be only 31 years old in 1463 and not 33. As soon as he acceded to the throne, the king elevated his 25 year-old half-brother Srei Reachea to the rank of Maha Uparaja. The chronicles said that before Neareay Reachea's enthronement, his wife Kaev gave birth to a son named Srei Soriyotei in 1459/1460 (year of the Hare of the first decade, of Cula 821/822, of 2003 of Buddhist era).[29,p73,p24] Neareay Reachea I fell gravely ill after five years of reign. He passed away in 1468 (year of the Rat of the tenth decade, in the month of Pisak, of Cula 829/830, and 2012 Buddhist Era).

The Period of Usurpations and Fraticidal War: Three Kings Reigning Simultaneously

57   Srei Reachea (1468-1486) ស្រីរាជា

Transliterated Name: Srī Rājā
Other Name: Reamea Thipadei

Style Name: Samdach Preah Srey Reacheathireach Reameathipadey [7,p223]
Accession: 1468
Born: Circa 1439-1440/Deceased: 1487
Relationship: Son of Ponhea Yat and Half-brother of Neareay Reachea I
Mother: Chan
Wife: Mneang Kesar
Religion: Theravada/Hinayana Buddhism
Capital: Phnom Penh and Kampong Siem
Genealogy: Appendix 3

Srei Reachea was the son of Ponhea Yat and Mneang Chan. According to the chronicle, he was born eight years after his half-brother Neareay Reachea I (year of the Goat of the first decade), which would have been in 1439-1440. The chronicles stated that he succeeded Neareay Reachea I in 1468 at the age of 30.[29,p7] Because he was born in 1439-1440, he would have been only 29 years old at the most when he acceded to the throne.

In 1471, Srei Reachea ordered the construction of a stupa on the north-east side of Phnom Daun Penh to house the ashes of his deceased half-brother, King Neareay Reachea I. After seven years of reign, the king convened a meeting that included royal families, noble families, and high dignitaries to discuss the affairs of the state and its relationship with Ayutthaya. The chronicles said that this important meeting took place in 1475/1476 (year of the Goat of the seventh decade, in the month of Kartika, on the tenth day of the waning moon).[29,p76] Srei Reachea gave a speech and asked these important families for their support in a proposed war against Ayutthaya. He wanted to avenge his ancestors for the misery that Ayutthaya had inflicted on the Cambodian people during its occupation of Angkor. He also wanted to reclaim the lost provinces that Ayutthaya took from Cambodia,[29,p77] which stretched from Nokor Reach Seima (នគររាជសីមា — present-day Nokhon Ratchasima or Korat, Thailand) to Baschimborei (បស្ចឹមបុរី — present-day Prachinburi, Thailand). In addition to the above mentioned two provinces, the lost provinces would have included Srah Kaeo (ស្រះកែវ — present-day Sa Kaeo, Thailand), Chanborei (ចន្ទបុរី — present-day Chanthaburi, Thailand), and Rayang (រយ៉ង — present-day Rayong, Thailand), and Krat (ក្រាត់ — present-day Trat, Thailand). They all supported the king in his call to war with Ayutthaya. Afterward, the king conferred to his half-brother Thommo Reachea (also brother of Neareay Reachea I) the title Maha Uparaja.

The chronicle stated that the king divided his strategy to attack Ayutthaya into six forces.[29,p77] Srei Reachea himself would lead the land army. He nominated Chao Hva Tolahac Kaev (ចៅហ្វាទទ្បរ កែវ) to be in charge of the navy, with the responsibility to recruit 30,000 soldiers from the provinces of Bassac/Srok Khleang/Srok Trang (បាសាក់/ស្រុកឃ្លាំង/ស្រុកត្រាំង — present-day Bassac in Soc Trang, Vietnam), Preah Trapeang (ព្រះត្រពាំង — present-day Tra Vinh, Vietnam), and Kramuon Sar/Reachea (ក្រមួនសរ/រាជា — present-day Rach Gia, Vietnam). Oknha Chakrei Maen (ឧកញ្ញាចក្រី មែន) was in charge of the front guard forces; a royal family member named Aphey Tos (អភ័យទោស) was to lead the right flank forces; Preah Suktoat (ព្រះ សុទោត់) was in charge of the left flank forces; and Oknha Kralahom Ming (ឧកញ្ញាក្រឡាហោម មីង) was given the responsibility of commanding the rear guard forces.

After consulting with the royal astrologer, it was determined that the most favorable time to launch an attack on Ayutthaya would be in Cula 837, in the year of the Goat of the seventh decade, in the month of Bos (បុស្ស), and on the fifth day of the waxing moon, which would correspond to 2 December 1475. With his army, the king left Phnom Penh in 1475 in the direction of Pursat (ពោធិ៍សាត់) and going through Battambang (បាត់ដំបង), Nong Sarikar (នោងសារិការ), Srah Kaeo, and Stung Ba Kraung (ស្ទឹងបាក្រុង). He left Thommo Reachea in charge of the capital. The king instructed Chao Hva Tolahac Kaev (ចៅហ្វាទទ្បរ កែវ) to retake Chanborei and Rayang (Krat was not mentioned because it may still be part of the Khmer provinces at the time). The general took the sea route by passing through Kampot (កំពត). He fought the battle at Rayang and killed the governor and all his subordinates. After the battle had been won, the Khmer population welcomed the Khmer forces that had liberated them from the control of Ayutthaya. After securing Rayang, the Khmer general continued his conquest over Chanborei. He gathered all the Khmer and Ayutthayan families to come under his control. On the other fronts, Oknha Chakrei Maen and his forces had reconquered the lost Khmer provinces of Nokor Reach Seima and Baschimborei (presumably Srah Kaeo also even though it was not specifically mentioned in the Cambodian Chronicles.[29,p77] The governors and their subordinates were captured. Four thousand Ayutthayan families were gathered and put under the control of the Khmer forces. Oknha Chakrei Maen waited for the king forces to join him.

The king arrived in Baschimborei and set his camp there in preparation for an offensive against Ayutthaya. Finally, he launched an attack against Ayutthaya and had the capital city surrounded. In an attempt to take over the city with five hundred of his soldiers, Oknha Chakrei Maen got too close to the rampart and was killed. Unable to take the city after many attempts, the king ordered his forces to fall back and return to Baschimborei to regroup.

In the meantime, the nephew of the king named Srei Soriyotei (son of Neareay Reachea I) who resided in Phnom Penh took advantage of the king's absence to mount a rebellion. He gathered his supporters and recruited trusted slaves (probably slaves working in the royal palace) to form his own rebellion forces. They went on to oppress the population living in the provinces of Thbong Khmum (ត្បូងឃ្មុំ), Romduol (រំដួល), Svay Teab (ស្វាយទៀប), Ba Phnom (បាភ្នំ), and Prey Veng (ព្រៃវែង); all located on the eastern side of the Mekong River. After he subdued the population, Srei Soriyotei assigned his own governors to form an army. With his new recruits he attacked the provinces north of Phnom Penh. He took over the provinces of Kampong Siem (កំពង់សៀម — present-day Kampong Cham), Stung Trâng (ស្ទឹងត្រង់), Cheung Prey (ជើងព្រៃ — present-day Kampong Cham), and Baray. It is my belief that Srei Soriyotei's betrayal toward the king may be partly due to jealousy because he thought he should have succeeded his father Nearay Reachea I.

Learning of Srei Soriyotei's betrayal, Thommo Reachea made a decision to dispatch his forces from Phnom Penh to take control of the provinces west of Tonlé Sap and Bassac River. Because the governors of the provinces of Peam Mé Sâ (ពាមមេស — present day Tien Giang, Vietnam), Prei Kor (ព្រៃគរ — present-day Gia Dinh/Cho Lon/Tan Anh/Tay Ninh province surrounding Saigon/Ho Chi Minh City), Baria/Preah Suorkea (បារៀ/ព្រះស្គួត — present-day Ba Ria-Vung Tau, Vietnam), and Daung Nay (ដូងណាយ — present-day Dong Nai and Phuoc Long, Vietnam) were on a campaign with the king against Ayutthaya, Thommo Reachea assigned his own governors to replace them. Thommo Reachea sent his emissary to inform the king, who camped at Baschimborei, about the decision he made to secure the country. He also told the king about Srei Soriyotei's rebellion and his control of the provinces northeast of Phnom Penh. He recommended the king to attack Srei Soriyotei from the north.

Before embarking on a campaign against his nephew, the king gave the final instructions to his generals in the war against Ayutthaya. He told Chau Hva Tolahac Kaev to stand his ground in Rayang and Chanborei in preparation for the Ayutthayan forces coming from the sea. He ordered the governor of Battambang, Oknha Mnometrei Phim (ឧកញ៉ាម្នោមេត្រីភិម), to take 5,000 soldiers to Neang Rong (នាងរង — present-day Buriram, Thailand) to prevent the Ayutthayan army from crossing into Khmer territory. Having given his instructions, the king marched toward Amrak Kirinbaur (អម្រាក់គិរិន្ធបុរ — present-day Kampong Chhnang) to face the forces of Srei Soriyotei in the month of Phalkun (ផល្គុន) in 1475. Unable to overcome the stronger forces of the king, Srei Soriyotei withdrew his forces and went to camp in Srei Santhor. I believe the chronicler made an error concerning the name Srei Santhor, because at that time the place was still called Basan. Chronologically, Srei Santhor did not exist yet. The name was changed to Srei Sâ Chhor — white lady standing — by Srei Sokontha Bat, son of Thommo Reachea, in honor to his favorite concubine Neang Sâ, who was better known as Neak Mneang Peou. Subsequently, the name was changed one more time to Srei Santhor. Srei Reachea defeated Srei Soriyotei and regained all the north provinces that were under the control of his nephew. Realizing that he would not be able to win a battle against the king, Srei Soriyotei resorted to a campaign of terrors. He went searching to punish the mothers, fathers, wives, and children of the soldiers who served under the king.

At that time, it was very fortunate for Cambodia that the king of Ayutthaya could not take advantage of the civil war between Srei Reachea and Srei Soriyotei. Ayutthaya itself was at war with the Môn kingdom of Hangsavati (located in present-day Myarnma/Burma). The campaign of terrors that Srei Soriyotei inflicted on the families of the soldiers serving the king had finally affected the king's soldiers. Fearing for the safety of their loved ones, the king's soldiers started to leave their positions and joined the army of Srei Soriyotei. Because of a great number of soldiers leaving his army, Srei Reachea knew that he could not continue the war against his treacherous nephew effectively. He asked his generals to hold the position while he would go to Phnom Penh to recruit more soldiers to replenish his army. Because Ayutthaya was busy fighting the kingdom of Hangsavati, Srei Reachea felt that Ayutthaya would not be a threat against Cambodia. The king asked Chao Hva Tolahac Kaev to bring his forces and all the boats from Bassac and Preah Trapeang to join him in Kampong Siem.

While the king was planning his war strategy against his nephew, Thommo Reachea who was acting as regent in Phnom Penh had a plan of his own. He ordered his ministers and generals to protect the capital and royal palace with troop reinforcement to prevent any unforeseen attack from Srei Reachea. He worried that he may anger the king because he had sent all the king's jewelries, wives, concubines, and servants back to the king, except for the *Preah Khan Reach* (Sacred Sword) and the royal regalia. Thommo Reachea ordered his generals to position their troops in Oudong to defend against an attack from the north; in Khsach Kandal (ក្សាច់កណ្ដាល) to protect against an attack from the east; and in Stung Kreang Ponlai (ស្ទឹងគ្រាំ ៨ពន្លៃ) to stop an attack coming from the water. Thommo Reachea dispatched his emissary to deliver a letter he wrote to the king about the royal jewelries, wives, and servants he sent to him. He did not want the king to come back to Phnom Penh. In a subtle way, he wrote a letter to the king informing him that if he were to come back to the city, he would not be able to withstand the attack by Srei Soriyotei from the north. He also told the king not to worry about the provinces in the south and in the west, because he had the situation under control by ordering his generals to defend them. He added a caveat saying that he gave a specific order to the soldiers on both sides not to communicate with each other. Thommo Reachea's message to the king was clear. He wanted to convey to the king that he was in charge. He implicitly told the king that he would not be welcomed into the capital anymore. It was an act of rebellion and betrayal on the part of Thommo Reachea. It was obvious that now Thommo Reachea had a taste of real power, he wanted to be king of Cambodia. The king was so incensed after reading the Uparaja's letter that he wanted to immediately mount a campaign against his half-brother. He calmed down after listening to the advice of his generals telling him that it would be foolish to fight Thommo Reachea and Srei Soriyorei at the same time. It would be even worse if the two princes decided to join forces fighting against the king.

In preparation for a possible long grinding war, the king ordered his soldiers to build a fortress in Kampong Siem to serve as his headquarters. He told the governors to control the western provinces of Ralā Ph-īe (រលាផ្អៀ], Rolea Pha-ea in the present-day district by the same name located in the province of Kampong Chhnang), Amrak Kitinbaur, Pursat, Battambang, Neang Rong, and all the way to the provinces taken by Ayutthaya. For the northern provinces, he told them to look after Kampong Siem, Choeung Prey, Kauk Seh (គោកសេះ, it later became Baray), Stung Trâng (ស្ទឹងត្រង់), Kampong Svay, and all the way to Kauk Khan (គោកខ្ជ, present-day Sisaket in Thailand), Soren (សុរិន្ទ), Singkeak (សិង្កាក់), and the frontier of Laos. The Cambodian chronicles mentioned the following additional provinces that were in preparation for the war:[29,p247] Longvek (លង្វែក), Ammaroat Borei (អំមរតបុរី), Krako (ក្រកូ), Krâng (ក្រង), Mong (មោង), Reussei Ñor (ឫស្សីញ៉ូរ), Peam (ពាម), Seima (សីមា), Mongkolborei (មង្គលបុរី), Rayang (រយ៉ង), Barin (បារិន), Kauk Kar Nong (គោកការនាង), Anlong Reach (អន្លង់រាជ), Prohm Tep (ព្រំទេព), Prey Kdei (ព្រៃក្ដី), Staung (ស្ទោង), Chikreng

(ជីព្រែង), Roluous (រលួស), Siem Reap (សៀមរាប), Mlou Prei (ម្លូព្រៃ), Sangkat (សង្កាត់), Thnot (ត្នោត), Teuk Cho (ទឹកជោរ).

The chronicles said that Srei Soriyotei was crowned king in Srei Santhor in 1477.[29,p82] It was an error on the part of the chronicler to use the name Srei Santhor because in 1477 the place was still called Basan. Not to be outdone, the ministers of Thommo Reachea organized for the enthronement of the prince. The chronicles said that he was crowned king in Phnom Penh in 1478 (year of the Dog of the tenth decade).[29,p82] For the first time Cambodia had three kings reigning simultaneously. The legitimate king, Srei Reachea, controlled the northern territory with its capital in Kampong Siem. The rebelled nephew, King Srei Soriyotei, controlled the eastern and southeastern territories with its capital in Basan (Srei Santhor). The treacherous half-brother, King Thommo Reachea, controlled the western and southern territories with its capital in Phnom Penh. Cambodia was thus divided into three zones where nephew and brothers were fighting to rule the country.

In 1480 (year of the Rat of the second decade), Mneang Kesar bore Srei Reachea a son. He was named Chau Ponhea Ong. The war for control of the country between the three kings had gone on for too long with no end in sight. The war started between Srei Reachea and Srei Soriyotei in 1476 (year of the Monkey of the eighth decade) and then spread to include Thommo Reachea. By 1486 (year of the Snake of the seventh decade) the war was still raging. The war brought a lot of misery and hardship to the people. Realizing that the war may not end any time soon, Thommo Reachea decided to appeal to the king of Ayutthaya, the enemy of Cambodia, to come to rescue the country. The Ayutthayan king was mentioned in the chronicle as Mahā Cakrabattrādhirāja. I have identified him as Borommatrailokanat (also known as Ramesuan II). Thommo Reachea invited Borommatrailokanat to bring his army to Cambodia. He was asked to play the role of arbiter between the conflicts of the three Khmer kings. Thommo Reachea claimed that he asked for Borommatrailokanat's help because he was concerned for the suffering of the Khmer people that lived miserably under the unending civil war. He wanted the Ayutthayan king to help stop the war and restore the country back to its prosperity. In lieu of Thommo Reachea's claim, it is necessary to analyze why he asked for Borommatrailokanat's help. Before she was married to Ponhea Yat, Thommo Reachea's mother was the widow of Borommatrailokanat's son. Considering the above connection, Thommo Reachea must have had a closer relationship with Borommatrailokanat than Srei Reachea had with this Ayutthayan king. Srei Reachea had no relationship with Borommatrailokanat from his Khmer mother's side, except through his father Ponhea Yat. As mentioned earlier, Ponhea Yat came from the side of his great grandmother, a Khmer princess from Suphanburi who married U-Thong. According to the *2/k.125 Fragment*, Ponhea Yat's father was King Ramaracha who was exiled to Chaktomouk by Intharacha, the grandfather of Borommatrailokanat. In this context, Ponhea Yat was enemy with Borommaracha II as well as Borommatrailokanat. By asking the Ayutthayan king for help and be the arbiter to resolve the Khmer conflict, Thommo Reachea knew that he would be the favorite to come out better than his half-brother and his nephew.

After Borommatrailokanat arrived with his army in Phnom Penh, Thommo Reachea and the Ayutthayan king took their forces to Kampong Siem to surround the fortress where Srei Reachea resided. After accepting the terms and explanations from Srei Reachea's emissaries, Borommatrailokanat and Thommo Reachea invited Srei Reachea to join them to discuss and resolve the problems. They asked each other for forgiveness. They instructed for the construction of a fortress in Oudong to be used for a conference to settle the war problem. After the construction had finished, the three kings went to meet at Oudong in 1486 [year of the Snake of the seventh decade, in the month of Meak (មាឃ), on the second day of the waning moon]. They convened a meeting in the fortress and they all agreed that Srei Soriyotei needed to be present also. The three kings sent an emissary to invite Srei Soriyotei to join them at Oudong, but in his grand illusion Srei Soriyotei wanted to continue the war because he thought he could beat the Ayutthayan army. Because his generals did not support his decision, Srei Soriyotei finally came to his senses and agreed to meet the other three kings at Oudong.

Srei Soriyotei was well received by the three kings, but as soon as the meeting started Borommatrailokanat demanded to take Srei Reachea and Srei Soriyotei back with him to Ayutthaya. He wanted Thommo Reachea the sole ruler of Cambodia. He concluded that leaving Srei Reachea and Srei Soriyotei in Cambodia would not be in the best interest of Cambodia. He said that troubles would start again once the Ayutthayan army returned home. It caught the two Khmer kings by surprise, especially Srei Reachea because in his naivety he thought that Borommatrailokanat may restore him as king of Cambodia again. Without Srei Reachea knowing it, but he should have suspected it, Thommo Reachea had an understanding with Borommatrailokanat that he would be chosen to reign as the sole ruler in Cambodia. The trap had already been set and it was too late for either Srei Reachea or Srei Soriyotei to do anything against Borommatrailokanat's decision. The Ayutthayan king took Srei Reachea, Srei Soriyotei, their families, their servants, and all their ministers back with him to Ayutthaya. He also demanded Thommo Reachea to return all the Ayutthayan families that Srei Reachea had brought to Cambodia during his campaign against Ayutthaya. Thommo Reachea complied with all the demands.

According to the Cambodian chronicles, Srei Reachea did not live long after he arrived in Ayutthaya. He died of grave illness from a broken heart as he felt humiliated by the dupery of Borommatrailokanat and Thommo Reachea. However, foul play could not be ruled out because Srei Reachea was not known to have any health issue when he left Cambodia. The chronicles said that he died in 1487, corresponding to the year of the Horse of the eighth decade, in the month of Phalkun, and on the eighth day of the waxing moon.[29,p94] In his last will before he died, Srei Reachea asked Borommatrailokanat to take good care of his son Chau Ponhea Ong. The chronicles said that the Ayutthayan king took the Khmer prince under his wing and gave his daughter, from his concubine Preah Tepi, away in marriage in 1490 (year of the Dog of the second decade).[29,p94] He was renamed to Preah Sithean Reachea. The chronicles said that he was twenty three years old. The royal chronicler must have made a mistake concerning either the age or the year of the marriage of the Khmer prince. If he were married in 1490, then Chau Ponhea Ong would have been only ten years old, which was not unusual in ancient time because the marriage was meant only to assign the couple to get married in the future. For Chau Ponhea Ong to be twenty three years old the marriage had to occur in the year of the Dog of the fourth decade and not of the second decade, which would have occurred after the death of Borommatrailokanat and under the reign of Ramathibodi II.

58   Srei Soriyotei (1477-1486) ស្រីសុរិយោទ័យ

Transliterated Name: Srī Suryodǎy
Other Name: Chao Ponhea Tieraraja
Accession: 1477
Born: Circa 1458/Deceased: 1488
Relationship: Son of Neareay Reachea I and nephew of Srei Reachea
Religion: Theravada/Hinayana Buddhism
Capital: Srei Santhor
Genealogy: Appendix 3

Srei Soriyotei was the son of Neareay Reachea I. He took advantage of King Srei Reachea's absence from Phnom Penh during his campaign against Ayutthaya to rebel against his uncle. With his rebelled army he controlled the eastern and southeastern territories of Cambodia. He was crowned king at Basan (present-day Srei Santhor) by his supporters in 1477 (year of the Rooster of the ninth decade). He reigned under the style name *Preah Bat Samdech Preah Srei Soriyotei Reacheathireach*. He ordered his generals to defend the provinces of Sambaur (សំបូរ), Thbong Khmum, Ba Phnom, Baria, Daung Nay, and other provinces neighboring Champa.

After ten years of battles between the forces of Srei Soriyotei, Srei Reachea, and Thommo Reachea, the war was still at a stalemate. It required the intervention of the Ayutthayan king, Borommatrailokanat, by the invitation of Thommo Reachea to terminate the war. With his army, Borommatrailokanat landed in Phnom Penh as a show of force to end the war, but in reality it was to support Thommo Reachea to remain on the throne of Cambodia. Even though Srei Soriyotei came from the same family branch as Thommo Reachea (with Srei Srangiem as the mother of Thommo Reachea and grandmother of Srei Soriyotei), it could be speculated that Borommatrailokanat may be in better and closer relationship with Thommo Reachea than with Srei Soriyotei.

As a condition to end the war, Thommo Reachea agreed to allow Borommatrailokanat to take both Srei Reachea and Srei Soriyotei back to Ayutthaya. Soon after the death of Srei Reachea that Srei Soriyotei fell gravely ill also. According to Khin Sok, Srei Soriyotei died of cholera. The chronicle said that he died in 1488, corresponding to the year of the Monkey of the tenth decade, in the month of Pisak (ពិសាខ), and on the first day of the waning moon.[29,p94] Like Srei Reachea, foul play could not be ruled out for the death of Srei Soriyotei. He was not known to have any health issue when he was taken prisoner to Ayutthaya. Srei Soriyotei dying of cholera must be viewed with great reservation for the fact that the chronicles were written under Thommo Reachea. Also, some of the versions of the Cambodian chronicles were borrowed from the Ayutthayan Chronicle.

59   Thommo Reachea (1486-1504) ធម្មរាជា

Transliterated Name: Dhammarājā
Other Name: Malivan Bukkalo Svami
Style name: Samdech Preah Thommo Reacheathireach Reameathipadei
Accession: 1486
Born: Circa 1442/Deceased: 1504
Relationship: Son of Ponhea Yat and Brother of Neareay Reachea I
Mother: Srangiem (Ayutthayan)
Religion: Theravada/Hinayana Buddhism
Capital: Phnom Penh
Genealogy: Appendix 3

Thommo Reachea was the younger brother of Neareay Reachea, whose mother was Ayutthayan and former widow of the Ayutthayan prince (Chau Ponhea Preah Nokor Eynt) who ruled Angkor in 1431. He is the half-brother of Srei Reachea. Not content being a regent in charge of Phnom Penh while the king was on a campaign fighting Ayutthaya, and not to be outdone by his nephew Srei Soriyotei, Thommo Reachea also decided to rebel against the king. The chronicles said that he was crowned king in 1478 (year of the Dog, in the tenth decade).[29,p82] He reigned under the style name Samdech Preah Thommo Reacheathireach Reameathipadei. He controlled the western and southern territories of Cambodia covering the provinces of Samrong Tong (សំរោង ទង), Thpong (ថ្ពង), Kampong Som (កំពងសោម), Kampot (កំពត), Treang (ទ្រាំង), and Peam Kancheu (ពាមកញ្ចើរ).

The queen bore Thommo Reachea two sons. The first son was born in 1479 (year of the Pig, the first of the decade). He was named Baña Tāmkhatti, but he was better known as Srei Sokonthor Bat. The second one was born in 1481 (year of the Ox, the third of the decade) with a given name Chan Kreas Reachea, but he was better known as Ang Chan I.[29,p83]

After ten years of war with no ending in sight, Thommo Reachea decided to appeal to the king of Ayutthaya, Borommatrailokanat, to come to Cambodia's rescue. After debarking in Phnom Penh in 1486 with his army, the Ayutthayan king and Thommo Reachea concocted a plan to bring Srei Reachea and Srei Soriyotei to come to a conference to resolve the war problem in the fortress of Oudong that was completed just for that occasion. Srei Reachea and Srei Soriyotei thought they went to the conference with the hope of bringing peace to Cambodia, but they never expected to be cornered into submissions to the will of the Ayutthayan king. With Thommo Reachea's approval, Borommatrailokanat took the two kings and their entourages back with him to Ayutthaya. A few months later upon arriving in Ayutthaya, Srei Reachea fell gravely ill with shame and a broken heart due to the duplicity of Borommatrailokanat and Thommo Reachea. According to the chronicles, he died shortly thereafter in 1487. Srei Soriyotei lived a year longer. He finally succumbed to an illness and died in 1488. Thommo Reachea sent his minister to Ayutthaya to retrieve the corpses of the two defunct Khmer kings. He also asked the Ayutthayan king to send back Chau Ponhea Ong so he could attend and perform a proper memorial and burial services in Cambodia for them. They were cremated in Phnom Penh with the full rituals dignified for kings. After the ceremony had been completed, Chau Ponhea Ong returned to Ayutthaya as was agreed between Thommo Reachea and Borommatrailokanat.

The chronicles said that Thommo Reachea was a fervent Buddhist. He learned the Buddhist canons of scriptures, the Tripitaka, by heart. To gain merits as well as to promote Buddhism in Cambodia, Thommo Reachea asked his generals, ministers, and religious leaders of the court to go to India to obtain some ashes of the Buddha. Emperor Asoka and Moggaliputta Tissa had buried the Buddha's ashes under 84,000 stupas that the emperor built and scattered all over India. Tissa Kumara was Asoka's brother; and when he entered monkhood he took the name of Moggaliputta Tissa. He was asked by Asoka to conduct the Third Buddhist Council convened around 250 BCE to purify the Sangha (the Buddha's community or assembly). The Sangha was corrupted by the greed and heretical views of monks who took advantage of Asoka's generosity through his largess to promote Buddhism. With his great wealth Asoka was able to build 84,000 pagodas and support the livelihood of monks throughout India.

In 1494 (2038 Buddhist Era, 1416 Grand Era, 856 Cula Era, year of the Tiger of the sixth decade, in the month of Pisak, on the fifth day of the waning moon), Thommo Reachea ordered the construction of a stupa in the village of Khvav Preah Theat (ខ្វាវព្រះ:ធាតុ) near the hill of Asantuk (អសន្ទុក) to house the sacred ashes of the Buddha.[29,p9] This village is presently called Phum Khvav located on National Highway No. 6 at 152 km from Phnom Penh and about 15 km from Kampong Thom.[29,p254] After the stupa was built and the ceremony to house the sacred ashes of the Buddha was completed, Thommo Reachea cleansed himself and entered monkhood to obtain merits. According to Khin Sok,[29,p96,p254] Thommo Reachea was ordained as a monk with the name Braḥ Goṇṇasāmī phala bhiraṃm parama viriyādhikabodhisambhāra mahāparipāla Indipras saṃriddhī (Venerable master of qualities where the fruits are excellent, superior due to the effort, bodhisambhara "possessing necessary conditions to attain supreme knowledge," the great protector of Indipras, and success). After three months he left the Sangha and returned to his royal palace in Phnom Penh. Upon arriving to his royal palace, the king received good news from his minister of defense that the Pursat governor had captured a big white elephant measuring about 2 meters in height. Because of its rarity, a white elephant was believed to bring luck and prosperity to the country. The king was very happy but his joy turned to sorrow when the elephant fell ill and died in 1502, only three years after it had been captured. The elephant may have died of sorrow because it was probably deprived of its freedom to roam freely in the forest. The confined environment in the royal elephant stable may not be suitable for this pride elephant that used to live in the wild.

To obtain good merits, the king ordered the digging of a pond in 1503 to give as a royal gift to the people of Samrong Tong. On his trip to the location he fell ill, and it continued to get worse after he returned to his royal palace. He finally passed away in 1504 in the year of the Rat of the sixth decade, in the month of Chais, and on the second day of the waning moon.[29,p99] He had reigned for eighteen years.

Sokonthor Bat's Favorite Concubine and Sdach Kân's Usurpation of Power

60   Srei Sokonthor Bat (1504-1512) ស្រីសុគន្ធបទ

Transliterated Name: Srī Sugandhapad
Other Names: Dang Khateya (Kshatriya) Reachea, Baña Tāmkhatti

Style Name: Preah Bat Samdach Sdach Preah Reach Ang Preah Srey Sokonthor Bat Prohm Prith Reacheathireach Reameathipadey [4,p23]

Accession: 1504

Born: 1479/Deceased: 1512

Relationship: Eldest son of Thommo Reachea

Purohita: Samdech Preah Eysei Phoat Suos (សម្ដេចព្រះឥសីភទ្ទសួស)

Mother: Tep Srei Thida Ksatrei

Wife: Neak Mneang Pcou (Concubine of 1st Rank)

Son: Chau Ponhea Yuos Reachea

Religion: Theravada/Hinayana Buddhism

Capital: Phnom Penh, Basan (Srei Santhor)

Genealogy: Appendix 3

Key Names and Places

Baña Tāmkhatti (ពញាតាំខត្តិ) = Srei Sokonthor Bat

Boeung Tea/Totea/Toteung (បឹងទា/បឹងទទា/បឹងទទឹង) = Duck/Partridge/Unconventional Lakes

Braḥ Bijai Nāga (ព្រះពិជ័យនាគ) = Preah Pichey Neak; father of Neak Mneang Peou and Kân

Campak' (ចំបក់) = Châmbâk; a tree with a scientific name Irvingia Malayana or Parinari Anamensis Hance

Cau Baña Yosarājā (ចៅពញាយោរាជា) = Chau Ponhea Yuos Reachea; son of Srei Sokonthor Bat and Neak Mneang Peou

Kân (កន) = Brother of Neang Peou

Khvav Preah Theatuk (ខ្វាវព្រះ៉ធាតុ) = Location where the Buddha's ashes were enshrined (near Kampong Thom)

Nāṅ Bau (នាងៅ៧) = Neang Peou; daughter of Neang Ban and Neay Kim; concubine of Srei Sokonthor Bat

Nāṅ Pān (នាងបាន) = Neang Ban; mother of Neang Peou

Nāy Gim (នាយគិម) = Neay Kim; father of Neang Peou

Neak Mè Ban (អ្នកម៉ែបាន) = Mother of Neak Mneang Peou; elevated from Neang Ban

Neak Mneang Peou = First rank concubine of Srei Sokonthor Bat; daughter of Preah Pichey Neak and Neak Mè Ban

Pādī (បាទី) = Bati; located in present-day Takeo

Pichey Neak (ពិជ័យនាគ) = Father of Neang Peou and Kân

Pol (ពល) = Slave

Preah Ratanaktrey (ព្រះរតនត្រៃ) = Triple Jewels (Buddha, Dharma, Sangha)

Preah Snâm Êk = First rank concubine

Samṭec Braḥ Īsī Bhădda Suos (សម្ដេចព្រះឥសីភទ្ទសួស) = Samdech Preah Eysei Phoat Suos; Chief Brahman

Samṭec Braḥ Sugandhādhīpatī (សម្ដេចព្រះសុគន្ធាធិបតី) = Venerable Samdech Preah Sukunthea Thipadei (Kân's guru)

Srei Sa (ស្រីស) = Nickname for Neang Peou; meaning white lady

Srī Sa Jhar (ស្រីសឈរ) = Srei Sa Chhor, which means white lady standing; formely name was Basan. It was renamed to honor Neak Mneang Peou

Sdịṅ Saen (ស្ទឹងសែន) = Stung Saen; located in the province of Kampong Svay

Srī Sandhar (ស្រីសន្ធរ) = Srei Santhor; changed from Srei Sa Chhor; meaning pleasant lady

Sū (សូ) = Student of the Chief Brahman

Uk Luoṅ Mantrī Snehā (ឧកល្វងមន្ត្រីស្នេហា) = Uk Luong Montrei Sneha; title given to Preah Pichey Neak

Ukñā Mḭn Snehā Comcitta (ឧកញ៉ាម៉ឺនស្នេហាចោមចិត្ត) = Oknha Meun Sneha Chom Chith; title given to Kân

Vatta Braḥ Nibbāna (វត្តព្រះនិព្វាន) = Vat Preah Nippean; meaning nirvana temple (built after Mneang Peou recovered from illness)

Vatta Brai Pāṃṅ (វត្តព្រៃបាំង) = Vat Prey Bang; meaning temple hidden by forest; changed from Vat Preah Nippean

After he succeeded his father Thommo Reachea in 1504, Baña Tāmkhatti (ពញាតាំខត្តិ) took the name of Srei Sokonthor Bat for his coronation. He was twenty five years old. He resided in the Chaktomouk Royal Palace in Phnom Penh for a year before deciding to move to Basan. In 1506, he removed his father's ashes from Chaktomouk to place them near the Buddha's ashes that were enshrined in Khvav Preah Theatuk.

The first few years of his reign were uneventful, but things started to change after he took on a new concubine named Nāṅ Bau (នាងពៅ, Neang Peou), the daughter of a *pol* (slave) woman and of a low ranking official. The ensuing events resulted in Kân, the younger brother of Neang Peou, rebelling against the king and then killed him to take over the throne. This story is well known among the populace, but people dared only whispering and not talking openly for generations. This story was recorded in the Cambodian Royal Chronicles, but it had been clamped down due to the danger and embarrassment it posed to the Cambodia crown. It was one of the darkest moments in the royal history of Cambodia. It came out to light only when the French Colonial administrations wanted to create a comprehensive genealogy of the Khmer kings.

The story recorded in the chronicles[6; 29] included some myths such as the royal servants opening up the fish belly to find a baby still alive. This baby happened to be Kân (កន), the son of Pichey Neak (ពិជ័យ នាគ). Also, the birth of Kân could not have occurred under the reign of Srei Sokonthor Bat because Kân was sixteen years old when he served the king. I will weed out the mythology aspect of the story such as a Naga came to Kân's rescue as he was drowning when the fishing net was cast over him; or wild birds stood on Kân's head to hide him from being discovered by the king's soldiers; or a Naga stood in front of a menacing soldier to protect Kân. I will report only the events that were believed to be historical in nature and relevant to the period of Srei Sokonthor Bat and Kân.

A free man named Nāy Gim (នាយគិម, Neay Kim) married Nāṅ Pān (នាងបាន, Neang Ban), a *pol* woman of Preah Ratanaktrey (ពលព្រះរតនត្រៃ, slave woman with the status of a Triple Jewels) working in a pagoda. Preah Ratanaktrey is the three precepts that define the foundation of Buddhism, which consist of Buddha, Dharma (law), and Sangha (priesthood community). People are called *Prachea Pol Roth* (ប្រជាពលរដ្ឋ) in Khmer, with the root word *pol* in the compound name. The word *Prachea Pol Roth* must have its origin from the fact that people — with the exception of royal offsprings, Brahmans, monks, and families of nobility backgrounds — were considered "slaves" of the state. Because Neang Ban was a Triple Jewels slave and not a common slave, she was allowed to marry a free man. Due to the stigma attached to it, normally a free man would not marry a slave. Because she had the status of a Triple Jewels slave working in a pagoda and not a regular slave working for a commoner, Neang Ban had a better chance for her children to move upward in status if she were to marry a free man. She must have been a pretty woman for Neay Kim to marry her and be unconcerned about any ramifications he might receive for his action. They produced a daughter and named her Neang Peou, but she was also known as Neang Sâ,[29,p258] which suggested that she had a clear complexion (because Sâ means white in Khmer). They produced a second child and named him Kân. The above event had to occur a few years prior to Srei Sokonthor's accession to the throne because Neang Peou and Kân were already teenagers, to becoming young adults when they served the king.

The beauty of Neang Peou must have been talked about within the compound of the royal palace because Srei Sokonthor Bat inquired about her after he became king. He called Neay Kim [note: the chronicle said that Neay Kim was a low ranking minister. Due to the stigma attached to a man marrying a slave who could ruin his career, I do not believe Neay Kim was a low ranking minister but rather one of the workers in the royal palace] and asked him to bring his daughter to the royal palace to serve him personally. It was a signal to Neay Kim that the king was interested in his daughter and intended to make her his concubine. Neang Peou must have been of exceptional beauty and Srei Sokonthor Bat must have loved her so much because soon after, the king honored her to the rank of Neak Mneang Peou and to the status of Preah Snâm Êk; which meant she was his mistress/concubine of the first rank. She was ranked only below the queen, but she got all the affection from the king. The king was so much in love with her that he renamed Basan to Srei Sâ Chhor (ស្រីសឈរ, white lady standing), which later became Srei Santhor (ស្រីសន្ធរ, pleasant lady).[29,p259] The king also gave Neay Kim a new name. He was called Braḥ Bijai Nāga (ព្រះពិជ័យនាគ, Preah Pichey Neak) with a title of Uk Luoṅ Mantrī Snehā (ឧកលួងមន្ត្រីស្នេហា Uk Luong Montrei Sneha), which elevated him to the rank equivalent to a lord. Neang Ban was also given a new name. She was called Neak Mè Ban (អ្នកម៉ែបាន, Lady Mother Ban), a name that was more dignified than Neang Ban.

The king wanted to give her a title and free her from slavery, but he was opposed by all his ministers due to the tradition and historical implication it would entail if he were to do so. His ministers explained that these slaves were offered by great kings in ancient times to the Triple Jewels (Buddha, Dharma, and Sangha) under oath, and that they would remain slaves for 5,000 years (end of Buddhism period). The oath was sacred and could not be taken lightly. To free Neak Mè Ban from the slavery bondage would be to mock and bring dishonor to the Triple Jewels. With a heavy heart and great disappointment, the king agreed not to go against the advice of his ministers.

In the meantime, Kân had also grown up to be a handsome teenager. He was a diligent and bright student. When he reached sixteen, the requirement age to work in the royal palace, his father and mother brought him to the palace to serve the king. The chronicles did not specify the year of his service, but it would probably be around 1505-1506. He rose rapidly in rank as the king accorded him the title of Ukñā Mīn Snehā Comcitta (ឧកញ៉ាម៉ឺនស្នេហាចោមចិត្ត, Oknha Meun Sneha Chom Chith), which meant beloved lord. Meun was an ancient official ranking that is no longer used. With their new found status, the family became very powerful and well sought after. The country was at peace and people were generous. Preah Pichey Neak and Neak Mè Ban built a temple and a study center for the monks that are now still standing. It is called Vat Mè Ban. The pagoda is located north of Srei Santhor and north of present-day National Road No.8.

After three years on the throne, the king decided to elevate his half-brother Chan Kreas Reachea, popularly known as Ang Chan, to the position of Maha Uparaja. The king instructed his brother to go installed himself in the Chaktomouk Royal Palace in Phnom Penh so that he could be close to the people.

The king was happy and the country was prosperous and at peace. Everything went as well as the king could hope for, but suddenly his favorite Snâm Êk, Neak Mneang Peou, fell gravely ill. The king was very worried as no medication could nurse her back to good health. The king prayed that he would erect a temple as an offering to the Almighty, and that Neak Mneang Peou herself would take care of the temple according to the tradition if she were healed back to good health. By miracle she recovered completely a week later. As promised, the king built a royal temple in dedication to the Sangha order and had Neak Mneang Peou removed weeds from the temple ground on holy days. Because the ground surrounding the temple was sparsely covered with trees, the king ordered that more trees be planted to shield Neak Mneang Peou from public eyes when she worked to remove the weeds. The temple was officially named Vat Preah Nippean (វត្តព្រះនិព្វាន), which means nirvana temple. After the trees had fully grown and hidden the temple from public view, people started to call it Vat Prey Bang (វត្តព្រៃបាំង), which means temple hidden by forest.[29,p105] The pagoda is located north of Srei Santhor and south of Vat Mae Ban, next to present-day National Road No.8.

On the same year, in 1507, Neak Mneang Peou gave birth to a son. He was named Cau Baṅā Yosarājā (ចៅពញាយោរាជា, Chau Ponhea Yuos Reachea). The king was feeling happy. He thought of nominating Kân to be a high-ranking minister, but because his mother was a slave of the Triple Jewels the king was afraid that he would be highly criticized for his action. Instead, the king decided to give Kân an honorific title *Ghun Luoṅ Braḥ Sṭec Samuha Senādhipatī* (ឃុនលួងព្រះស្ដេចសមុហាសេនាធិបតី, Khun Luong Preah Sdach Samuha Senathipadei). He had the power to command and use the slaves for the service of the Triple Jewels. The king cleverly did not assign his ranking to equate any of his ministers. Because of the power the king invested in him, Kân had the right to punish anybody who offended the Triple Jewels. Ministers and all officials who served the king were afraid of Kân. Being the brother of the king's favorite concubine and with the new power he gained, Kân became arrogant. He was not afraid of the king's ministers who were not only his seniors but also of noble families with much more experienced in the affairs of the state.

One night, after the first day of Khmer New Year in 1508, the king dreamt that his kingdom was in trouble. It must be noted that in ancient time, the New Year was not celebrated in the month of April like nowadays. According to Zhou Daguan who visited Angkor in 1296, the New Year was celebrated in November. It is believed it was the French that changed the New Year to April to allow people to celebrate after the harvesting season. In his dream the king was running away from a big dragon spitting venoms and flames that destroyed his capital. The dragon seized the royal parasol with his mouth and fled east. The king was very troubled by this dream. The next day he gathered his royal families and high dignitaries in the deliberation room. As they proceeded with the ceremony, the king saw two dragons, one male and one female, hovering above Kân's head. At that moment the governor of Battambang informed the king that the water from the cave of Phnom Banan (located in khum "sub-district" Kantuk (កន្ទុ) of srok "district" Sangker and in the province of Battambang), reserved for the king's bath, had become red like lacquer. The king was very worried when he returned to his room. He called the Chief Brahman and the royal foreseer/astrologer to come to his room to interpret the meaning of his dream, and of what he had seen in the deliberation room. At that moment the Chief Brahman told the king that the blade of *Preah Khan Reach* (Royal Sacred Sword) was covered with rust in its entirety — which, according to tradition was a bad omen indicating bad things to come. The royal astrologer interpreted the dream to mean that a person born in the year of the dragon would dispute his throne and would reign in the east. He specifically named Kân as the person who would dispute his throne, because he was born in the year of the dragon. The king agreed with the royal astrologer because it confirmed what he had seen and dreamt about, but he hesitated to punish Kân without any good reasons for fear of criticism from the people and also of angering Neak Mneang Peou, his favorite concubine and sister of Kân, who had just bore him a son. Finally, the king came up with a plan that would not draw any suspicions. He would organize a fishing expedition the next morning. They would cast a net into the water on purpose to get it tangled up in rocks. They would ask Kân to go into the water to free the net, and while he was in the water they would let go of multiple hawks to attack him. They would expect Kân to panic and get tangled up in the net and drowned. The death of Kân could not be blamed on the king. The two ministers agreed with the king's plan. The chronicles said that while the king was discussing his plan with the two ministers, Neak Mneang Peou came to listen to them at the door but she could not hear what was said clearly. She heard only the last part about asking Kân to dive into the water and letting the hawks lose to attack Kân so that he got entangled and drowned.

Fearing for her brother's life, Neak Mneang Peou warned Kân about the king's intention to drown him. She wrote a letter and told her brother that if the king asked him to dive into the water to untangle the net, he must swim under the water as far away as he could and never come back. The next morning the king executed the plan he had discussed with his two counselors. Because Kân was warned ahead by his sister, he was able to escape by swimming under water to a safe place. The lake where this event took place was called Boeung Tea (បឹងទា), which means Duck Lake; then it changed to Boeung Totea (បឹងទទា),

which means Partridge Lake; and finally to the present-day name Boeung Toteung (បឹងទទឹង), which means Untraditional/Unconventional Lake.[29,p109]

I would like to make some observations concerning the above story. The royal chroniclers had no knowledge of Neak Mneang Peou listening at the door when the king was discussing his plan with his counselors. Because only the king and his two counselors knew about the plan, the royal chronicler must have guessed that the only way Kân knew about the intention of the king to kill him was that he got the information from his sister who lived in the royal palace. I believe that Kân, being a clever man, would probably see through the king's motive to kill him on his own. He would then become very suspicious. Why would the king ask him to dive into the water to free the net while there were servants of much lower ranking than him who could also do the job? Kân probably believed that the court officials as well as other people may be jealous of him and wanted to see him dead. If he were a clever man as the chronicles said, he had to feel and sense the negative vibes around him. Because he had risen to power too fast, especially for a person of his background that did not deserve such an entitlement. He attracted the ire and jealousy of high-ranking officials and other princes. He had alienated the high-ranking ministers who were his seniors and presumably served the king well. Most of the officials had probably served the king's father even before Kân was born. It is conceivable that Kân received constant advice from his parents and his sister, and that they watched each other's backs. They ought to be always vigilant and alert if they wanted to survive in the world of politics. Concerning women in ancient times, it would be very unusual for them to know how to read and write because they were rarely allowed to go to school. For Neak Mneang Peou, unless she learned to read and write after she became the king's favorite concubine, she would never have the means or opportunities to learn those lessons when she was younger. Also, in ancient times there were no schools like in the present-day. Students learned from monks in temples. It is unconceivable that women were allowed to stay close to monks on a daily basis to learn lessons instead of staying at home helping their parents. If Neak Mneang Peou had heard the conversation like the chronicles said, and assuming she was illiterate, then she could not have written the letter to her brother unless she asked a learned man to write it for her. It is also possible that she asked her father to write the letter to his son to warn him about the trap the king had set for him. If this were the case, then the story of her listening at the door and heard of the concersation could have come from the person who wrote the letter for Neak Mneang Peou.

After the escape, Kân took refuge in the pagoda where he was raised and taught by his master, Saṃṭec Braḥ Sugandhādhīpatī (សម្ដេចព្រះសុគន្ធាធិបតី, Venerable Samdech Preah Sukunthea Thipadei). The monk listened to Kân's story and told him to escape to the east because he would not be safe staying in the pagoda. After gathering some weapons and supporters, they left the pagoda and moved east. With audacity, Kân showed up at the residence of the Ba Phnom governor. Right away the governor recognized Kân and was happy to receive him. As the governor bowed his head to greet, Kân took out his sword and with one sweeping motion he cut off the head of the governor. Kân's action stunted the officials standing in the room. He declared that he did it in the name of the king. He accused the governor of conspiring with the king's younger brother, the Uparaja, to take over the throne. He continued and said that those who were not in the conspiracy were ordered by the king to help him raise an army to fight the Uparaja in Phnom Penh. Officials in Ba Phnom were not aware that Kân was cunning them. Because of the power and authority that Kân used to wield and of the closeness he had with his sister, the king's favorite concubine, officials had no cause to doubt him. They obeyed his command because they believed it was the king's command. Kân was able to raise an army very fast. He went to the other provinces and repeated the same story. Very quickly he was able to raise a powerful army through his deception. The news of Kân building an army spread fast and reached the king. Alarmed, Neak Mneang Peou and Pichey Neak wrote to Kân asking him to stop his rebellion and to disband his army. They begged him to return to the capital. Kân responded with a deception by saying that he would return to the capital as soon as he finished letting everybody return home. In the meantime, the king decided not to attack Kân and waited for him to finish disbanding his army. That turned out to be a mistake because it was all that Kân needed to buy times to recruit more soldiers into his army. Knowing that he was able to fool his parents and the king, Kân seized on the opportunity to reinforce his army and told people that he did so under the king's order to fight the rebel Ponhea Chan Kreas Reachea, who resided in Phnom Penh. Words spread out and people started to talk about it. Very soon, the prince himself thought that the king was concocting a plan with Kân to get rid of him. Knowing that Kân and his sister were very close and that she was the king's favorite concubine, the prince got scared and decided to leave Phnom Penh in 1508 for Ayutthaya. Kân was very happy when he learned that the prince had fled to Ayutthaya. The prince was the only person Kân feared the most. When the king was told of his brother fleeing to Ayutthaya, he lamented that his brother should not have left him in the time when he needed him the most. The king was not aware of Kân's manipulative and mischievous action.

Pichey Neak, who was still loyal to the king volunteered to fight his own son. He promised and swore his loyalty to the king. Upon much consideration and with caution, the king agreed to Pichey Neak's request and gave him a small army of 1,000 men to command. The king was probably cautious not to give Kân's father a big army to command because he was not comfortable yet about Pichey Neak's complete loyalty to him. Pichey Neak's small army was no match to his son's big army of 50,000 men strong. At the end he was captured and made prisoner by his son. Finally, Kân was able to convince his father to switch his allegiance to him. Pichey Neak had betrayed his oath that he gave to the king. In an ironic twist of fate, he was killed as a result of an accident. It was reported that he fell on a sword with his throat badly injured. However, rumors spread that Kân had slashed the throat of his own father (the same way he had slashed the throat of the governor of Ba Phnom) as he was trying to convince his son to have a change of heart and stop fighting the king.

Kân was able to raise a large army that may even surpass the army of the king. Even with his big army, Kân was not able to defeat the king until he resorted to treachery. He lured Uk Mīn Surinda (ឧកម៉ឺនសុរិន្ទ, Uk Meun Surin) into his camp with a promise to award him a position of Yomareach (Chief of Justice) in his government. Uk Meun Surin was the son of Chau Ponhea Yuthea Sangkream (Minister of War). He blamed the king for the death of his father because the king sent him to fight Kân with only a small army. Uk Meun Surin deceived the king by feigning his alliance and entering the royal palace with his army of 200 men. He succeeded by assassinating the king in 1512 (year of the Monkey of the fourth decade, in the month of Chais, and on the fifth day of the waxing moon). The king died in the fortress of Sdiṅ Saen (ស្ទឹង ែសន, Stung Saen) in the province of Kampong Svay. Uk Meun Surin was captured during his treachery. He was beheaded with his head planted outside the fortress for people to view. The death of Srei Sokonthor Bat provided the opportunity for Kân to take over the throne. Realizing that the enemy was closing in, the five-year old Prince Yuos who was also Kân's nephew, left Stung Saen with his entourage and headed in the direction of Ayutthaya. In the meantime, the Chief Brahman Samṭec Braḥ Īsī Bhădda Suos (សម្ដេចព្រះ ឥសីភទ្ទសួស, Samdech Preah Eysei Phoat Suos) — the guardian of the Royal Sacred Sword — removed the Sword and all the royal regalia with him to join the prince. After thinking it over, the Chief Brahman and his student Sū (សូ) decided not to join the prince. They feared that the king of Ayutthaya may not let them return to Cambodia and that they might end up dead in Ayutthaya. They carried the Sacred Sword, the Victory Spear, the Scared Bow and Arrows, and Sacred Statues as far away from Stung Saen. After an exhaustive journey they arrived in Pādī　(ពទី, Bati) in present-day Takeo. Because Kân's army could be anywhere, the Chief Brahman and his student did not want to risk having the Sacred Sword and royal regalia falling into Kân's hand. They decided to hide them in a trunk of a Campak' tree (ចំបក់, Chambak) growing near a river.[29,p116] According to Khin Sok, the royal chronicle belonging to Madame Porée Maspéro did not mention the location of where the royal regalia were hidden. It only said that the Chief Brahman and his student lived a quiet life out of sight, and that nobody knew of the royal regalia whereabouts. The location of the Chambak tree was probably added at a later time in a different royal chronicles after the Royal sacred Sword had already been discovered.

[Kân (1512-1525) កន]

>Other Names: Sdach Kân
>Style Name: Preah Srei Chettha Thireach Reameathipadei[7,p252]
>Usurpation: 1512
>Relationship: Son of Preah Pichey Neak; Brother of Neak Mneang Peou (favorite concubine "Snâm Êk" of Srei Sokonthor Bat)
>Mother: Neang Mè Ban
>Construction: Srâlop Pichey Neak
>Capital: Srei Santhor, Chamlok Preah Srei, Thbong Khmum (in Kampong Cham)
>Born: Circa 1489/Deceased: 1525

Kân's Origin and Manipulative Plan to Raise an Army to Take over Power

Kân was the son of Neay Kim and Neang Ban. He was the younger brother of Neang Peou, who later became Srei Sokonthor Bat's concubine of the first rank (Snâm Êk). The baby found in the belly of a fish attributed to the birth of Kân cannot be taken seriously. The birthplace of Kân was never mentioned in any royal chronicles. However Kân's birthplace could be inferred based on the event described in the chronicles. Neay Kim was assumed to have married Neang Ban when he was serving King Sokonthor Bat at Srei Santhor. If this were indeed the case, then Kân must have been born at Srei Santhor.

According to the chronicles, King Srei Sokonthor Bat adored Neang Peou so much that he honored her with the title Neak Mneang Peou. He also accorded her father a new name and title. He was called Uk Luong Montrei Sneha Preah Pichey Neak. Her mother was also elevated in rank with the name Neak Mè Ban. Kân entered into the service of the king at the age of sixteen, probably around 1505-1506, the requirement age to serve in the royal palace. He rose rapidly in rank because of his close relationship with his sister and also because he was very intelligent and cunning.

At first, the governors of different provinces did not realize that Kân was manipulating them into raising an army for him. They believed that Kân had the mandate from the king to order them to raise an army to fight the Maha Uparaja Ponhea Chan Kreas Reachea. When Kân started to fight the king's army that the governors realized they were being duped. Kân had anticipated that his diabolic scheme would be discovered sooner or later. In order to control the recruits under his command, he resorted to another scheme by being both ruthless and generous at the same time. He would not tolerate any dissensions and disobediences, but he would reward those who supported him. He declared that those who sided with him would be well rewarded and placed in high positions in his government. All the pols would be set free and no longer be slaves. Very soon people started to join Kân, lured by his promise of high positions in his government.

As Kân's popularity started to spread, people by ignorance or by cultural tradition, believed that he received good merits and had great karma. His army swelled to a sizable proportion, equivalent or even surpassed the army of King Srei Sokonthor Bat.

In the meantime, Ang Chan who resided in Phnom Penh debated with his officials whether to raise an army of his own to fight Kân. After much deliberation, he decided not to do it for fear of being misunderstood by the king, which would confirm Kân's accusation. Knowing Kân's mischievous character, Kân would use the opportunity to justify his action to raise a bigger army if Ang Chan were trying to recruit soldiers to fight him. Ang Chan decided to leave Phnom Penh with his family and entourage. They headed in the direction of Ayutthaya.

Without having to deal with the threat coming from the Uparaja, Kân concentrated all his effort fighting the king. After the success of Uk Meun Surin's mission (he switched side to support Kân after blaming the king for the death of his father, the War Minister, that the king sent to fight Kân) to kill the king, Kân expanded his war to fight the other provinces. He entrusted his uncle Cau Hvā Kau (ចៅហ្វាកៅ, Chau Hva Kav) with the command of an army. He conquered the northern provinces, up to the frontier of Laos; the western provinces, all the way to the frontier of Ayutthaya; the eastern provinces, reaching to the frontier of Champa; and the southern provinces, leading tall the way to the sea.[29,p117] Kân assigned governors who supported him to be in charge of those provinces. Having secured the territories he had conquered, Kân returned to Srei Santhor in triumph.

Upon hearing of his brother's death, Ang Chan asked permission from the Ayutthayan king to return to Cambodia but the king refused to grant the prince's request.

Realizing that the Royal Sacred Sword and regalia had disappeared from the royal palace, Kân issued a reward of 500 damloeung gold (approximately 18.5 kg) and a high position in his government to the person who would find the Sword. Without the Sword, Kân could not accede to the throne in a traditional and legitimate way. Unable to find the Sword, Kân in his false glory had a fake sword made to imitate the real Royal Sacred Sword. With the new fake sword in display, all the ministers invited Kân to take possession of the throne.

The chronicles said that Kân was consecrated as king of Cambodia in 1512 (2056 of the Buddhist era, 1434 Saka, 875 Cula, in the year of the Monkey of the fourth decade, in the month of Bos, on the eleventh day of the waxing moon, at seven o' clock in the morning[29,p119]). Now known as Sdach Kân, the chronicles stated that he was twenty nine years old when he acceded to the throne. He could not have been this old because he was only sixteen when he started his service for King Srei Sokonthor Bat. Because Kân was awarded the title Oknha Meun between the start of Srei Sokonthor Bat's reign in 1504 and Neak Mneang Peou's delivery of her son in 1507, an estimate of Sdach Kân's age could be deduced. If the chronicles were correct, then Sdach Kân would have been only between twenty one and twenty four years old when he became king (16 + (1512-1507) = 21 and 16 + (1512-1504) = 24). Sdach Kân was consecrated as *Braḥ Srī Jetthādhīrāja Rāmādhīpatī* (ព្រះស្រីជេដ្ឋាធិរាជរាមាធិបតី, Preah Srei Chettha Thireach Reameathipadei). He resided in the same royal palace in Srei Santhor that Srei Sokonthor Bat had occupied.

The chronicles mentioned the death of Chief Brahman Eysei Phoat Suos, but it did not mention the date. I believe his death must have occurred around the time Kân acceded to the throne. The chronicles said that after the death of Eysei Phoat Suos, his student Sū (Sok) disobeyed his master and tried to retrieve the Sacred Sword from the tree to get the reward promised by Sdach Kân. While attempting to retrieve the Sacred Sword, he was bit by a cobra that lived in the trunk of the tree. When Sok died he also took away with him the secret location of the hidden Royal Sacred Sword. The Chief Brahman probably died of old age in combination with the exhaustive journey he took to avoid Kân's army.

At the beginning, Kân just wanted to escape from the trap that Srei Sokonthor Bat had set to kill him. However, after the escape his survival instinct took over. He started to rebel and take revenge on the king, which ultimately turned into a revolution. His first act as a king was to give everybody a tax exempt for one season [note: Khin Sok said one season,[29,p119] which I interpreted to be between three to six months, but Adhémard Leclère[7,p252] specifically said one year]. He awarded and honored his uncle Chau Hva Kav, brother of his mother, to the position of high dignitary (prime minister) in charge of royal services and the slaves of the Triple Jewels.

Kân Proclaimed Himself King and Built Himself a Palace Fortress

Sdach Kân proclaimed in 1514 that his reign would be considered the first dynasty under his family line. He ordered the construction of a new royal palace away from Srei Santhor. He stayed in Caṃlak' Braḥ Srī (ចំឡក់ព្រះស្រី, Chamlok Preah Srei) for five months before he found a terrain in the village of Dī Sraḷap' (ទីស្រឡប់, Ti Sralop) in the province of Thbong Khmum (present-day Kampong Cham near Ba

Phnom in Prey Veng) that he considered suitable for his taste. The village was located approximately 22 km east of the residence of the Prey Veng governor. The terrain was located on an elevated plateau with a dimension of about 2,000 meters on each side.[7,p253] Pleased with his choice, Sdach Kân ordered the construction of his new royal palace as a fortress in anticipation of a war. His fortress included temples, gardens, parks, enough space for recreation, and a square pond measuring 50 meters on each side.[29,p120,p270] The royal palace fortress was completed in two years. The chronicles said that Sdach Kân moved into the royal palace in 1516 (2060 of the Buddhist era, 878 of the Cula era, 1438 of the Grand era, in the year Rat of the eighth decade, in the month of Bos, on the tenth day of the waning moon[29,p120]). He named his new city Sraḷap' Bijai Nagara (ស្រឡប់ពិជ័យនគរ, Srâlop Pichey Neak). According to Khin Sok,[29,p270] the Veang Thioun Chronicle called it Srâlop Pichey Neak Boran Reach Theani (ស្រឡប់ពិជៃនាគ បុរាណរាជធានី) while other chronicles called it Srâlop Pichey Neak Bovor Reach Theani (ស្រឡប់ពិជៃនាគបវរាជ ធានី). What were the meaning and/or reason behind the name of the city? Did Kân dedicate the city to his fallen father Pichey Neak or to himself since he was born in the year of the dragon? After three years, the city was more populated than the old city of Srei Santhor. He issued new coins with the image of a dragon.

While Sdach Kân was living a life of pleasure and luxury surrounded by women in his royal palace, the two princes, Chan and Yuos (brother and son of Srei Sokonthor Bat, respectively), who were guests of the king of Ayutthaya (Ramathibodi II, son of Borommatrailokanat and brother of Intharacha II, would be the reigning king during that period) were living a life of restlessness and anguish. They were concerned about the fate of Cambodia, and were frustrated that Ramathibodi II would not allow them to return to Cambodia to liberate their country from the usurper Sdach Kân. What was the intention of Ramathibodi II to forbid the two princes to go back to Cambodia to fight Sdach Kân? Was the king afraid that war may spill over to Ayutthaya or was it something more calculating? Was the king waited for the right moment to attack Cambodia so he could claim credits for installing Ang Chan on the throne? If this would happen, then Cambodia would be a vassal state of Ayutthaya and Ang Chan would be forever indebted and in gratitude toward Ayutthaya.

Ang Chan's Escape Scheme out of Ayutthaya

Even though Ang Chan was living in Ayutthaya, he still kept contact with his supporters in Cambodia. The chronicles not only mentioned that Ang Chan lived in Debva Mahā Nagara (ទេពមហានគរ, Tep Maha Nokor or present-day Bangkok) since 1510 (year of the Snake of the first decade), but also said that Tā Mīoeń (តាមឿង, Ta Moeung) sent his men to bring messages to the prince very often to keep him abreast of the situation in Cambodia. Ang Chan must have lingered in Cambodia or in Ayutthaya for two years before he decided to seek refuge in Tep Maha Nokor because according to the same chronicles he left Phnom Penh in 1508.

In the meantime, there was a white elephant of two meters in height roaming in the province of Kanchanapuri, located in the northwest of the Ayutthayan capital city. As hard as they tried, the king's elephant hunters could not capture the prized elephant. Having learned of the failed attempt to capture the elephant, Ang Chan volunteered his service and promised the king he would capture the white elephant for him. The king was pleased to hear that. Because the Khmer prince wanted to return to Cambodia, he had to devise a plan to show that the white elephant was heading in the eastern direction. Very astute, Ang Chan asked fifteen trusted servants to sculpt true sizes of four wooden elephant feet. They would be used to imitate the marches of the elephant in the direction toward the east. To make the process more believable they collected elephant excrements and placed them along the steps of the elephant. From time to time, they placed white hairs resembling those of the white elephant on tree trunks to indicate that a white elephant had passed through. They implemented this process to indicate that the white elephant had reached the forest of Nāṅ Raṅ (នាងរង, Neang Rong) of present-day Buriram [note: Khin Sok said it was Nokor Reach Seima[29,p122]]. After completing their jobs, Ang Chan instructed his fifteen servants to spread the news to the people living in Neang Rong, Nāṅ Ph-aek (នាងផ្អែក, Neang Phaek), Cuṅ Kāl' (ចុងកាល Chong Kal), Ḍamnuk Ḍuṅtae (ទំនុកទុងតែ, Tumnuk Tongte), Ḍik Jor (ទឹកជោរ, Teuk Cho), Maṅgala Pūrī (មង្គលបុរី, Mongkol Borei), Pāt' Taṃpaṅ (បាត់ដំបង, Battambang), and Sīem Rāp [សៀមរាប, Siem Reap; note: I believe the chroniclers may have inadvertently made a mistake because the name Siem Reap did not exist yet at the time]. Afterward, they were to meet the prince in Pandāy Chmār (បន្ទាយឆ្មារ, Banteay Chhmar).

After one month, the news of a white elephant roaming in the area had reached the ears of the governor of Nokor Reach Seima. He wrote a letter to the king of Ayutthaya informing that a white elephant had been spotted in his province. Upon receiving the letter from the governor, the king convened a meeting. He asked the advice of his generals and ministers, whom would be the best person to send to capture the elephant. The high officials all answered that Ang Chan would be the most qualified person to do the job. According to Adhémard Leclère, Ang Chan had captured a white elephant once for the king.[7,p254] That was the reason why the high officials were all in agreement in assigning the job to the prince. The king agreed with his ministers. Ang Chan asked the king to provide him soldiers, elephants, and equipments to use to capture the white elephant. Being a Khmer prince, he did not have the same authority as an Ayutthayan prince. For this reason, he asked the king to grant him the power to command the soldiers as he wished. The king agreed and gave Ang Chan a royal sword (Preah Saen). The prince could use it to punish anybody who refused to obey his command. Khin Sok and Adhémard Leclère differed in the numbers of soldiers that the king gave to the prince. While Khin Sok said it was 5,000 soldiers,[29,p122] Leclère said it was only 500.[7,p254] I believe that 500 would be more sensible. Using 5,000 soldiers to capture an elephant would seem a little bit farfetched. I do not believe the Ayutthayan king would agree to give so many soldiers to Ang Chan to command.

Before he left on his mission, Ang Chan went to pay homage to his elder cousin Chau Ponhea Ong (the son of Srei Reachea) that King Borommatrailokanat had adopted in 1486. Borommatrailokanat gave away one of his daughters in marriage to Chau Ponhea Ong. He took on the name Braḥ Siddhānarājā (ព្រះ សិទ្ធានរាជា, Preah Sithean Reachea). Ang Chan reminded his elder cousin that he was a Khmer. He tried to convince his cousin to return to Cambodia with him to fight the usurper Sdach Kân. Prince Sithean Reachea said that he was well treated by the king, presumably King Ramathibodi II (grandson of Borommatrailokanat), and that he was given the province of Suvaṇṇagāloka (សុវណ្ណការលោក, Sawankhalok which is now part of the Sukhothai province) to govern. He was content and very grateful to the Ayutthayan king. Because Sithean Reachea was raised in Ayutthaya since he was six years old and well treated, he may not have the same attachment to his birth country as Ang Chan did. Sithean Reachea said that he would leave the duty to fight Sdach Kân entirely to Ang Chan. Without responding, Ang Chan bid farewell to his elder cousin but he felt sad that Sithean Reachea had forgotten about Cambodia and forsaken his duty as a Khmer prince to retake the country from a usurper.

With the 500 soldiers and 50 elephants, Ang Chan along with his cousin Prince Yuos and their entourages left Tep Maha Nokor in 1516 (year of the Rat of the eighth decade, in the month of Phalkun, and on the tenth day of the waning moon). They travelled days and nights for a week until they arrived at the frontier of Cambodia. Knowing he had put enough distance from Tep Maha Nokor, Ang Chan felt safe enough to send soldiers to deliver a message with some samples of the elephant dumps to the Ayutthayan king. Right away, the king suspected the true intention of Ang Chan when he learned the prince was close to the Cambodian frontier. The king gave a mandate to Mīn Bejjaṇā Bijitra (ម៉ឺនពេជ្ជពិចិត្រ, Meun Pich Pichith) with 30 soldiers on horsebacks to stop Ang Chan and asked him to return to the capital.

As soon as the prince crossed into Cambodia, he was able to recruit 800 people to join him right away. With his small army of new recruits he continued to the province of Teuk Cho. He found 2,200 former royal servants of men and women living in the province. His army swelled to 3,000, not counting the 500 Ayutthayan soldiers. With his army of untested fighters, the prince was able to mount a victory and took over the citadel in the province of Siem Reap [as mentioned earlier, the chronicler made an inadvertent mistake because the name of Siem Reap did not exist yet]. As to the king's envoy, he reached Ang Chan in the citadel and threatened to arrest him if he refused to return to Tep Maha Nokor. The prince pulled the royal sword that the Ayutthayan king gave him and in turn threatened to execute anybody who dared to stand in his way. Outnumbered by the 3,000 Khmer soldiers and facing with the authority of the royal sword, the king's envoy and his soldiers kneeled down in front of the prince and begged for forgiveness. The prince told the envoy to relay the message to the king that he was very grateful for the king's gracious treatment of him during his stay in Ayutthaya, and that he would one day pay it back after he had gotten rid of the usurper Kân. The prince released the 500 soldiers of their duties and let them go back to Ayutthaya.

After a few days of rest, he marched his army to Battambang. Governor Ukñā Mno Metrī (ឧកញ៉ាម្នោ មេត្រី, Oknha Mnometrei) was so happy when he learned that Ang Chan had arrived in his province. The governor brought 1,000 soldiers to join the prince. Afterward the prince continued his march toward the province of Pursat. Having got wind of the prince approaching his province, Ukñā Suorgāloka Kaev (ឧក ញ៉ាសួគ៌លោកកែវ, Oknha Suorkealoka Keo) placed 1,000 soldiers to protect the citadel and wrote a letter to inform Sdach Kân about the situation. When Ta Moeung learned that the prince was in the region, he gathered 3,000 volunteers to attack the citadel of Oknha Suorkealoka Keo under the cover of darkness. The governor was immediately killed during the attack. Ta Moeung greeted the prince when he arrived at the citadel the next morning. With the riches of the Pursat governor in abundance, the prince distributed them to his soldiers to keep them happy. The prince gave the title Oknha Suorkealoka to his trusted ally Moeung. He nominated him the new Governor of Pursat and also Chief of the army. Oknha Suorkealoka Moeung nominated his four sons to spearhead the army to attack the provinces of Kragar (ក្រគរ, Krakor), Khluṅ (ខ្លុង, Khlung), and Kraṅ (ក្រង, Krâng).

Ang Chan's victory gave Sdach Kân a great concern. Kân ordered Oknha Chakrei to recruit soldiers from the western provinces and utilized them to stop the advancing army of the prince in Longvek. He ordered his uncle Chau Hva Kav to support Oknha Chakrei in Kampong Siem. On his way to Kampong Siem, his uncle met the governor of Asantuk, Oknha Udaidhirāja (ឧកញ៉ាឧទៃធិរាជ, Outeythireach). They all marched to Longvek. After the three groups had been assembled they marched on to Krâng. Ta Moeung was not intimidated even though he was facing with a superior army of Chau Hva Kav. He ordered his eldest son to take 2,000 soldiers and go on the offensive. He charged on the enemies and killed Oknha Outeythireach. It was a fierce battle between the two forces, but because his troop was outnumbered the eldest son of Ta Moeung decided to fall back and return to Pursat. Because their leader was killed, the troop of Oknha Outeythireach also decided to return to their camp to report the bad news to Oknha Chakrei and Chau Hva Kav. They regrouped and decided to pursue the army of Ta Moeung all the way to the Citadel of Pursat. The citadel was now under siege and all escaped routes were cut off.

The Legend of Neak Ta Kleang Moeung

This is where the legend of Neak Ta Kleang Moeung started. Because they were greatly outnumbered by the enemy's forces, Ta Moeung offered a solution to Ang Chan to get out of the impossible situation. He volunteered to sacrifice himself so that he could bring the army of phantoms to fight the enemies. Ang Chan would not accept this foolish proposal because it was not only incredulous but it was also absurd. Ta Moeung was serious and wanted to commit suicide in front of the prince if he refused to accept his proposal. The prince finally gave in and allowed Ta Moeung to perform the intricate suicide ritual according to his wish.

Ta Moeung instructed the soldiers to dig a square hole of eight hatthas deep (Approximately 4 meters. One hattha is a distance from the point of the elbow to the tip of the middle finger) and fill it with a lot of weapons. He asked them to prepare offerings in all eight directions. He summoned his friend named Chan (not to be confused with Ang Chan) and gave him a specific instruction as follows:[29,pp275]

> *You will be the Me Smiṅ in my place. You will be the intermediary between the king and me so that he does not talk to me directly. Also, tomorrow will be a night of full moon in the month of Pisak. The night when you hear a very loud noise in the sky, you will lead the army to attack the citadel of the enemy.*

The above instruction needs to be clarified. The word king was intended to mean Prince Chan Kreas Reachea. According to Khin Sok, *Me Smiṅ* (មេស្មិង, Me Smeung) is a person in charge of performing a cult ceremony. According to the Cambodian tradition, *Me Smeung* believes in the occult and he represented the "genie" as he goes into a trance taking on the personality and soul of that "genie." He is the medium acting as an intermediary between human beings and the supernatural being represented in the "genie." Prior to the above statement, the personality of Ta Moeung had never been clarified. The above statement indicated that Ta Moeung was a *Me Smeung,* the head of the cult. Traditionally, this person is well respected because he possesses magical power. There still exists that kind of "genie" today and it is commonly called "គ្រូស្មិត, Krou Sathit."

 After he gave his instruction to his friend, Ta Moeung took a bath to cleanse and purify his body. He called his soldiers to gather around him. He performed the ritual ceremony to prepare for his self-sacrifice. He knelt down and with his hand joined, he called on the Triple Jewels and all divinities to help the king (Prince Chan) defeat his enemies. He told the soldiers to faithfully serve the king and not be afraid of the traitor. He said that he would leave them to go to assemble an army of phantoms, and that he would come back in time to help them defeat the enemies [note: Ta Moeung must have truly believed he could summon the dead to lead an army of phantoms because of the fact that he lived the life of a Smeung, Medium/Genie]. After finishing his speech and without hesitation he jumped into the pit. His neck was severed. After seeing their father sacrificed himself, the second and third sons also jumped into the pit to join him. The oldest and youngest sons were ready to jump into the pit also but they were stopped by the Chief of the army. The chronicles also said that Neak Mneang Kiev (the wife of the prince) asked permission from the prince to jump into the pit also as required by the ritual. After the completion of the ritual, drums were beaten out loudly like a sound of a thunder. The soldiers yelled with a scream of victory. They filled the pit back and built mounds for the four heroes who sacrificed their lives to bring the army of phantoms to lead the fight against the enemies. Ta Moeung left an instruction to call him Neak Ta Khleang Moeung. The prince was informed of the death of Ta Moeung after the ritual was completed. With great sadness, he cried for the loss of the four lives. He nominated the oldest son of Ta Moeung to replace his father and transferred the title Oknha Suorkealoka to him. He gave the title Oknha Sena Sangkream to the youngest son. He also made him Governor of the province of Amrak Kirinborei as well as chief of the army in charge of the citadel for that night. In the meantime, the forces of Chau Hva Kav and Oknha Chakrei that were camping outside the citadel for two days were waiting for the arrival of the army of Oknha Decho to launch a final attack against the citadel.

The chronicles said that in 1518 (year of the Ox of the ninth decade, on the month of Pisak, of the fifteenth day of the waxing moon), when the moon was at its zenith, Ang Chan was preparing for an offensive against the enemy. He was going to lead an army of 10,000 soldiers while Oknha Suorkealoka and Oknha Senathipadei were in charge of the front forces of 5,000 soldiers to spearhead the attack against Oknha Chakrei. Ang Chan asked Prince Yuos and Oknha Veung to guard the citadel with 3,000 soldiers.

Before going into the battle, the prince performed a ritual ceremony calling on the Triple Jewels, Indra, Brahma, the supernatural forces, the spirits of his ancestors, and Neak Ta Khleang Moeung to protect his army and lead them into victory against the enemy. As the prince was climbing on his white elephant ready to leave the citadel, he heard a blasting underground noise which shook the ground to its core. All the prince's soldiers heard the noise very clearly. The prince ordered his soldiers to beat the drums and gongs as loud as they could. As his soldiers shouted a war cry, the prince charged ahead toward the enemy. Caught by the sudden outburst and daring surprised attack, the forces of Chau Hva Kav and Oknha Chakrei went into disarray. Oknha Suorkealoka pursued Oknha Chakrei and killed him in a combat on elephant backs. He brought the enemy's head back to the citadel to present to the prince.

A critical analysis is in order concerning the above story. To understand the legend of Neak Ta Khleang Moeung, the story must be viewed in the context of the mind set of people living in the 16th century. Because Ta Moeung was a *Me Smeung,* he was not only respected but also worshipped by his soldiers for the fact that he possessed magical power that could summon supernatural beings.

Ta Moeung was very astute and understood psychology because he was practicing it throughout his life. He knew how to use it as a weapon in his favor. In ancient times and to a certain extent now, people believed in the power of magic. Realizing that the prince's army would not be able to defeat the enemy with an army that was far more superior, Ta Moeung had to resort to a psychological warfare that would boost the morale of the soldiers. His first act before his self-sacrifice was to instruct people to call him *Neak Ta Khleang Moeung.* This may seem trivial but the significance of the words *Neak Ta* was not only very important, but also crucial from a psychological point of view. There is no exact translation in English for these words, but it is equivalent to the word genie.

Neak Ta is an abstract concept buried deeply in the belief system in the Cambodian society, as well as in the Southeast Asian society in general. It portrays an image of a powerful genie in the realm of the non-living who can be called upon to the world of the living in time of needs. The soldiers must have felt restless after the self-sacrifices ritual. Witnessing how heroic their chief with two of his sons and the prince's wife gave up their lives to help them win the war, the soldiers in turn would not be afraid to sacrifice their lives fighting for the prince to achieve victory. The soldiers must have built up their emotions into its crescendo, and when the full moon came they were ready to charge into the enemy's frontline. The loud noises described in the chronicles must have come from the war cry of the restless and emotional soldiers. The surprise attack by the prince's army with the soldiers full of adrenaline and ready to erupt gave a definite advantage over the superior army of the enemy. History is full of examples of smaller forces winning battles over superior forces, based on strategies, surprised attacks, courage, and emotion. The shocking and inspiring psychological tactic used by *Ta Moeung* is reminiscent of the one employed by the legendary gladiator Spartacus that occurred around a century B.C. when he killed his personal horse to boost the morale of his followers when they faced the army of the Roman general Marcus Licinius Crassus. As recounted by the Greek historian Plutarch, Spartacus called for his horse to be brought to him for sacrifice when he faced an overwhelming Roman army of Crassus: "'When his horse was brought him, he drew out his sword and killed him, saying, if he got the day he should have a great many better horses of the enemies,' and if he lost he would 'have no need of this.'"[131]

After the battle had been won, the prince took a survey the next morning to gauge the results of the victory. The enemy left war equipment, elephants, horses, domestic animals, and food supply in the battlefield. The prince marched toward the province of Krakor, Krâng, and Khlung without any resistance. Sdach Kân sent his forces to stop the advancement of the prince's army but they were defeated on all fronts.

As the wet season was approaching, Sdach Kân sent an emissary to ask the prince for a ceasefire to allow people to work on their fields. Even though the momentum of the war turned in his favor, the prince agreed to the ceasefire because he knew his soldiers were tired and they needed a rest. It was during this time that the royal families and high officials asked Prince Chan Kreas Reachea to take the royal title of King of Cambodia. The prince accepted the honor but agreed to postpone the consecration ceremony until he had vanquished Sdach Kân first. The chronicles did not state the exact date this event took place but Adhémard Leclère said it was in 1516.[7,p262] Based on the chronology of the event, I have calculated that the ceasefire took place in 1518 between May and October.

The Defeat and End of Sdach Kân's Reign

The battles between King Ang Chan's army and Sdach Kân's army continued with no end in sight. Sdach Kân offered the king to divide the country into two equal regions and that each one would reign in his territory. It was an absurd proposal and the king rejected it right away. Ang Chan considered Sdach Kân a usurper and a thief who had stolen the kingdom of his ancestors. Unable to convince the king to accept his proposal and frustrated for not able to beat the king's army on the battlefields, Sdach Kân resorted to trickery one more time.

Sdach Kân chose 100 soldiers and instructed them to desert to the king's army. After gaining the trust of Ang Chan, Kân's soldier attempted to assassinate the king in 1520 while he was taking a bath in a river in the province of Paripūrṇa (បរិបូណ៌, Boribaur in present-day Kampong Chhnang). The assassination attempt failed. The king's soldiers killed eight enemies and captured ten others while the rest escaped into the forest.[29,p136] The war between Ang Chan and Sdach Kân continued for another five years before it came to a conclusion.

Cambodia history rarely mentioned about the banners used in wars. It was somewhat of a revelation when the chronicles described the banner used by Ang Chan during his battle against Sdach Kân's army at a place called Khñūṅ Mahā Sīek (ខ្មួមហាសៀក, Knhuong Maha Siek), which I believe to have occurred probably around November 1522 [the chronicles did not mention the specific date]. The chronicles said that the banner carried the images of a dragon and a Makara fish.[29,p141,p280] The Makara fish is also called Chlām Makara (ឆ្លាមមករ) and sometime Chlām or Trī Thkar (ត្រីថ្ករ), a kind of shark or swordfish. The fish was portrayed in Khmer arts in the middle of the seventh century of the style of Sambor Prey Kuk.

The battles between Ang Chan and Kân's armies continued until 1525. The king's army pursued Sdach Kân and his army all the way to his Citadel of Srâlop Pichey Neak. After three months of siege, the king's army was still not able to take over the citadel because it was well built on a mount that would not be easy to conquer.

The king had to resort to a ruse to flush out soldiers from the citadel. He announced to all people living in the citadel that he would not lift off the siege until he vanquished Sdach Kân. He said that once he became victorious he would declare everybody in the citadel slaves of the state. The prince also announced that the Ayutthayan king was on his way with his large army to help him get rid of Sdach Kân. After hearing the announcement, the soldiers in the citadel as well as their families living outside the citadel were very troubled. When nighttime came, Ang Chan ordered his soldiers to burn the dry grass around the city to fool people in the village, as well as in the citadel, that the fires were the camp fires coming from the Ayutthayan army. The villagers showed up at the gate and urged their husbands and children who were serving Sdach Kân to leave the citadel. Ang Chan's ruse worked to perfection because people started to panic. They opened the gate and ran out of the citadel. Seizing on that opportunity, the king's army made a final assault and entered into the citadel. With all the commotions going on, Chau Hva Kav grabbed his sword and spear and came face to face with Oknha Chakrei, the king's general. Without hesitation, the general thrust forward and cut off the head of Chau Hva Kav. At the same moment, Oknha Veang and his soldiers went into the interior of the palace and found Sdach Kân with his concubines. The general threw his spear and pierced the arm of Sdach Kân. They captured him and kept him under guard all night. The next day, Oknha Veang amassed all the goods and all five hundred of Sdach Kân's concubines. After the prisoners were presented, the king decided to condemn to death all Sdach Kân's children and the wives who bored those children. The immediate conspirators who supported Sdach Kân were also condemned to death. After parading for three days, Sdach Kân was beheaded. His head was planted on the east gate of the citadel.

The chronicles said that Sdach Kân died at the age of forty in 1525 (year of the Rooster, the seventh of the decade, which corresponded to 2069 of the Buddhist era) after reigning for fourteen years. I believe that the chronicles were in error concerning the age of Sdach Kân. Because Kân was sixteen between 1505 and 1506, he would have been only 35 to 36 years old when he died.

THE LONGVEK PERIOD (1525-1594)

The Longvek period started from Borom Reachea III, better known as Ang Chan I, and ended during the reign Chey Chetha I (1586-1594). The construction for the Citadel of Longvek was commissioned by Ang Chan I in 1527.[29,p14] Ang Chan I and his royal families moved into the royal palace in the Citadel of Longvek in 1529, with the exact date stated as the year of the Ox of the first decade, in the month of Bisākha (ពិសាខ, Pisak).[29,p144] It must be noted that different sources gave different dates, but those dates do not seem to correlate very well with the historical events.[29,p291]

Based on the Khmer Inscription K.27 of Vatta Romlok[132,p84,p259,note11] that was discovered by Étienne Aymonier,[7,pp288-289,note1] David Chandler stated that Naresuan laid an unsuccessful first siege on Longvek in 1587. Khin Sok, on the other hand, never considered the Ayutthayan attack on Longvek to be a siege on the citadel itself. From the inscription, Khin Sok interpreted that the army of King Naresuan only attacked the city of Longvek from the south. He did not consider this attack to be the first siege of Longvek.[29,p342]

Naresuan started his campaign against Cambodia in 1592. The first siege of the Citadel of Longvek took place in 1593, but it ended in failure. He returned to Ayutthaya with a sense of shame because he had never lost a battle before. Naresuan was better prepared on his second attempt to take over the Citadel of Longvek. The attack of Longvek near the end of 1593 was more successful. As the army of Naresuan moved toward Longvek, Srei Soriyopor was left to protect the citadel in 1594 after King Satha I and his son King Chey Chetha I left the royal palace to the province of Srei Sa Chhor (formerly Basan and precursor to Srei Santhor that covered the present-day province of Kratié). With the overwhelming force of the Ayutthayan army surrounding the city for a month, Srei Soriyopor finally surrendered to Naresuan with the terms set by the Ayutthayan king in order to save his starving soldiers.

The date for the fall or rather surrender of Longvek cannot be determined exactly because different sources give different dates. George Coedès stated that Longvek fell in January 1594.[19,p197] Coedès must have come up with this date based on Bernard Philippe Groslier's *Angkor et le Cambodge* that said Longvek fell in January 1594, which he in turn based his study on the Annals of Ayutthaya.[29,p34] Khin Sok, on the other hand, said that Naresuan entered into the Citadel of Longvek in the year of the Goat of the seventh decade, in the month of Caetra (ចេត្រ), on Saturday of the third day of the waxing moon.[29,p212]

The above year, which corresponded to 1595, would seem to be too far in the event timeline. In subsequent paragraphs, Khin Sok stated that Naresuan appointed an Ayutthayan minister and ordered him to administer the country of Cambodia in 2139 of the Buddhist year, 1594 of the Christian year, 1517 of the Grand Era (Saka year), 957 Cula, the fifth day of the waning moon, the month of Caetra, year of the Goat, and seventh of the decade.[29,p213] Based on the Buddhist, Saka, and Cula years mentioned above, the corresponding Christian year should be 1595 and not 1594 as cited by Khin Sok. Adhémard Leclère said that the fall of Longvek occurred on 27 September 1593. His assumption was based on the letter, dated 27 September 1593, that the Portuguese adventurer Diego Veloso (also written as Diego Belloso) received from the Governor of the Philippines.[7,p187] He mentioned that after receiving the letter from the governor, Veloso found out that Longvek had just fallen a few weeks prior to his arrival in Cambodia. This date stated by Leclère seems to be too premature. The date of Veloso's receiving the letter from the Governor of the Philippines and his arrival in Cambodia are in contrast with the account written by Father Friar Gabriel Quiroga de San Antonio of the Dominican Order. Father Gabriel who was sent to Manila by King Philippe II of Spain said that Veloso and Ruiz left Manila in February 1594 and were captured by the Ayutthayan army as soon as they arrived in Phnom Penh.[133,pxvi] This seems to indicate that Phnom Penh was in the hand of the Ayutthayan army around the time when Naresuan laid siege at the Citadel of Longvek. David Chandler was non-committal to the precise date but he stated that Longvek fell in 1594.[132,p84] Like Chandler, John F. Cady stated that Longvek was captured in 1594.[16,p193] Other sources give different dates for the fall and/or surrender of Longvek. Most historians seem to concur that Longvek fell in 1594. I believe the fall of Longvek occurred in June 1594 based on the following reasoning: 1) It has to be after Naresuan entered Pursat triumphantly, which was January-February 1594 based on the date given in the Cambodian chronicles as the year of the Horse of the sixth decade, in the month of Meak (មាឃ), and on the fifth day of the waning moon;[29,p204] 2) Frankfurter mentioned in his paper, *Events in Ayuddhya from Chulasakaraj 686-966*,[127,p24] that Naresuan attacked Longvek in 955 Cula, in the year of the Snake, on Friday the 10th of the 2nd waxing moon, which according to my calculation would have corresponded to 10 May 1594; 3) According to the Cambodian chronicles, Naresuan laid one month of siege at the Citadel of Longvek before Srei Soriyopor agreed to surrender to the Ayutthayan king;[29,p210] 4) Adding one month to the date of the attack of Longvek which occurred in May 1594, I deduce that the fall or surrender of Longvek occurred in June 1594.

When Louis Delaporte visited Longvek in 1873 he said that the city was abandoned and in ruin. He saw some remaining ramparts, some streets of the palace, a stepped pyramid landlocked with six gigantic sandstone feet surrounded by carved stelae, and debris of the Preah Keo pedestal.[134,p38]

61   Ang Chan I/Chan Reachea or Borom Reachea III (1516-1567)
អង្គចន្ទ (ទី១)/ចន្ទរាជា ឬ បរមរាជា (ទី៣)

Transliterated Names: Paramarājā III or Cand Rājā
Other Names: Cau Bañā Cand, Chan Kreas Reachea

Style Name: a) Braḥ Pāda Saṃṭec Braḥ Rāja Oṅkāra Braḥ Paramarājādhīrāja Rammādhipatī[29,p149];
b) Dhammika Varottama Parama Cakrabattra Mahāddhipdin-dhara[29,p149]; c) Narindhara;[29,p149]
d) Visuddhi Santhit Jā Īsū Kuṃbūl Raṭha Rāstha Kambujā Sirī Yasodhara Mahā Indipata Guru
Raṭha Rājadhānī Mandīra Selā Mahāsthāna Parama Nātha Parama Pabitra;[29,p149] e) Jā
Aṃmcās;[29,p149] f) Jīvit Loe Thpūṅ Kruṅ Kambujādhipatī Gaṅ' Braḥ Rāja Vāṃṅ Laṅvaek;[29,p149]
Brah Rajaonkara Paramarajadhiraja Ramadhipati Paramachakravartiraja[81,p34]; b) Samdach
Preah Boromneat Chan Reacheathireach Serey Chey Chesda Moha Krasath Ammachas Krung
Kampuchea[7,p262]

Accession: 1516
Crowned: Thursday, 10 March 1530
Born: 1481/Deceased: 1567
Relationship: Son of Thommo Reachea; younger half-brother of Sokonthor Bat
Mother: Maya Tep Bosba
Wife: Srei Tep Thida
Religion: Theravada/Hinayana Buddhism
Capital: Longvek
Construction: Citadel of Longvek
Genealogy: Appendix 3

The Search for a Location to Build the Royal Palace/Citadel

As mentioned previously, members of the royal family and high officials asked Ang Chan I in 1516 to accept the royal title King of Cambodia. Ang Chan I graciously accepted the honor but he asked to postpone the consecration ceremony until he had vanquished Sdach Kân. Now that the usurper was dead, Ang Chan I's priority was to find a suitable location to build his royal palace. The chronicles said that during the period of war with Sdach Kân, Srei Tep Thida bore Ang Chan I a son named Borom Reachea (IV) in 1518 (year of the Tiger of the tenth decade) and a daughter named Tevi Ksatrei in 1522 (year of the Horse of the fourth decade).

After the death of Sdach Kân in 1525, Ang Chan I returned to Longvek with his army. He wanted to build a royal palace to mark his reign and his victory over Sdach Kân. He found a very suitable location on a mound surrounded by lakes and forests. The mound was also situated near present-day Tonle Sap River. Pleased with the location, the king asked his ministers to start the construction of his royal palace and of the citadel. The Cambodian chronicles said that Ang Chan I gave the orders to his ministers to start the construction of the Longvek Citadel in 1527 (year of the Pig, the ninth decade, the month of Phalguna (ផល្គុន, Phalkun), and the sixth day of the waning moon).[29,p143] After giving his order, the king returned to his Citadel in Pursat. To commemorate his victory over Sdach Kân, the king renamed the Citadel of Pursat to the Citadel Banteay Meanchey to signify the Citadel of Victory. It must not be confused with the province of Banteay Meanchey.

The Victory over the Ayutthayan Army and the Birth of Siem Reap

Without even given time for Ang Chan I to enjoy his victory over Sdach Kân, King Ramathibodi II [using the Cambodian ranking system, he was Ang Chan I's uncle but 4th cousin once removed if the western ranking system were applied] sent a message demanding that the Khmer king sent the magnificent white elephant that he possessed as a tribute to Ayutthaya. Ang Chan I refused to comply with the demand of Ramathibodi II. He reasoned that if he were to comply with the Ayutthayan king's demand, then he would agree to accept Cambodia as a vassal state of Ayutthaya. Ramathibodi II was furious after he learned that Ang Chan I refused to comply with his demand. Sensing that Cambodia was weakened after the exhausting civil war against Sdach Kân, the Ayutthayan king sent his fresh army to invade Angkor. Ang Chan I hastily recruited Khmer volunteers. They were very enthusiastic to fight the enemy. The

Ayutthayan army was fresh but the soldiers did not have much experience in a war. On the other hand, the Khmers had a lot of experiences fighting in battles for the last seventeen years. Even though they were exhausted after a long drawn-out war, the Khmers felt they were defending the country and fighting for the king they supported and loved. Ang Chan I himself led his army to meet the Ayutthayan forces at Angkor. Because of their experiences, the Khmers defeated the Ayutthayan army without much trouble. They chased the enemy all the way back to the frontier. The event was believed to have taken place in 1525. The Khmers took 10,000 prisoners. Because the defeat of the Siamese was so thorough, the Khmers commemorated the battlefield area by giving it a name "Siem Reap" to signify that the Siamese had been flattened. It must be remembered that even though Siam as a country did not exist yet but the people occupying Lan Na, Sukhothai, and Ayutthaya were called Siem (Siamese) by the Khmer people. Afterward, Ang Chan I returned to his Citadel of Banteay Meanchey.

The Passing of Prince Yuos

Two years later in 1527 (year of the Pig of the ninth decade), Prince Yuos fell gravely ill and he died in the same year. The chronicles said he was thirty three years old but Adhémard Leclère said he was only eighteen[6,p273] when he passed away. He could not have been thirty three years old because the same chronicles previously mentioned that he was born in 1507, three years after Sokonthor Bat became king. Prince Yuos left a daughter named Braḥ Sujāti Strī (ព្រះសុជាតិក្សត្រី, Preah Socheat Strei: Princess Socheat)[29,p14] or Ratna Reachea Tevi Ksatrei who would later marry her uncle Borom Reachea IV.[135]

The Construction of a Pagoda in Dedication to Buddha

The chronicles said that Ang Chan I left Banteay Meanchey with the royal families and his government in 1528 (year of the Rat of the tenth decade, in the month of Pisak (ពិសាខ), and on the third day of the waning moon) in the direction to the Citadel of Paripūrṇa (បន្ទាយបរិបូណ៌, Citadel of Boribaur). Baribaur was an old province name for present-day Kampong Chhnang. During this time, the king had a pagoda built in a region called Brai Naṅuy (ព្រៃងងុយ, Prey Ngo-nguy which means sleepy forest). He had a statue of the Buddha made from the core section of his boat, and the statue of Ananda (the Buddha's cousin and disciple) made from the bow of the boat. The king named the pagoda Vatta Braḥ Buddha Lāy Lakkhana (វត្តព្រះពុទ្ធលាយលក្ខណ, Vat Preah Puth Leay Leakhana), which according to Jean Moura still exists today in Kampong Chhnang.[29,pp290-291] The name of the pagoda was to signify the Buddha had signs of characteristic qualities such as those shown in his palm, in the bottom of his feet, etc. The ceremony for the completion of the pagoda was celebrated in the year of the Ox, the first of the decade, on the fifth day of the waning moon; in 2073 of the Buddhist era, in 1451 of the Grand era, in 891 of the Cula era, which corresponded to 1529.[29,p14]

The Citadel of Longvek

The king was informed that the construction of the Citadel of Longvek was completed. With his royal families and members of his government, the king left Baribaur in 1529 (year of the Ox, the first of the decade, the sixth of the month, on the first day of the waning moon). The king arrived in his royal palace in the Citadel of Longvek in the same year, in the month of Pisak.

The Citadel of Longvek was described in different sources as enormous. Even a horse would get exhausted galloping around its perimeter. It was estimated by some sources that the citadel was approximately 3-4 km long by 2-3 km wide. As a comparison, the dimension of the outer moat of Angkor Wat is 1.5 km by 1.3 km. Comparing the surface areas, the Citadel of Longvek was between three to six times larger than the surface area of Angkor Wat (up to the extremity of the outer edge of the moat). A map of the Citadel of Longvek was produced by the Dutch in 1747. The famous map was displayed in many books, but the drawing seems to differ somewhat from the description reported in the Cambodian chronicles. As history had indicated, Longvek fell to the Ayutthayan army in 1594. The citadel was apparently destroyed before the time the Dutch made the famous map. Apparently, the Dutch had never seen the full scale of the citadel in its glory day. The Dutch could not have known about the details of the citadel because the Cambodian chronicles were not made available to the public yet. It was only after 1863 under the French Colonial rules that the Cambodia Royal Chronicles were translated into French because they wanted to build the genealogy of the Khmer royal families. The Dutch must have made the map based on legend and on the creative imagination of the map maker of what the Citadel of Longvek would have looked like. The Dutch map of the Citadel of Longvek is reproduced in Figure 51 (Courtesy of Antiqueriaat Sanderus).

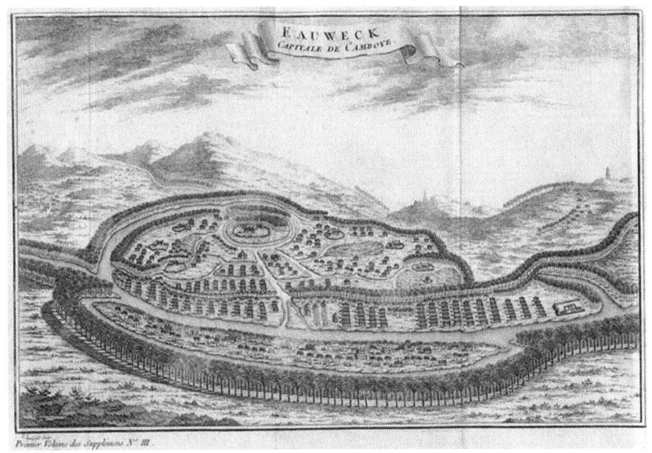

Figure 51. The 1747 Dutch Map of the Citadel of Longvek
(Courtesy of Antiquariaat Sanderus www.sanderusmaps.com)

According to the Cambodian chronicles, the citadel had walls on only three sides with the fourth side exposing to the river. The citadel was protected by five layers of walls, with the external one measuring approximately 11 meters wide at the base and 5 meters wide at the top. The wall was approximately 8.5 meters sitting on a foundation of stones with a depth of 3 meters. Canons were mounted on the citadel towers, eight at the gates and four at the corners, and guns were put along the first wall terrace to protect the citadel. Bamboos that could grow faster and could be grouped more densely than trees were planted to surround the citadel after its construction was completed. The chronicles stated that the bamboos were tightly planted to cover a width of 80 meters. The first enclosure (between the first and second walls) was the living quarter reserved for the artillery soldiers. The soldiers using firearms were patrolling in the second enclosure. A conference hall and a justice hall were also located in the second enclosure. Soldiers carrying swords lived in the third enclosure. They were probably placed there to act as a buffer zone to give the king an extra layer of protection, with the bodyguards living and patrolling in the fourth enclosure. The king lived in the fifth enclosure. Soldiers with guns were probably deemed to be a little too dangerous to be placed directly next to the king's bodyguards. Also, it would be strategically more advantageous to place soldiers with guns in the second enclosure to support the artillery soldiers in case of an attack by the enemies. The king's bodyguards were placed in the fourth enclosure for a quick response to the king's call. They were more privileged than the other soldiers because there was a theater to entertain them. It must be assumed that the families of the soldiers were probably also living within the enclosures where those soldiers were assigned for duties. Because of the enormous size of the citadel, there would be enough space to accommodate the families of the soldiers. The chronicles described that there were galleries in the fourth enclosure. The galleries were probably intentionally built to make the navigation in the enclosure very hard for people who were not familiar with the area. In case of enemies or potential traitors breaking through the other three enclosures, they would have very difficult times finding entrances to the fifth enclosure. There were also galleries in the fifth enclosure to keep the royal treasures as well as to house the purohita (Chief Brahman), and probably also the royal astrologer next to the treasures. Because the Chief Brahman was given the responsibility of guarding the royal regalia, his residence was assumed to be located next to the treasury rooms. Galleries were probably intentionally built to make the navigation through the maze difficult. In an emergency when the Chief Brahman had to remove the royal regalia from falling into the wrong hands, he would have a better chance to evade the enemies and escape to a safe place. The royal palace for the king and the residence for the queen, as well as that for the prince, were all located in the fifth enclosure. The king's palace was very large because it was also used to house his concubines, which could be numbered in the hundreds. There were royal hangars and boats as well as floating houses on the river. Food supplies and ammunitions were stored in 25 buildings behind the fifth wall. Ten buildings were constructed to store ammunitions and gun powders. The buildings were probably placed at strategic locations for a quick access when needed. They were probably not located in one place, but scattered all over the area to prevent any potential explosions that would destroy the entire supply. They were probably placed far away from the royal residences. Food supplies were stored in fifteen buildings. They were probably stored near the royal residences. The chronicles did not mention about the king's bodyguards living in the fifth enclosure, but it must be assumed there were probably a lot of them living within a calling distance from the king's palace. The chronicles did not mention about the citadel having a wall facing the river either, but it must be assumed there was probably one. The wall was probably of medium size and not as high as those facing the bamboo forest. Stables for elephants and horses were built outside the first wall, but they were able to roam freely because they were enclosed by the bamboo forest. There were parks for the elephants and horses to enjoy. There were stone platforms next to the river to use for washing the elephants and horses. As described above, the Dutch map does not seem to match the descriptions given in the chronicles. It must be assumed there were probably hidden gates within the bamboo forest leading to the outside world.

Instead of relying on the Dutch map, I have drawn a general floor plan of the Citadel of Longvek based on my interpretation of the Cambodian chronicles. I placed the locations of items discussed in the chronicles based on my explanations above. The general floor plan of the Citadel of Longvek is shown in Figure 52.

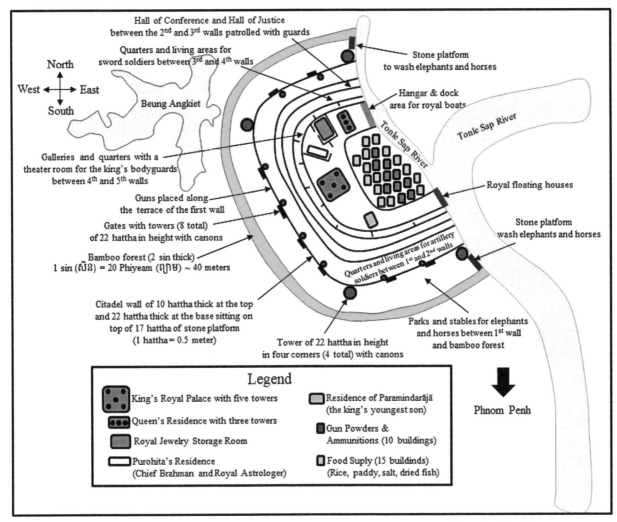

**Figure 52. Plan of the Citadel of Longvek as Interpreted by the Author
(Map created by Kenneth So; based on Ref. 29, pp. 143 and 288-289)**

The descriptions of the Citadel of Longvek are translated below in English for the benefits of the readers.[29,pp288-289]

The soil was dug to six hattha deep [my note: approximately 3 meters] and then filled with stones on all three sides. It was then compacted with soil to raise it to 17 hattha. The wall was then built on top of it to 10 hattha thick at its highest point and 22 hattha thick at the base. There were eight gates and each one had a tower with canons. Each tower had a height of 22 hattha. On the four corners of the citadel there were also four towers with canons. Guns were placed all along the terrace of the first wall. In front of the first enclosure [my note: outside the citadel rampart and behind the bamboo forest] there were elephant parks and stables [my note: including horses]. Within the first enclosure [my note: between the 1st and 2nd walls] lived the artillery soldiers and within the second enclosure there were soldiers with guns, a conference hall, and a justice hall. The sword soldiers lived within the third enclosure. In the galleries within the fourth enclosure there were bodyguards and a theater room. Within the fifth enclosure there were galleries with rooms to keep the royal treasures; and the residences of the purohita were also inside [my note: he was not just the Chief Brahman but he was also the guardian of royal regalia]. There was a royal palace with five towers for the king and his concubines. The residence for the queen had three towers. Food supplies containing rice, paddy, salt, and dried fish were stored in fifteen buildings behind the fifth wall. Ammunitions and gun powders were stored in ten buildings behind the fifth wall also. The residence for the king's youngest son, Samdech Preah Paramindaraja, was built inside the royal palace [my: probably within the fifth enclosure instead of the royal palace]. Hangars and docks for royal boats and floating houses were also built [my note: probably located in the fifth enclosure]. The king also ordered that platforms in stones be built for the washing and cleaning of the elephants and horses [my note: probably between the first wall and the bamboo forest]. The king ordered that bamboos be planted very tightly outside the citadel to make it impregnable as a defense against an enemy attack. He instructed that the bamboo forest be two sin deep [my note: one sin was equaled to 20 phiyeam, which were equivalent to 40 meters] and that nobody was allowed to cut them down. The chronicles also mentioned that the residence for the king's oldest son, Samdech Preah Reamea Thipadei, was built in Tuol Leap [my note: location undetermined].

The Discovery of the Hidden Preah Khan Reach and the Coronation of Ang Chan I

After Ang Chan I had settled down in his royal palace, all the high officials proposed to have a consecration ceremony for the king's accession to the throne. Ang Chan I reminded his ministers that traditions required the Rāja Pañca Kakudha Bhaṇta (រាជបញ្ចកកុធភណ្ឌ, Reach Pahnjak Kakkuth Phon) — the five royal paraphernalia — to be present before the ceremony could be performed. The five royal objects differed depending on the chronicles. According to Khin Sok, there are two lists. The first list includes the royal crown, the sacred sword, the royal white parasol, the royal shoes, and the royal flyswatter. The second list includes the royal crown, the sacred sword, the royal shoes, the royal cane, and the royal fan. The most important item among those five items is the sacred sword. Because only the Chief Brahman Suos and his student Su knew of the hidden location of the royal regalia, the secret also disappeared with them when they died. Now, the search for the royal regalia became a priority. The king ordered the governors in all provinces to look for the sacred sword. The chronicles said that a Krālā Bās (ក្រឡាពាស, Kralapeas) named Suos (no relation to the Chief Brahman Suos and his student Su), a dutiful son of a fisherman, from Bati discovered the sacred sword in the trunk of the Chambak tree near the river. Kralapeas was a title of a deputy chief overseeing the slaves Bal Cūl Ven (ពលចូលវៃន, Pol Chaul Ven; slave to do temporary works).[29,p292] He reported his finding to the governor and a ceremony took place to retrieve the sacred sword from the tree trunk. A procession carrying the sacred sword from Bati to the Citadel of Longvek was organized by the governor of Bati. The king went out of the citadel to greet the crowd. He had the sacred sword stored in a special room. He decreed the place to be called *Ho Pahnjak Khsetra.* "Ho" (ហោ) means "pavilion, hall, or room" in Khmer and "Khsetra" signified "the five Indian deities."

After the royal regalia and the *Preah Khan Reach* (Royal Sacred Sword) had been found, the consecration ceremony to coronate Ang Chan I was set up. The chronicles said that Ang Chan I acceded to the throne as King of Cambodia in 2073 of the Buddhist era, 1451 of the Grand era, 891 of the Cula era; in the year of the Ox of the first decade, in the month of Phalkun, on Thursday of the eleventh day of the waxing moon. Khin Sok reported the corresponding Christian year to be 1529,[29,p149] but according to my calculation it would fall on Thursday, 10 March 1530.

Ang Chan I had a full consecration ceremony at the age of forty nine [my note: he would have been only forty eight years old]. He reigned under the style name *Preah Dat Samdech Preah Reach Ang Preah Borom Reacheathireach Reameathipadei.* He issued a decree that he would be addressed as *Braḥ Pāda Anak Jā Amcās'* (ព្រះបាទអ្នកជាអម្ចាស់, Preah Bat Neak Chea Ang Mchas) from that day on. The term could be translated as *August feet of the one who is the master.* The king honored his queen with the title Samṭec Braḥ Bhagavatī Srī Deba Dhitā (សម្តេចព្រះភគវតីស្រីទេពធីតា, Samdech Preah Pheakavatei Srei Tep Thida). He nominated Braḥ Dhammaridhī Jai (ព្រះធម្មរិទ្ធិជៃ, Preah Thommo Rithy Chey) Chief Brahman Braḥ Īsī Bhāda

(ព្រះតសិកទ្ធ, Preah Eysei Phoat). As to Suos who found the Royal Sacred Sword, he became a lord and was awarded the title Chau Hva Tolaha. The other officials who fought in the war with the king from the beginning were also rewarded with the governorships or high positions in his government. Coincidentally, King Ramathibodi II of Ayutthaya passed away in 1529. He was succeeded by his son No Phutthamgkun. He reigned under the name Borommaracha IV for four years before dying of smallpox in 1533. He was succeeded by his five years old son Ratsada. The young king's reign lasted only five months before he was killed by his half-brother Chairacha who usurped the throne from him in 1534. Chairacha reigned from 1534 to 1547.

The Cambodian chronicles mentioned that Ang Chan I awarded five governorships of the following provinces to his loyal supporters shown below:[29,pp293-294]

- The Asantuk (អសន្ទុក) province that included the following twenty four counties was awarded to Cau Bañā Udaidhirāja (ចៅពញាឧទ័យធីរាជ, Chau Ponhea Outeythireach): Sdoṅ (ស្តោង, Staung), Jīkraeṅ (ជីក្រែង, Chikreng), Braṃ Deb (ព្រហ្មទេព, Prohm Tep), Prāsāda Ṭap' (ប្រាសាទដប់, Prasat Dorp), Brai Kṭī (ព្រៃក្តី, Prey Kdei), Sraṅae (ស្រងែ, Sra-ngè), Jhoe Dāl (ឈើទាល, Chheu Teal), Ṅan (ងន, Ngaun), Kaṃbaṅ Laeṅ (កំពង់លែង, Kampong Leng), Koḥ Ker (កោះកេរ្តិ៍ or គាស់កែ, Koh Ker), Braḥ Kān (ព្រះកាន, Preah Kan), Bodhi Roṅ (ពោធិរោង, Puthi Raung), Sen (សែន, Sén), Nagara (នគរ, Nokor), Mlū Brai (ម្លូ ប្រៃ, Mlu Prey), Jāṃ Ksānt (ជាំខ្សាន្ត, Choam Ksant), Vārī Saen (វារីសែន, Veari Saen), Brai Saṃpuor (ព្រៃសំបួរ, Prey Sombuor), Kaṃbūl Bejra (កំពូលពេជ្រ, Kampoul Pich), Braḥ Trasap' (ព្រះត្រសប់, Preah Trasap), Tpaeṅ (ថ្បែង, Tbèng), Braḥ Ghlāṃṅ (ព្រះឃ្លាំង, Preah Khleang), and Gok Seḥ (គោកសេះ, Kauk Seh).
- The Bodhisāt (ពោធិសាត់, Pursat) province that included the following six counties was awarded to Cau Bañā Suorgāloka (ចៅពញាស្វរគាលោក, Chau Ponhea Suorkealauk): Kragar (ក្រគរ, Krakor), Kraṅ (ក្រង, Krorng), Thbaṅ (ថ្បង, Thporng), Khluṅ (ខ្លុង, Khlong), Tāṃṅ (តាំង, Tang), and Saṃrae (សំរែ, Samrè).
- The Tpūṅ Ghmuṃ (ត្បូងឃ្មុំ, Thbong Khmum) province that included the following five counties and four sub-counties was awarded to Cau Bañā Ar Jūn (ចៅពញាអរជុន, Chau Ponhea Aur Chune): Duol Aṅguñ (ទួលអង្គុញ, Tuol Angkunh), Taṃpae (តំបែ, Dambè), Bhnaṃ Braḥ (ភ្នំព្រះ, Phnom Preah), Dvār Lo (ទ្វារលោ, Tvear Lo), Dvār Bjakṭī (ទ្វារភក្ដី, Tvear Pheakdei), Joeṅ Guor (ជើងគួរ, Cheung Kuor), Jrai Prahār (ជ្រៃប្រហារ, Chrey Prahar), Dvār Rūṅ (ទ្វាររូង, Tvear Raung), and Dvār Rīel (ទ្វាររៀល, Tvear Riel).
- The Pā Bhnaṃ (បាភ្នំ, Ba Phnom) province that included the following seven counties was awarded to Cau Bañā Dhammā Tejo (ចៅពញាធម្មតេជោ, Chau Ponhea Thommo Decho): Koḥ (កោះ, Koh), Mecuṅ (មេចុង, Mechong), Mekaṅ (មេកង, Mekorng; possibly Mesang), Svāy Dāp (ស្វាយទាប, Svay Teap), Raṃduol (រំដួល, Ramduol), Kaṇṭāl (កណ្ដាល, Kandal), and one undetermined county.
- The Drāṃṅ (ទ្រាំង, Treang) province that included the following six counties was awarded to Cau Bañā Bisṇuloka (ចៅពញាពិស្ណុលោក, Chau Ponhea Pisnuklauk): Bāṃ (ពាម, Peam), Brai Joeṅ (ព្រៃជើង, Prey Cheung), Jān' Juṃ (ជាន់ជុំ, Choan Chum), Pandāy Mās (បន្ទាយមាស, Banteay Meas), Srae Ranoṅ (ស្រែរនោង, Srè Ronaung), and Tāpuor (តាបួរ, Tabour).

According to the chronicles,[29,p150] the king ordered to have Vatta Traḷaeṅ Kaeṅ (វត្តត្រឡែងកែង, Vat Traleng Keng), which signified four-faced pagoda, built in 1530 in Longvek. The pagoda was built to house the statue of the Buddha made from the branch of a gagī (គគី, koki) tree and a block of stone that the king found sitting on that tree. The statue was carved with the Buddha having four faces and four backs fused into one body sitting on the stone. The king also had another pagoda built. He named it Vatta Braḥ Inda Deba Nimitta (វត្តព្រះឥន្ទទេពនិមិត្ត, Vat Preah Eynt Tep Nimitt) but people shortened it to the present-day name Vat Preah Eynt Tep. The king was a fervent Buddhist who believed in receiving merits for performing good deeds. He had a third pagoda built on the hill of Bhnaṃ Braḥ Rājadrabya (ភ្នំព្រះរាជទ្រព្យ, Phnom Preah Reach Troap) in the province of Saṃroṅ Daṅ (សំរោងទង, Samrong Tong). The name of the hill, which signified the mount of the king's wealth, is still preserved to this day. The pagoda was built to house one of the biggest statues of the Buddha, with a height of eighteen hattha, approximately equivalent to nine meters. In Buddhism, the number eighteen is considered a sacred number because it represents the eighteen qualities of Braḥ Bhagavānt Buddha (ព្រះភគវន្ត, Preah Pheakavant). The statue was named Buddha Aṭṭhārasa (អដ្ឋារស្ស) to signify the Buddha with eight corners. The statue was placed facing the northern side. There were statues of the Buddha's disciples, Arahant (អរហន្ត), sitting around the Buddha. The king also had a pond built to supply the pagoda with water. The pond was named Sraḥ Braḥ Dhammakerti (ព្រះធម្ម កេរ្តិ៍, Srah Preah Thommoker) to signify a heritage pond because Ang Chan I wanted to remind people that his father, Thommo Reachea, had the work started when he was alive. The king also had another pond built on the western side of the hill and a Bodhibritka (ពោធិព្រឹក្ស, Pothipreuk) tree planted next to it.

While the king was occupied with the social and religious programs, he nevertheless did not neglect his duty in preparing the country to be militarily ready. He ordered a lake dug to support an iron smelting plant that was built on the northern side of the hill. The Kouys were assigned to be in charge of the plant. Since the dawn of history, the Kouys had been known to work on metal and they became experts in their trades. They knew how to extract iron and gold from iron and gold ores. They were masters in building weapons. The lake was named Piṅ Phsār Ṭaek (បឹងផ្សារដែក, Boeung Phsar Dek; meaning Iron Market Lake). The king ordered a second lake dug in the northeast to support the foundry for the fabrication of guns and other objects made of bronze. The lake was named Piṅ Saṃrid (បឹងសំរិទ្ធ, Boeung Samrith; meaning Bronze Lake). The king had the land from Boeung Samrith to the river cleared for rice fields. The king proclaimed the river (present-day Tonle Sap) to be named Sdiṅ Roṅ Dūk (ស្ទឹងរោងទូក, Stung Raung Touk; meaning Hangar Boat Lake) because a hangar was built on the river to store the royal boats. Another land near the village of Bodhi Orām/Urāl (ពោធិឱរាម/ពោធិឱរាល, Puth Oream/Ureal) was cleared on the order of the king as an offering to the monastery of Srah Preah Thommoker. The king had a pagoda built in 1535 in Bati (present-day Kandal Stung district) near the Chambak tree to commemorate the discovery of the Royal Sacred Sword. The pagoda was named Vatta Dăb Bāt' Caṃpak' (វត្តទ័ពពាត់ចំបក់, Vat Toap Poat Chambak was to signify the monastery encircled by the army) and the location was called Bhūmi Dāna (ភូមិទាន, Phum Tean), which means the Village of Offerings.

Cambodia had been relatively at peace after the death of Ramathibodi II in 1529. While Cambodia was a stable country under Ang Chan I, Ayutthaya on the other hand was in turmoil and had three kings replaced prior to the war in 1536. Borommaracha IV succeeded his father Ramathibodi II, but his reign was short because he died of smallpox four years later. His infant son Rasatda, who was only five years old, succeeded him in 1533. His reign lasted only five months because he was murdered by his half-brother Chairacha who usurped the throne in 1534. After being on the throne for two years, Chairacha was emboldened and demanded that Ang Chan I sent him the white elephant that the Khmer king had in his possession. The Cambodian chronicles said that Ang Chan I was very upset at the Ayutthayan king. He wrote a letter to the Ayutthayan king which contained the following message:[29,pp297-298]

Cette noble parole de S.M. Braḥ Paramarājā Mahā Candarājā, s'adresse, au nom de la royale amitié, à S.M. Braḥ Cau Cakrabatti, le roi de Kruṅ Deba Srī Ayudhyā, l'auguste oncle (a), et S.M. est priée d'en prendre connaissance.

Or nous, le neveu, après avoir lu le message royal, trouvons qu'il y a beaucoup d'erreurs toutes contraires à la tradition des anciens règnes. Le pays du Grand Kambujā, la grande cité, est un très grand pays; la cité de Srī Ayudhyā était jadis soumise (au Kambujā) et lui offrit le tribut pendant plusieurs règnes. Pendant que nous étions accupés avec Ṣṭec Kan, le Siam ne nous a pas aidé; cela rend impossible pour les Khmers d'apporter le tribut à l'auguste oncle. Nous avons tenu conseil avec les membres de la famille royale, les grands généraux, les généraux, les grands et petits ministres et les serviteurs royaux et nous pensons que le Siam n'est pas un pays qui mérite notre reconnaissance; d'autre part, les Siamois sont venus clandestinement avec leur armée piller les biens des gens du peuple de notre pays, sans qu'aucun message royal n'eût déclaré la guerre; c'est pour cela que les Khmers ne peuvent pas traiter le Siam comme un pays ami. [(a): Le mot "oncle" marque ici non pas la parenté, mais la classe d'âges. Il s'agit d'un homme moins âgé que le père]

Translation:

This noble speech of His Majesty Preah Borom Reachea Maha Chan Reachea, addressing in the name of the royal friendship, to His Majesty Preah Chau Chakrabatti, King of Krung Tep Sri Ayutthaya, the august uncle (a), and to His Majesty is requested to take note.

But we, nephew, after having read the royal message, find that there are many errors all contrary to the tradition of the ancient kingdoms. The country of the Great Kambuja, the great city, is a very large country; the city of Sri Ayutthaya was in the past a vassal (of Kambuja) and had offered tributes to Kambuja under the reigns of several kings. While we were busy fighting Sdech Kan, Siam did not help us; it makes it impossible for the Khmers to bring tribute to the august uncle. We held a consultation with the members of the royal family, with the generals and high ranking generals, with the ministers and high ranking ministers, and with the royal caretakers and we agree that Siam is not a country that deserves our recognition; On the other hand, the Siamese came with their army illegally to plunder the property of the common people of our country, without any royal message for a declaration of war; that's why the Khmers cannot treat Siam as a friendly country. [(a): The word "uncle" does not indicate a relative, but a relationship based on ages. It indicates a man who is younger than a father].

Khin Sok stated that the word uncle used in the message above did not mean that Ang Chan I and Preah Chau Chakrabati (Ramathibodi II) were related, but the term was merely used as an expression of respect from a younger person to an older one. I would argue to the contrary, based on the fact that Khin Sok may not be aware or may not take into consideration about the relationship between Ponhea Yat and Borommaracha II that was described in the *2/k.125 Fragment*. The letter that King Ang Chan I made to the Ayutthayan king (Chairacha), stating that *His Majesty Preah Chau Chakrabatti, King of Krung Tep Sri Ayutthaya* (King Ramathibodi II) was his uncle, tends to support and reinforce the *2/k.125 Fragment* saying that Chau Ponhea Yat was the son of Ramaracha. As in the custom in Asia, but particularly in Cambodia and Thailand, the concept of family relationships is different than that used in the West. Because Chau Ponhea Yat was the son of King Ramaracha (from the branch of the Khmer princess from Suphanburi who married U-Thong/Ramathibodi I), then according to the Cambodian concept, King Ramathibodi II (from the branch of Pha-ngua/Borommaracha I, the Khmer prince from Suphanburi and brother of the Khmer princess) would be considered his nephew in the ranking order. Ang Chan I who was the grandson of Chau Ponhea Yat would therefore be considered as the nephew of Ramathibodi II. The Western concept ignores this important relationship where the younger generation must be respectful of the older generation. In the Western concept, Ang Chan I and Ramathibodi II would be considered as fourth cousins once removed with no emphasis to indicate the ranking order of seniority. Continuing on this line of Khmer ranking system, Ang Chan I would be considered the uncle of Chairacha. It may be partly for this reason that Ang Chan I wrote the letter to Chairacha with a tone that was less respectful.

After receiving the letter from Ang Chan I, Chairacha was very upset. He wanted to teach a lesson for refusing to obey his demand. He was acting as if Cambodia was a vassal state of Ayutthaya. To make the matter worse, he decided to send Preah Sithean Reachea to attack Cambodia. Preah Sithean Reachea was born as Chau Ponhea Ong. When he was six years old he was sent into exile to Ayutthaya with his father King Srei Reachea of Cambodia. He was adopted by King Borommatrailokanat and given in marriage to one of his daughters. He was given the province of Sawankhalok (present-day district of the province of Sukhothai in Thailand) to govern. From the Khmer royal lineage, Sithean Reachea could also be considered Characha's uncle. At first, Ang Chan I thought that the Ayutthayan king himself was leading the army to fight him until he realized to his sadness that the Ayutthayan king had sent Preah Sithean Reachea to fight him. Ang Chan I tried to talk his cousin out of fighting each other. He tried to reason with his elder cousin that they were from the same branch of family and that Ayutthaya's goal was to dominate Cambodia. Ang Chan I offered his cousin a way out by asking him to request the Ayutthayan king to send another prince to fight him in a dual combat on elephant backs. Sithean Reachea would not hear any of it and still wanted to engage the Ayutthayan army to fight the Khmer army. Because of Sithean Reachea's intransigence, Ang Chan I agreed to set the date for the battle to take place. On the appointed date of the battle, the two forces were engaged and at the end Sithean Reachea was killed. He died in the battle field on the back of his elephant in 1536 (year of the Monkey of the eight decade). The Khmer army pursued the Ayutthayan army and killed their generals. Bañā Mahā Mantrī (ពញ្ញាមហាមន្ត្រី, Ponhea Moha Montrei), Bañā Bahula Debva (ពញ្ញាពហុលទេព, Ponhea Pahul Tep), Bañā Bijai Naruṅga (ពញ្ញាពិជៃណរុង្គ, Ponhea Chey Norong), and Bañā Rāma Lekkhaṇa (ពញ្ញារាមលក្ខណ, Ponhea Ream Lekhanak) were all killed in the battle fields. The Khmer victory was complete. Half of the Ayutthayan army soldiers were made prisoners and most of the war equipments, elephants, horses were captured.

King Borom Reachea (III), popularly known as Ang Chan I, passed away in 1567 (year of the Hare of the ninth decade, in the month of Chais). The king's ashes were place in the stupa built on the eastern side of the Preah Reach Trop hill next to the Nirvana pagoda.

According to the Cambodian chronicles, Ayutthaya had not attacked Cambodia from 1536 until the end of Ang Chan I's reign. On the other hand, David K. Wyatt mentioned that Ayutthaya had a brief war with Cambodia in 1549 that lasted only a few months under the reign of Chakkraphat. The war with Cambodia was short-lived because Ayutthaya was attacked by Burma during that time. The war with Cambodia resumed from 1555 to 1556 when Ayutthaya attacked Longvek both by land and by water.[104,p79]

Based on the inscriptions carved on the panels, the bas-reliefs on the North Wing of the East Gallery and on the East Wing of the North Gallery were added or completed under the reign of King Ang Chan I. For the Battle of Pragiyotisha (North Wing, East Gallery), the inscription says that the carving was completed on Wednesday 8 September 1546.[81,p35] For the Battle of Shonitapura (East Wing, North Gallery), the inscription says that the carving was completed on Sunday 27 February 1564.[81,p35] It was reported that Ang Chan I noticed the incomplete work on the two panels during his campaign at Angkor around 1525 against the invading army of the Ayutthayan King Ramathibodi II. It was also reported that it was during Ang Chan I's returned trip to Angkor to check on the work progress of the two panels that he discovered the existence of Bayon, which at the time was deeply covered in the jungle and hidden from public view.[81,p35] The official chronicle of the Portuguese named Diogo do Cuoto dated 1585-1588, which mentioned a Khmer king ordering to have the jungle of Angkor cleared by *a force of 5,000-6,000 men* in 1550-1551 after he came from an elephant hunting trip,[136,p13] seems to correspond to the time when Ang Chan I discovered Bayon. Diogo do Cuoto who is considered as the first European to visit

Angkor, described Angkor Wat in this fashion:[136,p13] "it is of a construction so strange that one can hardly describe it with the pen, nor can one compare it to any other monument in the world." His account remained unpublished until only now.

According to a different chronicle,[29,pp305-306] Ang Chan I had two sons and one daughter. The chronicle said that his oldest son Preah Reamea Thipadei slept with his beautiful daughter named Ang Chan Mealea. He was heir to the throne but history did not mention about him. It was Borom Reachea (IV), his younger brother, who succeeded his father.

62   Borom Reachea IV (1568-1579) បរមរាជា (ទី ៤)

Transliterated Name: Paramarājā IV
Other Name: Borom Intho Reachea I
Style Name: Preah Bat Samdach Preah Borom Intho Reacheathireach Reameathipadey Borom Baupit[7,p278]
Accession: 1568
Born: 1518/Deceased: 1579
Relationship: Son of Ang Chan I/Borom Reachea III
Mother: Srei Tep Thida
Wife: Preah Sucheatei Strei or Ratna Reachea Tevi (Daughter of Ponhea Yuos); Kesar Mealea; Vaung (Vani).
Religion: Theravada/Hinayana Buddhism
Capital: Longvek, moved government to Kampong Krasang
Genealogy: Appendix 3

The Battle of Royal Elephants and the Campaign against Ayutthaya to Retake the Lost Khmer Province

Before Borom Reachea IV succeeded his father, Ang Chan I, in 1568 he already had three sons and one daughter with three different wives. He took his niece, Socheat Strei, as his first wife. She was the daughter of Ponhea Yuos, the only son of Srei Sokonthor Bat and Mneang Peou whose mother was a slave of the Triple Jewels and sister of the usurper Kân. Socheat Strei bore Borom Reachea IV a son named Satha (I) in 1543 and a daughter named Srei Socheat Ksatrei (also called Preah Cheat Ksatrei) in 1555. When Borom Reachea IV became king he elevated her to the style name Samdech Preah Pheakaveaktei Srei Ratanak Reachea Tevi. His second wife named Kesar Mealea bore him a son named Srei Soriyopor in 1548. His third wife named Vaung bore him a son named Ponhea An in 1555.

Borom Reachea IV had not forgotten about the Khmer provinces that were lost to Ayutthaya. Seizing on the death of the Ayutthayan king Chakkraphat (1548-1569) and on his weak son Mahin who was put on the throne by King Bayinnaung (1550-1581) of the Toungoo Dynasty, which had conquered the more powerful Môn Kindom of Pegu of Hanthawaddy (or Hamsavati) in mid-1541, Borom Reachea IV convened a meeting in 1569 with his generals, the noble families, and members of the royal families to attack Ayutthaya and retook the lost Khmer provinces. For simplicity and also to avoid confusion, I will refer King Bayinnaung and all his descendants as kings of Burma (present-day Myarnma). Borom Reachea IV ordered Ukñā Pudesarāja Kau (ឧញ្ញាបូទេសរាជិកៅ, Oknha Botes Reach Kau = Oknha Kau) and Ukñā Mahādhirāja Ut (ឧញ្ញាមហាធិរជ៌ឧិត, Oknha Moha Thireach Ut = Oknha Ut) to recruit 20,000 men from the provinces of Bassak, Preah Trapeang, Kramuon Sâ, Treang, and Banteay Meas. They were to attack Ayutthaya from the sea. He ordered Ukñā Mahāsenā Mịṅ (ឧញ្ញាមហាសេនាម៉ឹង, Oknha Moha Sena Meung = Oknha Meung) to raise an army of 20,000 men from the provinces of Thbong Khmum to Prohm Tep; they were to lead the land attack. As to Ukñā Yodhāsaṅgrāma Suos (ឧញ្ញាមហាយោធាសង្គ្រាមសួស, Oknha Moha Yuthea Sangkream Suos = Oknha Suos), he was ordered to raise an army of 20,000 men from the provinces of Bati to Battambang; they were to spearhead the attack from the middle.[7,p278; 29,p207] The attack from the sea by the Khmer forces was a complete success. They retook Chanborei, Rayang, Sak Sieng Sav, and Na Roeung from Ayutthaya (present-day Chanthaburi, Rayong, Chachoengsao or Paet Rio; according to Adhémard Leclère, Na Roeung was a neighboring province of Chachoengsao which could possibly be the present-day Sa Kaeo). In the course of the battles, the four Ayutthayan governors as well as Oknha Ut of Cambodia were killed. The land attack by the forces of Oknha Meung and Oknha Suos captured the provinces of Baschimborei and Neang Rong (present-day Prachinburi and Buriram). Cambodia took 70,000 prisoners and sent them to live in other provinces. The three Khmer generals pushed their forces to Ayutthaya and encircled the city. The Ayutthayan king left the city and fled to the province of Sawankhalok (district of the present-day province of Sukhothai). The Khmer forces could not take the city after one month of siege. The Khmer soldiers ran out of food supplies and became sick with fever as the rainy season started. Unable to take the city, Borom Reachea IV ordered his army to fall back.

In 1572 (year of the Monkey of the fourth decade), the king decided to move his government to Kampong Krasang in the province of Angkor Wat and left his oldest son, Satha, to take care of the royal palace at Longvek.[29,p163] Bernard P. Groslier had determined in his study that the village of Kampong Krasang (កំពង់ក្រសាំង) was located in the Angkor region,[29,p314] but the chronicle during the reign of Chey Chetha III specifically said that the village was located in Samrong Tong, which is in present-day Kampong Speu.[29,p312] The map of Cambodia produced by the National Geographic in 1967 shows that Kampong Krasang is located in the province of Banteay Meanchey at about 20 km southeast of Mongkol Borei. With an army of 20,000 men the Khmers easily conquered Nokor Reach Seima (present-day Nakhon Ratchasima or Korat).

In the same year, the ambitious Malean (ម៉ាលាន, Laos) king named Srī Sattaṇā Guṇhut (ស្រីសត្តនាគុណហុត, Si Sattana Kunhut) came up with a plan to conquer Cambodia. Malean, a Khmer word, is a direct translation of the words Lan Xang (Laos) which means a million elephants. The Laotian king challenged the Khmer king in a battle of elephants. The stake for the challenge was high. The loser would become a vassal state. The Laotian king sent two of his ministers, accompanied by an army of one thousand soldiers, and the combat elephant named Phlāy Siṅ Tū (ផ្លាយសិនតូ, Phlay Sing Tuk) to deliver a message to Borom Reachea IV. The Laotian king proposed to have his most powerful elephant, Phlay Sing Tuk of seven hattha in height (3.5 meters), fighting the best elephant the Khmer king had in his possession. Borom Reachea IV was indignant after reading the message from the Laotian king. He knew that Laos could never win a war against Cambodia. Borom Reachea IV understood the challenge and the arrogance of the Laotian king. The Laotian king showed his arrogance when he issued the challenge. He believed his elephant was the most powerful one without having even seen the elephant of the Khmer king. The Khmer king had an advantage because he saw the Laotian elephant and he was able to judge whether his elephant would be able to beat the enemy's elephant. He knew that Phlay Sing Tuk was a very powerful elephant, but the Khmer king had a ruse of his own. Borom Reachea IV knew that after traveling such a long distance, the Laotian elephant would not be in its best physical condition. The food, the terrain, and the environment in Cambodia were different than those in Laos. The king knew that he had his own best combat elephant in his stable that was well rested, well tested in combat, and as tall as the Laotian elephant. Instead of showing his anger, the Khmer king told the two Laotian ministers that he accepted the challenge.

According to the Cambodian chronicles,[29,p166] the Khmer king set up the elephant battle to take place in 1572 (2116 Buddhist era, 1494 of Grand era, 934 of Cula era, the seventh day of the waning moon, in the month of Phalkun, in the year of the Monkey of the fourth decade) on the hill of Asantuk across the river from the Citadel of Longvek. The Khmer king chose the most powerful elephant from the stable named Gujja Vai Hān Klā (គុជ្ជវៃហានក្ល, Kuch Vey Han Khla) that had the same height as the Laotian elephant for the challenge. While the Laotian elephant had to take the long route to reach the hill, the Khmer elephant was well rested traveling by a special house boat crossing the river from the Citadel of Longvek to the other side of the bank. The Khmer soldiers on the other side of the river were boisterous and yelling as the boats transporting the elephant, the horses, and the soldiers were crossing the river to join them. This place was known to this day as Kaṃbaṅ' Hau (កំពង់ហៅ, Kampong Hav which means the calling shore). A laborious ceremony of incantation was performed before the battle of the elephants started. Before accepting the challenge, Borom Reachea IV must have realized that the tusks of the Khmer elephant were longer than those of the Laotian elephant. The chronicles said that with its longer tusks, the Khmer elephant launched toward the Laotian elephant and pierced it in the neck (the chronicles said it pierced the other elephant in the area under the tusks). The wound prompted the Laotian elephant to withdraw from the combat. The Khmer elephant chased the Laotian elephant and gave it two more shots in the rump as its opponent ran away into the forest.[29,pp166-167] After the victory the king called on the two Laotian ministers and asked them whether they would fulfill their promises as agreed before the challenge. The two ministers asked the king's permission to allow them to return home so that they could report the defeat of the elephant Phlay Sing Tuk to the Laotian king. Borom Reachea IV let the two ministers and ten soldiers with the elephant go back to Laos. The remaining Laotian soldiers were given to serve the governor of Asantuk. As an astute king, Borom Reachea IV did not want to leave the country unprepared for any unforeseen attacks from the enemies. He went to the province of Kaṃbaṅ Svāy (កំពង់ស្វាយ, Kampong Svay which means mango shore) and ordered the governor to build a citadel and be vigilant. As the king descended the bank to embark on his royal boat to go back to his royal palace, he ordered that the place be called Kampong Thom (big shore/port).

During that time, Cambodia was still at war with Ayutthaya that occurred mostly on the western frontier of Cambodia. For the next few days, Borom Reachea IV ordered the governors of all provinces of the eastern and western shores to build citadels and recruit soldiers in preparation for a war with Ayutthaya that may spill over to the middle of the country. In the meantime, the two Laotian ministers arrived in Vientiane. They reported to the king that their elephant had been beaten by the Khmer elephant. They also delivered the message from the Khmer king demanding that the Laotian king kept his promise of sending tributes to Cambodia as a sign of his country's vassalage. After listening to his two ministers, the Laotian king became even more belligerent and proclaimed that he would never submit his country to be vassalage of Cambodia. Instead of doing nothing, the Laotian king decided to raise an army to bring war to Cambodia. As he reasoned, he would beat Cambodia because the country would be too occupied fighting a war with Ayutthaya and would not have enough strength and manpower to fight Laos. In 1573 (year of the Rooster of the fifth decade), the Laotian king ordered his Maha Uparaja (Chau Ream) who was his second in command to take 50,000 men by waterway toward Sambor. The king himself led an army of 70,000 men by land toward the province of Prohm Tep. After learning of the movements of the Laotian army, Borom Reachea IV devised a plan of attacks against the enemies. He put his oldest son, Satha, to be in charge of fighting the Laotian Uparaja's army by waterway. Prince Satha was able to raise an army of 30,000 men from Longvek to the provinces of Preah Trapeang. Srei Soriyopor, the king's second son, was put in charge to attack the enemies from the rear by following the route of Kampong Svay (Kampong Thom) to Angkor Wat. The prince was able to raise an army of 20,000 men that included one hundred fifty elephants, five hundred horses, and one hundred buffalos from the provinces of Pursat and Battambang. As to the king himself, he recruited an army of 50,000 men from the western side of the river that included five hundred elephants and two thousand horses.

In his march southward, the Laotian Uparaja started to become very suspicious because he did not encounter any resistances when he moved deeper and deeper into Cambodia. They were caught up by a strong wind when they arrived at Srei Sâ Chhor. Too dangerous to move forward, they decided to park their boats in a Prèk (ប្រែក, an affluent of a smaller river merging to a bigger river) to shelter themselves from the strong wind. The Cambodians had an advantage over the Laotians due to their familiarity with the territory. Learning that the Laotian army was resting and taking refuge in a Prèk from the strong wind, Prince Satha ordered his general to attack the enemies from the rear while he blocked the Prèk exit to trap the enemies in a confined place with no way out. The enemies were thoroughly defeated and many corpses were floating in the river. A great number of the Laotian soldiers were captured but the Laotian Uparaja was able to escape and returned to Laos. The above battle took place at Chhlong (ឆ្លូង). People commemorated the cleverness of the Khmer victory over the Laotian army by calling the place Prèk Prasab (ព្រែកប្រសប្, which means clever river) that still exists to this day. The actual river where the battle took place may be happening in Prèk Chhlong. In the meantime, the Laotian king pressed forward day and night with his army to reach the province of Kampong Svay. After spotting the Laotian army and realizing how tired the soldiers were, the Khmer king devised a plan to trap the advancing Laotian army from the rear with the forces of Srei Soriyopor, on the left and right flanks with the forces of his two generals, and on the front with the forces of the king himself. The Laotian army was massacred with corpses filling the forest. Unable to defend against the attacks from the Khmer army, the Laotian king fled with his remaining forces (estimated to be about five thousand) to Laos. He was pursued by the Khmer forces but they were unable to capture him.

While the Khmers were occupied fighting the Laotians, Maha Thammaracha took advantage of Khmer's trouble by retaking the provinces of Chanborei, Rayang, Sak Sieng Sau, Na Roeung, and Nokor Reach Seima from Cambodia in 1574 (year of the Dog of the sixth decade). After getting rid of the Laotian's threat, Borom Reachea IV decided to concentrate all his effort to regain the lost Khmer provinces back from Ayutthaya. With 70,000 soldiers, the king took the sea route to attack Ayutthaya. He conquered the provinces of Chanborei, Thonborei (near present-day Bangkok), and Phetborei (Present-day Petchaburi). The three Ayutthayan governors were killed in the battlefields. Maha Thammaracha who was installed as king of Ayutthaya by Burma in 1569 could not afford to have a continuous war with Cambodia if he wanted to liberate his country from the grips of the Burmese. In 1576 (year of the Rat of the eight decade), the Ayutthayan king wrote a letter to the Khmer king saying that the war between the two countries had brought tremendous sufferings to the people on both sides. He wished to make an alliance of friendship between the two countries to bring the war to an end. Borom Reachea IV was pleased after reading the message of peace from Maha Thammaracha. The Khmer king accepted the Ayutthayan king's friendship. He proposed that Cambodia would keep the territory east of the provinces of Baschimborei, Chanborei, and Nokor Reach Seima that were under Cambodia's control and that Ayutthaya would keep the territory west of the above mentioned provinces.[29,pp324-32] To reinforce the bond of friendship, he added that if one of the countries were attacked by an enemy the other country would come to her rescue. Maha Thammaracha was pleased to accept the offer. He hurriedly sent a message to the Khmer king because Ayutthaya was on the verge of fighting a war with Burma and Cambodia's help would be sorely needed. He proposed to have a demarcation ceremony of the borders with high officials and religious leaders from both countries to witness and bless the event with holy water. The Cambodian chronicles stated that the event for the demarcation of the borders occurred in 1577 (2121 Buddhist era, 1499 Grand era, 939 Cula, year of the Ox of the ninth decade). The chronicles recorded that both countries sent representatives to witness and commemorate the demarcation event that took place in Ro Ang Seila Bat (រោងសីលាបាទ, present-day Sa Keo in Thailand), which remained in place until 1883.[29,pp174-175; 87,p30] Cambodia was represented by Chau Hav Tolha (ចៅហ្វាទល្ហ), Oknha Thommo Decho (ឧកញ៉ាធម្មតេជោ), Oknha Chakrei Ratana (ឧកញ៉ាចក្រីរតន:), Preah Srei Phuri Preichea (ព្រះស្រីភូរីប្រិជា), Preah Reach Vireak Nukol (ព្រះរាជវិរនុកូល), Luong Reachea Meathyak (លួងរាជាមាត្យ), Moeun Sneha Phirum (ម៉ឺនស្នេហាភិរ), Venerable Samdech Preah Maha Prohm Moni (សម្តេចព្រះមហាព្រហ្មមុនី), Venerable Preah Thommo Moni (ព្រះធម្មមុនី), Venerable Preah Thommo Odom (ព្រះធម្មឧត្តម), Venerable Preah Ariyak Prithicha (ព្រះអរិយក្រឹទ្ធចារ្យ), Venerable Preah Vineaythirak (ព្រះវិន័យថេរ:), and many Khun (ឃុន) and Moeun (ម៉ឺន). Ayutthaya was represented by Ponhea Chakrei (ពញាចក្រី), Ponhea Phimuk Montrei (ពញាភិមុខមន្ត្រី), Ponhea Tep Rongg Rong Lor Chei (ពញាទេពរ្ទ្រង្រងឡូរ៉ៃ), Preah Buhul Tep (ព្រះបុហុល្លទេព), Venerable Samdech Preah Sangkhareach Keam Veasei (សម្តេចព្រះសង្ឃរាជគាមវាសី), Venerable Aran Reasei (អរញ្ញវាសី), the (king's) Left and Right Gurus, Brahman Preah Mahinreachea Sutheavatei (ព្រះមហិនរាជាវត្តី), Brahman Preah Boromchakriya (ព្រះបរមចរិយា),

Brahman Preah Tepchakriya (ព្រះទេពចរិយា), Brahman Horathipadei (ហោរាធិបតី), twenty more monks, and ten Brahman chaplains.

Borom Reachea IV who had defeated King Si Sattana Kunhut twice thought that Laos would not dare attacking Cambodia again. Unable to accept defeat, the Laotian king planned another attack on Cambodia in 1578 (year of the Tiger of the tenth decade). While one chronicle said that Laos sent an army of 20,000[29,p175] by waterway to attack Cambodia, another chronicle said that the Laotian forces numbered 200,000 men.[29,p326] It would seem unlikely that an army of 200,000 soldiers would be able to maneuver through the river (the Mekong River) easily. After learning that the Laotian army had crossed the province of Sambor, the Khmer governor sent a messenger to inform the king about the intention of the enemies. Without hesitation, Borom Reachea IV ordered his generals to form an army composed of two corps. One corps of 50,000 men were recruited from the provinces of Treang (ទ្រាំង), Banteay Meas (បន្ទាយមាស), Bati (បាទី), and Samrong Tong (សំរោងទង) to spearhead the attack; another corps of 70,000 men were recruited from southern and eastern sides of the Mekong River to attack the Laotian army from the banks. With five hundred boats, the king led the Khmer forces to meet the Laotian forces at Koh Phos (កោះផុះ, emerged island) in the region between present-day Kampong Cham and Phnom Penh. The Laotians were attacked by boats and by the river banks from the Khmer forces. The enemies were massacred with bodies floating everywhere in the river. Realizing that his forces were completely decimated, the Laotian Uparaja debarked to the island of Koh Phos. He was able to escape with half of his army to safety in a disguise. The Khmer forces were pursuing the enemies to the frontier of Laos but they were unable to capture the Uparaja. A great numbers of Laotian families were brought back to Cambodia and sent to live in Tuol Kreang (ទួលក្រាំង), near the village of Prey Puon (ព្រៃពួន) in the province of Samrong Tong. To this day, the village is called Kreang Leav (ក្រាំងលាវ). It is located in present-day district of Rolea Pha-ea (រលាផ្អើរ) in Kampong Chhnang. Other Laotian prisoners were sent to live in the provinces of Bati, Ba Phnom, Romduol, Svay Teab, Thbong Khmum, and Prey Veng (present-day Bati located in Takeo; Ba Phnom located in Prey Veng; Romdoul located in Siem Reap; Svay Teab located in Svay Rieng; Thbong Khmum located in Kampong Cham). To this day, there are a lot of Laotian descendants living in the above mentioned provinces.[29,p177]

In 1579 Borom Reachea IV fell gravely ill. He passed away soon after at the age of sixty two at midnight, in the first day of the waning moon, of the month of Asach, in the year of the Hare of the first decade.

The Violation of the Royal Protocol which Led to Instability and the Fall of Longvek

In the Cambodian folktale, the fall of Longvek was attributed mainly to the Ayutthayan's ruse and Khmer's greed. That theory was too simplistic.

According to the Khmer Inscription K.27 of Vatta Romlok (see p. 517 and Ref. 29, p. 342), the army of Naresuan attacked Longvek in 1587. Unlike David Chandler who stated this date to be the first siege of Longvek,[132,p84,p259] Khin Sok on the other hand considered it only to be an attack on the city of Longvek that came from the south. He did not view this attack to be the first siege of the Citadel of Longvek.[29,p342] The first siege of Longvek took place in early 1593 when King Naresuan of Ayutthaya started his campaign in 1592 to attack Cambodia. In his attempt to take Longvek, Naresuan decided to employ a new strategy. He had silver coins molded into bullets to fire into the bamboo forest that were planted to protect the citadel as the first line of defense. The Ayutthayan king used this strategy in the hope that Cambodian villagers would cut down the bamboos in search of the silver bullets, thus leaving the citadel vulnerable. Before Naresuan had a chance to see the result of his ruse, his army was defeated by a coordinated attack organized by the Khmer Upayuvaraja Srei Soriyopor. Naresuan who never lost a battle before returned to Ayutthaya humiliated. For almost the entire year he meticulously planned revenge on Cambodia. Before he conducted his second campaign against Cambodia and the Citadel of Longvek, Naresuan set up

Cambodia to fall into a trap. He transformed two "magicians" into two fake monks and sent them to Cambodia. One monk was to use poison to make people sick while the other monk was to heal them back to good health. Their reputations as great healers started to spread and finally reached the king. They were invited to live within the compound of the citadel. One day they poisoned the king but they used an antidote to get the king back to good health. Their duplicities were repeated many times until the king asked their advice what he needed to do to get rid of the sickness. They advised the king to get rid of all the statues of the Buddha in the pagodas. Because the king was not of sound mind, he ordered all the statues of the Buddha destroyed. Harm had already been done when Srei Soriyopor discovered too late that the two monks were fakes and that the king had been duped by them. After the two fake monks accomplished their mission, Naresuan launched his second campaign against Cambodia. It was a decisive campaign and Naresuan had his revenge. He defeated the Khmers everywhere. According to Khin Sok, Srei Soriyopor surrendered the Citadel of Longvek to Naresuan in the year of the Goat of the seventh decade, in the month of Chetra (ចេត្រ), on Saturday of the third day of the waxing moon.[29,p212] I do not concur with this date because it would correspond to 1595, which was too far removed from the event timeline to be considered for the fall of Longvek.

It is too simplistic to just attribute the fall of Longvek to the dupery and ingenuity of Naresuan. I suggest that the fall of Longvek was paved by the unwise actions that King Satha took during the course of his reign, such as abdicating to put his young son on the throne, which weakened the institution of the monarchy. Satha's action had alienated the royal families as well as the high officials, which in turn had Naresuan taking advantage of the situation that enabled him to launch his second attack on Longvek successfully. The destruction of the sacred statues of the Buddha ordered by Satha had also angered the populace. Probably in his desperation to save his throne, he agreed to convert to Christianity if Spain would agree to have the Governor of the Philippines send his troops to help Cambodia in the fight against Ayutthaya. Satha's desperate action may not only displease the people but may even lose their support all together.

Before going into the historical events that led to the fall of Longvek, it is first necessary to establish the timeline of the reign of Maha Thammaracha of Ayutthaya during this troublesome period. There are some discrepancies between different sources for the reigning period of King Maha Thammaracha. The confusion date of Maha Thammaracha's death may be caused by the manuscript that Prince Vasukri (aka Somdet Phra Paramanujit) wrote about the history of Ayutthaya in 1840. This manuscript was revised by Dr. Dan Beach Bradley under the tutelage of King Mongkut in 1865. Oskar Frankfurter produced a translation of this version, called *Events in Ayuddhya from Chulasakaraj 686-966*.[127] The translation mentioned the dates of accessions and deaths of all Ayutthayan kings except for the death of King Maha Thammaracha. The translation said that Maha Thammaracha was put on the throne in 931 by the King of Pegu. The years mentioned in the translation were all reported in Cula era, which in this case would make 931 corresponding to 1569/1570 AD. However, there was no mention of the date of Maha Thammaracha's death. After the accession of Maha Thammaracha, it mentioned that King Narayana reigned at Phitsanulok in 946 (Cula). By King Narayana, the translation must have meant King Naresuan because this king went on to attack Longvek in 955, in the year of the Snake, on Friday the 10th of the 2nd waxing moon, which would have corresponded to 10 May 1594.[127,p24] The translation never mentioned the date of King Narayana succeeding his father but it mentioned the death of Somdet Phra Vridharaj in 952 (Cula), which corresponded to 1590/1591 AD,[127,p2] By Somdet Phra Vridharaj did Prince Vasuki intend to mean Maha Thammaracha? It may be due to this ambiguity that George Coedès were uncertain at first about the exact date of the death of Maha Thammaracha. Khin Sok said that the official Annals of Siam[29,p338] recorded the death of Maha Thammaracha to be in 1579, but George Coedès who had originally agreed with that date changed his mind and reported that the death of the king occurred in 1590. David K. Wyatt also placed the death of Maha Thammaracha in 1590. The Cambodian Chronicles said that his death occurred between 1580 (year of the Naga of the second decade) and 1581 (year of the Snake of the third decade).

Maha Thammaracha was still alive in the year of the Naga because he sent an ambassador to King Satha for help fighting the invading army of Burma.[29,p181] Naresuan succeeded his father Maha Thammaracha.[29,p185]

The decisions that Kings Borom Reachea IV and Satha I made during their reigns had big ramifications on the future of Cambodia. King Satha I made an unwise decision that disregarded the royal protocol, which infuriated the royal families, the noble families, and the high-ranking officials. Concerned that his two young children, ages six and eleven, may never become kings if something were ever to happen to him, King Satha decided to step down and crown his oldest son, king, and his youngest son, Uparaja. Satha's younger half-brother, Srei Soriyopor, that the king appointed to the position of Uparaja after he acceded to the throne was changed as a result the king's two sons elevated to become king and Uparaja. Srei Soriyopor was promoted to the position of Upayuvaraja. This title, which is an honorific position reserved for a former king, suggested that Soriyopor would not be considered heir to Satha I anymore. Satha's action led to instability. Srei Soriyopor and the high officials felt a sense of betrayal on the part of the king. The ambitious Naresuan was keen to observe and understand the dire situation in Cambodia and learned to exploit it to his advantage when he became king of Ayutthaya. Prior to Satha succeeding him, Borom Reachea IV made an alliance with Maha Thammaracha of Ayutthaya to come to each other's aid in case of an attack by another country. Maha Thammaracha who was put on the throne of Ayutthaya by Burma could no longer take orders from his benefactor and decided to fight back. Seizing on the alliance he made with Cambodia, Maha Thammaracha asked Satha to send Khmer's soldiers to help Ayutthaya in its war against Burma. With the Khmer's army Maha Thammaracha was able to chase the Burmese out of Ayutthaya. Instead of being grateful, Naresuan became arrogant and disdainful toward Cambodia when he succeeded his father. Naresuan was an ambitious king and he seized on the turmoil in Cambodia and the weakness of Satha and his son, Chey Chetha, to attack Longvek and made Cambodia its vassal state. As explained earlier under "The Longvek Period," I believe the fall of Longvek occurred between January and February 1594.

63 Satha I or Borom Mahind Reachea (1579-1586) សត្ថា (ទី១) ឬ បរមមហិន្ទរាជា

Transliterated Name: Saṭṭhā I or Parama Mahindarājā

Other Name: Borom Intho Reachea II

Style Name: Preah Bat Samdach Preah Borom Intho Reacheathireach Remeathipadey Borom Baupit[7,p281]

Accession: 1579

Born: 1543/Deceased: 1596

Relationship: Eldest Son of Borom Reachea IV

Mother: Preah Sucheatei Strei or Ratna Reachea Tevi (Daughter of Ponhea Yuos)

Wives: 1. Srei Chakrabatei (Peou); 2. Bopha Pong (Bec Mai Sav, Laotian)

Religion: Theravada/Hinayana Buddhism

Capital: Longvek

Genealogy: Appendix 3

Satha was 36 years old when he succeeded his father, Borom Reachea IV, in 1579. He reigned under the name of Borom Mahind Reachea, but he is better known as Satha (I). His first wife named Peou was given the title of Samdach Preah Pheakavadei Srei Chakrapotireach (Chakrabatei). Satha had two sons with Mneang Peou before he became king. Their union produced Chey Chetha and Ponhea Tan. Satha had another son named Ponhea Nhom from his Laotian wife Bec Mai Sav, also known as Bopha Pong.[137] Even though Satha abdicated in 1586 in favor of his oldest son, Chey Chetha, he still retained all the power and controlled the government until the fall of Longvek. Because of this reason, the events that occurred under the reigns of King Satha I (from 1579 to 1586) and King Chey Chetha I (from 1586 to 1594) will be combined in this section.

As soon as he became king, Satha elevated his younger half-brother Srei Soriyopor to the rank of Uparaja (Vice King), essentially making him his heir. Srei Soriyopor who was four years younger than the king was intelligent and courageous as he had demonstrated during the battle against the Laotian army that invaded Cambodia during the reign of Bororm Reachea IV. He was loved by the people as well as by the king's ministers.

During this time, Maha Thammaracha who was put on the throne of Ayutthaya by Burma in 1569 started to have some problems with his benefactor. After eleven years, the relationship between Ayutthaya and Burma started to deteriorate. Maha Thammaracha wanted to strengthen the city wall and wanted Ayutthaya to be the master of its own security. Burma saw Maha Thammaracha's plan as a threat for two reasons. Burma was concerned because Maha Thammaracha would have to mobilize the population for manpower to build the wall, which in turn could be transformed into an army to fight the Burmese. The second concern for Burma was that the city of Ayutthaya would be hard to conquer once the wall was strengthened. The wall was completed in 1580.[104,p87; 127,p21] The years reported in the Cambodian chronicles and those reported by David K. Wyatt in his book, *Thailand, a Short History,* as well by Oskar Frankfurter[127] were different by about seven to eight years concerning the events that followed about the war between Ayutthaya and Burma. As stated in his paper, Frankfurter based his writing on the work of Prince Vasuki (aka Somdet Phra Paramanujit) who wrote the history of Ayutthaya in 1840; and on Dan Beach Bradley who revised the manuscript under the tutelage of King Mongkut in 1865. The confusion of the dates may be due to unspecified date of the death of King Thammaracha and the accession of his son, King Naresuan. The manuscript said that "… on Sunday the 11th of the 9th waxing moon in 931, the year of the snake, at about 6 o'clock Ayuddhya fell into the hands of the King of Pegu. On Friday the 6th day of the 12th waxing moon the Somdet Mahadharmarājādhirāj was crowned by right of conquest in Ayuddhaya."[127,p20] The year was recorded in Cula year, and 931 corresponded to 1569 AD.

I will use the events reported in the Cambodian chronicles to keep the years relevant to the historical events pertaining to the reign of the Khmer kings.

The Cambodian chronicles said that in 1580 (year of the Dragon of the tenth decade), Maha Thammaracha requested King Satha to send an army to help Ayutthaya in its war against Burma as agreed by the treaty signed between Cambodia and Ayutthaya. The Cambodian chronicles differed in the numbers of soldiers Cambodia sent to Ayutthaya. One chronicle gave the numbers as 2,000[29,p181] while the other chronicle stated that they were 20,000.[29,p336; 7,p282] Srei Soriyopor was leading the Khmer army. The battle that ensued between the Burmese forces and the allied forces (Cambodia and Ayutthaya) provided a glimpse of the behaviors and characters of the two headstrong princes, Srei Soriyopor of Cambodia and Naresuan of Ayutthaya. Srei Soriyopor who was born in 1547 was eight years older than Naresuan who was born in 1555.[104,p88]

The following events are retold and interpreted from Khin Sok's book *Chroniques Royales du Cambodge.*[104,pp181-183] Some of the events injected in this story were also taken from Adhémard Leclère's book, *Histoire du Cambodge;*[4] John F. Cady's book, *Southeast Asia, its Historical Development;*[16] David K. Wyatt's book, *A Short History of Thailand;*[104] *and Gabriel Quiiroga de San Antonio's book, A Brief and Truthful Relation of Events in the Kingdom of Cambodia.*[133] The allied forces were led by Srei Soriyopor (to be in charge of the left flank), by Ekathosarot (younger brother of Naresuan; he was in charge of the right flank), and by Naresuan (to be in charge of the front assault). As the Burmese army advanced and got to the proximity to the firing range, Srei Soriyopor ordered his soldiers to shoot at the Burmese soldiers. At the same time, the forces of Ekathosarot attacked the enemies from the right flank. When Naresuan heard that the battle had started, he sent his soldier to tell the Khmer prince to pull back and feign that his forces had been beaten by the enemies. Naresuan told the Khmer prince to flee toward him and let the enemies pursued him so that he could finish the battle. After receiving the message, Srei

Soriyopor told the soldier that he was sent by the Khmer king to fight and help Ayutthaya win the war and it would be dishonorable for him to feign the defeat. When Naresuan got the message back from the soldier he was very angry at Srei Soriyopor for refusing to listen to his command. The attacks by Srei Soriyopor and Ekathosarot's forces caught the enemies by a complete surprise. The Burmese soldiers were killed in great numbers and they were unable to fight back. The remaining soldiers fled the battlefield and returned to Burma. Naresuan was furious after the battle was over. The strategy of having Srei Soriyopor's forces feigning defeat to allow Naresuan to attack the enemies may work if the army was made up entirely of Ayutthayan forces; but it would become a problem duc to the trust issue when the forces were a combination of Khmer and Ayutthayan's soldiers. It would be of great consequences if Naresuan were to take full credits for the victory and were to claim that he had saved the Khmer forces from being destroyed. After the defeat of the enemies, Naresuan left the battlefield and returned to Phetborei (present-day Petchaburi) with his army to embark on their boats at Kampong Touk (place not identified). On his way to Ayutthaya, Naresuan saw the boat of Srei Soriyopor. He was annoyed when he saw Srei Soriyopor sitting on a chair nonchalantly with his feet dandling as the two boats were approaching. Probably still fuming from how the battle had ended, Naresuan started to get very angry because he thought that Srei Soriyopor did not give him enough respect. With a fit of anger, he ordered Luoṅ Bijaya Sirindra (លួងពិជ័យ សុរិន្ទ, Luong Pichey Surind) to cut off the head of a Burmese prisoner and had it exposed in plain view for Srei Soriyopor to see. The Khmer prince was very disgusted with the action of the Ayutthayan prince. Instead of being grateful for the Khmer's help, Naresuan acted as if Srei Soriyopor was his enemy.

The above conflict between Srei Soriyopor and Naresuan was told by Adhémard Leclère a little bit differently.[7,p282] According to Leclère, the event took place not on the sea but on land under a Banyan tree (ដើមពោធិ៍ដើមប៊ី). Noticing that Srei Soriyopor did not kneel down in front of him like all the high officials while sitting under the tree, Naresuan made some rude and condescending comments to the Khmer prince. Srei Soriyopor, who was of equal rank to Naresuan, responded that he was an Uparaja and a commander in Chief of the Khmer army sent by the Khmer king to assist Ayutthaya in its war against Burma. He was representing the Khmer king and he was expected to be treated as such. Without giving a response, Naresuan took one of the enemy soldiers captured by the Khmer army and slashed his throat. Then, Naresuan had the head of soldier planted on a bamboo pole to be displayed in front of Srei Soriyopor's boat. Naresuan's ruthless and disrespectful action disgusted the Khmer prince so much that Satha decided to annul the alliance between Cambodia and Ayutthaya after he had listened to his brother's story.

Because Naresuan played a crucial role in the future destruction of Longvek, it is necessary to mention his background in order to have a sense of understanding of his personality. His father was King Maha Thammaracha who married the daughter of his predecessor King Chakkraphat. Naresuan was kept hostage in Burma in 1564 when he was only nine years old. It may be that Maha Thammaracha offered his daughter in marriage to King Bayinnaung of Burma that Naresuan was returned to Ayutthaya in 1571.[104,p88] Naresuan gained fighting experience at an early age when his father sent him to Phitsanulok into battles at the age of sixteen. At the end of 1581, Maha Thammaracha sent Naresuan to Burma to pay respect to King Nandahayin who succeeded his father King Bayinnnaung who had just passed away. Naresuan's prowess as a young warrior prince was legendary. His conquest over the Shan state, which may be exaggerated, was well publicized. While conducting a campaign against the Shan state alongside the Burmese troop, he was able to take the enemy's city while the Burmese crown prince failed to do so. Naresuan's success brought the ire and jealousy of the Burmese crown prince, which resulted in an attempt by the Burmese king to ambush and kill him during the campaign against the Ava kingdom. Naresuan was able to escape the assassination attempt and returned with his troops to Phitsanulok and then to Ayutthaya.[104,p88] From that moment on, Naresuan became the enemy of Burma. He was able to repulse and beat back all Burmese's attacks against Ayutthaya. His early successes in the battlefields at such a young age had hardened his character and may embolden him to be pompous and arrogant.

Maha Thammaracha was not aware of the feud between his son and the Khmer prince that took place during the battle against Burma. After paying respect to the king, Srei Soriyopor left the city of Ayutthaya to return to Cambodia. When he arrived in the province of Chongkal, Srei Soriyopor convened a meeting with his generals and took a calculated risk by proposing to deport families living in Ayutthaya to Cambodia. Even though the action may anger both King Maha Thammaracha and King Satha, which could destroy the alliance of friendship between the two countries, Srei Soriyopor reasoned that Ayutthaya needed Cambodia more than the other way around because Ayutthaya was at that moment fighting the invasion army of Burma. All the generals concurred with the prince and would accept any punishments King Satha may inflict on them. With that decision, they gathered 5,000 families living in Ayutthaya and deported them to Cambodia.[29,p183] The prince asked the Khmer governors to be vigilant and be prepared for a reprisal from Ayutthaya. As soon as he arrived in Longvek, Srei Soriyopor reported all the events to the king and told him how he was treated with disdain by Naresuan. The king was very angry and felt that Naresuan forgot Cambodia was still a great country. The king ordered to relocate the Ayutthayan families that his brother brought in the province of Baribaur. The news of the evacuation of the Ayutthayan families to Cambodia reached King Maha Thammaracha. He was puzzled of the Khmer conduct because he thought that the two countries were allies. After an inquiry he found out that his son Naresuan treated Srei Soriyopor with contempt when the Khmer prince was in Ayutthaya as an ally fighting Burma. Naresuan wanted revenge but his father persuaded his son to calm down because Ayutthaya could not afford to have Cambodia as an enemy while the country was still fighting Burma. Soon after, Maha Thammaracha passed away and he was succeeded by his son Naresuan. According to the official Siamese annals, Maha Thammaracha died in Cula 941 which corresponded to 1579 AD;[29,p338] but George Coedès placed his death in 1590 AD;[29,p338] and David K. Wyatt also mentioned that he died in June 1590 AD.[104,p88] I decided to use the official date because the events described in the Cambodian chronicles are correlated better with 1579 as the date for the death of King Maha Thammaracha.

When King Satha learned that Naresuan succeeded his father as king of Ayutthaya, he ordered his generals and governors to be prepared for a possible attack from Ayutthaya. King Satha knew that Naresuan had a grudge against Cambodia. Naresuan also had a reputation of being an aggressive warrior since he was a prince. It was his father who restrained him from being too hotheaded and impulsive. Now that he became king there was nobody that could stop him from his ambition.

In 1581 (year of the Snake of the third decade), news of Burma preparing to attack Ayutthaya spread across the countries. Seizing on the occasion, Cambodia raised an army of 30,000 soldiers and attacked Ayutthaya. The Khmer army marched across the village of Laṃbaeṅ Khvāy (លំបែងខ្វាយ, Lompeng Khvay) and conquered all the Ayutthayan territories along its path. The Khmers retook the provinces of Baschim (បស្ចឹម), Nokor Reach Seima (នគររាជសីមា), and Nokor Noyok (នគរនោយក). After learning that the three provinces had fallen, Naresuan made a bold move by attacking Cambodia with his forces of 40,000 men and ignored about the threat coming from Burma. The Khmers could not defend against the surprise attack because they had only 2,500 soldiers to protect the provinces as the main forces had been withdrawn. The Ayutthayan army retook the three provinces. Learning of the bad news, King Satha mounted a counter-offensive with an army of 80,000 men. The Cambodian chronicles described the attack against Naresuan's army as follows:[29,pp339-340] the governor of Asantuk (អសន្ទុក) Ponhea Outey Thireach was in charge of the frontal assault with the forces of 20,000 men; Ponhea Chakrei was responsible for the right wing attack with the forces of 10,000 men; Ponhea Suorkealok was to attack from the left wing with the forces of 10,000 men; Governor Ponhea Decho from the province of Samrong Tong was assigned to lead the attack from the rear with the forces of 10,000 men; Oknha Preah Khleang, Head of the administration, was in command of 5,000 men; The king had 25,000 men [Khin Sok said it was 35,000 men] with more than 300 elephants and 1,500 horses under his command to spearhead the attack. The Khmer forces marched with that formation and crossed Pursat before finally taking a rest in Battambang for four days. Because Governor Ponhea Mnometrei Ros (ម្នោមេត្រីរស់) of Battambang knew the region better than anybody, the king gave him 20,000 men to attack the province of Baschimborei. With the province under the Khmer control, the king installed himself at Ra-ang Seila (រាងសីលា). From that command post, the king ordered Oknha Chakrei to attack Nokor Reach Seima with 30,000 men and Ponhea Suorkealok to assault the provinces of Chanborei and Nokor Noyok. The three provinces fell to the Khmer forces in 1581 (year of the Snake of the third decade, on the eleventh day of the waning moon, and in the month of Bos). Cambodia was relatively at peace for a short period of time while Naresuan was preoccupied fighting the Burmese army.

After eight years of reign and seeing that his children had grown up, Satha had a change of heart about making Srei Soriyopor his heir. He was concerned that his two sons may never be crowned kings if something were ever to happen to him. He decided to abdicate and crown his two sons to take over. Upon making his decision, the king convened a meeting with his generals and let them know about his wish to crown his two young sons. The royal and noble families, the generals, and the high officials were stunt when they heard the king.[29,p186] The king's action had disgusted his generals, his government ministers, as well as his two brothers, Uparaja Srei Soriyopor and Ponhea An. According to tradition, the ministers as well as Srei Soriyopor and Ponhea An had to bow or kneel down to the eleven-year old king. This had happened or not, the chronicles did not say anything about it. The two princes and high officials felt repulsive and betrayed by the king's action. They felt that King Satha had violated all royal traditions for the crowning of a king. The crowning of Chey Chetha and elevation of Ponhea Tan to Uparaja were only Satha's strategy of securing his two sons the throne after he died. Satha was still in charge of the government and conducted everyday affairs even though he had abdicated already. Having secured his son's reign, Satha elevated his brother Uparaja Srei Soriyopor to the title of Upayuvaraja, a ranking usually reserved for a former king. Even though this title was considered more honorific than that of Uparaja, however it essentially eliminated Srei Soriyopor as heir to the throne.

I have extracted and interpreted the following events from Khin Sok's book, *Chroniques Royales du Cambodge*,[29,pp187-193] and from the same sources mentioned earlier.[7; 16; 104; 133] From the moment Satha put his oldest son on the throne, the country started to descend into the state of turmoil and lawlessness. Thieves robbing people were occurring daily. Seizing on the unfortunate circumstances in Cambodia, Naresuan decided that the time was right for Ayutthaya to take revenge and launch an attack on Cambodia. According to the Khmer Inscription K.27 of Vat Romlok (see p. 517 and Ref. 29, p. 342), the Ayutthayan army attacked the city of Longvek in 1587, but resulted in failure to take over the city. Without giving up on his revenge, Naresuan and his army took back the provinces of Nokor Reach Seima and Baschimborei in 1588 (year of the Rat of the tenth decade).

Not content with the small victory that he gained, Naresuan carefully prepared his army for the next four years to conquer Cambodia. In 1592 (year of the Dragon of the fourth decade), Naresuan mounted a campaign against Cambodia with an army of 100,000 men that included 800 elephants and 1,800 horses. It was the biggest army Ayutthaya had ever formed to attack Cambodia. He gave an army of 5,000 men to his uncle Braḥ Rājamā Nūv (ព្រះរាជមាន្តរី, Preah Reachmea Nouv) to probe the situation in Cambodia before he launched an assault. Getting wind of the Ayutthayan advancing troops, Satha ordered Ukñā Nāyaka Im (ឧកញ៉ាបវរនាយកអិម, Oknha Bovor Niyuk Im = Oknha Im) to take 20,000 men to reinforce the forces of Ukñā Mnometrī Ras' (ឧកញ៉ាម្នោមេត្រីរស់, Oknha Mnometrei Ros = Oknha Ros), the governor of Battambang. He also gave 20,000 men to Ukñā Sraen Khāṅ Hvā Srī (ឧកញ៉ាស្រែនខាងហ្វាស្រី, Oknha Sren Khang Hva Srei = Oknha Srei) to go supporting the forces of Ukñā Suorgāloka (ឧកញ៉ាស៊ូតាលោក, Suorkalok), the governor of Pursat. Srei Soriyopor was assigned the duty to maintain the Citadel of Boribaur with 20,000 men. Ponhea An, Satha's youngest half-brother, was assigned the duty to recruit 15,000 men and used them to intercept the Ayutthayan army that was advancing toward Angkor. To his elder son, King Chey Chetha who was then seventeen years old, Satha ordered him to gather the population and food supplies from the provinces of Bati, Treang, Thbong Khmum, Ba Phnom, Bassak, and Preah Trapeang and to take them to the Citadel of Longvek. The generals and governors that Satha assigned to defend the country and fight the army of Ayutthaya were performing their duties without enthusiasm. They lost faith in Satha's leadership who was still acting as king and commanding his son, King Chey Chetha, like a puppet. The Khmers were in a defensive position while the Ayutthayans were in an offensive attack defeating the Khmers everywhere. Battambang, Angkor (Siem Reap), and Pursat fell, except the Citadel of Boribaur. After three months of encirclement and assault on the citadel, the Ayutthayan army still could not take over the citadel.

Fearing for his defeat, Satha enlisted in 1593 the help of Portuguese and Spanish adventurers named Diego Veloso (also spelled Diego Belloso) and Blas Ruiz, respectively. Satha used the help of foreign mercenaries in the same way Burma and Ayutthaya used the Portuguese. Veloso was 34 years old and had been living in Cambodia for ten years. He spoke Khmer fluently. Unlike Veloso, Ruiz was a new arrival. He had experience fighting in Peru before he moved to Manila, Philippines.[16,p196] He was 22 years old when he sailed from the Philippines to Cambodia in 1592. He was captured by the Cham when his boat had an accident, but he was able to escape and finally arrived in Cambodia in 1593. With two other adventurers named Antonio Marchado and Pantaleon Carneiro along with a Dominican Father d'Azevedo, Ruiz joined Veloso to serve the Khmer king.[7,pp325-326; 16,p196] Satha was so fond of Veloso that he offered his cousin in marriage and put him in charge of the royal guard protecting the court. Due to the clear and present danger posed by the Ayutthayan army, Satha sent Veloso and Ruiz to petition the Governor of the Philippines, Gómez Pérez Dasmariñas, to intervene in Cambodia. Unfortunately, they arrived in the Philippines on 19 October 1593 on the same day the governor was murdered at sea, on his way to Moluccas, by the Chinese slaves employed by the governor.[133,pxiv] Because Don Luis Pérez Dasmariñas replaced his father as an interim governor, he could not make a decision to send troops to Cambodia without the support from the Knight of the Order of Alcántara.[133,pxiv] Veloso who represented the king as the Khmer ambassador, tried in vain to convince the governor that the Khmer king would be willing to convert to Christianity if military aids were sent to Cambodia.

While Veloso tried to get help from the Spanish in the Philippines, Naresuan pressed his attack on Cambodia. Naresuan's goal was to capture the Citadel of Longvek, which was the center seat of power for the Khmer monarchy. With most of the Khmer forces defeated or concentrated only in the Citadel of Boribaur and Citadel of Longvek, Naresuan ordered his uncle Nouv to encircle Longvek with the plan to conduct a final assault on the citadel. Learning that the Citadel of Longvek was surrounded by the Ayutthayan army, Srei Soriyopor sent a message to Satha and asked him to pray and make offerings to the statue of the Buddha Kāy Siddhi (ពុទ្ធកាយសិទ្ធិ, Buddha Kaye Sitthik) in the pagoda Vatta Braḥ Inda Deba (វត្តព្រះឥន្ទទេព, Vat Preah Eynt Tep); to the statue of the Buddha in the pagoda Vatta Traḷaeṅ Kaeṅ (វត្ត ត្រឡែងកែង, Vat Traleng Keng); and to Neak Ta Khleang Moeung that were believed to have supernatural powers. Satha had the ceremony set up with prayers directed toward all eight directions lasting for a period of seven days. Either by coincidence or due to fatigue and malnutrition, the Ayutthayan army that had encircled the citadel for three months started to have all sorts of problems. The soldiers were short on food supplies. Naresuan was worried about the conditions of his soldiers because they were getting abnormally sick and weak. Knowing that it would be almost impossible to take over the citadel due to the impenetrable thick bamboo forest surrounding it, Naresuan resorted to a different strategy to win the war. He came up with a strategy to take over the impregnable citadel. He ordered his uncle Nouv to mold silver coins into bullets and used them as projectiles to bombard toward the bamboo forest that surrounded the citadel. With this strategy he hoped that people in the village would cut down the bamboos in search of the silver bullets, thus leaving the citadel vulnerable for an easy assault.

At this point, the Cambodian chronicles inexplicably placed Srei Soriyopor (the Upayuvaraja) in the Citadel of Longvek and not in the Citadel of Boribaur. Information was not given how Srei Soriyopor and his army left Baribaur and entered the Citadel of Longvek. It was Srei Soriyopor who gave orders and planned war strategies instead of Satha. While Naresuan gave the assignment to his uncle Nouv to fabricate silver bullets, Srei Soriyopor also had a plan of his own to beat back the Ayutthayan army that surrounded the citadel. Srei Soriyopor knew that the Ayutthayan soldiers were weak and sick. He wanted to take advantage of the situation. He convened a meeting with his generals and devised a plan to attack the Ayutthayan army. He instructed Luoṅ Jai Senā Uk (លួងដៃសេនាអ៊ុក, Luong Chey Sena Uk = Luong Uk) to inform Ponhea An and Chey Chetha who were in the command of the Khmer forces in Kampong Svay and Bati, respectively to attack the Ayutthayan army from the south and east on an agreed date. Srei Soriyopor would come out of the citadel to launch a frontal assault on the Ayutthayan army. The date of the attack was set for the fifth day of the waxing moon (៥ កើត), in the month of Chaitra (ចេត្រ, Chaet), in the year of the Serpent of the fifth decade (បញ្ចស័ក), which corresponded to 1593.

Without being detected by the Ayutthayan army, Luong Uk left the citadel under the cover of the night to inform Ponhea An and Chey Chetha of the plan. Ponhea An recruited more soldiers from the provinces of Kampong Svay, Baray (បារាយ៍), and Cheung Prey to fill in his army. With his army they marched toward the northern direction. Chey Chetha and the governors from the provinces of Bati, Treang, Banteay Meas, Bassak, Preah Trapeang, Kramuon Sâ, Ba Phnom, and Thbong Khmum moved their forces toward the eastern and southern shores (of the Tonle Sap/Mekong Rivers).

On the fixed date of the attack, the armies of Ponhea An, Chey Chetha, and all of the above governors arrived on an agreed location and launched their assaults on the Ayutthayan army. As the assault started, Srei Soriyopor rushed out of the citadel with his forces and attacked the Ayutthayan army. The Khmer coordinated attacks caught the army of Naresuan by surprise. The Ayutthayan soldiers who were already weak due to sickness and lack of food could not fight back effectively. Many Ayutthayan soldiers were killed in the battlefield. Naresuan left Cambodia in defeat with his remaining soldiers back to Ayutthaya.

After the victory, the Khmer people celebrated with abundance. Now that Cambodia was safe and after learning that silver bullets were scattered all over the bamboo forest, people from the village rushed out to cut down the bamboos to collect the silver bullets laying on the ground. Within a very short time the forest was stripped bare of bamboos, leaving the citadel vulnerable without its first line of defense.

In the meantime, Naresuan who had never lost a war before felt very humiliated. He wanted revenge and was planning a campaign against Cambodia. During his first campaign, Naresuan already tried to find out all about Cambodia. He ordered the arrest of two village chiefs for interrogation.[29,pp345-346] Chief Chan from Bati in present-day Takeo and Chief Peou from Leach in present-day Pursat were brought to Naresuan. The two old village chiefs said that during the reign of Ponhea Yat, the Khmer king had powerful Neak Ta (genies) installed in Phnom Penh, on the hill of Preah Reach Trop (ព្រះរាជទ្រព្យ), in Kien Svay Khnong (កៀនស្វាយក្នុង), in the pagoda of Ka-ngok Meas (ក្ងោកមាស), in the pagoda of Chrouy Ampil (ជ្រោយអំពិល), in Tvea Kampot (ទ្វារកំពត), in Prèk Bangkâng (ព្រែកបង្កង), and in Vihear Suorkea (វិហារស្វគ៌) for protection. Continuing the tradition, King Ang Chan I had the statue of Neak Ta Khleang Moeung erected, the statue of the Buddha Attharasa installed in the pagoda Vat Traleng Keng, and another statue of the Buddha installed on the hill of Preah Reach Trop.[29,p346] During that first campaign he learned that the Khmers had powerful statues of Neak Ta and of Buddha to protect them. It was customary in ancient time to believe in supernatural power. Before mounting a second campaign against Cambodia, Naresuan decided that he would not leave anything to chances. To combat the powerful forces protecting Cambodia, Naresuan involved the collaboration of two Ayutthayan "magicians" that he had in his royal palace for his service.[29,pp191-193,p348] He had the two men disguised as monks and then had both of them traveled to Laos first and then from Laos they went to Cambodia as not to raise any suspicions. The fake monk named Tikkapañño (តិក្កបញ្ញ, Tikkapagno) was to make people sick while the other fake monk Suppagno (សុរប ញ្ញ) played the role of a healer. Unbeknownst to people was that Tikkapañño used poison to make people sick. He then called on Suppagno to heal people with his antidote. The reputation of the two monks started to spread as they traveled through Cambodia healing people. Their reputations as healers reached the king's ears. The Cambodian chronicles was not specific about the identity of the Khmer king because the king's name was not mentioned. I will assume that it was Satha I even though Chey Chetha was officially the king. The Khmer king invited the two monks to reside in the pagoda Preah Eynt Tep Nimitt (វត្តព្រះឥន្ទ ទេពនិមិត្ត) within the citadel compound. As the two monks started to gain the king's trust, they were allowed to approach the king and provided him with their advice on his health. One day, one of the monks put poison in a betel nut and offered the king for consumption. As the king became sick after eating the betel nut, the other monk healed him back to good health. They used this scheme to get the king sick and then heal him on many occasions. After many times of being sick and then back to good health with the help of the two monks, the king sought their advice on what he needed to do to be completely cured of his sickness. The two monks told the king that his sickness was caused by the statue of Preah Traleng Keng and all the statues in the pagoda Preah Eynt Tep Nimitt. Not being of sound mind due to his sickness, the king agreed to have the statue of Preah Ang Traleng Keng thrown in the northern pond in the citadel. The statue of the Preah Kaye Sitthi (ព្រះកាយសិទ្ធិ) that Naresuan was afraid of due to its reputation of being powerful, and all the bronze statues of the Buddha from the pagoda Preah Eynt Tep Nimitt were thrown into the river Chroy Banh Leah (ជ្រោយបាញ់លៈ). Another chronicle confounded the statue of Preah Ang Traleng Keng with the statue of Preah Ang Attharasa. However, according to folktale, the two fake monks had the statue of Preah Ang Traleng Keng burned to ashes. As to the statue of Preah Kaye Sitthi and the bronze statues of the Buddha, they were all destroyed. After the statues of the Buddha had been destroyed, Srei Soriyopor and the people in the royal palace realized that the two monks were fakes but harms had already been done. They tried to arrest the two fake monks but they had already escaped because their mission had been accomplished.

From the time that Satha had the holy statues of the Buddha destroyed, Cambodia went into calamity with bad news occurring everywhere.[29,p193] It was reported that water in the pond of Phnom Banan (ភ្នំបា ណន្ត) had dried up; the blade of the Sacred Sword (*Preah Khan Reach*) had rusted in its entirety and chipped to the size of a corn grain; the statue of the Buddha in the pagoda Suorkea had broken; the leaves on the chrey tree had all fallen; and people had caught cholera and were starving.

In the meantime, the two fake monks arrived in Ayutthaya and reported their accomplishment to Naresuan. The bad news in Cambodia was good news to Ayutthaya. Naresuan was preparing his army of 100,000 men that was supported by 800 elephants and 1,500 horses to invade Cambodia one more time. The Cambodian chronicles reported the story of the Ayutthayan invasion in great details, which led to the fall of the Citadel of Longvek. I have reproduced the account from Khin Sok's book[29,pp193-217] in combination with Adhémard Leclère's book[7,pp286-292] and Father Gabriel Quiroga de San Antonio's book.[133,ppvii-xxx,pp3-12] Naresuan devised his plan of invasion of Cambodia as follows: 1) he nominated his uncle Nouv as Chief of the army and he gave him 10,000 men to command; 2) he ordered Ponhea Pich Borei (ពញាពេជ្រប្ញេរី) and the governors of Nokor Srei Thommareach (នគរស្រីធម្មរាជ), Sang Khla (សង់ខ្លា), and Maha Thai (មហាថៃ) to take 20,000 men and 450 boats through the sea route to attack the province of Bassak (present-day Soc Trang in Vietnam). Another army traveling by boats was to attack the provinces of Peam and Banteay Meas (present-day Ha Tien in Vietnam) neighboring Kampot; 3) he assigned his younger brother Ekathotsarot with the duty to protect the city.

Naresuan started his campaign against Cambodia in 1594 (year of the Horse of the sixth decade, on the eleventh day of the waxing moon, of the month of Meakasé). He ordered his two maritime armies to leave Ayutthaya in the direction of Cambodia. Naresuan conducted his land army in the direction of the bridge of Teuk Traeng (ស្ពានទឹកត្រែង, bridge of the water reed), with the goal to start his attack from Battambang. He ordered Ponhea Nokor Reach Seima to march his army of 30,000 men through Angkor in the direction of the province of Kampong Svay (present-day Kampong Thom). Getting wind of Naresuan raising a large army to invade Cambodia, the Khmer ministers reported the bad news to the king (presumably Satha and not Chey Chetha who was officially the king). Cambodia was not prepared for the war. Hastily, the king ordered all soldiers to bring their families and food supplies to move into the citadel.

He also instructed governors on all provinces to be prepared from the attacks by the Ayutthayan armies, both by land and by sea. The king convened a meeting with his generals. He ordered them to have sharp spikes planted around the citadel and to tell the soldiers that surrendering to the enemies would not be tolerated and would be punishable by death.

Having issued the above orders, the king charged Srei Soriyopor to take 30,000 men to occupy the Citadel of Boribaur in Pursat. They were to defend against the advancing army of Ayutthaya. Ponhea An and Ponhea Cin Cuṅ Tuk (ពញាចិនចុងតុក, Ponhea Chin Chung Tuk = Ponhea Tuk) were given only a small army of 1,500 men to defend the province of Banteay Meas also known as Peam (present-day Ha Tien in Vietnam) against the Ayutthayan army. As to Chey Chetha, the king gave him an army of 20,000 men to fight against the Ayutthayan army in Bassak. Ukñā Kralāhom Bau (ឧកញ៉ាក្រឡាហោមពៅ, Oknha Kralahom Peou = Oknha Peou) was given 20,000 men to protect the province of Kampong Svay and prevent the Ayutthayan army from moving farther down south. The king gave 20,000 men to Ukñā Vipulrāja Naṅ (ឧកញ៉ាវិបុលរាជនង, Oknha Vibolreach Norng = Oknha Norng) to occupy Angkor and stop the Ayutthayan army from advancing farther. Ukñā Pavara Nāyaka Im (ឧកញ៉ាបវរនាយកអិម, Oknha Bovor Niyuk Im = Oknha Im) was given 20,000 men to support the forces of Ukñā Mnometrī Ras' (ឧកញ៉ាម្នោមេត្រីរស់, Oknha Mnometrei Ros = Oknha Ros) in Battambang.

The first attack by the Ayutthayan army was directed toward the provinces of Kampong Som and Preah Trapeang (present-day Tra Vinh, Vietnam). The governors of Kampot and Kampong Som were not able to defend the provinces against the powerful attack of the enemies. With their defeated armies the two Khmer governors regrouped their soldiers to join the army of Ponhea An in Banteay Meas. Boldly, the Aytthayan army pursued the Khmers all the way to Banteay Meas. Ponhea An instructed his general Ponhea Tuk to take 5,000 soldiers to fight the Ayutthayan army at Touk Meas. The Khmer general was killed in the battle and without its leader the Khmer soldiers fell back and returned to the citadel. Realizing that they may be trapped in the citadel and seizing on the opportunity of the Ayutthayan army being exhausted in the battle, Ponhea An ordered his army and all the families to leave the citadel. They were able to make a push and escape from the citadel to take refuge in the province of Treang and set up a defense against the Ayutthayan army.

In the meantime, Preah Trapeang fell to another Ayutthayan army. Afterward, the army marched toward the forces of Chey Chetha in Bassak. The prince-king ordered his soldiers to fight the enemies but again, the Cambodian army was defeated. Chey Chetha decided to withdraw and took his army to join Ponhea An at Treang. Because of the lack of food supplies, Chey Chetha and Ponhea An decided to move their forces one more time to the province of Bati. Either they were also exhausted or by caution, the Ayutthayan army decided not to pursue the Khmer army. There were no food supplies left at Bati because they were all moved to the Citadel of Longvek. Finally, they decided to settle down at Srei Sâ Chhor (Srei Santhor) because of the fertile land. In the meantime, the Cambodian forces in Baria or Preah Suorkea (present-day Ba Ria-Vung Tau, Vietnam), Daung Nay (present-day Dong Nai, Vietnam), and Prey Nokor could not come to the rescue of the two princes because they have to defend their provinces against an impending invasion by the Vietnamese army. Vietnam seized on the opportunity of the Cambodian weakness for an invasion of Cambodia. The Ayutthayan army that had occupied Banteay Meas and Bassak was ruthless. They captured Cambodian citizens who hid themselves in the forest, took all their belongings and food supplies, and burnt their houses to ashes. The destructions of their villages were complete.

Naresuan led his land army toward Battambang to fight the Khmer army of Oknha Ros and Oknha Im. The two Khmer lords ordered their generals to take 7,000 men to meet the Ayutthayan army at Stung Thnot, near the hill of Preah Netra Preah.[29,p197] The Ayutthayan army of Naresuan's uncle launched his attack from Kbal Krabei (ក្បាលក្របី) in the province of Vattana. The Khmers were defeated with the provinces of Sisophon and Saṃnāt (សំណាត់, Somnat) fallen to the Ayutthayan army. The enemies occupied the Citadel of Thnot. Learning of the Khmer defeat, the two Khmer lords decided to make a stand and fight the powerful army of the Ayutthayan king in Battambang. The Khmers put up a fierce battle but they were no match against the overwhelming forces of the enemy. Oknha Im was killed in the battle. Without one of his leaders, Oknha Ros decided to fall back and moved his troops into the citadel. He gave a final speech to his soldiers that even though the Cambodian forces were a provincial army fighting against the king's army of Ayutthaya, Cambodians must show the enemies they were capable of putting up a brave fight. After finishing his speech, Oknha Ros mounted on his elephants and went out to face the enemies. He fought the enemies with all his might until he succumbed to exhaustion. His bravery was being noticed by Naresuan. He was finally captured and presented as prisoner to Naresuan. The Citadel of Battambang fell in 1594, with the exact date stated as the year of the Horse of the sixth decade, in the month of Meak (មាឃ), on the second day of the waxing moon.[29,pp201-202] The ensuing conversation took place between Naresuan and Oknha Mnometrei:[29,p200]

> *Voyant (l'Ukña Mnometrī), le roi se réjouit et lui demanda : "Quel est votre titre ?".*
>
> *L'Ukña Mnometrī lui répondit : "J'ai le titre d'Ukña Mnometrī, gouverneur de cette province de Pāt' Ṭampaṅ".*
>
> *Sa Majesté lui demanda encore: "Ne savez-vous point que nous sommes roi ? Est-ce (cette ignorance) qui fait que vous avez osé conduire une armée pour nous combattre ?".*
>
> *L'Ukña Mnometrī lui répondit : "Je pense que d'ordinaire le serviteur d'un royaume doit être reconnaissant envers son maître, qu'il doit engager sa vie pour s'acquitter des augustes bienfaits et moi qui suis quelqu'un de capable, si je m'étais attaché à la vie comme (le fait) une femme, je ne serais pas un homme. Tous les serviteurs royaux sont nés pour mourir un jour. Ce qui nous arrivera de bien ou de mal depend de nous, bonnes ou mauvaises actions. Une guerre implique nécessairement victoire ou défaite. Je me dois d'échanger ma vie contre le royaume pour mériter ma dignité de ministre."*

Translation:

> *At the sight (of Okña Mnometrei), the king is delighted and asked: "What is your title?"*
>
> *Okña Mnometrei answered: "My title is Okña Mnometrei, governor of the province of Battambang."*
>
> *His Majesty asked him again: "Don't you know that I am the king? Is it {by ignorance) that you dare fighting us?"*
>
> *Okña Mnometrei answered: "Usually the servant of a kingdom should be grateful to his master; he must commit his life to pay for the good deeds he benefitted from his master and I would not be a man if I cling on to my life like a woman. All royal servants were born to die one day. What happens to us, good or bad depends on us, good or bad actions. A war necessarily implies victory or defeat. I must sacrifice my life for the kingdom to be deserving of my dignity as the minister."*

Naresuan was satisfied after he heard the answers. He found dignity in the Cambodian governor and decided to spare his life with the condition that he brought all the dignitaries and Cambodian families to have them kneeled down in front of him with obedience. The governor had no choice but to agree to the king's request. He thanked the king for sparing his life but he also made a request to the king to tell his soldiers not to harm the people. Naresuan agreed to the governor's request. After all the people were brought in front of the Naresuan, he then said the following in a cleverly way:[29,p201]

> *Nous venons ici, non pas pour vous faire du mal, mais parce que nous avons entendu dire que le roi du pays de Kambujā ne pratiquait pas les dix règles royales, qu'il détruisait toutes les statues de Buddha de l'époque ancienne, qu'il rendait la religion bouddhique impure. Nous venons avec*

une armée afin que les royaumes des deux nobles cités soient liés par la noble amitié comme auparavant, cela rendra la religion bouddhique prospère. Rentrez tous dans vos villages et dans vos maisons.

Translation:

We come here, not to hurt you, but because we heard that the king of the country of Kambuja did not practice the ten royal rules; he destroyed the statues of the Buddha of ancient time which made the Buddhist religion becoming impure. We come with an army, so that the kingdoms of the two noble cities are bound by the noble friendship as before, and this will make the Buddhist religion prosperous again. Go back to your villages and your homes.

Naresuan's purpose was clear. He wanted people to turn against the Khmer king and see goodness in his deed. He was acting as the savior of the religion that had been trampled by the Khmer king.

After hearing that Battambang had fallen, the governor of Siem Reap Oknha Vibolreach and his generals lost all wills to fight. People were becoming very upset when they learned or became aware that the Khmer king was not respecting the rules of royal tradition and was the person who ordered the destruction of the sacred statues of the Buddha. The generals were rebelling and did not want to fight anymore to protect the throne. When the Ayutthayan army arrived, the governor and his generals decided not to engage into battle. They moved their soldiers to the other side of the river in an effort to join the forces of Srei Soriyopor at the Citadel of Boribaur. Without spilling a blood, the Ayutthayan army entered Angkor in 1594, with the exact date stated as the year of the Horse of the sixth decade, in the month of Meak (មាឃ), and on the first day of the waning moon.[29,p202] Srei Soriyopor was enraged upon hearing the news that Vibolreach did not put up a fight against the Ayutthayan army. He wanted to arrest the governor and had him executed. Srei Soriyopor's generals pleaded with the prince and convinced him to change his mind because the generals who served the governor refused to fight. Also, as they explained to the prince they did not want Naresuan to exploit the situation by making the matter worse. After hearing the advice from his generals, Srei Soriyopor calmed down and pardoned the governor and his generals. Learning that the Ayutthayan army attacked Pursat, Srei Soriyopor put Oknha Vibolreach in charge of an army of 5,000 men to help the forces of the governor Oknha Suorkealoka. After conquering Battambang, Naresuan sent his uncle with an army of 10,000 men to attack Pursat. Oknha Suorkealoka sent combined forces of 17,000 men to meet the Ayutthayan army north of Boeung Khnar (បឹងខ្នារ). A fierce battle took place between the two forces with many soldiers from both sides killed in the battlefield. As the battle was raging, the royal army of Naresuan arrived and the Khmer army had to split in two groups to fight the enemies. The army of Oknha Vibolreach with his 5,000 men also arrived to help the Khmer forces. Oknha Vibolreach fought with courage because he wanted to redeem his reputation and dignity. He fought to exhaustion and killed many enemies. He was finally killed by an enemy bullet. Unable to defend against the more powerful army of Naresuan, Oknha Suorkealoka withdrew his forces and escaped into the forest to rejoin the army of Srei Soriyopor in Baribaur. Naresuan entered into Pursat with his army triumphantly in 1594, with the exact date stated as the year of the Horse of the sixth decade, in the month of Meak (មាឃ), and on the fifth day of the waning moon.[29,p204] After occupying Pursat, Naresuan ordered his uncle Nouv to continue his march toward the provinces of Kragar (ក្រគរ, Krakor in present-day Pursat) and Kraṅ (ក្រង, Krang in present-day about 10 km east of Pursat). People fled at the sight of the Ayuthhayan army. Learning of the advancement of the enemy troops, Srei Soriyopor ordered his army of 10,000 men to meet the enemies at Sdiṅ Tnot (ស្ទឹងថ្នោត, Stung Thnot) in the provinces of Krakor and Krang. As the battle between the two forces was raging, Naresuan's army arrived to tip the balance. Outnumbered by the overwhelming forces of the enemies, the Khmer army retreated. After being informed of the superiority of the Ayutthayan army, Srei Soriyopor sent reinforcements of 15,000 men under the command of Ukñā Bhimuta Vaṁsā (ឧកញ៉ាភិមុត

វង្ស, Oknha Phikmuth Vongsa = Oknha Vongsa) to help the retreated Khmer army. The help arrived too late because the Khmer army was retreating in disarray and there was no way to organize them on time to get into formation to fight the enemies. Oknha Vongsa decided to set his camp there and waited to launch an attack on the Ayutthayan army. Again, as the Khmer army was battling with the Ayutthayan army of Reachmea Nouv, Naresuan and his powerful army came to the rescue of the army of his uncle one more time. The outcome was the same, with the Khmer army retreating against more powerful forces. When Oknha Vongsa informed Srei Soriyopor of the defeat and his retreat, the prince was terribly angry and wanted to punish his general but he realized it was unwise to do so in this situation. Naresuan pursued the Khmer army to the Citadel of Boribaur. It was reported in the chronicles that he set up his camp at a distance of 500 sin (equivalent to about 1,000 meters) from the citadel in 1594, with the exact date stated as the year of the Horse of the sixth decade, in the month of Māgha (មាឃ, Meak), and on the ninth day of the waning moon.[29,p205]

The defeat of the Khmer armies in the provinces of Kampot, Treang, Bassak, Preah Trapeang, Banteay Meas, Battambang, Pursat, and Siem Reap was bad news to King Satha. In a last effort to stop the advancement of the Ayutthayan armies, Satha ordered Ukñā Cakrī Sūr (ឧកញ្ញាចក្រីស្ងួរ, Oknha Chakrei Saur = Oknha Sor), Ukñā Rāja Tejā Sau (ឧកញ្ញារាជតេជាសៅ, Oknha Reach Decho Sao = Oknha Sao), and Ukñā Mahā Mantrī Saṃ (ឧកញ្ញាមហាមន្ត្រីសំ, Oknha Moha Montrei Sam = Oknha Sam) to take their armies to meet the enemies in the province of Bati at the shore of the river Braek Tūc (ព្រែកតូច, Prèk Touch in present-day Kampong Speu, west of Phnom Penh) and in the province of Saṃroṅ Daṅ (សំរោងទង, Samrong Tong in present-day Kampong Speu).

While the Ayutthayan army was camping outside the Citadel of Boribaur, Srei Soriyopor was more concerned about his brother King Satha who was residing in his royal palace in the Citadel of Longvek than for himself. Worrying that his brother would not be able to withstand the attack by the Ayutthayan forces, and knowing the determination of Naresuan to win the war at all cost, Srei Soriyopor wrote a letter to his brother asking him to temporarily leave Longvek to join Chey Chetha and Ponhea An who resided in the Citadel of Basan,[29,p206] in the province of Srei Sâ Chhor.[29,p196] He told Satha to let his generals defend the Citadel of Longvek in his absence. It must be noted that Srei Sokonthor Bat renamed the province of Basan to Srei Sâ Chhor[29,p259] in honor to Mneang Peou (his concubine of the first order) who was also called Neang Sâ[29,p258]. Srei Soriyopor felt that the king would be safer in Srei Sâ Chhor because of its proximity to the forest. It turned out that after receiving the letter, the king felt suspicious about his half-brother's motive. The king reminded his generals of Thommo Reachea's duplicity toward King Srei Reachea, when he concocted a plan with Borommatrailokanat to have the king exiled to Ayutthaya. It must be reminded that Thommo Reachea and King Srei Reachea were half-brothers like Srei Soriyopor and King Satha I. The generals were surprised at the king's remark because they thought that Srei Soriyopor's letter was sincere. However, before making a final decision the king needed to consult his astrologer/foreseer first. After consulting the astrologer, the horoscope fell on the story of Braḥ Rām (ព្រះរាម, Preah Ream) exiling himself voluntarily to the forest for fourteen years to avoid a dispute with his half-brother Braḥ Bhirut (ព្រះភិរុត, Preah Phiruth) for the succession to the throne of their father Dasaratha (ទសរថ, Tusaroth).[29,p207,p353] Another part of the horoscope said that a comet fell in the royal palace and wild animals entering into a village killing and eating people.[29, p207] The bad presages convinced the king to leave the Citadel of Longvek. In 1594 — corresponding to the year of the Horse of the sixth decade, in the month of Māgha (មាឃ, Meak), and on the fourteenth day of the waning moon (probably 9 February 1594) — Satha with his wife Braḥ Devī Khsatrī (ព្រះទេវីក្សត្រី, Preah Tevi Ksatrei), his second son Braḥ Paramarājā Bañā Tan' (ព្រះបរមរាជាពញាតាន់, Preah Borom Reachea Ponhea Tan), his youngest son Cau Bañā Ñom (ចៅពញាញោម, Chau Ponhea Nhom), his concubines, all his entourage, and five hundred of his bodyguards in red uniform left Longvek for the direction of Srei Sâ Chhor.[29,p20] It is my belief that Preah Tevi Ksatrei was Satha's mother and not his wife. Satha's first wife and mother of Chey Chetha I and Ponhea Tan should be Srei Chakrabatei. According to another text,[29,p353] Satha left Longvek not because he received a message from Srei Soriyopor but because of the approaching army of Ayutthaya. After Satha had left, his generals who were in charge of defending the citadel sent a message to Srei Soriyopor asking him to come to Longvek because the king had abandoned the citadel. After receiving the message, Srei Soriyopor left his citadel in the province of Ralā Ph-īe (រលាផ្អែ, Rolea Pha-ea in present-day district by the same name located in the province of Kampong Chhnang) for Longvek. King Satha arrived at Srei Sâ Chhor to meet his oldest son Chey Chetha and his youngest brother Chau Ponhea An in the year of the Horse of the sixth decade, in the month of Phalguna (ផល្គុន, Phalkun), and on the second day of the waxing moon,[29,p207] which corresponded to March-April 1594.

In his account during his time serving King Philip II of Spain (and then his son King Philip III after the death of his father) in the Philippines from June 1595 to 1608, Father Friar Gabriel Quiroga de San Antonio of the Dominican Order said that Satha left Longvek to Srei Santhor around February 1594.[133,pxvi]

While the Citadel of Boribaur was still being besieged, Naresuan made a bold decision to divide his army in two groups. He gave 40,000 men from his army to his uncle Nouv and ordered him to take the Citadel of Longvek where King Satha I resided.[29,p208] Srei Soriyopor had anticipated this move because he had placed Khmer soldiers in strategic positions along the route to Longvek to attack the Ayutthayan army. Prince Nouv could not accomplish his mission because the Khmer soldiers were attacking and harassing the Aytthayan army on every opportunity they could. Learning of their failure to reach Longvek, Naresuan believed that the key to win the war was to capture Srei Soriyopor. Naresuan ordered an all-out attack on the Citadel of Boribaur but the Khmers repelled every enemy's assault by firing bullets and cannon balls which killed many Aytthayan soldiers. Srei Soriyopor knew that the Khmer victory was only temporary as long as he and his army stayed in the citadel. Considering how powerful the army of Naresuan was, Srei Soriyopor knew that eventually the citadel would fall. After consulting with his generals, Srei Soriyopor decided to make an exit out of the Citadel to Longvek where its citadel was more defensible because it was built to withstand for strong enemy's attacks. He organized his exit by assigning the duties to his generals as follows:[29,p208] 1) Ukña Yodhā Saṅgrāma Duy (ឧកញ៉ាយោធាសង្គ្រាមទុយ, Oknha Yuthea Sangkream Tuy) and Braḥ Rāja Vara Nukūla Mī (ព្រះរាជវរនុកូលម្មី, Preah Reach Voreak Nokul Mi) were given 5,000 soldiers to command the front guard to spearhead the front assault; 2) Luoṅ Dibva Senā Kau (លួងទិព្វសេនាកៅ, Luong Tep Sena Kav), Luoṅ Rājamātya Sek (លួងរាជាមាត្យសេក, Luong Reachea Mityak Sek), Ukña Vaṅsādhipatī Mā (ឧកញ៉ាវង្សាធិបតីម៉ា, Oknha Vongsa Thipadei Ma), Ukña Kosādhipatī Som (ឧកញ៉ាកោសាធិបតីសោម, Oknha Kosa Thipadei Som), and Luoṅ Dhanukā Juṃ (លួងធនុកជុំ, Luong Thanuk Chum) were given 5,000 soldiers to take care of the rear guard to defend against the enemies' pursuit. Srei Soriyopor would be in charge of the elite army.

In 1594 — the year of the Horse of the sixth decade, in the month of Phalguna (ផល្គុន, Phalkun), and on the first day of the waning moon — under the cover of darkness Srei Soriyopor made an exit out of the citadel with his army. The Khmers were swift and took the Ayutthayan by surprise with their bold exit. They arrived at the Citadel of Longvek the same month probably around the ninth day of the waning moon because that was the date that Naresuan ordered his army to surround the citadel.[29,p209] The citadel was well fortified with a lot of soldiers but there was not enough food to sustain them for a long siege because King Satha I had taken most of the food supplies with him to Srei Santhor..

Naresuan knew that it would result in great casualties from both sides if he were to launch an assault and try to take the citadel by force. His objective was to win the war and fulfill his revenge, especially on Srei Soriyopor whom he had a dislike since they were fighting alongside against the Burmese army in 1580. After one month of siege without any outcome, Naresuan decide to write a letter to Srei Soriyopor after consulting with his generals. Naresuan's letter was recorded in the Cambodian chronicles as follows:[29,p210]

> *Le noble message de Sa Majesté Braḥ Narendrasūra, roi de la ville de Srī Ayudhyā, le Maître du peuple, par la voie de la noble amitié royale, à Sa Majesté de prendre connaissance. Moi, le roi de la ville de Srī Ayudhyā, j'ai conduit une armée et assiégé votre citadelle pendant un mois pour deux raisons; d'une part je voulais reconnaître les soldats d'élite, d'autre part (je voulais) protéger la religion bouddhique. Pourquoi ne vous voit-on pas sortir pour combattre ? Si le roi de la ville de Kambujā n'ose pas sortir pour faire la guerre, liez les armes et puis sortir pour vous prosterner docilement devant les deux Nobles Pieds afin que les soldats ne soient pas malheureux. Quant aux histoires anciennes, nous n'en parlerons plus, que Sa Majesté ne se fasse pas de souci. D'autre part, en ce moment la ville de Kambujā semble bien être entre nos mains. Nous pouvons donner l'ordre à notre armée de la détruire immédiatement. Qu'en pense le roi de la ville de Kambujā ? Veuillez nous répondre le plus tôt possible afin que nous en prenions connaissance.*

Translation:

> The noble message of His Majesty Brah Narendrasura, king of the city of Srī Ayudhyā, the Master of the people, through the noble royal friendship, to His Majesty the King of Great Kambujā, begs Your Majesty to take notice. I, the king of the city of Srī Ayudhyā, I led an army and besieged your citadel for a month for two reasons; on the one hand I wanted to recognize the elite soldiers, on the other hand (I wanted) to protect the Buddhist religion. Why do not we see you out to fight? If the king of the city of Kambujā dares not come out to fight a war, tie up your arms and then come out to kneel yourself down submissively to both Nobles Feet to avoid misery to the soldiers. As for ancient histories, we will not talk about them, and may His Majesty not to worry anymore. On the other hand, at this time the city of Kambujā seems to be in our hands. We can give the order to our army to destroy it immediately. What does the king of the city of Kambujā think? Please answer us as soon as possible so that we can make a decision.

According to the message above, Naresuan treated Srei Soriyopor as a king instead of a prince. It was probably proper because Srei Soriyopor was an Upayuvaraja which was a title normally reserved for a former king. As mentioned earlier, Satha elevated his brother to this position as a political move to make room for his son to succeed him. Even though Srei Soriyopor had never occupied the throne, Satha decided that giving his brother the title of Upayuvaraja may be the only way to atone for his brother's disappointment for making his son Chey Chetha the king of Cambodia.

After receiving the message from Naresuan, Srei Soriyopor asked his generals to give their opinions in this matter. Cau Hvā Daḷha (ចៅហ្វាទ័ឡ្ហ, Chau Hav Tolha) was the first one to start. He summarized his opinion by saying that the statues of the Buddha protecting the citadel were all destroyed, the best Khmer soldiers had been mostly captured, the food supplies were fallen to the enemies, the citadel that was covered by the bamboo forest had been cleared by the people who looked for the silver bullets, and that the citadel was under siege by a powerful enemy army. He advised that it would be better to accept the terms imposed by Narusean but he left the final decision to the Upayuvaraja. The other generals concurred with Chau Hav Tolha. Srei Soriyopor took the advice given by his generals. He had a letter written that contained the following message and had it delivered by Ukña Mahāsenā (ឧកញ៉ាមហាសេនា, Oknha Muha Sena) and Ukña Dhirājavaṅsā (ឧកញ៉ាធិរាជវង្ស, Oknha Thireach Vongsa) to King Naresuan:[29,p211]

> *Noble message, surgi du noble coeur de l'auguste Braḥ Srī Suriyobarṇa dhammika varottama parama mahā Ubhayorāja, qui vient, par la voie de la noble amitié, auprès de Sa Majesté l'auguste*

Braḥ Narendrasūra, roi de la ville de Srī Ayudhyā, l'excellent roi, et don't il est prié de prendre connaissance.

Puisque Sa Majesté a fréquemment conduit l'armée et foulé le sol du pays de Kambujā le Grand dans l'intention d'agrandir les provinces royales, et avec beaucoup de compassion pour les moines, les brahmanes et le peuple du pays de khemarā, et sans rancune à l'égard de ce qui s'est passé auparavant, moi l'auguste Mahā Ubhayorāja, je suis heureux de ce que Sa Majesté renoue ainsi la noble amitié royale selon l'antique et royale tradition. J'accepterai la royale amitié. D'autre part, l'auguste Seigneur Mahindarāja, le grand souverain, mon auguste et noble aîné s'est éloigné depuis plusieurs jours et je ne sais pas où il est allé. Si le roi de la ville Srī Ayudhyā est réellement venu avec la noble amitié, que son armée se retire et n'encercle plus la citadelle.

Translation:

Noble message, leaping out of the noble heart of the august Braḥ Srī Suriyobarṇa dhammika varottama parammahā Ubhayorāja, which comes by way of the noble friendship, to His Majesty the august Braḥ Narendrasūra, king of the city of Srī Ayudhyā, the great king, and he is requested to take notice.

Since His Majesty has frequently led the army and marched on the land of the country of the Great Kambuja with the intention to expand the royal provinces, and with great compassion for the monks, the Brahmans, and the people of the country of Khemarā, and without a grudge against what has happened in the past, I, the august Mahā Ubhayorāja, am very pleased that His Majesty revives the noble royal friendship in the ancient and royal tradition. I accept the royal friendship. On the other hand, the august Lord Mahindarāja, the great king, my august and noble elder brother has moved out for a few days and I do not know where he has gone. If the king of the city of Srī Ayudhyā is really coming with the noble friendship, may your army withdraw and not surround the citadel any longer.

Naresuan was please after he received the letter from Srei Soriyopor. He agreed to withdraw his army and not having the citadel surrounded any more. Srei Soriyopor was at first very cautious. He would let starving people in the citadel go out first to look for food and observed how the Ayutthayan army would do to them. As promised by Naresuan, his army did not do any harm to the people. With the consent of his generals, Srei Soriyopor ordered that a hall of reunion be prepared to receive King Naresuan. He asked his ministers and fifty of his chiefs of the army along with the Ayutthayan chiefs of the army to look for the oath water to be used for the ceremony. Naresuan was invited to come in the citadel.

In the year of the Goat of the seventh decade, in the month of Caetra, and on Saturday of the third day of the waxing moon, King Naresuan entered in the Citadel of Longvek.[29,p212] This year which corresponded to 1595 could not have been correct because it placed the fall of Longvek too far in the event timeline. Based on the account written by Father Gabriel Quiroga de San Antonio during his service to Kings Philippe II and Philippe III of Spain in the Philippines, Valeso and Blas Ruiz were taken prisoners by the Ayutthayan army as soon as he arrived in Phnom Penh after his voyage from Manila. They left Manila on February 1594. John F. Cady reported that Ruiz was able to escape from Cambodia on a boat he seized from Ayutthaya and arrived in Manila in June 1594.[16,p196] The above account seems to indicate that Valeso and Blas Ruiz were captured by the Ayutthayan army around the time Naresuan laid siege around the Citadel of Longvek. Based on my analysis of available sources, I believe the surrender of Longvek occurred in June 1594.

As Naresuan was meeting Srei Soriyopor at the gate of the citadel, he said: *"We have already conducted two times our army and it is only now that we arrive at the gate of the citadel."* Graciously, Srei Soriyopor responded: *"Twice, three times, I drove the army to the city of Srī Ayudhyā, I saw only the gate of the citadel, but I was not able to walk inside. You come only twice and you can enter the citadel; therefore, you are more powerful than me.*" After having said that, Srei Soriyopor invited Naresuan to come into the citadel and enter into the hall of reunion. Naresuan then gave the following speech:[29,p213]

Je suis venu avec l'armée pour renouer l'amitié royale comme auparavant, car le pays de Kambujā le Grand n'a pas tenu sa parole d'honneur; il a interrompu la noble amitié royale et a conduit son armée pour assiéger le noble pays siamois, sous le règne de mon auguste père, alors qu'il était en train de combattre avec le Man. Je voulais que les deux pays soient amis, qu'ils ne se battent plus dorénavant. Or Braḥ Mahindarājā, le noble aîné s'est enfui; cela n'est pas pas conforme à ce que j'avais projeté. C'est pouquoi je vous invite à vous render d'abord dans la ville de Srī Ayudhyā, je préparerai votre retour dans ce pays pour le gouverner.

Translation:

I came up with the army to renew the royal friendship like in the past, because the country of the Grand Kambujā has not kept its word of honor; it interrupted the noble royal friendship and led its army to besiege the noble Siamese country, under the reign of my august father, while he was fighting against the Burmese. I wish the two countries to be friends that henceforth will no longer be fighting each other. Now, Braḥ Mahindarājā the noble elder has fled; this does not conform to what I had planned. That is why I invite you to come to the city of Srī Ayudhyā first; I will prepare your return to this country to govern.

The above message from Naresuan was a diplomatic way of saying to Srei Soriyopor that he would be taken to Ayutthaya as a royal prisoner. Because no date was given for Srei Soriyopor's return to Cambodia, it was a gentle way of telling the Upayuvaraja that he may be living as a guest prisoner in Ayutthaya indefinitely. After saying that, Naresuan ordered the Upayuvaraja to assemble his wives, the princes and princesses, the nobles, and the ministers. Srei Soriyopor gathered his ministers and all his royal servants and told them that they had no choice but to follow the Ayutthayan king's order. He told them that they would try to find a way to return to Cambodia. Then, Srei Soriyopor called on his wife, his two sons Chey Chetha and Outey (note: not to be confused with Chey Chetha, the son of Satha and crowned king who resided at Srei Sâ Chhor with his father), his daughter Preah Ang Chan Bopha, and all the royal servants who wanted to accompany him.[29,p213]

Not content to take Srei Soriyopor and his family as prisoners, Naresuan ordered his army to capture all the Khmer families living on both sides of the Tonle Sap River from Samrong Tong to Neang Rong, a total of 120,000 people, to repopulate Ayutthaya.[7,p288; 29,p213] The Khmer prisoners rebelled when they arrived in Battambang because they did not want to go to Ayutthaya. Half of the families were separated forever. Adhémard Leclère declared that Cambodia never recovered from this depopulation policy that Naresuan implemented. He said that the fall of Longvek and its occupation by the Ayutthayan army for a couple of years had reduced Cambodia not only to a vassal state, but had also destroyed people's spirit and put Cambodia in the background to the point of non-existence by the eyes of Europeans in the forthcoming centuries. Naresuan was not only content to sack Longvek but he also burnt the citadel to ashes. As a victor, Naresuan took along with him all the Khmer treasures, sacred manuscripts, chronicles, books of code of laws, custom, and tradition.[7,p289] Leclère mentioned that in 1692 Chey Chetha III had to ask his aunt to recall to him about certain Khmer customs and rule of laws because there were no manuscripts left to read.[7,p292]

With the Ayutthayan army occupying Longvek in proximity to Srei Sâ Chhor, Satha I did not feel safe. According to Adhémard Leclère, Satha I decided to flee to Stung Treng but his aunt Tevy Ksatrei (Leclère was mistaken in this relationship. I believe that Tevy Ksatrei was Satha I's mother) and his two sons, presumably Ponhea Tan and Ponhea Nhom, decided not to follow him. He said they went to Phnom

Peam Cheang, present-day Kampong Cham.[7,p325] This account is contrary to M. Cabaton who specifically said that Satha I fled to Vientiane in Laos,[7,pp324-325] and to Father Gabriel Quiroga de San Antonio who said that Satha I and his two sons fled to Laos. The Dominican Friar even said that Satha I's elder son, presumably Ponhea Tan, was married to the daughter of the Laotian king.[133,pp10-11] In this instance, Father Gabriel may be possibly mistaken between Satha I (the king who abdicated but retained all the power when he was ruling Cambodia) and Ponhea Tan (the son who was put on the throne by his father but did not have any ruling power). It was Satha I who married a Laotian named Bec Mai Sav (aka Bopha Pong) and their union produced a son named Ponhea Nhom. According to Leclère, Géraerd Van Wusthof of the Netherland who navigated the Mekong River in 1641-1642 all the way to Vientiane indicated that the frontier of Cambodia during that period was higher up north, between the present-day Khong and Basak, districts of Champassak, Laos.[7,p325]

There may be some confusion concerning the above event. According to the chronicles, Satha, his wife Tevi Ksatrei (Khin Sok said she was Satha's wife; Leclère said she was his aunt; but I believe she was Satha's mother), Ponhea Tan (Satha's second son), and Ponhea Nhom (Satha's youngest son from his marriage with a Laotian) left Longvek to join Chey Chetha (Satha's oldest son whom he was crowned king) and Ponhea An (Satha's half-brother) in Srei Sâ Chhor. Leclère and Father Gabriel may be confused about the names and relationships between Satha and all the rest. I believe that Ponhea Tan and Ponhea Nhom fled with their father Satha to Stung Treng (mistaken as Vientiane) and that Tevi Ksatrei, Chey Chetha, and Ponhea An decided not to go to Stung Treng with them but to go to Phnom Peam Cheang instead. Tevi Ksatrei may have decided to follow her grandson Chey Chetha than going with her son Satha.

John F. Cady said that Veloso and Ruiz went searching for Satha, around 1596, and upon arriving in Vientiane discovered that the king had passed away.[16,p243] However, according to the Cambodian chronicles he died in Stung Treng of malaria in 1596.

64   Chey Chetha I (1586-1594) ជ័យជេដ្ឋា (ទី១)

Transliterated Name: Jayajetthā I
Style Name: Preah Chey Chethathireach Remeathipadey Borom Baupit[7,p283]
Accession: 1586
Born: 1575/Deceased: 1596
Relationship: Eldest Son of Satha I
Mother: Srei Chakrabatei (Peou)
Religion: Theravada/Hinayana Buddhism
Capital: Longvek
Genealogy: Appendix 3

As mentioned earlier, Chey Chetha I was crowned king in 1586 at the age of eleven by his father King Satha I. Chey Chetha I was king in name only because his father was still the person who governed the country and issued all the orders.

After the fall of Longvek, not much was heard about Chey Chetha I. According to some accounts, Chey Chetha I died of malaria in Stung Treng with his father in 1596. Could it be possible he died in Phnom Peam Cheang instead? The full account of the reign of Chey Chetha I was combined under the reign of Satha I.

AYUTTHAYA'S OCCUPATION OF CAMBODIA (1594-1595)

Diego Veloso and Blas Ruiz were sent on a mission by Satha in late 1593 to secure the help of the Spanish governor of the Philippines to support Cambodia in its war against the Ayutthayan army of Naresuan.[16,p196] According to Father Gabriel Quiroga de San Antonio, they left Manila in February 1594.[133,pxvi] When they arrived in Cambodia in early 1594, they found out that King Satha had already left Longvek.[16,p196] They were captured and made prisoners by Naresuan as soon as they arrived in Cambodia. However, Ruiz managed to escape and seized a boat to sail back to Manila. He arrived in Manila in June 1594.[16,p196] Concerned about Ruiz's escape, Naresuan made a deal with Veloso. He allowed the Spaniard to travel back to Manila to appeal to the governor of the Philippines to stay neutral and not interfere in Cambodia. Naresuan was concerned because he did not want the Spanish to get involved in Cambodia due to the impeding threat of another attack by the Burmese. It would be hard for him to fight a war in two fronts. He wanted the Cambodian problem to be resolved so that he could concentrate all his effort fighting Burma. Veloso feigned his acceptance of Naresuan's proposal, but as soon as he arrived in Manila he pleaded with the Philippines governor to intervene in Cambodia. There were two opposing forces in play in the Philippines. The Lieutenant-Governor Antonio de Morga and his allies were against sending Spanish soldiers to Cambodia to help the Cambodian king regained his throne. On the other hand, the Dominican priests were in favor of helping Cambodia because they felt it would be a great opportunity to evangelize a Khmer king and establish a Catholic foundation in Cambodia. The Dominican priests won out the argument. The interim governor, Don Luis Pérez Dasmariñas, agreed to intervene in Cambodia.[133,pxxi]

Khin Sok mentioned that Naresuan assigned an Ayutthayan with the title of Moha Montrei to administer Cambodia in 2139 of the Buddhist year, 1517 Saka, 957 Cula, year of the Goat of the seventh decade, in the month of Caetra of the fifth day of the waning moon,[29,p213] which corresponded to 1595 AD. According to Adhémard Leclère, Narusean ordered that the capital of Longvek be burnt to ashes.[7,p289] Afterward, Moha Montrei moved his headquarters to Oudong.[29,p216]

In the meantime, the occupation of Cambodia by the Ayutthayan forces ran into complications. Cambodia was left without any leaders. Sotha and his sons had escaped to Stung Treng. Srei Soriyopor and his sons were taken prisoners to Ayutthaya. With this void emerged a member of the royal family nicknamed Reamea Cheung Prey. He was able to raise an army and with audacity he attacked and defeated the Ayutthayan army. According to Adhémard Leclère, 20,000 Ayutthayan soldiers were killed[7,p327] but Khin Sok said that Naresuan left only 2,000 soldiers for Moha Montrei to govern Cambodia.[29,p217] The event took place in 1595. The defeat ended the Ayutthayan occupation of Cambodia.

REFERENCE

1. Coedès, George. (1968). *The Indianized States of Southeast Asia*. Honolulu: University of Hawaii Press.
2. *Kingdom of Funan*. Retrieved January 10, 2009 from http://en.wikipedia.org/wiki/Kingdom _of_ Funan.
3. Coedès, George. *Le Royaume du Founan*. Extract from Les Peuples de la Péninsule Indochinoise, Chapter 3. Retrieved January 15, 2009 from http://www.refer.org/cbodg_ct/ tur/hist/founan.html.
4. Pelliot, Paul. (1925). Quelques Textes Chinoise Concernant l'Indochine Hindouisée. *Études Asiatiques*, Paris, **2**:243-263.
5. Vickery, Michael. (2003). Funan Reviewed: Deconstructing the Ancients. *Bulletin de l'Ecole Française d'Extrême-Orient*, Tome 90-91, pp. 101-143.
6. Briggs, Lawrence Palmer. (1951). *The Ancient Khmer Empire*. The American Philosophical Society, New Series – Volume 41, Part 1, Philadelphia.
7. Leclère, Adhémard. (1914). *Histoire du Cambodge depuis le 1er Siècle de Notre Ère*. Librairie Paul Geuthner, Paris.
8. Coedès, George. (1911). Études Cambodgiennes: La Légende de la Nagi. *Bulletin de l'École Française d'Extrême Orient*, 11: 391-393.
9. *Khmer Chankitek Calendar*. Retrieved July 12, 2010 from http://www.cam-cc.org/calendar /calendardata .php.
10. Khoo, James C. M. (2003). *Art & Archaeology of Fu Nan: Pre-Khmer Kingdom of the Lower Mekong Valley*. Orchid Press, Bangkok.
11. Wang, Gungwu. (1958). The Nanhai Trade. *Journal of the Malayan Branch of the Royal Asiatic Society*, 31/2.
12. White, Peter P. and W. E. Garrett. (1971, March). Southeast Asia 1 – Mosaic of Cultures. *National Geographic*, 295-329.
13. Conner, Jacob E. (1912, March). The Forgotten Ruins of Indochina. *National Geographic*, 209-272.
14. Aymonier, Étienne. (1999). *Khmer Heritage in Thailand*. Bangkok: White Lotus Co, Ltd.
15. Petithuguenin, Paul. (1905). A Propos des Origines et de l'Histoire Ancienne du Siam. *The Journal of the Siam Society*, Volume II, Bangkok.
16. Cady, John F. (1964). *Southeast Asia, its Historical Development*. New York: McGraw-Hill, Inc.
17. Foucher, Alfred. La vieille Route de l'Inde de Bactres a Taxila. *Paris: Les editions d'art et d'histoire*, 2 vols., 1942-1947.
18. Austroasiatic Languages. Retrieved November 1, 2010, from Wikipedia, http://en. wikipedia.org/wiki/Austro-Asiatic_languages.
19. Coedès, George. (1966). *The Making of South East Asia* (H. M. Wright, Translator). Berkeley and Los Angeles: University of California Press.
20. Rouer, Jérôme. (1996). Les Ethnies du Cambodge. *Source de References: Anthropologie Des Cambodgiens par le Dr Georges Olivier, EFEO 1968*.
21. Olivier, Georges. Les Tribus du Cambodge. *Etude Extraite d'Anthroplogie des Cambodgiens, EFEO*.
22. *Mnong People*. Retrieved November 26, 2013, from http://en.wikipedia.org/wiki/Mnong_ people.
23. Coedès, George. (1936). Études Cambodgiennes, XXXII. La plus ancienne inscription en pāli du Cambodge. *Bulletin de l'École Française d'extrême-Orient*, XXXVI: 14-21.
24. Pelliot, Paul. (1903). Le Fou-nan. *Bulletin de l'École Française d'Extrême Orient*, Tome 3, pp. 248 -303.
25. Daniels, Peter T. & William Bright. (1996). *The World's Writing Systems*. New York: Oxford University Press.
26. *Pan Localization Cambodia (PLC)*. 2nd Asian Regional Training on Local Language Computing, Prince d'Angkor Hote, Siem Reap, Cambodia, 20-24 June 2005, Retrieved February 15, 2008, from http://www.panl10n.net/Presentations/Cambodia/Chea/Collation Asian%28Cambodia%29.pdf.
27. Pelliot, Paul. (1993). *The Customs of Cambodia by Chou Ta-Kuan*. (J. Gilman d'Arcy Paul, Translated from Pelliot's French Translation of the Chinese version of Chou Ta-Kuan). Bangkok: The Siam Society.
28. *Calendar for Year 1530 (Cambodia)*. Retrieved June 24, 2016 from http://www.timeanddate.com/ calendar/?year=1530&country=140.
29. Khin, Sok. (1988). *Chroniques Royales du Cambodge (de Bañā Yāt à la Prise de Laṅvaek) (de 1417 à 1595)*. Paris: École Française d'Extrême-Orient.
30. Bernhard, Peter. Kalender und Zeitrechnung: Zählung von Jahren im Khmer-Kalender. Retrieved June 10, 2012, from http://www.bernhardpeter.de/Kalender/seite492.htm.
31. *Khmer Chhankitek Calendar*. Cambodian Coordinating Council. Retrieved June 10, 2012 from http://www .cam-cc.org/calendar/chhankitek.php.
32. Coedès, George. (1944). *Histoire Ancienne des États Hindouisés d'Etrême-Orient*. Hanoi: Imprimerie d'Extrême-Orient.
33. Cravath, Paul. (2007). *Earth in Flower*. Holmes Beach, Florida: DatASIA, Inc.

34. Vickery, Michael. Coedès' Histories of Cambodia. Retrieved July 12, 2014, from http://www.Thaiscience. info/journals/Article/Coedes%20histories%20of%20cambodia.pdf.

35. Coedès, Georges. (1931). A propos de l'origine des chiffres arabes. *Bulletin of the School of Oriental Studies, University of London*, Vol. 6, No. 2, pp. 323-328.

36. Maspero, Georges. (1904). *L'Empire Khmèr*. Phnom Penh: Imprimerie du Protectorat.

37. Coedès, George. *Études Cambodgiennes XXV: Deux inscriptions sankrites du Foun-nan*. pp. 2-8.

38. *Kingdom of Funan*. Retrieved August 18, 2014, from http://en.wikipedia.org/wiki/ Kingdom _of_ Funan.

39. *Lapis Lazuli Texts: Mahāprajñāpāramitā Mañjuśrīparivarta Sūtra*. (Translation from Taishō Tripitaka, Volume S, Number 232). Retrieved August 8, 2014, from http:// www.lapislazulitexts. com/translations.html.

40. *Buddhism in Cambodia*. Retrieved August 15, 2014, from http://khmerratana.blogspot. com/2010/04/ Buddhism-in-cambodia.html.

41. *Taishō Tripitaka*. Retrieved January 3, 2017 from https://en.wikipedia.org/wiki/Taish%C5%8DTripi%E1% B9%ADaka

42. Jao, Hui. Eminent Monks of the Liang Dynasty: The Life of Sanghavarman. Retrieved September 21, 2014 from http://santifm.org/santipada/2010/the-first-chinese-bhikkhunis.

43. Chakravarti, Adhir. (1982). *Royal Succession in Ancient Cambodia*. Calcutta: The Asiatic Society.

44. Jessup, Helen Ibbitson. (2004). *Art & Architecture of Cambodia*. London: Thames & Hudson Ltd.

45. Coedès, George. (1941). La Stèle du Práḥ Khǎn d'Aṅkor. *Bulletin de l'École d'Extrême-Orient*, Tome 41, pp. 255-302.

46. Chapuis, Oscar. (1955). A *History of Vietnam: From Hong Bang to Tu Duc*. Westport, CT: Greenwood Publishing Group, Inc.

47. Barth, Auguste. (1885). Inscriptions Sanscrites du Cambodge. *A.I. & B.I., N.E.M.* 1-180.

48. Aymonier, Étienne. (1900-1903). *Le Cambodge. 3 Volumes. I. Le Royaume Actuel; II. Les Provinces Siamoises; III. Le Groupe d'Angkor et l'Histoire*. Paris: Ernest Leroux.

49. Aymonier, Étienne. (1878). *Edification d'Angkor Wat, ou Satra de Prea Ket Mealea. Textes Khmèrs. Publiés Avec Une Traduction Sommaire*. 68-84. Saigon: E.A.

50. Groslier, Georges. (1924). Amarendrapura dans Amoghapura. *Bulletin de l'École Française d'Extrême- Orient*, 24: 359-372.

51. Elliot, Charles. (1927). *Hinduism and Buddhism: An Historical Sketch, 3 Volumes, Notes d'Épigraphie de Louis Finot*. London: Arnold.

52. Guy, John. (2014). *Lost Kingdoms: Hindu-Buddhist Sculpture of Early Southeast Asia*. The Metropolitain Museum of Arts, New York. New Haven: Yale University Press.

53. Wolters, O. W. (2002). *North-Western Cambodia in the Seventh Century. Classical Civilizations of South-East Asia: key papers from SOAS*. London: Vladimir Braginsky.

54. The Khmer Invention of Number Zero Published in the Smithsonian Magazine (Sotheara Vong, personal communication by E-mail, November 25, 2014).

55. Dupont, Pierre. (1943). I. La Dislocation du Tchen-la et la Formation du Cambodge Angkorien (VIIe-IXe Siècle). *Bulletin de l'Ecole Française d'Extrême-Orient*, Tome 43, pp. 17-55.

56. Sharan, Mahesh Kumar. Studies in Sanskrit Inscriptions of Ancient Cambodia. *Abhinav Publications*.

57. *Chenla*. Retrieved November 10, 2014, from http://en.wikipedia.org/wiki/Chenla.

58. Ooi, Keat Gin. (1959). *Southeast Asia: A Historical Encyclopedia From Angkor Wat to East Timor*. Santa Barbara.

59. *Zhuang People*. Retrieved November 15, 2014, from http://en.wikipedia.org /wiki/Zhuang _people.

60. Mémoire sur les coutumes du Cambodge. (1902). *Bulletin de l'Ecole Française d'Extrême-Orient*, Tome 2, pp. 123-177

61. *Sailendra*. Retrieved December 16, 2014, from http://en.wikipidia.org/wiki/sailendra.

62. Casey, Robert J. (1920, September). Four Faces of Siva: The Mystery of Angkor. *National Geographic*.

63. Vickery, Michael. (1986). Some Remarks on Early State Formation in Cambodia. *Institute of Southeast/Asian Studies*, Singapore, pp. 95-115.

64. Stone, Richard and Robert Clark. (2009, July). Angkor: Why an Ancient Civilization Collapsed. *National Geographic*, 26-55.

65. Candee, Helen Churchill. (2008). *Angkor the Magnificent*. Holmes Beach: DatASIA Press.

66. Day, Mary Beth, et al. (2011, November 22). *Paleoenvironmental History of the West Baray, Angkor (Cambodia)*. La Jolla, California: University of San Diego.

67. Golzio, Karl-Heinz. *Considerations on the Chronology and History of 9ᵗʰ Century Cambodia*. Retrieved January 8, 2015 from http://www.khmerstudies.org/download-files/publications/siksacakr/no2/ consideration. pdf?lbisphpreq=1.

68. Jacques, Claude. (1972). La carrière de Jayavarman II. *Bulletin de l'École Française d'Extrême-Orient*, nᵒ 59.

69. Vickery, Michael. (1998). Society, Economics, and Politics in Pre-Angkor Cambodia: the 7th-8th Centuries. *Toyo Bunko, Centre for East Asian Cultural Studies for Unesco*, 486 p.

70. Khy, Phanra. *Angkor: Essai de Lecture de la Civilisation et de l'Histoire*.

71. Jacques, Claude. *History of the Phnom Bakheng Monument.* Retrieved March 20, 2015 from http: //www.khmerstudies.org/download-files/events/conferences/Phnom%20Bakheng%20Workshop/Claude%20 Jacques% 20-%2023-40.pdf?lbisphpreq=1

72. Freeman, Michael and Claude Jacques. (2003). *Ancient Angkor.* Trumbull, CT: Weatherhill Inc.

73. Coedès, George. *Études Cambodgiennes, Bulletin de l'École Française d'Extrême-Orient*:
    1. 1911-1940. Les Traditions Généalogiques des Premiers Rois d'Angkor, d'Après les Inscriptions de Yaçovarman et de Rājendravarman, 28: 124-140.
    2. La Stèle de Fondation de Pre Rup, 73-142.

74. Coedès, George. (1908). L'Inscription de Baksei Chamkrong. Études Cambodgiennes, *Journal Asiatique*, Paris, Scr. 10, 9 (13): 467-515.

75. Vickery, Michael. (2004, June). Cambodia and Its Neighbors in the 15th Century. *Asia Research Institute*, Working Paper Series No. 27.

76. Jacobsen, Trudy. (2008). *Lost Goddesses: The denial of Female Power in Cambodian History.* Malaysia: NIAS Press.

77. Coedès, George. (1911-1940). Études Cambodgiennes; La Stèle de Palhal, 13 (VI):27-36. *Bulletin de l'École Française d;Extrême-Orient.*

78. Jacques, Claude and Michael Freeman. (2003). *Ancient Angkor.* USA: Weatherhill Inc.

79. Leroux, Ernest. (1883). *Éthnographie des Peuples Étrangères à la Chinois...Méridionaux ...Ouvrage Composé du XIII Siècle de Notre Ère, par Ma Touan Lin (Traduit par le marquis d'Hervey de Saint-Denys.*

80. Walker, Veronica. (2016, September-October). Angkor Wat: Seeking the Hidden Temples of Cambodia. *National Geographic – History*, pp. 90-94.

81. Maxwell, S. Thomas and Jaroslav Poncar. (2006). *Of Gods, Kings, and Men: The Reliefs of Angkor Wat.* Germany: Silkworm Books.

82. Mannikka, Eleanor. (2006). *Angkor Wat: Time, Space, and Kingship.* Pittsburgh, PA: University of Hawaii Press.

83. Hancock, Graham. (1996). *Lost Star of Myth and Time.* Honolulu: St. Lynn's Press.

84. Meeus, Jean. (1998). *Astronomical Algorithms.* Richmond, VA: Willmann-Bell, 2nd Edition.

85. Slater, Ken. *Equinox & Solstice Calculator.* Retrieved March 8, 2016, from https:// stellafane.org/ misc/equinox.html.

86. Hancock, Graham. (2012, September 30). *Quest for the Lost Civilization* (Channel 4 Television and The Learning Channel). Retrieved February 18, 2016 from https://www. youtube.com/watch?v= T5DNvYMtkyk.

87. Khin, Sok. (1991). *Le Cambodge entre le Siam et le Vietnam (de 1775 à 1860).* Paris: École Française d'Extrême-Orient.

88. Bower, Bruce. (2016, April 29). Lasers Unveil Secrets and Mysteries of Angkor Wat. *Science News*, Retrieved August 19, 2016 from https://www.sciencenews.org/article/lasers-unveil-secrets-and-mysteries-angkor-wat.

89. Goonatilake, Hema. (2003, July). Sri Lanka-Cambodia Relations. *Journal of the Royal Asiatic Society of Sri Lanka*, 1988, New Series, Volume XLVIII, Special Number.

90. Sharrock, Peter. (2015). *Banteay Chhmar, Garrison-Temple of the Khmer Empire.* Bangkok: River Books Co., Ltd.

91. Maspero, Georges. *Le Royaume de Champa.* Paris, les Editions G. Van Œst.

92. Hirth, Friedrich, and W. W. Rockhill. Chau Ju-qua on his work entitled "Chu-fan-Chi" regarding the Chinese and Arab trade in the twelfth and thirteenth centuries. *St. Petersburg, Imperial Arcade of Sciences.*

93. Cunin, Olivier. (2010, October 24). The Small Citadel: Reconstructing the Ruined Buddhist Complex of Banteay Chhmar. *Lecture at the Smithsonian's Museums of Asian Art*, Retrieved January 12, 2015 from http://www.visitbanteaychhmar.org/the-temples.

94. *Anavapata.* Retrieved July 12, 2015, from http://en.wikipedia.org/wiki/ Anavatapta.

95. Article on Banteay Chhmar in Asian Review (Michael Vickery, personal communication by e-mail, March 26, 2016).

96. Davis, Kent. (2010, January 2). *Banteay Chhmar in 1937 Ancient Khmer City in Cambodia.* Retrieved January 10, 2016, from http://www.devata.org/banteay-chhmar-in-1937-ancient-khmer-city-in-cambodia/# .WGsOnVxdL5s.

97. Romano, Michele. (2014, December). *Action Plan for Banteay Chhmar 2014. Commissioned by Ministry of Culture and Fine Arts in Collaboration with UNESCO, Phnom Penh.*

98. Roeder, Eric, (1999, Fall). The Origin and Significance of the Emerald Buddha. *Journal of The Southeast Asian Studies Student Association*, Vol. 3.

99. Fickle, Dorothy. (1989). *Image of the Buddha in Thailand.* Oxford University Press.

100. Jacques, Claude. (1999). Les Derniers Siècles d'Angkor. *In: Comptes-rendus des Séancesde l'Académie des Inscriptions et Belles-Lettres*, 143e Année, N. 1, pp. 367-390.

101. White, Peter T. and Wilbur E. Garrett. (1982, May). The Temples of Angkor: Ancient Glory in Stone. *National Geographic*, pp. 552-589.

102. Im, Odom (2010, 27 April). អ្នកស្រាវជ្រាវរកឃើញអំបូរជនជាតិខ្មែរ១ក្រុមកំពុងរស់នៅប្រទេសចិន (Researchers discovered ethnic Khmer group living in China). [Interview with Sum Chhum Bun]. *Radio Free Asia.* Retrieved December 7, 2015 from http://www.rfa.org/ khmer/indepth/kh-small-group-found-living-in-china-04262010232759.html.

103. Coedès, George. (1921). The Origins of the Sukhodaya Dynasty. *The Journal of the Siam Society*, Volume XIV, Bangkok.
104. Wyatt, David K. (2003). *Thailand: A Short History*. New Haven: Yale University Press.
105. Leroux, E. (1904). *Nan Tchao Ye-Tche: Histore Particulière du Nan-tchao, traduction d'un histoire de l'ancien Yunnan par Camille Sainson*. Paris.
106. Wolters, O.W. (1966). *The Khmer King at Basan (1371-3) and the Restoration of the Cambodian Chronology during the Fourteenth and Fifteenth Centuries*. Retrieved March 20, 2009, from www.ihp.sinica.edu.tw /~asiamajor/pdf/1966/1966-44.pdf.
107. Uk Solang, and Beling UK. (1999). *A Record of Cambodia's Land & Customs*. England: A Bright Pen Book.
108. Vickery, Michael. (1977, January 1). The 2/k.125 Fragment, a Lost Chronicle of Ayutthaya. *Journal of the Siam Society*, 65, pp. 1-80.
109. Le Boulanger, Paul. (1931). *Histoire du Laos Français*. Paris: Librairie Plon.
110. Mak, Phoeun. (2002). Essai de Tableau Chronologique des Rois du Cambodge de la Période Post-Angkorienne. *Journal Asiatique*, 290.1, 101-161.
111. Khanittanan, Wilaiwan. Khmero-Thai: The Great Change in the History of the Thai Language of the Chao Phraya Basin. *Department of Linguistic, Faculty of Liberal Arts, Thammasat University*.
112. Baradat, R. (1941). Les Sâmrê ou Péâr. Population Primitive de l'Ouest du Cambodge. *Bulletin de l'Ecole Française d'Extrême-Orient*, Tome 41, pp. 1-150.
113. Rémusat, J.P. Abel. (1819). *Description du Royaume de Cambodge par un Voyageur Chinois qui a Visité cette Contrée à la Fin du XIIIᵉ siècle*. Paris: Imprimerie de J. Smith.
114. Goodrich L. Carrington and Chaaying Fang. (1976). *Dictionary of Ming Biography 1368- 1644, Volume II*. Columbia University Press.
115. Stark, Miriam T. *From Funan to Angkor: Collapse and Regeneration in Ancient Cambodia*. Retrieved June 18, 2013, from http://www.anthropology.hawaii.edu/people/ faculty/Stark/pdfs/ From_Funan_to_Angkor. pdf.
116. Stadner, Donald M. (2008). The Golden Rock at Kyaik-Hti-Yo. *SOAS Bulletin of Burma Research*, Volume 6.
117. Buckley, Brendan M., et al. (2010, March 29). Climate as a Contributing Factor in the Demise of Angkor, Cambodia. *Proceedings of the National Academy of Sciences USA*.
118. Thongchai, Winichakul. (1997). *Siam Mapped: A History of the Geo-Body of a Nation*. Honolulu: University of Hawaii Press.
119. Khun Borom. (Based on Thailand: A Short History by David K. Wyatt, New Haven, Yale University Press, 2003). Retrieved March 25, 2010, from http://en.wikipedia.org/wiki/ Khun_Borom.
120. Coedès, George. (1919). L'Inscription de Nagara Jum. *The Journal of the Siam Society*, Volume 13.3, Bangkok.
121. Coedès, George. (1918). *Nouvelles Notes Critiques sur l'Inscription de Rāma Khamhaeng*.
122. Chamberlain, James R. (1991). The Ram Khamhaeng Controversy, Collected Papers. The Siam Society Under Royal Patronnage, Bangkok.
123. Krairiksh, Piriya. (1993). A Historiography of Sukhothai Art: a Framework in Need of Revision. *The Journal of the Siam Society*, Vol. 81.1.
124. Gossling, Betty. (1995). On the 'Strangeness' of Inscription 1: Comments on Michael Wright's 'A Pious Fable: Reconsidering the Inscription 1 Controversy: A 'Demonic' View;' and Michael Vickery's 'Piltdown 3: Further Discussion of the Ram Khamhaeng Inscription'. *The Journal of the Siam Society*, Vol. 83 (1 & 2).
125. Wright, Michael. (1995). A Pious Fable - Reconsidering the Inscription 1 Controversy: A 'Demonic' View. *The Journal of the Siam Society*, Vol. 83.0.
126. Cornellius Beach. (1913). The Proximate Source of the Siam Alphabet. *The Journal of the Siam Society*, Vol X, Bangkok.
127. Frankfurter, O. (1909). Events in Ayuddhya from Chulasakaraj 686-966. *The Journal of the Siam Society*, Vol. 6.3.
128. Hennequin, Laurent. *George Coedès' Chronology of the Kingdom of Haripunjaya*.
129. Van der Cruysse, Dirk (2001). Introduction to *The Diary of Kosa Pan: Thai Ambassador to France, June-July 1686, by Ok-phra Wisut Sunthon*. Translated by Visudh Busyakul. Edited by Michael Smithies. Bangkok: Silkworm Books.
130. Marshall, Andrew MacGregor. (2012). *Medical Committee Report on the Death of Rama VIII*. Retrieved August 8, 2014, from http://www.zenjournalist.org/2012/02/09/medical-committee-report-on-the-death-of-rama-viii/.
131. Redonet, Fernando Lillo. (2015, August-September). Spartacus. *National Geographic History*, pp. 52-63.
132. Chandler, P. David. (2000). *A History of Cambodia*. Colorado: Westview Press.
133. Quiroga, Gabriel de San Antonio. (1998). *Brief and Truthful Relation of Events in the Kingdom of Cambodia*. Bangkok: White Lotus Co. Ltd.
134. Delaporte, Louis. (1880). *Voyage au Cambodge – L'Architecture Khmer*. Paris: Librairie CH. Delagrave.
135. Buyers, Christopher. *The Royal Ark: Royal and Ruling Houses of Africa, Asia, Oceania and the Americas: Cambodia*. Retrieved May 1, 2010, from http://4dw.net/ royalark/ cambodia.php.
136. Coe, Michael D. (2003). *Angkor and the Khmer Civilization*. London: Thames & Hudson Ltd.

137. Suszynski, Henry. The Genealogical Gleanings. Retrieved February 2, 2008, from http://freepages.genealogy.rootsweb.ancestry.com/~royalty/.

138. *Cambodia Town's Team — Founders. City of Long Beach, California.* Retrieved December 16, 2012 from http://kafv.wordpress.com/2010/09/29/cambodia-towns-team-founders-city-of-long-beach-california/.

BIBLIOGRAPHY

1. Bhagavan, Sri Sathay Sai Baba. (1977). *The Rama Story.* Sri Sathya Sai Education and Publication Foundation, Bangalore District, Karnataka, India.
2. Bercholz, Samuel and Sherab Chodzin Kohn. (1993). *Entering the Stream.* Shambhala, Boston, MA.
3. Chakravarti, Adhir. (1973). *New Light on Saiva Tantrika Texts Known in Ancient Cambodia.* Journal of The Asiatic Society, Vol XV, Nos 1-4, Calcutta, India.
4. Chakravarti, Adhir. (1982). *Royal Succession in Ancient Cambodia.* The Asiatic Society, Calcutta, India.
5. Chandler, David P. (1972). *The Land and People of Cambodia.* J. B. Lippincott Company, New York.
6. Coulson, Michael. (1992). *Sanskrit: A Complete Course for Beginners.* NTC/Comtemporary Publishing, Chicago, IL.
7. Delaporte, Louis. (1880). *Voyage au Cambodge, l'Architecture Khmer.* Librairie Ch. Delagrave, Paris.
8. Eyewitness Travel. (2011). *Cambodia und Laos.* Dorling Kindersley Limited, London.
9. Eyewitness Travel Guides. (1997). *Thailand.* DK Publishing Inc., New York.
10. Faraut, Félix Gaspard. (2015). *Astronomie Cambodgienne, Vol. I.* Fascimile Publisher, Delhi, India.
11. Garrett, E. Wilbur. (1982, May). The Temples of Angkor: Will They Survive. *National Geographic*, 548-551.
12. Giteau, M. (1957). *Histoire du Cambodge.* Libraririe Marcel Didier, Paris.
13. Groslier, George. (2016). *Water and Light.* (Pedro Rodriguez, Translated from George Groslier's 1931 Edition, Eaux et Lumière). DatAsia Press, Holmes Beach, FL.
14. Groslier, Bernard Philippe. (1961). *Indochine – Carrefour des Arts.* Éditions Albin Michel, Paris.
15. Handley, Paul M. (2006). *The King Never Smiles: A Biography of Thailand's Bhumibol Adulyadej.* Yale University Press, New Haven, CT.
16. Long, Seam. (1997). *Toponymie Khmère (d'après les Inscriptions du Cambodge (du VIe. – XIVe. Siècles).* Édition de l'Institut Bouddhique, Phnom Penh, Cambodia.
17. Manac'h, Étienne M. (1977). *Mémoires d'Extrême Asie – La Face Cachée du Monde.* Libraririe Arthème Fayard, France.
18. Marchal, Henri. (1928). *Guide Archéologique aux Temples d'Angkor.* Les Éditions G. Van Oest, Paris.
19. Maspero, Georges. (1904). *L'Empire Khmèr.* Imprimerie du Protectorat, Phnom Penh, Cambodia.
20. Moore, Robert. (1960, April). Angkor, Jewel of the Jungle. *National geographic*, 517-569.
21. Overy, Richard. (2007). *Complete History of the World.* Times Books, Milan.
22. Ronglier, Jacques. (2005). *Parlons Kouy.* L'Harmattan, Paris.
23. *The Encyclopedia of Eastern Philosophy and Religion.* (1994). Shambhala, Boston, MA.
24. Thiounn, Oknha Veang. (1921-1926). *Preah Khan - L'Epée Sacrée du Cambodge.*
25. *The Encyclopedia of Eastern Philosophy and Religion.* (1994). Shambala, Boston, MA.
26. Van, Sok. (1959). *Résumé d'Histoire du Cambodge.* Sokcheavit Printing, Phnom Penh, Cambodia.
27. Vong, Sotheara. (2003). *Seila Chareuk Ney Pratés Kampuchea Samay Mon Angkor.* Buddhist Institute Printing House, Phnom Penh, Cambodia.
28. White, Peter P. and Wilbur. E. Garrett. (1971, March). Southeast Asia 1 – Mosaic of Cultures. *National Geographic*, 295-329
29. Winichakul, Thongchai. (1994). *Siam Mapped.* University of Hawaii Press, Hawaii.

INSCRIPTION

Baksei Chamkrong: K.286

Stanza 27: Mentioned Yasovarman (I)'s territory (His domain was much larger than his predecessors).

Stanza 27: Praising Yasovarman (I) and mentioning the important work that he had done such as the constructions of Eastern Baray, the temples of Phnom Bakheng and Lolei. It was engraved under the reign of Rajendravarman (II) around 950.

Stanza 35: Mentioned that Jayavarman (IV)'s wife was a sister of Yasovarman (I).

Sdol Kak Thom: K.235 (BEFEO XLIII, PP. 56-134)

The inscription was engraved under the reign of Udayadityavarman II in 1050. It mentioned that Yasovarman (I) had built the temple *Vnam Kantal*, now identified by experts as Phnom Bakheng. Because the way he was praised (pan....), expert misidentified Vnam Kantal and thought that it was Bayon. They realized only until 1930 that it was Phnom Bakheng.[71,p27]

Prasat Pram Lveng (Tháp Mười): K.5

The inscription which is now displayed at the Museum Vietnam of History in Ho Chi Minh City mentioned that a prince named Guṇavarman, younger son (*nṛpasunu—bālo pi*) of a king Jayavarman], was *"the moon of the Kauṇḍinya line (... kauṇḍi[n]ya[vaṅ]śaśaśinā ...) and chief "of a realm wrested from the mud"*.

Inscription de Vatta Romlok: K.27 (Khin Sok, BEFEO, KXVII, Paris: 125-133)

The inscription, written in Khmer on wood, was discovered by Étienne Aymonier in Vat Romlok in Angkor Borei in the province of Takeo.[4,p289] The inscription was translated by Khin Sok as follows:[29,p342,note759]

Au moment de la construction de cette pagoda (la pagoda de Romlok), en l'année du Porc, 949 de l'ère (Culla), quand l'armée de l'auguste Naressakhassa vint attaquer la ville de Laṅvaek, à ce moment nous nous sommes séparés.

The inscription mentioned that the army of Naresuan attacked the city of Longvek in the year of the Pig, 949 Cula (corresponding to 1587 AD). David Chandler picked up on Aymonier's theme cited 1587 AD as the first siege of Longvek.[131,p84,note11 on p259] Unlike Aymonier and Chandler, Khin Sok interpreted 1587 AD as only an attack on the city of Longvek by the Ayutthayan army coming from the south. The Ayutthayan army never laid siege to the Citadel of Longvek itself. He did not consider this attack to be the first siege of Longvek.

The following inscriptions were my translation from French into English from Pierre Dupont's paper "I. La dislocation du Tchen-la et la formation du Cambodge angkorien (VIIe-IXe siècle)."[55] Adhir Chakravarti's translation from his book "Royal Succession in Ancient Cambodia"[43] will be included as a comparison only when there are great discrepencies between the two texts. Adhir Chakravarti's translation is quoted and placed in brackets.

Inscription of Angkor[55,p19]

Stele of Western Baray: K.904

The princess Sobhajaya — daughter of the king (deceased) Jayavarman (I) and the queen Jayadevi — wife of the Brahman Sakrasvamin, built a foundation at Siva Tripurantakesvara. Jayadevi joined in. It referred to bad times. The posthumous name of Jayavarman I seemed to be *vraḥ kamratāṅ añ ta dau Sivapura, 635/713* (Cf. BE, XXXIX, 341. Unedited translation of George Coedès' work).

Inscription of Angkor[43,p51]

Stele of Eastern Baray: K.904 (My note: Adhir Chakravarti was in error by calling the stele Eastern Barray because on page 23 in his book, he was in agreement with Pierre Dupont by calling the stele Western Barray).

["Śobhājayā is the daughter of the deceased king Jayavarman I-Śivapura and wife of the Brāhmaṇa Śakrasvāmin. Śobhājayā, in concert with Jayadevī, the reigning queen, founds a Śiva-Tripurāntakeśvara. Queen Jayadevī, whose relationship with king Jayavarman is not indicated, complains of the wickedness of the time. The transcription is dated in A.D. 713"]

Inscription of Indravarman I[55,p19]

Stele of Práḥ Kó Foundation: K.713 (799-877); Stele of Bàkoṅ: K.826 (803/881); Stele of Phnoṃ Bàyàṅ: K.14; Lintels of Práḥ Kó: K.310 and K.317 (801/879); Right door-pillars of Bàkoṅ: K.304-308 (810/879)

Stanza III: Indravarman I acceded to the throne in 799/877.

Stanza IV: His mother, "born in a family where kings were succeeding each other," had as father, Sri Rudravarman, as maternal grandfather, King Sri Nripatindravarman [II], and as husband, King Sri Prithivindravarman, "born of a family of *ksatriya.*"

Inscription of Yasovarman I[55,pp20-21]

Digraphic inscriptions commemorating the foundations of Yasodharasvama of Phnoṃ Práḥ Bàt (K.95); Pràsàt Tà Siev (K.323); Práḥ Kó (K.309); Pràsàt Nǎk Buos (K.346); Práḥ Thāt Práḥ Srěi (K.101); Práḥ Thāt Khtom (K.110); Vat Hà (K.57); Vat Kandàl (K.47); Práḥ Oṅkàr (K.42); Kŭhâ Práḥ (K.45); Huei Thà Mô (K.362); Texts dated 811/889.

Stanza II: Sri Pushkaraksha, a descendant [son?] of the Lord of Aninditapura, acceded to the throne of Sambhupura; he was the maternal uncle of the maternal uncle of the mother of Jayavarman II.

Stanza III: Rajendravarman I, a descendant [son?] of Pushkaraksha, and king of Sambhupura belonged to the line of great kings (*adhirāja*) of Vyadhapura from his mother's side.

Stanza IV: Had Nripatindradevi as a wife and Mahipativarman as a son.

Stanza V: On the other hand, the Brahman Agastya, from Aryadesa, married the royal princess Yasomati.

Stanza VI: Had as a son, King Narendravarman, father of Narendralakshmi.

Stanza VII: Which, she married King Rajapativarman and had Rajendradevi as a daughter.

Stanza VIII: This latter married Mahipativarman [cf. st. IV] and had Indradevi as daughter.

Stanza IX-X: On the other hand, Jayavarman II had Jayavarman III = Jayavardhana as son.

Stanza XI: The younger brother of the mother of the mother of Jayavarman III was Sri Rudravarman.

Stanza XII: Sri Rudravarman had as his nephew (the son of a sister), King Sri Prithivindravarman.

Stanza XIII: "In that race of Kshatriya," Sri Rudravarman, *avanipālaka*, married the daughter of Sri Nripatindravarman [II] and had a daughter.

Stanza XIV: Sri Prithivindravarman married the daughter of Sri Rudravarman and had King Sri Indravarman as son.

Stanza XVI: Indravarman and Indradevi [cf. st. VIII] had Sri Yasovarman as son.

Inscription of Yasovarman I[43,p5]

["Inscription of Práḥ Kô. 815 Śaka = A.D. 893". Coedès, *loc. Cit.*, p. 32 ff. Engraved on the back of the stlèle of Indravarman I. Foundations made for the benefits of the temples of Parameśvara (Jayavarman II) and Śrī Pṛthivīndradevī (spouse of Pṛthivīndravarman)"]

Inscription of Rajendravarman II[55,pp21-22]

Stele of Prè Rup Foundation: K.806 (866/944)

Stanza VI: There was a king Sri Baladitya, a descendant of Kaundinya and Soma.

Stanza VII: His sister had a daughter, Sarasvati, who married the Brahman Visvarupa.

Stanza VIII: This Brahman and this *Kshatriya* had in their offspring [as a daughter?], Vedavati, who married Dvivedabhatta.

Stanza IX: King Nripatindravarman, brother of the mother of the mother of Vedavati [therefore, also descendant of Sarasvati and Visvarupa?], was the father of King Sri Pushkaraksha, himself the maternal uncle of the maternal uncle of the mother of Jayavarman II.

Stanza XI: In the family of Vedavati, coming from the line of kings, was born Mahendradevi.

Stanza XII: The father of Vedavati had as descendant, Sri Mahendravarman.

Stanza XIII: Mahendravarman and Mahendradevi had Rajendravarman II as son.

Stanza XIV: Vedavati and Visvarupa had kings in their offspring.

Stanza XVII: The father of Rajendravarman II was the Lord (*Isvara*) of Bhavapura.

Stanza C: Paramesvara [Jayavarman II] married a "girl of the mount."

Stanza CCLXXX: Jayadevi, mother of King Harshavarman II, was the sister of Mahendradevi.

Stanza CCLXXXI: ["Harṣavarman II is called a younger brother *(anuja)* of Rājendravarman II (Dupont believes that St. C of this inscription records the marriage of Jayavarman II-Parameśvara with a daughter of the mountain (*loc. Cit.*, *p. 22*) but the text does not conatin any thing like that)"[43,p54]

Stele of Baksei Chamkrong Foundation: K.286 (869/947)

Stanza XXI: ["Jayavarman III was the son (*atmaju*) of Jayavarman II (st. XIX)"[43,p55]

Stanza XXIV: The maternal uncle of Jayavarman II = [Prithivindravarman] had a son named Sri Indravarman (my note: this is a mistake. It should say Jayavarman III instead of Jayavarman II).

Stanza XXIV: ["The son of the maternal uncle of Jayavarman III was Indravarman." (Adhir Chakravarti's note: "Dupont thinks that Indravarman was the son of the maternal uncle of Jayavarman II (*loc. cit.* p. 22) but the mention of Jayavarman III before the introduction of the name of Indravarman makes it little likely."[43,p55]

Stele of Eastern Mébon Foundation: K.528 (874/952)
Stanza VIII: Baladitya, a descendant of Kaundiniya and Soma, was king of Aninditapura.

Stanza X: Sarasvati, a daughter of his daughter, married the Brahman Visvarupa.

Stanza XI-XII: In this race, was born Mahendradevi, a daughter of a king, who married Mahendravarman, son of a king of kings of … pura [if Mahendravarman has inherited from his father, he would be king of Bhavapura. Cf. no 19, St. XVII].

Inscription Pertaining to Various Dignitaries[55,p22]
Stele of Pràsàt Kandól Dò'm (North): K.809 (Foundation built by the *purojita* Sivasoma in 80x saka, which corresponded to 878/887 AD)
Stanza XXX: (Sivasoma) was the son of King Sri Jayendradhipativarman, maternal uncle of Jayavarman II.

Stanza XXX: ["Śivasoma, the *guru* of Indravarman, was the grandson of king Jayendrādhipativarman (*yaś = śrī jayendrādhipativarmaṇas = tanay-ātmajaḥ*), maternal uncle of Jayavarman II." (Adhir Chakravarti's note: "Dupont (*loc. cit.*) is again mistaken in holding Śivasoma as the son of Jayendrādhipativarman."[43,p55]

Stele of Práḥ Ěinkosěi: K.263 (890/968 and 892/970) and Pràsàt Kǒmphu's: K.669 (894/972) — Foundations built the Brahman Divakarabhatta.
Stanza V: Baladitya, a descendant of Kaundinya and Soma, was king of Aninditapura.

Inscription of Doubtful Attribution[55,p22]
Stele of Lovék: K.136 (undated)
Stanza VII: Punnagavarman was the son of Rudravarmana and Narendralakshmi (a descendant, born from this line, is in the service of Jayavarman II).

Inscription of Banteay Chhmar (Displayed at the National Museum in Phnom Penh):
K.227 (Inscriptions du Cambodge, vol VIII' by George Cœdes in 1966)
The inscription mentioned the names of four Sanjaks (royal servants) — Arjuna, Sri Dharadevapura, Sri Deva, and Sri Vardhana — who sacrificed their lives to protect the Crown Prince Samtac Srindrakumara on two different occasions [according to the inscriptions of Prasat Chrung and Phimeanakas (Ref. 6, p. 207), Yasovarman II was overthrown and killed in 1165 by an ambitious high-ranking officer of the court named Tribhuvanaditya. He usurped the throne and ruled under the name of Tribhuvanadityavarman before he was killed by the Chams in 1177. It is believed that Samtac Srindrakumara and his four Sanjaks lost their lives between 1160 and 1165 in defending king Yasovarman II against either Bharata Rahu or Tribhuvanaditya].

ABOUT THE AUTHOR

I studied at the Université Scientifique et Médicale de Grenoble in France; earned my B.S. in Chemical Engineering at the University of Tennessee; my M.S. in Systems Management at the University of Southern California (USC); and Certificate degrees in space related fields at the California Institute of Technology (Caltech) and at the University of California, Los Angeles (UCLA). I am a member of Alpha Chi Sigma (ΑΧΣ), of the honor societies Phi Kappa Phi (ΦΚΦ) and Tau Beta Pi (ΤΒΠ), and of the National Association of Rocketry.

I was a Senior Rocket Scientist with over 35 years of experience with aerospace companies and NASA in the fields of manned and unmanned space vehicles. I was the recipient of the NASA Langley Research Center's (NASA LaRC) Chairman Certificate of Appreciation for my support of the Critical Evaluation Task Force (CETF) investigating the causes of the 1986 Space Shuttle Challenger accident during my special assignment working at NASA LaRC from 1986 to 1987 (Figure 53). My vast experience in aerospace involved the NASA Lunar Base and Mars projects (Figure 54); the development of Technical manual published in the NASA Tech Brief magazine (Figure 55); and the launching and/or returning of manned and unmanned space vehicles safely back to earth (Figure 56); as well as calculating the sun position during the year and its impact on the earth, space vehicles, and satellites. My familiarization of the celestial mechanics enabled me to understand the method used to produce the lunar-solar calendar that the Khmer calls *chankitek*, discussed in Chapter III of Book I. Outside of my job, my main interest and passion is historical research about Southeast Asia, particularly about Cambodia. I have dedicated the last 25 years writing about events related to Cambodia. Among my works, my writings include:

- Memories of my Childhood (April 2014)
- The Last Khmer God-King (Phnom Penh Post, October 2012)
- Yuon: What's in a Xenonym (Phnom Penh Post, February 2010)
- Preah Vihear: A Khmer Heritage (2008)
- Temple Tensions (Phnom Penh Post, June 2008)
- Preah Khan Reach and the Genealogy of Khmer Kings (2008)
- Prince Sisowath Youtevong (Contribution to Wikipedia, 2008)
- Without Economic Freedom, There is No Freedom (2006)
- Is Using the Word "Yuon" Justified and Beneficial to Khmer? (2006)
- The First Cambodian New Year Parade in Long Beach (2005)
- A Time to Heal and Unite (2005)
- The Road to Khmer Independence (2003)
- The Khmers (2002)
- The Calm Before the Storm (2000)
- Are We Solely to Blame for All of our Problems? (1999)
- Quo Non Ascendet (1999)
- The Khmer Home in Southeast Asia: A Wider View (Phnom Penh Post, August 1999)
- Nationalism and the Genesis of the Khmer Language (1998)
- Is Karma Moving Like a Straight Arrow or Like a Heat Seeking Missile? (1998)
- Rubicon: Khmer Style (1998)
- Democracy and Consensus (1998)
- The Convenient Death of Pol Pot (1998)
- A Brief History of Buddhism, Including That of Cambodia (1997)

- Puddh Tomneay (1996)
- Khmer Conscience (1991-1993, during UNTAC)

In addition to my research and writing on Khmer history, I had been actively involved in the Cambodian communities for over 20 years during my time living in California. I was on the Board of Directors of the United Cambodia Community (UCC) in Long Beach, California in the 1990s. My proudest achievements for the Cambodian community were the founding of the Cambodia Town Initiative Task Force (CTITF) with the other nine members (Figure 57);[138] http://kafv.wordpress.com/2010/09/29/cambodia-towns-team-founders-city-of-long-beach-california/) and the completion of the proposal for Cambodia Town that was submitted to the Long Beach City Council on 15 January 2002 (Figure 58). Consequently, on 3 July 2007 the Long Beach City Council officially approved Cambodia Town as a landmark in Long Beach.

My well-rounded understanding of Cambodian history and my quest to present it in the most accurate of light can be reflected in my analytical, historical, methodological, and multi-cultural research and approach. My ability to correlate events is strengthened by my engineering background as a senior rocket scientist and the knowledge I gained from working with the brightest minds in the world at the NASA LaRC during the CETF that was formed to investigate the root causes of the Orbiter Challenger accident. I had written six technical papers that can be accessed at the following websites: http://papers.sae.org/881035/; http://papers.sae.org/881081/; http://arc.aiaa.org/doi/abs/10.2514/6.1990-2816;http://ntrs.nasa.gov/search.jsp?R=19850000427; http://papers.sae.org /871427/; and http://papers.sae.org/871417/.

My experience during that period came out to be personally very useful, as well as gratifying, and served me well in my research and investigation of Cambodia history. My understanding and pursuit of Khmer spirituality through my monkhood experience in 1996, under the tutelage of Preah Kru Chum Choeum, for a short period of time to pay homage to my parents, at the San Jose Pagoda in California, enabled me to comprehend Cambodia history in a manner that I could have never achieved otherwise.

I have retired from the aerospace industry since 2014 and am currently a Board Adviser for the Cambodia Historians Association (CHA) headquartered in Phnom Penh, Cambodia.

**Figure 53. NASA Langley Research Center
Certificate of Appreciation for the Support
of the Critical Evaluation Task Force
to Determine the Cause of the
Space Shuttle Challenger Accident**

**Figure 54. NASA Langley Research Center
Certificate of Appreciation for Outstanding
Contribution to the Projects of Lunar Base
& Environmental Control Life Support System**

**Figure 55. NASA Certificate of Recognition
for the Development of a Technical Innovation
Published in the NASA Tech Brief**

**Figure 56. Rockwell International
Award for Outstanding Achievement
for the Project Assured Crew**

Rescue Vehicle

Names of Cambodia Town Founding Members

The names from left to right shown in Figure 57 are as follows: Pasin Chanou (Proposal), Rosana Chanou (Administration), David Kar (Public Relations, Lead), Solange Kea, Esq. (Legal), Annie H. Lee (Public Relations), Harrison T. S. Lee (Administration, Lead), Morakod Lim, M.D. (Public Relations), Kenneth T. So (Proposal, Lead), Philip T. Thong (Finance, Lead), Sovuthy Tith (Finance).

Figure 57. Cambodia Town Founding Members

Cambodia Town Initiative Task Force
555 East Pacific Coast Hwy,
Suite #218
Long Beach, CA 90806
(562) 489-1780

March 7, 2002

City Hall
The Long Beach City Council
333 W Ocean Blvd
Civic Center Plaza
Long Beach 90802
(562) 570-6555

Subject: Request for Official Recognition of Cambodia Town

The Honorable Mayor and Members of the Long Beach City Council:

The Cambodia Town Initiative Task Force (CTITF) respectfully requests that the city of Long Beach consider officially designating a section of Anaheim Street between Temple Avenue and Long Beach Blvd. as **Cambodia Town**. This request is the result of several meetings held over the past 8 months with interested citizens, community leaders, and various Cambodian associations and organizations from Long Beach and the surrounding area.

Cambodian Americans from greater Los Angeles County, Orange County, and as far away as San Diego, Fresno, Stockton, Oakland, San Jose, and San Francisco come to this area on a regular basis to shop, eat, and do business. Long Beach is known throughout the world as being home to the largest population of Cambodians outside of Cambodia and holds tremendous significance for Cambodians everywhere as the heart of the Cambodian diasporic experience. We believe that official recognition of this section of Long Beach as **Cambodia Town** will attract more businesses and tourists, increase civic pride, and help to improve and enhance the area for everyone.

We have attached articles from the Press Telegram, Los Angeles Times, and The Bayon Business News, published in Lowell, Massachusetts for your review. Each of these articles speak to the significance Long Beach holds for Cambodians, the pride we feel for our adopted city, and our hope to continue growing and prospering here. We have also attached the names of Cambodian organizations that are supporting the effort initiative for the formal recognition of Cambodia Town in Long Beach.

We wish to thank you in advance for your careful consideration of our request. We look forward to working with you on developing **Cambodia Town** and building it into a model community.

Sincerely,

Kenneth T. So
CTITF Proposal Team Leader

Solange Kea, Esq.
CTITF Legal Team Leader

**Figure 58. Letter Submitted to the Long Beach City Council for the
Official Recognition of Cambodia Town**

APPENDIX 1

**Letters of Encouragement and Appreciation from King Father Norodom Sihanouk,
Queen Mother Norodom Monineath Sihanouk, and King Norodom Sihamoni
Concerning my Effort to Write the Book on the Khmer Kings**

 នរោត្តម សីហនុ
នៃកម្ពុជា
និង
សម្តេចព្រះមហាក្សត្រី ព្រះមហេសី
នរោត្តម មុនិនាថ សីហនុ
នៃព្រះរាជាណាចក្រកម្ពុជា

ជូន   លោក Kenneth T. So

kenneth. aryasatya@gmail.com

លោកជាទីរាប់អាន និងស្រឡាញ់ដ៏ជ្រាលជ្រៅ

យើងខ្ញុំបានទទួលហើយនូវនិតិផ្សាយ របស់លោក នៅក្នុងឱកាសពិធីបុណ្យចូលឆ្នាំថ្មី ប្រពៃណីជាតិយើង ត្រូមទាំងអត្ថបទ " The Khmer Kings, chapter II "។

យើងខ្ញុំសូមថ្លែងអំណរគុណដ៏ជ្រាលជ្រៅ និងសូមសរសើរដើកក់ត្រៃចំពោះការនិពន្ធរបស់លោក ក្នុងការស្រាវជ្រាវដើម្បីផ្សព្វផ្សាយអំពី Khmer Traditional Calendar ។ ខ្ញុំមជូន ពរលោក ត្រូមទាំងក្រុមគ្រួសារ បានប្រកបតែនឹងបុទ្ធទាំងបួនប្រការ អាយុ វណ្ណៈ សុខៈ ពលៈ កុំបីឃ្លៀងឃ្លាតឡើយ។

សូមលោក ទទួលនូវសេចក្តីរាប់អាន និងស្រឡាញ់ដ៏ជ្រាលជ្រៅ អំពីយើងខ្ញុំ។

នរោត្តម សីហនុ   នរោត្តម មុនិនាថ សីហនុ
ភ្នំពេញ ថ្ងៃទី២៤ ខែមេសា ឆ្នាំ២០១១

His Majesty Preah Bat Samdech Preah Boromneath
NORODOM SIHAMONI
KING of CAMBODIA

To Mr Kenneth T. So and Family

Dear Compatriots,

Thank you very much indeed for your handwritten letter of warm wishes along with a most interesting sample of your first draft on Chapter 3 of your book about the Khmer Kings.

Please accept, dear Compatriots, with my best wishes for a Happy and Prosperous New Year 2011, the assurances of my high and cordial consideration.

avec mes affectueuses pensées,

Norodom Sihamoni

Phnom Penh, 20 January 2011

Note: My personal address was edited out from the above letters.

APPENDIX 2

Ancient Khmer Coins

**Coins found at Angkor Borei and are believed to be used during the Funan period
(Personal Collection)**

Obverse side: Sunset/Sunrise casting its reflection on the ocean (1.1 inch dia.)	Reverse side: King stretching his arms with his children to protect his kingdom (1.1 inch dia.)	Obverse Side: Galloping Horse (1.4 inch dia.)	Reverse Side: Royal Crest? (1.4 inch dia.)

Obverse Side: Serpent coiling around a fruit tree (1.9 in. dia.)	Reverse Side: Dancing Garuda (Krut) (1.9 in. dia.)	Obverse Side: Mahout riding an elephant? (0.8 in. dia.)	Reverse Side: Symbol representing a royal palace? (0.8 in. dia.)

Obverse Side: Seal in the ocean (1.9 inch dia.)	Reverse Side: Representation of the distance/separation between earth and moon? (1.9 inch dia.)	Obverse Side: Hanuman (Monkey King) (0.7 inch dia.)	Reverse Side: Lotus Flower (0.7 inch dia.)

Coins found at Angkor Borei and are believed to be used during the Funan period
(Personal Collection)

| Obverse, Convex Side: Territory of Funan with moon above? (1.0 in. dia.) | Reverse, Concave Side: Representation of distance/separation between earth and stars? (1.0 in. dia.) | Obverse, Convex Side: Dog barking at night (1.0 inch dia.) | Reverse, Concave Side: Insignia or Trident (1.0 inch dia.) |

| Obverse Side: Bird with symbol on top left the same as shown on the reverse side (0.8 inch dia.) | Reverse Side: Symbol that could be a Funan writing (0.8 inch dia.) | Hanuman (Monkey God) | Hindu god (Probably Shiva) |

Coins used during the Angkor period (Personal Collection)

| Dancing Apsara (1. 2 inch dia.) | Leafly Design (1. 4 inch dia.) | Flower (1. 2 inch dia.) | Leafly Design (0.6 inch dia.) |

APPENDIX 3

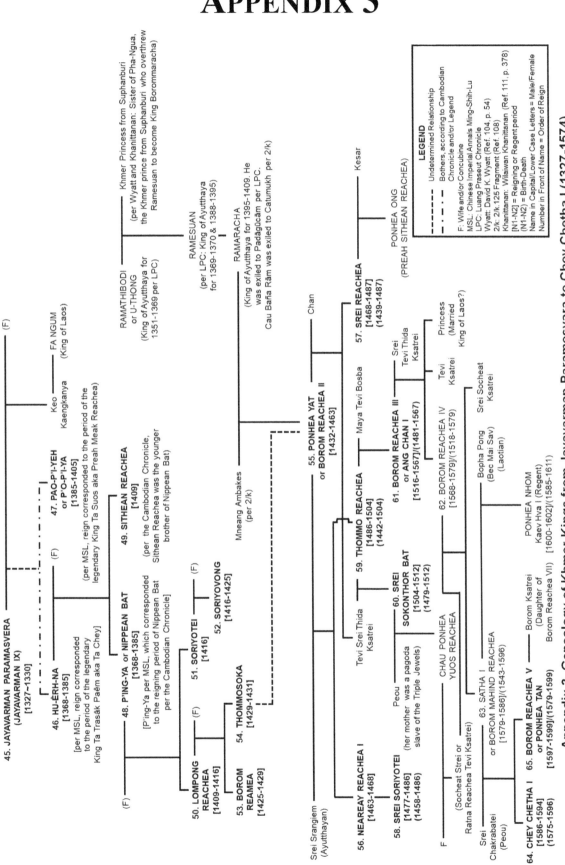

Appendix 3. Genealogy of Khmer Kings from Jayavarman Paramesvara to Chey Chetha I (1327-1574)

APPENDIX 4

English Translation of Ram Khamhaeng Inscriptions
(Reference 121, pp. 445-450)

[Face 1/Lines 1-3]:
My father was named Sri Indraditya, my mother was named Nang Süang, my elder brother was named Bang Müang. There were five of us born from the same womb: three boys and two girls. My eldest brother died when he was stll a child.

[Face 1/Lines 3-10]:
When I was nineteen years old, Lord Sam Chon, the ruler of Müang Chot, came to attack Müang Tak. My father went to fight Lord Sam Chon on the left; Lord Sam Chon drove forward on the right. Lord Sam Chon attacked in force; my father's men fled in confusion. I did not flee. I mounted my elephant, opened [a way through] the soldiers, and pushed him ahead in front of my father. I fought an elephant duel with Lord Sam Chon. I fought Lord Sam Chon's elephant, Mas Müang by name, and beat him. Lord Sam Chon fled. Then my father named me Phra Ram Khamhaeng because I fought Lord Sam Chon's elephant.

[Face 1/Lines 10-18]:
In my father's lifetime I served my father and I served my mother. When I caught any game or fish I brought them to my father. When I picked any acid or sweet fruits that were delicious and good to eat, I brought them to my father. When I went hunting elephants, either by lasso or by [driving them into] a corral, I brought them to my father. When I raided a town or village and captured elephants, young men or women of rank, silver or gold, I turned them over to my father. When my father died, my elder brother was still alive, and I served him steadfastly as I had served my father. When my elder brother died, I got the whole kingdom for myself.

[Face 1/Lines 18-35 and Face 2/Line 1-8]:
In the time of King Ram Khamhaeng this land of Sukhothai is thriving. There is fish in the water and rice in the fields. The lord of the realm does not levy toll on his subjects for traveling the roads; they lead their cattle to trade or ride their horses to sell; whoever wants to trade in elephants, does so; whoever wants to trade in horses, does so; whoever wants to trade in silver or gold, does so. When any commoner or man of rank dies, his estate — his elephants, wives, children, granaries, rice, retainers, and groves of areca and betel — is left in its entirety to his son. When commoners or men of rank differ and disagree, [the King] examines the case to get at the truth and then settles it justly for them. He does not connive with thieves or favor concealers [of stolen goods]. When he sees someone's rice he does not covet it; when he sees someone's wealth he does not get angry. If anyone riding an elephant comes to see him to put his own country under his protection, he helps him, treats him generously, and takes care of him; if [someone comes to him] with no elephants, no horses, no young men or women of rank, no silver or gold, he gives him some, and helps him until he can establish a state [of his own]. When he captures enemy warriors, he does not kill them or beat them. He has hung a bell in the opening of the gate over there; if any commoner in the land has a grievance which sickens his belly and gripes his heart, and which he wants to make known to his ruler and lord, it is easy: he goes and strikes the bell which the King has hung there; King Ram Khamhaeng, the ruler of the kingdom, hears the call; he goes and questions the man, examines the case, and decides it justly for him. So the people of this müang of Sukhothai praise him. They plant areca groves and betel groves all over this müang; coconut groves and jackfruit groves are planted in abundance in this müang, mango groves and tamarind groves are planted in abundance in this müang. Anyone who pants them gets them for himself and keep them. Inside this city there is a marvelous pond of water which is as clear and as good to drink as the water of the [Me] Khong in the dry season. The triple rampart surrounding this city of Sukhothai measures three thousand four hundred fathoms.

[Face 2/Lines 8-23]:
The people of this city of Sukhothai like to observe the precepts and bestow alms. King ram Khamhaeng, the ruler of this city of Sukhothai, as well as the princes and princesses, the young men and women of rank, and all the noble folk, without exception, both male and female, all have faith in the religion of the Buddha, and all observe the precepts during the rainy season. At the close of the rainy season they celebrate the *kathin* ceremonies, which last a month, with heaps of cowries, with heaps of areca nuts, with heaps of flowers, with cushions and pillows: the gifts they present [to the monks] as accessories to the *kathin* [amount to] two million each year. Everyone goes to the Araññika to the parade-ground. They repeatedly pay homage together, accompanied by the music of instruments and singing. Whoever wants to make merry, does so. As this Sukhothai has four very

big gates, and as the people always crowd together to come in and watch the King lighting candles and setting off fire-works, the city is filled to the bursting point.

[Face 2/Lines 23-27]:
Inside this city of Sukhothai, there are viharas, there are golden statues of the Buddha, there are statues eighteen cubits in height; there are big statues of the Buddha and medium-sized ones; there are big viharas and medium-sized ones; there are monks, Nissayamuttas, Theras, and Mahatheras.

[Face 2/Lines 27-33]:
West of this city of Sukhothai is the Araññika, built by King Ram Khamhaeng as a gift to the Mahathera Sangharaja, the sage who has studied the scriptures from beginning to end, who is wiser than any other monk in the kingdom, and who has come here from the Müang Sri Dhammaraja. Inside the Araññika there is a large rectangular vihara, tall and exceedingly beautiful, and an eighteen-cubit statue of the Buddha standing up.

[Face 2/Lines 33-35]:
East of this city of Sukhothai there are viharas and ponds, there is the large lake, there are groves of areca and betel, upland and lowland farms, homesteads, large and small villages, groves and mango and tamarind. [They] are as beautiful to look at as if they were made for that purpose.

[Face 3/Lines 1-3]:
North of this city of Sukhothai there is the bazaar, there is the Acan statue, there are the *prasadas,* there are groves of coconut and jackfruit, upland and lowland farms, homesteads, large and small villages.

[Face 3/Lines 3-10]:
South of this city of Sukhothai there are kuti with viharas and resident monks, there is the dam, there are groves of coconut and jackfruit, groves of mango and tamarind, there are mountain streams, and there is Phra Khaphung. The divine sprite of that mountain is more powerful than any other sprite in the kingdom. Whatever lord may rule this kingdom of Sukhothai, if he makes obeisance to him properly, with the right offerings, this kingdom will endure, this kingdom will thrive; but if obeisance is not made properly or the offerings are not right, the sprite of the hill will no longer protect it and the kingdom will be lost.

[Face 3/Lines 10-27]:
In 1214 saka, a Year of the Dragon [AD 1292], King Ram Khamhaeng, lord of this kingdom of Sri Sajjanalai and Sukhothai, who had planted these sugar-palm trees fourteen years before, commanded his craftsmen to carve a slab of stone and place it in the midst of these sugar-palm trees. On the day of the new moon, the eighth day of the waxing moon, the day of the full moon, and the eighth day of the waning moon, [one of] the monks, theras, or mahatheras goes up and sits on the stone slab to preach the Dharma to the throng of laypeople who observe the precepts. When it is not a day for preaching the Dharma, King Ram Khamhaeng, lord of the kingdom of Sri Sajjanalai and Sukhothai, goes up, sits on the stone slab, and lets the officials, lords, and princes discuss affairs of state with him. On the day of the new moon and the day of the full moon, when the white elephant named Rucasri has been decked out with howdah and tasseled head cloth, and always with gold on both tusks, King Ram Khamhaeng mounts him, ride away to the Araññika to pay homage to Sangharaja, and then returns. There is an inscription in the city of Chaliang, erected beside the Sri Ratanadhatu, there is an inscription in the cave called Phra Ram's Cave, which is located on the bank of the River Samphai; and there is an inscription in the Ratadhara Cave. In this sugar-palm Grove there are two pavilions, one named sala Phra Masa, one named Buddhasala. The slab of stone is named Manangasilabat. It is installed here for everyone to see.

[Face 4/Lines 1-4]:
All the Ma, the Kao, the Lao, the Tai of the land under the vault of heaven and the Tai who live along the U and Khong came and do obeisance to King Sri Indraditya's son King Ram Khamhaeng, who is lord of the Kingdom of Sri Sajjanalai and Sukhothai.

[Face 4/Lines 4-8]:
In 1207 saka, a Year of the Boar [AD 1285], he caused the holy relics to be dug up so that everyone could see them. They were worshipped for a month and six days, then they were buried in the middle of Sri Sajjanalai, and a cetiya was built on top of them which was finished in six years. A wall of rock enclosing the Phra Dhatu was built which was finished in three years.

[Face 4/Lines 8-11]:
Formely these Tai letters did not exist. In 1205 saka, a Year of the Goat [AD 1283], King Ram Khamhaeng set his mind and his heart on devising these Tai letters. So these Tai letters exist because that lord devised them.

[Face 4/Lines 11-27]:

King Ram Khamhaeng was sovereign over all the Tai. He was the teacher who taught all the Tai to understand merit and the Dharma rightly. Among men who live in the lands of the Tai, there is no one equal him in knowledge and wisdom, in bravery and courage, in strength and energy. He was able to subdue a throne of enemies who possessed broad kingdoms and many elephants. The places whose submission he receive on the east include Sra Luang, Song Khwae, Lum Pa Cai, Sakha the banks of the Khong, and Viang Can-Vieng Kham, which is the furthest place. On the south, [they include] Khanthi, Phra Bang, Phraek, Suphannaphum, Ratchaburi, Phetchaburi, Sri Dharmaraja, and the seacoast, which is the farthest place. On the west, [they include] Müang Chot, Müang …n, and Hamsavati, the seas being their limit. On the north, they include Müang Phlae, Müang man, Müang N[an], Müang Phlua, and, beyond the banks of the Khong, Müang Sava [Luang Phrabang], which is the farthest place. All the people who live in these lands have been reared by him in accordance with the Dharma, every one of them.

INDEX

CPSIA information can be obtained
at www.ICGtesting.com
Printed in the USA
BVHW05s2106090318
510098BV00030B/307/P

9 781934 431368